TExES™ CORE SUBJECTS EC-6 (291)

By Luis A. Rosado, Ed.D.

Contributing Authors
Ann Cavallo, Ph.D.
Mary Curtis, Ph.D.
Diane M. Lange, Ph.D.
Larry P. Nelson, Ph.D.
Kathleen C. Tice, Ph.D.
Jason Wardlaw, Ph.D.

Research & Education Association

Research & Education Association
258 Prospect Plains Road
Cranbury, New Jersey 08512
Email: info@rea.com

TExES™ Core Subjects EC-6 (291)

Published 2019

Printed in the United States of America

Library of Congress Control Number 2015959980

ISBN-13: 978-0-7386-1199-0
ISBN-10: 0-7386-1199-9

The competencies presented in this book were created and implemented by the Texas Education Agency and Pearson Education, Inc., or its affiliates. Texas Examinations of Educator Standards and TExES are trademarks of the Texas Education Agency. All other trademarks cited in this publication are the property of their respective owners.

Cover image: ©istockphoto.com/iofoto

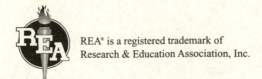

Contents

CONTENTS

About the Author

Dr. Luis A. Rosado is a Professor of Bilingual Education and the Director of the Center for Bilingual and ESL Education in the College of Education and Health Professions at the University of Texas at Arlington. He holds degrees from the University of Puerto Rico, Boston State College, and Texas A&I University, now Texas A&M–Kingsville. Prior to coming to UT Arlington, Dr. Rosado held academic appointments at Pontifical Catholic University of Puerto Rico, Texas Southern University, and Texas Woman's University. Dr. Rosado has more than three decades of teaching experience at the elementary, high school, and college levels. He has taught in Puerto Rico, Massachusetts, and Texas.

In 2011, Dr. Rosado was the co-recipient of a $1.9 million grant from the U.S. Department of Education's Office of English Language Acquisition to improve preparation for teachers serving English learners. In total, Dr. Rosado has received more than $5.6 million in state and federal funding to prepare bilingual and ESL teachers as well as school administrators, and to provide services to support high school students.

Dr. Rosado has written extensively in the areas of pedagogy and professional responsibilities, parental involvement, cross-cultural communication, preparation for teacher certification exams, and Spanish for bilingual teachers. Among his publications are a series of books to prepare pre-service teachers for certification tests, including REA's best-selling *TExES Bilingual Generalist EC-6 (192)*, and *Desarrollo del Español para Maestros en Programas de Educación Bilingüe* (Spanish Development for Teachers in Bilingual Education Programs), for which, with co-author Lidia Morris, he earned first place in the 2014 International Latino Book Awards in the category of Best Reference Book—Spanish or Bilingual. The book, which is intended, Dr. Rosado says, "to polish Spanish, not to teach Spanish," is being used by several universities and a number of Texas school districts.

Author's Dedication

This book is dedicated to Kelly, Koko, and Alex because through their natural behavior and development, they guided me to see the connection between theory and practice.

About the Contributing Authors

English Language Arts and Reading

Dr. Kathleen Copeland Tice is the Program Coordinator for Literacy Studies in the Department of Curriculum & Instruction at the University of Texas at Arlington. She also teaches courses in literacy studies at both the undergraduate and graduate level. Her research has focused upon teacher knowledge development and service-learning in teacher preparation. She has served as the annual conference Program Chair for the Service-Learning & Experiential Education–Special Interest Group of the American Educational Research Association. She is a co-editor of the *International Journal of Research on Service-Learning in Teacher Education*. Dr. Tice won a 2015 Literacy Grant from the Honor Society of Phi Kappa Phi, the nation's oldest and most prestigious collegiate honor society for all academic disciplines. Her teaching awards include the University of Texas System Regents' Outstanding Teacher Award. She received her master's degree in reading education from the University of Houston, and earned her Ph.D. in reading and in English/language arts education from the University of Texas at Austin.

Health and Physical Education

Dr. Larry P. Nelson is an Associate Professor in the Department of Kinesiology at the University of Texas at Arlington. He holds a Ph.D. in Sport & Exercise Science from the University of Northern Colorado; an M.S. in Physical Education Pedagogy from Colorado State University; and a B.S. in Exercise and Sport Science from Colorado State University. His research interests include physical education program assessment and evaluation, developing service-learning models that improve preservice teachers' efficacy, and testing active-learning strategies for critical thinking development. Dr. Nelson is a co-founder of Dancing Classrooms North Texas 501(c)(3) and is the Research Coordinator for Dancing Classrooms (National Network). He was awarded the *Fort Worth Star-Telegram*'s Community Service-Learning Award in 2008, the inaugural UT Regents' Outstanding Teaching Award in 2009, and was named Citizen of the Year by the YMCA of Arlington in 2011. Dr. Nelson enjoys coaching soccer in the Arlington community.

Mathematics

Dr. Jason Wardlaw is an analog integrated circuit design engineer. He received a B.S. and a Ph.D. in Electrical Engineering from Texas A&M University. Dr. Wardlaw was a Teaching Assistant and Assistant Lecturer for the Department of Electrical and Computer Engineering at Texas A&M University from 2005 to 2008. From June 2008 to December 2010, he was involved in a National Science Foundation GK–12 program for enhancing STEM awareness in rural middle school classrooms.

Music

Diane Lange is Professor and Area Coordinator of Music Education at the University of Texas at Arlington, where she oversees the music education area and teaches undergraduate and graduate courses in Early Childhood and Elementary Music Education. She also teaches early childhood music at her private studio, The Musical Treehouse. Dr. Lange has taught elementary music for ten years in both Michigan and Nevada. She received her Orff Levels and Master Class at Memphis State University and GIML Level I and II at Michigan State University. She is a certified faculty member where she teaches GIML Level I around the country. Dr. Lange received both her Bachelor of Music in Education and Master of Music from Central Michigan University, and earned her Ph.D. from Michigan State University. She has presented clinics and workshops at multiple state, national, and international conferences. She has published *Together in Harmony: Combining Orff Schulwerk and Music Learning Theory, Together Again in Harmony: Combining Orff Schulwerk and Music Learning Theory,* a chapter on combining Music Learning Theory and Orff Schulwerk that appeared in *Music Learning Theory: Theory in Practice* and several articles on combining Orff Schulwerk and Music Learning Theory. In addition, she is a co-author for *Jump Right In: The Elementary Music Curriculum*, Grades Kindergarten and 5. Dr. Lange has held executive board positions with the Gordon Institute for Music Learning, North Texas chapter of AOSA, and Early Childhood Music and Movement Association.

Science

Dr. Ann Cavallo is Associate Dean for Research and Graduate Studies, Co-director of UTeach Arlington Science and Mathematics Education program, and Professor of Science Education at UT Arlington. Dr. Cavallo earned her B.S. from Niagara University, and her M.S. in Science Education/ Biology, M.S. in Natural Science, and Ph.D. in Science Education from Syracuse University. She holds secondary teacher certification in Biology, Chemistry, Earth Science, and General Science, and taught middle and high school science prior to earning her graduate degrees. She has held faculty appointments at the University of Oklahoma, the University of California–Davis, and Wayne State University. She joined the faculty at the University of Texas at Arlington in 2006 as Associate Professor and earned the rank of Professor in 2009 in her field of Science Education. Dr. Cavallo received the 2015 Distinguished Record of Research or Creative Activity Award from UT Arlington. She is Principal Investigator of three National Science Foundation grants totaling over $3 million. Dr. Cavallo's research has investigated high school and college students' learning approaches and strategies, scientific reasoning, self-efficacy, and their acquisition of conceptual understandings of science. Dr. Cavallo has over 40 publications in internationally and nationally refereed journals and proceedings, as well as several books and book chapters, including co-authoring REA's top-selling *TExEs Generalist 4–8* test prep. In total, she has secured more than $9 million in grants from various funding agencies to support her work.

Social Studies

Dr. Mary D. Curtis is Visiting Assistant Professor, Coordinator of Secondary and EC–12 Education Programs, and Director, Center for Social Science Education at the University of Texas at Arlington. Dr. Curtis earned her B.A. in political science from Texas A&M University, M.S. in instructional technology from the University of Houston–Clear Lake, and Ph.D. in Geography Education from Texas State University. She worked 10 years as a Social Studies teacher in the Clear Creek Independent School District, League City, Texas. In 2007 Dr. Curtis received the K–12 Distinguished Teaching Award from the National Council for Geography Education. In 2008 and again 2010, she was named a Gilbert M. Grosvenor Scholar, the only candidate to earn this distinction twice. Grosvenor Scholars manage political outreach to build geography awareness and conduct research in conjunction with the National Geographic Education Foundation and Education Program division of the National Geographic Society.

About REA

Founded in 1959, Research & Education Association (REA) is dedicated to publishing the finest and most effective educational materials—including study guides and test preps—for students of all ages. Today, REA's wide-ranging catalog is a leading resource for students, teachers, and other professionals. Visit *www.rea.com* to see a complete listing of all our titles.

Publisher's Acknowledgments

SVP and Publisher: Pam Weston

VP, Editorial Services: Larry B. Kling

VP, Technology: John Paul Cording

Managing Editor: Diane Goldschmidt

Copywriter and Proofreader: Kelli A. Wilkins

Copyediting: John Kupetz, Miriam Perkoff, Sandra Rush, and Stu Schwartz

Indexing: Terry Casey, Casey Indexing and Information Service

Composition Services: Caragraphics

Page and Cover Design: Eve Grinnell

Getting Started

Congratulations! By taking the TExES Core Subjects EC-6 (291) test, you're on your way to a rewarding career as a teacher of young students in Texas. Our book gives you everything you need to succeed on this important exam, bringing you one step closer to being certified to teach in Texas.

This TExES Core Subjects test prep includes:

- Complete overview of the TExES Core Subjects EC-6 (291) test

- Comprehensive review for all five subject tests in the TExES Core Subjects test battery

- Full-length practice test based on the official exam, complete with detailed answer explanations

HOW TO USE THIS BOOK

About Our Review

The review chapters in this book are designed to help you sharpen your command of all the skills you'll need to pass the Core Subjects EC-6 test. The test is composed of five domains and 47 competencies. Each of the skills required for all five domains is discussed at length to optimize your understanding of what the test covers.

Keep in mind that your schooling has taught you most of what you need to know to answer the questions on the test. Our content review is designed to reinforce what you have learned and show you how to relate the information you have acquired to the specific competencies on the test.

Studying your class notes and textbooks together with our review will give you an excellent foundation for passing the test.

About Our Practice Test

The best way to personalize your study plan is to get feedback on what you know and what you don't. This book gives you a full-length practice test based on the official TExES Core Subjects EC-6 exam, along with detailed answer explanations.

After reviewing with the book, take the practice test to ensure that you have mastered the material and are ready for test day. Review the detailed answer explanations to identify any areas where you need extra study, and read those sections of the review chapters again.

AN OVERVIEW OF THE TEST

What is assessed on the Core Subjects EC-6 test?

The TExES Core Subjects EC-6 test is a criterion-referenced examination constructed to measure the knowledge and skills that an entry-level educator in Texas public schools must have. The test is a requirement for candidates seeking a Core Subjects EC-6 certificate. Because it's a computer-administered test, the Core Subjects EC-6 exam is available throughout the year at numerous locations across the state and at select locations nationally. To find the test center near you, visit *www.tx.nesinc.com*.

Candidates are limited to five attempts to take any of Texas's teacher certification tests, but in the event you don't pass the Core Subjects EC-6 test, you need to retake only the individual subtest(s) where your score falls short.

On the next page are the five domains that correspond with the Core Subjects exam's five subject tests. The table covers the percentage and number of questions in each domain, as well as the time allocated for each section of the test. These domains and the competencies rooted in them represent the knowledge that teams of teachers, subject area specialists, and district-level educators have determined to be important for beginning teachers.

A Snapshot of the TExES Core Subjects EC-6 Test

Subject Test	Competencies	Percentage	Total Items	Time
English Language Arts and Reading & the Science of Teaching Reading (801)	13	28%	75	1 hour and 45 minutes (105 minutes)
Mathematics (802)	6	18%	47	60 minutes
Social Studies (803)	5	16%	41	35 minutes
Science (804)	18	19%	52	40 minutes
Fine Arts, Health, and Physical Education (805)	5	19%	52	40 minutes
TOTAL	47	100%	267	4 hours and 40 minutes

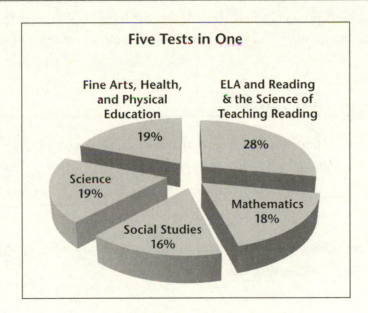

What is the format of the TExES Core Subjects EC-6 test?

The test includes a total of 267 items, with 230 scorable multiple-choice items, and 37 non-scorable items used for field testing. You won't know which is which, so they surely aren't worth worrying about. Your final scaled score will be based only on the scorable items. The test is organized into five subject tests.

Multiple-Choice Questions

Though all the questions on the test are multiple-choice, they may not all be the type of multiple-choice question with which you're familiar. The majority of questions on the Core Subjects test are standard multiple-choice items. The questions are not intended merely to test your command of facts but also your critical-thinking skills. For example, you may be asked to analyze information and compare it with knowledge you have, or make a judgment about it. To acquaint yourself with all the standards and competencies covered on the test, be sure to download Pearson's test framework at *www.tx.nesinc.com*.

Some multiple-choice questions are self-contained while others are clustered, branching off a common stimulus. Each question will generally have four choices: A, B, C, and D. (Some questions may have five options.) In most cases, the correct answer will require you to identify the single best response. Some questions, however, will require you to select *all* the responses that answer the question correctly. In such instances, you will click check boxes instead of ovals. Also be aware that this test occasionally presents non-traditional formats for multiple-choice items, both to present the information and to allow you to select the best answer. A rundown of these new formats follows.

Unfamiliar Question Types

There are several unfamiliar question types that may show up on the Core Subjects test. First, let's look at the kind of question that asks test-takers to identify more than one correct response option to a question.

Example

1. Which of the following led to the American Revolution? Select *all* that apply.

   A. the French and Indian War

   B. the Intolerable Acts

   C. the French Revolution

   D. the Articles of Confederation

Answer and Explanation

Options (A) and (B) are correct. The French and Indian War (A), fought from 1754 to 1763, served as a powerful vehicle by which the British Empire extended its reach in North America. The British sought to impose taxation on the colonists to finance the defense of the newly acquired territory, which aggravated growing discontent with British governance. The Intolerable Acts (B) embraced measures enacted by the British Parliament in 1774 to strike back at the colonists' defiance (e.g., the Boston Tea Party in 1773) of British rule. The move backfired, spawning the First Continental Congress later that year. Simple chronology helps you root out the French Revolution (C) as an incorrect option. The French Revolution, fought from 1787 to 1799, is an anachronistic response that could not have led to the American Revolution, which ended in 1783. Finally, the Articles of Confederation instead of leading to the American Revolution actually *resulted from* it. The Articles were drafted in 1776-77 and adopted by Congress on Nov. 15, 1777, as the first U.S. constitution.

According to Pearson, the Core Subjects EC-6 test may use interactive questions that may include audio or video clips instead of, say, a static map or reading passage.

Item formats may ask you to select the correct answer(s) by any of these means:

1. Click on a sentence or sentences, or on parts of a graphic representation, such as a map, chart, or figure – sometimes termed a "hot spot."

2. Drag and drop answer options into "target" areas in a table, piece of text, or graphic.

3. Use a drop-down menu.

More than anything, these innovative item types require that you read the instructions carefully to be sure you are fully responsive to the question.

The TExES Core Subjects test is scored based on the number of questions you answer correctly. With no penalty for guessing, you won't want to leave any item unanswered.

When should the test be taken?

Traditionally, teacher preparation programs determine when their candidates take the required tests for teacher certification. These programs will also clear you to take the examinations and make final recommendations for certification to the Texas State Board for Educator Certification (SBEC).

A candidate seeking EC-6 certification may take the appropriate Core Subjects test at such time as his or her Educator Preparation Program (EPP) determines the candidate's readiness to take the test, or upon successful completion of the EPP, whichever comes first. The EPP will determine readiness through benchmarks and structured assessments of the candidates' progress throughout the preparation program.

For those seeking certification right out of college, the TExES 291 Core Subjects EC–6 is generally taken just before graduation. Taking TExES examinations is a requirement to teach in Texas, so if you are planning on being an educator, you must take and pass these tests.

How do I register for the test?

To register for the TExES 291 test, you must create an account in the Pearson online registration system. Registration will then be available to you online, 24/7, during the regular, late, and emergency registration periods. Visit Pearson's TExES website at *www.tx.nesinc.com* and follow the instructions.

The TExES Registration Bulletin provides information about test dates and locations, as well as information on registration and testing accommodations for those with special needs. The registration bulletin is available at *www.tx.nesinc.com.*

Registration bulletins are also available at the education departments of Texas colleges and universities. To address issues that cannot be solved at the teacher preparation program level, you can contact the offices of SBEC at (888) 863-5880 or (512) 469-8400.

You must pay a registration fee to take the TExES tests, and you will also incur additional late fees if registering after the scheduled date.

What's the passing score?

There are 267 multiple-choice questions on the TExES 291 test. Your score on each of the TExES 291's subtests (test codes 801 to 805) will be reported on a 100-300 scale. A scaled score of 240 is set as the minimum passing score. To put this in context, you want to be confident you can answer between 70% and 80% of the questions correctly. To achieve the 70% level, you must get 190 questions correct; to reach the 80% level, you need to get 214 questions correct. As you work your way through our practice tests, scores in this range will suggest that you are sufficiently absorbing the test content. On the actual test, 32 of the 267 questions are being field-tested and thus will not be scored. There is no holistic score for the full Core Subjects EC-6 battery; overall results are reported as "pass" or "not pass" because, as Pearson puts it, "there is no total scaled score for the overall exam."

If you do not get a passing score on the practice test, study the detailed explanations for the questions you answered incorrectly. Note which types of questions you answered wrong, and re-examine the corresponding review content. After further review, you may want to retake the practice test.

When will I receive my score report?

As part of the registration process to take TExES examinations, test candidates set up an account with Pearson in which they are assigned a username and password. Use this account to access your score report information on Pearson's TExES website. Score reports will be posted by 5 p.m. CT on the score reporting date and will be available for 90 days.

What if I don't pass each subject area subtest?

You must pass all parts of the Core Subjects EC-6 test in order to meet the examination requirement for Texas's Core Subjects EC-6 certificate. If you don't do well on every part of the Core Subjects test, don't panic. You can retake the entire test or any individual subject area subtests up to four times. Both options require a 45-day waiting period after the first and subsequent attempts. You are given four attempts to retake all portions of the Core Subjects exams. After the first attempt, each testing session counts as another try, regardless of whether the session includes the entire exam or one of the subject area subtests. Candidates retaking the entire Core Subjects battery must literally view (but not answer) all of the test questions in each subtest, "even if they have previously passed one or more of the subject area subtests," says the Texas Education Agency.

How should I prepare for the test?

It is never too early to start studying for the TExES. The earlier you begin, the more time you will have to sharpen your skills. Do not procrastinate. Cramming is not an effective way to study, since it does not allow you the time needed to learn the test material. It is important for you to choose the time and place for studying that works best for you. Be consistent and use your time wisely. Work out a study routine and stick to it.

When you take REA's practice test, simulate the conditions of the actual test as closely as possible. Turn your television and radio off, and go to a quiet place free from distraction. Read each question carefully, consider all answer choices, and pace yourself.

After completing the test, thoroughly review the explanations to the questions you answered incorrectly. But don't overdo it. Take one problem area at a time; review it until you are confident that you have mastered the material. Give extra attention to the areas giving you the most difficulty, as this will help build your score.

Because the TExES 291 test covers content areas in grades EC-6, you should review the state curricula for these grades (Texas Essential Knowledge and Skills) available at *http://www.tea.state.tx.us*.

It is also important to familiarize yourself with the released examinations that students in grades 3 to 6 take to demonstrate mastery of the state curriculum. These tests are released after each administration. The released tests for grades 3 to 6 are available at *http://www.tea.state.tx.us*.

TEXES CORE SUBJECTS EC-6 (291) STUDY SCHEDULE

Week	Activity
1–3	Study the review chapters. Useful study techniques include highlighting key terms and information and taking notes as you read the review. Reinforce your mastery of the competencies by making flashcards that target your weakest areas.
4	Take the practice test battery. Score your tests and identify topics where you need more review.
5	Reread all your notes, refresh your understanding of the test's competencies and skills, review your college textbooks, and read class notes you've taken. This is also the time to consider any other supplementary materials that your advisor or the Texas Education Agency suggests. Review the agency's website at *http://www.tea.state.tx.us/*.
6	Retake the practice tests in the subjects in which you need to lift your performance. Score your test and restudy the appropriate review section(s) until you are confident you understand the material.

Are there any breaks during the test?

Although there is no designated break during the Core Subjects test, you do have a little time to use for the restroom or snacking or stretching outside the testing room. As you can see from the table on page 3, the total time allotted for all the subtests is 4 hours and 40 minutes. But the grand total for the entire testing period is 5 hours. That leaves you 20 minutes to make your own break.

Bear in mind the following:

- You need to get permission to leave the testing room.

- You cannot take a break during any of the subtests – only between tests.

- The overall test clock never stops.

- The timer for individual subtests starts only when you begin a test.

- Consult your test admission materials for further details, including updates from Pearson.

What else do I need to know about test day?

The day before your test, check for any updates in your Pearson testing account. This is where you'll learn of any changes to your reporting schedule or if there's a change in the test site.

On the day of the test, you should wake up early after a good night's rest. Have a good breakfast and dress in layers that can be removed or added as the conditions in the test center require.

Arrive at the test center early. This will allow you to relax and collect your thoughts before the test, and will also spare you the anguish that comes with being late. As an added incentive to make sure that you arrive early, keep in mind that no one will be admitted into the test center after the test has begun.

Before you leave for the testing site, carefully review your registration materials. Make sure you bring your admission ticket and two unexpired forms of identification. Primary forms of ID include:

- Passport

- Government-issued driver's license

- State or Province ID card

- National ID card

- Military ID card

You may need to produce a supplemental ID document if any questions arise with your primary ID or if your primary ID is otherwise valid but lacks your full name, photo, and signature. Without proper identification, you will not be admitted to the test center.

Strict rules limit what you can bring into the test center to just your ID; we recommend that you consult the Texas Education Agency's "Texas Educator Certification Registration Bulletin" for a complete rundown. You may not bring watches of any kind, cellphones, smartphones, or any other electronic communication devices or weapons of any kind. Scrap paper, written notes, books, and any printed material is prohibited.

No smoking, eating, or drinking is allowed in the testing room. Consider bringing a small snack and a bottle of water to partake of beforehand to keep you sharp during the test.

Good luck on the TExES Core Subjects EC-6 test!

Proven Test-Taking Strategies for TExES Core Subjects

1. Guess Away

One of the most frequently asked questions about the TExES Core Subjects test is: Can I guess? The answer: absolutely! There is no penalty for guessing on the test. That means if you refrain from guessing, you may lose points. To guess smartly, use the process of elimination (see Strategy No. 2). Your score is based strictly on the number of correct answers. So answer all questions and take your best guess when you don't know the answer.

2. Process of Elimination

Process of elimination is one of the most important test-taking strategies at your disposal. Process of elimination means looking at the choices and eliminating the ones you know are wrong, including answers that are partially wrong. Your odds of getting the right answer increase from the moment you're able to get rid of a wrong choice.

3. All in

Review all the response options. Just because you believe you've found the correct answer—or, in some cases, answers—look at each choice so you don't mistakenly jump to any conclusions. If you are asked to choose the *best* answer, be sure your first answer is really the best one.

4. Choice of the Day

What if you are truly stumped and can't use the process of elimination? It's time to pick a fallback answer. On the day of the test, choose the position of the answer (e.g., the third of the four choices) that you will pick for any question you cannot smartly guess. According to the laws of probability, you have a higher chance of getting an answer right if you stick to one chosen position for the answer choice when you have to guess an answer instead of randomly picking one.

5. Use Choices to Confirm Your Answer

The great thing about multiple-choice questions is that the answer has to be staring back at you. Have an answer in mind and use the choices to *confirm* it. For the Math test, in the cases in which you're given a problem to solve, try to find the match among the choices. Or try the opposite: *backsolving*—that is, working backwards—from the choices given.

6. Watch the Clock

Among the most vital point-saving skills is active time management. The breakdown and time limits of each section are provided as you begin each test. Keep an eye on the timer on your computer screen. Make sure you stay on top of how much time you have left for each section and never spend too much time on any one question. Remember: Most multiple-choice questions are worth one raw point. Treat each one as if it's the one that will put you over the top. You never know, it just might. The last thing you want on test day is to lose easy points because you ran out of time and focused too much on difficult questions.

7. Read, Read, Read

It's important to read through all the multiple-choice options. Even if you believe answer choice A is correct, you can misread a question or response option if you're rushing to get through the test. While it is important not to linger on a question, it is also crucial to avoid giving a question short shrift. Slow down, calm down, read all the choices. Verify that your choice is the best one, and click on it.

8. Take Notes

Use the scratch paper provided to you to make notes to work toward the answer(s). If you use all the scratch paper you're initially given, you can get more.

9. Isolate Limiters

Pay attention to any limiters in a multiple-choice question stem. These are words such as *initial*, *best*, *most* (as in *most appropriate* or *most likely*), *not*, *least*, *except*, *required*, or *necessary*. Especially watch for negative words, such as "Choose the answer that is *not* true." When you select your answer, double-check yourself by asking how the response fits the limitations established by the stem. Think of the stem as a puzzle piece that perfectly fits only the response option(s) that contain the correct answer. Let it guide you.

10. It's Not a Race

Ignore other test-takers. Don't compare yourself to anyone else in the room. Focus on the items in front of you and the time you have left. If someone finishes the test 30 minutes early, it does not necessarily mean that person answered more questions correctly than you did. Stay calm and focus on *your* test. It's the only one that matters.

11. Confirm Your Click

In the digital age, many of us are used to rapid-clicking, be it in the course of emailing or gaming. Look at the screen to be sure to see that your mouse-click is acknowledged. If your answer doesn't register, you won't get credit. However, if you want to mark it for review so you can return later, that's your call. Before you click "Submit," use the test's review screen to see whether you inadvertently skipped any questions.

12. Creature of Habit? No Worries.

We are all creatures of habit. It's therefore best to follow a familiar pattern of study. Do what's comfortable for you. Set a time and place each day to study for this test. Whether it is 30 minutes at the library or an hour in a secluded corner of your local coffee shop, commit yourself as best you can to this schedule every day. Find quiet places where it is less crowded, as constant background noise can distract you. Don't study one subject for too long, either. Take an occasional breather and treat yourself to a healthy snack or some quick exercise. After your short break—5 or 10 minutes can do the trick—return to what you were studying or start a new section.

13. Knowledge is Power

Purchasing this book gave you an edge on passing the TExES Core Subjects test. Make the most of this edge. Review the sections on how the test is structured, what the directions look like, what types of questions will be asked, and so on. Take our practice tests to familiarize yourself with what the test looks and feels like. Most test anxiety occurs because people feel unprepared when they are taking the test, and they psych themselves out. You can whittle away at anxiety by learning the format of the test and by knowing what to expect. Fully simulating the test even once will boost your chances of getting the score you need. Meanwhile, the knowledge you've gained will also will save you the valuable time that would have been eaten up puzzling through what the directions are asking As an added benefit, previewing the test will free up your brain's resources so you can focus on racking up as many points as you can.

14. B-r-e-a-t-h-e

Anxiety is neither unusual nor necessarily unwelcome on a test. Just don't let it stifle you. Take a moment to breathe. This won't merely make you feel good. The brain uses roughly three times as much oxygen as muscles in the body do: Give it what it needs.

Now consider this: What's the worst that can happen when you take a test? You may have an off day, and despite your best efforts, you may not pass. Well, the good news is that this test can be retaken. Fortunately, the TExES Core Subjects test is something you can study and prepare for, and in some ways to a greater extent than other tests you've taken throughout your academic career. In fact, study after study has validated the value of test preparation. Yes, there will be questions you won't know, but neither your teacher education program nor state licensing board (which sets its own cut scores) expects you to know everything. When unfamiliar vocabulary appears or difficult math problems loom, don't despair: Use context clues, process of elimination, or your response option of the day (i.e., choose either A, B, C, or D routinely when you need to resort to a guess) to make your choice, and then press ahead. If you have time left, you can always come back to the question later. If not, relax. It is only one question on a test filled with many.

Take a deep breath and then exhale. You know this information. Now you're going to show it.

Subject Test I: English Language Arts and Reading & the Science of Teaching Reading (801)

COMPETENCY 001: ORAL LANGUAGE

The teacher understands the importance of oral language, knows the developmental processes of oral language, and provides the students with varied opportunities to develop listening and speaking skills.

When children come to school, virtually all of them will be able to speak and listen in at least one language. In acquiring oral language, children gain mastery of the sounds of the language, the **phonemes**, and how sounds can be combined. Children also will gain a knowledge of **semantics**, or the ways meaning is generated in a language, which includes not only the meanings of words, but also the way words, phrases, and sentences combine in ways that make sense. Additionally, children learn how words can be placed together, or the **syntax** of the language.

In learning how to speak and listen, children do more than imitate the words they hear. Children learn the underlying principles for how words can be combined, which makes it possible for language learners to understand sentences they have never heard before and to produce sentences they have never said before. However, parents, caretakers, and others play an invaluable role in children's language acquisition. Children hear language being used, or are provided modeling. Also, children are provided real reasons to communicate.

Language acquisition results from the combination of three main components: innate abilities and mechanism of the learner, exposure to the speech of caretakers and parents, and the interaction of children in their immediate linguistic environment. The way that children acquire language suggests that humans are born with the abilities and mechanism to do so. Linguist Noam Chomsky called this mechanism a Language Acquisition Device (LAD). Chomsky said humans possess an **"internal grammar,"** or set of linguistic principles, that are activated potentially for all languages. The LAD is considered universal. It adapts to the language(s) being exposed or learned. However, linguists have argued that language only emerges if this internal mechanism is triggered by stimuli from people in the child's environment.

Young children frequently do replicate someone's behaviors, actions, and language usage. In language acquisition, young learners produce language by observing and replicating their caregiver's phrases and words. However, such **imitation** alone does not account for the complexity of children's language development. Toddlers test language rules on their own to figure how language works. Imitation alone cannot explain such idiosyncratic statements as "I 'goed' out yesterday." These nonstandard utterances show that the child is field-testing language rules. In this case, the child is testing the rule for forming the regular past tense and has applied it to an irregular verb. Such overgeneralization characterizes first language acquisition during most early childhood, and these show how children assume an active, constructive role in language acquisition. Direct language instruction and/or correction does not account for the complexity of the acquisition of oral language. Instead, through meaningful interactions with others and real reasons for using language, children figure out how language works.

Language Is Learned in Social Settings

Participation in conversation provides children with the vocabulary and the format of conversations they need to develop oral language (Stewig & Jett-Simpson, 1995). Parents and others do not always engage in direct language teaching but instead help the child's language acquisition by communicating with the child. Because of this linguistic support, virtually all children acquire at least one language before they come to school. However, differences exist among children because some children have richer oral language experiences in their homes and communities. These differences in oral language experiences can account for differences in their oral language abilities. A shy or reticent child may have a strong level of oral language development, so shyness should not be confused with ability. At the same time, teachers need to know that some children will rely more upon schooling to develop further their oral language abilities. Children who are brought up in a society in which participation in adults' conversations is restricted might not have the same language development and most likely will begin school behind their classmates.

Children Are Concerned with Meaning

Children quickly understand that the main purpose of language is communication. Attempts to correct grammar usage have little impact in language development in early childhood. Young learners expect language to make sense and rely on sympathetic listeners to understand them. Therefore, modeling and avoiding error correction is always the best way to support language development in young children. In other words, children will gain an understanding of how to use language by engaging in meaningful language situations. By providing a model of conventional language or standard language, children will gain understanding.

Language Components

Teachers must develop a clear understanding of language to support the formal linguistic development of young children. To accomplish this goal, teachers ought to develop a clear understanding of the six key components: phonology, morphology, syntax, lexicon, pragmatics and semantics.

Phonology is the study of the sound system of a language. The basic units of sound are called phonemes. **Graphemes** or individual letters represent **phonemes**. For example, the word *through* has seven graphemes (i.e., letters) that represent only three sounds /th,r,u/. Teacher candidates should be able not only to differentiate these two terms, but they should also make their students aware of the difference between letters in a word and the sounds that the letters represent. English has 26 graphemes to represent about 44 phonemes. Consequently, children must be able to connect these letters to identify sounds of individual words, phrases, and sentences.

Morphology is the study of the structure of words and word formation. Morphemes are the smallest representation of meaning. For example, the word *cars* is made up of two **morphemes**: the basic word or root word "car" and the plural morpheme "s." Having an understanding of the morphology of a language will help students when they are required to decode and understand printed information.

Syntax entails the ways in which words are organized and arranged in a language. English has specific basic sentence structures. Examples of the four most common sentence patterns in English can be found in Table 3-1.

Table 3-1. Basic Sentence Patterns

Noun	Verb	Predicate
Katrina (Subject)	was (Intransitive Verb)	a hurricane (Predicate Nominative)
The hurricane (Subject)	was (Intransitive Verb)	destructive (Predicate Adjective)
FEMA (Subject)	provided (Transitive Verb)	lodging to the people. (Direct Object) (Indirect Object)
Spike Lee (Subject)	won (Transitive Verb)	an award. (Direct Object)

Lexicon refers to the vocabulary of a language. Because the meanings of words change based on context and historical framework, vocabulary is said to be one of the most variable and rich components of a language. For example, the word *hot* can have several meanings. These include high temperature, sexy, fashionable, and lucky (e.g., a "hot streak"). In a few years, any of the meanings might change or become obsolete.

Pragmatics describes how context can affect the interpretation of communication. Pragmatics describes the hidden rules of communication understood by native speakers of the same language. Native speakers often call these rules "common sense rules." However, these rules might be only common to native speakers. These rules are not immediately evident to ELLs. Thus, teachers should again introduce these rules within context.

Take, for example, a greeting exchange. In English, one person greets another with such routine statements as "How are you?" Pragmatically, the receiver is expected to answer with such generic statements as "Not bad," "I'm OK," or "Fine." When such an exchange of words is completed, the conversation is expected to end. However, ELLs and people new to the culture might misinterpret the routine question as a literal inquiry and try to answer it directly. They will often provide more information than the greeter expected.

Semantics refers to how meaning is conveyed in a language through the use of its vocabulary. The meaning of words is also based on culture as well as the context of the conversation taking place. Connotation and denotation are used in a language to convey meaning.

Connotation refers to the implied meaning of words and ideas, and speakers must have knowledge of the culture to understand an expression's implied meaning. Idiomatic expressions are an example of how usage implies meaning as a communication tool. Having this prior knowledge often presents a challenge to ELLs because they lack the familiarity with American culture that native speakers generally have. For instance, the idiom "it's raining cats and dogs" may confuse ELLs who do not have the cultural knowledge to be familiar with this. Thus, teachers should teach idioms in context so that students can understand them and learn to use them. Teachers also must describe the idiom, especially its intended meaning, so that students fully understand its use.

Denotation refers to the literal meaning of words and ideas. For instance, a sign that reads "Dog contained by invisible fence." might be confusing for those not aware of this new technology. They might try to touch to see if they can find the "invisible fence." However, pragmatically, this phrase requires people to go beyond the literal meaning of the phrase and understand that whoever posted the sign meant that the dog is contained with an electronic device, not necessarily with a fence.

The *Amelia Bedelia* series written by Peggy Parish is about a character who understands everything only literally (i.e., denotation). Her limited understanding creates many communication problems and comedic situations.

Stages of First Language Development

First language acquisition is characterized by stages of development and maturation. These stages are influenced by the learner's level and quality of exposure to the native language. Therefore, assigning an exact age for each language-development stage can be challenging. However, linguistic milestones can identify these stages and develop a working framework for readers. A description of these stages follows.

Babbling or Pre-Language Stage (0–6 months)

Children at the **pre-language stage** send and receive messages and use reflexive crying to communicate with caregivers. They play vocally by producing multiple linguistic and nonlinguistic sounds (e.g., mmm, dada). Infants (0–2 years) can identify the voices of parents and family members, and they can follow certain commands. They also begin understanding the intonation patterns used to convey anger or excitement and the patterns used to ask questions.

Holophrastic or One-Word Stage (11–19 months)

Children at the **one-word stage** imitate the inflections and facial expressions of adults. They recognize their name and follow simple instructions presented in context. Children use adults as tools by pointing to objects and requesting help. They understand **word concepts** and use these to conceptualize complete ideas.

Two-Word Stage (13–24 months)

At the **two-word stage**, children produce rudimentary phrases. These constructions are characterized by a combination of two types of words—pivot and open words. Pivot refers to words that can accomplish multiple functions, i.e., no, up, all, see, more, and gone. The open class contains words that refer to one concept. Words like home, milk, doggy, juice, pants, and shoe are used, mainly to refer to one situation. Based on the vocabulary limitations of this stage, children use combinations of these two classes to create the subject and the predicate of the sentence. Some possible examples of utterances produced at this stage are "See baby," "See mommy," "No more," and "All gone."

Telegraphic Stage (18–27 months)

The **telegraphic stage** represents a higher degree of linguistic development in which the child goes beyond the use of two-word communication in their speech. Most words used at this stage are content words with high semantic value (convey more meaning) that can be used in multiple situations. Function words include nouns, adjectives, and verbs. At this stage children use content words as they have heard them used. The use of such function words as prepositions and articles, however, is limited at this stage because they do not convey as much information as content words.

The typical sentence at this stage consists of subject, verb, object or adjective format. Some possible examples of utterances produced at this stage are "hello there," "milk all gone," and "that's not nice."

Ages Two to Three

At age two, children have about 200 to 300 words in their linguistic repertoire and can produce short sentences. At this point, children use prepositions and pronouns with some inconsistency. The vocabulary of 3-year-olds grows to about 900 to 1,000 words. Three-year-olds begin creating three- or four-word sentences. They can follow two-step commands and engage in short dialogues about familiar topics. In schools with programs for 3-year-olds, children get exposed to informal and formal registers, variants of a language used for a particular purpose depending on the social setting. Children at this age, request instead of demand, use courteous vocabulary, and follow conversation formats.

Age Four

Four-year-olds have about 1,500 words in their speaking repertoire. They use more complex sentence structures, but their speech still contains pronunciation problems as well as overgeneralizations.

Four-year-olds understand more than what they can verbalize. They can answer factual questions in contextualized situations but have difficulties explaining the rationale for their answers.

Age Five

Five-year-olds have a vocabulary of about 2,100 words and a working knowledge of the grammar of the language. They may have problems dealing with compound sentences and sentences with embedded meaning. They are learning to understand time and use verbs accordingly. Most children at this stage have mastered the use of the progressive (-*ing*), regular past tense (-*ed*), and plurals (-*s*). Irregular verbs still constitute a challenge for 5-year-olds. They can identify and produce specific sounds and blends (combinations of phonemes such as in the word *block*). The vocabulary continues to increase as children have more contact with peers and teachers in school.

Ages Six and Seven

Six- to 7-year-old children have a speaking vocabulary of about 2,100 words and a comprehension vocabulary of more than 20,000 words. Children use well-constructed sentences using all parts of speech. They still might have problems with certain words and structures, but their speech is fluent and clear. However, speakers at this age might still have problems with words containing sounds like /v/, /th/, /ch/, and /sh/. Some children will use the sound of the /w/ in place of the required /r/ and /l/ sounds. They can separate words into syllables and decode written language. They can understand and address questions that call for reasons for an action. For example, they can explain their actions and answer such questions as "Why did you pick number five as the answer?" After age six, children continue to polish their language skills and add new and more sophisticated vocabulary.

Ages Eight to Twelve

The speaking repertoire of 8- to 12-year-olds continues to grow and to improve as their communication changes from using language to have their needs met to becoming language makers in academic settings. Eight-year-olds begin using relative pronoun clauses (i.e., The boy whom you met yesterday is my friend). They also use subordinated clauses that begin with *when, if,* and *because* (i.e., If you bother me, I am going to tell the teacher). At age nine, the use of the gerund has become common for speakers (i.e., Cheating is bad). Children use more complex sentences, vocabulary, and verb construction. Their speech is more coherent through the use of connectors and transition words.

At ages 10 through 12, students can make use of roots, prefixes, and suffixes to understand new words in the language.

The Connection Between Speaking, Listening, and Reading

In any given language, meaning is created through socially shared conventions. During the first months of life, babies are active listeners. Long before they can respond orally, however, they communicate nonverbally by waving their arms, smiling, or wiggling. They are also capable of communicating their needs and wants through nonverbal communication, including body language and crying. Through listening, they develop the receptive language needed to communicate orally.

Although listening is used extensively in communication, it does not get much attention at school. Although no well-defined model exists for teaching listening skills, some theorists link listening skills to reading skills. Reading and listening both entail receiving language and making use of similar language comprehension. Listening and reading both require the use of skills in phonology, syntax, and semantics as well as knowledge of the structure of text. Both language skills also seem to be controlled by the same cognitive processes. Several studies suggest that the teaching of listening can be done by engaging in activities similar to those used to develop speaking, reading, and writing proficiencies. For example, teachers can guide students' listening activities by setting a purpose for listening, providing questions before and after the listening activity, and encouraging children to forge links between the new information just heard and the knowledge already in place.

Children also need to be coached in the use of appropriate volume and speed when they speak and in the rules required to participate in discussions as well as the culturally defined rules for maintaining a polite conversation. In American culture, such rules include staying on a topic and taking turns without interrupting speakers.

Effective listening experiences can be integrated into all areas of the curriculum to enhance learning while also building children's listening abilities. Teachers also can provide additional listening experience by having children listen as the audience in different formats, with another individual, in small groups, and in whole-class situations. Teachers also can expand listening experiences by providing listening experiences in formal and informal contexts and by varying the purposes for listening, such as to gain information, solve problems, and/or interact with classmates.

Teachers can read aloud quality literature daily to provide different purposes for listening and to enhance learning throughout the curriculum. All grade levels should hear their teacher read aloud to them daily. Reading aloud is among the most effective ways to build academic vocabulary because written words can exceed those used in daily oral communication. Reading aloud also builds listening comprehension, which then provides for reading comprehension. In oral communication, children most often are exposed to shorter segments of language as they talk and listen. If children do not get experience at listening to someone reading aloud to them, they will be unprepared for the longer, more sophisticated written texts they will encounter in their education. All these activities can guide students to listen, which can also improve their speaking ability.

Activities to Promote Oral Communication

The best way to promote oral communication is to guide students into using language in meaningful situations. In the classroom, teachers can organize activities to resemble real-life situations to promote communication among students. The previous discussion of listening comprehension provides ways to incorporate oral language development as part of teaching across the curriculum. Other valuable examples of activities are described as follows.

Dramatic Play

Dramatic play using prompts is an ideal activity to develop communication. In dramatic play, students get opportunities to role-play in simulations of real life. Students may get either a specific role to play or be asked to improvise roles. For example, one child can play the role of a parent, another the role of a student in trouble, and a third the role of a teacher.

Language Play

Language play involves the use of language in rhyme, alliteration, songs, and repetitive patterns to amuse children. Tongue twisters are commonly used to practice pronunciation and language patterns. Through these activities, children acquire language knowledge in a relaxed and fun environment. Teachers can also use nursery rhymes, poems, and stories that contain rhyme to introduce these language features.

Show-and-Tell

In **show-and-tell**, children bring artifacts and personal items to class. Children show objects and describe them to the class. In addition to the benefit of oral communication, this activity can promote both home and cultural pride as well as multicultural awareness.

Puppet Show

Hand, finger, and string puppets can promote communication and confidence among children. **Puppet shows** let students communicate orally by using the puppet as a tool to convey information. The use of puppets is also an enjoyable and motivating activity for learners, especially young ones.

"Turn and Talk"

Traditionally, teachers have asked the entire group a question or set of questions as part of providing learning experiences. Many children are reluctant to share because they are not confident in talking in a whole-group setting in school, but they could gain in confidence and ability when given the opportunity to talk and listen with another classmate first. "Turn and Talk" can be used when the teacher would like students to think more about a topic or experience. Rather than an individual child answering the teacher's question, children turn and talk to a partner to help crystallize their thinking and develop their oral language abilities. After talking with a partner, the children then can share what they talked about with the whole group. For example, after the children have learned about the function of the bark of the tree one day in science, the teacher could ask the children to turn and talk about one thing they learned. Then the children could share and talk as a whole group. The teacher also could write to record a list of ideas that could be reviewed in later lessons of the unit on trees.

"Turn and Talk" works best when the teacher makes sure all students have partners who can help them grow in speaking and listening. For example, it may be best to place a reticent child with a child who is confident but also supportive. Teachers also should help students learn about how to be a polite listener. Providing a demonstration of how to "turn and talk" also provides invaluable help for students. Many teachers use this strategy in situations where the children can address what needs to be addressed in 30 to 60 seconds, or through a brief talking situation. However, letting students talk with a partner or work together could be a part of classroom learning also for longer periods of time.

Interviews

Pair interview is an additional strategy that can promote oral communication. This strategy pairs children to learn information from each other and then report their findings to the class. Depending on the children's age, the responses gathered during the pair interview can also be recorded in writing to be used later in the children's presentation. This strategy can be used throughout the year and for different classroom activities. For example, students need to get to know each other on the first day of school, and they could interview each other. Interviews also could be used for other projects where students interview people in their family or community to learn more about a topic or time period. Teachers can help students succeed by modeling and by providing examples of questions that can be used.

Oral Presentations

Preparing children to communicate what they think and know is common practice in classrooms. Depending on the children's age, the expectations surrounding the ways in which they share this information orally will vary. For instance, kindergarten teachers should not expect their students to deliver a 20-minute presentation. Instead, giving their students an opportunity to deliver presentations in a nonthreatening environment and activity (e.g., show-and-tell) can lead them to appreciate the art of public speaking from a young age. As children advance in elementary school, the expectations change. For instance, elementary students are expected to use correct language when speaking and have accurate information when creating a presentation. Students thus are expected to find reliable information and sources when investigating a topic of their choice or one that has been assigned. Elementary students also learn that the topic of a presentation can be delivered to different audiences. Students must get opportunities to understand how a presentation should be modified to meet the needs of their audience. For example, children can be led to prepare a short presentation to inform other children at their school why recycling is important to the environment and ask them to start a recycling project in their classrooms. These same students then could be asked to revise their presentation to deliver it to members of the school board and/or the school principal so that they can receive the resources needed to start the recycling project in their school. Students also can learn ways to create presentations (e.g., incorporating electronic media). Regardless of the presentation, students should be able to communicate to different audiences.

Assessing Speaking Ability

Intelligibility

A child's speaking ability is assessed informally in class as part of daily activities and conversations. First, teachers must determine whether the child's speech is intelligible and can be understood by native speakers with minimum effort. Developmental issues, the use of dialectical variations, and speech disorders can cause intelligibility problems for native speakers. To assess the child's speech, teachers need an understanding of the developmental patterns in language mastery and use these patterns as a foundation for assessing the child's performance. Teachers should also develop an understanding of the features of dialects spoken in the community to avoid confusion with features that contrast with Standard English. For example, speakers of **African American Vernacular English** (AAVE) and speakers of the **Boston dialect** drop the /r/ after a vowel. One example of this is in the statement ". . . park the car in Harvard yard," which, spoken by a Bostonian may sound more like "[Pahk the kah in Hahvud yahd.]" In this case, the omission of post-vocalic

/r/ cannot be identified as a pronunciation problem. Teachers thus need a working knowledge of the dialects used in the community to make accurate assessments of children's speech.

Language Interference

Teachers must account for how the first language of an ELL may interfere in the pronunciation of English. Phonologically, language interference can happen at the word or sentence level. The most noticeable language interference happens when students use the phonology of their first language to pronounce words in English. For example, most Spanish dialects do not use the /v/ sound and instead replace it with the /b/ sound. This feature creates semantic problems when native Spanish speakers pronounce the English word "vowel" as "bowel," which can discomfit the speaker. Korean and Japanese speakers might also experience language interference when using the English /r/ sound because this sound is not present in their language. Chinese has both the /r/ and /l/ sounds, but native Chinese speakers may still experience problems with these two sounds when learning English. They sometimes substitute the /r/ with the /l/ sound. This feature can create semantic problems when native Chinese, Korean, and Japanese speakers pronounce the English word "rice" as "lice." A second interference can be caused by the application of incorrect word stress in English. For example, in Standard English most speakers will place the primary stress of the word *composition* on the second-to-last (penultimate) syllable \,käm-pə-'zi-shən\. However, Spanish speakers and speakers of Caribbean English might place the primary stress on the last syllable \,käm-pə-zi-'shən\, resulting in nonstandard English pronunciation. Thus, teachers must become aware of conflicting language sounds and provide appropriate language support to ELLs.

Communication Style and Culture

Culture plays an important role in how people communicate orally as well as in writing. In written and oral communication, English uses a linear rhetorical pattern that allows little flexibility to deviate from the topic. Other languages such as Spanish, Russian, and Arabic allow for a more flexible progression to convey information. This flexibility is identified as a curvilinear or associational style because it allows speakers the option of deviating from the main topic without being penalized. This cultural and linguistic difference can create problems in assessing the speaking and writing capabilities of children who are native speakers of languages other than English. Teachers must be vigilant to determine how the first language (L1) and culture affect the performance of children in the second language (L2).

Speaking Checklist

Students' speaking abilities can also be assessed in the classroom with a structured checklist identifying specific features that teachers want to observe. Lapp et al. (2001) developed an instrument to assess speaking ability called the Speaking Checklist. A summary of key elements is presented on the next page.

1. Sticks to the topic

2. Builds support for the subject

3. Speaks clearly

4. Takes turns and waits to talk

5. Talks so others in the group can hear

6. Speaks smoothly

7. Uses courteous language

8. Presents in an organized and interesting way

9. Supports the topical thesis

10. Answers questions effectively

11. Is comfortable speaking publicly

12. Maintains listeners' interest

13. Volunteers to answer in class

The Texas Education Agency (TEA) developed an instrument to comply with the accountability system of the Elementary and Secondary Education Act (i.e., No Child Left Behind). Termed the Texas English Language Proficiency Assessment System (TELPAS), this instrument is designed to assess the language development of ELLs in listening, speaking, reading, and writing (TEA, 2014–2015). TELPAS contains a checklist to assess the speaking component based on a four-point scale: Beginning, Intermediate, Advanced, and Advanced High. The checklist uses a holistic rating to assess not only the speaking ability, but also the listening and writing abilities in grades K–12 (TEA, 2014–2015). Students must score at the Advanced High level to be considered fully fluent. To receive the Advanced High rating in the speaking subtest of TELPA, students should be able to:

1. participate in extended discussion in social and grade-appropriate academic topics;

2. communicate using abstract and concrete content-based vocabulary during classroom instruction;

3. use complex English grammar structures and complex sentences at a level comparative to native speakers; and

4. minimize pronunciation or linguistic errors that interfere with overall communication.

Communication Disorders

A **communication disorder** occurs when a person's speech interferes with his or her ability to convey messages during interactions with others. The four classifications of language disorders include those in voice, fluency, articulation, and language processing (Piper, 2006).

Voice Disorders

Voice disorders refer to any distortion of the pitch, timbre, or volume of spoken communication. The two types of voice disorders are phonation and resonance. **Phonation disorder** describes any abnormality in the vibration of the vocal fold. For example, hoarseness or extreme breathiness can interfere with comprehension. **Resonance disorder** describes abnormalities created when sound passes through the vocal tract. The most common resonance disorder occurs when the sound passing through the nasal cavity changes oral sounds to nasal. These are called hypernasal sounds. This disorder should not be confused with the nasal quality of Southern dialects such as the Texas twang.

Fluency Disorders

Fluency disorders refer to any condition that affects the child's ability to produce coherent and fluent communication. Stuttering and cluttering cause the most common fluency disorder. **Stuttering** is characterized by multiple false starts or the inability to produce the intended sounds. **Cluttering** occurs when children try to communicate too fast and thus make comprehension difficult. Teachers should be cautious when assessing ELLs who might experience such temporary fluency dysfunction as hesitations, false starts, and repetition, which can be attributed to anxiety or confusion with the two languages. For instance, ELLs may stutter because they cannot find or might not know the appropriate word in English. Allowing students to code-switch from English to their first language or providing them more wait time can be used as temporary remedies to stuttering. Additionally, children new to the language often use the intonation pattern and delivery speed of their native language. Thus, the delivery might become incomprehensible and be mistaken as cluttering.

Articulation Problems

The most common articulation disorder is lisping. **Lisping** is a term used when speakers produce the sound /s/, /sh/, /z/, and /ch/ with their tongue between the upper and lower teeth. Other sounds that can present challenges to children are the /w/, /l/, and /r/. Children may have problems with specific sounds that can cause unintelligibility and the production of aesthetically displeasing sounds. Some problems might be developmental and will eventually be eliminated, but others might require speech therapy. Elmer Fudd and Sylvester the Cat, two popular cartoon characters, exhibit these speech features (i.e., Sylvester's lisp and Elmer's difficulty with the /r/ sound as in "wabbit").

Language Processing Disorders

Language processing disorders are caused by a brain-based disturbance called **aphasia**. Three types of aphasia are known: receptive, expressive, and global. **Receptive aphasia**, or "sensory aphasia," results from a lesion to a region in the upper back part of the temporal lobe of the brain. Receptive aphasia creates problems with listening comprehension and retrieval of words from memory. People affected with this condition often repeat formulaic phrases and produce unintelligible sequences of words or sounds. **Expressive aphasia** results from damage to the lower back part of the frontal lobe. This damage affects speaking ability and causes specific problems with articulation and fluency. The speech is often slow and includes multiple hesitations as well as problems with the suprasegmental features of language, such as intonation, rhythm, and stress. The sentences are short and contain only the necessary features to convey the message. The speech resembles that of children at the telegraphic stage of first language development. **Global aphasia** is another brain-based disorder; it affects the receptive and expressive features of language. Children with this severe impairment of articulation and fluency produce minimal speech, and their comprehension is limited. This language disorder is also known as "irreversible aphasia," which suggests that little can be done to help children with this condition.

COMPETENCY 002: PHONOLOGICAL AND PHONEMIC AWARENESS

The teacher understands phonological and phonemic awareness and employs a variety of approaches to help students develop phonological and phonemic awareness.

Importance of Phonemic and Phonological Awareness for Reading and Writing

Phonemic and phonological awareness constitutes the foundation for the development of the metalinguistic awareness that children need to become successful language learners and effective readers, in a language that uses an alphabetic writing system, like English. When children read, they are required to segment, or separate sounds, such as in b-a-t when encountering a word, and readers also must blend, or combine sounds when saying *bat*. Children also must be aware of sounds of words when spelling a word. Children who are aware of the sounds of words will be better able to account for those sounds when they read and spell.

Phonological Awareness and Phonemic Awareness

Phonological awareness is the ability to recognize and manipulate components of the sound system and the structure of words. It includes the ability to segment words into syllables and phonemes. It also encompasses the ability to discriminate, remember, and manipulate words in sentences as well as sounds within a word. It also includes the ability to identify lexical stress in individual words as well as sentence stress.

Phonemic awareness refers to a child's ability to understand that words have smaller components called sounds (phonemes). It is a component of a large concept: phonological awareness. This awareness constitutes the basic linguistic principle required for the development of oral and written communication. When children understand this principle, they begin "cracking the linguistic code" and discover more sophisticated linguistic principles like phonological awareness. Children who have developed phonemic awareness can dissect a word into each phoneme and put it back to recreate the word. The ability to manipulate spoken words has been linked to successful reading development.

Syllabication

Syllabication is an important component of phonological awareness. It refers to the ability to conceptualize and separate words into syllables, which are their basic pronunciation components in English. Syllables can be as simple as one vowel or can be a combination of vowels and consonants. For example, the word *elegant* contains three syllables (el/e/gant), one of which is a vowel alone. Vowels are the heart of a syllable, and syllables constitute the basic unit of pronunciation. Syllables thus influence the rhythm of the language, poetic meter, and word stress. Syllabication can be taught using the appropriate voice intonation to indicate the beginning and end of a syllable. Teachers often clap to indicate syllable boundaries.

Lexical and Sentence Stress

English uses different stress levels to convey meaning at the word level (lexical) and at the phrase or sentence level (prosodic stress). An analysis of these levels of stress follows.

Lexical Stress

English has at last four levels of word stress—primary, secondary, tertiary, and quaternary. The identification of the primary and secondary stress is vital to produce a standard pronunciation. For example, if we examine the pronunciation of an uncommon name like *Copernicus,* most English speakers will have to think twice to identify the primary and secondary stress in the word. In this case, the name has four syllables \kō-'pər-ni-kəs\, and the primary stress is in the antepenultimate (third from right).

Phonemic Stress

Phonemic stress is a form of lexical stress in which the location of the stress in a word can change its meaning. For example, the word *present* has two meanings depending on how it is pronounced. With the stress on the first syllable \'pre-zənt\, it becomes a noun, but if the stress is placed on the last syllable \pri-əzent\, it becomes a verb.

Sentence Stress

Sentence stress and the intonation pattern used in sentences create another challenge for young learners and ELLs. In a typical sentence, content words (nouns, verbs, adjectives, and adverbs) are emphasized more than function words (articles, prepositions, and conjunctions). Sentence stress and the intonation pattern are commonly used to highlight a segment of the sentence or to modify the sentences. English speakers can use the same sentence to change the meaning. For example, in the sentence "She is BUYING the house," the speaker emphasizes the word BUYING. She does so to clarify that she is buying, not leasing, the house. In the same sentence, the speaker can emphasize or stress the word SHE, to imply that *she* and not anyone else is the one buying. Sentence stress also can change the classification of the utterances. For example, in the example below, when emphasizing the verb *are* makes the utterance a question, while a slight change of intonation to the pronoun *you* changes the utterance to the reply to the question.

EXAMPLE

Question: How **are** you?   Reply: How are **you**?

With time and appropriate instruction, lexical and word stress can be internalized. However, it requires adequate time and appropriate instruction. For young learners, teachers can use nursery rhymes, short poems, or stories like Humpty Dumpty of the Mother Goose nursery rhymes. The use of these rhythmic patterns in an enjoyable and relaxed environment introduces children to the sounds and music of language. Eventually, children will notice the ending of the words and how specific sounds relate to each other. Moreover, rhymes help ELLs as they develop phonemic awareness, as well as prosodic stress in phrases and sentences.

Alliteration is a technique to emphasize phonemes by using successive words that begin with the same consonant sound or letter. Tongue twisters are the best-known form of alliteration. Children can repeat tongue twisters for fun, and simultaneously develop an awareness of the sound-symbol correspondence. In the following example, the /p/ sound is emphasized:

Peter Piper picked a peck of pickled peppers.

Special Considerations when Teaching Phonemic and Phonological Awareness

It is easier to break sentences into words and break words into syllables than to break syllables into phonemes. This component constitutes the cornerstone of further language development. For that reason, instructors are advised to introduce phonological awareness first with simple concepts like rhyming and recognizing syllables before asking children to recognize and manipulate sounds of words. Instructors should consider using the following sequence when teaching phonological awareness.

- Guide children to recognize rhyming words heard in nursery rhymes and poems.

- Introduce syllable using counting, tapping, blending, or segmenting words into syllables.

- Introduce onset and rimes blending the two components in words like *b-at,* and *s-ad*.

- Guide children to identify initial sounds in words like *bed* /b/ and *cat* /c/.

- Model blending sounds and repeat the word slowly to see if students recognize them.

- Guide students to stretch the sounds to segment words like /b/ /e/ /d/.

- Begin teaching phonemic awareness by using short monosyllabic words. Introduce words with a consistent structure like consonant-vowel-consonant, i.e., *bat* and *cat*, before introducing more difficult ones.

- Begin segmenting short words into phonemes. When children understand this component of phonemic awareness, introduce syllabication and other components of phonological awareness.

- Introduce sounds in initial position, then sounds in final position, and finally (the most difficult ones) the phonemes in medial position.

- When teaching sound-symbol correspondence, introduce sounds that present the least chance for distortion. Sounds like the nasal /m/ and sibilant /s/ represent easier sounds for the child than the brief sounds created with stop sounds like /p/, /t/, and /k/.

Additional Strategies to Teach Phonemic and Phonological Awareness

Teachers can promote phonemic and phonological knowledge using the following list of strategies:

- Read poetry aloud to children to expose children to the music and cadence of language. Librarians can help teachers locate poetry that meets the interests and needs of students. Reading poetry aloud is among the best ways to develop phonemic and phonological awareness because students acquire these language components in an enjoyable and relaxed environment.

- Organize a writing center where students can write daily. When children write and use invented spelling, they develop phonemic awareness as they try to account for the sounds they hear. Even if the child's early efforts are unconventional, the child gains by accounting for sounds in the word. This is critical in learning to spell.

- Teach the child to isolate phonemes. Follow a pattern from the simplest to the most difficult. Begin with initial and final sounds and then add phonemes in middle position. Ask such questions as "What is the first sound of the word boy?"

- Guide children to blend sounds and come up with rhymes. Ask the child, "What word can you create when you blend the sounds *t* and *ake*, or *l* and *ake*."

- Introduce blending by guiding children to identify the word created when the following sounds are blended: /b/, /a/, and /t/.

- Guide children to identify a word like *tape* and then remove the onset (the first letter) and ask the class: "What word is left when we remove the first letter (*t*)?" (Answer: *ape*) Then ask students, "Is this a word?"

- Teach word segmentation by saying a word and then guiding children to identify the sounds they hear. Teachers can begin with simple monosyllabic words like *car* and then expand to more sophisticated words.

- Use onsets and rimes to teach the sound-symbol relationship. Guide children to create new words by substituting the first letter of monosyllabic words. For example, using the word *ring* the child can replace the initial sounds to create additional words *sing, king,* and *spring*. An activity like this can emphasize phonemic awareness and teach how word families can support vocabulary development.

- Introduce minimal pairs, which are sets of words that differ in only one phoneme like *pat* and *bat* to guide students to notice the difference. Teachers should pronounce both words and ask students if the words are the same or different. Start by contrasting words with initial consonant sounds, as in *pat* and *bat*. Then expand to include more sophisticated contrasting pairs, as in *bit* and *beet*.

Balanced Reading Program

The development of phonemic and phonological awareness is vital to prepare students for formal reading instruction. However, a reading program must go beyond these components to incorporate a balanced reading program (National Reading Panel, 2000). The balanced reading program encompasses best teaching practices from two traditionally opposing reading instruction programs: the skills-based approach, which emphasizes phonics instruction, and the meaning-based approach, which promotes reading comprehension and enrichment. The researchers concluded that a balanced reading program that incorporates the best principles of phonics (skills-based) and whole language (meaning-based) instruction can best address the reading needs of all children.

COMPETENCY 003: ALPHABETIC PRINCIPLE

The teacher understands the importance of the alphabetic principle for reading English and provides instruction that helps students understand the relationship between spoken language and printed words.

The alphabetic principle has been described as the ability to connect letters with sounds, and to create words based on these associations. Children learning to read also must develop an understanding that letters and letter patterns represent the sounds of spoken English (University of Oregon, n.d.). Understanding the ways in which these sound-symbol relationships are created helps them conceptualize that predictable connections exist between phonemes and graphemes.

How Is the Alphabetic Principle Learned?

Traditionally, children go through specific stages in learning new words and mastering the alphabetic principle (Ehri, 1998). Preschoolers are exposed to components of the alphabetic principle through their environment. They can identify the logo of stores like Walmart or Burger King by their design instead of by the specific letters contained in the logo. But because they are not connecting the letters and the sounds of the logo, this stage is considered a pre-alphabetic phase (University of Oregon, n.d.). At home, children might also be exposed to the alphabet song, which most of them learn subconsciously. Eventually, children engage in a partial alphabetic phase as they play with alphabet blocks and other concrete letter objects typical in early childhood programs. Children connect the shape of the letters with the sound they represent. Children are also often exposed to children's literature and books in which the sound-symbol correspondence is controlled. Children also connect initial letters with the sound of the names of peers, like the *N* of Nancy and *A* of Alex.

The next phase of learning new words is identified as the full alphabetic stage. At this stage, children connect the letters with the sounds they represent as well as the meaning of the word. Children get excited during this stage because they are beginning to "crack" the written code of the language. In the final and last stage of development, called the consolidated alphabetic stage, children conceptualize that they can use components of words they know to decode new words. They discover how they can create new words with onsets, rhymes, and other letter sequences.

One of the main purposes of phonics instruction at this stage is to guide children into understanding the connection between the grapheme and phoneme and the sequence that they create to form words and sentences. This knowledge enables students to expand the number of words they recognize instantly (sight words), and this prepares them for literacy.

Teaching the Grapheme-Phoneme Correspondence

The introduction of the grapheme-phoneme correspondence can be presented through games, songs, and other engaging activities, but eventually the correspondence should be presented explicitly. Teachers must bring the skills to the surface and make students aware of the concepts and skills they need to become effective readers. Teachers should account for the complexity of the language and the maturity level of the children when introducing them to the alphabetic principle. A list of considerations and strategies for teaching the grapheme-phoneme connection follows.

- The introduction of the letter-sound correspondence should be guided by the potential support of the children's efforts to become a reader. Introduce the spelling of the letters that the child is most likely to encounter in text. For example, the letters *m, a, t, s, p,* and *h* are used more frequently in writing than letters like *x* or *q* or consonant digraphs like *kn* or *gn*.

- Begin instruction in the grapho-phonemic relationship by using sounds that present the least possible distortion or confusion with other sounds. Sounds that are easier to perceive are the nasals /m/ and /n/, the fricative /f/, the sibilant /s/, and the English retroflex /r/.

- Teachers should postpone the introduction of less clear phonemes like the nasal /ng/, the distinction between the sibilants /s/ and /z/, the troublesome sounds in English like the voiced *th* in the word *them,* and the unvoiced counterpart in the word *think*.

- Introduce words with one or two consonants and one short vowel sound, such as in the words *on* and *car*. Later, long vowel sounds can be introduced.

- Add consonant blends like "try" next, followed by digraphs like *th, sh,* and *ch* in words such as *thanks, show,* and *chop*. Digraphs can lead students to recognize such common words as *this, she,* and *chair*. Introduce single consonants and consonant blends or clusters in separate lessons to avoid confusion.

- Avoid voiceless-stop sounds (/t/, /p/, /k/) at the beginning or middle of words because the short duration of these phonemes makes them difficult to perceive. Teachers should postpone the introduction of conflicting letter-sound correspondence of phonemes like the /b/ and v/ or /i/ and /e/ or visually confusing graphemes like the *b* and *d* or *p* and *g*.

Types of Writing Systems

Several classifications exist for writing systems. Three of the most commonly known writing systems are logographic, syllabic, and alphabetic writing. In logographic writing systems, words, ideas, and concepts are represented with a visual or graphic symbol. **Logographic writing** was the first type of written language developed in the history of civilizations. The multiple variations of the Chinese language are the best known example of a logographic writing system. The logograms (pictograms and ideograms) used in Mandarin Chinese are common to all dialectical variations of Chinese, including Cantonese. Around the world, simplified pictorial symbols are used as international symbols on roads and in public facilities. For example, a fork and a knife stand for food or a restaurant, and the figure of a man or woman identifies restroom facilities by gender. In **syllabic writing** systems, syllables are depicted through the use of unique symbols. Each symbol represents a syllable instead of a single phoneme. Some of the best known syllabic languages are: Cherokee, Japanese, Hmong, Thai, Lao, and Tibetan. The **alphabetic writing** system uses the sounds of the language as a basic unit for writing. English and most European languages use an alphabetic writing system based upon phonetic signs. Theoretically, each symbol represents one unit of sound in this system. However, this principle works better with languages that have consistent sound-symbol relationships. Many alphabetic languages like Spanish are more phonetically consistent than English. An analysis of the grapheme-phoneme correspondence of English follows.

The Grapheme-Phoneme Correspondence of English

The connection between graphemes and phonemes in English is not always consistent. English has 26 graphemes to represent about 44 phonemes. The consonant system is more consistent than the vowel system. English has five letters to represent 14 vowel sounds, including the diphthongs. This grapheme-phoneme correspondence makes decoding and pronunciation challenging for young learners as well as students new to the language. This inconsistency is partially caused by the evolution of the English language and the influence of multiple languages in the development of modern English. Teachers must be proactive and identify these troublesome areas and organize instruction to address them. Some potential concerns are as follow:

1. Graphemes can represent multiple phonemes. For example, the grapheme *s* can represent multiple phonemes: cars-/z/, calls-/z/, sugar-/sh/, mission-/sh/, and walks-/s/. This grapheme-phoneme inconsistency represents a challenge when trying to use a phonic approach to teach reading.

2. English has graphemes that represent a sound in some words, but remain silent in others. For example, often the graphemes *s* and *l* become silent without giving readers a reliable clue for this change: *island*, *calm*, and *palm*. (Some speakers will make an attempt to pronounce the /s/ and /l/ in these words.)

3. English has multiple vowel and consonant digraphs in which two letters represent one sound. This inconsistency presents a challenge to native English speakers as well as ELLs. Table 3-2 presents examples of common English digraphs.

Table 3-2. Vowel and Consonant Digraphs

Consonants Digraphs	Examples	Vowel Digraphs	Examples
Ch	Chair	oo	Book
Sh	Shirt	ea	Beach
Gh	Ghost	ee	Sheet
Pn	Pneumonia	ie	Pie
Ps	Psychology	oe	Toe
Wr	Write	ue	Blue

4. English speakers use multiple contractions in daily communication. These can create listening comprehension problems for students, especially ELLs. Teachers should introduce contractions together with the long version of the words to avoid confusion. Table 3-3 presents a few examples of the confusion contractions can cause.

Table 3-3. Contractions in English

Contractions	Regular Form	Possible Confusion
they're	they are	there and their
he's	he is	his
he'll	he will	hill, heel, heal
you're	you are	your

5. English has multiple words with consonant clusters beginning with *s*. Examples of these initial clusters are in the following words: speak, spring, splash, state, string, slate, smoke, snow and scripture. These clusters require students to blend the sounds while also recognizing the sounds of individual phonemes. These sounds represent a challenge for all ELLs, especially native Spanish speakers because Spanish has no words beginning with these letter sequences. In Spanish, these clusters occur only in medial positions and are always preceded by the vowel e. Examples can be found in the words *espero*, *escapar*, e*sprimir, escalar, estrategia,* and *estar*. Based on these features, Spanish-speaking English language learners will place the vowel *e* in front of English words with these initial consonant clusters, creating nonstandard pronunciation.

6. Several words in English end in consonant clusters (e.g., *rant, cord, first,* and *card*). Both young native English-speaking children and ELLs may have difficulty blending clusters at the end of the words. For native Spanish speakers, these clusters represent a unique challenge because Spanish does not have words ending in consonant clusters. Based on this feature, Spanish-speaking children, and possibly most children in early childhood, may simplify a final consonant cluster in English. For example, the word *board* might become *boar*.

COMPETENCY 004: LITERACY DEVELOPMENT

The teacher understands that literacy develops over time, progressing from emergent to proficient stages, and uses a variety of approaches to support the development of students' literacy.

Literacy development begins at home when parents read stories and create literacy opportunities for their children (Heath, 1983). Through such activities, parents help their children to hear the similarities and differences in the sounds of words. Because of linguistic stimulation, children manipulate and understand sounds in spoken language. Learners will practice this understanding by making up rhymes and creating words on their own. When children can follow the written text with the oral production, they learn the names of the letters and the different sounds that each letter represents. Finally, children link the letters of the alphabet with the sounds of the words they speak. At this point, children develop the phonemic and phonological awareness needed to become emergent readers.

Stages of Reading Development

Much research has been conducted on the stages of reading development. Three widely used labels for these stages include emergent readers, early readers, and fluent readers. Researchers have concluded that these stages are cumulative (Chall, 1983). Children thus must develop the skills and knowledge in each of these stages to use them in subsequent ones.

Emergent Readers

Emergent readers understand that print contains meaningful information. Emergent readers also show abilities such as the following:

1. Display basic reading readiness skills such as directionality movement (eye movement from left to right, top to bottom, and return sweep).

2. Point to words to make voice-print match.

3. Locate unknown and known words.

4. Use some initial and final consonant sounds in reading words.

5. Use illustrations, or picture clues, to support identifying words and comprehension.

6. Use story structure to make connections to print.

7. Use repeated phrases or patterns to read.

Early Readers (or Progressing Readers)

Early readers have mastered reading readiness skills, and they are beginning to read simple text with some success. They are also developing an internal list of high-frequency words in print. Their reliance on picture clues has decreased now that they can get more information from print. Children at this stage also can show abilities such as the following:

- Use the cuing system to confirm information in the text.

- Engage in self-correction when text does not make sense to them.

- Rely on grapho-phonemic information to sound words as a decoding strategy, using beginning, middle, and ending letter-sound correspondences.

- Read familiar texts with fluency, including appropriate phrasing and intonation.

- Notice features, such as punctuation and capitalization, from language and text as well as the use of bold print and variation in format.

- Retell stories read to them with detail and accuracy.

- Engage in discussion of stories read.

Newly Fluent Readers or Transitional Readers

Newly fluent readers can read with relative fluency and comprehension. They can use several cuing systems (semantic, structural, visual, and grapho-phonemic) to get meaning from print. Newly fluent readers also can show abilities such as the following:

- Self-monitor their reading, and can identify and correct simple errors with minimum external support. They ask clarification questions to develop an understanding of the content.

- Summarize the part of the story they have read and make inferences about the content.

- Handle more challenging vocabulary by using context clues.

- Use literary terms and grammatical concepts.

- Enjoy reading from several genres for information and pleasure.

Children at this stage are not totally independent readers, but with practice and support from teachers, they soon become fluent and independent readers.

Literacy Development in School

As children enter school, formal reading instruction begins. How children should be taught to read stirs debate that comes down to a discussion about where to start and how to proceed with instruction. The two most common approaches used to teach reading in public schools are skills-based and meaning-based. The skills-based approach is also called the bottom-up approach, and the meaning-based is also known as the top-down approach.

Bottom-up Approach (Skills-based)

The **bottom-up approach** (Gough, 1972) proceeds from the specific to the general, or from the parts to the whole. This approach begins with phonemes and graphemes and continues by expanding to the syllable, words, sentences, and paragraphs, and then, to whole reading selections. The best representation of this approach is phonics instruction. Phonics is a method of teaching beginners to read and pronounce words by teaching them the phonetic value of letters, letter groups, and syllables. Because English has an alphabetic writing system, an understanding of the letter-sound relationship may help the beginning reader. However, this view of reading instruction maintains that these relationships should be taught in isolation, in a highly sequenced manner, followed by reading words that represent the regularities of English in print. Children are asked to read decodable texts by sounding the words. Typically, this approach uses reading programs that offer stories with controlled vocabulary made of letter-sound relationships and words with which children are already familiar. Thus, children might be asked to read such a passage as:

The cat sat on a mat.

The cat saw the rat in the pan. The rat saw the cat.

The rat and the cat ran and ran.

Writing instruction follows in the same way. Children are asked to write decodable words and fill in the blanks with decodable words in sentences in workbooks. This is based on the assumption that when children progress past this initial reading instruction time frame, meaning will follow. Phonics instruction was widely used in the late 1960s and 1970s, and it is still promoted today. The flaw in this instruction is that many English words, including the highest frequency words, are not phonetically regular. Comprehension of text also can be limited in phonics because there is little to comprehend in texts such as "pig did a jig."

Modern approaches to phonics instruction have made the stories more enjoyable and interesting. The assumption is that textual meaning will become apparent in time. However, children do need to build comprehension and word recognition abilities from the outset. Furthermore, teaching phonics is not the same as teaching reading. Reading and spelling also require much more than just phonics. Spelling strategies and word analysis skills are equally important. Asking children to memorize phonics rules also will not ensure application of those rules. Even if that were true, the word the child is trying to decode is frequently an exception to the stated rule. Teaching children to use phonics differs from teaching them about phonics. In summary, the skills-based approach begins reading instruction with a study of single letters, letter sounds, blends and digraphs, blends and digraph sounds, and vowels and vowel sounds in isolation, and it does so in a highly sequenced manner. The children read and write decodable words, with a great emphasis on reading each word accurately, as opposed to reading to comprehend the text as a whole.

Top-Down Approach (Meaning-based)

Another approach to promoting literacy is the **top-down approach**. This approach begins with the whole and then proceeds to its individual parts. The top-down approach begins with whole stories, paragraphs, sentences, words and then proceeds to the smallest units of syllables, graphemes, and phonemes. The approach that best represents this view is the Whole Language Approach. The Whole Language Approach grew out of the work of Dr. Kenneth Goodman, who was a leader in the development of the psycholinguistic perspective. This approach suggests that to derive meaning from text, readers rely more on the structure and meaning of language than on the graphic information from the text. Goodman and other researchers showed that literacy development parallels language development. Goodman's contributions to the field include miscue analysis, which begins with a child's reading a selection orally while an examiner notes variations between the oral reading and the printed text. Each variation from the text is called a miscue and is analyzed for type of variation. Previously, teacher candidates were urged to read and reread texts with a young child until the child could read every word in the text perfectly. Goodman suggested that only miscues that altered meaning should be corrected, while unimportant miscues could be ignored.

The whole-language approach contrasts with the emphasis on phonics that is promoted in the skills-based approach. The meaning-based approach to reading emphasizes comprehension and meaning in texts. Children focus on the wholeness of words, sentences, paragraphs, and entire books and seek meaning through context. Whole-language advocates stress the importance of reading high-quality children's literature and extending the meaning of the literature through conversation, projects, and writing. Instead of fill-in-the-blank workbooks, children are encouraged to write journals, letters, and lists and to participate in writing workshops. Word recognition skills, including phonics, are taught in the context of reading and writing and are taught in relation to the text. Children are taught the four cueing systems and to ask themselves, "Does it look right? Does it sound right? Does it make sense?" Children are taught that people read books to make meaning. Thus, the focus of this approach is on comprehension as well as making connections.

Balanced Reading Program

Many classrooms are places where young children enjoy learning to read and write in a balanced reading instructional program. Research into best practices suggests that the teaching of reading requires solid skill instruction, including several techniques for decoding unknown words. These techniques include phonics instruction embedded in interesting reading and writing experiences with whole and authentic literature-based texts to facilitate the construction of meaning. This approach to instruction combines the best skill instruction and the whole language approach to teach both skills and meaning as well as to meet the reading needs of individual children. Some of the reading strategies used in a balanced literacy program include:

Teacher-directed/reading to students (read aloud)

- Shared reading, guided reading, and reading workshops

- Student-directed reading and independent reading

- Teacher-directed writing, writing to/for students as part of the classroom routines, and process writing

- Shared writing as in language experience/interactive writing

- Writing workshop and independent writing activities

Children's Literature

Classifications give the reader a general idea of what to expect in a text. Teachers today are expected to share a wide range of texts with children. All literature can be divided into three major categories: fiction, nonfiction, and poetry. Genres of fiction include realistic fiction, historical fiction, science fiction, fantasy, and traditional literature. Traditional literature encompasses folktales, fables, myths, epics, and legends. Nonfiction includes informational books, biography, and autobiography.

The most common books for young children are picture books. However, picture books are written for older students, too. In fact, many picture books are based upon stories for older students but have been adapted to include illustrations. Picture books can feature all genres. In picture books, illustrations and the text work together to communicate the story. Therefore, teachers should make sure children can view the illustrations as the teacher reads the words. Teachers can read aloud to the entire class. They also can read aloud to small groups of children, and this works best if the illustrations are not easily seen from a distance. If a teacher reads aloud to one small group of children one day, the teacher can read aloud a story to other groups on other days so that all have the opportunity to participate in this format over the course of the week.

Traditional literature comprises the stories that have their roots in the oral tradition of story-telling and have been handed down through generations. This genre also includes modern versions of these stories. Teachers can read and share multiple versions of these stories, and then compare and contrast them. Teachers also might read a number of folktales and keep track of the elements that these stories have in common and guide children toward noticing where these tales show up in their daily lives. Children enjoy sharing what they notice. Some examples of folk literature are:

- Animal tales in which the characters are animals exhibiting human characteristics, e.g., *Anansi the Spider*.

- Fables in which the main characters are animals and present a moral, e.g., *The Tortoise and the Hare*.

- The Pourquoi tales comprise creation stories from around the world. Every culture may have a different version of the way things were created, e.g., *How the Sea was Created* or *The Legend of the Bluebonnet*.

- Wonder tales describe stories of enchantment in faraway lands. Traditionally, they present the themes of good vs. evil, e.g., *Snow White*.

- Noodle head tales are stories of lovable fools. They include individuals who are not very bright but survive and often succeed, e.g., *Puss in Boots*.

- Cumulative tales are stories in which the information is presented in a sequence and all the events in the sequence are repeated, e.g., *The Gingerbread Man* and *The Three Little Pigs*.

- Tall tales describe the stories of legendary people or fictitious characters who accomplish great things, e.g., *Paul Bunyan*, *John Henry*, and *Pecos Bill*.

- Ghost stories have traditionally been used to regulate the behavior of children, such as *El Cucuy* in the Puerto Rican culture.

Multicultural literature acknowledges the importance of sharing literature from various cultures so that students learn about other cultures and so that students are more apt to see their culture featured in books. Multicultural literature for youth can be written by people from countries throughout the world. The term *authentic multicultural* has been used to describe literature written by members of a cultural group to represent their own historical development and culture.

Modern fantasy presents make-believe stories. These tales are so beyond reality that the stories can't be true. Extraordinary events take place within the covers of these books. Fantasy allows a child to move beyond the normal life in the classroom and speculate about a life that never was and may never be. Fantasy sparks intense discussions and provides opportunities to illuminate the author's craft.

Historical fiction is set in the past and lets children live vicariously in times and places they cannot experience in any other way. This fiction often depicts real people and events, with fiction laced around them. Historical fiction enhances social studies.

Nonfiction has the real world as its point of origin. These texts help expand children's knowledge when they are studying a topic, but these readings must be evaluated for accuracy and authenticity as well as inclusion of important facts.

Nonfiction can support the teaching of content and promote higher-level comprehension skills.

Biography describes the lives of real people. Autobiography describes the life of the author. These books also can enhance social studies because they often include information that transforms a name in a textbook into a person that children may like to know better.

Poetry is difficult to define for children, except as "not prose." Poetry uses words to capture something: a sight, a feeling, or perhaps a sound. Poetry should be chosen carefully for a child because it should elicit a response from the child that connects with the experience of the poem or the author. All children need poetry in their lives. Poetry should be celebrated and enjoyed as part of the classroom experience, and a literacy-rich classroom will always include a collection of poetry to read, reread, savor, and enjoy.

Teachers can choose from an overwhelming variety of children's literature. When selecting books for the classroom, a teacher must consider several issues: Are the facts accurate? Is the book aesthetically pleasing? Is the book engaging? All children deserve to see positive images of children like themselves in the books they read, and illustrations can have a powerful influence on their perceptions of the world. Children also need to see positive images of children who are not like themselves because who is or is not depicted in books can influence a child's perception of the world. Teachers should provide children with literature that depicts an affirming, multicultural view, and the selection of books should show many different protagonists. Both boys and girls, for example, should be depicted as able and strong.

To teach all components of all genres, teacher candidates should know the terminology to analyze stories. They should also guide children to use appropriate terms to describe different literature. Thus, teachers can introduce most of the terminology to study literature by using words familiar to their students.

When students can understand a concept, teachers can introduce standard terminology used in describing literature. These terms can be used as teachers read aloud a book or as part of continued discussion about a book.

Students can learn information about the story including the author and illustrators, the publishing company, dedication page, and even the International Standard Book Number (ISBN).

Teachers can help students learn terms used to describe the characters of the story, such as the protagonist and the antagonist or villain.

A story's point of view can be first person (where the author is one of the characters of the story and the narrator), the omniscient point of view (where the narrator is an outsider who knows what the characters are thinking or feeling), or the limited point of view, or subjective consciousness (where the narrator is not a character in the story).

The setting refers to the geographical location and the general environment and historical circumstances of the story.

The plot tells us what happens and the theme tells us why it happens, or is a message that is not explicitly stated but emerges from the plot. Some examples of themes are: problems of growing up and maturing, linguistic and cultural adjustment, love and friendship, family issues, and achieving one's identity.

Exposition: It is usually used to introduce the background information and to understand or introduce characters.

Dialogue: Communication between and among the characters.

Vocabulary: Word choice, use of concrete vs. abstract terminology (i.e., Is the vocabulary appropriate for the intended audience?)

Imagery: The use of words to create sensory impressions. It conveys sights, sounds, textures, smells, and tastes. Imagery includes the collection of images used to create an emotional response in the reader.

Tone: The author's mood and manner of expression. It might be humorous, serious, satirical, passionate, sensitive, childlike, zealous, indifferent, poignant, or warm.

Analysis of the story: It might be multicultural or traditional, or include possible stereotypes, sexism, religious issues, controversial elements, or words or ideas that might create controversy.

Fostering the Home–School Connection

Teacher candidates must understand the impact that fostering the home–school connection can have on student learning. Teachers also must know that developing connections between home and school can enhance students' long-term achievement in their classroom (Heath, 1983). Working with families and other professionals to promote student learning is crucial to meeting the needs of all students.

Ethnographic research conducted by Shirley Brice Heath showed that home literacy and the expectations surrounding literacy opportunities and events can differ from those provided at school (Heath, 1983). Teacher candidates must therefore work with parents to identify commonalities and differences in literacy practices and build on both to establish a stronger home–school connection. When parents and families are included in the teaching and learning, students and their families feel valued and welcome. Likewise, when parents see their child's literacy learning experiences at home surface in the classroom (e.g., a child writes a poem about his or her family and it is shared in a poetry reading), it reinforces their work as "primary teachers." Strategies to develop the home–school connection include:

- Parents should feel comfortable when coming to the classroom, and they should feel they can contact the teacher when they have a question or concern. Parents should feel welcomed.

- Select readings and displays (e.g., banners) to let students and their families see portrayed in literature.

- Develop activities that value students' cultural, linguistic, and ethnic background.

- Create a home-school journal in which the teacher and the families can share ideas about the child's development and progress. This journal also can be used as a formative assessment tool to have parents track their child's progress throughout the year.

- Display signs (e.g., murals) using languages other than English in an assigned area in the classroom.

- Give parents and families an opportunity to share their personal, cultural, and linguistic experiences in the classroom. Don't use these shared experiences simply as an occasional "cultural diversity" lesson; use them consistently to guide the teaching.

- Provide parents with flexible meeting times to accommodate their schedules.

Teacher candidates must also show parents and families the value of the home-school connection and the impact their role has on their child's learning. For instance, teachers should explain to parents that when they point to objects and labels in the grocery store, it helps young children develop the foundation for reading. As children grow older, teachers can provide parents with additional activities to integrate literacy with other content areas. With a unit on saving money, for example, the teacher might complement the lesson by asking parents to have children make a grocery list. After writing the list, the child's task is then to record the prices of the products on their list. This activity will require the child and parent to collaborate. The child later can bring the grocery list to school and discuss ways in which his or her family can save on groceries for their home while reinforcing the skills taught in school.

COMPETENCY 005: WORD ANALYSIS AND IDENTIFICATION SKILLS

The teacher understands the importance of word identification skills (including decoding, blending, structural analysis, sight word vocabulary, and contextual analysis) and provides many opportunities for students to practice and improve word identification skills.

Word analysis refers to the way that children approach a written word to decode and obtain its meaning. Word analysis should be practiced daily in class. Its goals include helping children become skillful in rapid word recognition. Research suggests that fluent word identification must be accomplished before a child can readily comprehend text. If a child must take pains to analyze many words in a text, the memory and attention needed for comprehension are absorbed by word analysis. The pleasure in a good story is also lost. Beginning readers typically decode each word as they read it, but repeated exposure to the same words increases the instant-recognition vocabulary. Developing readers must learn to recognize words that occur often. Those words are called sight words.

Students identify/recognize words in four major ways: sight vocabulary, phonics analysis, words parts or structural analysis, and context clues. Proficient readers use these strategies to decode and understand words. Teachers should make sure students master all four ways rather than relying upon one or two. Teachers also should provide explicit, systematic instruction in each skill and enable students to read independently and/or with reading buddies to practice their word analysis skills.

Sight Words

Words a student can recognize without hesitating are sight vocabulary. As students read more, their sight vocabulary increases. Students also should learn how to spell these words so that they can use them when they write. In 1948, Edward W. Dolch identified 220 of the most frequent words in the English language. He believed that if children were exposed to these words and learned to recognize them as sight words, they would become fluent readers. Examples of Dolch words include *a, an, am, at, can, had, has, ran, the, after, but, got,* and *away.* The introduction of these sight words can expedite decoding and develop fluency in early readers.

Phonic Generalizations

Phonic generalizations describe strategies used to introduce word recognition and decoding skills for emerging readers. The rules are not 100 percent applicable, but they help in many cases. A list of these rules follows (Center for Applied Research in Education, 1988):

1. Words with double *ee* usually represent a long sound. Example: *beet*.

2. The letter *y* in final position usually has a vowel sound, e.g., *by* /ay/.

3. When the *C* is followed by the vowels *e* or *i*, the sound of the *c* is /s/. Examples: *Cesar, city.*

4. When the *C* is followed by the vowels *o, u* or *a,* the sound of the *c* is /k/. Examples: *Cord, cult,* and *car.*

5. In the cluster *ght,* the *gh* is silent. Example: thou*ght*.

6. When a word has a double consonant, only one is pronounced. Example: *Call.*

7. In most two-syllable words, the first syllable is accented. Example: *carton.*

8. In words with two adjacent vowels, only the first vowel is pronounced, creating a long sound (The first vowel does the talking). Example: *beach.*

9. In words containing two vowels, one of which is a final *e*, the first vowel produces a long sound, and the *e* is silent. Example: *cape*.

10. In the syllable structure consonant-vowel-consonant, the sound of the vowel is short. Example: *cat*.

Structural Analysis/Word Parts

Another strategy for readers to get clues is to pay attention to the structure or parts of a word: base/root words, affixes (prefixes, infixes, and suffixes) of derivational morphemes, and suffixes in inflectional endings. Morphemes are the smallest units of meaning. These units can be taught. Common derivational morphemes in the form of prefixes, infixes, and suffixes, and inflectional endings should be shown to students. An analysis of derivational and inflectional morphemes follows.

Most **derivational morphemes** come from foreign languages like Greek and Latin, and they represent consistent meanings. For example, in the prefixes *pre-, anti-,* and *sub-,* each has consistent meaning in English and other languages, namely *pre-* (before), *anti-* (against), and *sub-* (under). Many English prefixes are common to such Western languages like German, and all Romance languages. Derivational morphemes can also change the syntactic classification of the word. For example, the word *care* is a free morpheme representing a verb or a noun. However, when the suffix *-ful* is added, it changes to an adjective, and the adjective becomes an adverb when the morpheme *-ly* is added, giving us *carefully*. Using this or similar examples, teachers can teach morphemes as well as parts of a sentence.

See Table 3-4 for examples in English and Spanish. Derivational morphemes can change a word's the syntactic classification. Adding a morpheme to a word can change it from a verb to a noun or from an adjective to an adverb. Children guided to recognize derivational morphemes will have an advantage in decoding words.

Table 3-4. Examples of Common Prefixes in English and Spanish

Roots	Meaning	Words in English	Words in Spanish
bio	life	symbiosis	simbiosis
phobia (fobia)	fear of	xenophobia	xenophobia
phono (fono)	sound	phonetics	fonética
photo (foto)	light	photography	fotografía
chrono/crono	time	chronology	cronología

Inflectional morphemes only happen in final position in a word. They typically follow derivational morphemes in a word, and do not change the syntactic classification of the word. English has the following eight inflectional morphemes:

1. Short and long plural -*s*, e.g., two cars, three pens. Long plural -*s*. Use long plurals after *ch, sh, s, z,* and *x,* e.g., *churches, washes, cases,* and *boxes.*

2. Third person singular -*s*, e.g., Mary walks quickly.

3. Possessive *'s,* e.g., Martha's boy

4. Progressive -*ing,* e.g., She is walking. The gerund is not included in this group, i.e., Walking is good for your health.

5. Regular past tense -*ed*, e.g., He worked hard.

6. Past participle -*en* or -*ed,* e.g., She has beaten the system, or It has been ruined.

7. Comparative (-*er, better, worse, farther, less,* and *more*), e.g., Basketball players are generally taller than baseball players.

8. Superlative (-*est, best, worst, furthest, least,* and *most*), e.g., Soccer is the most popular sport in the world.

Understanding the meaning of these morphemes can enhance students' decoding and comprehension skills. The ability to associate sounds rapidly and accurately with a cluster of letters leads to more rapid and efficient word identification. As young readers build an increasing repertoire of words they recognize with little effort, they can use the words they know to help them recognize other, possibly related, words that are unfamiliar. The best way to help students gain skill in word-recognition is through reading and writing activities.

As children read and reread texts of their own choice, they have many opportunities to decode a word. For example, they will realize that each time a letter combination such as *c-a-t* is found in the selection, it's read as *cat*. With each exposure to that word, the child reads it more easily. A child who writes a sentence with that word develops a greater sensitivity to meaning or context clues. The child trying to spell that word reviews and applies what he or she knows about letter-sound associations.

Context Clues

Contextual clues can help students identify unknown words and information. Context clues can use pictorial information, knowledge, and experience as well as information about the type of speech. The cultural framework of the writing can also help clarify meaning. However, the child must understand the culture to benefit from that framework.

Semantic Clues

When using **semantic cues**, readers think about the meaning, or what would make sense, as they encounter a word. Semantic clues require a child to think about the meanings of words – as well as what – he or she knows about the topic being read. For example, when reading a story about hawks, teachers can help children activate prior knowledge about the bird. The children then can develop an expectation that the reading may contain words associated with hawks, including such words as *predator, carnivorous, food chain,* and *wingspan.* This discussion might help a child gain a sense of what to expect in a sentence. For ELLs who might not be familiar with hawks, teachers should identify equivalent species from these students' geographical area.

Syntactic Clues

The word order in a sentence might also provide clues to readers. For example, in the sentence, "Hawks are _____," the order of the words in the sentence indicates that the missing word must be an adjective or a noun, even if the reader is not conscious of the term adjective, or noun. This open-ended sentence can lead students to words such as *carnivorous, predatory,* or other words that expand information about the subject. Furthermore, illustrations in the book can often help identify a word. A picture of a hawk eating its prey can lead students to the words *predator* or *carnivorous.*

Context clues are often not specific enough to enable students to predict the exact word, but when combined with such other clues as phonics and structural clues, a student can often identify the word.

Words That Can Create Comprehension Problems for Children

Children can decode some words while still having problems identifying the intended meaning. These difficult words include homonyms, homographs, and homophones. Homonyms are words that have the same sound and the same spelling but differ in meaning. Homonyms are common in the content areas and can create comprehension problems. The context will determine the meaning of the words. Examples of homonyms are presented in Table 3-5.

Table 3-5. Examples of Homonyms

Word	Meaning 1	Meaning 2
Club	A place to socialize	A wooden stick
Fine	To imply good or okay	A penalty
Bank	A place where money is stored	Margins of a river
Rock	A stone	Type of music

Homophones sound the same but are spelled differently and have different meanings. Examples of homophones are *blew* and *blue; heir* and *air; wait* and *weight; hear* and *here; eight* and *ate; to, two,* and *too; there and their; deer and dear;* and *hair* and *hare.*

Homographs are spelled the same way but have more than one pronunciation and different meanings. For example, the word *bow* has two pronunciations. The first refers to the front part of a ship as well as the way people bend to salute. The second refers to a weapon as well as the decorative knot used in clothing or the device used to play string instruments. Consider the use of the word in the following sentence: The warrior wore a red bow, stood on the bow of the ship, put away his bow and arrows, and graciously bowed to the audience.

Compound words are created when two independent words join to create a new word. Knowing the meaning of the two words often will guide students to understand the meaning of the compound word. For example, the compound word *birdhouse* is composed of the words *bird* and *house*. With this information, children can understand that the new word refers to a refuge or a house for birds. However, some compound words can confuse children. Examples of deceptive compound words are *butterfly, nightmare,* and *brainstorm.*

COMPETENCY 006: READING FLUENCY

The teacher understands the importance of fluency for reading comprehension and provides many opportunities for students to improve their reading fluency.

Reading fluency is the ability to decode words quickly and accurately to read text with the appropriate word stress, pitch, and intonation pattern (or prosody). Reading fluency requires automaticity of word recognition and reading with prosody to facilitate comprehension. Automaticity is the quick and accurate recognition of letters, words, and language conventions. Automaticity is achieved through continuous practice using texts at the child's reading level.

Fluency and Comprehension

Fluency is a prerequisite for language comprehension. Children struggling with fluency devote their time to mastering their language skills. This effort detracts from the concentration they should be placing on reading comprehension. When students read aloud in class, the main purpose of the activity is to develop fluency. If the teacher asks the child comprehension questions after the child has read aloud, the child will most likely have to read the same passage silently to respond. Teachers thus should separate these two activities and have children read silently for comprehension and read aloud for fluency.

Speed: What Is the Expectation?

Chapter 110.3 TEKS for English language arts and reading suggests that the typical child in first grade should read about 60 words per minute (wpm). The rate should increase by 10 words in each grade, i.e., second grade (70 wpm), third grade (80 wpm), and fourth grade (90 wpm). To determine the wpm, a simple formula is used. The words read in a minute, minus errors, equals the wpm (UT system/TEA, 2002). The expectation is that children in the first to fourth grade should read independently with minimum difficulty, i.e., finding no more than one in 20 words difficult.

How Do We Teach Fluency?

Teachers can use several strategies to promote reading fluency. Descriptions of these strategies follow.

Repeated Readings

Teachers can promote opportunities for repeated reading using text at the reading level of the child. Teachers, parents, and peers can provide support and feedback for these students. Allow the child to read the same story repeatedly to develop fluency.

Choral Reading

Reading "in group" is another activity used to promote reading fluency. Here, students read a text together. This activity is ideal for ELLs and struggling readers because pronunciation and fluency problems will not be publicly noticed and they can use the model provided by fluent readers.

Pairing Students

Pairing proficient readers with ELLs or struggling readers can benefit both groups—the proficient child gets additional practice reading, and the ELLs and struggling readers can listen to fluent readers. ELLs and struggling readers can also read to their partners and get input.

Interactive Computer Programs

Interactive reading programs can provide individual reading support for children. These computer programs often contain colorful pictures and interesting stories. The child should have the option of clicking on the words or pictures to have the selected word read aloud or to get animation of the word's meaning. The program can also read a story at normal speed while the child follows the highlighted words in print.

Silent Sustained Reading (SSR)

The primary goal of silent sustained reading (SSR) is to boost reading comprehension, but guiding the child to read silently and continuously for about 20 minutes a day also can improve reading fluency. This activity can also teach the child to read silently without moving his or her lips.

Readers' Theatre

In Readers' Theatre, a story is modified so that characters have to read portions of the text. Students rehearse their reading part and then create a theatre format to present the reading. Students can read the script, perform actions or do both. The intent is for the children to read, not to memorize the lines. The story comes alive for the audience through the children's voices. Students gain in fluency and comprehension as they read and reread their parts to read accurately, smoothly, and with intonation. As they become a character or the narrator, students decide how the person would sound in the circumstance, which fosters comprehension. Teachers can create scripts by rewriting guided reading stories or informational selections to develop a script.

Developing Reading Fluency

Pointing to words while reading helps students see the letter-sound correspondence, but this practice can affect the development of reading fluency. Second graders should be guided to discontinue this practice. Continuous monitoring of reading fluency is required to insure that children develop and maintain reading fluency when they are exposed to more challenging texts. To be sure that students maintain reading fluency, teachers can conduct individual assessment using teacher-developed checklists or more standardized processes like running records.

Assessing Reading Fluency

A running record is an assessment strategy designed by Mary Clay (2002) to assess students' word identification skills and fluency in oral reading. The teacher listens to a student read a page and uses a copy of the page to mark each word the child mispronounces. The teacher writes the incorrect word over the printed word, draws a line through each word the child skips, and draws an arrow under repeated words. Teachers can identify the type of error and then provide additional support to individual learners.

COMPETENCY 007: READING COMPREHENSION AND APPLICATIONS

The teacher understands the importance of reading for understanding, knows the components and processes of reading comprehension, and teaches students strategies for improving their comprehension, including using a variety of texts and contexts.

Helping students read for understanding is the central goal of reading instruction. Comprehension is a complex process involving the text, the reader, the situation, and the purpose for reading. Several factors come into play as a child tries to understand a passage. First, students cannot comprehend texts if they cannot read the words. To improve students' comprehension skills, instructors must teach them to decode well. Children need time during the school day to read texts that are easy for them and have time to discuss what they have read. Children need to read and reread easy texts often so that decoding becomes rapid, easy, and accurate. Children who comprehend well have bigger vocabularies than children who struggle with reading. This is partly because vocabulary develops through contact with new words as children read text rich in new words. It has also been suggested that teaching vocabulary in isolation does not automatically enhance comprehension.

Background Knowledge

Reading comprehension can be affected by prior knowledge, and readers with rich prior knowledge about the topic of a reading often understand the reading better than classmates with less prior knowledge. A discrepancy between the schema intended by the author and the schema that the reader brings to the reading can create confusion and comprehension problems. This is especially important for students from linguistically and culturally diverse backgrounds because they might not have the cultural information necessary to understand stories written in view of the background of experiences of American students. For example, students need to know the original version of *The Three Little Pigs* before they can understand the humor of a fractured story tale version, such as *The True Story of the Three Little Pigs,* a book where the story is told from the wolf's viewpoint.

Guided Practice and Independent Practice

Through a gradual release of responsibility (Pearson & Gallagher, 1983) and careful and strategic scaffolding, teachers can guide students to practice and apply specific reading strategies in their independent reading. In guided practice, teachers provide support and resources. Scaffolding learners with guided support means working within their zone of proximal development or what the students can do with the help of a peer or adult (Vygotsky, 1978). In independent practice, students have opportunities to apply the skills and strategies they learned during modeling and guided practice. In independent practice, students practice reading skills with text that is at their instructional and independent reading level. Teachers should continuously reinforce reading strategies and skills through both guided and independent practice.

Pre-Reading Activities

Prior knowledge affects students' interest in what they read and what they want to read. Students like to read about familiar topics, and teachers should identify interests in children and find appropriate stories to match those interests. A teacher can also make an unfamiliar topic familiar through pre-reading activities that activate prior knowledge, form new knowledge, and thus stir imagination. Teachers of ELLs often must spend more time in pre-reading activities than the time devoted to reading the stories. They must review unknown vocabulary, assess students' understanding of terminology and then build on this new knowledge to increase students' interest in what they are about to read.

Setting the Purpose for Reading

Teachers should set a purpose for reading and ask the students to predict what the purpose of the reading is. The teacher and the students can both thus obtain and draw on students' prior knowledge about the topic. Making predictions about the upcoming text and then reading based on those predictions lets students identify key points to pay attention to while reading. Children should be encouraged to generate questions about the text while reading.

Linking Prior Knowledge to New Knowledge

Teachers should help readers to process text containing new facts through reading strategies and then relate the new information to prior knowledge. Questioning is a simple but powerful mechanism to guide children to link prior knowledge to new knowledge. Through questioning, teachers guide children to question the facts and the intent of the author as well as check their answers through text verification. Conversation lets children compare their predictions and expectations about the content. Conversations also help children see the need to revise their prior knowledge when they encounter compelling new ideas that challenge prior knowledge. As part of these ongoing conversations, teachers will become alert to students who are applying incorrect schema as they read and will then encourage the use of more appropriate knowledge. These conversations also help children determine the meanings of unfamiliar vocabulary based on context clues and others' opinions as well as through the use of such appropriate source materials as glossaries, dictionaries, and other texts. After reading activities, teachers should encourage children to revisit the text—to reread and make notes and paraphrase—to remember important points, interpret the text, evaluate its quality, and review important points. Children should also be encouraged to think about how they might use ideas encountered in the text. As children gain competence, they enjoy showing what they know.

Story Grammar

Children should be encouraged to be aware of the components and structure of stories, or story-grammar. Through discussion students can be aware of the setting and characters, as well as problems encountered by characters, attempted solutions to the problems, the successful solution, and the ending. Teachers can use graphic organizers to present a visual clue of these components. Story frames can be modified to introduce components of literature as well as provide an assessment tool to check comprehension.

As children's comprehension grows more sophisticated, they move from trying to comprehend the text to reading critically. They grow in understanding that comprehension can go beyond the denotative components of the facts in a text. With skillful instruction, children read not only what a text says but also how it portrays the subject. Students recognize how every text is the unique creation of a unique author, and they learn to compare and contrast the treatment of the same subject in different texts. For example, teachers can introduce the multiple versions such stories as Cinderella to discuss how stories can represent similar themes using unique settings and situations. To see different versions of the Cinderella story, visit the Children's Literature Web Guide (Brown, 1997). Examples of variations on Cinderella are *Mufaro's Beautiful Daughters: An African Tale* by John Steptoe; *Yeh-Shen, a Cinderella Tale from China* by Ai-Ling Louie; and *The Egyptian Cinderella* by Shirley Climo. Teachers can help students grow in comprehension through stages.

When students retell the story together or on their own, teachers can determine if the students understood what took place. Understanding what is said or what took place is literal comprehension and is basic. However, students also need to be able to comprehend at higher levels by making inferences and understanding messages that emerge from the story. Further discussions can focus upon literary elements as students gain in ability. Students can attain the skill set needed to engage in text interpretation and thus detect and articulate tone and persuasive elements as well as discuss point of view, and recognize bias.

Over time and with good instruction, children learn to infer unstated meanings based on social conventions, shared knowledge, shared experience, or shared values. They make sense of text by recognizing implications and drawing conclusions, and they move past believing something simply because it was in print.

Monitoring Comprehension

Children must be taught to monitor their own comprehension and to decide when they should exert more effort or apply a strategy to make sense of text. To model monitoring techniques, teachers can read passages aloud, stopping frequently for comprehension checks. Through questioning and clarification of concepts, teachers can guide students to determine whether they understand the text. Another way to facilitate monitoring comprehension is to state the purpose of the reading so that students can focus on that component of the content. The goal of comprehension instruction is for the child to read at a level where the application of strategies becomes automatic.

Teachers should allow time for in-school reading and recognize that good texts are comprehended on a deep level only through rereading and meaningful discussions.

Comprehension is maximized when readers are fluent in all the processes of skilled reading, from the decoding of words to the articulation and easy application of the comprehension strategies used by good readers. Teaching of comprehension strategies must be viewed as a long-term developmental process, and the teaching of all reading strategies succeeds more when they are taught and used by all teachers on a staff.

Monitoring Reading Comprehension in Pre-Literate Children

Story retelling is a strategy used with young children to assess listening and reading comprehension. This strategy can also assess knowledge of syntax and vocabulary as well as speaking ability and knowledge about the structure of stories. Informal or structured checklists can be used to assess a student's comprehension, sentence structure knowledge, and vocabulary development as he or she retells a story. Any checklist for retelling should assess the child's ability to (Lapp et al., 2001):

- Retell the story with details.

- Show evidence of comprehension of the story line and plot, including the characters, setting, author's intention, and literal and implied meaning.

- Show evidence that the child understood major ideas and the ideas that support them.

- Bring background information to the selection.

- Analyze and make judgments based on facts.

- Retell the selection in sentences that make grammatical sense.

- Retell the story using sentences that include standard usage of verbs, adjectives, conjunctions, and compound sentences.

- Use a rich and meaningful vocabulary with minimal use of slang and colloquial expressions.

- Adapt spoken language for audience, purpose, and occasion.

- Listen to evaluate a speaker's message and to enjoy and appreciate spoken language.

Reading Strategies

Identifying strategies used by proficient readers can help teachers make skillful choices of activities that will maximize student learning. Anne Goudvis and Stephanie Harvey (2000) offer the following suggestions for useful activities.

Activating Prior Knowledge

Readers pay more attention when they can relate to the text. Readers bring their knowledge and experience to reading, but they comprehend better when they think about the connections that link the text, their lives, and the larger world. This strategy is especially important when teaching children from diverse cultural and linguistic backgrounds.

Teachers must explore the schemata necessary for children to understand the story—as well as the knowledge that children bring to the reading. One strategy to explore a child's background is the KWL chart. This chart asks students to describe what they know, want to know, learned and still want to learn or areas that the students did not understand well. Because this is a class activity, children can benefit from what others already know, what others want to learn, and what areas were difficult for others.

Predicting or Asking Questions

Questioning keeps readers engaged. When readers ask questions, even before they read, they clarify understanding and forge ahead to make meaning. Questions are at the heart of thoughtful reading. A variation of this strategy is to give students true or false questions about the content to be read. When students answer the questions, they then read to check their responses.

Visualizing

Active readers create visual images based on the words they read. These images enhance understanding. Guiding children to draw these visual images can help in retaining the most important component of the story.

Drawing Inferences

Inferring occurs when the readers take what they know, garner clues from the text, and think ahead to make a judgment, discern a theme, or speculate about what is to come. Readers should analyze ideas explicitly stated as well as those expressed implicitly to develop a clear understanding of the text to improve the accuracy of their inferences.

Determining Important Ideas

Readers should grasp essential ideas and important information when reading. Readers must differentiate between less important ideas and ideas central to the meaning of the text. Analyzing pictorial and graphic clues as well as the repetition of ideas and the theme of the story can guide students to determine key ideas in the text. When working with expository writing, teachers can guide students to identify how information is organized in this writing. Students should be guided to notice the main heading, subheadings, and bold or italicized letters because these features are used to communicate the most important ideas.

Synthesizing

Synthesizing information combines new information with existing knowledge to form an original idea or interpretation. Reviewing, sorting, and sifting important information can lead to new insights that change how readers think.

Metacomprehension

Capable readers are aware of how well they are understanding as they read. If they get confused, readers should stop to clarify their understanding.

Confirming Predictions

As part of pre-reading activities, young learners are guided to study the title and subsection as well as the available visual input to make predictions about the story. Students later read the story to confirm or reject their predictions. This activity has no wrong answer. Students confirm negatively or positively. With practice students become better at predicting the content of stories, but the goal is determining whether a prediction is correct.

Students should use such parts of a book as the charts, diagrams, indexes, and table of contents to improve their understanding of the content.

Reflecting

An important strategy is for students to reflect on what they have just read. Reflection can be simply thinking, or it can be more formal, such as a discussion or writing in a journal. While providing instruction in a subject, the teacher determines whether the reading is at the students' level. If not, the teacher should accommodate either in the material or in the presentation of it.

Assessing Comprehension

A frequent device for assessing comprehension is the use of oral or written questions. Convergent questions have only one correct answer, while divergent questions have more than one correct answer. Most tests include a combination of these types. Assessing comprehension also can be based upon whether students can understand at the literal level and remember ideas stated explicitly in the text. However, writers do not explicitly state all their ideas. Readers must make inferences, which calls for them to put together clues from what is stated explicitly. These inferences can entail putting together ideas suggested from a pair or group of sentences. Readers also must relate the text to their knowledge and experience to reach such high understanding as grasping implicit themes or lessons.

Teachers can help students develop comprehension via discussions with them after they have read the material or after the material has been read aloud to them. During the discussion, teachers can model thinking about the story, chapter, or selection. Teachers also can introduce implicit ideas to show students how competent readers think about what they read.

Teachers also can help students understand different writing by including fiction, nonfiction, and poetry in what they read aloud. Discussions also can have the students take notes together to organize and remember information.

Another activity for checking comprehension is a cloze test. This test presents a reading passage with omitted words that the student must supply. The test-maker must decide whether to accept only the exact word or to accept synonyms as well. If assessing reading comprehension is the goal, the teacher might accept synonyms and not demand the exact word.

The speed at which a student reads helps determine the level of comprehension, up to a point. The faster a student reads, the better the student comprehends, with some limitations. The slow reader who must analyze each word does not comprehend as well as the fast reader, but someone can read too fast. Most students have had to reread material. For example, a student reading a chapter to prepare for a test might read more slowly than when reading a short story for pleasure or reading a text to get the main idea.

Students can also use semantic mapping to connect the vocabulary they learn in class with what they have previously seen, heard or learned. The strategy works as follows:

1. The teacher puts a word or phrase representing the story in the middle of the board/paper/transparency. The teacher can have preselected categories related to the central word (three to five categories).

2. The teacher asks students to brainstorm related words in each category. The teacher also introduces words related to the text.

3. Students also can look through the text to locate more words that may fit with the key word or phrase. Related words that may appear in future readings can be included.

4. In discussing the words, students can talk about their personal connections with the book.

COMPETENCY 008: VOCABULARY DEVELOPMENT

The teacher knows the importance of vocabulary development and applies that knowledge to teach reading, listening, speaking and writing.

Vocabulary development is the key foundation for further development in all four language skills—listening, speaking, reading, and writing. Listening comprehension relies on the recognition of key vocabulary and concepts. If the child does not recognize spoken words, he or she will not be able to understand oral messages. Oral communication relies on the development of receptive and productive vocabulary. The larger the productive vocabulary of the child, the easier it is to communicate orally and in writing. Becoming a proficient reader depends upon immediate recognition and understanding of words. Vocabulary development is the single most important component of successful reading (*The Report of the National Reading Panel*, 2000).

When readers recognize and understand individual words, they can devote attention to creating meaning or comprehending information. Students also rely upon understanding the meanings of words to comprehend instruction that relies upon listening, speaking, reading and writing. Vocabulary development begins at home, even before children enter school. Pre-school age children begin developing their speaking and listening vocabularies through meaningful interactions with others. Even without being taught directly, children acquire and refine their knowledge of social words. Schooling provides opportunities for students to expand their social and academic language. With formal schooling, students develop their speaking and listening vocabulary while also getting opportunities to expand their reading and writing skills. Although students continue to gain in vocabulary development through their interactions in school, explicit instruction plays a decisive role in helping students develop the academic vocabulary needed to succeed in school.

Vocabulary Levels

Beck, McKeown, and Kucan identified four tiers of vocabulary words (2002). Three (level 1, 2 and 3) are highly relevant to the development of vocabulary in elementary school and successful completion of high school. An analysis of these levels follows.

Tier 1 words are used in daily speech. This tier includes basic vocabulary words, simple idioms, and speech connectors (Calderon, 2007). Most native English speakers from middle class backgrounds bring many of these words to school. However, children of poverty as well as ELLs might lack these words. This initial discrepancy creates an academic that can only be met through meaningful vocabulary development at the social and academic levels for ELLs and children of poverty.

Tier 2 words are more formal and academic and are learned in school through direct instruction or during reading. Children need these words to succeed in school. These words are used to explain processes and academic concepts in the content areas, and students need them for specificity and precision when discussing concepts (Calderon, 2007). Calderon organized these words based on the required speech acts. A few examples follow:

- Cause and effect (*because, due to, as a result, since, on the other hand…*)

- Proving examples (*that is, for example, for instance, to illustrate this point…*)

- Compare and contrast (*or, but, however, despite*)

Tier 3 words describe the technical vocabulary used in the content areas. This register is developed through direct instruction and through reading and discussion in the content area. Some words come from the Latin and the Greek languages, and they contain multiple affixes (prefixes, infixes, and suffixes) and root words that can be taught through structural analysis. These Latin- and Greek-based words contain morphemes that have specific meaning in isolation, and they can be presented to children through their original meaning. For example, the Greek-based word *democracy* can be structurally separated in two main components: *demo* (–people), and *cracy* (–government). With these two components, students can understand that democracy is a government by the people and for the people. Words that follow similar patterns include: *photograph, telephone, microscope, intravenous,* and *hydrophobia.* From these five words teachers can teach 10 different concepts: (1) photo (light), (2) graph (form), (3) tele (distance), (4) phone (sound), (5) micro (small), (6) scope (vision), (7) intra (inside), (8) venous (veins), and (9) hydro (liquid), and (10) phobia (fear). Using these morphemes students can recognize multiple words that contain them.

Since most content words in English come from the Latin and the Greek, most tier 3 words have cognates (similar words) in most Indo-European languages and more so in Latin-based languages like Spanish, Italian, Rumanian, French, and Portuguese. Moreover, these fancy words (level 3) of Latin origin are often words of regular usage in Spanish and perhaps in other Romance languages.

Tier 4 words represent sophisticated vocabulary that learners need to succeed beyond the elementary years. These words are rare and do not constitute part of the vocabulary of children in K-6, but, teachers should introduce them as part of academic vocabulary development. Children who compete in spelling bees often get exposed to this vocabulary. Examples include: apothecary, mortified, nocturnal, philanthropy, canonized, juxtaposition, and panacea.

To support language development in school and provide access to content area instruction, teachers should provide explicit instruction in levels 2 and 3. Instruction in Level 1 words might also be necessary for children who come to school with limited vocabulary development as well as children who are new to the language, i.e., ELLs.

Semantic Clusters

Robert Marzano proposed the teaching of vocabulary organized around semantic clusters. He developed 420 semantic clusters of words, organized via complexity and grammatical function (2010). The complexity of the terms were identified by a scale ranging from 1 to 5, with numerals from 1 to 3 identifying basic vocabulary and 4 to 5 identifying more advanced terms.

To illustrate this point, one of his semantic clusters—**Reptiles/Mythical Animals** (Marzano, 2010, p. 108)—follows:

Level 1:   None

Level 2:   alligator, snake, turtle, and dragon

Level 3:   dinosaur, mermaid, and monster

Level 4:   cobra, crocodile, rattlesnake, and unicorn

Level 5:   nymph and serpent

Because of the academic complexity of the cluster, no Level 1 words are listed. Instead, the bulk of the words falls in Levels 2 to 4. Level 5 presents words not common in daily speech. The term *nymph* is rarely used unless the topic is mythology, and the term *serpent* is substituted for the common term—*snake*. However, if students learn the term *serpent,* they can learn about semantic word families like *serpentarium* and *serpentine*.

Some other examples of semantic clusters presented in Marzano (2010) follow:

- **Modals** (can, could, may, might, ought to, used to, shall…)

- **Dwelling for animals** (nest, aquarium, beehive, cocoon, birdhouse…)

- **Chemical concepts** (helium, oxygen, cholesterol, compound, sodium, enzyme…)

- **Woodlands and Forest** (jungle, glade, grove, woodland)

- **Crops and Soils** (fertilize, cultivate, irrigate, plow, harvest…)

Vocabulary Development and Instruction

Vocabulary development entails **connecting a word** (or label) **with concepts.** If students understand a concept, they can remember it and use the word linked to it. Learning how to use dictionaries is important and can help, but, gains in vocabulary development do not take place best when students stop reading to look up words and memorize definitions. Instead, teachers are encouraged to guide students to use word decoding and contextual analysis to get meaning. Teachers also must prepare students to identify words that can be understood through contextual clues and to recognize when the use of a dictionary is absolutely required.

Instruction will vary depending upon what students need. A brief example may suffice if students understand a concept and are learning a new word for that concept. On the other hand, students will need more experiences if they understand a concept but are learning a word in a language other than their native language. It can be especially challenging for students to understand a concept while learning new words.

The vocabulary and concepts students encounter in some content areas will be abstract or foreign to some of them. Explicit instruction thus is needed to build an understanding of the concepts, and the instruction also must help students acquire the productive vocabulary used to participate in class discussions.

When students understand a concept at a deeper level, they understand how the concept relates to others. Students also improve conceptual development when concepts and vocabulary are presented in class, readings and discussions. When teachers let students participate in hands-on activities using these terms, students also develop a better understanding of the vocabulary and the concept they represent. For example, if a teacher wants to present the concept of *buoyancy,* instead of simply defining it, he or she can do experiments in "float and sink" in which students link the concept with an activity.

Reading Aloud and Independent Reading

Teachers can help students improve vocabulary development through reading aloud as well as independent reading. In reading, students encounter words and concepts not likely to be a part of their oral language experiences. Students also learn new words through the use of **contextual analysis** in which they use surrounding words and illustrations to help them understand the meanings of words. Although instructors are not teaching words directly, students make gains through their engagement with reading. The words that become a part of their reading vocabulary (receptive vocabulary) can become part of their listening (receptive) and speaking and writing (productive) vocabulary. If teachers make sure students encounter different literature, students will be more likely to make extensive vocabulary gains.

Systematic Vocabulary Instruction

Vocabulary development also should include systematic instruction that helps students learn strategies for gaining vocabulary. Teachers can provide instruction before, during, and after reading to show students how to rely upon context clues in understanding unknown words.

Teachers can also help students learn how to use **word structure** to understand and remember new words. Morphemes are the smallest units of meaning in language, and these can have meaning of their own (free morphemes). For example, the word *happy* is a free morpheme with its own meaning, while the word *happily* contains one free morpheme (*happy*) and the adverb—bound morphemes—*ly*. Guiding students to understand the function of these morphemes can help in their vocabulary development and in improving their listening, speaking, reading and writing skills.

Learning Latin and Greek roots and derivations as well as morphemes in general can also help students understand and remember new words. The following table presents examples of derivational morphemes—those able to change the syntactic classification—that can be explicitly taught to students. The table also shows Latin and Greek morphemes that in context or in isolation have specific meaning in English and other Indo-European languages.

Table 3-6. Greek and Latin Morphemes

Morphemes	Meaning	Words in English	Spanish Cognates
mega	Big	Megaton	Megaton
Chrono.crono	Time	Chronometer	Cronómetro
Metro	Measure	Altimeter	Altímetro
Micro	Small	Microorganism	Microorganismo
Scope	Look carefully	Microscope	Micrócpio
Phobia	Fear	Claustrophobia	Claustrofobia
Hydro	Liquid	Hydrocephalic	Hidrocefálico

Teaching derivational morphemes and their meaning can increase children's academic vocabulary. When students learn the vocabulary in one language, teachers can introduce cognates in other languages, such as Spanish. Guiding students to recognize cognates in other languages can increase vocabulary development in English learners.

Dictionary and Thesaurus

Teaching the use of dictionaries and thesauri can also help students identify words and their meaning, but merely asking students to look up words and copy definitions does not help understanding. However, dictionary skills must be taught explicitly so that students can make appropriate use of this resource. When students learn to identify the word, they also should be taught how to decide which definition fits the sentence they are reading or writing. Teachers thus must guide students to study the different entries in the definition and decide on the one that fits the context of the sentence. The use of electronic dictionaries and especially an electronic thesaurus can increase accessibility of definitions and synonyms. Using an electronic thesaurus can improve vocabulary development in speaking, reading, and writing.

Teaching Vocabulary for Understanding and Learning in Content Areas

Teaching all new words of a reading selection is often unnecessary and may not work. Teachers and students must decide which words are critical to understanding the selection. Teachers also should decide whether all students can gain enough understanding by how a word is used in the selection. For example, a word that a native speaker could figure by using context clues may not be one that an English learner could. Teachers also must determine how much instruction is needed without disrupting the enjoyment and understanding of the reading or the reading aloud. However, vocabulary often does require direct instruction because the concepts are new to students. Students also must be shown how concepts relate to one another to understand each concept fully and to understand the concepts collectively.

Vocabulary development can take place **before reading** to help students encounter new concepts and words. Teachers should consider students' different backgrounds so that they can relate new concepts to a student's previous learning and background knowledge. Rather than ask students to look up a word in a glossary of the textbook, teachers should provide examples, illustrations or visual diagrams. Learning how to use a dictionary is an important skill for students to learn, but dictionary definitions rarely help students understand an unfamiliar concept. Teachers also should show students how to use any illustrations or diagrams the text provides to help them with vocabulary and associated concepts.

Vocabulary development can take place **after reading** to help students retain what they have learned. Students may understand what they have read but may not remember how the concepts presented in a chapter relate to each other. **Diagrams** and **word maps** can illustrate a concept and connections among concepts.

Vocabulary development constitutes the foundation for further development in other areas. Teachers thus must emphasize vocabulary. Simple sight words as well as the use of dictionaries and thesauri, affixes and root words, and cognates can help develop vocabulary.

COMPETENCY 009: READING, INQUIRY AND RESEARCH

The teacher understands the importance of research and inquiry skills to students' academic success and provides students with instruction that promotes their acquisition and effective use of those study skills in the content areas.

Transition from "Learning to Read" to "Reading to Learn"

Children from pre-K to second grade spend most of the language arts portion of their day trying to decode and make sense of written language. The main purpose of this stage is to read for pleasure. Traditionally, illustrated short stories with a specific structure and predictable story line are used to guide the child in "learning to read." However, in the upper elementary grades, children's needs go beyond decoding and reading for pleasure. "Reading to learn" becomes the main task. The "reading to learn" stage requires students to decode written language and understand the content and get vital information from it. An important component of "reading to learn" is to understand how text is organized in the content areas. Children must recognize key components of the organizational format and identify the type of information offered. Teachers should guide children to notice and study the structure of text, including the table of contents, titles, subtitles, and headings.

Structure of Text

Students must examine the structure of the text to comprehend it. To help students reach this goal, teachers should guide students through a picture, table, and graphic walk-through of the text while asking questions and pointing out useful text features to the students. Most texts have titles, subtitles, headings, glossaries, and bolded words. What techniques were used to make important ideas stand out? Figuring the structure of a text helps students to read more efficiently. Children can anticipate what information a selection will reveal when they understand textual structure. Understanding the pattern of the text helps students organize ideas, and authors choose from a short list of organizational patterns. The following are the most common:

- Chronological order relates events in a temporal sequence from beginning to the end

- Cause-and-effect relationships between events, with the causes identified or implied

- Problem description, followed by solutions

- Comparisons and/or contrasts to describe ideas

- Sequential materials, presented as directions to be followed in a prescribed order

Becoming More Efficient Readers

Students with strong comprehension skills and decoding ability are ready to become more efficient readers by practicing the techniques of scanning and skimming to get content information. To help students with scanning, the teacher shows them how to look for specific information by using the headings, indices, boldface and italics to guide them to specific words or content. In skimming, students are shown how to read major headings, table of contents, bold letters, graphic materials, and summary paragraphs to get the main idea of the content.

Study Skills

Students must know how to study information presented to them in texts and other media. Graphic organizers help students review material and see the relationships between one bit of information and another. For example, a Venn diagram helps students identify how things are alike and different. A Venn diagram can also help students recognize how a single topic is treated in two readings or how two books, animals, or ecosystems are alike and different. The student labels the two overlapping circles and lists items unique to each one in each respective circle. In the center where the circles overlap, the student records the items common to each.

Note-taking is a skill that is rarely taught explicitly in school. Teachers assume incorrectly that taking notes is a skill that students will learn naturally. Learning this skill can have multiple cognitive advantages for students. Taking notes help students identify and summarize relevant information. In the process of note-taking, students receive and process information, and write it in their own words Moreover, taking legible and relevant notes will guide students to develop a better understanding of the content, and thus, able to ask meaningful questions in class to corroborate information and to expand on it. A key challenge in note-taking is to decide what information is relevant. To teach this concept, teachers have to share with students the purpose of the lecture or class. In elementary schools, teachers use the "statement of objectives" where they explain the purpose of the lesson. If students know the rationale for the lesson and what is expected from them, they will have better change to identify relevant materials.

Teachers should also think of a task that requires students to accomplish higher-level manipulation of the information. First, help the children form a researchable question. Second, have them highlight key words that might be used to search for information. Third, put students in groups and have them brainstorm other key words. Next, ask them to list appropriate sources. Finally, as they skim articles, they can fill in the chart with chunks of information.

Graphic Organizers

Graphic organizers help students improve organizational skills and provide a visual representation of facts and concepts as well as their relationships within an organized framework. The ability to organize information and ideas is fundamental to effective thinking. To increase reading comprehension among ELLs, let students share information about the story or passage. Through this activity, students can help each other via conversation and peer scaffolding. Semantic mapping can be used before and after readings to organize materials in new ways by highlighting connections among ideas.

Think-Aloud

Think-alouds let the teacher and students problem-solve together. The teacher poses a question to students. Then, the teacher, group of students, or entire class responds. This strategy can increase reading comprehension in the content areas. In modeling a think-aloud, the following steps are used (Wilhelm, 2001).

1. The teacher explains *what* the strategy is and what it is used for.

2. The teacher explains *why* the strategy is important for improving reading comprehension.

3. The teacher explains *when* to use the strategy.

4. The teacher models *how* to use the strategy with an **authentic text.**

5. The teacher guides student practice using authentic text.

6. The teacher gradually releases responsibility for doing the think-aloud to students.

7. Students practice the strategy in pairs or independently.

8. The teacher asks that students do a think-aloud in which they explain and articulate their thinking for using the strategy.

Summarizing and Organizing Content

When children are guided to summarize and organize content, they are using reading comprehension and taking this content to a higher level of thinking that includes evaluation, analysis, and synthesis. Going beyond the literal meaning and reorganizing content requires students to develop a deeper understanding of that content. Teachers should guide students to reorganize content (study skills) by creating their own tables, charts, and graphs. For example, students can develop a chart containing the longest rivers of the world organized by regions and countries. When children are required to present information using a new structure, their comprehension and knowledge of the content area increases, and their retention is enhanced.

Study Plans

To increase content comprehension, teachers might acquaint students with several study plans to help them read content materials. Many plans are easily accessed, and the teacher and the students can select the plan(s) that works best for them within subjects. Students may use mnemonic, or memory-related, devices, to help them remember the steps in reading a chapter effectively.

SQ4R

Students often use plans such as SQ4R when reading text in content areas. The acronym stands for survey, question, read, reflect, recite, and review (Thomas & Robinson, 1972). An explanation of the different components of the SQ4R follows:

- **Survey:** During the survey (S) part, readers examine the headings, illustrations, bold letters, and major components of the text to develop predictions and generate questions (Q) about the topic.

- **Question:** Students may wish to devise some questions that the chapter will probably answer. Through these questions, students establish the purpose for reading, and the questions serve as a reading guide. If the chapter has questions at the end, students can also study these before reading the chapter.

- **Read (1R):** During the next stage, students read while looking for answers to their generated questions and/or those questions written by the publishers, which are usually located at the end of the section.

- **Write (2R):** Students monitor their comprehension as they write a summary of the story or text. Creating a summary, allows students provide opportunities to internalize and make their own interpretation of the content.

- **Recite (3R):** Students try to answer orally or in writing the student-developed questions or the questions at the end of the chapter.

- **Review (4R):** Finally, students review the text to evaluate the accuracy of their answers and to show how much they learned about the content.

Reciprocal Teaching

Reciprocal teaching is an instructional activity designed for struggling readers in which the teacher engages students in a dialogue about specific portions of a text (Palinscar & Brown, 1984). The main purpose of this activity is to monitor reading comprehension and guide children to build meaning. The dialogue is structured to elicit four components:

1. Summarizing the content of a passage

2. Asking a question about the main idea

3. Clarifying difficult parts of the content

4. Predicting what will come next

DRTA

DRTA stands for Directed Reading/Thinking Activity. This teacher-directed strategy helps students establish a purpose for reading a story or expository writing from a content book (Reuzel & Cooter, 1992). The teacher models the how to create and correct predictions as the story progresses to strengthen comprehension. DRTA has three main steps:

1. **Sample the text to develop background:** Children are guided to read the title, look at pictures or any kind of visual representations, and read some sample lines from the text to develop a hypothesis about the content of the text.

2. **Make predictions:** Students make predictions based on a sample of the text.

3. **Confirm or correct predictions:** Children read the text and engage in follow-up activities to check the predictions.

Reading Comprehension in the Content Areas

To help children and especially ELLs in reading material that may be beyond their reading level, teachers can incorporate the following strategies:

- Record selected passages that students can listen to, while reading along with the text. Teachers can also use adult volunteers and fluent readers in the group to read to children unable to read it for themselves.

- Pair children into a tutor/tutee arrangement or in a small group reading format. Teachers should pair children of different linguistic levels and degrees of achievement to create a peer-support system.

- Introduce the technical vocabulary of the content areas before reading. Introduce such elements as connotation (implied meaning), denotation (literal meaning), and idioms as they are used in text. For example, the word *right* can have multiple meanings depending on the content area or the activity. In mathematics, *right* is an angle of 90 degrees, but in social studies *right* can be used to provide directions or to declare correctness.

- Teach content vocabulary through direct, concrete experiences rather than by definitions. Definitions can lead to misinterpretations because additional words are required to define the term. Teaching vocabulary in a contextualized situation is especially important for ELLs because they often rely on translations that do not always represent the intended concept. For example, in English the word *bayou* is used extensively in Texas and Louisiana. However, *bayou* is hard to define for someone who has never seen one. What is the difference between a bayou, a creek, a swamp, or a marshland? How big is a bayou? If an adult has difficulty answering these questions, imagine how young children may struggle.

- Introduce instructional strategies for self-monitoring reading comprehension. In this strategy, students read a passage aloud and then pause to question themselves about its meaning.

Strategies for Developing Critical-Thinking Skills

Critical-thinking skills include analysis, synthesis, and evaluation. Benjamin Bloom (1956) created a taxonomy for categorizing levels of thinking. The taxonomy presents a structure to categorize the levels of thinking required to ask and answer questions. These questions have been used to guide children from the recalling of information (knowledge) and understanding information (comprehension) to using such higher order thinking skills as analysis, synthesis, and evaluation. Recalling and understanding are important parts of reading comprehension, but teachers must help children move from literal comprehension and explicit ideas to figurative comprehension and implicit ideas. Teachers must guide children to analyze (analysis) the ideas presented in text and then make inferences (analysis), to assess their inferences (evaluation), to draw conclusions about the ideas (synthesis), and perhaps to apply the ideas to new situations (application). Children who can go beyond the literal and explicit information in text develop a deeper understand of the content areas and manipulate the content at higher levels of thinking.

Linguistic Accommodation Testing for ELLs and Special Education Students

Texas provides for linguistic accommodation for ELLs and special education children taking the content portion of the State of Texas Assessment of Academic Readiness (STAAR) examination in grades 3–8 and 10 to ensure that reading comprehension does not interfere in assessing content mastery. Based on specific recommendations from the Admission, Review, and Dismissal (ARD) and/or the Language Proficiency Assessment Committee (LPAC), districts can allow linguistic accommodations for special education and ELL students when taking the basic skills test (STAAR). A list of allowed linguistic accommodations follows (TEA, 2015):

1. Presenting the information in two languages side by side.

2. Allowing the test administrator to read the questions or translate words, phrases, and sentences.

3. Using dictionaries to find translations.

4. Allowing the use of bilingual or English-language glossaries.

5. Allowing the test administrator to present the information using simple language.

6. Using visual and nonverbal communication to make content clear.

COMPETENCY 010: WRITING CONVENTIONS

The teacher understands the conventions of writing in English and provides instruction that helps students develop proficiency in applying writing conventions.

The transition from oral language development to written communication requires students to develop an awareness of the following concepts (Peregoy, Boyle and Cadiero-Kapplan, 2008):

1. Print carries meaning and conveys a message.

2. Spoken words can be written and preserved.

3. English reading and writing follows a specific direction; that is, from left to right and top to bottom.

4. Spoken language is composed of phonemes, and these sounds can be represented by specific letters of the alphabet (alphabetic principle).

5. As an alphabetic language, English has a sound-symbol correspondence, but it is often inconsistent.

6. Spoken language can be used as a foundation for spelling (phonics).

Spoken and Written English

The productive skills of language (speaking and writing) are interconnected. A strong oral development can facilitate the development of written communication. Also, showing students how they can talk about something and then put what they say on paper can help. However, because spoken language is usually less formal than written language, teachers must be sure that students use more formal language when writing. In speaking, the words used are often more elliptical because people can rely upon asking questions and gestures to establish meaning. However, when writing, people must rely solely upon words to establish meaning.

English favors active voice as opposed to passive voice in both oral and written communication. For example, the sentence "Hurricane Katrina devastated New Orleans" works better than "New Orleans was devastated by Hurricane Katrina" because it uses the active voice. Teachers should guide students to work with a partner in converting passive sentences to active sentences and then guide them to discuss how these changes affect the tone and meaning of the sentences.

Developing Readiness for Writing

A visit to an early childhood classroom shows children singing, drawing, and painting as well as playing with blocks, clay, puzzles, and cutting figures with scissors. Although some visitors might question the value of instruction in early childhood, children are doing intensive work. They are developing the fine motor skills needed to master such pre-reading skills as pencil grip and paper position as well as the first strokes of representing the shapes of letters and words.

Spelling Stages

As children name letters and read print, they also write letters and words. Writing development occurs about the same time as reading development, not afterward, as traditional reading readiness assumed. Whole language seeks to integrate the language arts rather than sequence them. Change has marked educators' beliefs about reading instruction and how reading develops, and change has marked the methods and philosophies behind the teaching of writing.

Drawing begins children's attempts to convey a message in written form. Teachers can use this interest to introduce writing skills by guiding children to add words to drawings to supplement the information. Children first can dictate the story to teachers until they feel comfortable enough to write it on their own. The development of written communication follows a predictable sequence that starts with scribbling and then develops pseudo letters and invented words until conventional spelling is achieved. An analysis of the stages of spelling follows:

Scribbling

Children pretend they are writing. Eventually, they develop letter-like symbols. This stage represents an awareness of the difference between writing and drawing to communicate. Scribbling differs from drawing because the child purposely scribbles from left and often also follows the top-to-bottom progression.

Pseudo Letters

In this phase, children try to create forms that resemble letters, but these forms cannot always be identified as such. They become aware that the alphabet contains characters of different shapes, and they try to reproduce these randomly. The child's writing shows not or little evidence of letter-sound relationships.

This stage is when the appearance of "invented spelling" is shown, or where children try to connect the sounds (phonemes) and the letters (graphemes) to create words, and the result is non-standard writing. The child's writing often relies upon a letter name strategy (e.g., *R* for *are*). The writing shows recognition of letters representing sounds in words, such that the main sounds in words are represented, but spelling is abbreviated with one to three letters being used to spell a word. Initial and final sounds are most often represented. Consonants are used more than vowels.

Phonetic

In this stage, the child is able to represent all major sounds with letters, and the spellings show the sequence of sounds in pronunciations. The surface sounds of words are represented, and the letters are used on the basis of sound alone, such as in *BABES* for *babies*. The way a child discerns a sound may not be conventional, such as *GR* for *dr*.

Transitional Spelling

Eventually, children discontinue over-reliance on phonetic spelling, notice visual clues, and develop a knowledge of using morphological information, or word structure. Sight-word training becomes important at this stage. Students produce more standard spelling and try self-correction. Writing samples might become difficult to read because students erase often to self-correct. Some inflectional endings (plurals, comparative, superlative, past tense, and present progressive) may appear in writing samples. Students may still have problems with words with double vowels, such as *book* and *feed,* and words containing consonant digraphs like *through* or *charm*.

Conventional Spelling

Children spell most words using conventional spelling. They still may have problems in spelling some less typical words and fail to see these when proofreading their work. At this stage, students do have almost complete mastery of the most complex sound-symbol relationships and are increasingly proficient in proofreading their spelling.

Writing Stages

In addition to the traditional spelling stages, students also go through specific stages of writing. Lapp et al. (2001) divided the process into three stages: emerging writers, early writers, and newly fluent writers. A summary of these stages follows:

Characteristics of Emerging Writers

Students at the emerging stage of writing development can:

- Dictate an idea or a complete story.

- Use initial sounds in their writing.

- Use pictures, scribbles, symbols, letters, and/or known words to communicate message.

- Understand that writing symbolizes speech.

Educational Implications

Read stories to children and ask them to retell the story while you record it. Then read the story again to emphasize the connection between speech and print. When children write words or pseudo words, ask them to read what they have written to you, and if necessary, provide conventional spelling as an alternative. Use the **Language Experience Approach** to guide children to connect spoken words with their written representations. Guide children to dictate words and sentences while you record them on the board. Read the words while pointing to them. Then ask students to copy the sentences. The next day, review the written sentences and use them for additional language development. Introduce writing for functional tasks like labeling objects and places in the classroom, writing the plan of the day, taking notes, and listing names or things to remember.

Characteristics of Early Writers

Typically, children at the early stage of writing exhibit the following behaviors:

- Understand that a written message remains the same each time it is read.

- Use their knowledge of sounds and letters as they progress through the stages of spelling development.

- With modeling and help, incorporate feedback in revising and editing their writing.

- Use conventional grammar, spelling, capitalization, and punctuation.

Educational Implications

Guide children to read and reread the same information to establish a connection between letters and sounds. Identify specific words and divide them into syllables to establish a connection between the sounds within a syllable. Take expressions commonly used in children's literature and oral communication and guide students to hear word boundaries. For example, children might write the statement "Once upon a time" as "Oncesoponditim," which represents how the expression is produced orally without word boundaries. Model the writing with an LCD projection system or the traditional chalkboard. Think aloud while you are writing and ask for guidance from students. "Do we need a comma here or a final period? Do we need a capital A in the word "American?" With children's writing samples, use peer input for editing and guide students to self-correct. Instead of correcting errors directly, ask questions leading children to examine grammar and syntax and make their own corrections.

Characteristics of Newly Fluent Writers

Newly fluent writers can:

- Use prewriting strategies to achieve their purposes.

- Address a topic or write to a prompt clearly and independently.

- Organize writing to include a beginning, middle, and end.

- Consistently use conventional grammar, spelling, capitalization, and punctuation.

- Revise and edit written work independently and/or collectively.

- Produce many genres of writing.

Educational Implications

Use prewriting activities to plan for writing. This activity is especially important for children whose native language does not require the linear progression used in English writing. The thinking and planning will guide children to comply with this linear rhetorical pattern. Provide interesting writing prompts to children to guide their writing. You may use the prompt given on the STAAR released tests available online. The Texas Education Agency typically releases the tests used in its yearly administrations. For information on released STAAR tests, search "STAAR released test questions" at the Texas Education Agency website at *http://tea.texas.gov*.

Continue using peer editing and encourage self-corrections. Guide students to produce such different writing as response to literature as well as journals, narrative and expository writing.

Writing Expectations

Children in kindergarten through sixth grade are expected to progress through the stages of writing and develop conventional spelling and coherent compositions. The fourth-grade STAAR examinations require students to develop coherent writing free of major errors. It is also expected that children produce and refine compositions for general and specific audiences. Children must edit their work and the work of others based on clarity of ideas, coherence, and the conventions of writing.

Strategies for Using Writing Conventions

The main objective of writing is to convey what the writer intends to communicate. When this is accomplished, students must check for writing conventions (grammar, punctuation, spelling, and capitalization). Various strategies can help students master writing conventions.

Modeling

Modeling is one of the best tools to introduce effective writing. To model effective writing, teachers can introduce writing samples that use conventions appropriately. Teachers also can present a writing sample that contains typical errors in English conventions and ask students to provide corrections.

Sentence Builders

A typical problem in children's writing is the use of sentence fragments, instead of complete sentences. To guide children to produce complete sentences, teachers can use a technique called "sentence builders." The teacher provides students with a list of words by syntactic categories (articles, adjectives, nouns, verbs, and conjunctions) and guides children to produce sentences using each component. As a follow-up, children are asked to identify the subject and the predicate, and specifically the verb. They are also asked to read the sentence to see whether it contains a complete idea.

Punctuation Exercise

To teach the importance of punctuation, teachers can use sentences in which commas or periods are necessary to communicate the ideas and guide students to use punctuation to clarify the message. Consider this sentence: "This season's fashions use these fabric blends: polyester and cotton, linen, silk and spandex and cotton and wool." In this sentence, without a comma after *spandex,* it is not clear what fabrics constitute the blends. Use the serial comma to avoid confusion.

Identifying Common Spelling Problems

Assess students' writing to identify common problems across the group and design lessons to address the problems. For example, if students are producing words like *bred* and *sale boat* in place of *bread* and *sailboat,* provide instruction to guide students to standard spelling. Spelling instruction can also address high-frequency words students are apt to use and words that are often misspelled. Some examples of this type of word are: *there-their-they're* or *to-too-two.*

Connecting Discourse

Connecting discourse is a definite challenge to students in the early grades. Children often produce choppy sentences without transition words or phrases to connect ideas or paragraphs. Most of these connectors are not used in daily speech unless students have had some speech training or academic preparation in the area. Teachers thus must teach connectors explicitly. Teachers can provide a list of possible sentence connectors and guide students to use them. These connectors include such words or phrases as "as long as," "moreover," "even though," and "furthermore."

Dependent and Independent Clauses

Another way to minimize choppy sentences is to guide children to combine sentences by choosing from the following options:

1. Use such conjunctions as *and, but, or, nor,* or *yet.* For example, "My car is beautiful, but it is getting old." The sentence has two independent clauses joined by the coordinate conjunction *but.* A comma is required before the conjunction.

2. Join two complete sentences with a semicolon. For example, "Maricela is a highly intelligent student; she was the valedictorian of the class of 2015." The lowercase is used after the semicolon.

3. Use dependent and independent clauses. For example, "Although Damian is a bright young man, he is having problems in college." The dependent linking word *although* at the start of the introductory dependent clause made the independent clause necessary to complete the whole idea. The last statement in the independent clause makes sense by itself, but it gains context when combined with the dependent clause.

Strategies to Promote Written Communication

Reading to students provides multiple benefits. It develops print awareness and an understanding of the intonation pattern of the language. A discussion on the content of a story enhances comprehension and lets student practice speaking. It also provides a model of fluent reading with the appropriate intonation pattern of the language. Reading together can be enjoyable. Students laugh and talk about the story and the characters. Children can also sample such different writing as poetry, fiction, and nonfiction. Finally, they are exposed to the story framework of setting, characters, plot, climax, and resolution.

Dictated Materials—The Language Experience Approach

Children's individual or group-dictated stories guide children to connect spoken language with its written representation. If working with a group of children, the dictation may be presented on a chart, board, or projection screen. This could take place as the children discuss events of the day or what happened on a field trip. If working with an individual child, the teacher can ask the child to draw a picture representing the events of the day. Then, ask the child to tell the teacher what actually happened. The teacher can write students' dictations.

With a whole group, a similar process is followed. The teacher will record the story on the board or projection screen, so everyone can see the writing. When the teacher records the story, it is helpful if the teacher says each word aloud while writing it. Following the writing of what the children dictate, the teacher reads it in a natural tone of voice, pointing to each word as it is pronounced. To help students develop knowledge of clauses and phrases, the teacher can read the story while placing a hand under each phrase as it is read. Students can also read the story in choral reading, by pairs, or individually.

Interactive Journals

As discussed earlier in the chapter, writing in journals provides students with opportunities to use language in literary contexts. Teachers and students can have a designated time for journal writing to communicate daily. This gives students the freedom to use their own mechanics and phonetic spellings. Because the purpose of written journals is to communicate, teachers should not correct children's journal writing. Instead they should write comments on content, model standard writing, and provide encouragement and reassurance.

Using Routines as Literacy Events

Several routine activities can be modified to develop reading and writing. These activities include:

- Use a chart with students' names on it to take attendance. In the morning, students get their card and move it to the chart to show they are present. Students' names can also be placed in alphabetical order, which uses indirect teaching to deal with that concept.

- Do a daily weather report that uses pictures and words representing the weather conditions, such as cloudy, clear, and rainy. Students can move the cards to show the prevailing weather conditions for the day.

- Show today's day and date by having students select the appropriate card to show the days of the week and the date.

- Organize a calendar of events for the day or the month. Review the plan of the day in the morning.

- Use written notes to communicate with students. Use these written notes to praise them or to discuss behavior and their performance in class.

COMPETENCY 011: WRITTEN COMMUNICATION

The teacher understands that writing to communicate is a developmental process and provides instruction that promotes students' competence in written communication.

Writing is a developmental process that requires students to go through a series of steps to complete a written product. These steps include brainstorming, semantic mapping, outlining, reading, and researching. Students must also learn to write for different audiences and purposes (e.g., expressive, informative, persuasive). They also will be required to use their knowledge of text genres, structures (e.g., letter, poem, narrative, and expository), and strategies (e.g., peer conferences) for completing a written piece. The steps students must go through include drafting, editing, revising, proofreading, and publishing. However, students should know that writing is recursive, and opportunities always exist to keep improving what they are writing.

Children also must know English grammar and mechanics to revise their writing. This attention to grammar and mechanics includes checking sentence construction and revising run-on sentences and misplaced modifiers; revising subject-verb and pronoun-antecedent agreement; revising pronouns, adverbs, adjectives as well as verb forms and plural and possessive nouns; and revising capitalization, punctuation, and spelling. Students also should analyze and revise written work for style, clarity, organization, audience, and purpose. This includes adding transition words and phrases, reordering sentences or paragraphs, deleting unnecessary information, and adding a topic sentence, if it is missing as well as improving clarity, precision, and effectiveness through word choices.

Dr. Donald Graves, a professor of education at the University of New Hampshire, developed an approach to writing instruction called writing workshop or process writing (1983). His idea was simple, teach children to write the way professional writers write. What do writers do? They write about what they want or need to write. They may read about the subject, talk about the subject, take notes, or study the topic before they compose. Then they may write a draft, knowing they are not done. Writers may share the draft with others and write notes all over it. They may also check every sentence, thinking about word choice and looking for vagueness as well as places where the piece falls off the subject. Writers may then revise the draft, share it, revise it, and keep doing so until they are satisfied with the product. Then they publish it.

In a writing workshop, students select topics rather than have the teacher assign them. They thus have ownership of their writing by selecting the topic and content. Similarly, professional writers save scraps of writing in a journal. They may save a turn of phrase, a comment overheard on a bus, a new word, good quotes, or an interesting topic until they decide on their topic. Students can follow a similar path. They can take notes, keep a writer's notebook, and use it to begin writing.

Teachers do teach in a writing workshop. The writing workshop has a predictable structure, and students write on a daily basis. Students first write rough drafts and focus upon establishing content. In final drafts, the teacher helps students learn about proofreading, and there the focus is on spelling, punctuation, and usage.

Mini-lesson

They often use a mini-lesson that takes place at the beginning of a writers' workshop. The mini-lesson can focus upon procedures or the workshop, such as how to use the writing folder, where students keep their rough drafts or work in progress.

The mini-lesson also focuses upon such strategies and techniques as how to select a topic, write a rough draft, revise a piece, and create a picture with words. The mini-lesson also can be used to model different writing. Students often begin with personal narratives or informal reports. Over the school year, students can be shown how to write formal reports, fiction, and poetry.

Writing and Conference

After the mini-lesson, writing and conference time takes place. The students write, and the teacher writes. After about 10 minutes, the teacher circulates among students to support their writing as they write. Writers often share drafts of their work with spouses, colleagues in a writing group, and/or an editor. Similarly, teachers have brief conferences with students as, they write a rough draft. Teachers do not tell the students what to say, but they have conferences to encourage the child to discover what he or she wants to write.

In a writing conference, the teacher helps the child discover what he/she wants to say:

1. Ask the child to read aloud what he or she has written.

2. Tell the student what the teacher heard or liked, using the writer's words rather than general praise (e.g., "That's great").

3. Ask genuine questions seeking clarification of the ideas expressed.

Students also have whole-class conferences. That is, the writing workshop concludes with whole-class sharing, or author's chair, where children are invited to share their work with the class. After young authors read their piece, classmates can offer affirmations and suggestions. With the teacher's guidance, students follow the same structure that the teacher uses for conferences.

Publishing Conferences of the Writing Workshop

After a specified time, students select a piece to publish from their rough-draft folders. The teacher reads the pieces before having a publishing conference with a small group. Other students continue writing at their desks/tables.

During a publishing conference, the teacher calls a group of students together to use a proof-reading list. The teacher shows students how to use the proofreading list, which becomes more sophisticated as students learn more about punctuation and usage.

The teacher provides guidance and selects one or two skills to teach each child. Students are not expected to find all the errors in spelling, punctuation, and usage. The teacher will later use a different color of ink to correct remaining errors.

The teacher or the students type a final draft for publication. Outlets for publication can be books published for classroom libraries or gifts, Lucite frames, and bulletin boards.

The children have a writing folder for rough drafts, and the teacher develops a system for passing out folders for the writing workshop.

A cumulative folder is kept for each child and includes a copy of rough and final drafts dated to show progress. Through the process approach, students write daily, select topics, write rough drafts, revise their work, and share writing with others.

Other Approaches

Besides process writing, teachers can try approaches that focus upon specifics of the writing process. The best-known system is called the 6+1 Trait Writing. Developed by the Northwest Regional Educational Laboratory (NREL), this system emphasizes seven elements of writing (n.d.). They are:

1. Organization—the internal structure of the sample.

2. Ideas—how ideas are presented in the sample.

3. Voice—the uniqueness of the author and how ideas are projected.

4. Word Choice—the vocabulary used to convey meaning.

5. Sentence Fluency—the flow of ideas and the use of connectors.

6. Conventions—the use of capitalization, punctuation, and spelling.

7. Presentation—how the final product looks in print.

The Texas Education Agency developed a similar writing program emphasizing comparable components:

1. Focus and Coherence—how the main idea is introduced and supported in the composition.

2. Organization—the organization of ideas, including connectors.

3. Development of Ideas—how the ideas are presented and supported.

4. Voice—the uniqueness of the author and how ideas are projected.

5. Conventions—the use of capitalization, punctuation, and spelling.

Both the 6+1 Trait Writing and the TEA writing programs guide children to show knowledge of writing traits. To assess students' performance, both programs develop a four-point rubric for each writing trait.

Identifying the Characteristics of Modes of Writing

Writing serves different functions. The main functions are to narrate, describe, explain, and persuade. Students must know these functions, though these four categories are neither exhaustive nor mutually exclusive.

The narrative is a story or an account. It may recount an incident or a series of incidents. The account may be autobiographical to make a point. The narrative may be fiction or nonfiction.

Descriptive writing provides information about a person, place, or thing. Descriptive writing can be fiction or nonfiction. Description is a powerful tool in advertisement. Advertisements describe items using factual information, but the information is presented to persuade prospective buyers.

Expository writing explains and clarifies ideas. Students are probably most familiar with this writing. The expository essay may have a narrative, but the storytelling or recounting is minor and serves the explanation. Expository writing is found in textbooks. For instance, a textbook on the history of Texas would likely be expository.

Persuasive writing tries to convince the reader of something. Persuasive writing fills magazines and newspapers and permeates the Internet. The writer may be trying to push a political candidate, convince someone to vote for a zoning ordinance, or promote a diet plan. Effective persuasive writing presents a point and provides factual and/or anecdotal evidence to support it. The structure may be formal and should include counterarguments. Whatever the organization, the writer's intent is to persuade the reader. Nearly all essays include persuasion.

Authors choose their form of writing not only to tell a story but also to present ideas. Whether choosing the narrative, descriptive, expository, or persuasive format, writers have something on their minds that they want to convey to readers.

Writing for Audiences, Occasions, and Purposes

The writer must consider the audience, occasion, and purpose when choosing the writing mode. The teacher should designate an audience for students' writing. When they know the intended audience, the can modify their writing to suit the intended readers. For instance, a fourth-grade teacher might suggest that the class take their compositions about a favorite animal to second graders and let the younger children read them. To address second graders, the writers will have to use manuscript and not cursive writing, choose a simple vocabulary, and omit complex sentences for their young audience.

The occasion also helps to determine the elements of writing. The language should fit the occasion. Students should remember that words have such effects as evoking sympathy or raising questions about an opposing view. The students and teacher might try to determine the likely effect a word or words might have on an audience of a writer's choice.

The purpose helps determine the format (narrative, expository, descriptive, or persuasive) and the language of the writer. For instance, students might consider the appropriateness of writing for such purposes as a business letter, a communication with residents of a retirement center, or a thank-you note to parents. The teacher and students also might try to identify the persuasive techniques a writer uses in a passage.

In selecting the mode of writing for a persuasive writing, the writer might need to consider the following:

1. What would the audience need to know to believe you or to accept your position? Imagine someone you know listening to you presenting a position or opinion and then saying, "Oh yeah? Prove it!" What evidence do you need to prove your idea to this skeptic?

2. With what might the audience disagree?

3. What common knowledge does the audience share with you?

4. What information do you need to share with the audience?

The teacher might have the students practice selecting the mode and the language by adapting forms, organizational strategies, and styles for different audiences and purposes.

Types of Writing

Teachers should encourage children to write for meaningful purposes. Meaningful writing can be incorporated into daily classroom activities and enhance not only writing skills but also content area mastery. Functional writing and journal writing can be incorporated into the classroom.

Functional Writing

Functional writing describes activities in which writing is used to achieve a specific purpose. For example, labeling areas and objects in the classroom is a meaningful and useful activity for all students, especially ELLs. Note-taking or developing a grocery list or list of holiday gifts becomes a meaningful activity and will motivate children to write.

Journal Writing

Journals can be used in elementary grades for various purposes. Some of these are:

1. Personal journals can record personal information and encourage self-analysis of experiences. This is a personal document and should be up to the child whether to make it available to others.

2. Dialogue journals promote written communication among students and between the teacher and students. The main purpose is to communicate, not to teach writing skills. Teachers can model writing when they reply to children.

3. Reflective journals respond in writing to specific situations or problems and are often shared with the teacher for input.

4. Learning logs are used in content areas to record ideas discussed in class. Students describe what they have learned and what gives them difficulty. Teachers read the document and act on the requests for help.

COMPETENCY 012: VIEWING AND REPRESENTING

The teacher understands skills for interpreting, analyzing, evaluating and producing visual images and messages in various types of media and provides students with opportunities to develop skills in this area.

According to the TEKS (1998), students in EC-6 grades must develop the skills needed to create and understand images and messages presented in different media. The skills increase in complexity as students move from lower to upper elementary grades. For instance, students in grades 1–3 must produce visual representations of what they learn as well as of the tasks they do (e.g., create an image summarizing a story they have read). Students also must know how to discuss the visual representations they have created. In grades 4–6, students must understand, interpret, analyze, critique, and produce these visual representations as well as discuss their meaning or significance through the multiple media, including newsletters, charts, and electronic presentations. Students also should understand an author's purpose and choice of elements used to get his or her message across via multiple media. The characteristics and functions of the different media are explained below.

Types and Characteristics of Media

A medium is considered to be any means used to convey information to others. At least three main media are available: print, visual, and electronic. Print media disseminate information in print form and include newspapers, magazines, and direct mail. Print media are static; that is, once the information is published, it cannot be changed. Visual media incorporates visual imagery to complement or supplement the message. Visual media can also stand alone. For example, photographs and paintings can convey meaning without text. Moreover, visual media are also an integral part of print media to illustrate messages. As such, visual media can take many forms, including photography, film, and even cartoons. Visual media can be static (e.g., still photograph) or dynamic, as seen in movies or videos.

Besides incorporating print and visual imagery, electronic media require such external devices as a television, computer, or personal assistant device to display the information and images. Electronic media are used in different fields, including journalism, fine arts, commerce, education, and communications. A primary electronic medium that encompasses different electronic tools is the Internet, which contains photographs, videos, blogs, email, and multiple articles. Electronic books are available on the web.

When using these electronic media, teachers must remember that technology changes fast. Many tools for presenting information are improved and refined almost daily. For instance, photography has evolved from being created on photographic plates and then film to now being created digitally. Teachers should realize a vast array of possibilities to create and display information is available via existing media. As the need for using and sharing massive amounts of information with others becomes necessary, some media will take precedence over others. For example, the use of online information has become so pervasive that static media, like print media, are now being channeled electronically (e.g., newspapers and books). The use of online resources and Web sites has become a staple. Students expect those around them to know how to use these tools. Students seek opportunities to use and produce different products through different media.

Representing Messages and Meanings through Media

Charts, tables, graphs, pictures, and print and non-print media are examples of materials used to present or summarize information and/or to complement messages. For instance, a chart can summarize much information without written explanations. Students should understand that visual representations are important and that their purpose is to present information and facilitate communicating the message. Visual images should also be used to make information more understandable. A graphic can expand or illustrate a concept, support points, summarize data, organize facts, add a dimension to the content (such as a cartoon adding humor), compare information, show change over time, or furnish additional information. Through graphics, the reader can interpret, predict, and apply information with careful observation. Questioning students as they create visual images (e.g., asking what they are trying to convey or how they think someone will interpret their image) as well as providing ongoing feedback may help students to focus and clarify the information they are presenting with graphics.

Understanding How Students May Interpret and Evaluate Visual Images

Teachers should realize that even a graphic that looks uncomplicated may challenge a reader's interpretive skills. Many inferences may be necessary for even the simplest visual aid or graphic. Students may first skip the graphics or skim them without interpreting them. Students also may just focus on the graphics without paying attention to the written explanations. Even students with training in the use of graphic information may fail to transfer that knowledge to other content areas or have trouble going from print to graphic and then back to print. In either case, students may not have been taught how to use multiple representations of information. Teachers can help students use multiple representations of information via open-book and guided reading. A teacher can also show how to use a chart or graph via electronic tools, including overhead projectors and interactive whiteboards. Examples of effective presentations and how to create them can be shared with the students. Resources and software to improve their writing (mentor texts) (Dorfman & Cappelli, 2007) can give students examples of how to select images to use with text (e.g., consideration of how the image parallels or complements the text).

Visual design can be viewed as containing its own grammar (Kress & van Leeuwen, 2001). Teachers can help students to understand and apply such visual grammar by teaching its component parts (Wysocki, Johnson-Eilola, Selfe, & Sirc, 2004). Some of these key components are:

- Visual impact: how the overall visual design appeals to the reader (e.g., through detail, layout, color).

- Visual coherence: how the design creates unity and wholeness (e.g., via shapes, line, imagery).

- Visual salience: using design features to generate a desired effect (e.g., through varying size, colors, clip art, etc.)

- Organization: how the layout of the page creates a unique pattern understandable to the reader (e.g., through consideration of how items in the layout might be arranged on the page).

These features of visual literacy overlap and can guide students toward an awareness of the visual literacy.

Teachers should model how to read, complement, and interpret visual images whenever students are required to create them. Pictures and other graphics can arouse interest and stimulate thinking. Graphics also can add clarity, prevent misunderstanding, show step-by-step development, and exhibit the status of things, events, and processes, as well as demonstrate comparisons and contrasts (Vacca and Vacca 1989).

Integrating Technology for Producing Communications

Teachers should provide students with opportunities to use state-of-the-art technology and tools. Doing so will motivate children to read and write as well as monitor their writing and enable them to communicate with different media. For instance, one could assume that the goal of word-processor software is simply to record written information. With technological advances, such software now offers writers help with the editing their documents. Other uses for this software include creating semantic maps, tables, charts, and graphs. Such writing-related elements as spell check, definitions of terms, thesaurus, and even suggestions for sentence constructions are commonly available in programs like Microsoft Word. A spell checker not only helps identify misspelled words but also frees students from the pressure of spelling things right, at least at the drafting stage. Students should be encouraged to put their ideas in writing without stopping to check spelling. When they finish writing, they address other important concerns like spelling. Students also should be reminded that the spell checker won't always work. Therefore, children should be guided to pay attention to corrections and learn from them.

Teachers should show children how to take advantage of programs available for communicating and creating electronic products. The products they can create include a classroom newsletter, a multimedia presentation, and a video response to a group project. Students should keep their audience and purpose in mind when they create their pieces. Doing so will also help them make sure the language they use is appropriate and understandable for their audience.

COMPETENCY 013: ASSESSMENT OF DEVELOPING LITERACY

The teacher understands the basic principles of literacy assessment and uses a variety of assessments to guide literacy instruction.

Knowledge and Use of Literacy Assessment

The two main types of assessment are formal and informal. Each has a place in the classroom, especially the literacy classroom. Teachers understand the importance of ongoing assessment as an instructional tool and use both informal and formal assessment measures to assess students' learning in their classroom. Teachers should never group children permanently because of one assessment, either formal or informal. Any grouping should come about after the considering several assessments, and the grouping should be flexible to recognize differences among the students in each group.

Informal Assessments

Teachers can learn valuable information by observing their students at work. Many school districts use an inventory/report card to inform adults at home about children's progress. Through trial and error, teachers usually develop their own means of assessing their students' skills. Almost every book on teaching reading and writing includes informal tests. Teachers can also develop their own informal reading assessment. The purpose of these assessments is to collect information about what students can and cannot do. One such assessment is the running record. A running record assesses students' word identification skills and fluency in oral reading. In a running record, the teacher uses a copy of the page to mark each word the child mispronounces as the teacher listens to a student read a page. If the student misses a word, the teacher writes the incorrect word over the printed word, draws a line through each word the child skips, and draws an arrow under repeated words.

Reading Levels

Reading specialists have identified three reading proficiency levels, independent, instructional, and frustration. If the student reads 95% of the words correctly, the child is reading at the independent level. If the student reads 90% to 94% of the words correctly, the child is reading at the instructional level, which means the child can perform satisfactorily with help from the teacher. If the student reads 89% or fewer words correctly, the child is reading at the frustration level.

These reading levels are determined based on children's ability to answer comprehension questions after reading passages. Proficiency levels are assessed through informal reading inventories.

Informal Reading Inventories

Informal reading inventories are assessment instruments designed to identify children's proficiency levels. Most basal reader books contain an informal reading inventory. These passages are graded by reading levels, via comprehension questions. Teachers begin with a passage at the reading level of the child and continue increasing the complexity until the child is unable to respond to the comprehension questions.

Story Retelling

Asking a child to retell a story is another informal assessment. The ability to retell a story is useful to the teacher, parent, and the child. Informal assessment measures can also include observations, journals, conversations, and written drafts.

Structured Informal Observations

The teacher may also observe individual or group work. Usually, the teacher makes a checklist of competencies, skills, or requirements and then uses the list to check those for student or group displays. A teacher wishing to emphasize interviewing skills could devise a checklist that includes personal appearance, mannerisms, and confidence as well as addressing the questions asked. A teacher who wants to emphasize careful listening might observe a discussion with a checklist that includes paying attention, summarizing others' ideas, asking questions, and not interrupting.

Checklists let teachers capture behaviors that cannot be measured with a paper-and-pencil test, such as following the correct sequence of steps in a science experiment or including all important elements in a speech in class. The structure of a checklist is both an advantage and a disadvantage. The structure, provides consistency but lacks flexibility. An open-ended comment section at the end of a checklist can help overcome this disadvantage.

Anecdotal Records

Anecdotal records sometimes help. For example, they can capture how a group of students solves a problem. The anecdotal records can be useful when giving feedback to the group. Students can also be taught to write explanations of the procedures they use for their projects or science experiments. An anecdotal record can include all relevant information, but its disadvantages include how much time it takes. Assigning a grade for it also can be difficult, but if the anecdotal record is used solely for feedback, no grade is necessary.

Portfolio Assessment

Portfolios collect students' best work. They can be used in any subject in which the teacher wants students to take more responsibility for planning, carrying out, and organizing their own learning. Like a portfolio created by an artist, model, or performer, a student portfolio provides a succinct picture of the child's achievements over time. Portfolios may contain essays or articles written on paper, videotapes, multimedia presentations on computer disks, or a combination of these. Language arts teachers often use portfolios to collect the best samples of student writing over a year. Because it is unrealistic to include every piece of a student's work in one portfolio, teachers should provide or help students develop guidelines for what to include. Portfolios require students to devise a way to evaluate their own work. A portfolio should not be a scrapbook for collecting handouts or work done by others, but it also can include work by a group in which the student participated.

Portfolios can provide a clear picture of students' progress, and they are not affected by one inferior test grade. They also help develop students' self-assessment skills. Portfolios require time to teach students how to develop them, but the time is well spent when students learn valuable skills. Another concern is how much time teachers must spend to assess portfolios. However, as students become more proficient at self-assessment, the teacher can spend more time in coaching and advising students throughout the development of their portfolios and less time evaluating them at the end. Because parents may not understand how the teacher will grade the portfolios, the teacher should devise a system that students and parents understand before work on the portfolios begins.

Miscue Analysis

Miscue analysis is an assessment procedure to assess oral reading. Miscues refer to any deviation from text made during oral reading. The procedure for its implementation follows:

1. Select reading material a bit above the current reading level of the child. The complete story should be about 500 words.

2. Provide a copy of the selection to the child.

3. Use a triple-spaced copy of the selection to allow room to write comments.

4. Record the reading.

5. Provide instructions to the child and tell him or her that you cannot help during the reading.

6. Ask questions about the story.

7. Let the reader listen to the recording and then analyze it.

8. Look for consistent miscues and pay special attention to first and final clusters/blends and digraphs.

Running Records

Running records are ongoing assessments designed to analyze the reading performance of early readers. As the student reads aloud, the teacher uses a checklist to record the performance. The teacher uses specific symbols to represent substitutions, omissions, insertions, repetitions, and self-corrections. The teacher calculates how many words the child read correctly to arrive at a percentage to determine whether the selection is at the student's independent, instructional, or frustration level. The teacher also can analyze miscues to determine whether the child is relying upon visual, semantics and/or syntactic cues while reading. The teacher can use this information to help the student during word study.

Formal Assessments

Formal measures may include teacher-made tests, district exams, and standardized tests. Formative and summative evaluations are part of effective instruction. Formative evaluation occurs when the teacher or the students monitor progress while instruction can still be modified. Summative evaluation occurs at the end of a specific time or course of study. Usually, a summative evaluation applies a single grade or score to represent a student's performance.

Teachers should use a variety of formal assessments. Teacher-made instruments should be developed when planning goals and outcomes rather than after the completion of the lessons. Carefully planned objectives and assessment instruments guide lesson development for the teacher. Paper-and-pencil tests are the most common method for evaluating progress.

Criterion-Referenced Tests

In criterion-referenced tests (CRTs), the teacher tries to measure each student against uniform objectives or criteria (standards). CRTs allow the possibility that all students can score 100% on the test because they understand the concepts being tested. Teacher-made tests should be criterion-referenced because the teacher should develop them to measure the achievement of predetermined course outcomes. If teachers have properly prepared lessons based on the outcomes and if students have mastered the outcomes, scores on CRTs should be high. Students are not competing with each other for a high score because this test does not limit the number of students who can score well. Some commercially developed tests are criterion-referenced, but most are norm-referenced.

The State of Texas Assessments of Academic Readiness (STAAR) is a criterion-referenced basic skills test for children in grades 3 to 12. This criterion-referenced test assesses the implementation and the mastery of the Texas Essential Knowledge and Skills (TEKS), the Texas state curriculum.

Norm-Referenced Tests

A norm-referenced test (NRT) is designed to compare the performance of groups of students. This test is competitive because a limited number of students can score well. A plot of NRT scores resembles a bell-shaped curve, with most scores clustering around the center and a few scores at each end. The midpoint is the average of test data, and half will score above average and half below. The bell-shaped curve is a mathematical description of the results of tossing coins. It represents the chance or normal distribution of skills, knowledge, or events across the general population. A survey of the height of sixth-grade boys will result in an average height, with half the boys above average height and half below. A small number will have heights far above average, and a small number will have heights far below. However, most heights will cluster around the average. A percentile score (not to be confused with a percentage) is a way of reporting a student's NRT score. The percentile score indicates the percentage of the population whose scores fall at or below the student's score. For example, if a group of students score at the 80th percentile, it means that the group scored as well as or better than 79% of the students who took the test. A student with a score at the 50th percentile has an average score. Percentile scores rank students from highest to lowest.

By themselves, percentile scores do not indicate how well the student has mastered the content objectives. Raw scores indicate how many questions the student answered correctly and are thus useful in computing a percentage score.

The Texas Education Agency (TEA) has a comprehensive list of approved norm-referenced tests from which districts can choose to assess students' achievement in the state. This list includes the California Achievement Test (CAT), Stanford Achievement Test, and the Iowa Test of Basic Skills (ITBS).

Authentic Assessments

Paper-and-pencil and essay tests are not the only methods of assessment. Assessments include projects, observations, checklists, anecdotal records, portfolios, self-assessments, and peer assessments. Although these assessments often take more time and effort to plan and administer, they often provide a more authentic measurement of progress. Portfolio is a form of authentic assessment because students gather the materials without thinking about the assessment process. They are just carrying out activities that later can be used for assessment.

Performance-Based Assessment

Some states and districts are moving toward performance-based tests, which assess students on how well they perform certain tasks. Students must use higher-level thinking skills to apply, analyze, synthesize, and evaluate ideas and data. For example, assessing content using a performance-based test might require students to read a problem, design and carry out a laboratory experiment, and then write summaries of their findings. The performance-based assessment would evaluate both the process students used and the output they produced. An English performance-based test might ask students to read a selection of literature and then write a critical analysis. A mathematics performance-based test might state a problem, require students to invent one or more methods of solving the problem, use one of the methods to arrive at a solution, and then write the solution and an explanation of the processes they used.

Performance-based assessments let students create solutions to problems or questions and require them to use higher-level skills. This approach has weaknesses, however. It can be time consuming, and it often requires multiple resources, which can be expensive. Teachers also must get training in how to apply the test. However, many schools consider performance-based testing to be a more authentic measure of achievement than traditional tests.

Constructing Classroom-Based Tests

Teachers must consider professional and technical factors when designing tests. They first must recognize that test construction is as creative, challenging, and important as the rest of their teaching. The planning and background that contribute to teaching are incomplete unless evaluation of student performance provides accurate feedback to the teacher and the student about the learning.

Good tests stem from careful planning, creative thinking, and hard work as well as technical knowledge about the methods of measuring student knowledge and performance. Classroom tests that accomplish their purpose result from the development of a pool of items and the constant revision of those items based on feedback. This process makes the evaluation of students valid and reliable. Tests provide a valuable instructional aid because they help determine student progress and provide feedback to teachers about their own effectiveness. The tests reveal misunderstanding and problems that can help the teacher recognize areas that need instructional development. This information also provides the basis for the remediation of students and the revision of teaching procedures. The construction, administration, and proper scoring of classroom tests are thus among the most important activities in teaching.

Essay Tests

There are advantages and disadvantages to essay tests. Advantages of essay questions include the possibility for students to be creative in their answers, the opportunity for students to explain their responses, and the potential to test for higher-level thinking skills. Disadvantages of essay questions include the time students need to formulate meaningful responses, and the time teachers need to evaluate the essays. In addition, language difficulties can make essay tests extremely difficult for some students, including ELLs. Consistency in evaluating essays can also be a problem for some teachers, but an outline of the acceptable answers—a scoring rubric—can help a teacher avoid inconsistency. Teachers who write specific questions and know what they are looking for are more likely to be consistent in grading. Also, if there are several essay questions, the effective teacher grades all student responses to the first question, then moves on to all responses to the second, and so on.

Using Rubrics for Assessment

A rubric is a checklist with assigned point values. To create a rubric, a teacher uses the lesson objectives. Students should get an explanation of the rubric when they get their writing assignment so that they can use it as a guide while they work. The teacher then uses the rubric to evaluate the completed assignment. Rubrics help teachers provide clear, well-planned instructions and guidelines for activities and can decrease student frustration. When teachers model what they expect and state clear objectives or goals for each assignment, students perform better.

Scoring Compositions

Holistic scoring is used to evaluate the writing of students in Texas. The scoring of the whole writing sample is based on a pre-established criteria contained in a rubric. The writing rubric used to score the performance on STAAR is based on four levels. Students need to score at level three or four to pass the test.

Ongoing Assessment

Ongoing assessment describes any assessment done as part of the teaching cycle. It provides teachers with updated information about students' progress as well as the challenges that children face. This information can then be incorporated into daily instruction. All informal assessments are considered ongoing assessments.

Assessing English Language Learners

The Texas English Language Proficiency Assessment System (TELPAS) is the Texas assessment instrument for English language learners (ELLs). This instrument was designed to comply with the accountability requirements of the federal Elementary and Secondary Education Act. This instrument assesses the progress of ELLs in grades K–12 in the four language domains, listening, speaking, reading, and writing. The federal legislation requires that all ELLs be assessed yearly in all four language areas to document progress toward English language mastery. Students begin taking TELPAS in kindergarten and stop only when they are reclassified as fluent English speakers (TEA, 2011).

For students in grades K–1, TELPAS uses a holistic approach and classroom observations to assess the four language domains. In grades 2–12, TELPAS uses a multiple-choice format to assess reading comprehension and uses holistically rated instruments based on classroom observations to assess listening, speaking, and writing.

The TEKS and the English Language Proficiency Standards

TELPAS is aligned with the K–12 Texas state curriculum and the English Language Proficiency Standards (ELPS) mandated by state legislation (TAC Chapter 74.4). When instruction to ELLs is delivered in English, the ELPS are implemented as part of an ongoing content area support for ELLs. To implement this support, teachers delivering content instruction in English are required by law to add language proficiency objectives to their daily lesson plans (TAC Chapter 74.4). The implementation of the ELPS objectives requires content-area teachers to select the appropriate ELPS objective for the lesson so that ELLs can develop the academic proficiency to benefit from instruction and master the state curriculum.

Diversity in the Classroom

Teachers appreciate diversity. An instructor recognizes how diversity in the classroom creates an environment in which everyone accepts and celebrates the diversity and the uniqueness of individuals. In that environment, the teacher and the students view the race, ethnicity, religion, national origin, learning style, and gender of learners and the teacher as strengths that foster learning with and from each other.

References

Beck, I. L., McKeown, M. G., and Kucan, L. (2002). Bringing words to life: Robust vocabulary instruction. New York: Guilford.

Bloom, B. S. (1956). Taxonomy of educational objectives: The classification of educational goals: Handbook I, cognitive domain. New York: Toronto: Longmans, Green.

Brown, D. K. (1997). The children's literature web guide. Retrieved from *http://www.ucalgary. ca/~dkbrown/cinderella.html*.

Calderon, M. (2007). Teaching reading to English language learners, Grades 6-12: A framework for improving achievement in the content areas. Thousand Oaks, CA: Corwin Press.

Chall, J. S. (1983). Stages of reading development, New York: McGraw-Hill.

Clay, M. M. (2002). An observation survey of early literacy achievement (2nd ed.). Portsmouth, NH: Heinemann.

Dorfman, L. R., & Cappelli. R. (2007). Mentor texts: Teaching writing through children's literature, K–6. Portland, ME: Stenhouse Publishers.

Ehri, L. (1998). Grapheme-phoneme knowledge is essential for learning to read words in English. In J. Metsala and L. Ehri (Eds.), Word recognition in beginning literacy (pp. 3–40). Mahwah, NJ: Erlbaum.

Goudvis, A. & Harvey, S. (2000). Strategies that work. Portland, ME: Stenhouse Publishers.

Gough, P. B. (1972). One second of reading. In Ed. H. Singer & R. B. Ruddell (Eds.), Theoretical models and processes of reading (3rd ed.) (pp. 661–686). Newark, Delaware: International Reading Association.

Graves, D. H. (1983). Writing: Teachers and children at work. Portsmouth, NH: Heinemann Educational Books.

Heath, S. B. (1983). Ways with words: Language, life and work in communities and classrooms. Cambridge: Cambridge University Press.

Kress, G. & Van Leeuwen, T. J. (2001). Multimodal Discourse: The modes and media of contemporary communication. London, England: Oxford University Press.

Lapp, D., D. Fisher, J. Flood, & Cabello, A. (2001). An integrated approach to the teaching and assessment of language arts. In S. Rollins Hurley & J. Villamil Tinajero (Eds.), Literacy assessment of second language learners (pp. 1–24). Boston, MA: Allyn and Bacon.

Marzano, R. (2010). Teaching basic and advanced vocabulary: A framework for direct instruction. United States: Heinle Cengage Learning

National Reading Panel (2000). Teaching children to read: An evidence-based assessment of the scientific research literature of reading and its implications for reading instruction. Accessed at *http://www.nichd.nih.gov/publications/pubs/nrp/pages/smallbook.aspx*.

Palinscar, A. S. & Brown, A. L. (1984). Reciprocal teaching of comprehension-fostering and comprehension-monitoring activities. Cognition and Instruction (1): 117–175.

Peregoy, S. F., O. F. Boyle, & Cadiero-Kapplan, K. (2008). Reading, writing and learning in ESL: A Resource Book for K–12 Teachers (5th ed.). New York: Pearson.

Piper, T. (2006). Language and learning: The home school years. (4th ed.). Columbus, Ohio: Merrill Prentice Hall.

Regional Education Laboratory (n.d.). 6+1 Trait writing. Retrieved from *http://educationnorthwest. org/traits*).

Reuzel, R. D., & Cooter, R. (1992). Teaching children to read: From basals to books. New York: Macmillan Publishing Co.

Snow, C. E., Burns, M.S., & Griffin, P. (1998). Preventing reading difficulties in young children. Washington, DC: National Academy Press.

Stewig, J. W. & Jett-Simpson, M. (1995). Language arts in the early childhood classroom. Belmont, CA: Wadsworth.

TEA (2015) Linguistic Accommodations for ELLs Participating in the STAAR Program. Retrieved from *http://www.seguin.k12.tx.us/users/0020/docs/2015_Linguistic_Accommodations.pdf*.

TEA (n.d.). TELPAS Resources Student Assessment Home. Retrieved from *http://www.tea. state. tx.us/student.assessment/ell/telpas*.

TEA (2011). Educator Guide to the Texas English Language Proficiency Assessment (TELPAS). Student Assessment Division, TEA, Austin, Texas. Retrieved from *http://www.seisd.net/common/pages/DisplayFile.aspx?itemId=2069345*.

TEA (2014-2015) Rater Training for 2014-2015 –TELPAS. Division of Student Assessment. Retrieved from *http://tea.texas.gov/student.assessment/ell/telpas*.

TAC chapter 74 (n.d.). Curriculum Requirements. Subchapter A. Required Curriculum. Online *http://ritter.tea.state.tx.us/rules/tac/chapter074/ch074a.html*.

The Center for Applied Research in Education (1988). Phonics generalizations. Retrieved from *http://www.thegrowingroom.org/page.cfm?p=1747&eid=275*.

Thomas, E., & Robinson, H. (1972). Improving reading in every class: A source book for teachers. Boston: Allyn and Bacon.

University of Oregon (n.d.). Center for Teaching and Learning. Big Ideas in Beginning Reading. Retrieved from *http://reading.uoregon.edu/big_ideas/au/au_what.php*.

Vacca, R. T., & J. A. Vacca, J. A. (1989). Content area reading. Glenview, IL: Scott Foresman.

Wysocki, A. F., Johnson-Eilola, J., Selfe, L., & Sirc, G. (2004). Writing new media: Theory and applications for expanding the teaching of composition. Logan, UT: Utah State University Press.

Subject Test II: Mathematics (802)

The teacher understands how students learn mathematical skills and uses that knowledge to plan, organize, and implement instruction and assess learning.

In 2000, the National Council of Teachers of Mathematics (NCTM) published the *Principles and Standards for School Mathematics*. The national organization's goals include the development and improvement of mathematics education. In the NCTM publication, the association identified six principles and ten standards that children in kindergarten through grade 12 should be able to master. The document guides states and district curricula development and specifies the mathematics content knowledge students should develop.

Principles of Mathematics

The NCTM (2000) identified six principles that should guide mathematics instruction. These include equity, curriculum, teaching, learning, assessment, and technology.

- **Equity**—Excellence in mathematics education requires equity: high expectations and strong support for all students.

- **Curriculum**—A curriculum must be coherent, focused on important and well-articulated mathematics concepts across the grades.

- **Teaching**—Effective mathematics teaching requires understanding what students know and need to learn while challenging and supporting students to learn it well.

- **Learning**—Students must learn mathematics with understanding, actively building new knowledge from experience and previous knowledge.

- **Assessment**—Assessment should support the learning of important mathematics concepts, and furnish useful information to both teachers and students.

- **Technology**—Technology is essential in teaching and learning mathematics; it influences the teaching of mathematics while enhancing and facilitating students' learning.

Mathematics and English Language Learners

Contrary to popular belief, mathematics is not a universal language. It is a language with special nomenclature and unique concepts. Even the way that people perform mathematical processes is often different across cultures. For example, the processes used for division in Mexico and the Dominican Republic differ from the process used in the United States. In Mexico, the problem is set up in a similar fashion but most of the steps are done mentally, as opposed to the American way in which students write every step as part of the process. As an example, for the problem "11 divided by 2," children in Mexico are taught to multiply 2 by 5 to obtain 10, but they do not write the 10 under the 11—they do it mentally and write the remainder below the 11. In the Dominican Republic, children do not use the division bracket traditionally used in the United States and Mexico; instead, they use a bracket similar to an elongated **L**, and they place the **divisor** inside the bracket and the **dividend** outside. Thus, children from Mexico and the Dominican Republic might experience confusion when asked to perform division "the American way."

Table 4–1 illustrates three different processes used to perform division.

Table 4-1. Division in Three Cultures

American	Mexican	Dominican Republic
$\begin{array}{r} 5 \\ 2\overline{)11} \\ -10 \\ \hline 1R \end{array}$	$\begin{array}{r} 5 \\ 2\overline{)11} \\ 1R \end{array}$	$\begin{array}{r} 11 \ \lfloor 5 \\ -10 \ \ 2 \\ 1R \ \ 0 \end{array}$

The use of Arabic numbers does not present problems for English language learners (ELLs). The real challenge is to comprehend the **explanation** of the process in a language that ELLs have not yet mastered. Providing examples of the mathematical process and modeling while describing the process can definitely improve comprehension. Students who enjoy **inductive teaching**—learning through examples—will definitely benefit from this approach. However, students who enjoy the **deductive approach**—learning step by step—might experience comprehension problems.

The Nomenclature of Mathematics

In addition to the obvious English communication problems, ELLs face a number of challenges with the technical vocabulary or the nomenclature of mathematics for at least three reasons. First, the mathematics classroom tends to abound in assumptions concerning students' prior knowledge of specialized terms, such as **denominator**, **subtraction**, **minuend**, **divisor**, and **subtrahend**, among others. Second, the terms having one meaning in one subject domain can take on an entirely different meaning in the vocabulary of mathematics; these terms include **quarter**, **column**, **product**, **rational**, **even**, and **table**. Third, the vocabulary tends to encompass a variety of homophones (words pronounced the same way but having different meanings), which can be troublesome for English learners who are unaccustomed to the new language. **Table 4-2** lists various mathematics terms, and **Table 4-3** presents unfamiliar structures that may be confusing for all students.

Table 4-2. Terminology of Mathematics

Terminology	Generic Meaning	Mathematical Meaning
Even	Equal amount, same level	Numbers divisible by 2 yielding no remainder
Face	Front of human head	Surface of a geometric solid
Plane	Flat surface, aircraft, or without adornment (plain)	A two-dimensional surface
Mean	Not nice, or to express a particular message	Arithmetic average of a set of values
Right	Correct, proper, or a direction	Forming a 90° angle
Some/Sum	A small amount (some)	Answer to addition problem
Volume	Loudness of sounds	Quantity of liquid

Table 4-3. Unfamiliar Structures

Technical terms (e.g., equation, exponents, inequalities, quotient)
Varied degrees of focus on problem solving versus computation and notation
Use of passive voice for most problem-solving questions and statements
Use of various mathematical symbols unfamiliar to ELLs (e.g., π, $\$$, $<$, $=$, $\pm$, and $\neq$)
Multiple words or phrases indicating the same operations (e.g., fractional parts, divide, separate, equivalent parts, etc.)
Unclear "if . . . then . . ." problem statements
Specific examples in word problems drawn from culturally unfamiliar situations
Focus on problem solving using cultural bias strategies or context unfamiliar to ELLs
Multiple words with similar meanings (e.g., sum, total)
New information that does not fit with prior knowledge of subject matter (e.g., time, temperature, money, measurement, use of manipulatives in the classroom)

Developmentally Appropriate Instruction

Children develop a basic understanding of numbers at two years of age or even younger. Infants and toddlers understand the concepts of "one" or "more," usually within the context of food. Rote counting, or the verbal repetition of numbers, begins around the age of two to three years. This rote memorization can be used as a foundation for building an understanding of the number concepts of combining, separating, and naming amounts using concrete objects as soon as language develops. In their effort to develop the idea of amount, children must first know the language of number words (Fuson & Hall, 1983). Sometimes children appear to be counting when, in fact, they are naming the objects. For example, when a child has eight red blocks and begins to count out loud, "One, two, three, four, five, six, seven, eight," pointing to each block as he/she goes, and then says, "Eight," we need to ask questions. "How do you know?" or "Can you show me eight?" will tell us whether the child recognizes that the entire set makes up "eight" or that the last block is named "Eight." They need to understand that the idea of amount is inclusive of all the previously counted blocks, not just the name of the last block.

Children should be encouraged to think about numbers and the quantity of objects in meaningful situations. For example, children may be asked to hold up five crayons or hand out five crayons to each student. Kamii (2000) states that, to deepen quantification knowledge, students should compare sets in real-life situations rather than just counting out objects. It is important for children to use movable objects, moving to larger quantities, in order to create their own internal mental relationships while interacting with various types of objects (Pepper & Hunting, 1998).

In making the move from quantification to computation, it is helpful to pose an addition question by using concrete objects. Using a context for the objects helps children make their own sense and helps them to develop their own autonomy about the operation of addition. For example, a simple addition problem can be introduced by putting beads on a string and asking children to add or subtract the various colors to create a necklace or bracelet. Many times children will prefer to "use paper and pencil" instead of objects, so they can externalize their own ideas and use drawings instead. This is probably why children do not choose to use counters to solve word problems (Kamii, 2000).

Several materials or concrete objects can be used to help children demonstrate the mathematics of the problems. It is important to distinguish between **discrete models** (e.g., counters) and **continuous models** (e.g., number lines that children might choose for solving problems). Personal algorithms can grow directly from meaningful experiences acting out problems, whether through direct modeling or counting until the mathematics concepts make sense to the child.

Cognitive Development and Mathematics

The cognitive development of children in pre-kindergarten (pre-K) through grade 6 represents a special challenge when attempting to learn the symbolic and abstract representation used in mathematics. Children are expected to learn an entire organized discipline, usually represented in symbolic form. They may learn to deal with symbols well enough to perform arithmetic operations. However, having learned arithmetic procedures is not sufficient for real understanding of the concepts that symbolic manipulations represent. There is no guarantee that children will be able to use those concepts to solve problems.

Learning mathematics requires children to create and recreate mathematics relationships in their own minds. Children need direct and concrete interaction with mathematical ideas; these ideas are not accessible from abstractions and symbols. Continuous interaction between a child's mind and concrete experiences in the real world are necessary to learn concepts in math.

As a developmental biologist, **Jean Piaget** (1896–1980) observed and recorded the intellectual abilities of infants, children, and adolescents. His stages of intellectual development were related to brain growth and led him to conclude that the thinking and reasoning of children were dominated by preoperational thought—a pattern of thinking that is egocentric, centered, irreversible, and nontransformational (Piaget & Inhelder, 1969). His theory concerned the growth of intelligence, the emergence and acquisition of schemata, or schemes of a child using "developmental stages," to explain how children acquire new information. Piaget divided the schemes children use into four main stages:

- Sensorimotor stage (birth–2 years)
- Preoperational stage (years 2–7)
- Concrete Operational stage (years 7–11)
- Formal Operational stage (years 11–adult)

The importance of these stages of development as conceptualized by Piaget is the recognition of the child's ability to integrate symbolic referents (objects or experiences) and to interpret the mathematical concept. Children around six years old (first graders in the Preoperational stage) tend to fix their attention on a single aspect of a relationship. For example, if two rows of the same number of coins are lined up, one-to-one, equally spaced, and children are asked whether the number of coins in the two rows are the same, they are likely to judge the two to be equal. When the appearance of one of the rows is changed, either by spreading the coins out farther or stacking them, children are more likely to judge them as being unequal. Their response is not based on logical reasoning but on their own perception.

According to Piaget, the **Preoperational stage** of development includes the processes of symbolic functioning, centration, intuitive thought, egocentrism, and inability to conserve. Children in the **Concrete Operational stage** exhibit the developmental processes of decentering, reversibility, conservation, serialization, classification, and elimination of egocentrism. The **Formal Operational stage** of cognitive development begins around eleven years of age (puberty) and continues into adulthood. The characteristics of this stage focus on the ability to use symbols and think abstractly.

Sperry Smith (2008) reports that children in the Preoperational stage experience problems with at least two perceptual concepts—centration and conservation.

- **Centration**—Focusing on only one aspect of a situation or problem. For example, let's say we take two 5″ × 8″ cards and roll each into a tube, rolling one the short way and the other the long way. We then tape them to make cylindrical containers, and fill each tube with beans to compare how much each holds. When presented with the two cylinders, a preschool child might judge the quantity of beans in the tall cylinder to be more than the shorter, based on his or her perception of tall and short as opposed to the actual volume of the container.

- **Conservation**—Understanding that quantity, length, or number of items is unrelated to the arrangement or appearance of the object or items. This limitation can affect children's ability to measure volume and to understand the value of money. For example, children may think a nickel is worth more than a dime because the coin is larger, or that five nickels are more than a quarter.

During the Concrete Operational stage of cognitive development (grades 2 to 7) children experience rapid growth in cognitive development. This stage is characterized by the ability to think logically about concrete objects or relationships. Some of the characteristics of children at this stage are as follows:

- **Decentering**—The child can take into account multiple aspects of a problem to solve it; the child can form a conclusion based on reason rather than perception.

- **Reversibility**—The child understands that the objects can be changed and then returned to their original state; the child can determine that $4 + 4 = 8$ and $8 - 4 = 4$, the original quantity.

- **Conservation**—The child understands that quantity, length, or number of items is unrelated to the arrangement or appearance of the object; the child can discern that if water is transferred from a filled cup to a pitcher, it will conserve the quantity and be equal to the original filled cup.

- **Serialization**—The child is able to arrange objects in an order according to size, shape, or any other attribute; the child can arrange geometric forms by shape, size, color, and thickness of the form.

- **Classification**—The child can name and identify sets of objects according to appearance, size, or other characteristics; the child can arrange objects based on characteristics.

- **Elimination of Egocentrism**—The child is able to view things from another's perspective; the child can retell a story from another child's perspective.

Since Piaget completed his work, contemporary researchers (often referred to as neo-Piagetian and post-Piagetian researchers) found that Piaget had underestimated the abilities of children in the preschool and early elementary years. Even before the second or early third grade, some students develop more sophisticated thinking and reasoning skills, especially if they have had adequate instruction and opportunities to interact with adults and competent peers (Vygotsky, 1986). Children's intellectual development appears to proceed continuously, and their cognitive development is influenced by their culture and by instruction (Santrock, 2003). This relates to cognitively guided instruction (CGI) (Carpenter, Fennema, Franke, Levi & Empson, 1999; Flavell, 1985; Kamii, 2000). The CGI model depends heavily on a well-developed structure of how children learn a given topic and on the ability of the teacher to assess the knowledge of each child and provide appropriate experiences. Kamii's work and CGI's researchers connect their respective research to understanding how children learn mathematics concepts and how to recognize different strategies young children use when they execute operations.

Mathematics in Real-Life Situations

Mathematical concepts are an integral part of our daily life. Children should be encouraged to pay attention to daily activities and identify the mathematical principles used to perform the activity or the task. A simple visit to the local supermarket requires some level of mathematical development to communicate effectively. For instance, reading product labels requires an understanding of weights and measurements. It also requires knowledge of the standard and metric systems and the value of money. Without this kind of knowledge, it would be practically impossible to make product comparisons.

Consider the following situation:

> A consumer is trying to decide between two products—a kilogram of coffee for $3.99 or 2 pounds of the same coffee for $3.99. What item represents the best value?

In order to make this decision, the consumer must have an understanding of the **standard** and **metric** systems of measurement. Most consumers in the United States will probably go with 2 pounds because they are familiar with the **standard** system of measurement. However, this option is not the best value for the money because 1 kilogram is equivalent to 2.2 pounds. Parents can present this kind of problem to children and ask them to help in the decision-making process. When mathematics is used in real-life situations, it becomes more meaningful and easier to internalize.

As seen in this example, it is important for children to learn to use mathematical principles to assist with their day-to-day lives. As children reach adulthood, they should already understand some basic real-life situations and meanings, such as the purpose of banks, different taxes and to what they apply, and how to use credit responsibly. One method of teaching the students these topics is to allow them to balance a budget for a family. They would understand the cost of groceries, bills for a home, and how much money it takes to raise children.

Manipulatives in Mathematics

Children can benefit from group instruction and the use of concrete objects and manipulatives. Manipulatives can be used to provide "hands-on-learning" for kindergarten to high school students. Manipulatives enhance student understanding, enable students to have conversations that are grounded in a common model, and help students to recognize and correct any misconceptions they may have.

Manipulatives also are an excellent way for students to develop self-verbalizing learning strategies. As they use the senses of sight, touch, and hearing, students should be encouraged to talk their way through each problem, either with peers or to themselves. Physical materials can model the situation and illuminate some of the aspects of the processes of various operations, such as multiplication and division. It is important that the concept is understood by the student and that the manipulative is appropriate for the concept so the materials can be used in ways that make sense. It is important that students first develop relationships that are mental abstractions about the mathematics being represented by the physical materials and then develop a corresponding symbolic representation. Teachers have to ask appropriate questions and listen to students explain their thinking to know whether they have abstracted the idea from the physical models.

In addition to the manipulatives used in mathematics, the typical classroom contains a variety of instructional materials to support children in the learning process (see **Table 4-4**). Teachers should be encouraged to use these aids to make mathematics more engaging and meaningful to children.

Games are highly motivational for children in pre-K through grade 6. A simple game using dice can be used to teach counting, place value, probability, and fractions. Color tiles, unifix cubes, two-color counters, and pattern blocks can be used to teach sequencing, patterns, odd and even numbers, probability, and statistics. Children learn best when they can manipulate materials to check their understanding and link what they are learning to real-life situations. In fact, they learn about fractions initially outside the school. For example, children often hear adults use fractions in various conversations : "You can have half of my cookie." "My gas tank is half full." "The recipe calls for two-thirds of a cup of cereal."

Table 4-4. Types of Manipulatives and Instructional Materials Used in the Mathematics Classroom

Grades K-1	Grade 2	Grade 3	Grade 4	Grade 5	Grade 6
Beads, string, sewing cards	Blocks	Base-ten blocks	Geometric Solids	Cuisenaire rods	Cuisenaire rods
Snap cubes, straws	Cubes	Tangrams	Geoboards	Virtual manipulatives	Virtual manipulatives
Color tiles	Chips	Pattern blocks	Calculators	Calculators	Calculators
Two-color counters	Measuring cups	Playing cards	Protractors	Graduated cylinders	Attribute logic blocks
Macaroni, beans, cereal, candy, raisins, crackers	Attribute shapes	Scales: customary and metric	Tangrams	Timers	Algebra tiles
Buttons, sticks, stones, shells	Money models	Magnetic numbers, chalk boards	Pentominoes	Metric beaker set for volume	Video games
Paper clips	Number lines	Spinners, dice	Graphing paper	Metric trundle wheel	Math software games
Toothpicks	Dominoes	Calendar	Fraction kit	Fraction tower cubes	iPods
Legos	Unifix cubes	Fractional shapes	Platform scale	Connecting cubes	Balance metric weight set
Egg cartons	Clock faces	Games	Customary weight set	Board games	Computer/Internet
Teddy bear counters	Ruler, yard stick, metric stick	Measuring tape	Metric weight set	Fraction tiles	Smart boards
Board games	Balance scales	0–99 charts	Graphing boards	Geoboards	Digital cameras, camcorders
Pictographs	Linear graphs	Bar graphs	Scatter plot graphs	Pie charts and graphs	Computer templates

Numbers and fractions represent a challenge to elementary students. A number of ideas about fractions take shape informally in children's minds from their experiences. They may have heard of one-half, one-fourth, and one-third of a unit—but not two-thirds or three-fourths. Therefore, their understanding may be incomplete and confused. Children think of "half" as any part of a whole, rather than one of two equal parts, and refer to one-half being larger than another. For example, they may say, "Your half is bigger than mine." Additionally, they may not understand relationships, such as three-fourths of an inch is one-fourth less than one inch. Classroom instruction should build on children's previous experiences and focus within the context of real life before moving to the symbolic representations. Fractions may be taught using fraction kits, where students cut and label the pieces to relate the fractional notation to the concrete pieces and compare the sizes of the fractional parts. They are able to see that $\frac{1}{4}$, for example, is larger than $\frac{1}{8}$, and they can measure to prove that two of the $\frac{1}{8}$ pieces are equivalent to $\frac{1}{4}$. **Table 4-5** presents an analysis of fractions.

Table 4-5. Equivalent Fractions

One Whole = $\frac{1}{1}$							
One-half = $\frac{1}{2}$				One-half = $\frac{1}{2}$			
One-fourth = $\frac{1}{4}$		One-fourth = $\frac{1}{4}$		One-fourth = $\frac{1}{4}$		One-fourth = $\frac{1}{4}$	
$\frac{1}{8}$	$\frac{1}{8}$	$\frac{1}{8}$	$\frac{1}{8}$	$\frac{1}{8}$	$\frac{1}{8}$	$\frac{1}{8}$	$\frac{1}{8}$
$\frac{1}{16}$ $\frac{1}{16}$	$\frac{1}{16}$ $\frac{1}{16}$	$\frac{1}{16}$ $\frac{1}{16}$	$\frac{1}{16}$ $\frac{1}{16}$	$\frac{1}{16}$ $\frac{1}{16}$	$\frac{1}{16}$ $\frac{1}{16}$	$\frac{1}{16}$ $\frac{1}{16}$	$\frac{1}{16}$ $\frac{1}{16}$

Use of Technology

As rapidly as technology is changing and improving, educators are challenged to keep up with those advances and learn how to use technology to improve instruction. Clearly, changes need to be made in how schools acquire access to these new advances. These changes must be equitably implemented so that students who live in poverty have the same access to technology and challenging mathematics as their affluent peers. The newest advancements in hand-held computers present educators with both opportunities and responsibilities. The primary opportunity is that of allowing access to challenging mathematics for every student, regardless of the student's past mastery of arithmetic or rote skills.

Digital videos provide opportunities for students to evaluate their own explanations of problem solutions. Students may present their videos and discuss similarities and differences in approaches to solving problems. These may be uploaded onto a website to allow for online discussions using discussion board tools, blogs, and various communication tools with other students. Students can develop effective presentations, online resources, wikis, and other projects for sharing with learners around the world. Additional digital presentation tools may help students to develop effective presentations that communicate mathematical ideas. Programs such as PowerPoint and HyperStudio allow students to integrate graphics, digital images and video, and text into their presentations.

Learning Environment

The *Professional Standards for Teaching Mathematics* (NCTM, 2007) presents standards for the teaching of mathematics, organized under four categories: tasks, discourse, environment, and analysis. These four strands are integrated and interdependent, and are crucial in shaping what goes on in mathematics classrooms.

- Tasks—the projects, questions, problems, constructions, applications, and exercises in which students engage

- Discourse—the manner of representing, thinking, talking, agreeing, and disagreeing that teachers and students use to engage in these tasks

- Environment—the setting for learning

- Analysis—the systematic reflection in which teachers engage

The mathematics teacher should create a learning environment that fosters the development of each student's mathematical ability by doing the following:

- Providing and structuring the time necessary to explore sound mathematics and grapple with significant ideas and problems

- Using the physical space and materials in ways that facilitate learning mathematics

- Providing a context that encourages the development of mathematical skill and proficiency

- Respecting and valuing students' ideas, ways of thinking, and mathematical dispositions

Included in the *Professional Standards for Teaching Mathematics* are five major shifts in the environment of mathematics classrooms from current practice to teaching for the empowerment of students. These major shift areas include:

- Treating classrooms as mathematical communities rather than simply a collection of individuals

- Students using logic and mathematical evidence as verification rather than students relying solely on the teacher for correct answers

- Students employing mathematical reasoning rather than merely memorizing procedures

- Emphasizing problem solving rather than an emphasis on mechanistic answer-finding

- Students connecting mathematics, its ideas, and its applications rather than viewing mathematics as a body of isolated concepts and procedures

The Texas Essential Knowledge and Skills

The Texas Essential Knowledge and Skills (TEKS) is the state's required curriculum. The implementation of TEKS for mathematics requires a well-balanced curriculum beginning in kindergarten and continuing through grade 12. (See: 19 TAC Chapter 111. Texas Essential Knowledge and Skills for Mathematics.)

Pre-kindergarten content has been aligned with the TEKS and may be found in the Texas Education Agency's Pre-kindergarten Curriculum Guidelines (2008) at *http://tea.texas.gov.*

Both the TEKS and the pre-K Curriculum Guidelines incorporate the NCTM principles and standards, which provide early experiences and exploration of number concepts using concrete objects to learn about one-to-one correspondence. In the first and second grades, students continue exploring number concepts and begin learning basic computation skills. In the third through fifth grades, they continue developing number concepts to include multiplication, division, fraction and decimal representations, geometric principles, and algebraic reasoning. **Table 4-6** presents the focal points from pre-K through grade 6.

Table 4-6. Mathematics Curriculum: Number Concepts Strand for Pre-K through Grade 6

Grade Level	Numbers and Operations
Pre-K	1. Explores concrete models and materials; begins to arrange sets of concrete objects in one-to-one correspondence; counts to 10 or higher by ones, by fives or higher; combines, separates, and names "how many" concrete objects. 2. Begins to recognize and can describe the concept of zero (meaning there are none); identifying first and last in a series; compares numbers of concrete objects by using language (e.g., "same" or "equal," "one more," "more than," or "less than").
Kindergarten	1. Uses whole number concepts to describe how many objects are in a set (through 20) by using verbal and symbolic descriptions; uses sets of concrete objects to represent quantities given in verbal or written form (through 20); uses one-to-one correspondence and language such as "more than," "same number as," or "two less than" to describe relative sizes of sets of concrete objects; names the ordinal positions in a sequence, such as first, second, third, etc. 2. Begins to demonstrate the concepts of "part of" and "whole" with real objects. 3. Sorts to explore numbers; uses patterns; and is able to model and create addition and subtraction problems in real situations with concrete objects.

Grade Level	Numbers and Operations
First Grade	1. Has the ability to create sets of tens and ones using concrete objects to describe, compare, and order whole numbers; reads and writes numbers to 99 to describe sets of concrete objects; compares and orders whole numbers up to 99 (e.g., "less than," "greater than," or "equal to") by using sets of concrete objects and pictorial models. 2. Separates a whole into two, three, or four equal parts and uses appropriate language to describe the parts, such as "three out of four equal parts." 3. Models and creates addition and subtraction problem situations with concrete objects and writes corresponding number sentences. 4. Identifies individual coins by name and value and describes relationships among them.
Second Grade	1. Uses concrete models of hundreds, tens, and ones to represent a given whole number (up to 999) in various ways; begins to use place value to read, write, and describe the value of whole numbers to 999; uses models to compare and order whole numbers to 999; records comparisons using numbers and symbols ($<$, $=$, $>$). 2. Uses concrete models to represent and name fractional parts of a whole object (with denominators of 12 or less). 3. Models addition and subtraction of two-digit numbers with objects, pictures, words, and numbers; solves problems with and without regrouping; is able to recall and apply basic addition and subtraction facts (to 18). 4. Determines the value of a collection of coins up to one dollar; describes how the cent symbol, dollar symbol, and decimal point are used to name the value of a collection of coins.
Third Grade	1. Uses place value to read, write (in symbols and words), and describe the value of whole numbers; compares and orders whole numbers through 9,999. 2. Uses fraction names and symbols to describe fractional parts of whole objects or sets of objects; compares fractional parts of whole objects or sets of objects in a problem situation using concrete models 3. Selects and uses addition or subtraction to solve problems involving whole numbers through 999; uses problem-solving strategies; is able to use rounding and compatible numbers to estimate solutions to addition and subtraction problems. 4. Applies multiplication facts through 12 by using concrete models and objects (up to two digits times one digit); uses models to solve division problems; uses number sentences to record solutions; identifies patterns in related multiplication and division sentences (fact families).

(continued)

Grade Level	Numbers and Operations
Fourth Grade	1. Uses place value to read, write, compare, and order whole numbers through 999,999,999 and decimals involving tenths and hundredths, including money, using concrete objects and pictorial models. 2. Uses concrete objects and pictorial models to generate equivalent fractions. 3. Uses multiplication to solve problems (no more than two digits times two digits); uses division to solve problems (no more than one-digit divisors and three-digit dividends). 4. Uses strategies, including rounding and compatible numbers, to estimate solutions to addition, subtraction, multiplication, and division problems.
Fifth Grade	1. Uses place value to read, write, compare, and order whole numbers through 999,999,999,999 and decimals through the thousandths place. 2. Identifies common factors of a set of whole numbers; uses multiplication to solve problems involving whole numbers (no more than three digits times two digits); uses division to solve problems involving whole numbers (no more than two-digit divisors and three-digit dividends), including solutions with a remainder.
Sixth Grade	1. Compares and orders nonnegative rational numbers; generates equivalent forms of rational numbers, including whole numbers, fractions, and decimals; uses integers to represent real-life situations. 2. Is able to write prime factorizations using exponents; identifies factors of a positive integer, common factors, and the greatest common factor of a set of positive integers.

Analysis of Teaching and Learning

The teacher of mathematics should engage in ongoing analysis of teaching and learning by doing the following:

- observing, listening to, and gathering other information about students to assess what they are learning

- examining the effects of the task, discourse, and learning environment on students' mathematical knowledge, skills, and dispositions in order to ensure that every student is learning sound and significant mathematics and is developing a positive disposition toward mathematics

- challenging and extending students' ideas

- adapting or changing activities while teaching

- making both short- and long-range plans

- describing and commenting on each student's learning to parents and administrators as well as to the students themselves

Making Connections with the Real World

The U.S. Department of Labor (2012) developed a list of the top professions that require a strong knowledge of mathematics. Some of the most prominent jobs are as accountants and auditors, computer programmers, computer scientists, computer engineers and system analysts, economists and marketing research analysts, managers, mathematicians, operations research analysts, statisticians, and financial planners.

The preceding list of professions is useful for emphasizing the importance of mathematics in our lives; however, most children in early childhood might not be aware of, and cannot relate to, these kinds of jobs. The best way to link mathematics to real jobs or activities is to guide students to develop a list of jobs available in their community. For example, a unit about community helpers will yield a large list of occupations, such as nurses, physicians, sanitary workers, home builders, landscapers, plumbers, carpenters, and tile installers. Teachers can assign readings about these professions and invite community sources to describe and demonstrate how they use mathematics in their profession. The interactive and concrete approach can easily present the need for mathematics in our daily lives.

One of the key challenges in promoting interest in mathematics is to convince children that mathematics plays an important role in their lives. Based on this assumption, teachers need to introduce mathematics concepts in a problem-solving format using real-life situations. Some examples for pre-K through grade 6 are the following:

- Purchase inexpensive items at the dollar store and set up a "classroom store" where the students can purchase items using play money. Children can earn play money as part of the classroom management program, which can reward students with play money for good behavior.

- Organize cooking activities at home or in school using recipes requiring specific units of measurement; this activity can also be linked to science, particularly to chemistry.

- Guide students to identify the most appropriate measuring system to compute the size of objects and the area of spaces in the classroom or school.

- Plan a field trip for which students have to estimate the cost of the trip. Children have to use computation skills to determine the cost of the activity.

- Plan a road trip using an Internet program (e.g., *mapquest.com*) to calculate distances between places and then use distance to calculate travel time and gas expenses based on mileage.

- Create tables or graphs of the expenses versus travel time to estimate costs associated with taking shorter or longer trips based on the average daily costs from the previous examples.

Thematic Instruction

Thematic instruction is the organization of curriculum content based on themes or topics. Thematic instruction integrates basic disciplines (e.g., reading, math, music, art, and science) with the exploration of broad subjects, such as *American Indians*, *Six Flags over Texas*, *state symbols*, *river systems in Texas*, *the rain forest*, *recycling resources*, and so on. The selection of the theme can be done school-wide, by grade, or by individual teacher.

Thematic planning provides opportunities for the students to hear similar information in various instructional segments and from a variety of sources. Additionally, it allows opportunities for students to apply cognitive processes and creativity through content-area instruction based on real-life situations.

Planning and Organizing Thematic Units

Teachers must consider several important elements when planning and organizing thematic units. The basic steps are selecting the theme, designing the integrated curriculum, gathering materials for the unit, and arranging thematic activities (Fredericks, Blake-Kline, and Kristo, 1997).

Selecting the Theme

Identify a theme, taking into account its interest to children, the relevance of the topic, and the connection to the state curriculum. The theme should be broad enough to allow the integration of content areas. For example, a topic such as "our solar system" is broad enough to cover every content area in the curriculum. However, the topic of "goldfish" might be too limited in scope to allow the easy integration of subjects.

Designing the Integrated Curriculum

The state curriculum (TEKS) should be the guiding force in the organization of the integrated curriculum. Once this connection is established, teachers must identify the main principles or generalizations about the theme. Using these generalizations, teachers need to identify the key objectives to involve each content area and the materials needed to implement instruction.

Thematic instruction minimizes the artificial boundaries created through traditional course scheduling. The fixed course scheduling for the content areas can now be combined into larger segments where multiple content areas are delivered in an integrated manner. When designing instruction for children in the early grades, teachers must take into account the developmental characteristics of the children to keep them focused and engaged.

Gathering Materials for the Unit

Gathering materials for the unit can be challenging for first-year teachers. They should request input from veteran teachers and from the school librarian. Some of the key considerations when selecting materials are as follows:

- The materials should focus on the same set of generalizations and principles in each of the content areas.

- Materials should include narratives, expositions, drama, poems, and a variety of materials and resource books, magazines, newspapers, movies, Internet materials, videotapes, and audiotapes.

- Materials should also represent a range of thinking abilities and literacy development, including materials written in a language other than English.

- Materials should represent the home as well as the school culture and language of the students.

Arranging Thematic Activities

Traditionally, thematic units are organized into three main segments—introduction to the unit, presentation of the content, and a closing activity. The opening activity is designed to motivate children and to get them interested in the theme. Children are exposed to the goals and the steps in the presentation of the theme. The presentation of the content is done through various coordinated lessons and activities. The closing activity is designed to review and pull together the concepts learned and to celebrate the mastery of the content.

Types of Questioning Strategies

Clearly, all teachers should use open questions that do not have simple yes/no answers. Questions should focus students' thinking, require them to think critically, and help them to "clarify or justify their ideas orally and in writing." Good questions "elicit language and challenge each student's thinking" (NCTM, 2000, p. 35). Teachers need to model these questioning strategies. The NCTM Professional Standards propose five categories of questions that teachers should ask to elicit justification and reasoning, as shown in **Table 4-7**, along with sample questions.

Table 4–7. Questioning Strategies for Mathematics Discourse

Category 1—Questions that help students learn how to make learning math meaningful.

"Do you agree (disagree) with the correct answer?"

"Does anyone use a different strategy to get the correct answer? Explain it."

Category 2—Questions that help students to become self-reliant and determine whether something is mathematically correct.

"Does that make sense?"

"Tell me what makes this a reasonable solution to the task?"

Category 3—Questions that help students learn to reason mathematically. "What have you tried that has worked or not worked?"

"How could you explain this in your own words?"

Category 4—Questions that help students learn to solve problems. "What would happen if...?"

"What would happen if not . . . ?"

"What pattern do you see, and how would you explain your answer?"

Category 5—Questions that relate to helping students connect mathematics, its ideas, and its applications.

"Have we solved a problem that is similar to this one?"

"Can you write another problem like this one?"

Source: Adapted from Charles Al. Dana Center, Mathematics TEKS Toolkit. UT-Austin. Available online at: http://www.utdanacenter.org/mathtoolkit/support/questioning.php

Using Formal and Informal Assessment

The State of Texas Assessments of Academic Readiness (STAAR) is the state assessment for reading, math, writing, science, and social studies. The STAAR test evaluates student learning based on the state-required curriculum, the Texas Essential Knowledge and Skills. STAAR is a "high-stakes" testing system that provides accountability for districts, schools, administrators, teachers, and students. By law, Texas students must pass the STAAR test to be promoted at certain grade levels and to graduate from high school.

COMPETENCY 002: NUMBER CONCEPTS AND OPERATIONS

The teacher understands concepts related to numbers, operations and algorithms, and the properties of numbers.

Number Concepts

One of the key challenges in mathematics education is the teaching of technical vocabulary and concepts. Teachers as well as students need to have an understanding of the key terms used in mathematics to communicate effectively in the classroom. A summary of key mathematical terms and concepts follows.

Integers

An **integer** is a whole number that includes all positive and negative numbers, including zero. This may be represented on a number line that extends in both directions from 1. You might have −45, −450,000, 0, 234, or 78,306. Integers do not include decimals or fractions. The members of the set {..., −6, −5, −4, −3, −2, −1, 0, 1, 2, 3, 4, 5, 6...} are all integers.

Many real-life situations are represented with integers.

Natural Numbers

A **natural number** is a positive integer or a nonnegative integer. There is a small difference because nonnegative integers also include "0." A list of positive integers would include whole numbers but not zero. Natural numbers include 1, 2, 3, 4, 5 ... ∞, where ∞ is the symbol for infinity. Natural numbers are all whole numbers. They do not include negative numbers, fractions, or decimals.

Rational Numbers

A number that can be expressed as a ratio or quotient of two nonzero integers is known as a **rational number**. Rational numbers can be expressed as common fractions or decimals, such as $\frac{3}{5}$ or 0.6. Finite decimals, repeating decimals, mixed numbers, and whole numbers are all rational numbers. Nonrepeating decimals cannot be expressed in this way, and are said to be irrational.

Irrational Numbers

An irrational number is a number that cannot be represented as an exact ratio of two integers. The decimal form of the number never terminates and never repeats. Examples include the square root of 2 ($\sqrt{2}$) and pi (π).

Real Numbers

A **real number** describes any number that is positive, negative, or zero and can be used to measure continuous quantities. A real number also includes numbers that have decimal representations, even those with infinite decimal sequences, such as π.

Place Value

Place values are the basic foundation for understanding mathematic computation. The simple number 1984 can be explained based on the positions of the numbers in the value scale. See the example in **Table 4-8**.

Table 4-8. Place Values

Thousand	Hundred	Ten	One
1000	900	80	4
1	9	8	4

Basic Operations and Their Algorithms

This section discusses some of the basic operations covered in the EC-6 curricula, as well as the algorithms for these operations. An **algorithm** is an established and well-defined step-by-step problem-solving method used to achieve a desired mathematical result.

Addition

Addition is the mathematical operation of combining two or more quantities into a sum. The quantity is often a number with one or more digits. The term **digit** in mathematics is a number symbol (e.g., 1, 2, or 3) used in numerals to represent numbers (these are real numbers or integers) in positional numeral systems. In addition of whole numbers, the key element is to align the numbers based on place value—ones, tens, hundreds, thousands, and so forth. Following the alignment, proceed to add beginning with the ones—in a right to left progression.

25 Step 1: Add the numbers in the ones place (5 + 2 = 7)
+ 32 Step 2: Add the numbers in the tens place (2 + 3 = 5)

57

Subtraction

Subtraction is the process/operation of removing objects from a larger group, or finding parts of a whole. It is the opposite of addition. Subtraction is indicated by the minus sign (–). When a number (formally called a *subtrahend*) is subtracted from another number (formally called a *minu-*

end), the resulting number (the *difference*) is smaller than the minuend. As an example, see the following operation:

25   minuend
–20 subtrahend
<u>   </u>
05 remainder or difference

Step 1: Beginning with the ones, subtract the bottom number from the top number.

Step 2: Subtract the tens by using the same process to get the result.

A typical subtraction problem would be: "From a group of 25 cars, 20 were sold. How many are left?" The child might know the operation but may not understand that the word "left" in the problem calls for subtraction. Teachers need to develop a list of key words linked to each of the four basic operations.

Like addition, subtraction is a process in which children must see their learning task as one of making sense of whatever they are studying. It is not appropriate to teach children how to do a procedure without teaching them how to reason. Students should not be expected to do things by rote or be made to say things they do not honestly understand.

Additionally, the complexity of the language can create problems for all children, especially for English Language Learners (ELLs). For example, some common phrases used in forming subtraction word problems include: (1) How many are left (or left over)? (2) How many more are needed? (3) How many less (or fewer)? (4) How many more than . . .? (5) How many would you have if half were subtracted? Words and phrases used for explaining subtraction include: *minus, take away, decrease, reduce, deduct, remove, less than,* and *how many do you need to take away to get* a certain number.

Children need to make sense of the procedure. The most obvious message to a child is that addition and subtraction require that you follow the "rules." Teaching "what to do" in mathematics is a widespread practice in the classroom. However, it is important to understand that just teaching procedures and teaching procedures in relation to their meaning are two very different approaches to teaching mathematics. When students do not have the broader understanding, they may lack the cognitive flexibility to deal with situations that may differ (even slightly) regarding the format of the problem or question from the particular situation learned. Have children describe their thinking processes and explain why their answers make sense. When children know the "why" of what they are doing, their understanding and skills can be applied more easily to new tasks.

Multiplication

Multiplication is a mathematical operation of combining groups of equal amounts. Multiplication may be described as repeated addition or the inverse of division (discussed next). Traditionally, multiplication requires students to learn the multiplication facts and develop computation facility. After learning all the "times tables," children learn to multiply with paper and pencil, first practicing with one-digit multipliers ($24 \times 5 =$) and progressing to two-digit and three-digit multipliers, and so on. Word problems provide a way for children to apply the concepts of multiplication in various situations. An example of the steps in the process is shown below.

$$
\begin{array}{r}
\overset{3}{95} \quad \text{factor} \\
\times 7 \quad \text{factor} \\
\hline
665 \quad \text{product}
\end{array}
$$

Step 1: Multiply $7 \times 5 = 35$.

Step 2: Since the number has more than one digit (i.e., 3 tens and 5 ones), place the 3 at the top of the tens column and the 5 in the ones column of the product.

Step 3: Multiply the digit in the tens place (9) by the factor (7) to get $7 \times 9 = 63$.

Step 4: Add the 63 to the 3 placed in the tens place; this equals 66.

Step 5: Place the 66 to the left of the ones column to obtain the final result of 665.

Teachers should link multiplication to real-world contexts. Having children explore with groups of objects helps them link the idea of multiplication as repeated addition. Children need to interact with the concept of multiplication pictorially by drawing sets of objects, symbolically by writing the multiplication sentences ($4 \times 6 = 24$), and verbally by reading the sentences (4 sets of 6 equals 24; 4 groups of 6 equals 24; 4 times 6 equals 24). Children need opportunities to see mathematics in their daily lives, not as existing in the classrooms or on the pages of their textbooks.

Division

Division is a mathematical operation involving two numbers that tells how many groups there are or how many are in each group. It may be thought of as the inverse of multiplication. The symbol for division is $\div$ or /. For example, $58 \div 8$ or $\dfrac{58}{8}$, which both can be set up in long division as

$$
\begin{array}{r}
7 \text{ R2} \\
8\overline{)58} \\
-56 \\
\hline
2
\end{array}
$$

Step 1: Place the **divisor** (number doing the dividing) outside the division bracket on the left-hand side and the **dividend** (number being divided) inside it.

Step 2: Examine the first digit of the dividend. If this is smaller than the divisor, then use the first two digits of the dividend.

Step 3: Identify how many times the divisor (8) can fit into the dividend (58).

Step 4: Place the result (7) on top of the 8 in 58.

Step 5: Multiply the quotient (7) by the divisor (8), which equals 56.

Step 6: Subtract the 56 from 58 to identify a possible remainder.

Step 7: Place the remainder (i.e., R2) in the **quotient** (answer).

Fractions

A **fraction** is a number that represents part of a whole, part of a set, or a quotient in the form $\frac{a}{b}$, which can be read as "a divided by b." The number above the fraction bar is called the numerator, and the number below the fraction bar is called the denominator.

Finding Equivalent Fractions, or Simplification of Fractions

To identify an equivalent fraction, follow these steps, using the example $\frac{2}{4}$.

Step 1: Find a number that can be divided evenly into the numerator and the denominator. For example, in the fraction $\frac{2}{4}$, the number 2 can be divided evenly into 2 and 4.

Step 2: Divide the numerator and denominator by 2 and get the result:. $\frac{2}{4} = \frac{1}{2}$.

Adding and Subtracting Homogeneous Fractions

When adding or subtracting fractions with the same denominator (**homogeneous** fractions), add or subtract the numerators and keep the denominator the same. For example,

$$\frac{2}{5} + \frac{1}{5} = \frac{3}{5} \qquad \frac{7}{9} - \frac{5}{9} = \frac{2}{9}$$

Changing Improper Fractions to Mixed Numbers

To change an improper fraction, such as $\frac{5}{2}$, to a mixed number (a number with a whole number part and a fractional part), divide the numerator by the denominator and represent the remainder as a fraction. For example:

$$\frac{5}{2} = \frac{4+1}{2} = \frac{2\times 2+1}{2} = \frac{4}{2} + \frac{1}{2} = 2\frac{1}{2}$$

Adding and Subtracting Mixed Numbers

To add and subtract mixed numbers, follow the algorithm provided in the example below.

$$\begin{array}{r} 2\frac{5}{10} \\ +1\frac{4}{10} \\ \hline \end{array} \qquad \begin{array}{r} 7\frac{9}{12} \\ -5\frac{4}{12} \\ \hline \end{array}$$

$$3\frac{9}{10} \qquad 2\frac{5}{12}$$

Add or subtract the fractions, then add or subtract the whole numbers.

If necessary to complete the operation, change the top mixed number by "borrowing" from the whole number part. Reduce the whole number part by 1 and increase the fraction part by adding a fraction that is equivalent to 1. For example,

$$5\frac{2}{7} = 4\frac{2}{7} + \frac{7}{7} = 4\frac{9}{7}$$

Reduce = 5 to 4, add $\frac{7}{7}$ to $\frac{2}{7}$, then proceed as usual.

$$-3\frac{4}{7} = -3\frac{4}{7} = -3\frac{4}{7}$$

$$1\frac{5}{7}$$

Changing Mixed Numbers to Improper Fractions

To change a mixed number to an improper fraction (a fraction with the numerator greater than the denominator), multiply the denominator by the whole number; then add the result to the numerator to obtain the new numerator. For example,

$$2\frac{3}{4} = \frac{2 \times 4 + 3}{4} = \frac{8 + 3}{4} = \frac{11}{4}$$

Adding Fractions with Different Denominators

To work with fractions with different denominators, it is necessary to rewrite the fractions using a **common denominator**, or a number that is a multiple of the original denominators. For example, to rename the fractions $\frac{1}{2}$ and $\frac{2}{3}$, it is necessary to find a common denominator for both of them. In this case the lowest common denominator is 6 because 6 is a multiple of both of the original denominators. Another way to say this is that both original denominators are factors of 6. So, by multiplying each original fraction by $\frac{6}{6}$ (which equals 1 and thus doesn't change the value of the original fraction), $\frac{1}{2} \times \frac{6}{6} = \frac{6}{12} = \frac{3}{6}$ and $\frac{2}{3} \times \frac{6}{6} = \frac{12}{18} = \frac{4}{6}$. The fractions now have the same denominator. Thus,

$$\frac{1}{2} + \frac{2}{3} = \frac{3}{6} + \frac{4}{6} = \frac{7}{6}.$$

Multiplying Fractions

Multiplying fractions involves multiplying the numerators together and the denominators together (horizontally), then simplifying the product (note that the term used is **simplify** and not *reduce*, the value of the fraction remains unchanged). For example,

$$\frac{2}{3} \times \frac{3}{4} = \frac{2 \times 3}{3 \times 4} = \frac{6}{12} = \frac{1}{2}$$

If the numbers to be multiplied are mixed fractions, first rewrite them as improper fractions, such as $\frac{6}{2}$, and then proceed to multiply as described earlier.

Dividing Fractions

To perform this operation, take the reciprocal of the second fraction (the one doing the dividing) and multiply the numbers as just described for multiplying fractions. A **reciprocal** is a fraction with the numerator and denominator switched.

For example, to perform $\frac{1}{5}$ divided by $\frac{3}{8}$, follow these steps. Obtain the reciprocal of the second fraction, so $\frac{3}{8}$ is changed to $\frac{8}{3}$. Then proceed to multiply:

$$\frac{1}{5} \div \frac{3}{8} = \frac{1}{5} \times \frac{8}{3} = \frac{8}{15}$$

Decimal Numbers

Decimal numbers are fractional numbers that are written using base ten. A mixed decimal number has a whole number part as well; for example, 0.28 is a decimal number and 3.9 is a mixed decimal number.

Decimal numbers are fractions whose denominators are powers of 10 (i.e., 10, 100, 1000, and so forth). For example, 0.098 is equivalent to $\frac{98}{1000}$.

Adding and Subtracting Decimals

To add or subtract decimal numbers, arrange them vertically, align the decimal points, inserting zeros if necessary for the alignment, then add or subtract the same as done for whole numbers. The decimal point remains in the same location. For example, for 23.5 + 237.04,

```
   23.50
 +237.04
  260.54
```

Multiplying Decimals

Multiplication of decimals does not require aligning decimal points; the numbers can be arranged vertically, with right sides aligned. The numbers can then be multiplied as if they were whole numbers. The numbers of digits to the right of the decimal point in the product should be equal to the sum of the number of digits to the right of the decimal point in the two factors. For example,

$$
\begin{array}{ll}
1.25 & \text{Two numbers to the right of the decimal point} \\
\times\,0.6 & \text{One number to the right of the decimal point} \\
\hline
0.750 & \text{Therefore, three numbers to the right of the decimal point.}
\end{array}
$$

Dividing Decimals

Division of decimals is done like traditional whole number division. The number of digits to the right of the decimal point in the divisor (number doing the dividing) is how far the decimal point in the dividend (number being divided) should be moved to the right. Then the decimal point in the quotient (answer) will appear above this point. For example, when dividing 1.44 by 0.3, since the divisor (0.3) has one digit after the decimal point, the decimal point in the dividend (1.44) is moved one digit to the right, and the decimal point in the quotient (4.8) is aligned above it.

$$0.3\overline{)1.44} = 03.\overline{)14.4}^{\,4.8}$$

Percents

Percent is another way of expressing a fractional number. Percent always expresses a fractional number in terms of $\frac{1}{100}$, or 0.01. Percents use the "%" symbol. For example, 40 parts out of 100 is 40%.

A percent is easily converted to a common fraction or decimal representation. To convert a percent to a common fraction, place the percent in the numerator and use 100 as the denominator (simplify as necessary). To convert a percent to a decimal fraction, divide the percent by 100, or move the decimal point two places to the left. Thus,

$$100\% = \frac{100}{100} = 1.0 \qquad 25\% = \frac{25}{100} = 0.25 \qquad 150\% = \frac{150}{100} = 1.5$$

The fraction equivalents of a percent often can be simplified by dividing by a common factor. Thus, $25\% = \frac{25}{100} = \frac{\frac{25}{25}}{\frac{100}{25}} = \frac{1}{4}$.

To convert a common fraction to a percent, follow this procedure: Carry out the division of the numerator by the denominator of the fraction to get the decimal equivalent. Then, to convert the decimal to a percentage, move the decimal point two places to the right (adding 0's as placeholders, if needed) and round as necessary. For example,

$$\frac{1}{4} = 1 \div 4 = .25 = \frac{25}{100} = 25\%$$

$$\frac{2}{7} = 2 \div 7 = .286 = \frac{286}{1000} = 28.6\%, \text{ which can be rounded to } 29\%$$

To find the **percentage** of a known quantity, change the percent to a common fraction or a decimal fraction, and multiply the fraction times the quantity. The percentage is expressed in the same units as the known quantity. For example, to find 25% of 360 books, change 25% to 0.25 and multiply times 360, or $0.25 \times 360 = 90$. The result is 90 books.

Mathematical Terms and Operations

Exponential Notation

Exponential notation is a symbolic way of showing how many times a number or variable is used as a factor. In the notation 5^3, the exponent 3 shows that 5 is a factor used three times, calculated in the following way: $5^3 = 5 \times 5 \times 5 = 125$.

A negative exponent indicates a reciprocal. Therefore, $5^{-3} = \frac{1}{5^3} = \frac{1}{5 \times 5 \times 5} = \frac{1}{125}$.

Absolute Value

Absolute value is the distance of a number from zero on the number line. This action ignores the + or – sign of a number. The notation for absolute value is two vertical lines, so $|x|$ is the graphic used to describe the action of absolute value. For example, $|-5| = 5$ or $|5| = 5$.

Expanded Form

The expanded form of numbers shows the place value of each digit. For example: $263 = 200 + 60 + 3$, which is equal to 2 hundreds, 6 tens, and 3 ones.

Expanded Notation

Expanded notation, just as expanded form, shows place value by multiplying each digit in a number by the appropriate power of 10. For example,

$$523 = 5 \times 10^2 + 2 \times 10 + 3 \times 1 \textit{ or } 5 \times 10^2 + 2 \times 10^1 + 3 \times 10^0$$

Scientific Notation

Scientific notation is a form of writing a number as the product of a power of 10 and a decimal number greater than or equal to 1 and less than 10. For example,

$$2,400,000 = 2.4 \times 10^6; \quad 240.2 = 2.402 \times 10^2; \quad 0.0024 = 2.4 \times 10^{-3}$$

Estimation and Rounding

Estimation is used to make an approximation that is still close enough to be useful. When using estimation, use the leading or the left-most digit to make an estimate.

Rounding may be used to estimate a sum, difference, or product and to make mental approximations. Look at the digit to be rounded and use the following rules for rounding.

- If the digit is 0, 1, 2, 3, or 4, leave the digit as is.

- If the digit is 5, 6, 7, 8, or 9, round up (e.g., 5 is changed to a 6).

- All of the digits after the rounded digit become zeros.

For example, an estimation can be obtained by rounding up or down:

$$532 + 385 + 57 = 500 + 400 + 60 = 960.$$

The result certainly is less precise than doing the actual addition, but it is easier to perform mentally in most cases. This example is sometimes referred to as **front-end estimation** because it uses the leading, or left-most digit to make an estimate quickly and easily.

Rounding may also be used to reduce the number of digits in a number. Rounding is especially useful to have fewer digits in the answer when dividing numbers with remainders. For example, to divide a 20-cm-long wire into 3 equal pieces and to find the length of each piece, divide 20 by 3 to get the length of each piece.

$$\frac{20}{3} = 6.66666666666666\ldots$$

The 6 repeats an infinite number of times. This is known as a **repeating decimal**. Typically, the answer is based on the required number of decimal places. Decimal places here refers to the number of digits to the right of the decimal point. Usually rounding to the tenths or hundredths place is sufficient. To round the answer (6.666 . . .) to the nearest hundredths place, the next digit in the thousandths place is 6, so the 6 in the hundredths place is rounded up, giving 6.67 as the desired answer.

A decimal in which one or more digits repeat infinitely is indicated by a bar over the repeating digits; for example: $0.3333\ldots$ or $0.\overline{3}$ and $5.272727\ldots$ or $5.\overline{27}$.

Number Theory

Teacher candidates have to have a solid command of basic number theory. This section discusses some of the elements required for the EC-6 curricula.

Prime Factorization

Prime factorization involves knowledge of two sets of numbers:

- **Prime numbers** are natural numbers greater than 1 that are divisible only by themselves and 1. The first eight prime numbers are {2, 3, 5, 7, 11, 13, 17, 19}.

- **Composite numbers** are natural numbers greater than zero that are divisible by at least one other number besides 1 and themselves. Composite numbers have at least three factors; for example, 9 is a composite number because it has three factors: 1, 3, and 9.

Every composite number can be written as a product of prime numbers. This is called the **prime factorization** of the number. To perform prime factorization, start by factoring a known prime number into the given number. Then repeat this procedure on all factors until no more factorization can take place. When a factor is repeated in a prime factorization, express the repeated factor by using an exponent.

A factor tree can also help in finding the prime factorization of a composite number. It does not matter which factor pair is used first, as long as factoring continues until there are only prime numbers.

The prime factorization of 48 follows. Note the use of an exponent for repeat factors.

$48 = 3 \times 16$	Start by factoring 48 by a known prime, 3.
$48 = 3 \times 2 \times 8$	Factor 16 by 2, the lowest divisible prime of 16.
$48 = 3 \times 2 \times 2 \times 4$	Factor 8 similarly.
$48 = 3 \times 2 \times 2 \times 2 \times 2$	Factor 4 similarly.
$48 = 3 \times 2^4$	Express $2 \times 2 \times 2 \times 2$ as 2^4.

The exponent 4 shows how many times the base number 2 is used as a factor. The factor 3 is used only once. It has an exponent of 1. Exponents of 1 do not need to be written because they are implied. Prime factorizations are usually written in order from least to greatest base number. The prime factorization of 48 is usually written as $2^4 \times 3$.

Greatest Common Divisor

The **greatest common divisor** (GCD) of two or more nonzero integers is the largest positive integer that divides into the numbers without producing a remainder. Sometimes the term used is "divides evenly into." This is useful for simplifying fractions into their lowest terms. For example, to simplify $\frac{42}{56}$, find the GCD of 42 and 56, which is 14, and factor it out of the numerator and denominator: $\frac{42}{56} = \frac{3 \times 14}{4 \times 14} = \frac{3}{4}$.

Note that although 42 and 56 are each divisible by larger numbers (21 and 28, respectively), the largest number that is a factor of *both* 42 and 56, is 14.

Common Multiple

A common multiple is a whole number that is a multiple of two or more given numbers. For example, the common multiples of 2, 3, and 4 are 12, 24, 36, 48 . . .

Numbers and their Properties

Numbers have basic properties that can help simplify mathematics problem solving and reasoning skills. Some of these are:

Commutative Property

The order of the **addends** (terms being added) or **factors** (in multiplication) do not change the result.

$a + b = b + a$ and $a \times b = b \times a$

Addition: $6 + 8 = 14$ is the same as $8 + 6 = 14$

Multiplication: $5 \times 8 = 40$ is the same as $8 \times 5 = 40$

Associative Property of Multiplication and Addition

The order of the addends or factors will not change the sum or the product.

$(a + b) + c = a + (b + c)$ and $(a \times b) \times c = a \times (b \times c)$

Addition: $(2 + 3) + 5 = 10, 2 + (3 + 5) = 10$

Multiplication: $(2 \times 3) \times 5 = 30, 2 \times (3 \times 5) = 30$

Property of Zero

The sum of a number and zero is the number itself, and the product of a number and zero is zero.

Addition: $8 + 0 = 8$

Multiplication: $8 \times 0 = 0$

Distributive Property

The distributive property says that everything within the parentheses needs to be multiplied by the number on the outside.

You can add and then multiply or multiply and then add.

$$a(b + c) = a \times (b + c) \qquad \text{or} \qquad a(b + c) = (a \times b) + (a \times c)$$

$$8(5 + 2) = 8 \times 7 = 56 \qquad \text{or} \qquad 8(5 + 2) = (8 \times 5) + (8 \times 2) = 56$$

The distributive property also works with subtraction, so that $4(8 - 5) = 4(8) - 4(5) = 32 - 20 = 12$, Again, if the quantity in the parentheses is evaluated first, $4(8 - 5) = 4(3) = 12$.

Students may first learn the distributive property when they are learning order of operations, which is discussed next.

Order of Operations

The solutions of many problems in mathematics involve a series of calculations, or steps. Consider the equation $3 + 2 \times 6 = n$. Should this be calculated "left to right" by doing the + first and get 30? Or should the multiplication be calculated first and get 15? To avoid confusion and to obtain the correct answer, mathematicians decided long ago that all calculations should be done in the same order.

An arithmetic expression is evaluated by following these ordered steps, called the **order of operations:**

1. Simplify within grouping symbols, such as parentheses or brackets, starting with the innermost.

2. Apply exponents—powers and roots.

3. Perform all multiplications and divisions in order from left to right.

4. Perform all additions and subtractions in order from left to right.

You may have learned this order of operations as being

Please Excuse My Dear Aunt Sally!

The words in this sentence stand for *Parentheses, Exponentiation, Multiplication, Division, Addition*, and *Subtraction*, or generally, using the first letter of the order, as **PEMDAS**. So what is the correct answer for our problem? The order of operations would say that in the absence of parentheses, multiply 2×6 first, and then add 3, so the answer should be 15. If you were to add $3 + 2 = 5$, then multiply 5×6 that would be 30, a very different (and wrong) answer! If the $3 + 2$ were supposed to be added first, the problem should be written $(3 + 2) \times 6$ because then PEMDAS says to do the operations in the parentheses first.

COMPETENCY 003: PATTERNS AND ALGEBRA

The teacher understands concepts related to patterns, relations, functions, and algebraic reasoning.

Problem-Solving Situations

The role of operations in problem solving involves developing critical thinking and rational powers. The uses of operations in problem solving include applications, study of patterns and relationships, translation of word problems with a variety of structures and situations into symbolic representations using equations, and the selection of problem-solving strategies, all of which are topics covered in this competency.

Linear and Nonlinear Functional Relationships

Many functions can be represented by pairs of numbers. A real-valued function assigns to each real number x in a specified set of numbers, called the domain of f, a single real number designated as $f(x)$. The variable x is called the independent variable. If $y = f(x)$, we call y the dependent variable. Then, $f(0)$ is the value of the function when $x = 0$.

A function can be specified in the following ways: (1) numerically by means of a table, (2) algebraically by means of a formula, or (3) graphically by means of a graph. A **numerically specified function** is shown in **Table 4–9**, which shows the values: $f(0) = 3.01$ and $f(1) = -1.03$.

Table 4–9. Numerically Specified Function

x	0	1	2	3
$f(x)$	3.01	−1.03	2.22	0.01

Suppose an algebraically specified function f is specified by

$f(x) = 3x^2 - 4x + 1$.

Then by substituting 2 for x,

$f(x) = 3x^2 - 4x + 1$

$f(2) = 3(2)^2 - 4(2) + 1$

$f(2) = 12 - 8 + 1 = 5$

Likewise, $f(-1) = 3(-1)^2 - 4(-1) + 1 = 3 + 4 + 1 = 8$.

The graph of a **linear function** is a straight line (that is why it is called "linear"). A linear function is one of the most fundamental and important relationship concepts used as a foundation for advanced mathematics. A linear function is one that always satisfies the following: $f(x + y) = f(x) + f(y)$ and $f(\alpha x) = \alpha f(x)$. In this definition, x and y are input variables and α is a constant.

For example, consider the function $f(x) = 2x$. For any two input values a and b, suppose $x = a + b$. The function now becomes $f(x) = f(a + b) = 2(a + b) = 2a + 2b$. We see that if we substitute, $x = a$ and then $x = b$, we obtain $f(a) = 2a$ and $f(b) = 2b$ and $f(a + b) = f(a) + f(b)$, which satisfies the first rule. Checking the second constraint, $f(\alpha x) = 2\alpha x$, which is equivalent to $\alpha f(x) = \alpha 2x$ due to the associative/commutative properties of multiplication.

A **nonlinear function** does not satisfy the constraints of a linear function. For example, the function $f(x) = x^2$ is nonlinear because $f(a + b) = (a + b)^2 = a^2 + 2ab + b^2$ is not equal to $f(a) + f(b) = a^2 + b^2$.

We will revisit the concept of linear and nonlinear functions later.

Function

Functions can be used to understand how one quantity varies in relation to (or is a function of) changes in the second quantity. For example, there is a functional relationship between the price per pound of a particular type of meat and the total amount paid for ten pounds of that type of meat. You can see that the values of one variable determine the values of another.

Patterns

A **pattern** can be a design (geometric) or sequence (numeric or algebraic) that is predictable because some aspect of it repeats and/or can be represented by an equation. For example, a numeric pattern that adds increments of 3 looks like this: 4, 7, 10, 13. . . . An algebraic pattern that adds one to the multiple: x, $2x$, $3x$ . . . ; or when students are asked to identify patterns using fact families. A fact family is a set of numbers that are related using different matematical operations. For example, 1, 2, and 3 are a fact family because of the following fact family relationships: $1 + 2 = 3$, $2 + 1 = 3$, $3 - 2 = 1$, and $3 - 1 = 2$. A fact family will always have at least four math facts relating the family. This can also be seen in the following example from the STAAR Objective 2, item (3.6) – Patterns, relationships, and algebraic thinking:

(C) Identify patterns in related multiplication and division sentences (fact families) such as $2 \times 3 = 6$, $3 \times 2 = 6$, $6 \div 2 = 3$, $6 \div 3 = 2$.

In the above example there is only a single fact family listed. However, there are many other fact family relationships that can be found that will allow students to identify patterns in addition, subtraction, multiplication, and division sentences.

Algebraic Pattern

An **algebraic pattern** is a set of numbers and/or variables in a specific order. An example would be a chart showing the distance in feet Max travels on his bicycle versus the time in seconds, as shown in the chart below. What is one way to find the number of feet Max travels on his bicycle in 1 second?

No. of seconds	6	8	9
No. of feet	90	120	135

First, students need to be able to understand the algebraic pattern presented in the chart and how the numbers are listed. Students should divide the number of feet by the number of seconds to find the correct answer. However, in this problem the answer 15 does not answer the test question, which asks which operation was used to derive the answer to the question.

Algebraic Expression

An **algebraic expression** is a mathematical phrase that is written by using one or more variables and constants, but does not contain a relation symbol (e.g., $5y + 8$).

A **variable** or an unknown is a letter that stands for a number in an algebraic expression.

A **coefficient** is the number that precedes the variable to give the quantity of the variable in the expression. Algebraic expressions are comprised of terms, or groupings of variables and numbers. An algebraic expression with one term is called a **monomial**; with two terms, a **binomial**; with three terms, a **trinomial**; with more than one term, a **polynomial**. When writing algebraic expressions, coefficients are always written before variables. For example, *2a* is correct, whereas *a2* is not.

For example, $2ab - cd$ is a binomial (two-term) algebraic expression with variables a, b, c, and d, and terms $2ab$ and $(-cd)$. The coefficient of ab is 2, and the coefficient of cd is -1. As another example, $x^2 + 3y - 1$ is a trinomial algebraic expression using the variables x and y, and terms x^2, $3y$, and (-1); likewise, $z(x - 1) + uv - wy - 2$ is a polynomial with variables z, x, u, v, w, and y, and terms $z(x - 1)$, uv, $(-wy)$, and (-2).

Operations with algebraic expressions are governed by various rules and conventions.

- For **addition and subtraction**, *only like algebraic terms (same variable bases with the same exponents) can be added or subtracted* to produce simpler expressions. For example, $2x^3$ and $3x^3$ can be added together to get $5x^3$ because the terms are *like* terms; they both are x^3 terms. In contrast, $7m^3$ and $6m^2$ cannot be added together because they have *unlike* exponents. (*Note*: To *evaluate* an algebraic expression means to simplify it by using conventional rules.)

- When **multiplying exponential terms** together, the constant terms are multiplied, but the *exponents of the terms with the same variable bases are added together*, which is somewhat counterintuitive. For example, $4w^2$ multiplied by $8w^3$ gives $32w^5$ (not $32w^6$, as one might guess).

- When like algebraic terms are **divided**, exponents are subtracted. For example, $\dfrac{2x^7}{5x^3}$ becomes $\dfrac{\frac{2x}{7-3}}{\frac{5x}{3-3}} = \dfrac{2x^4}{5}$.

Multiplication of Binomials

In algebra, it is frequently necessary to multiply two binomials. The FOIL method is one way to multiply binomials. FOIL stands for "first, outer, inner, last" or "first, outside, inside, last." Multiply the first terms in the parentheses, then the outermost terms, then the innermost terms, then the last terms, and then add the products together and simplify the expression by combining like terms. For example, to multiply $(x + 3)$ and $(2x - 5)$, multiply x by $2x$ (the first terms), x by -5 (outer terms), 3 by $2x$ (inner terms), and 3 by -5 (last terms). The four products ($2x^2$, $-5x$, $6x$, and -15) add up to $2x^2 + x - 15$. If the polynomials to be multiplied have more than two terms (trinomials, for instance), make sure that *each* term of the first polynomial is multiplied by *each* term of the second.

The opposite of polynomial multiplication is factoring. **Factoring** a polynomial means rewriting it as the product of factors (often two binomials). The trinomial $x^2 - 11x + 28$, for instance, can be factored into $(x - 4)(x - 7)$. (You can check this by "FOILing" the binomials.) When attempting to factor polynomials, it is sometimes helpful to first factor out any factor that might be common to all terms. The two terms in $5x^2 - 10$, for example, both contain the factor 5. This means that the expression can be factored as $5(x^2 - 2)$.

Algebraic Relationship

It is important to express the relationship between two or more numbers by using an algebraic expression. The algebraic relationship that represents 2, 4, 6, 8, . . . is $2n$ (where $n = 1, 2, 3, . . .$) and the algebraic relationship that represents 4, 7, 10, 13, . . . is $3n + 1$ (where $n = 1, 2, 3, . . .$).

Algebraic Solution

An **algebraic solution** is the process of solving a mathematical problem by using the principles of algebra.

Performing Operations with Negative and Positive Numbers

When performing operations on negative and positive numbers, the key component is to pay attention to the sign. Rules for multiplication and division are the same—two positives or two negatives make a positive, and mixing negative with positive makes a negative. See the following examples.

- negative × negative = positive (–6 × –5 = 30)

- positive × positive = positive (6 × 5 = 30)

- positive × negative = negative (6 × –5 = –30)

Graphs and Symbolic Representations

A graph is an image or chart representation used to show a numerical relationship. On the TExES, teacher candidates are required to study graphs, charts, and tables, and answer questions based on the information presented. A **table** is a systematic or orderly list of values, usually in rows and columns. Tables often are organized from a function or relationship. Four kinds of **graphs** are generally used in grades pre-K to grade 6—pictorial, bar, line, and pie.

Pictorial graphs are the most concrete representations of information. They represent a transition from the real object graphs to symbolic graphs (Sperry Smith, 2008). These graphs usually are used to introduce children to graphing in pre-K through grade 1. For example, the teacher can use pictures of pizzas and hot dogs to represent the number of children that prefer one food over the other.

Bar graphs are used to represent two elements of a *single* subject. For example, the bar graph that follows presents the number of books read by a group of students. This graph presents in a concrete fashion that student E was the top reader, with 5 books, and student A read the lowest number of books.

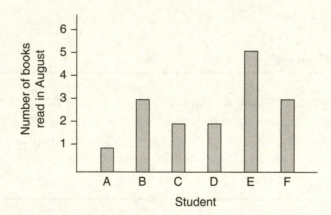

Line graphs present information in a fashion similar to bar graphs, but they use points and lines. This type of representation is more abstract for children and is therefore more challenging for them. A line graph tracks one or more subjects. One element is usually a time period over which the other element increases, decreases, or remains static. The following line graph depicts U.S. immigration statistics from 1820 to 2000.

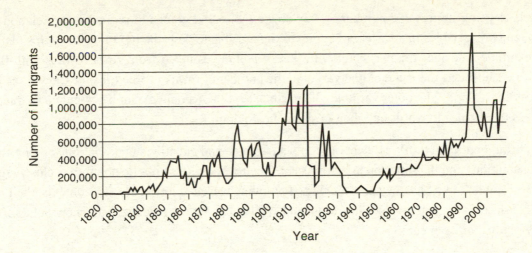

Pie charts are used to help visualize relationships based on percentages of a possible 100%. This graph appears to be easy to read, which is deceptive. It requires an understanding of percentages, which makes it inappropriate for children in the early grades. A pie graph representing food preferences follows.

Food Preferences

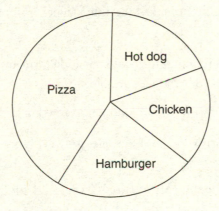

Identifying Patterns Using Concrete Models

Kindergarten students begin to use concrete models to construct, describe, extend, and determine what comes next in repeating patterns. To identify and construct repeating patterns, students must be able to identify the attributes of the objects in the pattern. Therefore, students sort objects by their attributes before they begin constructing their own patterns. Students construct patterns with two (AB, AAB, ABB) or three (ABC, ACB, BAC, BCA, CAB, CBA) elements. As students become more familiar with the structure of patterns they are able to begin to think about how two patterns are similar and different.

By grade 5, students continue their work from grades 3 and 4 by examining, representing, and describing situations in which the rate of change is constant. Students move from using concrete models to using figures and numbers. They create tables and graphs to represent the relationship between two variables in a variety of contexts and are able to describe the rules for each situation. For example, consider the perimeters of a set of rectangles made from rows of tiles with three tiles in each row. If the value of one variable (the number of rows of three tiles) is known, the corresponding value of the other variable (the perimeter of the rectangle) can be calculated. Students express these rules in words and then in symbolic notation.

Throughout their work, students use tables, graphs, and equations and relations among those representations and the situation they represent. Their work with symbolic notation is closely related to the context in which they are working. By moving back and forth between contexts, their own ways of describing general rules in words, and symbolic notation, students learn how notation can carry mathematical meaning.

Linear and Nonlinear Functions

As stated previously, a **linear function** is one whose graph is a straight line. The equation for a linear function, which is a first-degree polynomial function of one variable, can be written in the form of $y = mx + b$, called the **slope-intercept form** of the equation. The constant m is called the **slope** or **gradient**, and b is the **y-intercept**, or the point of intersection between the graph of the function and the y-axis. Changing m makes the line steeper or more gradual; changing b moves the line up or down.

The form of the equation in function form and equation form are given below. Note that x is the independent variable and y is the dependent variable.

$f(x) = mx + b$ (function form)   Example: $f(x) = 3x - 1$ ($m = 3$, $b = -1$).

$y = mx + b$ (equation form)   Example: $y = 3x - 1$

A partial table of values of the linear function $f(x) = 3x - 1$ follows.

x	−4	−3	−2	−1	0	1	2	3
y	−13	−10	−7	−4	−1	2	5	8

This linear equation has $m = 3$ (slope), $b = -1$ (y-intercept). Notice that $x = 0$ gives $y = -1$, the value of b. Numerically, b is the value of y when $x = 0$. On the graph, the corresponding point $(0, -1)$ is the point where the graph crosses the y-axis. The role of m in the equation $y = 3x - 1$ means that the value of y increases by 3 for every increase of 1 in x.

The graph of this function is a straight line rising by 3 for every 1 we go to the right. We say that we have a *rise* of 3 units for each *run* of 1 unit. Similarly, we have a rise of 6 for a run of 2, a rise of 9 for a run of 3, and so on. Thus we see that $m = 3$ is a measure of the steepness of the line. Geometrically, the graph of a linear function $f(x) = mx + b$ rises by m units for every 1 unit move to the right.

Examples of functions whose graph is a line include the following:

- $f_1(x) = 2x + 1$

- $f_2(x) = \dfrac{x}{2} + 1$

- $f_3(x) = \dfrac{x}{2} - 1$

The graphs of these equations are shown below:

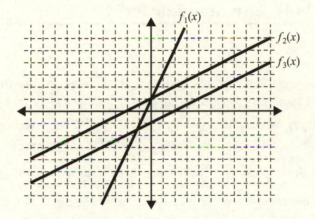

A **nonlinear** function, as the name implies, is not linear. An example is the quadratic $x^2 + x - 1 = 0$. Although nonlinear, this simple example may be solved exactly by using a formula (called the quadratic formula, a topic for higher grades) and is very well understood. To determine whether a function is linear or nonlinear, see the following examples.

$y = 4x$	$y = x^2 + x - 2$	$y = \dfrac{7}{x}$
Linear. $y = 4x$ can be written as $y = mx + b$	Nonlinear. $y = x^2 + x - 2$ cannot be written as $y = mx + b$ because it has an x^2 term	Nonlinear. $y = \dfrac{7}{x}$ cannot be written as $y = mx + b$ because x is in the denominator

Proportional Reasoning

Proportional reasoning is important in preparing students for algebra. Students in 5th grade begin to use a ratio chart to solve proportion problems. Proportions may present a challenge for students. Often they involve two unlike values that are related in a certain way. Students can be influenced by the context, so it is important to expose students to various examples, as in the following types of problems:

1. The office copier uses 5 reams of paper every 2 weeks. At the end of 6 weeks, how many reams of paper will the office copier have used?

2. Each table in the restaurant has a vase with three long-stem roses. The restaurant has 15 tables. How many flowers are there altogether?

3. The soccer coach orders new soccer balls for the team. She orders 3 out of 4 soccer balls in the school colors. If she orders 36 soccer balls, how many of these will be painted in the school colors?

Variables, Equations, and Inequalities

Equations

An equation is a mathematical sentence stating that two expressions are equal. Many mathematical expressions include letters called **variables**. Variables are classified as either independent (free) or dependent (bound). An expression may be evaluated for a given combination of values for the independent variables, although for some combinations, the value of the expression may be undefined. For example, the expression $\frac{x}{y}$ evaluated for $x = 10$, $y = 5$, will give 2; but it is undefined for $y = 0$. Thus an expression represents a function whose inputs are the values assigned to the independent variables and whose output is the resulting value of the expression.

The evaluation of an expression is dependent on the definition of the mathematical operators and on the system of values applied in the context of the expression. See Formal Semantics and Interpretation (logic) for the study of this question in logic.

Two expressions are said to be equivalent if, for each combination of values for the free variables, they have the same output, i.e., they represent the same function.

In equations, the '+' and '−' (addition and subtraction) symbols have their usual meanings. Division can be expressed as either $x/2$ or $\frac{x}{2}$ (like a fraction); both are perfectly valid. Multiplication can use the symbols $\times$, $\cdot$ (a multiplication dot), parentheses, or the sign can simply be omitted when multiplication is implicit. So $2 \cdot x$, or $2 \times x$, or $2(x)$, or $2x$ are all acceptable (notice how the "times" symbol resembles an "x" and also how the " $\cdot$ " symbol resembles a decimal point, so to avoid confusion it may be best to use one of the latter two forms depending on the problem).

An algebraic expression must be well formed. That is, the operators must have the correct number of inputs, in the correct places. As examples, the expression $2 + 3$ is well formed, but the expression $*2 +$ is not—at least, not in the usual notation of arithmetic.

Algebraic Inequality

An **algebraic inequality** is an algebraic statement about the relative size of one or more variables and/or constants. Inequalities are used to determine the relationship between these values. For example, taking x as a variable and saying, "x is less than 5," may be written as $x < 5$. An algebraic inequality also may use one or more variables and constants that shows a greater than or less than relationship, such as $2x - 8 > x + 24$.

Solving an algebraic inequality means finding all of its solutions. A "solution" of an inequality is a number or group of numbers that, when substituted for the variable (for example, x) make the inequality a true statement. As was the case for solving equations, certain manipulations of the inequality do not change the solution. Consider the list of manipulations shown below for the algebraic inequality $2x + 8 > 24$.

1. Adding or subtracting the same number on both sides: $2x + 8 > 24$ has the same solution as the inequality $2x > 16$. (The second inequality was obtained from the first one by subtracting 8 from both sides.)

2. Switching sides and changing the orientation of the inequality sign: $2x + 8 > 24$ has the same solution as $24 < 2x + 8$. (Merely switch the sides of the inequality and turn the ">" into a "<")

3a. Multiplying or dividing by the same *positive* number on both sides.

Last, the operation that is the source of all the trouble with inequalities:

3b. Multiplying or dividing by the same *negative* number on both sides *and* changing the orientation of the inequality sign.

This does not seem too difficult. The inequality $2x > 6$ has the same solution as the inequality $x > 3$ (dividing by +2 on both sides). The inequality $-2x \geq 4$ has the same solutions as the inequality $x \leq -2$ (dividing by (-2) on both sides and switching "$\geq$" to "$\leq$").

The inequality $x^2 > x$, however, does not have the same solutions as the inequality $x > 1$. Dividing both sides by x is not possible, because x can be either positive or negative). In fact, it is easy to check that $x = -2$ solves the first inequality but does not solve the second inequality.

COMPETENCY 004: GEOMETRY AND MEASUREMENT

The teacher understands concepts and principles of geometry and measurement.

Geometry and measurement are significant strands of mathematics. In the elementary classroom, children's experience in geometry should provide for the development of the concepts of direction, shape, size, symmetry, congruence, and similarity in using two-dimensional and three-dimensional shapes. Experiences for children should begin with exploring, playing, and building with shapes using familiar objects and a wide variety of concrete materials. Children must use these experiences to develop appropriate vocabulary and build on their understanding. Middle school students use formal generalizations to understand geometric relationships.

Concepts and skills in the measurement strand of mathematics deal with making comparisons between what is being measured and the standard for measurement. Children need first-hand experiences with measuring activities that require them to practice the skill. Additionally, children should be aware that measurement is never exact, but instead is actually an estimation. However, it is important that children learn to practice making estimates. Measuring gives children practical applications to apply their computation skills. It also provides a way to link geometric concepts to number concepts.

The Van Hiele Theory

Although the Van Hiele theory (Van Hiele, 1986) has been recognized for its role in describing the levels of thinking associated with the learning of geometry, it also has been developed as a general theory of mathematics education. In 1988, Fuys, Gedds, and Tischler interpreted much of that work. The Van Hiele theory is a stage theory, set out in levels. The theory does not stop at the description of "levels of thinking," but provides a foundation for understanding the movement between these levels, and the role of the teacher in assisting with this progression. The theory goes beyond the concerns of Piaget, who did not address the question of how students may be encouraged to progress from level to level. The Van Hiele theory, in addition to describing levels of thinking, offers an important addition. This is the notion of *stages of learning* as means by which the learner may be assisted to use higher-level thinking skills. Five such stages (levels 0–4) are specified in **Table 4-10** (Van Hiele, 1986).

Table 4–10. Van Hiele's Levels of Geometric Thinking

What the teacher needs to know	What the learner can do
Van Hiele's Levels **0—Visualization** Learners develop a mental picture of each shape; therefore, teachers need to provide a multitude of good physical examples and nonexamples for exploration.	**Learner is able to:** • Select a specific shape from a set of shapes • Sort and match shapes • Identify shapes in the environment • Point out shapes (e.g., a baseball diamond, etc.)
1—Analysis Learners begin to talk and notice the properties of the shapes. Teachers can focus on the various components of the geometric shape.	**Learner is able to:** • Predict a shape's final form after seeing only a part of it • List several attributes of each shape • Subdivide a shape into parts, describe the various pieces, and create a shape from parts
2—Informal Deduction Students stop relying on visualization, and now use relationships to make a conclusion. Focus is on the first two levels for students in K-8.	**Learner is able to:** • Recognize that squares belong in both the rectangle and rhombus category • Use "if" statements describing the shape • Divide a rectangle into two congruent triangles • Identify parallelograms based on the criteria regarding opposite equal angles
3—Formal Deduction Focus is on higher levels of geometry, using various theorems to teach how two triangles are congruent (e.g., side-angle-side (SAS) theorem).	**Learner is able to:** • Make deductions and support those deductions • Do high school–level geometry including construction of their own proofs involving quadrilaterals drawn on a sphere.
4—Rigor Rigor is associated with college-level geometry.	**Learner is able to:** • Compare different geometries at the proof level

Points, Lines, Angles, Lengths, and Distances

A fundamental concept of geometry is the notion of a **point**. A point is a specific location, taking up no space, having no area, and frequently represented by a dot. A point is considered to have no dimensions. In other words, it has neither length nor breadth (width) nor depth.

Through any two points there is exactly one **straight line**; lines are one-dimensional. **Planes** (think of flat surfaces without edges) are two-dimensional, meaning they have infinite length and width but no depth. From these foundational ideas one can move to some other important geometric terms and ideas.

- A **line segment** is any portion of a line between two points on that line. It has a definite start and a definite end, called the **endpoints**. The notation for a segment extending from point A to point B is $\overline{AB}$.

- A **ray** is like a line segment, except it extends forever in one direction. The notation for a ray originating at endpoint X through point Y is $\overrightarrow{XY}$.

An **angle** is formed when two rays (or lines) share an endpoint. Typically, a **degree** is the unit of measure of the angle created. If a circle is divided into 360 even pie-shaped slices, each slice has an angle measure of 1 degree. (Thus, a circle has 360 degrees.)

- If an angle has exactly 90 degrees it is called a **right angle**.

- Angles of less than 90 degrees are **acute angles**.

- Angles greater than 90 degrees but less than 180 degrees are **obtuse angles**.

- If two angles have the same size (regardless of how long their rays might be drawn), they are **congruent**. Congruence is shown by the symbol $\cong$ (e.g., $\angle m \cong \angle n$, which is read "angle m is congruent to angle n").

In addition, combinations of two angles can be classified as complementary and supplementary. The angles do not have to be adjacent (next to each other).

- **Supplementary angles** are two angles that add up to 180°.

- **Complementary angles** are two angles that add up to 90°.

If two lines intersect, they form two pairs of equal angles, called **vertical angles**. The measures of vertical angles (the angles across from each other) are equivalent; that is, vertical angles are congruent.

Parallel lines and **perpendicular lines** are important concepts in geometry. Parallel lines never cross. Consider the two parallel lines that follow, and a third line (a **transversal**) that crosses them. Note that among the many individual angles created, there are only two angle measures: 30° (noted in the figure) and the supplementary angle 150° (= 180° − 30°).

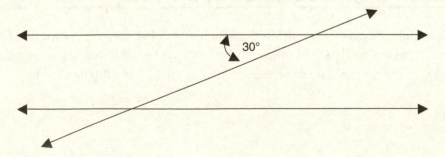

An example of perpendicular lines is shown in the figure below. When lines are perpendicular, the measures of the angles created at their intersection are all 90°, signified by the small square shown in the figure. We say *AB* is perpendicular to *CD*.

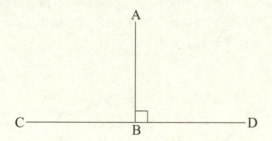

Polygons

A **polygon** is a many-sided plane (two-dimensional) figure bounded by a finite number of straight lines. An angle in a polygon is referred to as a vertex (plural is vertices).

Polygons are described based on the number of sides, which are equal to the number of vertices. Some of the most common are the following:

- Three-sided polygons are **triangles**.

- Four-sided polygons are **quadrilaterals**.

- Five-sided polygons are **pentagons**.

- Six-sided polygons are **hexagons**.

- Eight-sided polygons are **octagons**.

Triangles

Properties of Triangles

Triangles are three-sided polygons. There are three types of triangles according to their sides—isosceles, equilateral, and scalene.

- An **isosceles** triangle has two equal sides and two equal angles.

- If the measures of all sides of the triangle are equal, then the triangle is called an **equilateral** triangle (this means all sides are equal). This is also called an **equiangular** triangle (since all angles are also equal).

- A **scalene** triangle has three unequal sides.

Triangles can be named according to their angles:

- In an **acute** triangle, all three angles are acute.

- In a **right** triangle, one of the angles is a right angle.

- In an **obtuse** triangle, one of the angles is obtuse.

In the figure below, the base is *b* and the height, *h*, is the perpendicular distance from the base to the opposite vertex. Any side can be considered a base. Note that the height of a triangle is not necessarily the same as the length of any of its sides.

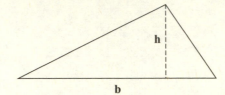

Using Triangles to Explore Geometric Relationships

A property of all triangles is that the sum of the measures of the three angles is 180°. If the measures of two angles are known, the third can be deduced.

Right triangles have several special properties. A chief property is described by the **Pythagorean theorem**, which states that in any right triangle with legs (shorter sides) *a* and *b*, and hypotenuse (the longest side) *c*, the sum of the squares of the legs will be equal to the square of the hypotenuse ($a^2 + b^2 = c^2$). Note that in the following right triangle, $3^2 + 4^2 = 5^2$.

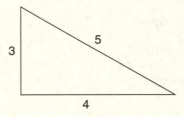

Sufficient evidence for congruence between two triangles can be shown through the following comparisons:

- **SAS** (Side-Angle-Side): If two pairs of sides of two triangles are equal in length, and the included angles are equal in measurement, then the triangles are congruent.

- **SSS** (Side-Side-Side): If three pairs of sides of two triangles are equal in length, then the triangles are congruent.

- **ASA** (Angle-Side-Angle): If two pairs of angles of two triangles are equal in measurement, and the included sides are equal in length, then the triangles are congruent.

- **AAS** (Angle-Angle-Side): If two pairs of angles of two triangles are equal in measurement and a pair of *corresponding* sides is of equal length, then the triangles are congruent.

Quadrilaterals

Parallelograms

A **parallelogram** is a four-sided polygon with two pairs of equal and parallel sides. In the figure below, one pair of parallel sides is designated as *b* and the height *h* is the perpendicular distance between the two bases. Note that, as with triangles, any side can be considered a base, the height of a parallelogram is not necessarily the same as the length of the other side. If it is, the figure is a rectangle.

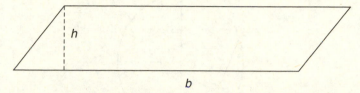

A rhombus is a special type of parallelogram in which all the sides are the same length.

Rectangles

A **rectangle** is a type of parallelogram with four right angles. The sides are designated *l*, which is the same as the base *b* for parallelograms, and *w*, which is the height of the rectangle.

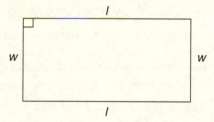

Squares

A **square** is a type of parallelogram with four right angles and four equal sides. The sides are designated *s*.

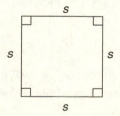

Circles

Circles are unique shapes in geometry because they have no angles. They are all the points that are equidistant from a point called the **center**. The **diameter** of a circle is a straight line segment that goes from one edge of a circle to the other side, passing through the center. The **radius** of a circle is half of its diameter (from the center to an edge). A **chord** is any segment that goes from one point on the edge of a circle to any other point on the edge. (All diameters are chords, but not all chords are diameters.)

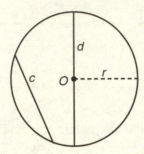

Formulas for Perimeter and Area

Finding the Perimeter

The **perimeter** of a two-dimensional (flat) shape or object is the distance around the object (think of a fence, for example). Perimeter is measured in linear units (e.g., inches, feet, and meters).

The **perimeter of a triangle** is found by adding the measures of the three sides of the triangle. This relationship can be represented by $P = s_1 + s_2 + s_3$, where s_1, s_2, and s_3 are the measures of the sides of the triangle. For example, if a triangle has three sides measuring 3 inches, 4 inches, and 5 inches, then the perimeter of the triangle is given by $P = 3$ inches $+ 4$ inches $+ 5$ inches $= 12$ inches.

The **perimeter of a rectangle** is found by adding twice the length of the rectangle to twice the width of the rectangle. This relationship is commonly given by the formula: $P = 2l + 2w$, where l is the measure of the length and w is the measure of the width. For example, if a rectangle has a length of 10 m and a width of 5 m, then the perimeter of the rectangle is given by $P = 2(10$ m$) + 2(5$ m$) = 30$ m.

The **perimeter of a square** is found by multiplying four times the measure of a side of the square. This relationship is commonly given by the formula $P = 4s$, where s is the measure of a side of the square. For example, if a square has a side of 5 feet, then the perimeter of the square is given by $P = 4(5$ feet$) = 20$ feet.

The **circumference** of a circle can be thought of as the perimeter of the circle. It is the distance around the circle, and is given by the formula:

$$C = 2\pi r \text{ or } C = \pi d$$

where π, or pi, is defined as the ratio of a circle's circumference to its diameter. The value of π is the same for all circles; it is an irrational number, 3.14159 . . . The approximation 3.14 is adequate for most calculations. In the formulas for the circumference, the d represents the diameter and the r stands for the radius of the circle.

Finding the Area

The **area of a parallelogram** is found by multiplying the measure of the base by the measure of the height, or $A = bh$.

If a diagonal is drawn on any parallelogram, it is divided into two congruent triangles, so one half the area of the parallelogram, is the **area of a triangle**, or $A = \frac{1}{2}bh$.

The **area of a rectangle** is similarly found by multiplying the measure of the length (or base) of the rectangle by the measure of the width of the rectangle, which is also its height. This relationship is commonly given by $A = l \times w$, where l is the measure of the length and w is the measure of the width. For example, if a rectangle has a length of 10 m and a width of 5 m, then the area of the rectangle is given by $A = 10 \text{ m} \times 5 \text{ m} = 50 \text{ m}^2$.

The **area of a square** is found by squaring the measure of the side of the square. This relationship is commonly given by $A = s^2$, where s is the measure of a side. For example, if a square has a side of 5 ft, then the area of the square is given by $A = (5 \text{ ft})^2 = 25 \text{ ft}^2$.

The **area of a circle** can be found by squaring the length of its radius, then multiplying that product by π. The formula is given as $A = \pi r^2$. The value of π is approximately 3.14, as discussed above for the circumference of a circle. The approximate area of the circle with a radius of 6 can be found by squaring 6 (giving 36), then multiplying 36 by 3.14, giving an area of $A \approx 113$ square units (the symbol ≈ means "approximately equal to").

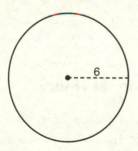

Similarity and Congruence

Geometric figures are **similar** if they have the exact same shapes, even if they do not have the same sizes. In the figure below, triangles A and B are similar. Corresponding angles of similar figures have the same measure, and the lengths of corresponding sides are proportional.

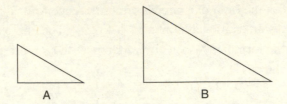

In the next figure, rectangles A and B are similar, but the corresponding sides are not only proportional, they are equal. Figures are **congruent** if they have the same shape *and* size. (Congruent figures are also similar, but similar figures are not necessarily congruent.)

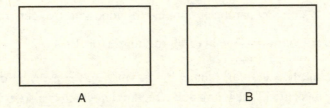

Three-Dimensional Figures

Three-dimensional figures have length, width, and height. Typical three-dimensional figures are

- a **rectangular solid** (think of a brick)

- a **cube** (a rectangular solid with all square sides)

- a **cylinder** (think of a can)

- a **prism**, a three-dimensional solid consisting of a collection of polygons, with two congruent, parallel faces (called bases) that are polygons and lateral (side) faces that are parallelograms

- a **sphere** (think of a ball)

Formulas for Three-Dimensional Figures

Volume refers to how much space is inside of three-dimensional, closed containers. It is useful to think of volume as how many cubic units could fit into a solid.

The **volume of a rectangular solid** is equal to the product of its length, width, and height; $V = l \times w \times h$. The **volume of a cube**, which has equal length, width, and height, is $V = s^3$.

The parts of a rectangular solid or cube are listed below and shown in the figure.

- A **vertex** is the union of two segments or point of intersection of two sides of a polygon.

- Each of the plane regions (sides) of a geometric body is a **face**.

- An **edge** is a line segment where two faces of a three-dimensional figure meet.

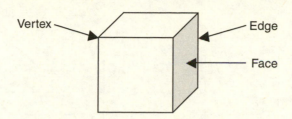

The number of faces, edges, and faces can be identified visually, or by the relationship among them: $F + V = E + 2$. A rectangular solid or cube has 6 faces, 12 edges, and 8 vertices.

The **volume of a prism** can be found by multiplying the area of the prism's base by its height. The volume of the triangular prism shown below is 60 cubic units. (The area of the triangular base is given as 10 square units, and the height is 6 units.)

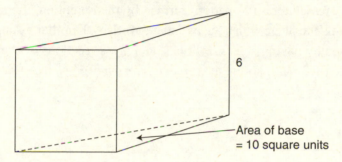

A cylinder is like a prism in that it has parallel faces, but its rounded "side" is smooth. The formula for finding the **volume of a cylinder** is the same as the formula for finding the volume of a prism: the area of the cylinder's base is multiplied by the height, or $V = \pi r^2 h$. The volume of the cylinder shown below is $V = (5 \times 5 \times \pi \times 8) \approx 628$ cubic units.

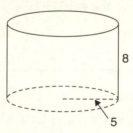

Symmetry

Symmetry is the correspondence in size, form, and arrangement of parts on opposite sides of a plane, line, or point. For example, a figure that has line symmetry has two halves that coincide if folded along its line of symmetry.

Polygons may have lines of symmetry, which can be thought of as imaginary fold lines that produce two congruent, mirror-image figures. Squares have four lines of symmetry, and non-square rectangles have two, as shown in the following figures. Circles have an infinite number of lines of symmetry.

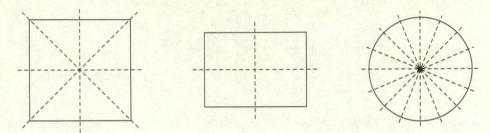

Tessellations

The arrangement of polygons that forms a grid is called a **tessellation**; however, other shapes may also tessellate. A tessellation is a pattern formed by the repetition of a single unit or shape that, when repeated, fills the plane with no gaps and no overlaps. Familiar examples of tessellations are the patterns formed by paving stones or bricks, and cross- sections of beehives, which are in the shape of hexagons. (See Math Forum at: *http://mathforum.org/geometry/rugs/symmetry/ grids. html.*)

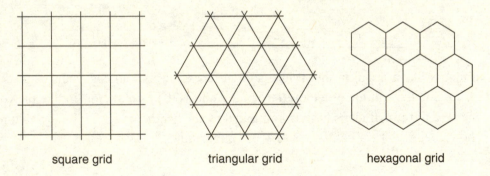

| square grid | triangular grid | hexagonal grid |

Ordered Pairs

Ordered pairs comprise a set of numbers listed as x and y values that are used to locate a point on a coordinate plane. An ordered pair is written as (x,y), where the first number tells how far to move horizontally from 0 and the second number (y) tells how far to move vertically from 0.

Coordinate Plane

A coordinate plane is a grid made of two main perpendicular lines, the **x-axis** and the **y-axis**. The x-axis runs horizontally and the y-axis runs vertically. The point of intersection of the two axes is called the **origin**. The origin is defined by the ordered pair (0,0). Sets of ordered pairs may be plotted on a coordinate plane to create different lines, rays, shapes, and so on.

Concepts of Measurement

Concepts and skills in the measurement strand of the math curriculum all deal with making comparisons between what is being measured and some suitable standard of measure. Measurement offers opportunities for interdisciplinary learning in social studies, geography, science, art, and music. Key to the development of skills in measurement is allowing for various types of measurement activities. Children need first-hand practice with measuring and making estimates in measurement.

The principles of measurement involve understanding the attributes of length, capacity, weight, area, volume, time, temperature, and angles. Being able to measure connects mathematics to the environment and gives children practical applications for computation skills. The ability to estimate by using measurement tools (e.g., rulers, thermometers, measuring cups, and scales) is a necessary skill for children to develop. According to Burns (2000), concepts in measurement include four stages in learning when developing classroom activities:

1. Comparing objects by matching—ordering items based on size.

2. Comparing a variety of objects for measuring—using body parts, blocks, cubes, etc.

3. Comparing objects using units in standard and metric systems.

4. Comparing using suitable units for specific measurements, taking into consideration the scale of the object being measured.

Time

The two basic kinds of clocks are **digital** and **analog**. The digital represents the time by using Arabic numbers, separating the hours from the minutes with a colon (12:45), which makes it relatively easy to read. The analog clock uses two hands to represent the hours and minutes based on 60 minutes for an hour and 60 seconds for a minute. Students must have a mathematical understanding of each of the numbers on a clock face when using analog clocks.

In addition, students should be aware of the time equivalents shown in Table 4-11.

Table 4-11. Time Equivalents

1 year = 365 days
1 year = 12 months
1 year = 52 weeks
1 week = 7 days
1 day = 24 hours
1 hour = 60 minutes
1 minute = 60 seconds

Temperature

Temperature is measured by using a thermometer, which is usually filled with mercury (a liquid metallic element that expands with heat). The **Fahrenheit** scale (°F) is used in the United States, whereas the **Celsius** scale (°C) is used in countries throughout the world. The Celsius scale is specifically useful in scientific experimentation. Water boils at 212°F or 100°C, and freezes at 32°F or 0°C.

Money

Teaching the concept of money involves understanding the concept of base ten. Children learn how to relate each denomination to pennies and understand the relationships among the other coins. Use real currency to introduce this concept. Children begin by observing the various coins and their attributes. They learn to associate the value for each of the coins and to make equivalences. Suggest that students begin by counting out a bag of coins and then trade out the various coins for larger denominations—for example, 5 pennies for one nickel.

Transformations: Translations, Rotations, and Reflections

Translation

Translation (also called a slide) simply means moving. Every translation has a direction and distance. This is known as a transformation that moves a geometric figure by sliding. Each of the points of the geometric figure moves the same distance in the same direction. This may be shown on a graph by moving the shape without rotating or reflecting it. The triangle in the following figure is translated down and to the left.

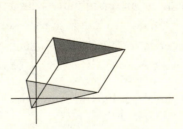

Rotation

Rotation (also called a turn) is known as a transformation that rotates or turns the shape around. Each rotation has a center and an angle for movement of a given number of degrees.

Reflection

Reflection (also called a flip) is known as a transformation that means to reflect an object or to make the figure/object appear to be backwards or flipped. It produces the mirror image of a geometric figure.

Conversions within and between Measurement Systems

Units of Measurement

TEKS requires that students in kindergarten through grade 6 become familiar with and apply knowledge of measurement using both U.S. Customary (standard) and metric systems.

Customary Units

- **Linear** measurement: Customary units of length include inches, feet, yards, and miles.

- Measurement of **mass**: Customary units of weight include ounces, pounds and tons.

- **Volume** measurement: Customary units of capacity include teaspoons, tablespoons, cups, pints, quarts, and gallons.

Metric Units

- **Linear** measurement: Metric units of length include millimeters, centimeters, meters, and kilometers. The centimeter is the basic metric unit of length, at least for short distances. There are about 2.5 centimeters to 1 inch. The kilometer is a metric unit of length used for longer distances. It takes more than 1.5 kilometers to make a mile.

- Measurement of **mass**: Metric units of weight include grams and kilograms. The gram is the basic metric unit of mass (which for many purposes is the same as weight). A large paper clip weighs about 1 gram. It takes about 28 grams to make 1 ounce.

- **Volume** measurement: Metric units of capacity include milliliters and liters. The liter is the basic metric unit of volume. A liter is slightly larger than a quart, so it takes more than four liters to make a gallon.

Table 4–12 provides relationships within these two units of measurement.

Table 4-12. Customary and Metric Systems

Customary System	Metric System
Linear 12 inches (in.) = 1 foot (ft.) 3 feet (ft.) = 1 yard (yd.) 1,760 yards (yds.) = 1 mile (mi.) 5,280 feet (ft.) = 1 mile (mi.)	**Linear** 10 millimeters (mm) = 1 centimeter (cm) 100 centimeters (cm) = 1 meter (m) 1000 meters (m) = 1 kilometer (km)
Capacity and Volume 1 gallon (gal.) = 4 quarts (qt.) 1 gallon (gal.) = 128 fluid ounces 1 quart (qt.) = 2 pints (pt.) 1 pint (pt.) = 2 cups (C.) 1 pint (pt.) = 16 fluid ounces (oz.) 1 cup (C.) = 8 fluid ounces (oz.)	**Capacity and Volume** 1 liter (L) = 1000 milliliters (ml)
Mass and Weight 1 ton =-2000 pounds (lbs) 1 pound (lb.) = 16 ounces (oz.)	**Mass and Weight** 1 kilogram (kg) = 1000 grams (g) 1 gram (g) = 1000 milligrams (mg)

Logical Reasoning

The development of **logical reasoning** is closely related to children's language development. Elementary mathematics instruction should help students learn to organize ideas, understand what they are studying, and explain their thinking as they solve problems. Activities should provide students with opportunities to make generalizations and conclusions, to justify them with logical arguments, and to be able to communicate their reasoning to others. Mathematics is a way of thinking, rather than a body of facts. This is an important distinction for children to understand. Critical thinking and logical reasoning aid students in clarifying their thought processes, and they may apply this skill in all curriculum areas.

In the early grades through grade 3, logical thinking should be introduced using an informal approach. There should be many opportunities for children to explore, manipulate, and experience concrete objects to identify their attributes, to make comparisons, to classify by their characteristics, and to make generalizations about their properties. The use of words such as *all, some, if, then,* or *not* helps children gain knowledge with the language used in logic. In upper elementary grades, students should be provided with learning activities involving deductive and inductive reasoning.

Deductive Reasoning

Deductive reasoning requires moving from an assumption to a conclusion. Deductive reasoning is reasoning from the general to the specific, and it is supported by deductive logic. Students use this type of reasoning in daily life, for example: "It is raining so I need to take my umbrella to school." Note that conclusions reached via deductive reasoning are sound only if the original assumptions are actually true.

An example of how deductive reasoning can be used to solve a geometry problem is the following.

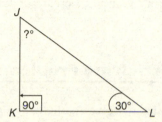

The sum of the measures of the three angles of any triangle is 180° (a general proposition). The sum of the measures of $\angle K$ and $\angle L$ is 120°; therefore, the measure of $\angle J$ is 60° (a specific proposition).

Inductive Reasoning

Inductive reasoning involves examining particular instances to come to some general assumptions. This type of reasoning is informal and intuitive. When thinking inductively, students make hypotheses, extend thought patterns, use analogies, and make reasonable conclusions from examining what appears to be a large enough body of evidence. Students use this type of reasoning regularly in life situations; for example, "If I do my homework all this week, I think my mother will take me to the concert on Saturday."

With inductive reasoning, a general rule is inferred from specific observations (which may be limited). Moving from the statement, "All fish that I have ever seen have fins" (specific but limited observations) to "All fish have fins" (a general proposition) is an example of inductive reasoning. Conclusions arrived using inductive reasoning are not necessarily always true.

Axiomatic Structure

An **axiom** is a mathematical rule. This basic assumption about a system allows theorems to be developed. For example, the system could be the points and lines in the plane. Then an axiom would be that given any two distinct points in the plane, there is a unique straight line through them.

COMPETENCY 005: PROBABILITY AND STATISTICS

The teacher understands concepts related to probability and statistics and their applications.

Statistics is the science or study of data. Statistical methods are used to describe, analyze, evaluate, and interpret information. The information is then used for predicting, drawing inferences, and making decisions. Data analysis involves both probability and statistics. Probability gives a way to measure uncertainty and is essential for understanding statistical methods. It explains data sets to give a type of generalized statistic, to make a prediction, or to infer something beyond the specific data collected. Probability is used to create experimental and theoretical models of situations.

Counting Techniques for Solving Problems

Students use counting techniques to solve mathematics problems. Some of the techniques include the following.

- Use networks, traceable paths, tree diagrams, Venn diagrams, and other pictorial representations to find the number of outcomes in a problem situation. For example, suppose a motel has 4 different elevators that go from Joan's room to the pool and 3 different doors to the pool area. Use a tree diagram to show how many different ways Joan can get from her room to the pool.

- Use the fundamental counting principle to find the number of outcomes in a problem situation. For example, a student can choose from 6 shirts, 4 pairs of jeans, and 3 pairs of shoes to wear to school. Ignoring color coordination, construct a tree diagram or other pictorial representation to show how many different outfits the student could assemble.

- Use combinatorial reasoning to solve problems. For example, a gym locker combination contains the numbers 2, 4, 6, and 8, but the gymnast has forgotten the order in which they occur. What is the maximum number of combinations the gymnast needs to try before the locker can be opened?

- Use counting techniques to solve probability problems. For example, what is the probability that the gymnast's locker from the problem above opens with the first combination?

- Use simulations to solve counting and probability problems. For example, a panel of 12 jurors was selected from a large group that was 70% male and 30% female. The jury turned out to be 11 men and 1 woman. Suspecting gender bias, the defense attorneys asked how likely it is that this situation, or even 12 men and 0 women, would occur purely by chance. Simulate this situation by using a random number generator to select 12 numbers, letting 0, 1, and 2 represent women and 3, 4, 5, 6, 7, 8, and 9 represent men. Note the number of times that 11 or 12 men are chosen.

Research on Teaching Data Analysis

There is some general agreement with regard to six underlying facts about the learning and teaching of data analysis. These include the following:

1. A problem-solving approach to teaching is consistent with how learners develop data analysis knowledge. (Lajoie, Jacobs & Lavigne, 1995).

2. Concept knowledge must be developed first before developing procedural knowledge. This can then be further developed by using problem solving, for example, understanding the concept of sample before gathering data to analyze a problem/situation. (Horvath & Lehrer, 1998).

3. Concepts and procedures are interdependent. (Konold & Higgins, 2003)

4. Statistical representations can become more sophisticated using technology and as students have more experience with data (Friel, Curcio & Bright, 2001).

5. Data organization can be improved by using technology tools. (Konold, 2002; Lehrer & Romberg, 1996).

6. Teachers must sequence instruction based on developmental age-appropriate situations, so students may examine certain types of situations before other types. For example, students should study situations in which all outcomes are equally likely before studying situations in which all outcomes are not equally likely. (Horvath & Lehrer, 1998).

Probability

Learning probability and statistics provides real applications of arithmetic. When basic computation skills are used in context, students have the opportunity to see the advantages and limitations of their calculations. Most arithmetic is done with a degree of uncertainty. Examples include estimating costs, making calculations of needed building materials, approximating estimated time of arrival (ETA) on trips, and estimating time for baking or cooking food.

A set of data can be described by its range, mean, median, and/or mode.

The **range** of a set of data is the difference between the greatest and the least numbers in the data set. Subtract these numbers to find the difference, which is the range.

The **mean** of a set of data is the average of the data values. To find the mean, add all the data values and then divide this sum by the number of values in the set.

The **median** of a set of data is the middle value of all the numbers. To find the middle value, list the numbers in order from the least to greatest or from greatest to least. Cross out one value on each end of the list until you reach the middle. If there are two values in the middle, find the number halfway between the two values by adding them together and dividing their sum by 2 (taking the mean of the two numbers).

The **mode** is the value (or values) that appear in a set of data more frequently than any other value. If all the values in a set of data appear the same number of times, the set does not have a mode. It is possible, however, to have more than one mode.

Studying probability and statistics should involve real problems and/or simulations. A theoretical or abstract approach is not appropriate for students in elementary mathematics. The approach should be based on experiments that draw on children's experiences and interests. Children's intuition needs to be challenged. Once they understand or can say what "should happen" in a situation, then they may be able to conduct experiments to test their predictions. Basic to probability and statistics are the following steps:

1. Data collection

2. Sampling

3. Organizing and representing data

4. Interpreting data

5. Assigning probabilities

6. Making inferences

Probability is a way of describing the likelihood of a particular outcome. An event is random when a selection is made without looking. A fraction can be used to describe the results of a probability experiment in this way. (1) The numerator of the fraction is the number of *favorable* outcomes for the experiment. ("Favorable" outcomes just refers to the outcome of interest in the probability; it can even be unfavorable in a social sense, such as the probability of death due to a disease.) (2) The denominator of the fraction is the number of all the *possible* outcomes for the experiment.

> Gabrielle is randomly choosing a marble from a bag containing three marbles—1 red marble, 1 blue marble, and 1 green marble. What is the probability that she will choose a green marble on a single pull?
>
> - There is 1 green marble in the bag. There is 1 favorable outcome.
> - There are $1 + 1 + 1 = 3$ marbles in the bag. There are 3 possible outcomes.
>
> $$\text{Probability of choosing a green marble} = \frac{\text{Number of favorable outcomes}}{\text{Total number of possible outcomes}} = \frac{1}{3}$$
>
> The probability that Gabrielle will choose a green marble on a single pull is $\frac{1}{3}$ or 1 out of 3.

Students need to demonstrate an understanding of probability and statistics and be able to do the following: (1) use experimental and theoretical probability to make predictions; and (2) use statistical representations to analyze data. A **sample space** is the set of all possible outcomes of an experiment. For example, a coin is flipped, it will land either heads or tails. Students learn to list the sample space, or all the possible outcomes: heads or tails. Sample spaces may also be listed on a chart or tree diagram.

Jones, Langral, Thornton, and Mogill (1999) have developed a four-stage framework that attempts to explain the learning process for probability. Learners begin at the subjective level, at which they are easily swayed by personal experiences when making probabilistic statements. At the second level, transitional learners begin to recognize the importance of organizing information. At the third level, students become informal quantitative thinkers. At the final level, students work at the purely numerical level in which they understand the nuances of numerical argument and use sophisticated procedures to determine numerical facts.

Students should learn to read graphs, making quick visual summaries as well as further interpretations and comparisons of data through finding means, medians, and modes. Students can use tables, line graphs, bar graphs, circle graphs, line plots, and pictographs to organize and display data. This is a helpful strategy used in problem solving.

For example, a **line plot** represents a set of data by showing how often a piece of data appears in that set. This plot consists of a number line that indicates the values of the data set and marks placed above the corresponding number each time that value appears in the data set. For example, suppose the heights of ten 12-year-old girls were measured and recorded. Then a line plot can be used to record the data from a chart, and students may make comparisons of the range of height, find the tallest or shortest girl, and interpret the data found.

In real-world problems, students may sample a part of a population. Students need to learn the difference between random and nonrandom samples and the importance this difference makes in statistical studies. As an example, to determine the percentage of people who are left-handed, students would not poll only famous athletes as a random sampling.

For students to fully understand data analysis, all frameworks and researchers agree that students should generate their own data. They should work with simulations that model real situations. They should use dice, spinners, two-color counters, and coins. As students begin to understand how to gather their own data, they need to be consciously aware of any graphical representations they might choose to use, recognizing the difference between discrete and continuous situations. Technology is a highly useful tool in data analysis and in making sense of the data, so students should be made aware of what is available in the ever-changing electronics world.

COMPETENCY 006: MATHEMATICAL PROCESSES

The teacher understands mathematical processes and knows how to reason mathematically, solve mathematical problems, and make mathematical connections within and outside of mathematics.

The National Council of Teachers of Mathematics (NCTM) and the Texas Essential Knowledge and Skills (TEKS) have emphasized the importance of teaching mathematical reasoning to children from kindergarten through grade 12. Teachers of the youngest students face a challenge because the ability to perform operations involving logical reasoning requires some level of cognitive maturity and the ability to think abstractly. From kindergarten to grade 2, children must understand the principles and patterns of the number system and the symbols used to represent numbers. Principles of measurement and basic geometry are also introduced early in the process. In grades 1 and 2, children begin to use quantitative reasoning and basic algorithms for addition and subtraction. From grade 3 continuing throughout elementary school, students continue to improve their basic knowledge of the number system and the abstraction of mathematical reasoning and begin to explore basic algebraic, geometric, and spatial reasoning. They also master multiplication facts and division. Word problems and mathematical reasoning are heavily emphasized in preparation for TEKS, which is offered in grades 3 to 12.

Logical Reasoning

Teachers must create opportunities to motivate children to engage in exploratory mathematics to develop logical thinking. For the early grades, this exploration can be done in **learning centers**, where children have the opportunity to work with blocks, shapes, and other manipulatives that are used to teach mathematical concepts in an indirect fashion through student-selected activities.

In addition to exposure to mathematics concepts in learning centers, teachers use instructional strategies to apply mathematics concepts in real-life situations. As an example, a role-play activity involving children ordering food in a restaurant on a given budget may be simulated in the classroom. This type of activity may guide children to understand basic mathematical concepts, including calculating sums of money, giving change, understanding percentages to determine an appropriate gratuity or sales tax, and the use of mathematics in daily life. Further extensions can be made with this scenario by teaching the students to understand the concept of budgeting and managing money based on a salary, including living within a budget and balancing a checkbook.

Solving mathematics problems involves logical reasoning, or thinking in a way that makes sense. Students can use logical reasoning to find patterns in a set of data and can then use those patterns to draw conclusions about the data that can be used to solve problems. They can identify characteristics that numbers or objects have in common, looking for patterns in different ways. For example, a group of geometric objects may have some property in common, such as all being quadrilaterals or all having right angles.

Problem-Solving Strategies

Solving problems involves more than just numerical computation; logical reasoning and careful planning also play important roles. Various methods can be used to solve word problems. Strategies may include, but are not limited to, acting the problems out, drawing a picture or graph, using logical reasoning, looking for a pattern, using a process of elimination, creating an organized chart or list, solving a simpler but related problem, using trial and error (guess and check), working backwards, or writing an equation. **Table 4-13** lists some of the steps used in solving problems.

Table 4-13. Steps in Solving a Problem

Understand the problem

Organize the given information and identify the question. Be aware that extraneous or irrelevant information may be given that is not needed to solve the problem.

Choose a strategy and/or make a plan

After you have organized the information, decide how to use this information to find an answer. Think about the math concepts that apply to the situation. Identify the order in which you will find new information and carry out your strategy.

Carry out the plan

After you have chosen a problem-solving strategy, use that strategy to work out the problem. Go step-by-step through your plan, writing down important information at each step.

Check your answer

Check your answer to see whether it answers the question. Is it stated in the correct units? Is it reasonable? Does it make sense? Estimate the solution and then compare the estimate to the computed answer. They should be approximately equal.

Developmental Considerations

Children in pre-K and kindergarten might have problems understanding basic number systems and how numbers are presented symbolically. They might have difficulties dealing with measurement activities that require them to master the principle of conservation. They might think that an apple split in half is more than a single apple, or a soda drink in a tall and narrow glass might be more than the same amount of liquid in a shorter and wider glass. These cognitive and reasoning limitations tend to disappear as children develop. By first grade, the principle of conservation is generally acquired.

Mathematics instruction in kindergarten through grade 6 involves not only knowing mathematical processes but also being able to determine when a given process is required.

Children must develop the ability to reason through word problems and understand the type of answer required. Most third graders can do addition, subtraction, multiplication, and even division. However, they might have difficulties with word problems and problem-solving activities that require them to identify the appropriate mathematical process. They might also have problems understanding questions involving multiple steps and deciding on the appropriate answer. The word problem that follows represents an example.

> Joe can place a maximum of 5 apples in a paper sack. If he needs to put 32 apples in sacks, how many sacks does he need?

In this example, most students will know that the problem calls for division—32 divided by 5—which will yield the expected number of 6.4. Some students will provide 6.4 as the answer, but the real question is: "How many sacks does Joe need?" Children will have to reason that the number of paper sacks can be only whole numbers; thus, the answer cannot be 6.4 sacks but rather 7 paper sacks.

Mathematical reasoning is crucial for understanding and using mathematics. This type of contextual or situational reasoning is certainly important, and questions such as the preceding one have a solid place in the curriculum and on state tests. Logical reasoning is the foundation for understanding mathematics and its use in life.

Historical Development of Mathematics

Every culture has developed some form of functional mathematics concept. In most cases, accomplishments of these civilizations have been transmitted to and enhanced by other groups. This transmission of knowledge and its cumulative effects have resulted in the creation of the modern-day mathematics used around the world. Some of the key civilizations that impacted the development of mathematics in the Western world are discussed in the following sections.

Egyptians and Babylonians

The first mathematicians that impacted the development of modern-day mathematics were from the ancient civilizations of Babylon and Egypt around 3000 BCE. The ancient Egyptians wrote numbers using hieroglyphs to represents the numbers 1, 10, 100, 1,000, 10,000, and 1,000,000. They used numbers into the millions for practical purposes like managing resources and for building large-scale public structures such as temples and pyramids.

The Babylonians made great advances in science, math, and, specifically, in astronomy. They also developed tables for multiplication and division as well as square and cube roots. One of the greatest accomplishments of Babylonian civilization was the development of a number system with a base of 60. This number system constituted the foundation for the advanced mathematics evolution that followed the Egyptians and Babylonians.

Greeks

The Greeks built on the accomplishments of the Egyptians and Babylonians and further developed the field of mathematics. Most historians believe that the formal study of mathematics as a discipline began with the Athenian Greek school of Thales and Pythagoras. Some authorities identify Thales and Pythagoras as the founders of Greek mathematics. Thales (640–550 BCE) was a merchant who traveled extensively and became acquainted with Egyptian mathematics. Some of his contributions include the following facts: a circle is bisected by the diameter, angles at the base of an isosceles triangle are equal, and an angle inscribed in a semicircle is a right angle.

Pythagoras, a former pupil of Thales, followed his teacher's ideas and eventually became one of the leading figures of Greek mathematics. Pythagoras taught that there is a basic relationship between harmony and mathematics. He developed the relationship of the sides of a right triangle, later named the Pythagorean theorem. After the early Athenian Greeks, the Alexandrian Greeks emerged as the leaders in the study of science and mathematics. Around 300 BCE, Ptolemy founded the university at Alexandria in Egypt, which became the center of learning for the Western world. This institution became the leading force in the study of mathematics, contributing multiple discoveries and some of the greatest thinkers of the time. Two of the leading figures that emerged during this period were Archimedes and Euclid.

Archimedes calculated the distances of the planets from the Earth and constructed a spherical planetarium imitating the motions of the Sun, Moon, and the six then-known planets. He also made multiple discoveries with scientific and military applications. Euclid was one of the most influential Greek mathematicians in the world. He is believed to have learned geometry from the students of Plato. Euclid is famous for providing a complete record of the mathematics accomplishments of Ancient Greece. He wrote several books on the elements of geometry. His mathematics knowledge has served as the standard mathematics textbook for over two thousand years (Euclidean geometry).

The Greeks also discovered that rational numbers could not accurately express all mathematical values. Based on this need, they developed the concept of irrational numbers. An irrational number cannot be expressed as a fraction. In decimal form, irrational numbers do not repeat in a pattern or terminate; they continue to infinity. Some examples of irrational numbers are $\pi = 3.141592654\ldots$ and $\sqrt{2} = 1.41421356\ldots$

Hindus

Around the fifth century, the Hindus developed a system of mathematics that allowed for astronomical calculations. They developed a technique of computation that later influenced the development of modern-day algebra.

Arab Contributions

The Arabs were the first civilization to solve sophisticated algebraic equations such as those currently used in science and engineering (e.g., quadratic equations). They also developed and perfected geometric algebra. Arab mathematicians used the work of the Greeks in geometry and improved the development of the field. They founded non-Euclidian geometry and made advances in trigonometry. The greatest contributions of the Arabs were the development of the numeric system, which resulted in the spread of the cumulative knowledge of mathematics to the world.

The Concept of Zero

Some historians believe that the concept of zero used today originated in India around the year 650 CE. Others suggest that it was perfected from the work of Greek astronomers. However, all seem to agree that eventually the Arabs used the concept of the zero to develop the current system of enumeration used in the world. The zero that we know today came from the Hindu tradition.

The Number System

The **number system** used in modern days is described as a Hindu-Arabic numeration system. It uses numbers from 1 to 9 and 0. Historians seem to agree that the Hindus contributed to the development of the base-10 digit system and the Arabs perfected and spread it throughout the world.

The cumulative knowledge of the Babylonians, Egyptians, and Greeks was translated from Greek into Arabic. At the same time, the mathematical accomplishments of the Hindus were also translated into Arabic. The collective knowledge of these civilizations and the improvement and innovations developed in the Arab world became the mathematics of Western Europe and, over a period of several hundred years of further development, became the mathematics of the world.

Other Civilizations

Other civilizations, such as the Mayans and the Aztecs, made significant progress in mathematics. The Mayan civilization around 700 BCE developed an elaborate calendar, and independently from the Arabs, the mathematical concept of zero. The Mayans also had highly advanced knowledge of astronomy, engineering, and the arts. The concept of zero was also developed separately by the Mayans in 700 CE; however, there is no evidence to suggest that the Mayan concept of zero impacted the development of mathematics beyond the Maya empire in Central America.

The Aztec civilization flourished around 1325 BCE. The Aztecs were also skilled builders and engineers, accomplished astronomers, and mathematicians. Like the Egyptians, they used mathematical principles for functional purposes to build pyramids, palaces, plazas, and canals.

Mathematicians from other places in the world developed significant accomplishments in mathematics. China, Japan, and several kingdoms from Africa are examples of civilizations that made sizeable progress in mathematics; however, their accomplishments did not have a direct impact on the development of mathematics in the Western world. For a detailed analysis of the historical development of mathematics and the contribution of various civilizations, see the "History of Mathematics" website, maintained by David E. Joyce of Clark University in Worcester, Massachusetts (http://aleph0.clarku.edu/~djoyce/mathhist/).

Key Developments in Mathematics Education in the United States

In the last half century, the U.S. education system has made important changes in the teaching of mathematics. Some of the key changes are listed below.

1950s to 1960s

- Significant changes in content of elementary mathematics programs
- New content added
- Standard content taught at earlier grade levels

1970s

- Slowing down of content changes
- Attention and focus on "system of delivery" of content

Late 1970s, early 1980s

- Back-to-basics movement
- Heavy emphasis on drill and practice

Late 1980s

- Increased emphasis on teaching concepts and problem solving

1990s

- Increased use of computers and calculators for computation
- Increased emphasis on estimation, problem solving, and higher-level thinking
- Release of Professional Standards for Teaching Mathematics (1991)

Early 2000s

- Increased emphasis on assessment, equity, technology, learning, teaching and curriculum standards

- Use of literature and cultural connections with mathematics and its implication in teaching

- Increased emphasis on research-based instructional strategies

References

Burns, M. 2000. *About teaching mathematics: A K-8 resource.* Sausalito, CA: Math Solutions Publications.

Carpenter, T.M., Fennema, E., Franke, M. L., Levi, L., & Empson. S. B. (1999). *Children's mathematics: Cognitively guided instruction.* Portsmouth, NH: Heinemann.

Flavell, J.H. (1985). *Cognitive development.* 2nd ed. Upper Saddle River, NJ: Prentice Hall.

Fredericks, A. D., Blake-Kline, B., & Kristo, J. V. (1997). *Teaching the integrated language arts: Process and practice.* New York: Longman.

Friel, S.N., Curcio, F.R., & Bright, G. W. (2001). Making sense of graphs: Critical Factors influencing comprehension and instructional implication. *Journal of Research in Mathematics Education*, 32(2), 124–158.

Fuson, K. C., & Hall, J. W. (1983). The acquisition of early number word meanings: A conceptual analysis and review. In *The development of mathematical thinking,* ed. H. P. Ginsburg, pp. 49–107. Orlando, FL: Academic Press.

Fuys, D., Gedds, D., & Tischler, R. 1988. The Van Hiele model of thinking in geometry among adolescent. *Journal of Research in Mathematics Education Monograph #3.* Reston, VA: NCTM.

Horvath, J.K., & Lehrer, R. (1998). A model-based perspective on the development of children's understanding of chance and uncertainty. In S.P. Lajoie (Ed.), *Reflections on statistics: Learning teaching, and assessment in grades K–12,* (pp. 121–148). Mahwah, NJ: Lawrence Erlbaum Associates.

Jones, G.A., Langrall, C. W., Thorton, C. A., & Mogill, A. T. (1999). Student's probabilistic thinking in instruction. *Journal for Research in Mathematics Education*, 30(5), 487–519.

Kamii, C. (2000). *Young children reinvent arithmetic: Implications of Piaget's theory.* New York: Teacher College Press.

Konold, C. (2002). Teaching concepts rather than conventions. *New England Journal of Mathematics Education, 34(2),* 69–80. Retrieved from *http://researchgate.net/publication/266339257 Teaching concepts rather than conventions.*

Konold, C., & Higgins, T. (2003). Reasoning about data. In J. Kilpatrick, W.G. Martin, and D.E. Schifter (Eds.). *A research companion to principles and standards for school mathematics*, Reston, VA: NCTM.

Lehrer, R., & Romberg, T. (1996). Exploring children's data modeling. *Cognition and Instruction, 14(1), 69–108.*

Lejoie, S.P., Jacobs, V. R., & Lavigne, N. C. (1995). Empowering children in the use of statistics. *Journal of Mathematics Behavior, 14(4), 401–425.*

National Council of Teachers of Mathematics (NCTM). (2007). *Professional standards for teaching mathematics.* Retrieved from *http://toolkitforchange.org/toolkit/view.php?obj=1039&menu=i*

National Council of Teachers of Mathematics (NCTM). (2000). *Principles and standards for school mathematics.* Reston, VA: NCTM.

Pepper, C., & Hunting, R. P. (1998). Preschoolers' counting and sharing. Journal for Research in Mathematics Education, 29(2), 14–183.

Piaget, J., & Inhelder, B. (1969). *The psychology of the child.* New York: Basic Books.

Santrock, J.W. (2003). *Children* (7th ed.), Boston, PA: McGraw-Hill.

Sperry Smith, S. (2008). *Early childhood mathematics,* 4th ed. Boston, MA: Allyn and Bacon.

Texas Education Agency (TEA). (2008). Pre-kindergarten curriculum guidelines. Online: *http://tea.texas.gov/index2.aspx?id=2147495508&menu_id=214783718.*

Texas Education Agency (TEA). (2007-2015). Texas Essential Knowledge and Skills by Chapter, online: *http://ritter.tea.state.tx.us/rules/tac/chapter iii/index.html..*

Texas Education Agency (TEA). (2014-2015). STAAR released test questions. Available online at http://tea.texas.gov/student.assessment/staar/math/

U.S. Department of Labor. (2012). Bureau of Labor Statistics, U.S. Department of Labor Occupational Outlook Handbook, 2008–09 edition, Bulletin 2700. Washington, DC: Superintendent of Documents, U.S. Government Printing Office. Retrieved from. *http://www.bls.gov/OCO/*

Van Hiele, P. M. (1986). *Structure and Insight.* Orlando, FL: Academic Press.

Vygotsky, L. S. (1986). *Thought and language* (new rev. ed.) Cambridge, MA: MIT Press.

Subject Test III: Social Studies (803)

The teacher understands and applies social science knowledge and skills to plan, organize, and implement instruction and assess learning.

Social Studies Curricula

Social studies is an umbrella term encompassing the disciplines of history, geography, civics and government, economics, and psychology. All five components are intertwined with the standards shown in Figure 5-1, which were developed by the National Council for the Teaching of Social Studies in 1997 (NCTSS, 2006). The Texas Education Agency (TEA) used these curriculum standards as a foundation to develop the state social studies curriculum for kindergarten through grade 12. Educators have a crucial responsibility because they lay the foundation of American core values, citizenship, democracy, and patriotism. Social studies often can be taught less than the intended state curriculum indicates. EC-6 teachers must learn to find ways to infuse their curricula with social studies lessons and recognize that social studies strongly supports literacy and other content areas. Understanding maps, diagrams, charts, and graphs as well as analysis of spatial patterns and relationships support students' spatial and mathematical reasoning capabilities.

Texas Essential Knowledge and Skills (TEKS) in Social Studies

The Texas Essential Knowledge and Skills (TEKS) is the state curriculum for kindergarten to grade 12. The TEKS organizes the social studies content inductively, from the known to the unknown. In this vertical alignment, children begin learning about the self in kindergarten and expand their knowledge with each successive grade, eventually encompassing the community, the state, the nation, and the world. Secondary grade-level social studies courses build and rely on the foundation laid by EC-6 teachers. A summary of the key components of the social studies curriculum covered in kindergarten through grade 6 follows.

Kindergarten—Child, Home, Family, and Classroom

- The child as an individual

- Home and families

- State and national heritage

- Patriotic holidays and the contribution of historical characters

Figure 5-1. Social Studies Strands

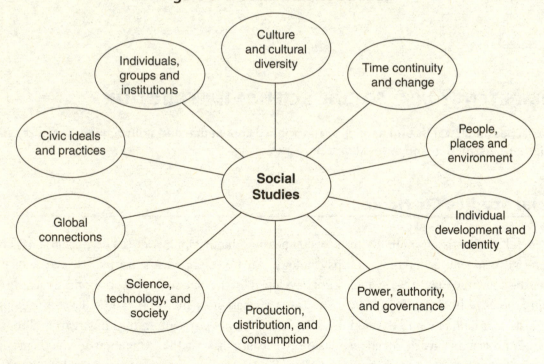

Grade 1—Child's Relationship to the Classroom, School, and Community

- The concept of chronology developed by distinguishing among past, present, and future

- Anthems and mottoes of Texas and the United States

- Relationship among the classroom, school, and community

Grade 2—Local Community

- Impact of significant individuals and events in the history of the community, state, and nation

- Concepts of time and chronology by measuring calendar time by days, weeks, months, and years

- Relationship between the physical environment and human activities

- Functions of government and the services it provides

Grade 3—How Individuals Change Their Communities and the World

- Past and present heroes and their contributions

- People who overcame obstacles

- Economic, cultural, and scientific contributions made by individuals

Grade 4—History of Texas

- History of Texas from its beginning to the present

- Events and individuals of the 19th and 20th centuries

- Human activity and physical features of regions in Texas and the Western Hemisphere

- Native Americans in Texas and the Western Hemisphere

- European exploration and colonization

- Types of Native American governments

- Characteristics of Spanish and Mexican colonial governments

Grade 5—United States History

- History of the United States from its beginning to the present

- Significant events and individuals of the late 19th and 20th centuries, including contributions of important inventors and scientists

- Regions of the United States that result from physical features and human activity

- Characteristics and benefits of the free enterprise system

- Roots of representative government

- Important ideas in the Declaration of Independence

- Meaning of the Pledge of Allegiance

- Fundamental rights guaranteed in the Bill of Rights

- Customs and celebrations of racial, ethnic, and religious groups in the United States

Grade 6—People and Places of the Contemporary World

- This part of the curriculum is designed to introduce students to the concepts of cultural geography. The discipline of geography explores patterns, relationships, and processes at local to global scale.

- People and places of the contemporary world

- Societies from the following regions in the world: Europe, Russia and the Eurasian republics, North America, Middle America, South America, Southwest Asia-North Africa, Sub-Saharan Africa, South Asia, East Asia, Southeast Asia, Australia, and the Pacific Realm

- Influence of individuals and groups from different cultures on selected historical and contemporary events

- Different ways of organizing economic and governmental systems

Integration of Social Studies

As mentioned, the teaching of social studies by definition implies integration of content from five disciplines: history, geography, civics and government, economics, and psychology. However, teachers can go beyond this integration and add components from other content areas. A literature-based approach is an ideal way to integrate social studies with language arts. Through the use of authentic multicultural literature, teachers can expose children to quality reading as well as the cultures of the many ethnic and linguistic groups living in the United States. Social studies is strongly linked with English Language Arts and Reading. It not only requires strong reading and writing skills but also supports reading by providing an understanding of the history as well as the physical and cultural characteristics of a place.

The use of thematic units can also help teachers to integrate the content areas. In this approach, a teacher or teachers select a theme and organize content area instruction around it. Thematic instruction can be done in a self-contained classroom or in a departmental format in which several teachers teach the content. However, units may be organized by key time periods in history or regions of the world with key themes serving as "big ideas" or "guiding questions" to drive instruction. This method allows learners to "chunk" the material historically or geographically while simultaneously analyzing major themes or "big ideas" that connect to other units of instruction. Some educators may prefer this method because it divides content into units familiar to both the educator and students.

Thematic instruction is ideal for English language learners (ELLs) because the use of a common theme in multiple content areas makes content more cognitively accessible for them. For example, in a unit on the **solar system**, the names of the planets and the terminology used to describe the system can be introduced and repeated in several subjects through the duration of the unit. The presentation and repetition of content in different subjects and under different conditions allow students the opportunity to develop English vocabulary while learning content.

Using Maps and Globes

Symbolic representation can pose challenges for children in kindergarten through grade 4 and occasionally in grades 5 and 6. Maps and globes are tools for representing space symbolically. Globes are a mathematical model of the Earth and show correct, unaltered (not distorted) distance, size, and shape of continents and bodies of water. Maps are a flat representation of the world and distort the distance, size, or shape of continents and bodies of water. This distortion can confuse the young learner. In the early grades, the main purpose of globes is to familiarize children with the roundness of the Earth help them develop a global perspective. Globes also can help in studying the proportion of land and water. In kindergarten through third grade, teachers should use a simplified 12-inch globe that uses no more than three colors to represent land elevation and no more than two to represent water depth. For this age group, the globe should include only the largest rivers, cities, and oceans. In grades 4 through 6, students can use a 16-inch globe containing additional details and usually seven colors to represent land elevation and three colors to represent water depth.

Activities for Students in Kindergarten through Grade 6

Teaching map concepts in kindergarten through grade 4 should include the following:

- Stress that the globe is a small representation of the Earth.

- Show how globes represent land and water.

- Identify major countries (e.g., the United States, Mexico, and Canada), their capitals and major cities.

- Identify major landforms and water bodies.

- Show and explain the location of the North Pole and the Northern Hemisphere, where most of the world's land is located.

- Show and explain the location of the South Pole and the Southern Hemisphere, where most of the world's water is located.

- Show the relationship and location of the Earth in the solar system.

- Use the globe to find the continent, the country, the state, and the city in which the children live.

- Encourage children to explore the globe to find places by themselves.

- Compare the size of the continents represented on a globe with their representation on a Mercator projection—the flat representation.

Teaching map concepts in fifth and sixth grade should include the following:

- Identify countries, capitals, and other major cities in the world

- Identify major landforms and bodies of water

- Create and interpret maps.

- Use maps and globes to pose and answer questions.

- Locate major historical and contemporary societies on maps and globes.

- Use maps to solve real-life problems, i.e., using road maps to plan a route to a specific destination.

Latitude and Longitude—Developmental Considerations

The concepts of **latitude** and **longitude** are generally covered in fourth grade and up. However, even fourth graders may have difficulty understanding the mathematics involved in the grid system. Children might get confused with these concepts:

- The length of the meridians of longitude and the parallels of latitude on a globe and Mercator projection look different.

- The meridians of longitude have a consistent length, but the parallels of latitude vary, becoming smaller as they move away from the equator. However, lines of longitude meet at the poles.

- Lines of latitude are measured in degrees based on the angle formed when measured from the equator, zero degrees latitude. Lines of longitude are measured in degrees based on time. (For more information on the history of measuring longitude, visit the *National Geographic* website at *http://education.nationalgeographic.com/encyclopedia/longitude*.)

They also might have trouble conceptualizing and separating the Western Hemisphere and the Eastern Hemisphere or the Northern and Southern hemispheres. Teachers should define the term "hemisphere" and use such concrete material as a ball to represent these concepts.

Using Technology Information in Social Studies

Research in social studies uses systematic inquiry. Engaging children in inquiry develops the ability to acquire and analyze information from sources. Inquiry also fosters the ability to design and conduct investigations, which helps students learn key content in social studies.

To gather information, students should learn about the sources used in social sciences research. They should learn to distinguish between primary and secondary sources as they become familiar with encyclopedias, almanacs, atlases, government documents, artifacts, and oral histories. Students should apply critical-thinking skills to organize and use information acquired from sources including electronic technology. Information about social studies is on the Internet, but students should learn to evaluate the scholarship of the sources and then use those with credibility. Students also can use commercially developed programs like *Oregon Trails* and *Where in the World is Carmen San Diego?* Digital globes, such as Google Earth (*https://www.google.com/earth/*) or National Geographic's Map Machine (maps.nationalgeographic.com/map-machine) are **geospatial**

technologies that provide a forum to analyze relationships and patterns at a local to global scale. These interactive programs expose students to problem-solving skills and social studies content in a fun and supportive environment.

Graphic Representations of Historical Information

Information in social studies can be presented in a visual form through the use of graphs and charts to make content accessible to all children, including ELLs.

Graphs

The most common graphs are the pictorial graph, the bar graph, the pie or circle graph, and the line graph. The **pictorial graph** is the most concrete graph because it uses a picture of the object it represents. **Bar graphs** are more concrete than pie graphs. Although **pie graphs** appear simple enough for children in the elementary grades, students must understand percentages to interpret them, and percentages aren't studied until late in the elementary grades. Teachers first can use real situations to guide students in the construction of graphs. For example, teachers can create a simple graph showing information about students in the classroom, such as the number of boys and girls or their preferences for color or food. Figure 5-2 shows the results of a poll on the favorite foods of first-grade boys and girls. A common bar graph in social studies is the population pyramid, which shows the number of males and females for each age group in a community. The population pyramid is appropriate for upper elementary because it uses percentages as well as whole numbers. Visit the Census Bureau's website for more information at *http://www.census.gov/population/ metro/data/pop_pyramid.html*. When possible, teachers should also incorporate such charts and graphs common to other disciplines as the dot plots in mathematics, to reinforce concepts and show that learning is continuous and can be applied in different ways.

Figure 5-2—Food Preferences for Children

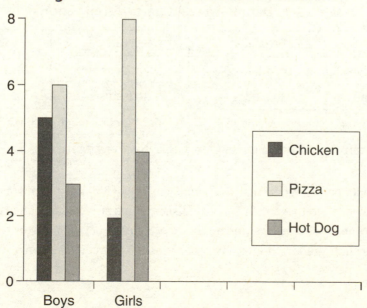

Figure 5-3. Pie Graph—Methods of Transportation

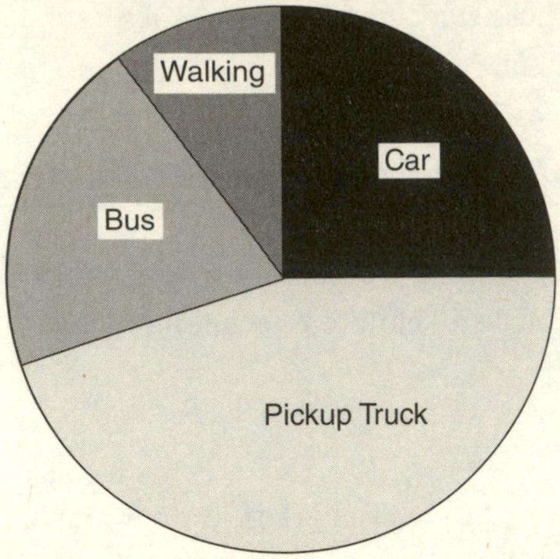

Teachers can use more sophisticated graphs like the pie to represent research information. For example, children can take five to 10 minutes a day to observe the transportation used by people in the neighborhood and prepare a graph similar to the one in Figure 5-3. Teachers can use this information to guide children to make inferences about the information contained in the graph. Why are so many people using pickup trucks for transportation? Why are few people walking?

Charts

Charts can record information and present ideas concisely. Charts are ideal for showing concepts concretely. **Data retrieval charts** can collect and track data gathered from research, observation, or experimentation. The chart allows easy comparison of two or more sets of data. For example, students could use the chart shown in Table 5-1 to record information about the foods of the ethnic groups represented in their classroom.

Table 5-1. Data Retrieval Chart—Ethnic Foods

Ethnic Group	Breakfast	Dinner	Special Days
Mexican American	Tortilla/eggs	Enchiladas/rice	Tamales/menudo
Puerto Rican	Bread/eggs	Pinto beans/rice	Roasted Pork/rice
African American	Grits/eggs	Collard greens/meat	Glazed smoked ham
Italian American	Frittata (omelet)	Spaghetti/meatballs	Special lasagna

Narrative charts can show events in a sequence. For example, students can develop charts showing the steps needed to make their favorite dishes. A narrative chart can also present a timeline of historical events. A simple timeline might show a child's personal history. Because children in kindergarten through grade 2 might have problems conceptualizing time, initial exposure to timelines should begin with what they did yesterday, what they are doing today, and what they will do tomorrow (See Figure 5-4b). Starting in third grade, children can introduce more challenging components, like those listed in Figure 5-4.

Figure 5-4a. A Timeline—My History

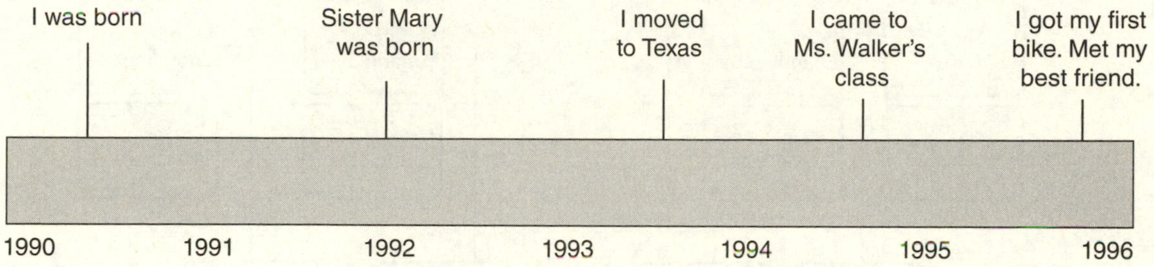

| I was born | Sister Mary was born | I moved to Texas | I came to Ms. Walker's class | I got my first bike. Met my best friend. |

| 1990 | 1991 | 1992 | 1993 | 1994 | 1995 | 1996 |

Figure 5-4b. A Timeline—My Day

Yesterday	Today	Tomorrow
I played with my dog	I went to school.	I will go to school.
I went to school.	I went to the library.	I am going to see a movie.

A tabulation or classification chart provides an orderly columnar display of information for comparison. For example, Table 5-2 compares data based on the 2010 United States census.

**Table 5-2. Tabulation or Classification Chart—
U.S. and Texas Populations by Group**

Race/Ethnic Group Population	Percentage of U.S. Population	Percentage of Texas Population
Caucasian/not Hispanic	62.6%	44.0%
African American	13.2%	12.4%
Asian	5.3%	4.3%
Hispanic or Latino	17.1%	38.4%
American Indian/Alaskan Native	1.2%	1.0%
Native Hawaiian/Pacific Is.	0.2%	0.1%

Source: U.S. Census Bureau (2013): online http://quickfacts.census.gov/qfd/states/00000.html Texas Quick Facts online: http://www.census.gov/quickfacts/table/PST045214/48,00

Using developmentally appropriate vocabulary, teachers can guide students to recall and infer data from the chart.

A **pedigree chart** shows the origin and development of something. Examples are a person's family, the pedigree line of a purebred dog, and the development of a political party. Figure 5-5 presents a pedigree chart.

Figure 5-5. A Pedigree Chart—My Family Tree

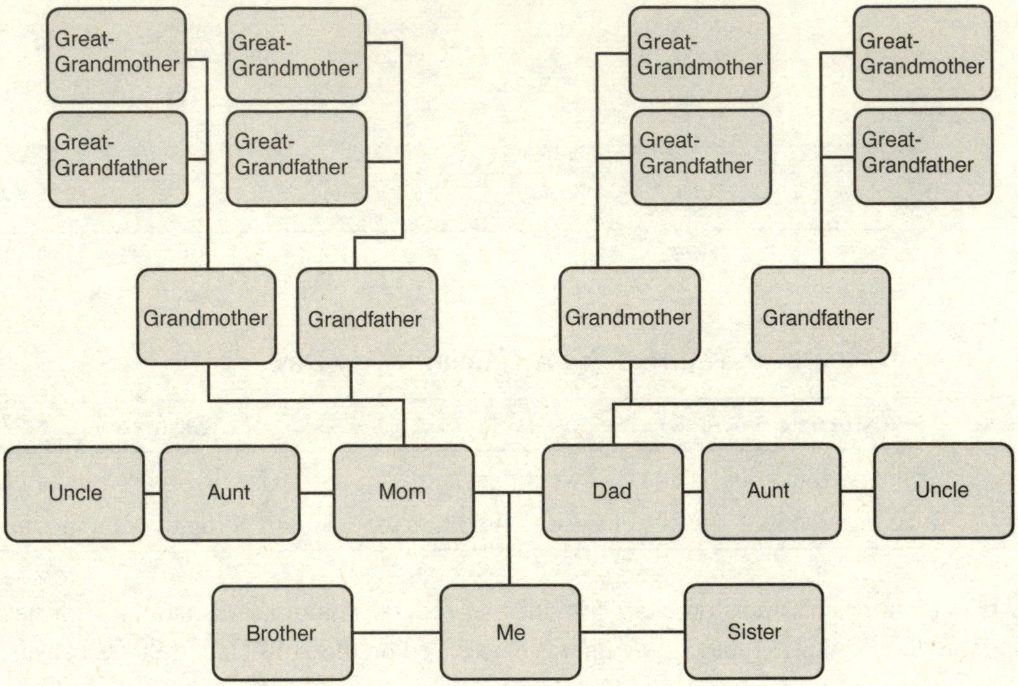

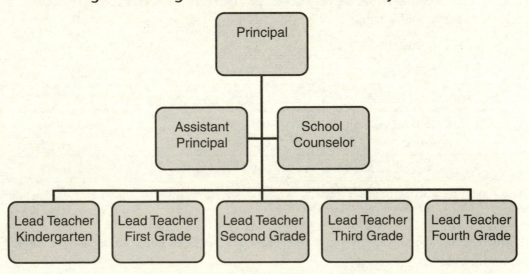

An organizational chart shows the structure of an organization, such as a school or business. Figure 5-6 is a chart showing the typical organization of an elementary school.

Figure 5-6. Organizational Chart—Elementary School

A **flowchart** shows a process at certain points. For example, Figure 5-7 shows the process to complete an academic degree.

Figure 5-7. Flowchart for Program Completion

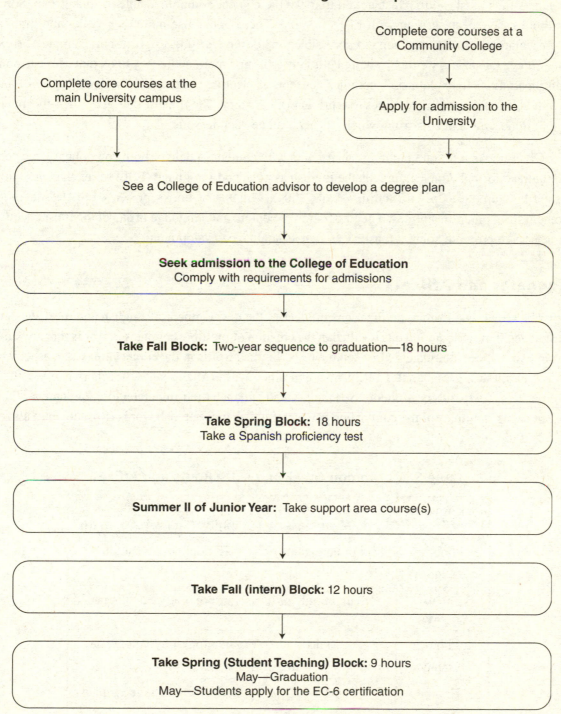

Addressing the Needs of English Language Learners

English language learners (ELLs) can find social studies instruction quite challenging. Teachers thus must modify instruction to make the content comprehensible for this group. Some textbooks have been written with ELLs in mind. These books use numerous visual and graphic representations to make the content accessible to children learning English. For example, *Adventure Tales of America*, written by Jody Potts (1994), is an American history book that uses cartoons and illustrations to explain such complex concepts as electing the president and making a bill into law. It also uses concrete timelines to represent U.S. history. The illustrations give ELLs the meaning of important concepts from which teachers can develop lessons.

Other books integrate language instruction with content to deliver both components in a contextualized format. One example is the English as a Second Language (ESL) series *Avenues*, published by Hampton Brown (Schifini et al., 2004). This set of books presents ESL lessons with content from other disciplines. The integration of content and language is one of the most effective strategies to promote content mastery as well as language development.

Cognates and Affixes

The Greek and Roman civilizations influenced the development of English and most Western languages. This association has resulted in the creation of multiple cognates— words that are similar in two or more languages. Most sophisticated English words in the content areas and, especially in social studies, are cognates of Spanish and other Western languages. Teachers can use these similarities to expand the students' vocabulary and enhance their understanding of content. Table 5-3 presents examples of the connection between English and Spanish words (Rosado and Salazar, 2002–2003).

Table 5-3. Common Greek and Latin Roots and Affixes

Roots/Affixes	Meaning	English/Spanish Cognates
Phobia Xeno	Fear of Foreigners or strangers	Xenophobia/Xenofobia
Phono Logy(ia)	Sound Study of	Phonology/Fonología
Photo Graphy	Light Graph, form	Photography/Fotografía
Homo Sapiens	Same, Man Able to Think	Homo sapiens/homo sapiens
Demo Cracy	People Government	Democracy/Democracia

Instructional Techniques to Support ELLs

Teachers should use different activities to teach the state curriculum to ELLs at the grade level and complexity required of native English speakers. Scaffolding was originally used to describe how adults support children's efforts to communicate in the native language (L1). The same concept can facilitate language and content development for ELLs. The term *scaffolding* alludes to the provisional structure that provides support during the construction of a building. This support is eliminated when the structure is complete. Following this analogy, ELLs receive language support to make content accessible to them until they achieve mastery in the second language (L2). When the mastery is accomplished, the language support is eliminated.

Graphic organizers are visuals that show relationships. These are the most common graphic organizers:

- A **semantic web** or **tree diagram** shows the relationship between main ideas and subordinated components.

- A **timeline** presents a visual summary of chronological events, and it is ideal for showing the events in a sequence.

- A **flowchart** shows cause-and-effect relationships and can show steps in a process, such as the process for admission to a school or program.

- A **Venn diagram** uses circles to compare common and unique elements of two or three distinct components, such as properties of numbers, elements of stories, or events or civilizations (like the Maya, Inca, and Aztec shown in Figure 5-8).

The **SQ4R** is a study strategy in which the learner engages in the entire reading process. The acronym stands for **survey**, **question**, **read**, **reflect**, **recite**, and **review**. During the **survey** part, readers examine the headings and major components of the text to develop predictions and generate questions. Through these **questions**, students establish the purpose for reading. As they **read**, students look for answers to the questions they generated. They monitor their comprehension as they **reflect**, write a summary, and **recite** the content they learned. Finally, they **review** to evaluate how much they learned about the content.

Figure 5-8. Venn diagram—Three Civilizations

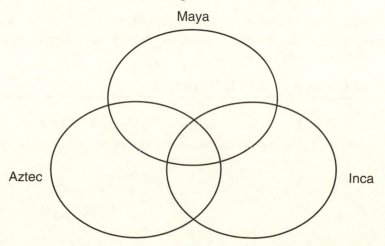

Strategies to Integrate Language Arts and Social Studies

Sheltered English

Sheltered English is an instructional approach designed to make content comprehensible for ELLs (Echevarria, Vogt, and Short, 2012). In the program, children are "sheltered" from the pressure of competing with native English learners. To deliver comprehensible input, content instruction is linguistically simplified through contextualized instruction, visual aids, hands-on activities, controlled vocabulary (guarded vocabulary), and body language. Some strategies teachers can use to modify language to make it comprehensible are:

- Control the length and complexity of the sentences. Children respond better to short, simple sentences.

- Introduce technical vocabulary before beginning the lesson.

- Use repetition, restatement, and paraphrasing to clarify concepts.

- Control the speed of delivery and use a different type of intonation to emphasize important concepts.

- Supplement oral presentations with diagrams, graphic organizers, and manipulatives to make content easier to understand.

- Help students use drawings and graphic organizers to visualize word problems and experiments, and as tools for communication.

- Guide students in using role-play to represent important concepts.

- Use such linguistic modifications as repetition and pauses during speech (Parker, 2001).

- Make the presentation of content more interactive with comprehension checks.

- Use cooperative learning strategies.

- Organize content around thematic units.

- Use graphic organizers to simplify and chunk content.

- Emphasize the gist of concepts instead of details.

Sheltered English is most effective in a classroom with students from many language groups who are at least at the intermediate level of English language development (Schifini, 1985).

Academic Vocabulary in Social Studies

Academic vocabulary is the vocabulary needed to understand the concepts of school. In other words, it is the vocabulary of teaching and learning. Standardized assessments, such as state tests, use academic language. It is imperative that teachers use the appropriate terminology to prepare students for state and district exams. Marzano and Pickering (2005) emphasize the importance of teaching academic vocabulary to English language learners and recommend a six-step systematic approach that includes direct instruction as well as practice and reinforcement. The steps to teach academic vocabulary are presented next.

- The teacher provides a description, explanation, or example of the new term.

- Students restate the description, example, or explanation in their own words.

- Students create a representation of the word by drawing a picture, symbol, or graphic.

- Students periodically participate in activities to add to their knowledge of terms.

- Students discuss terms with one another.

- Students participate in games and activities that reinforce the new term.

Cooperative learning is a teaching strategy designed to create a low-anxiety learning environment in which students work in small groups to achieve instructional goals. In cooperative learning, students with different levels of ability or language development collaborate to support each other to ensure that each member masters the objectives of the lesson. This approach can deliver content as well as language instruction. Traditionally, the strategy is delivered in specific steps (Arends, 1998):

1. **Present Goals**—The teacher goes over the objectives of the lesson and provides the motivation.

2. **Present Information**—The teacher presents information to students orally or with text.

3. **Organize Students into Learning Teams**—The teacher explains to students how to form learning teams and helps groups make an efficient transition.

4. **Assist Teamwork and Study**—The teacher-helps learning teams as they do their work.

5. **Test Students on the Content**—The teacher tests students' knowledge of learning materials as each group presents the results of their work.

6. **Provide Recognition**—The teacher finds ways to recognize individual and group efforts and achievements.

To emphasize the cooperative nature of the strategy, specific methods were developed to enrich the lessons such as Student Teams Achievement Division (STAD), Group Investigations, Think-Pair-Share, and Numbered Heads Together. These specialized methods are described in the sections that follow.

Student Teams Achievement Division (STAD)

1. The teacher presents new academic information to students.

2. Students are divided into four- or five-member learning teams.

3. Team members master the content and then help each other learn the material through tutoring and quizzing one another as well as conducting team discussions.

4. Each student gets an improvement score to show the growth he or she has made.

5. Daily or weekly quizzes are given to assess mastery.

6. Each week, through newsletters or a short ceremony, groups and individual students are recognized for showing the most improvement (Slavin, 1986).

Group Investigation

1. Students select a subtopic within a general area.

2. The teacher divides the class into groups of two to six students. Group composition should be ethnically and academically heterogeneous.

3. The students and the teacher plan specific learning procedures, tasks, and goals.

4. Students carry out the plan using sources. The teacher monitors the process and helps as needed.

5. The students analyze and evaluate information and plan to sum it in an interesting way for possible display or presentation to the class.

6. The students present their final product.

7. The teacher conducts individual or group evaluations (Thelen, 1981).

Think-Pair-Share

This activity was developed as a result of the wait-time research. Wait-time research suggests that pausing for a few seconds to allow children to reflect on the question can improve the quality of the response as well as the overall performance of children (Rowe, 1986).

1. **Think**—The teacher poses a question and asks students to spend a minute thinking alone about the answer. No talking or walking is allowed.

2. **Pair**—Students pair off and discuss what they have been thinking about, sharing possible answers or information.

3. **Share**—Students share their answers with the whole class. The teacher goes around the classroom from pair to pair until a fourth or a half of the class has a chance to report (Lyman, 1981).

Numbered Heads Together

This activity was designed to involve more students in the review of materials covered in class.

1. **Number**—The teacher divides the students into teams with three to five members each and assigns a number to each member.

2. **Question**—The teacher asks a question.

3. **Heads Together**—Students put their heads together to figure out the answer and to be sure everyone knows the answer.

4. **Answer**—The teacher calls a number, and students from each group with that number raise their hands and provide the answer (Kagan, 1985).

COMPETENCY 002: HISTORY

The teacher understands and applies knowledge of significant historical events and developments, multiple historical interpretations and ideas and relationships between the past, the present, and the future as defined by the Texas Essential Knowledge and Skills (TEKS).

World History

The World History Encyclopedia divides the history of the world into five periods: the Ancient World, the Middle Ages, the Age of Discovery, Revolution and Industry, and the Modern World (Ganeri, Martell & Williams, 1999). A summary and time line of key events in each period is presented here.

The Ancient World (4 Million Years Ago to 500 CE)*

Study of the ancient world focuses on the development of the first humans, the first farmers, and the first civilizations. It documents the critical change in human behavior from hunter-gather to agrarian societies, which occurred after man learned to domesticate plants and animals. This time period emphasizes the history of the ancient civilizations of Mesopotamia, Sumer, Assyria, Babylon, Egypt, the Indus Valley, megalith Europe, ancient China, Phoenicia, ancient America, ancient Greece, the Celts, the Romans, and empires in Africa and India.

---

* The terms "Before Common Era (BCE)" and "Common Era (CE)" are being used in place of the traditional "Before Christ (BC)" and "Anno Domini (AD)" to identify historical periods. These terms are more inclusive and eliminate religious references.

Timeline of the Ancient World

4000 BCE	*Homo sapiens* appear in different regions of the world
3500 BCE	The Sumerians of Mesopotamia invent writing and the wheel
3100 BCE	Egypt becomes unified
2800 BCE	Building begins in Stonehenge, England
2500 BCE	Indus civilization flourishes in India
1600–1100 BCE	Mycenaean control of Greece
1200–400 BCE	Olmecs civilization flourishes in western Mexico
1000–612 BCE	New Assyrian Empire flourishes
753 BCE	Foundation of Rome
605–562 BCE	King Nebuchadnezzar rebuilds the city Babylon
476–431 BCE	Golden age of Athens
336–323 BCE	Alexander the Great rules the world
1 CE	*Birth of Christ (Est.)*
27 BCE to 14 CE	Augustus rules as the first Roman emperor (some historians date the beginning of Augustus's reign to 31 BCE coinciding with the victory at Actium)
476 CE	Western Roman Empire falls

Note: The years in the timeline decrease from 4000 BCE until the common era (CE) begins, after which time the years increase.

The Middle Ages (500–1400 CE)

This period includes the Byzantine civilization, the rise of Islam, civilizations of the Americas, the Vikings, the feudal system, the Crusades, Genghis Khan and China, the African kingdoms, and the Hundred Years' War.

Timeline for the Middle Ages (CE)

500	Eastern Roman (Byzantine Empire) at its peak
600	Teotihuacán civilization is flourishing in Mexico
600	Rise of Islam

700	Mayan civilization at its height in Central America
700	Feudal system begins in Europe; peasants serve a lord in exchange for protection
711	Moors invade Spain
750	Abbasid dynasty is founded; Arab Empire at its peak
800	Charlemagne crowned emperor of the Holy Roman Empire
900	Rise of Toltec civilization in Mexico
1000	Vikings land in North America
1095	Muslim Turks take Jerusalem and ban Christian pilgrims from the city
1096–1270	Crusades try to rescue Jerusalem from the Muslims
1215	Genghis Khan and the Mongols invade China
1271	Marco Polo travels to China from Italy
1300	Renaissance begins in Europe
1325	Aztecs established Tenochtitlán near modern day Mexico City
1368	Foundation of the Ming dynasty in China

Age of Discovery (1400–1700)

This period includes the Renaissance, the development of the Aztec and Inca civilizations, voyages of discovery from Spain and Portugal, African empires, the Reformation, and the Ottoman Empire. It marks when European citizenry became more educated and questioned the power of the church and the monarchy.

Timeline for the Age of Discovery

1441	Portuguese begin slave trade from Africa to Europe
1448	Portuguese explorers reach the southern part of Africa
1453	Fall of the eastern Roman Empire (Constantinople)
1454	Gutenberg invents the printing machine
1492	Columbus sails from Spain to America
1492	Spain becomes unified and expels the Jews and Spanish Moors; Colonization of the Americas begins with Christopher Columbus in the Dominican Republic

1497	Portuguese reach India
1500	Inca Empire at its peak in Peru
1508	Begin the colonization of Puerto Rico
1511	Begin the colonization of Cuba
1517	Martin Luther begins the religious Reformation in Europe
1520	Suleiman rules the Ottoman Empire
1522	Magellan travels around the world (Portuguese)
1535	Spain completes the conquest of the Aztecs in Mexico and the Incas in Peru
1543	Copernicus suggests that the Sun, not the Earth, is the center of the universe
1571	Europeans defeat the Muslim Ottomans in the battle of Lepanto
1588	England defeats the Spanish Armada and becomes the greatest naval power in the world
1607	England begins the colonization of North America
1609	Galileo uses a new invention, the telescope, to study the universe
1618	Thirty Years' War begins (The key participants in the war included: The Holy Roman Empire, Great Britain, the Dutch Republic, Denmark, Germany, Sweden, France, Spain, and Austria)

Revolution and Industry (1700–1900)

This period includes the Russian Empire, the Manchu dynasty in China, the Enlightenment in Europe, the growth of Austria and Prussia, the birth of the United States, the French Revolution, the Napoleonic Era, the Industrial Revolution, the British Empire, the American Civil War, and the unification of Italy and Germany.

Timeline for the Age of Revolution and Industry

1644	The Manchu overthrow the Ming dynasty of China
1682–1725	Peter the Great rules Russia; Frederick the Great becomes king of Prussia; expanded territory, strong military
1756–1763	Seven Years' War ensues, with France, Austria, and Russia clashing against Prussia and England
1768	James Cook visits regions in the Pacific

1776	America declares independence from England
1789	French Revolution begins with the fall of the Bastille in Paris
1791	As part of the Enlightenment, Thomas Paine publishes *The Rights of Man*.
1804	Napoleon declares himself emperor of France, beginning the Napoleonic Era
1808	Wars for independence begin in Spanish America
1837–1901	British Empire at its peak under Queen Victoria I
1848	Year of revolution in all Europe
1861–65	American Civil War
1869	Union Pacific Railroad links the East and West coasts of the United States

The Modern World (1900–Present)

This period includes the struggle for equal rights for women, World War I, the Russian Revolution, the Great Depression, the rise of fascism, revolution in China, World War II, Israel versus Palestine, the Cold War, the space race, the Korean and Vietnam wars, and globalization. The early 1900s also saw some revolutions, the seeds for which were sown in the previous period.

Timeline for the Modern World

1910	Mexican revolution begins. Large numbers of Mexicans immigrate to the U.S.
1914	World War I begins when Austria declares war on Serbia and Germany on Russia
1917	Woodrow Wilson signs Jones-Shafroth Act into law, granting American citizenship to Puerto Ricans
	The United States declares war against Germany and the Central Powers.
	Russian Revolution starts when the Bolsheviks, led by Lenin, seize power from Czar Nicholas II.
1918	World War I ends; Europe is in ruins, and Germany is heavily punished
1929	Great Depression begins in the United States
1933	Adolf Hitler achieves power in Germany
1936–39	Spanish Civil War brings Francisco Franco to power
1939	World War II begins when Germany invades Poland and Czechoslovakia
1941	United States enters World War II
1945	Germany surrenders to the Allied Forces, and Japan surrenders after the United States detonates two atomic bombs in Hiroshima and Nagasaki
1947	Pakistan and India obtain independence from Great Britain
1948–49	State of Israel is founded in Palestine, and the Arabs declare war
1949	Communist Mao Zedong gains control of China

1959	Cuban Revolution; Communist Fidel Castro seizes power
1960	Many countries in Africa gain independence
1965–72	America participates in the Vietnam War
1969	American astronaut Neil Armstrong sets foot on the Moon
1973	U.S. pulls out of Vietnam; conflict ends
1974	U.S. President Nixon resigns because of Watergate scandal
1975	Cambodian genocide begins; Pol Pot becomes Communist dictator in Cambodia
1976	First Ebola virus outbreaks in Sudan and Zaire
1978	John Paul II becomes the Catholic Pope
1979	Ayatollah Khomeini becomes leader of Iran
1984	Indira Gandhi, Prime Minister of India, is assassinated
1986	Space Shuttle *Challenger* explodes
1988	Iranian airliner is shot down by the U.S.; the U.S.S.R. launches the *Mir* space station
1989	Berlin Wall falls; Chinese military massacres students who are protesting in Tiananmen Square
1990	Germany is reunited
1991	Soviet Union collapses, and the Cold War ends
1994	Free elections in South Africa and the end of apartheid
2001	9/11 terrorist attack in New York City and Washington D.C., and over Shanksville, Pennsylvania
2001	War in Afghanistan against the Taliban
2003	U.S. Space Shuttle *Columbia* disintegrates during re-entry on Feb. 1
	War in Iraq
2009	Barack Obama becomes the 44th president of the United States

For details about these historical periods, go to these websites: Kidipede—History for Kids (*www.historyforkids.org*) and Ancient Mesoamerican Civilizations, created and maintained by Kevin L. Callahan of the University of Minnesota, Department of Anthropology (*www.angelfire. com/ca/humanorigins*).

The Enlightenment—The Age of Reason

The Enlightenment refers to a period during the seventeenth and eighteenth centuries when people questioned religious dogmas and emphasized scientific reasoning and knowledge. This quest for knowledge resulted in the development of modern chemistry and biology. People questioned governments and demanded more individual freedoms. The search for freedom led countries to seek independence and fight tyranny. For example, the quest for freedom led to the American

War of Independence and the French Revolution. The American Revolution motivated the Spanish colonies to seek independence. Some of the leading thinkers of this period were Jean-Jacques Rousseau, John Locke, Charles Montesquieu, Voltaire, and Francis Bacon. Enlightenment ideas quickly reached the British colonies. Many leaders responsible for the writing of the Constitution were familiar with the leading Enlightenment thinkers, and framed the Constitution to protect the natural rights of the individual and limit the power of the government.

The Industrial Revolution and Modern Technology

The Industrial Revolution began in England in the mid-18th century. Inventions that made mining fossil fuel (coal) easier provided the energy needed to expand and promote industrial development. Improvement on the steam engine and industrial machines led to the mass production of goods as well as a better distribution system. The economic growth motivated people to leave the rural areas and move to the cities. The following timeline highlights inventions that supported the industrial revolution and modern life:

Timeline for Industrial and Technological Development

1769   Richard Arkwright patents the spinning machine powered by a waterwheel, which marks the beginning of industrial mass production of textiles

1810   A German, Frederick Koenig, invents an improved printing press

1831   An American, Cyrus H. McCormick, invents the mechanical reaper, which revolutionizes farming so that more crops can be harvested by machines. This allowed for greater food production, marking a move toward commercial farming. Mass food production supported urbanization by providing a food source for cities.

1836   Samuel Colt patents the first revolver in the U.S. to be able to be used as a practical weapon. Colt's manufacturing firm would later produce the pistols most widely used in the U.S. Civil War.

1837–1838   Samuel Morse invents the telegraph and the Morse code

1843   Alexander Bain invents the first fax machine, which evolves from the telegraph

1846   Ascanio Sobrero, an Italian chemist, invents nitroglycerin

1856   Louis Pasteur invents the process of pasteurization

1858   Jean Lenoir invents an internal combustion engine

1866   Albert Nobel invents dynamite

1876   Alexander Graham Bell patents the telephone

1885	Gottlieb Daimler invents the first gas engine motorcycle
1900	Ferdinand von Zeppelin invents a rigid dirigible airship called the zeppelin
1903	The Wright brothers invent the first gas-powered airplane
1905	Albert Einstein publishes the theory of relativity: $E = mc^2$
1914	Henry Ford introduces the assembly line and begins building the first American cars
1928	Biologist Alexander Fleming discovers penicillin
1930	Vannevar Bush at the Massachusetts Institute of Technology invents the analog computer
1940	Peter Goldmark invents modern color television
1946	The atomic bomb is invented
1952	The hydrogen bomb is invented
1955	The antibiotic tetracycline is invented
1959	Jack Kilby and Robert Noyce invent the microchip
1969	The predecessor of the Internet, called the ARPAnet, is invented
1971	Ray Tomlinson invents Internet-based e-mail; Engineer Ted Hoff develops the first microprocessor.
1974	Micro Instrumentation and Telemetry Systems (MITS) makes the Altair available, a mail-order personal computer building kit
1975	Paul G. Allen and Bill Gates form Microsoft
1985	Microsoft develops the Windows program
1988	Digital cellular phones are invented
1990	Tim Berners-Lee creates the Internet protocol HTTP and the World Wide Web language HTM

Settlements, Building Communities, and Understanding Culture

Historically, communities have formed to fulfill a number of needs. They include security, religious freedom, and material well-being as well as the protection provided by laws. For example, farmers and townspeople under feudalism during the Middle Ages would offer their allegiance to a noble who promised to protect them. As another example, immigrants throughout history have come to the United States to practice the religion of their choice as well as to have their rights and freedom protected under the law. As communities develop, they seek to meet their needs by such ways as educating their members, creating a system to govern and to protect the people, establishing communication and transportation systems, and providing recreation. Throughout history, certain members rise to meet or advocate for the needs and well-being of others within a community or for the community as a whole. These leaders are often recognized as patriots and become historical figures. They help shape societies and can even impact the development of a state or nation. Good members of the community include such people as political and military leaders (e.g., mayors, governors, presidents, generals), police officers, firefighters, educators (e.g., principals, teachers), doctors, inventors, scientists, athletes, doctors, artists, writers, activists, etc.). In the United States many individuals have shaped communities as well as the nation. They include George Washington, Benjamin Franklin, Harriet Tubman, Abraham Lincoln, Upton Sinclair, Susan B. Anthony, Ida Tarbell, Henry Ford, Steve Jobs, Franklin D. Roosevelt, Dwight Eisenhower, Harry Truman, Jonas Salk, Thomas Dewey, Mark Twain, Edward Hopper, Georgia O'Keeffe, Charlie Chaplin, Louis Armstrong, Billie Holiday, Booker T. Washington, W.E.B. DuBois, Martin Luther King, Daniel K. Inouye, Cesar Chavez, Jackie Robinson, and Lyndon Johnson (from Gillespie County, Texas) to name but a few. In Texas, many patriots and historical figures shaped our communities such as Sam Houston, Davy Crockett, Stephen F. Austin, Sarah Driscoll, José de Escandón, Capt. Anthony F. Lucas, James Stephen Hogg, Molly Ivins, and Ann Richards.

Culture is "the sum total of knowledge, attitudes, and habitual behavior patterns shared and transmitted by the members of a society" (De Blij & Murphy, 1999). Cultures change and adapt for a number of reasons. For example, cultural attire can be a simple adaptation to account for cold or hot weather, mild or harsh climates. For example, a parka may be worn in Alaska while light jackets are worn in Texas during the winter. Native Americans exemplified adaptation when some groups used grease from animal fat to ward off mosquitoes. Cultures may also change through modifications. For example, the extreme heat and humidity in the South are better withstood through the invention of air conditioning. Modifications, such as roads and railroads as well as steel frames for buildings, etc., allowed cultures to develop and expand their population and their geographic area over time. Moving to a new location and interacting with communities can also impact groups of people. For example, in Texas, many cultural groups (e.g., Hispanic, Germans, Polish, Czech, African-American, etc.) have learned from each other through cultural diffusion. **Cultural diffusion** is "the process of dissemination, the spread of an idea or innovation from its source area to other cultures" (De Blij, Murphy, Alexander 1999). This can be seen in Texas through many foods (e.g., tacos, burritos, pork rinds, cornbread, sauerkraut, and sausage) and cultural traditions (e.g., Oktoberfest, Cinco de Mayo, festivals and state fairs, Kwanzaa, Christmas, Hanukkah, etc.). These are also examples of a **cultural exchange**, whereby groups of people take on some of the traits of other cultural groups.

Ancient Civilizations of the Americas

Among the most developed ancient civilizations in the Americas were the Olmecs, Mayas, Toltecs, Aztecs, and Incas.

Mayas (1800 BCE to 900 CE)

One of the earliest civilizations of Mesoamerica was the Mayan, from regions of Mexico's Yucatán Peninsula, Guatemala, and Honduras. The Mayas developed a highly integrated society with elaborate religious observances for which they built stone and mortar pyramids. The center of the Mayan civilization was the city of Chichén Itzá and its religious centers, where human victims were sacrificed. The Mayas developed an elaborate calendar, a system of writing, and the mathematical concept of zero. They also had highly advanced knowledge of astronomy, engineering, and art. When the Spanish conquerors arrived, most Mayan religious centers had been abandoned, and the civilization was declining.

Zapotecs, Olmecs, and Toltecs

Farther north in Mexico, three highly sophisticated civilizations emerged: the Olmecs, Zapotecs, Teotihuacán, and Toltecs. Beginning with the Olmecs, who flourished around 1200 BCE and followed by the Toltecs and Zapotecs, these groups developed sophisticated civilizations. They used a ceremonial calendar and had built stone pyramids to perform religious observances. Teotihuacán is the best-known example of religious ceremonial sites built by these civilizations. They developed a partly alphabetic writing system and left codices describing their history, religion, and daily events. They also built pyramids starting in about 1000 BCE, which predates the pyramids in Egypt. Two of the most famous are the Pyramid of the Sun and the Pyramid of the Moon in Teotihuacan, Mexico, between 1 and 250 CE.

Aztecs (6th century to 1525 CE)

The Aztec civilization achieved the highest development in Mexico. The Aztecs had a centralized government headed by a king and supported by a large army. They were also skilled builders and engineers and accomplished astronomers and mathematicians. They built the city of Tenochtitlan, with many pyramids, palaces, plazas, and canals. At the peak of their civilization, the Aztecs had a population of about 5 million. According to the Native Languages of America, Classical Nahuatl, the administrative language of the Aztec empire, is practically extinct. However, modern Nahuatl varieties are still being used in Mexico, and used in their bilingual education programs (Rosado, Hellawell, & Zamora, 2011). For more information on native languages go to *http://www. native-languages.org.*

Incas—Children of the Sun

The Inca civilization covered the modern countries of Ecuador, Peru, and central Chile. Although they were not as advanced in mathematics and the sciences as the Mayans and Aztecs, the Incas had a well-developed political system. They also built a monumental road system to unify the empire. Their civilization was at its peak when the Spanish conquerors arrived in Cuzco, the capital of the empire. The Quechua are descendants from the Inca and still live in large numbers in South America, mainly in the Andes Mountains.

Mound Builders in North America

In North America, two major groups, known as the Woodland and Mississippian peoples, lived in the Great Lakes and Mississippi area. These people built burial mounds dated as early as 500 CE. The Mississippian people built flat-topped mounds as foundations for wooden temples dating from 500 CE. The chiefs and the priests of these groups lived in residences built on the top of the mounds, while the rest of the population lived in houses below. These mound-building civilizations declined gradually and disappeared by the 14th century.

Inhabitants of the South and Southwest

In the southwestern United States and northern Mexico, two ancient cultures developed: the Anasazi and the Hohokam. The Anasazi developed adobe architecture consisting of individual apartments, storage areas, and a central plaza. They worked the land, developed a system of irrigation, and made cloth and baskets. The Hohokam built separate stone and timber houses around a central plaza. Neither group developed a written language. Drought and attacks from rival tribes contributed to the decline of these civilizations. Historians believe that the Anasazi built the cliff dwellings at Mesa Verde, Colorado, during the 14th and 15th centuries to protect against these attacks.

Pueblo Indians

Evidence suggests that the Anasazi settled along the Rio Grande and intermarried with the local population, leading to the emergence of the Pueblo people. The Pueblo culture improved on the architectural tradition and farming techniques of their predecessors. The Pueblos produced drought-resistant corn and squash, which became the foundation of their diet. The Pueblo Indians survived the Spanish conquest and colonization.

Iroquois

The Iroquois inhabited the area of Ontario, Canada, and upstate New York for at least 4,500 years before the arrival of Europeans. They hunted and fished, but farming became the main economic activity for the group. The Iroquois had a matrilineal line of descent, with women doing most of the farming to support the community. They developed the Iroquois Confederation to discourage war among the groups and to provide a common defense.

American History

Colonization

In 1565, the Spaniards established the first successful European settlement in North America —Saint Augustine—near what is now Jacksonville, Florida. Following the Spaniards, the English tried to establish its first permanent colony on Roanoke (1586), an island off the coast of North

Carolina. This colony disappeared. Nearly 20 years later, the first permanent English settlement in North America was established on May 14, 1607, near present-day Williamsburg, Virginia. Further north, the Dutch settled colonies in the region of present-day New York and New Jersey. Following the Dutch, numerous private companies received royal charters, or patents, permitting them to begin colonization in North America. Three of the first and most successful were the Plymouth Company, the Massachusetts Bay Company, and the London Company. The London Company was the first to exercise this patent.

The English Colonies

Thirteen colonies were established on the Atlantic coastline. Three types of colonies developed and were based on three different charters: corporate colonies, royal colonies, and proprietary colonies. These were divided in three geographical regions: the New England Colonies, the Middle Colonies, and the Southern Colonies. The New England Colonies consisted of Massachusetts, Connecticut, Rhode Island, and New Hampshire. Their economy was based on farming and such small industries as fishing, lumber, and crafts. The Middle Colonies consisted of New York, New Jersey, Delaware, Maryland, and Pennsylvania. Their economy was based on farming, shipping, fishing, and trading. The Southern Colonies were: Virginia, North Carolina, South Carolina, and Georgia. Their economy, which was centered around agriculture, was based on tobacco, rice, and indigo as well as the cotton plantations. Plantations produced agricultural crops in large scale and exploited workers as well as the environment. Each colonial region had unique cultures, communities, and geographical settings that affected their political and economic development.

Virginia (1607)

The London Company established the first English colony in Jamestown, Virginia. The leader of the colony was Capt. John Smith. Natives of the area captured Smith and sentenced him to death. Pocahontas, daughter of the tribe's chief, intervened and saved his life. Contrary to popular belief, John Smith did not marry Pocahontas. She married John Rolfe, a tobacco farmer from the same colony. In 1619, the colony of Virginia established the first European-style form of government in North America, the **House of Burgesses**.

Massachusetts (1620)

The Puritans, who fled England to avoid religious persecution, founded Plymouth in 1620. Plymouth was the first permanent colony in New England. The group obtained a patent from the London Virginia Company. Among the Puritans were both separatists and non-separatists. The Pilgrims were separatists, a radical faction of Puritans who wanted to separate from the Church of England rather than merely purify it. The group obtained a patent from the London Virginia Company to finance their pilgrimage to America; hence the name *Pilgrim*. The ship used for the journey was called the *Mayflower*. Approximately two-thirds on board were non-separatist Pilgrims. Before arriving, they wrote the **Mayflower Compact**, a document containing rules to guide life in the community. This compact, signed November 11, 1620, established one of the first types of government in North America.

New Hampshire (1623)

Two groups founded the New Hampshire colony. The first group was led by Capt. John Mason, who established a fishing village in 1623. In 1638, a group led by John Wheelwright founded a second settlement called Exeter. That colony began as a proprietorship but became a royal colony.

New Jersey (1623)

The Dutch founded the New Jersey colony in 1623. After taking over the Dutch territory between Virginia and New England in 1664, King George II of England gave it to his brother, the Duke of York. The duke then gave the territory as a proprietary grant to Sir George Carteret and Lord Berkeley. In 1702, New Jersey became an English colony.

New York (1624)

New York was part of New Amsterdam, a possession of the Dutch government. In 1674, the British took control of the territory, and in 1685 New York officially became a royal colony.

Maryland (1633)

In 1632, King Charles I granted a Maryland Charter to Lord Baltimore (George Calvert). In 1633, the colony was established as a refuge for freemen, especially Catholics.

Rhode Island (1636)

Roger Williams founded the Rhode Island colony in 1636, and in 1638 Anne Hutchinson settled an additional part of the colony. Both Williams and Hutchinson had been banned from Massachusetts for their religious and political views and were looking for sanctuary. The colony was first a corporation and became a royal colony.

Connecticut (1636)

As early as 1633, Dutch traders had established a permanent settlement near Hartford. After the decline of the Dutch influence in the area, Thomas Hooker established the colony of Connecticut. Hooker and his followers were also seeking religious freedom after they were expelled from Massachusetts. In 1662, Connecticut obtained a Royal Charter under the leadership of John Winthrop Jr.

Delaware (1638)

The Dutch and Swedish first settled this colony. With the decline of the Dutch influence in the area, the English took control. In 1682, Delaware was awarded to William Penn.

North Carolina (1653)

By 1653, Virginia colonists began moving south and settling in the North Carolina region. In 1691, the region was officially recognized as a colony, and Charles I granted a royal charter in 1729.

South Carolina (1663)

In 1663, King Charles II created the colony of Carolina by granting the territory, of what is now North Carolina, South Carolina, and Georgia, to loyal supporters. It began as a proprietary colony and became a royal colony in 1719. Sir John Yeamans, a plantation owner from Barbados, founded the city of Charleston in 1670.

Pennsylvania (1682)

As early as 1647, Swedish, Dutch, and English settlers tried to establish permanent settlements in Delaware. In 1681, a large territory, which included Pennsylvania, was granted to William Penn. Penn was a Quaker, a religion persecuted in England. He made Pennsylvania a safe haven for Quakers, and a large number of German Quakers settled in the colony. In 1683, the first group of settlers arrived in Pennsylvania and formed Germantown near Philadelphia.

Georgia (1732)

The colony of Georgia was founded with two main purposes: establish a buffer zone from the Spanish settlement south of the colony and provide a safe haven for poor people. The British government had put many people in jail for being unable to pay their debts. These debtors were removed from jail and placed in this colony with the thinking that if the Spanish were to attack, it would give the other colonies time to prepare. Table 5-4 summarizes the key historical characters and events of the colonies.

Table 5-4. The Thirteen American Colonies

Colony	Year Established	Colonizer	Historical Features/ Characters
Virginia	1607	London Company	Capt. John Smith, John Rolfe, and Pocahontas
Massachusetts	1620	Puritans with a patent from the London Virginia Company	Puritans, Mayflower, Mayflower Compact, William Bradford

Colony	Year Established	Colonizer	Historical Features/ Characters
New Hampshire	1623	Proprietary colony	Capt. John Mason, John Wheelwright
New Jersey	1623	Dutch possession, then a proprietorship	Duke of York
New York	1624	Dutch possession, then a proprietorship	Purchase of the island of Manhattan, Duke of York
Maryland	1633	Proprietorship	George Calvert (Lord Baltimore), the colony served as a refuge for persecuted Catholics
Rhode Island	1636	Corporate colony	Roger Williams and Anne Hutchinson
Connecticut	1636	Corporate colony	Thomas Hooker and John Winthrop
Delaware	1638	Corporate colony	First, under the Dutch, Swedish, and finally under British control. William Penn
North Carolina	1653	Proprietorship	King Charles II
South Carolina	1663	Proprietorship, then a charter colony	King Charles II, Sir John Yeamans
Pennsylvania	1682	Proprietorship	William Penn and Quakers
Georgia	1732	Charter colony	James Edward Oglethorpe

Representative Government in Colonial America

The United States was settled by pioneers who wanted to experience freedom and have a voice in how they were governed. These settlers were influenced by such enlightened individuals as John Locke, Montesquieu, Thomas Hobbes, and Thomas Paine as well as by their experiences in establishing and governing their settlements. Colonists thus developed greater expectations for representation in their government. Actions and documents such as the Magna Carta (English Bill of Rights), the Mayflower Compact, the Virginia House of Burgesses, and the Fundamental Orders of Connecticut exemplify this belief.

The colonists were unique because they were English citizens who chose to move to the New World. They were not natives who were conquered and forced to become a colony. The colonists thus brought with them their tradition of hard work, individual freedom, and representative government that reflected English values and the influence of Locke and the Age of Reason. They believed in the right to elect the people who would represent them in deciding such important issues as taxation. The Virginia House of Burgesses was the first colonial assembly of elected representatives from the Virginia settlement. It was established in Jamestown to represent the colonists in Virginia in making laws.

The Mayflower Compact was drawn and signed by the Pilgrims aboard the Mayflower. They pledged to consult one another to make decisions and act by the will of the majority. It is one of the earliest agreements to establish a political body and to give that body the power to act for the good of the colony. Eventually, the lack of representation for colonists led to rebellions, like the Boston Tea Party, and to such meetings as the Continental Congress and the Second Continental Congress, which led to the Declaration of Independence July 4, 1776. After the colonists won the War for Independence, also called the Revolutionary War, their desire for representational government led to the development of the Articles of Confederation and then to the Constitution of the United States.

Indentured Servants

The indentured servant system was used to bring workers to the New World. In practice, the indentured servant would sell himself or herself to an agent or ship captain before leaving England. In turn, the contract would be sold to a buyer in the colonies to recover the cost of passage. Criminals and people in debt could be sold for life or until they paid their debts. In some cases, at the end of the service, servants remained as salaried workers, or in the best situations, the servants were given a piece of land for their services. This system of provisional servitude was not applied to Africans. Instead, permanent slavery was instituted.

The French and Indian War

The French and Indian War, the North American part of the Seven Years' War, began in 1754 as part of a larger imperial war in Europe between France and Britain. Both countries sought to expand their control in the Americas. Their poorly defined borders and attempts to militarily strengthen their claims caused increased tensions that led to war. The war officially ended with the Treaty of Paris in 1763 and a solid British victory. However, the conflict was expensive. Therefore, the British government levied heavy taxes on the American colonists to help pay for the war, adding to the rising tensions in the colonies. Coupled with limitations on colonists' westward expansion and increased war with the Indians, the colonists would soon rebel and fight for their independence.

American Revolution

The main reasons for the War of Independence, also known as the American Revolution, were economic. England and as other European nations had established *mercantilism* to exploit the colonies. This system had three main principles:

1. The wealth of the nation is measured in terms of accrued commodities, especially gold and silver.

2. Economic activities can increase the power and control of the national government.

3. The colonies existed for the benefit of England, the mother country.

England used mercantilism effectively in the 13 colonies, but after more than a century of British rule, the colonies were primed for independence, and war with England became inevitable.

Another reason for the rebellion was the cost of the war. It emptied the British coffers, and the British Crown needed a quick way to recover. The taxation system that followed the French and Indian War was unbearable for the colonies. They responded with civil disobedience and by boycotting the government of King George. In response to civil disobedience, the British sent troops to Boston, where the groups clashed and several colonists were killed. The event was called the **Boston Massacre**. One of the best-known boycotts was the **Boston Tea Party**, in which the colonists dumped tea in the Boston harbor to protest taxation. These events and the repression that followed led to the American War of Independence.

Continental Congress

Following the events in Massachusetts, representatives of the colonies met in Philadelphia to discuss the political and economic situation in the colonies. No clear solutions were reached at this congress. Once the hostilities started, the Second Continental Congress met to discuss preparations for war. George Washington was elected commander of the American forces, and war was declared against the British. The Congress named a committee, led by Thomas Jefferson, to prepare the Declaration of Independence, which was officially signed July 4, 1776.

The Declaration of Independence

The **Declaration of Independence** pronounced the colonies free and independent states. It consists of a preamble, or introduction, followed by three main parts. The first part stresses natural unalienable rights and liberties that belong to all people from birth. The second part consists of a list of specific grievances and injustices committed by Britain. The third part announces the colonies as the United States of America. This document provided the foundation to establish equal rights for all people. By signing this document, the colonists formally declared they were independent from English rule, thus officially beginning the American Revolution.

Revolution

The **American Revolution** began in Massachusetts in the outskirts of Concord and Lexington. In 1775, while the colonists were preparing for war, hundreds of British soldiers marched against them. Paul Revere warned the colonists of British troop movements, and minutemen took up arms to face the enemy. At Concord, the British were repelled and forced back to Boston. American sharpshooters ambushed and killed hundreds of British soldiers on their way back to Boston. After this colonial victory, the battle of Bunker Hill was fought near Boston. The British lost a large number of soldiers but managed to defeat the colonial troops. In Long Island, N.Y., the British later won another decisive victory over the Americans. In 1778, the French joined the war in support of the Americans, in retaliation for their defeat at the hands of the British in the Seven Years War. With the support of the French, the American troops defeated the British forces in Yorktown, Virginia, in 1781. The **Treaty of Paris**, officially signed in 1783, ended the war and gave independence to the new nation. For additional details about the American Revolution, go to the web page of HistoryCentral.com at *http://www.historycentral.com/Revolt.*

Establishing a New Nation

Articles of Confederation

During the Revolutionary War, the **Second Continental Congress** ran the government. After independence, the Articles of Confederation defined a new form of government. The new government was composed of representatives from 13 independent states with limited power. The Congress could not declare war or raise an army. It could ask the states for money or for soldiers, but the states had to agree to provide them.

Under this government, each state printed its own money and taxed imports from other states.

The new government provided common citizenship: citizens of the United States. It organized a uniform system of weights and measurements as well as a postal service. It also became responsible for issues related to Native Americans living within the borders of the new nation. The confederation served as the official government of the young republic until 1789, when the states ratified the Constitution.

United States Constitution

After six years under the **Articles of Confederation**, the leaders of the nation realized that the American government needed revision to bolster its strength and to improve its governing capabilities. To accomplish this goal, a constitutional convention was held in Philadelphia in 1787. The leaders of this initiative were George Washington, James Madison, Benjamin Franklin, and Alexander Hamilton. From this convention, a new form of government emerged. The **Constitution** was officially ratified in 1788, and in 1789 George Washington was selected to be the first president of the United States. The republic defined by the Constitution was composed of three branches— executive, judicial, and legislative—and included a system of checks and balances to regulate each branch.

To learn more about historical American documents, go to "A Chronology of U.S. Historical Documents," a website created and maintained by the University of Oklahoma Law Center, at *www.law.ou.edu/hist.*

Policies of the New Nation

Monroe Doctrine

In 1823, President Monroe made clear to European countries that the United States would not permit the establishment of colonies in the Western Hemisphere. Monroe also banned European countries from attacking the new American republics that were just becoming established in the early 19th century. The U.S. also was not going to involve itself in European affairs. This concept of "America for Americans" is known as the **Monroe Doctrine**.

Manifest Destiny

In 1844, President James K. Polk declared to the world that the United States would eventually become a world power and expand to its natural borders. Some of the borders mentioned were the Pacific to the west and Mexico to the south. Eventually, Polk's expectations became a reality as a result of the war between Mexico and the United States from 1846 to 1848. This prevailing nationalistic attitude in the 1800s was called **Manifest Destiny**, a term coined by newspaper editor John O'Sullivan in 1845 to describe this way of thinking. It was initially used as a Democratic slogan, but was later embraced by the Republicans. Many Americans believed it was the country's destiny to stretch from the Atlantic Ocean to the Pacific Ocean. This belief helped fuel and justify westward expansion, wars, land purchases, treatment of the Native Americans, and economic development. Yet, it was not a conviction supported by everyone. Some Americans, most notably the Whig party, did not believe that it was American's divine right to expand, but rather we should be a virtuous example of democracy for others to follow. However, Jefferson's purchase of the Louisiana territory in 1803 created conditions to support America's westward growth and development.

As America grew in the 19th century, so did its need for resources, land, and desire to expand. European settlers had originally claimed much of the terrain, although Native Americans had long established territories of their own. Therefore, when land was garnered through agreements (e.g., Louisiana Purchase from the French), annexation (e.g., Texas), and war (e.g., with Mexico), the American people expected that they had a right to the land. Acquiring more land made the country stronger economically. For example, more crops could be grown to provide a food source for American cities or to be exported to other countries. The natural resources fueled the country's industrial power. The **Transcontinental Railroad** was built to move resources and people across the nation and thus tied the nation together from the East Coast to the West Coast. The railroad was pivotal to the economic growth and development of the United States and to the rapid settling of the West.

However, this expansion came at great cost to the Native Americans. Some Native Americans may have coexisted peacefully with settlers if peace agreements were made and kept. Others groups, such as the Comanche and Apache, were more aggressive and given to war. The expansion of American settlements in the 1800s caused tensions to increase between Native Americans and settlers. In the end, Native Americans were forced to give up their lands and eventually their way of life. The American government set aside reservations, land specifically for these groups. However, this land was typically poor quality and unwanted by both Americans and Native Americans. This forced Native Americans into a state of dependency and poverty. If life on the reservation was refused, war ensued to compel them to comply. In many cases, Native Americans were killed in raids or in war. Native Americans also attacked settlers, which added to the distrust and increased military action. One of the most controversial actions occurred in 1830 when Andrew Jackson signed the **Indian Removal Act**, which basically forced Native Americans out of the southern cotton producing lands in the south east of the Mississippi. Although this action did not follow the legal process of negotiating the removal of a treaty fairly, Andrew Jackson's administration wanted all Native Americans out of the economically productive eastern part of the country. The Indian removal process, also known as the **Trail of Tears**, forced Native Americans to vacate their homes in the southeastern part of the United States to lands in the west, mainly in what is now Oklahoma.

As the nation grew, so did local, state, and national politics. The issue of slavery was a constant concern. Agreements were made to limit the number of states that did or did not allow slavery. Expanded territories became states as the population increased, thereby adding to the number of members of Congress in the Senate and House of Representatives. The influx of legislators affected laws and policies. These legislative decisions included laws about Native Americans, slavery, and big businesses (e.g., railroads, steel, meat packing industries, etc.).

Slavery in the United States

The Dutch brought the first African slaves to Virginia in 1619 to work on plantations. From 1640 to 1680, large numbers of slaves were brought to the Americas. With the invention of Eli Whitney's cotton gin, cotton became the economic mainstay of the South, and the demand for labor increased the slave trade. From 1798 to 1808, more than 200,000 African slaves were brought to America, mostly to the South.

Beginning in 1774, the North began regulating and eventually prohibiting slavery. By 1804, New York and New Jersey had passed gradual emancipation laws. Meanwhile, the slave trade in the South grew to meet the economic needs of the area. Eventually, slavery, along with other economic and ideological differences between the regions, resulted in the American Civil War. In 1862, Abraham Lincoln issued the *Emancipation Proclamation*, granting freedom to slaves in the South. After the war, the 13th Amendment to the Constitution officially abolished slavery. Additionally, in 1866 the 14th Amendment gave African Americans full citizenship, and the 15th Amendment granted voting rights to black men.

Civil War

The expansion of the United States brought additional problems for the young nation. Slavery divided the nation. By the 1800s, slavery had been virtually abolished in the North. The northern states' reasons for turning against slavery were primarily economic: the North had become more urban and industrialized than the South, and northern states received large numbers of immigrants who provided the necessary labor. Southern states remained mostly rural and received few immigrants, making slavery the foundation of their economy. With the nation's expansion west and the addition of new states, slavery became a contentious issue. Any new state would affect the balance between the free and slave states.

Slavery became the main topic of the presidential election of 1860. The candidates were clearly aligned either for or against slavery. The southern Democrats backed a strong proslavery candidate, John C. Breckinridge of Kentucky, while the new Republican Party selected a strong antislavery candidate in Abraham Lincoln. Lincoln's election resulted in the secession of the southern states from the union, the creation of the Confederacy, and the start of the American Civil War. The southern states created the Confederate States of America and selected Jefferson Davis as president.

The American Civil War in Texas

Initially Texas was divided about entering the war. Texas had fought hard to get into the Union, but many Texans did not like the northern legislators' control of the government. Texans also did not like the antislavery sentiment, although only about one-fourth owned slaves. Once in the war, the state provided many troops and was essential to westward expansion, protecting the Gulf Coast and supporting major battles in the Deep South. For more information visit the Texas State Historical Association, *https://www.tshaonline.org/handbook/online/articles/qdc02.*

Battle of Gettysburg

Several battles were fought in this war, but none was as memorable as the Battle of Gettysburg. Fought in 1863, this battle was the most disastrous event of the war and perhaps in the history of the United States. In this battle, more than 50,000 soldiers from the North and the South lost their lives. In a speech delivered on the battlefield in November 1863, President Lincoln eulogized the fallen Union soldiers in a speech known as the *Gettysburg Address*. After five years of fighting and the loss of thousands of lives and millions of dollars in property, in 1865 the commander of the Confederate army, General Robert E. Lee, surrendered to General Ulysses S. Grant, commander of the Union forces.

Reconstruction Era (1865–1877)

Because the war was fought primarily in the South, the region was devastated. Therefore, physical reconstruction focused on the South. However, the emotional reconstruction as well as the reconstruction of American unity had to be done nationwide, and admission of rebel states back into the Union was not automatically granted. The Reconstruction period was characterized by hatred and violence. Lincoln was assassinated shortly after the end of the war in 1865, and leadership of the reconstruction effort fell to Andrew Johnson, a southerner who was disliked by the North as well as the South. He was impeached and almost removed from power.

A major obstacle to the reunification of the nation resulted from the black codes. These restrictive laws were passed by southern legislatures to control former slaves. Some black codes restricted free assembly, while others restricted the jobs that former slaves could do. In 1867, the U.S. Congress, still composed entirely of northerners, passed legislation to eliminate the black codes. Additionally, Congress required southern states to ratify the **Fourteenth Amendment** of the Constitution prior to being allowed back into the Union. The Fourteenth Amendment gave citizenship to blacks. Finally, in 1870, the last two states (Texas and Florida) were allowed back in the Union.

Reconstruction in Texas

Reconstruction in Texas caused much political, economic, and social tension. The Union first moved a number of troops throughout the state to aid in the transition and to enforce Union rules. However, within a year most of the troops were sent to the frontier, allowing more former secessionists to have political power. After much turmoil and the removal of key state and local legislators throughout the state, Texas ratified the new constitution, established the Bureau of Refugees, Freedmen, and Abandoned Lands (the Freedmen's Bureau), and accepted the 13th, 14th, and 15th amendments. However, violence became a problem as some areas developed the black codes, rules to control the African American population, and the rise of the Ku Klux Klan (KKK). Other issues facing Texas included the economy as well as the situation with Native Americans. Railroads were a major part of economic development in Texas because they would allow quick access to agriculture and textile markets. This industry needed financial support after the war, which caused tension within and between political parties. Additionally, the influx of immigrants as well as migrants from the Deep South who came to Texas for a better life taxed the ability of already overburdened systems to support the increase in population. For more information go to *https://www. tshaonline.org/handbook/online/articles/mzr01*.

Ku Klux Klan

The **Ku Klux Klan** was among a number of secret societies established during Reconstruction to continue the implementation of the black codes and to terrorize African Americans. Klan members warned blacks not to vote or exercise individual freedoms. The Klan divided the South based on color lines. More subtle legislation was passed in the South to control the progress of African Americans. These new laws were known as Jim Crow laws. Racial separation characterized life in the South and other parts of the nation for most of the 20th century.

Economic Development

After the reunification of the country, energy was redirected to the economic development and growth of the nation. Inventions as well as the development of the railroad paved the way to economic recovery. The reconstruction that followed the war also played a vital role in the development of the United States as a solid economic and industrial nation.

In the late 19th and early 20th centuries Americans recognized opportunities in cities. Migration to urban areas caused the cities to grow exponentially in size and population as well as population density. This is called **urbanization**. The fast growth caused issues with housing, transportation, sanitation, and employment (De Blij & Murphy, 2005). People from diverse backgrounds were forced to live and work in proximity. The surrounding countryside was absorbed as an area grew. Poor areas, called **shantytowns**, sometimes developed on the periphery of the cities. The rapid increase in population provided more workers than needed for manufacturing, resulting in a surplus of labor. In Texas, the greatest examples of urbanization occurred in cities that serve as major transportation and economic centers. They include Galveston, Houston, Corpus Christi, El Paso, San Antonio, Austin, Dallas, Fort Worth, and Amarillo. Urbanization also led to urban sprawl, the multidimensional expansion of a city. Urban sprawl may not always coincide with proper coding and planning.

In the 19th and 20th centuries, American farmers used exploitive agricultural methods that rarely conserved the soil. Overgrazing as well as expanding farmland and using new mechanized practices increased production but created a problem. The land could not replete the nutrients at the same rate they were used. In the 1930s, the area encompassing the Texas and Oklahoma panhandles as well as parts of Kansas, Colorado, and New Mexico suffered from a strong drought. The thin, dry soil did not have enough plants to anchor the topsoil. Strong winds blew the topsoil into dust storms. The affected region was called the Dust Bowl.

Civil Rights Movement

Civil Rights for Freed Slaves

Civil rights are legal and political rights of the people in a particular country. In the United States, the Constitution and its Bill of Rights guarantee civil rights to American citizens and residents. The first 10 amendments to the U.S. Constitution are known as the Bill of Rights. As a result of the Civil War, three additional amendments were added. The 13th, 14th, and 15th amendments were passed during Reconstruction. The **13th Amendment** freed the slaves without compensation to slave owners. The **14th Amendment** declared that all people born in the U.S. were citizens (except Native Americans), that all citizens were entitled to equal rights, and that their rights were protected by due process. The **15th Amendment** granted black men the right to vote.

The civil rights movement sought equality for African Americans. Even after the 13th, 14th, and 15th amendments were added to the Constitution, blacks were denied full civil rights. Discrimination existed throughout the nation. Jim Crow laws enforced strict separation in the South. They were also kept from voting by poll taxes and literacy tests. In the North many qualified African Americans could not find good jobs. Segregation rules restricted blacks to separate facilities in public places such as theaters, restaurants, buses, restrooms, and schools. Discrimination also affected other minorities such as Latinos, Asians, and Native Americans. In 1896, *Plessy v. Ferguson* legalized segregation, allowing "separate but equal facilities" for black and white students.

The African American Civil Rights Movement

Several historic events marked the beginning of what is known as the **Civil Rights Movement**. In 1947, Jackie Robinson became the first African American to play baseball on a major league team. In 1948, President Truman ordered the integration of the armed forces and introduced civil rights legislation in Congress. The National Association for the Advancement of Colored People (NAACP) challenged the laws of segregation with the *Brown v. Board of Education of Topeka* case, and in 1954 the Supreme Court ruled that racial segregation in public schools was unconstitutional.

Another important event in the civil rights movement was the Montgomery Bus Boycott. In December 1955, Rosa Parks, an activist and respected resident of Montgomery, Alabama, refused to give up her seat on the bus to a white man as the state's Jim Crow laws required. She was arrested and sent to jail. Her actions prompted local community leaders of the NAACP to form the Montgomery Improvement Association.

The association chose a young Baptist minister, Dr. Martin Luther King Jr., to lead the organization and to direct a boycott of the Montgomery bus company. The boycott began in December 1956 and ended about a year later when the U.S. Supreme Court ruled segregation on buses unconstitutional. This victory gained national attention, and King became the most prominent figure of the civil rights movement. He founded the Southern Christian Leadership Conference (SCLC) with other African American leaders. The SCLC favored such nonviolent forms of protest as sit-ins, boycotts, and protest marches. King's "I Have a Dream" speech, delivered Aug. 23, 1963, took place during the march on Washington in support of the Civil Rights Act of 1964. The eloquent speech and orderly demonstration gained more supporters for the cause. King's work resulted in the Civil Rights Act in 1964. He was assassinated in 1968 in Memphis, Tennessee.

President John F. Kennedy proposed new civil rights laws as well as programs to help the millions of Americans living in poverty. After his assassination in Dallas in 1963, President Lyndon B. Johnson urged Congress to pass the laws in honor of Kennedy. Johnson persuaded the majority of Democrats and some Republicans. The **Civil Rights Act** passed in 1964 prohibited segregation in all public facilities and discrimination in education and employment.

The Mexican American Civil Rights Movement

During the 1960s Mexican Americans were engaged in the struggle for human rights, and Mexican American leaders started the Chicano Movement as part of that struggle. This movement was cultural as well as political (Rosales Castañeda n.d.). It embraced four main goals: the restoration of land grants, farm workers' rights, education, and political rights (Mendoza, 2001). The movement also sought to rescue the cultural and linguistic identity of Mexican Americans.

Activist Reies Tijerina started the Chicano Movement in New Mexico with the *land grant movement,* which sought to recover the land taken from the Mexican Americans as a result of the Guadalupe Hidalgo Treaty of 1848 and the eventual annexation of the American Southwest. In Colorado, Rodolfo "Corky" Gonzales founded the *Crusade for Justice* as a platform for the political movement (Mendoza, 2001). He also defined the movement through his epic poem "Yo Soy Joaquín/I am Joaquin." His poem described the historical development of Mexican American identity and described the struggles of Mexican Americans in the United States.

To support the rights of farm workers, human rights leaders Cesar Chávez and Dolores Huerta founded the United Farm Workers (UFW) union. Through the UFW they fought for better working conditions and fair compensation for agricultural workers.

In Texas, the movement focused its attention on the educational and political rights of Mexican Americans. In Crystal City, students took a leadership role organizing Mexican American voters and joining the political process. As part of this, the Mexican American Youth Organization (MAYO), under the leadership of José Ángel Gutiérrez and Mario Compean founded the Raza Unida Party (RUP) in 1970. Through the RUP, they sought to bring greater economic, social, and political autonomy to Mexican Americans (Acosta, n.d.). As a result of this movement, the RUP nominated candidates for mayor, city councils, and school boards in three South Texas cities—Crystal City, Cotulla, and Carrizo. The RUP won seats in those communities. This political awakening of the Mexican-American voters in Texas paved the way for better schools and programs for Mexican American and minority children in general.

Civil Rights in Texas

Texas civil rights issues center mainly on African Americans and Mexican Americans, the largest ethnic minority groups. Although both parties have fought for equal treatment since the mid-1800s, true change did not occur until the 20th century. This change was fraught with violence and intimidation from such factions as the Ku Klux Klan, the White Caps, community leaders, law officials, and the Texas Rangers. Such actions as the poll-tax and Jim Crow laws limited African American and Mexican American involvement in politics and society. Schools and communities were segregated by ethnicities until the *Brown v. Board of Education* (1954) decision started a change to integrated schools. Civil rights transformation was a long, arduous process. It required laws to change, and communities to modify their cultural customs, traditions, and mindsets. Much support for civil rights came from the middle class. After World War II, many Mexican or African American men pushed for equal treatment, which influenced the tumultuous 1960s when many men and women spoke out against inequalities. These ethnic groups have made gains in their struggle for civil rights and continue to work to ensure that they are treated equally by the law and within their Texas communities. To learn more, read the information contained in the following link: *https://www.tshaonline.org/handbook/online/articles/pkcfl*.

Women's Rights

While the 19th Amendment to the Constitution guaranteed women the right to vote in 1920, women remained subject to discrimination. The civil rights movement provided the impetus for the women's movement of the sixties. The women's movement attained better employment and professional opportunities for women. The Equal Pay Act of 1963 and the Civil Rights Act of 1964 prohibited discrimination based on gender. In 1966, Betty Friedan, author of *The Feminine Mystique*, and other leaders founded the National Organization for Women (NOW). This organization adopted the activist approach used by the African-American leaders of the civil rights movement. The Equal Rights Amendment of 1972 guarantees women's equal rights.

The Woman Suffrage movement in Texas was a long fight of determination that began in the 1860s. Although women worked and paid taxes like men, they did not have the right to vote for leaders and rarely participated in government and politics. Opponents of woman suffrage feared that allowing a change in women's status would challenge cultural customs and traditions. In fact, recent male immigrants could vote before women could. Women not only had to convince political leaders to stop the disenfranchisement of women. They also had to persuade people, including other women, that women's roles at home, in the community, and at work would not change simply because they could vote. The Texas legislature considered and/or voted on woman's suffrage multiple times from the 1860s to the early 1900s. In June 1919 the 19th Amendment giving the women the right to vote nationally was submitted to the states for ratification. On June 28, 1919, Texas became the ninth state to ratify it. To learn more, read the information contained in the following link: *https://www.tshaonline.org/handbook/online/articles/viw0.*

Temperance Movement—Prohibition

The temperance movement sought to prohibit alcohol consumption in the United States. This movement began in the 1830s, and by 1855 13 states had enacted legislation to prohibit the use of alcohol. In 1919 the U.S. Constitution was amended to prohibit alcohol consumption at the national level. This marked the adoption of the 18th Amendment. However, the ban was never fully enforced. Battles between law enforcements agents and organized crime characterized the Prohibition era. Al Capone and other leaders of organized crime made millions selling alcohol. After 14 years of Prohibition and unsuccessful attempts to enforce the law, it was repealed in 1933 with the 21st Amendment.

Texas politics was affected by the Prohibition movement for nearly a century (1840s-1930s). Initially, Prohibition resonated with fundamental Christians and later gained local and state support. Local communities determined whether they would be "dry" (that is, prohibit the production and sale of alcohol) or not. The Legislature passed laws limiting and disallowing alcohol before the 18th Amendment to the U.S. Constitution, which prohibited alcohol in the United States. After the repeal of the 18th Amendment, Texas reverted to allowing local governments to determine whether to allow the sale of alcohol in their communities. Texas still has some dry counties and cities. Since the 1980s, laws dictate when the legal drinking age begins, and warning labels are required on alcohol products. For more information, visit the Texas State Historical Association, *http://www.tshaonline.org/handbook/online/articles/vap01.*

Conflicts and Wars

Spanish-American War of 1898

The outbreak of war in 1898 between Spain and the United States made the United States a world power. Setting the tone for the **Spanish-American War** were blaring headlines accompanied by sensationalized reporting of the sinking of the *Maine*. Though it's too much to claim that the newspapers started the war, what came to be known as "yellow journalism" certainly helped sound the drumbeat for war.

As a result of this war, the United States established itself as a global power and with a strong spheres of influence in the Caribbean Sea and Pacific Ocean, which will also shape its role in the future European affairs. The U.S. helped Cuba become an independent nation, and it gained control of the Philippines, Guam, and Puerto Rico. Eventually, the Philippines became an independent nation, while Puerto Rico and Guam remained U.S. territories. In Cuba the United States took control of Guantánamo Bay and established a naval base. Five years later, Cuba signed a lease to allow the naval base to remain in place. In 1934 Cuba gave the United States a perpetual lease to the area. Eventually, the people of Guam and Puerto Rico became American citizens.

World War I

The first global war, which came to be known as **World War I**, began in Europe and involved two alliances: the **Allies** and the **Central Powers**. The Allies included the countries of England, France, Russia, and Italy, and toward the end of the war, the United States. The Central Powers included the countries of Germany, the Austria-Hungary Empire, Turkey, and Bulgaria. Initially, America remained neutral and benefited from trading with the Allies. America's neutrality was challenged, however, when the Germans developed the submarine, and used it to destroy Allied ships and to sink American merchant ships. In 1915, the Germans sank a British liner, the *Lusitania*, killing more than 1,100 passengers, including 128 Americans. Additionally, American cargo ships were sunk. This forced President Wilson to ask Congress to declare war against Germany and the Central Powers April 6, 1917. The influx of fresh American forces fostered the Allies' victory in 1918.

With the **Treaty of Versailles**, the war officially ended. In this treaty, the Central Powers were punished and forced to pay for the war. Additionally, the Austria-Hungary Empire was dismembered, and new countries were created. The punitive conditions of the Treaty of Versailles created the resentment of the Germans. This resentment helped lead to the second global confrontation, **World War II**.

The Bolshevik Revolution in Russia

In 1917, the Communists, led by Vladimir Lenin, took over the Russia Empire in what was called the **Bolshevik Revolution**. To address the unrest at home, Russia withdrew from World War I. As a result of this revolution, or civil war, the Russian Empire ceased to exist and the Union of Soviet Socialist Republics (USSR) was established (1922). The USSR underwent a period of governmental reconstruction to incorporate the communist philosophy. As a result of this revolution, Russia underwent a period of governmental reconstruction to incorporate the communist philosophy.

The Great Depression

After World War I, the United States enjoyed a period of prosperity during the 1920s. But it all ended abruptly October 29, 1929, when the stock market crashed, starting what was called the **Great Depression**. During the Depression, millions of people lost their capital and their jobs. Between 1933 and 1937, President Franklin D. Roosevelt implemented a series of government-sponsored programs, called the **New Deal**, designed to revitalize the economy and alleviate the poverty and despair caused by the Depression.

World War II

The emergence of totalitarian countries like the USSR, Germany, and Italy created instability in Europe and led to war. The Communist Soviet Union under Joseph Stalin became a threat to European countries. Italy was a fascist, belligerent state where individual liberties were ignored. Germany under Adolf Hitler was ready to avenge the humiliating treatment it suffered as a result of World War I. In the Pacific, Japan was building an empire that had already conquered parts of China. These conditions promoted the creation of military alliances that led to World War II. Germany, Italy, and Japan created the **Axis Powers**, and the USSR, France, and England became the Allies. The war started with the German invasion of Poland in 1939. Two days later, France and England declared war against Germany. Hitler conquered most of Europe in a short time. France was occupied, and England was brought close to submission. The United States supported the Allies with supplies and weapons but did not send troops. Although it remained neutral for the first few years of the war, the United States joined the Allies when Japan attacked its naval base in Pearl Harbor, Hawaii, in 1941. Three days later, Hitler declared war on the United States. Believing Germany to be the greater threat, the United States concentrated on the war in Europe before turning its attention to Japan.

D-Day

With Hitler in full control of Europe, the United States joined England and representatives of the French government to plan and execute the invasion of Europe in 1944. On June 6, Gen. Dwight D. Eisenhower, with a quarter of a million Allied soldiers, crossed the English Channel into France and launched one of the largest offensives against the German occupying forces. This large attack on Germany was known as D-Day. As a result of the collective effort of the Allies, France was freed from German occupation. With the combined forces of England, Russia, Canada, and the United States, Hitler and the Axis forces were defeated.

Yalta Conference

The Allies met in Yalta, Russia, to discuss the terms of the treaty to end the war. The Allied leaders—Winston Churchill, Joseph Stalin, and Franklin D. Roosevelt—discussed the peace. Under the terms of peace agreed to at Yalta, Germany was to be divided into four sections, each controlled by an Allied country—Britain, France, Russia, and the United States. The Germans were to pay the Russians for war reparations in money and labor. Poland was divided, and the Russians received control of one section (later they took full control of the nation). Finally, plans were set to organize the United Nations to prevent future conflicts in the world.

Hiroshima and Nagasaki

The United States was fighting the war on two fronts, and the Japanese appeared to be invincible. An island nation, Japan had gained control of much territory in the Pacific, most of it islands. Securing each island would take much time and cost many American soldiers' lives. The best available option was determined to be the atomic bomb. After asking for the Japanese to surrender, the United States by the order of President Harry Truman dropped two atomic bombs, one each on the cities of Hiroshima and Nagasaki. The death and destruction caused by these two bombs forced the Japanese government to surrender in 1945, which officially ended World War II.

Marshall Plan

The Marshall Plan was a U.S.-supported program to rebuild the economic infrastructure in Europe. The United States provided money and machinery for the reconstruction of the continent.

The Holocaust and Creation of Israel

During World War II, Hitler devised a "master plan" to exterminate the Jewish population. Germany placed European Jews in concentration camps and systematically killed millions. This act of genocide is known as the Holocaust. At the end of the war, under the leadership of Great Britain, the United States, and the United Nations, the state of Israel was created in Palestine. On that same day, the Arab Liberation Army (ALA) was created to fight the Jewish state. This liberation movement has resulted in several wars between Israel and the Arabs. Today, this war has expanded to include Europe and the United States, with many terrorist attacks committed during the new century.

Truman Doctrine

In response to the threat of the Soviets, Harry Truman issued a proclamation warning communist countries that the United States would help any nation in danger of falling under communist control. This declaration was called the Truman Doctrine. As a result of this doctrine, the United States fought two major military conflicts: the Korean War and the Vietnam War.

Cold War

As a result of the Yalta agreement, the Soviet Union became the most powerful country in Europe and Asia. Following Russia's taking over Poland and East Berlin and its building of the Berlin Wall, a new war emerged between the Soviet Union and the United States—the Cold War. Although war was never formally declared between the two nations, confrontations occurred from

1945 to 1991. In 1963, the two nations were on the verge of nuclear war after Premier Nikita Khrushchev ordered the deployment of nuclear missiles to Cuba. An intense negotiation between Premier Khrushchev and President Kennedy avoided war between the two countries. This intense confrontation was called the Cuban Missile Crisis.

The Cold War ended with the fall of the Soviet Union under the leadership of Mikhail Gorbachev. The fall of the Soviet empire resulted in the reunification of Germany and the independence of the republics that made up the Union of Soviet Socialist Republics (USSR).*

War on Terrorism

On September 11, 2001, terrorists from abroad attacked Americans on American soil in a series of murderous events. The assailants hijacked four domestic aircraft and used two of them as missiles to crash into the twin towers of the World Trade Center in New York and a third to strike the Pentagon just outside Washington D.C. A fourth plane crashed in Shanksville, Pennsylvania, as passengers tried to wrest control of the plane from the hijackers. The attacks killed nearly 3,000 people. As a result of the attacks, the United States declared war on terrorism and attacked and ultimately toppled the ultraconservative Taliban regime early in the course of the Afghanistan War (2001–2014). The Taliban had harbored al-Qaeda, the terrorist group that planned the 9/11 attacks. Al-Qaeda's leader, Osama bin Laden, the mastermind of the 9/11 attacks, was hunted for nearly a decade and was killed by U.S. special forces on May 2, 2011, in his Pakistani compound. Meanwhile, the search for alleged weapons of mass destruction (WMD), as well as Iraq's support of terrorist organizations, led the United States into the Iraq War (2003–2011). In 2015, the U.S. was still fighting to stabilize the region. WMD were never found, though this topic continues to stir debate. In hindsight, the American government came to recognize that faulty intelligence paved the way for the rationale for the Iraq invasion.

War in Syria

The recent war in Syria has given rise to the Islamic State, also known as the Islamic State of Iraq and Syria (ISIS), an extreme al-Qaeda faction from Iraq. The Syrian conflict began in March 2011 with pro-democracy protests that ended when demonstrators were shot by Syrian security forces. This action triggered protests across the nation, while some opponents fought back. The violence and fighting continued to escalate from 2012–2014, with 2014 being the deadliest year. The conflicts grew to be more than issues with President Assad. The Sunni majority was against the Shia Alawite sect supporting the president. Neighboring countries and key world powers were drawn in as well. The UN commission of inquiry found human rights violations on both sides. The Islamic State grew in power and was accused of intimidating the public, killing Syrian security forces, and engaging in the mass murder of religious minorities. Although President Assad agreed to destroy his chemical weapons, evidence indicated these weapons were used against his opponents. According to the BBC, the Islamic State capitalized on the turmoil

* Often *Russia* and *USSR* are used interchangeably. Teachers should be aware of this misconception and use these terms correctly.

to seize large amounts of territory in Iraq and Syria. "In September 2014, a U.S.-led coalition launched air strikes inside Iraq and Syria in an effort to 'degrade and ultimately destroy' ISIS." (BBC, 2015). In January 2014 a conference between the U.S., Russia, and the U.N. tried unsuccessfully to agree on the implementation of the 2012 Geneva Communiqué to establish a governing body in Syria. The conflict continues, with Iran and Russia supporting the Alawite-led government. Turkey, various Arab states, the U.S., the U.K. and France have been supporting the Sunni-led opposition. This war is continuing.

History of Texas

Before European Colonization

Several Native American groups inhabited the territory that became Texas. The three groups living in the coastal plains—the Coahuiltecans, Karankawas, and Caddos—were food gatherers, fishermen, and farmers. When the Spanish arrived in Texas, they made first contact with these groups. The name Texas came as a result of contact with the Caddos. Trying to communicate to the Spaniards that they were not hostile, some Caddos identified themselves with the word *taysha*, which in their language meant "friend" or "ally" (Fry n.d.). When the Spaniards heard the word *taysha*, they thought the Caddos were identifying the name of the region. From that exchange, the name Texas and the state motto, "Friendship," emerged. A fourth group, the Jumanos, lived in the mountains and basins of West Texas. The information about this group is limited because they virtually disappeared before the Spaniards arrived. The last two groups are the Comanches and the Apaches. These two groups coexisted with Europeans and resisted colonization. After they domesticated horses, which had been introduced by the Spanish, the Comanches and Apaches became fierce warriors and successful buffalo hunters. The domestication of the horse allowed the development of the culture of the buffalo. When buffalo were later annihilated in the area, these two groups became practically extinct. Table 5-5 presents a summary of Native American groups from Texas.

European Colonization

Cabeza de Vaca

The Spanish exploration of the territory that became Texas began in 1528, when Cabeza de Vaca and three companions landed. The four Spaniards made contact with the Caddo in the southeastern part of the state, near modern-day Houston. In his account of the meeting, de Vaca described the Caddo as a sophisticated Native American group. From there, de Vaca continued exploring the area that became New Mexico and Arizona (Sheppard n.d.). No other significant events happened in the region until 1541, when Francisco Vázquez de Coronado explored the region that became Texas.

Francisco Vázquez de Coronado

In response to reports of the mythical Seven Cities of Cibola, Coronado led an expedition of almost a thousand men in search of the golden cities. The expedition left Mexico City and explored the southwestern United States and northern Texas. In 1542, Coronado returned to Mexico empty-handed. For the next 140 years, the Texas region remained isolated, and no other attempts were made to colonize it.

Table 5-5. Native American Groups from Texas

Regions	Native Group
Coastal plains, flatland	**Coahuiltecan** (Rio Grande Valley) **Economic Activity:** Food gatherers and hunters—roots, beans of the mesquite tree, rabbit, birds, and deer **Features:** Lived in family groups
	Karankawa (Southeastern Texas) **Economic Activity:** Fishing and food gathering **Features:** Lived as nomads and used canoes for fishing
	Caddo (East Texas, Piney Woods) **Economic Activity:** Farming—squash, pumpkins, tobacco, and corn (good food supply) **Features:** Built villages and lived in groups
Central plains, flatland, and hills	**Apache** (Central and western Texas) **Economic Activity:** Farming and hunting **Features:** Lived as nomads, built portable housing called tepees, domesticated horses, and hunted bison
Great Plains, flatland, and hills	**Comanche** **Economic Activity:** Hunters **Features:** Lived as nomads and built portable housing; also domesticated the horse and hunted the buffalo
Mountains and basins	**Jumano** (West Texas) **Economic Activity:** Farming and hunting **Features:** Mostly sedentary and built homes of adobe

Juán de Oñate

In 1595, Oñate received permission from King Philip II of Spain to colonize New Mexico. In 1598, he founded the first European settlement west of the Mississippi in New Mexico.

First Mission in Texas

In 1682, the Spanish established the first permanent settlement in Texas—the mission of Ysleta del Sur near what is now El Paso. After this mission, no serious efforts were made to colonize the area until the French threatened the Spanish hegemony in East Texas.

French Influence in Texas

In 1682, Robert de la Salle established a French settlement in Fort Saint Louis in East Texas. A few years later, the Spaniards expelled the French and established a series of missions in East Texas to control the French threat in the region.

San Antonio

In 1718, the Spanish established a mission and a fort—San Antonio de Valero and Fort San Antonio de Bexar—near what is now San Antonio. These settlements were established to provide protection and support to settlements in East Texas.

Mexican Independence

During the first part of the 19th century, the Spanish empire began crumbling. Mexico obtained its independence in 1821 and took control of the colony of Texas.

Anglo-American Presence in Texas

In 1820, Moses Austin received permission from the Spanish government to bring Anglo-American families to settle in Texas. This agreement was voided when Mexico took control of the territory. Austin's son, Stephen, later negotiated with the Mexican government and obtained a similar agreement to let Anglo-Americans settle in Texas. By 1835, the settlers were the majority in the region, and this antagonized the Mexican government. The result was war.

Texas War for Independence

Conflicts between Texans and the Mexican government started as early as 1830. The colonists felt that the government was not providing adequate support and protection to Texas. Initially, they wanted to negotiate with the new president, Santa Anna, and sent Stephen Austin to Mexico City to represent the colony. The Mexican government was not willing to negotiate and jailed Austin for a year.

First Battle in Gonzales

The town of Gonzales had a cannon to protect the colonists from the Native Americans. By order of the government, Mexican soldiers came to take the cannon from the colonists in October 1835. The Texans refused to relinquish their weapon and fired it against the Mexican soldiers. The incident in Gonzales began the war for Texas independence.

Sam Houston

A delegation of Texans traveled to Washington, D.C., to secure support from the U.S. government. Sam Houston, a former governor of Tennessee, volunteered to fight for Texas and would become the commander-in-chief of the Texas army.

The Alamo and Goliad

The first meaningful battle of the Texas war for independence took place near what is now San Antonio in a small mission and fort called the Alamo. When the war began, fewer than 200 men, led by Col. William Travis, protected the Alamo. Such historical figures as James Bowie and Davy Crockett joined Travis in defending the Alamo. In 1836, Gen. Antonio López de Santa Anna and the Mexican army took the fort and killed all its defenders, including Texans of Mexican ancestry. Following this victory, Santa Anna continued marching against the rebels and took Goliad, where more than 300 rebels were killed. These two battles provided the patriotic emotion that resulted in the creation of an army and led to victory against Mexico.

Texas Declaration of Independence

A few days before the Battle of the Alamo, a group of Texans met at Washington-on-the-Brazos to issue a declaration of independence and to form the new government. An interim government for the Republic of Texas was established, with David G. Burnet as president and Lorenzo de Zavala as vice president.

Battle of San Jacinto

While the colonists were fighting the Mexican army at the Alamo and in Goliad, Gen. Sam Houston was strengthening the army of the new republic. The Texan army continued retreating ahead of the Mexican forces until they reached the San Jacinto River, near the city of Houston. In a battle that lasted less than 20 minutes, Houston's troops defeated the Mexican army and captured Gen. Santa Anna. Texas President Burnet and Mexican President Santa Anna signed the Treaty of Velasco, with Santa Anna agreeing to withdraw his troops from Texas in exchange for safe conduct back to Mexico, where he would lobby for recognition of Texas independence. Santa Anna's commitment never materialized, and the Mexican government refused to recognize Texas as an independent republic. Nevertheless, Sam Houston became the president of the new republic, and from 1836 to 1845, Texas was an independent nation. However, the Mexican government still considered it a rebellious province that it could reclaim (Barker & Pohl, 2009).

Republic Period

Despite the economic hardship typical of new nations, Texas remained independent for 10 years and was recognized by several nations, including the United States. However, unable to secure its borders and reverse its financial situation, the new nation sought the support of the United States.

Texas Joins the United States

In 1845, Texas became the 28th state of the American union. Immediately, the U.S. government sent troops to the Rio Grande, which Mexicans considered their territory, to secure the Texas border. The ensuing clashes between Mexican and U.S. forces resulted in Congress declaring war in May 1846.

Mexican-American War

Between 1846 and 1848, Mexico and the United States waged a war that ended with a decisive victory and tremendous land acquisitions for the United States. As a result of the Treaty of Guadalupe Hidalgo, Mexico withdrew its claim over Texas and established the Rio Grande, or Rio Bravo, as it is known in Mexico, as the official border between the two countries. Mexico also ceded California and the territory known today as the American Southwest to the United States. Figure 5-9 presents a timeline of important events in Texas from 1528 to 1861.

Confederacy Period (1861–65)

At the onset of the American Civil War, Texas left the Union and joined the Confederacy as a proslavery state. After five years of war, the Confederate army, led by Gen. Robert E. Lee, surrendered to Gen. Ulysses S. Grant, the leader of the Union forces. After the war, the Union forces occupied the South for 12 years (1865–1877) during Reconstruction.

Figure 5-9. Texas Timeline from 1528 to 1861

1528	1541	1682	1682	1690	1718	1820
Cabeza de Vaca lands in Texas	Coronado explores Texas	Mission founded in El Paso	La Salle (French) lands in Texas	First mission in East Texas San Francisco de los Tejas	Mission and fort founded in San Antonio	Austin arrives in San Antonio

1861	1848	1846	1845	1836	1835	1833
Texas secedes from the union	Treaty of Guadalupe Hidalgo	Mexican-American War begins	Texas becomes the 28th state in the union	Battle of San Jacinto; Texas declares independence	Battle of Gonzales marks beginning of Texas revolution	Santa Anna becomes president of Mexico

Reconstruction Period

Under Reconstruction, Texas was briefly occupied by U.S. troops. Texas was allowed to rejoin the union in 1870. The Ku Klux Klan became active then, terrorizing African-Americans in Texas and the southern states.

Economic Development after Reconstruction

After Reconstruction, the Texas economy flourished, largely based on the growth of the cattle industry. Barbed wire was introduced in 1880, and ranchers began using scientific cattle breeding to increase production and improve the quality of meat.

Boom or Bust Economic Cycles in Texas

As Texas developed in the latter part of the 19th into the 20th and 21st centuries, it experienced a number of "boom or bust" economic cycles. They included railroads, the cattle industry, oil and gas production, cotton, real estate, banking, and computer technology. A "boom or bust" economy undergoes sharp fluctuations from boom, a period of strength and wealth, to bust, a period of weakness and poverty. These variations affect the stability of the economy and the ability for the state to plan its future. In 1901, oil was discovered in the Spindletop Oil Field near Beaumont. The development of the oil industry made Texas the leading producer of oil in the United States. Because of this boom, cities like Houston and Dallas became large urban and industrial centers.

World Wars and Beyond

As a result of World War I, Texas emerged as a leading military training center. Several military bases were established, bringing economic growth. The rapid development of the aircraft industry and highly technological businesses led to rapid industrialization. By World War II, Texas was a leading state in the defense industry. The modern economy of Texas still relies on agriculture, ranching, and oil production, but new high-technology industries are becoming the state's top economic forces.

Six Flags over Texas

The phrase "Six flags over Texas" describes the different countries that have exerted control in Texas since 1519, when the first European exploration of the region by Cortés took place:

- Spain (1519–1821)
- France (1685–1690)
- Mexico (1821–1836)

- Republic of Texas (1836–1845)

- United States (1845–1861)

- Texas in the Confederacy (1861–1865)

- Back to the American union (1870–present)

State Facts and Symbols

Here's a snapshot of symbols and iconography associated with Texas:

- State flower   Bluebonnet

- State bird   Mockingbird

- State tree   Pecan

- State motto   Friendship

- Border states   Oklahoma, Louisiana, Arkansas, and New Mexico

- State song   "Texas, Our Texas," by William J. Marsh and Gladys Yoakum Wright

Here are the lyrics to "Texas, Our Texas":

Texas, our Texas!
All hail the
mighty State!
Texas, our Texas!
So wonderful so
great!

Boldest and grandest, withstanding ev'ry test;
O Empire wide and glorious, you stand supremely blest.

[Refrain]
God bless you Texas!
And keep you brave and
strong, That you may grow
in power and worth,
thro'out the ages long.

COMPETENCY 003: GEOGRAPHY AND CULTURE

The teacher understands and applies knowledge of geographic relationships involving people, places, and environments in Texas, the United States, and the world; and also understands and applies knowledge of cultural development, adaptation, diversity, and interactions among science, technology, and society as defined by the Texas Essential Knowledge and Skills (TEKS).

Geography

Geography studies the Earth's surface, the organisms that populate it, and their interaction within the ecosystem by examining spatial patterns, processes, and relationships from a local to global scale. Geography can be divided into two main areas: physical and cultural. *Physical geography* refers to the physical characteristics of the surface of the Earth and how those features affect life (e.g., plate tectonics, landforms, bodies of water, climate, biomes, weathering, erosion, etc.). *Cultural, or human, geography* deals with the interaction of humans with their environment and how that interaction produces changes. Humans can alter the physical environment of the Earth, but the physical environment can also shape humans and their culture. For example, the Incas built the capital of their empire, Cuzco, in the Andes Mountains in what is now Peru. This city has an altitude of 11,152 feet above sea level, where oxygen is scarce and agriculture is a challenge. However, the Incas managed to live and flourish. They carved the land for agriculture and built roads and cities. In turn, the environment changed the Incas, who had to evolve to tolerate the low levels of oxygen. Studies conducted on the Indians from Peru suggest that people of the Andes developed genetic adaptations for high-altitude living (Discovery Channel, March 10, 2004). By adapting to environmental conditions, the inhabitants not only survived but also flourished in less-than-ideal conditions.

Physical Geography Influences Settlement Locations

People typically settle where there is good land, good climate, and good, clean water. The location of such renewable and nonrenewable natural resources as fresh water, fossil fuels, fertile soils, and timber affect decisions about where to build a community. For example, the settlement patterns in Texas and in the United States show that people did not simply settle where the climate was good for crops or along the coast where land was easily accessed. People also settled away from the coast along waterways. This provided a fresh source of water as well as a resource for food and transportation. However, settlement decisions can also cause stress on the natural resource. For example, in San Antonio the Edward's Aquifer is one of the most prolific underground sources of water in the world. The demand for the water may become greater than the capacity of the aquifer, which will affect the livelihood of the people as well as the potential development of urban areas in the region.

Locating Places and Regions on a Map

Maps have two categories: reference and thematic. *Reference maps* show the locations of places, boundaries of countries, states, counties, towns, landforms and bodies of water. They are sometimes referred to as political and physical maps. A *physical map* shows the topography of the Earth, including land features and elevations. A *political map* shows how a country is organized. Atlases are examples of reference maps. *Thematic maps, or special purpose maps,* show such specific topics as population density or distribution of world religions as well as physical, social, economic, political, agricultural, or economic features. An *economic map* shows the important resources of a country or region. A *historical map* shows the location of historical events. *Population maps* show where people live.

A globe is a scale model of the Earth shaped like a sphere. Because a globe models the shape of the Earth, it shows sizes and shapes accurately. The Mercator projection map is a flat representation of the Earth, and it thus distorts the shape, size, and/or distance in some way. This projection, used initially for shipping, is most accurate nearest the equator. The portability of maps makes them more useful than globes. The position of people, places, and things can be identified using relative or absolute location. **Relative location** uses references to help describe where something is. For example, a house may be located next to a big soccer field. **Absolute location** provides the exact position of the destination. This could be as simple as an address for a house or the coordinates of the location using latitude and longitude. It is important to say "latitude and longitude" in that order because the coordinate system identifies latitude first. For example, Dallas is located at 33°N, 97°W.

The Grid System

A grid system is a network of horizontal and vertical lines used to locate points on a map or chart by coordinates. This grid shows the location of places. In this grid system, latitudinal and longitudinal lines form divisions that consist of geometrical coordinates used to designate the location of places on the surface of the Earth on a globe or map. The lines measure distances in degrees.

Latitudinal lines are horizontal and run parallel around the Earth measuring the distance north and south of the equator. The equator is identified as the 0 degree line of latitude, and it divides the Earth into the Northern and the Southern hemispheres. The United States is located in the Northern Hemisphere, while Brazil is located in the Southern Hemisphere. Longitudinal lines are vertical and run north and south going east and west. The 0 degree line of longitude is the first meridian known as the prime meridian. It goes through Greenwich, England, and it divides the Earth into the Eastern and Western hemispheres. The United States is in the Western Hemisphere, and Japan is in the Eastern Hemisphere.

Geographic Symbols

A compass rose is a design printed on a chart or map for reference. It shows the orientation of a map on Earth and shows the four cardinal directions (north, south, east, and west). A compass rose may also show intermediate directions (southeast, northeast, northwest, and southwest). Maps use symbols to contain a lot of information that can be easily understood. Common map symbols include dots, stars, and small pictures to represent cities or places. Some maps use different colors to represent such features as elevations and divisions. These symbols and colors are defined in the map's key, or legend. A map scale shows the distance between two places in the world. The scale to which a map is drawn represents the ratio of the distance between two points on the Earth and the distance between the two corresponding points on the map. When teaching cardinal and intermediate directions, teachers sometimes label walls with N, S, E, W to aid students when giving directions. Teachers need to take precautions to assure that each wall is labeled accurately. This means that the wall that faces north is labeled "North." If North is in a corner, label the corner North. The wall then can have a sign for the correct intermediate direction.

Time Zones

Time zones are established based on the lines of longitude, or meridians. These lines run from north to south. The prime meridian, or the meridian at 0 degrees, has been set in Greenwich, England. On the other side of the globe is the 180th meridian along which the International Date Line generally follows. The prime meridian divides the Earth into the Western and Eastern hemispheres. Following the sunlight as it travels along the rotating Earth, the time decreases moving from east to west. When people travel from China (east) to the United States (west), they save a day; that is, they might spend a day traveling but still arrive on the same calendar day.

The United States has six time zones of one hour difference each—Eastern, Central, Mountain, Pacific, Alaska, and Hawaii. Figure 5-10 represents the six time zones in the United States with a key city for each zone. Technically, the United States has four time zones in the contiguous 48 states, five in the continental U.S. (America) with the addition of Alaska, and when we add the Hawaii, we add the sixth time zone. For more information about time zones, go to the website provided by the National Institute of Standards and Technology (an agency of the U.S. Department of Commerce) and the U.S. Naval Observatory at *http://time.gov/aboutB.html*.

Figure 5-10. Times Zones in the United States

West ←					→ East
Hawaii	Alaska	Pacific	Mountain	Central	Eastern
1:00 PM	2:00 PM	3:00 PM	4:00 PM	5:00 PM	6:00 PM
Honolulu	Anchorage	Los Angeles	Phoenix	Dallas	New York City

Regions of the World

A world region is an area of the world that shares similar, unifying cultural or physical characteristics different from those of surrounding areas. The physical features refer to such topographic characteristics as elevation, rivers, and mountains. The cultural features include all the features that distinguish different groups of people. Examples of these features include language, religion, government, economics, food, architecture, shared values, and family life.

Geographers have divided the world into 10 common regions: North America, Central and South America, Europe, Central Eurasia, the Middle East, North Africa, Sub-Saharan Africa, South Asia, East Asia, and Australasia. These divisions are based on physical and cultural similarities. North America consists of Canada, the United States, and Mexico. The Europeans colonized the North American region. Table 5-6 presents an overview of the world regions by physical and cultural features. World region names and scope can vary depending on the purpose of those defining the area. For example, when discussing North America and Latin America, North America in this instance only refers to Canada and the United States, while Latin America consists of everything south of the United States (Mexico, Central America, the Caribbean, and South America).

Table 5-6. World Regions

World Region	Physical Features	Cultural Features
North America	• Consists of Canada, the United States, and Mexico. • The United States is the fourth largest country in the world. • Oil is an important resource in the U.S. • Most of the U.S. has a humid-continental or humid-subtropical climate • Most of Canada has a subarctic or tundra climate. • Over 75% of Canadians live along the Southern border. • The areas of greatest concentration of population in the U.S. are along the East Coast and California. • The climate of Mexico ranges from humid tropical and subtropical to desert and highland. • Mexico has rich mineral resources including oil.	• Europeans colonized this region. • Languages spoken are predominantly English, Spanish, and French. • Most people hold Christian beliefs.

(continued)

World Region	Physical Features	Cultural Features
Central and South America	• Includes the countries of Central America, the Caribbean islands, and South America. • The majority of this continuous mass of land is south of the Equator. • South America extends from Point Gallinas in Colombia to Cape Horn. • Part of South America lies closer to the South Pole than any other land mass of this size. • Venezuela is one of the world's leading exporters of oil. • Most of Eastern Central America and equatorial South America have a humid tropical climate.	• Most people speak Spanish, but many other languages are spoken: Portuguese, French, Dutch, English, and several Native American languages and dialects. • Christian beliefs, the Roman Catholic religion is predominant. • Architecture, law, religion, traditions, and language are strongly influenced by Europe's colonial rule of this region. • The many ethnic groups in this region are separated by geographical barriers such as the Andes and the Amazon.
Europe	• Western section of the Eurasian continent • Shares a mountain chain, the Alps. • Most of Europe has a temperate climate. • Europe's irregular coastline has many harbors that are important manufacturing and trade centers. • The rivers of Europe are important resources for trade, water, and hydro-electricity. • European population growth rates are the smallest in the world.	• Shares a common history in the Roman Empire and later the Catholic Church and Latin language. • English is the most spoken language in Europe, German and French are also widespread. • Cultural diffusion or shared cultural traits spread throughout Europe. • Ninety percent of all adults ages 15–24 speak a second language and some countries are considered multilingual. • Europeans practice many different religions. • Roman Catholicism is the predominant religion of many European countries. • Most of Northern and Central Europe is Protestant. • Jews live in many parts of Western Europe.
Central Eurasia	• Central Asia and Eastern Europe • United around one continuous mass of land located in the middle of the continent. • Little access to the sea • The borders of Eastern European countries have changed many times. • From WWII to the late 1980s, the Soviet Union controlled Eastern Europe and introduced communism to the region.	• Conquered at different times by the Persians, Mongolians, Tartars, the French, the Germans, and the Russians. • Slavic languages are predominant. • Most people in the Eastern part of the region follow the Eastern Orthodox church; people in the Northern area are mostly Roman Catholic.

World Region	Physical Features	Cultural Features
Middle East	• Consists of the area of southwest Asia and North Africa. • Access to sea water • The majority of the land is desert. • Rich in oil	• While the majority of people follow the religion of Islam there are also groups that follow Christianity and Judaism. • The religion defines the law in many places. • The most ancient of human civilizations. Egyptians, Assyrians, Babylonians, Persians, Greeks, and Romans have left their mark in this region. • This region has been the fighting ground for many religious battles.
North Africa	• Part of the African continent • Includes Egypt, Libya, Tunisia, Algeria, and Morocco • Extensive coastline • The Sahara desert and the Nile river are two important physical features of this area • Rich in oil • Egypt is undergoing rapid growth, urbanization, and industrialization	• The majority of people follow the religion of Islam. • People speak Arabic predominantly. • Religious issues influence the politics of this area.
Sub-Saharan Africa	• Consists of Africa south of the Sahara • Most of the area is a savanna • Has abundant rain • Extensive coastline • Fertile land • Most people live in the forest zone and the dry savannas • Agriculture is the predominant activity in West Africa • Livestock is the predominant economic activity in the northern area	• Cultural diversity reflects indigenous, Arab, and European influences. • Majority follows tribal beliefs, Christianity, or a combination of both. • Most people speak native African or European languages. • Over 500 ethnic groups live in this region.
South Asia	• Consists of a large Indian peninsula that extends into the Indian Ocean. • Abundant rainfall • Strong seasonal winds called monsoons • Rice is an important crop. • One of the most populated regions in the world. • The world's highest mountains are located in the northern area of this region. • Many major manufacturing and trade centers are located along the coast.	• People in South Asia speak many languages. • Predominant beliefs are of Eastern origins such as Buddhism and Hinduism. • Many South Asians are farmers who live in small villages. • Many cultural influences • Through the efforts of Mohandas Gandhi the region gained its independence from Britain in 1947.

(continued)

World Region	Physical Features	Cultural Features
East Asia	• Consists of China, Korea, Taiwan, and Japan. • It is the most densely populated region in the world. • Large expanse of coastline.	• Buddhism and Taoism are predominant religions. • Confucian philosophy • People speak Chinese, Japanese, Korean, Mongolian, and many other languages. • Chinese Script or characters influence many of the writing systems of these languages. • Culturally, China has had a major influence in this region.
Australasia	• It is composed of the Australian continent and surrounding islands. • South of the equator	• English is the predominant language of most of the nations in this region • Population is a large Christian majority.

Regions of the United States

The concept of regions facilitates the examination of geography by providing a convenient and manageable unit for studying the Earth's human and natural environment. The continental United States can be divided into eight broad physical geographic divisions:

- **Laurentian Highlands** are part of the Canadian Shield that extends into the northern United States and the Great Lakes area. This area has a hard winter, and agriculture is limited.

- **Atlantic–Gulf Coastal Plains** are the coastal regions of the eastern and southern states. It includes New York City in the North, the Mid-Atlantic states to Florida in the South, and all the way west to Texas on the Gulf Coast. It is sometimes referred to as two regions: Coastal Plains and Gulf Coastal Plains.

- **Appalachian Highlands** covers the Appalachian Mountains, the Adirondack Mountains, and New England—Connecticut, Maine, Massachusetts, New Hampshire, Rhode Island, and Vermont.

- **Interior Plains and the Great Plains** covers the interior United States. Included in this area are the states west of the Appalachians, south of the Great Lakes, and as far west as Montana, Wyoming, Colorado, New Mexico, and northwestern Texas. Most of the nation's wheat, corn, and feed crops are grown in this area.

- **Interior Highlands** is also part of the interior continental United States. This area includes the Ozark Mountains and Missouri, Arkansas, and Kentucky as well as part of Oklahoma and Kansas.

- **Rocky Mountain System** is in the western United States and Canada extending from British Colombia to Montana, Utah, Colorado, and New Mexico. The mountain range is called the **Continental Divide**, because it separates the eastward-flowing rivers from the westward-flowing rivers. The waters that flow eastward empty into the Atlantic Ocean, and those that flow westward empty into the Pacific Ocean.

- **Intermontane Plateaus** is a large region that includes the Pacific Northwest, the Colorado Plateau, and the basins of the southwestern United States. This area covers Washington, Oregon, Idaho, part of Utah, New Mexico, and Arizona. It also covers the Grand Canyon and Death Valley.

- **Pacific Mountain System** covers the West Coast. This area extends from the Cascade Mountains in the north down the entire West Coast through Washington, Oregon, and California.

Texas Regions and Economic Activity

Texas is the second-largest state in the United States, behind Alaska. Covering 268,601 square miles, the state contains five geographic regions within its boundaries. Table 5-7 lists the regions and the key cities and main economic activities of each.

Largest Rivers in the World

These are the three largest rivers in the world:

- The Nile (North and East Africa) is the longest river in the world. It originates in Lake Victoria, which is shared by Uganda, Kenya, and Tanzania. It flows north* following the downward slant of the land to its mouth at the Mediterranean Sea.

- The Amazon (South America) is the second-largest. The widest river in the world, it originates in Perú, and its mouth is at the Atlantic Ocean off the coast of Brazil.

- The Chang Jiang or Yangtze (China) is the third-largest river. Its source is the Tibetan Plateau, and its mouth is at the East China Sea.

For more information about the world's largest rivers, go to the Social Studies for Kids website at *www.socialstudiesforkids.com/articles/geography/longestriverstable.htm*.

---

* Students may have a misconception that rivers only run south. Due to gravity, rivers run downhill. This means that they can flow in a cardinal or intermediate direction, as long as it is toward lower levels of land.

Table 5-7. Regions and Economic Activity in Texas

Region	Key Cities	Main Economic Activities	Key Statistics
Coastal plains, flatland	Dallas, Houston, San Antonio, Austin, Corpus Christi, Laredo	Lumber—East Texas (Piney Woods) Oil—Refineries in Houston Farming—Rice, oranges, cotton, wheat, milo Ranching—Cattle in Kingsville Shipping—Houston	Population—High: 1 of 3 Texans Rainfall—High Distinguishing Mark—Hurricanes
Central plains, flatland and hills	Fort Worth, Arlington, San Angelo, Abilene	Ranching—Cattle, wool (mohair), sheep Farming—Grains	Population—High Rainfall—Medium Distinguishing Marks—Tornadoes, northerlies (cold winds), hailstorms; large ranches
Great Plains Flatland and hill country	Midland, Odessa, Lubbock, Amarillo, Texas Panhandle	Ranching—Cattle, sheep Minerals—Graphite Oil—Odessa and Midland Farming—Wheat	Population—Average Rainfall—Medium Distinguishing Marks—Snowstorms, dust storms, windmills, use of aquifers
Mountains and basins, Rocky Mountains, Davis, Chisos, and Guadalupe, Chihuahuan Desert	El Paso	Ranching—Limited large ranches Mexico-U.S. border economy based on trading of goods produced by the industries established in Mexico—maquiladoras.	Population—Low Rainfall—Low; hard rain wears out the rocks and land Distinguishing Mark—Big Bend National Park

Rivers in the United States

These are the largest and most important rivers in the United States:

- The Mississippi is the longest river in the United States and the 14th longest in the world. It begins in Minnesota and ends in the Gulf of Mexico.

- The Ohio River begins near Pittsburgh and runs southwest, ending in the Mississippi River on the Illinois and Missouri borders.

- The Rio Grande begins in the San Juan Mountains of southern Colorado and ends in the Gulf of Mexico. The river is the official border between the United States and Mexico, where it is known as the Rio Bravo.

- The Colorado River begins in the Rocky Mountains and ends in California.

- The Missouri River begins in the Rocky Mountains, flowing north first and then generally southeast across the central United States, ending at the Mississippi River, just to the north of St. Louis.

- For information about rivers in the United States, visit *WorldAtlas.com*. To view the most significant rivers of the continental United States, visit *www.worldatlas.com/webimage/ countrys/namerica/ usstates/artwork/rivers/uslayout.htm*.

Mountains in the World

With notable exception of the peak known as K2, which is part of the Karakoram Range, the tallest mountains in the world are located in the Himalayas, ranging across the countries of China, Pakistan, Nepal, and Tibet. Table 5-8 lists the top 10 tallest mountains. Compared with the world's tallest peaks, the United States' mountains are small. The highest mountain is Denali, formerly knows as Mt. McKinley, in Alaska. Alaska has the 16 highest peaks in the United States. A list of the mountains with 16,000 feet or above is presented in Table 5-9. For additional information about the world's mountains, go to the Infoplease.com website at *www.infoplease.com/ipa/A0001771.html*.

Deforestation

Deforestation can increase soil erosion and can lead to tragedies like the mudslides that occurred in 2006 in the Philippines, where thousands of people were buried alive. The rate of soil erosion is most likely to exceed the rate of soil formation in areas like Brazil, where people have cut forests to clear land for farming.

Table 5-8. Tallest Mountains in the World

Mountain	Location	Height (in feet)
Everest	Nepal/Tibet	29,035
K2	Pakistan/China	28,250
Kanchenjunga	India/Nepal	28,169
Lhotse I	Nepal/Tibet	27,940
Makalu I	Nepal/Tibet	27,766
Cho Oyu	Nepal/Tibet	26,906
Dhaulagiri	Nepal	26,795
Manaslu I	Nepal	26,781
Nanga Parbat	Pakistan	26,660
Annapurna	Nepal	26,545

Table 5-9. Tallest Mountains in the United States

Mountain	Location	Height (in feet)
Denali*	Alaska	20,310
Mt. St. Elias	Alaska	18,008
Mt. Foraker	Alaska	17,400
Mt. Bona	Alaska	16,500
Mt. Blackburn	Alaska	16,390
Mt. Sanford	Alaska	16,237

Deposition

Deposition is the carrying of soil from one place to another, usually by water or wind. This process is responsible for the creation of beaches as well as the sand dunes found in desert areas and the landforms created by glaciers.

Geographical Tools

Social scientists (e.g., geographers, historians, political scientists, and economists) use an assortment of geographical tools to help examine physical and cultural geographic data. First, the globe is recognized as a mathematical model of the world and is important to students' development of spatial thinking. It shows accurate distance, shape, and size of continents and bodies of water. As will be discussed, colors are used to symbolize elevation or other concepts. The complexity of the globe increases with the grade level. Maps are a flat representation of the world or a region of the world. As with globes, the complexity of maps increases developmentally with the grade level. Charts, graphs, and diagrams are also used to analyze data. Some mathematical representations, such as Dot Plots, offer an opportunity to reinforce mathematical concepts while examining cultural and historical data sets. Digital geospatial tools can offer teachers an alternative to paper maps and allow for more depth and rigor when used appropriately. These tools can provide an easy way to explore data spatially, such as in the Annie E. Case Foundation KIDS COUNT website (*http://datacenter.kidscount.org/*) and the Census Bureau webpage for kids (*http://www.census.gov/schools/census_for_kids*). Others provide interactive online maps such as *http://mrnussbaum.com/united-states/amwest/* or *http://mrnussbaum.com/united-states/southwest/*. A popular digital globe is Google Earth *https://www.google.com/earth/*), which allows users to add data layers and to spatially analyze data from a local to global scale. Finally, ArcGIS Online (*http://www.arcgis.com/features/*) offers an online tool that facilitates inquiry-based discussions and lets students and teachers explore data and create maps.

---

*Also called Mt. McKinley. Denali's official elevation was established by the U.S. Geological Survey in 2015.

Map Skills by Grade—Scope and Sequence

Kindergarten

Students should create and interpret maps of places and regions of the world that contain developmentally appropriate map elements and symbols. A compass rose and grid system should be used to locate places on maps and globes as well. Place location, or memorizing countries, cities, bodies of water, and landforms on a map, is critical to learning geography and other social studies. It provides lays foundation on which content about Texas, the United States, and the World can be built. Its importance is akin to the multiplication tables in mathematics. Maps may be provided through an online or desktop digital source or on paper. Paper maps may already have an outline of a region or require students to sketch the area. Sketch maps are important because they require students to create a mental image, or map, of the area. Doing so will help them visualize the region when learning about social studies, and it will also help them to make connections to other content, including literature and science.

In addition to the knowledge required in the Texas Essential Knowledge and Skills (TEKS), each student in kindergarten through grade 6 should learn the following geography skills and concepts.

- Understands and uses terms related to location, direction, and distance (*up*, *down*, *left*, *right*, *here*, *near*, *far*).

- Recognizes a globe as a model of the Earth.

- Recognizes and uses terms that express relative size and shape (big, little, large, small, round, square).

- Identifies school and local community by name.

- Recognizes and uses models and symbols to represent real things.

- Identifies bodies of water—oceans, seas, lakes, rivers, ponds, and bayous (TEKS).

- Identifies landforms—plains, mountains, deserts, hills, and canyons (TEKS).

- Identifies natural resources—water, soil, trees, metals, and fish (TEKS).

Grade 1

- Makes and uses simple classroom maps to locate objects.

- Knows geographical location of home in relation to school and neighborhood.

- Knows the layout of the school campus.

- Identifies state and nation by name.

- Follows and gives verbal directions (here, there, left, right, below, above).

- Distinguishes between land and water symbols on globes and maps.

- Relates locations on maps and globes to locations on the Earth.

- Observes, describes, and builds simple models and maps of the local environment.

- Knows the four cardinal points (TEKS).

- Identifies the physical characteristics of places—precipitation, body of water, landforms, types of vegetation, and climate (TEKS).

Grade 2

- Makes and uses simple maps of the school and neighborhood.

- Interprets map symbols using a legend.

- Knows and uses cardinal directions.

- Locates community, state, and nation on maps and globes.

- Identifies local landforms.

- Differentiates between maps and globes.

- Locates other neighborhoods studied on maps.

- Knows the continents of the world (TEKS).

- Identifies important landmarks—Statue of Liberty, Washington Monument, etc. (TEKS).

- Identifies natural resources (TEKS).

- Identifies aspects of the physical environment, from organisms to communities (TEKS).

Grade 3

- Uses distance, directions, scale, and map symbols.

- Compares own community with other communities.

- Compares urban and rural environments.

- Uses charts to record and present information (TEKS).

- Understands climate and such influences on climate as wind velocity, precipitation, and proximity to bodies of water.

- Uses the compass rose as a means of orientation on a map of the Earth (TEKS).

- Uses graphs (TEKS).

- Uses graphic organizers and diagrams to arrange items in meaningful way (TEKS).

- Understands that landforms change through erosion and deposition (TEKS).

- Understands that regions are areas of the Earth's surface (TEKS).

- Uses scale to represent distances (TEKS).

- Uses timelines to list events chronologically.

Grade 4

- Interprets pictures, graphs, charts, and tables.

- Works with distance, directions, scale, and map symbols.

- Relates similarities and differences between maps and globes.

- Uses maps of different scales and themes.

- Recognizes the common characteristics of the map grid system.

- Compares and contrasts regions on a state, national, or world basis.

- Understands such concepts of adaptation and modification as changing the landscape to meet survival needs and building to adjust to a new environment (TEKS).

- Identifies elements that affect the climate (TEKS).

- Uses a compass rose to find true directions.

- Identifies key explorers and their achievements (TEKS).

- Identifies how geography affects the settlement and development of places.

- Understands the connection between climate and vegetation.

- Identifies global divisions, like the prime meridian, the equator, and the four hemispheres (TEKS).

Grade 5

- Uses geographic tools to collect, analyze, and interpret data (TEKS).

- Applies such geographic tools as grid systems, legends, symbols, scales, and compass roses to make and interpret maps (TEKS).

- Translates geographic data into such formats as graphs and maps (TEKS).

- Understands the concept of regions and can describe regions in the U.S. that result from patterns of human activity, including political, population, and economic regions as well as from physical characteristics, including landform, climate, and vegetation regions (TEKS).

- Locates the 50 states on a map and identifies regions made by groups of states, such as New England and the Great Plains (TEKS).

- Understands and describes location and patterns of settlement as well as their distribution (TEKS).

- Analyzes the location of U. S. cities, including state capitals (TEKS).

- Understands how people adapt and modify their environment to meet human needs (TEKS).

- Analyzes the consequences of human modification of the environment in the United States (TEKS).

Grade 6

- Uses maps, globes, graphs, charts, models, and databases to answer geographic questions.

- Creates maps, graphs, models, and databases (TEKS).

- Poses and answers questions about geographic distributions and patterns from selected world regions and countries (TEKS).

- Compares selected world regions and countries by using data from maps, graphs, charts, databases, and models (TEKS).

- Understands the characteristics and relative locations of major historical and contemporary societies (TEKS).

- Locates major historical and contemporary societies on maps and globes (TEKS).

- Identifies and explains how geography affects patterns of population in places and regions (TEKS).

- Understands how geography influences the economic development, political relationships, and policies of societies (TEKS).

- Understands the impact of physical processes on patterns in the environment (TEKS).

- Understands the impact of interactions between people and the physical environment on the development of places and regions (TEKS).

Culture

The culture of a group is reflected in what its people write, create, and wear as well their government, decisions, customs and ceremonies, way of life, and dwellings. Humans share their culture through oral traditions, stories, real and mythical heroes, music, paintings, and sculptures. Significant historical periods represent cultural ideals at a given time and may continue to influence following generations as well as other regions of the world. For example, the Renaissance, Baroque, Classicism, Neoclassicism, and Romanticism are key historical periods that gave birth to influential literature, art, and music. The Renaissance, or "rebirth," was a time of great creativity. William Shakespeare's plays explored humanity in plays that are still read and performed. Leonardo de Vinci created inspiring painting and sculptures. He also was known as the "Renaissance Man" who learned about and pursued different disciplines that enabled him follow his interest in science and inventions as well. Literature and art often also reflect their time as well as the societies in which they were produced. The Renaissance also reflected reformation of attitudes toward political authority, which was mainly embodied in the church and monarchs. Society questioned and challenged decisions made by the church – as well as the monarch's rule. (For more information go to *http://www.britannica.com/EBchecked/topic/497731/Renaissance.*) In the United States, the American Renaissance occurred in literature from the 1830s through the Civil War and into the 1880s. As with the European renaissance, literature and the arts explored humanity and challenged current beliefs in the church, politics, and society. It was a period of time that was greatly governed by Transcendentalism. American Transcendentalism, a term derived from the philosopher Kant, was heavily influenced by the great minds of England and Germany. In America this philosophy, or belief, was idealistic in nature, rooted in faith, and had a visionary bent. It was a collection of complex beliefs such as "that the spark of divinity lies within man; that everything in the world is a microcosm of existence; that the individual soul is identical to the world soul, or Over-Soul, as Emerson called it. … By meditation, by communing with nature, through work and art, man could transcend his senses and attain an understanding of beauty and goodness and truth." (*http://www. pbs.org/wnet/ihas/icon/transcend.html*) This philosophy permeated American life through literature, poetry, art work (e.g., painting, sculpture), architecture, and music. Common authors include names such as Emerson, Thoreau, Hawthorne, Whitman, and Dickinson, just to name a few. The renaissance is just one example how creative expression is influenced by societal issues and how it can transcend the boundaries of societies with art, music, and literature and explore such universal ideas as religion, justice, and the passage of time.

Culture can also be also analyzed by the effects of race, gender, socioeconomic class, and status and stratification on the ways of life. Historically, individuals differentiate themselves, and this affects their societies. For example, race has been used as a way to segment society and to allow certain groups to achieve status or some reward over another group. Race groups people according to such common features as hair, eye, or skin color. Ethnicity identifies a group of people by cultural traits. During World War II, Adolf Hitler, the leader of Germany, identified Jews as the reason for the economic and social crisis Germany was facing. He gradually stratified society by Jew and non-Jew. Although he referred to the ethnic group, Jews were recognized by characteristics that Hitler identified as the Jewish race. In the United States, people have recognized race as both unifying and divisive. For example, enclaves developed in cities where people with similar ethnic backgrounds lived. In this way, the immigrants felt at home and could ease into American culture. However, cultural differences sometimes have divided people. After a series of potato famines in Ireland, Irish immigrants moved to America to find a new life—and were met with such signs as "Don't hire Irish" and such comments as "dirty Irish." Texas was settled by cultural groups who created towns to reflect their German, Polish, Mexican, and other heritages. At the same time, societies were often stratified by race, gender, and socioeconomic class.

Cultural Diffusion

Cultural diffusion describes the exchange or transmission of cultural information and lifestyles among people worldwide. For example, most people use cotton, a fabric developed in India, and silk, developed in China. Chicken and pigs were originally domesticated in Asia, but because of cultural diffusion, these animals are common in most countries. Many countries are predominantly

Christian today, but Christianity was born in the Middle East, where most people are Muslim. The Romans facilitated the cultural diffusion of Christianity around the ancient world. Travelers visiting Morocco, a Muslim country in North Africa, may be surprised to hear Puerto Rican salsa and Jamaican reggae music played in local nightclubs. The popularity of Latin and Caribbean rhythms in a predominantly Muslim country is an example of the powerful effect of cultural diffusion.

Cultural diffusion influences the development of multicultural societies, which may have unifying and divisive qualities. The influx of people can aid the social and economic development of a nation. All cultures have unique characteristics and knowledge that can add to a society. These include inventions, art, music, and technology as well as production techniques. However, tensions can rise when people compete for housing, jobs, and land. Large cultural groups also may seek to dominate and exploit smaller, weaker cultural groups. Conflict also may occur if cultural groups try to force their way of life on others.

Relationships among cultural groups are dynamic. The relationships are influenced by conflict, cooperation, and change and are based on such factors as race, ethnicity, and religion. For example, in the 1960s tensions among the Caucasian and African-American races in the United States brought about much change. Although in the South some conflicts occurred in the form of riots, protests, and attacks, both races also cooperated through marches, speeches, peaceful demonstrations, and, eventually, new laws. Religion can also cause tensions. For example, in Northern Ireland, Catholics and Protestants have fought for many years. Although both groups are Christian, their religion has come to symbolize geopolitical issues.

Improved communication, transportation and economic development can also impact cultural change. For example, the country of Malawi, on the continent of Africa, has a poor infrastructure resulting in a few people owning a telephone in their house or village. Telephones with landlines require electricity, wiring under or above ground, and other infrastructure. However, satellites allow farmers in this country to operate satellite mobile telephones that need little infrastructure. The people in Malawi, like many African cultures, have a strong oral tradition, meaning they learn by listening as experienced elders pass knowledge and traditions. Many cannot read and write. Satellite phones let members of this society gain new knowledge to improve their agriculture by using their oral traditions rather than written language.

COMPETENCY 004: ECONOMICS

The teacher understands and applies knowledge of economic systems and how people organize economic systems to produce, distribute, and consume goods and services.

Basic Principles of Economy

Economics is a social science that analyzes the principles that regulate the production, distribution, and consumption of resources in society. It emphasizes how these principles operate within the economic choices of individuals, households, businesses, and governments. Economics can be divided into two main areas: macroeconomics and microeconomics. *Macroeconomics* studies the economy at the world, regional, state, and local levels. The topics include reasons and ways to control inflation, causes of unemployment, and economic growth. *Microeconomics* deals with specific issues related to decision-making.

Theory of Supply and Demand

This theory of supply and demand maintains that prices vary based on balance between the availability of a product or service at a certain price (supply) and the desire of potential buyers to pay that price (demand). This balance of supply and demand can occur naturally or be created artificially. An example of an artificially created balance is the intentional destruction of a surplus of a given product on the world market to maintain the price. Another way is to control the production and availability of the product to create a scarcity. For instance, the Organization of Petroleum Exporting Countries (OPEC) often reduces its production of oil to increase the price.

Goods and Services

Machines increase the availability of goods and services. Machine, or industrial, production can decrease the cost of making the goods and consequently their price. For example, as a result of the division of labor and the use of assembly lines developed by Eli Whitney in 1799, production costs of manufactured goods decreased and productivity increased. Mass production that resulted from the Industrial Revolution made contemporary families and children more likely to become consumers rather than producers. Before the Industrial Revolution, especially in colonial America, children produced goods and contributed to the group.

Economic activities are categorized into five major categories: primary, secondary, tertiary, quaternary, and quinary. Primary economic activities directly use natural resources by such activities as farming, mining, logging, etc. Secondary economic activities take the primary goods and change, or manufacture, them in some way. For example, fresh vegetables are canned or put into a frozen dinner. Tertiary activities typically refer to the service industry. To carry the previous examples further, the grocery store where canned and frozen foods are bought is considered part of the tertiary sector. Quaternary activities typically require specialized knowledge or technical skills and refer to the "collection, processing, and manipulation of information and capital (finance, administration, insurance, legal services, computer services, etc.)" (de Blij & Murphy 1999, 320). Finally, the quinary sector "denotes activities that facilitate complex decision making and the advancement of human capacities (scientific research, high-level management, etc.)" required for jobs like "research professors, the heads of corporations, and top government officials" (de Blij & Murphy 1999, 320).

Major Economic Systems

The three main economic systems are: free enterprise (also known as market economy and/or capitalism), communism, and socialism.

Free Enterprise

Free enterprise is an economic and political doctrine of the capitalist system. The concept is based on the premise that the economy can regulate itself in a freely competitive market through supply and demand and with minimum governmental intervention. This economic system allows entrepreneurship, or individually owned and operated businesses. One of the main benefits of free enterprise is the competition among businesses. This results in a greater choice and better prices for consumers as well as in increased specialization and trade. Americans believe strongly in equal opportunities for all. All citizens are to be given an equal chance to succeed. Individual ownership and engagement in the free-market system comes with the responsibility and importance of employing moral and ethical business practices. The federal government is sometimes needed to protect workers, small businesses and the consumer. For example, business cannot discriminate, or treat someone differently, based on such things as skin color, ethnicity, and gender. The United States government is also supposed to safeguard small business by preventing monopolies, which occur when one business controls part of the market. The U.S. government tries to encourage small businesses to flourish. Additionally, regulations are laws that require businesses to use safe practices. For example, in the early 20th century, President Theodore Roosevelt pushed through a meat inspection act to make sure that meat is packaged properly to prevent people from getting sick. The Food and Drug Administration now requires such additional information as the expiration date to inform consumers about a product.

Free enterprise has greatly influenced globalization. *Globalization* can be defined as a continuous increase of cross-border financial, economic, and social activities. It implies some level of economic interdependence among individuals, financial entities, and nations. Because of globalization, trade barriers have been lessened and in some cases eliminated, and tariffs on imported products have been largely discontinued. In a global market, it is difficult to determine the origins of products. For example, Toyota from Japan and Ford from the United States joined forces to build cars using parts and labor from Mexico.

The concept of *economic interdependence* describes a close connection between producers and consumers of goods and services within a nation or across nations. This economic interdependence has guided nations to establish large markets of free trade zones like the European Union (EU) trade agreement and the North American Free Trade Agreement (NAFTA) for Canada, Mexico, and the United States. The European Union went a step further. In 2002 it adopted a common currency—the Euro—for the Union. This alliance has resulted in the Euro's ranking as one of the strongest currencies in the world.

Communism

Communism* is a system in which the state controls economic activity in the nation. The state rejects free enterprise and capitalism. Private ownership thus is discouraged and often prohibited. Usually the nation is ruled through a one-party system. In theory, communism maintains that the country should not have social classes as a way to avoid the oppressor–oppressed dichotomy. In reality, a small, elite, wealthy class controls the country. Typically, a large gap emerges between the rich and poor classes in this type of economic system. The middle class in this system is not well defined or large in size. In some cases, it is possible for a middle class may not exist.

Socialism

Socialism is a system of government in which the central government controls the production and distribution of goods, services, and labor. The goal is to promote an equitable distribution of resources among the people. In theory, the working class should take over and administer collectively the resources for their benefit and the benefit of the nation as a whole.

Money and Banking

Under the presidency of Woodrow Wilson, the Federal Reserve System was established in 1913. The main purpose of this institution is to keep the banking industry strong to ensure a supply of currency. The Federal Reserve is run by the Federal Reserve Board of Governors, a seven-member body appointed to a four-year term, with the option of being reappointed to a maximum of 14-year terms. The main function of the Federal Reserve Bank is to promote fiscal stability and economic growth and to regulate inflation and deflation. The Board of Governors controls the flow of money and sets the interest rate that banks use to lend money. The board increases the interest rate to control inflation and lowers the interest rate when business slows. To learn more about the Federal Reserve System go to (*http://www.federalreserve.gov*).

Economic Indicators

The health of an economy is determined by assessing indicators. An indicator is a statistic used to evaluate the strength of an economy to make economic predictions about the country or state. For example, a country's gross national product (GNP) or gross domestic product (GDP) explains the monetary value of the goods and services produced by a given country. Other indicators may include unemployment, number of doctors, life expectancy, number of imports and exports, inflation and deflation.

---

* Note: Although Communism is technically an economic term, it may be used to describe both an economic and political system in the context of strong government control, meaning that the government gives little power to the citizens of the country. This can be confusing for students. Be sure to be clear how you phrase your discussion with students.

Inflation and Deflation

Inflation reduces the purchasing power of money, which technically affects the value of the currency. Countries devalue their currency to keep up with inflation. Deflation is the opposite: the purchasing power of money increases, thereby lowering the prices of goods and services. In deflation, consumers benefit, but industry suffers. The Federal Reserve controls the flow of money and keeps a balance between inflation and deflation.

Government Regulations and Taxation

City, state, and national governments regulate businesses to ensure safe, fair, and consistent practices and create a framework for standardizing production of certain products. Taxes support regulations by providing the money to pay people to inspect products and practices as well as to enforce sanctions. Regulations are important to build consumer trust. For example, children's toys are not allowed to use lead-based paint because a child may put a toy in his or her mouth and become sick. Taxes pay for inspectors to monitor toy manufacturers as well as the people who take these cases to court. Buildings are also examined during construction to check that the frame and materials are up to code. When businesses fail to comply with regulations, the owners are fined or in some cases put in jail. However, if the regulations are viewed as burdensome to businesses, it can be said that the regulations will negatively affect business development or be too great of a tax burden for the community. There must be a careful balance between providing a safe, consistent product and being too restrictive and thereby cause a negative impact on businesses.

American Federal Income Tax System

In 1913, the 16th Amendment of the U.S. Constitution allowed the imposition of direct taxation of citizens. This direct taxation is known as the federal income tax.

Interdependence of State, National, and World Economies

The economy of Texas is based primarily on telecommunications, software, financial services, business products and services, semiconductors, biotechnology, and oil and coal. Agriculture and ranching are still viable economic activities, but they no longer carry the economy. A large percentage of these products is exported to members of NAFTA—Mexico and Canada—and to the world markets. According to the Texas Economic Update, if Texas were a nation, it would rank as the eighth-largest economy in the world (Strayhorn, 2004).

The Texas economy relies heavily on exports of goods and services. From 2002 through 2005, Texas was ranked as the No. 1 state in export revenues (BIDC 2006). Without its exports, the Texas economy could not sustain its growth. Because of the interdependence of state and global economies, political turmoil and economic problems in the world affect the Texas economy. For example, because part of Texas's economy is based on petroleum, OPEC's decisions have a direct impact on the state's economy.

COMPETENCY 005: GOVERNMENT AND CITIZENSHIP

The teacher understands and applies knowledge of concepts of government, democracy, and citizenship, including ways that individuals and groups achieve their goals through political systems.

Forms of Government

The U.S. Department of State identifies 26 forms of governments in the world (CIA, n.d).

Three of the most common forms of government are democracy, monarchy, and totalitarian. A description of these types of government follows:

1. **Democracy** is a form of government in which the majority rules. The governments' power is limited, meaning that a constitution, or agreement with the people, delineates the authority that the government is allowed. Citizens in this government enjoy an abundance of civil liberties. In the United States, these civil liberties are unique because they are called "inalienable rights," meaning that they cannot be ever taken away from the citizens by the government or any other entity. Although rare, pure democracies, a form of government where each individual votes on all decisions, exist in some places. In the United States, pure democracies are still used in some town hall meetings, where people meet to make decisions for their town. In practice, it becomes a representative democracy, in which the people elect candidates to represent them in the government. Democratic governments typically have either free enterprise or socialist economies.

2. **Monarchy** is a system in which a king or queen leads the nation. The monarch gains power by inheriting it from his or her parents. The monarch can have supreme powers and control the entire government, or he or she can have limited or ceremonial powers circumscribed by a parliament or a constitution, which occurs in a constitutional monarchy.

3. **Totalitarian** is a form of government in which one person or a few people have all of the governing power and authority. The central government controls nearly all aspects of its citizens' political, social, cultural, and economic lives, including education, employment, housing, reproduction, and movement. This form of government typically has either a communist or socialist economic system. Additionally, citizens have few individual rights, while the government has unlimited rights. Incidences of human rights violations, or abuses, are typically more frequent under this government.

The three main classifications for these forms of government are based on the number of people in power—government by one person, a group, or by many people:

Rule by One

In this government, one person becomes the supreme leader of the nation.

Some of the terminology and concepts linked to this type of government are:

- **Autocracy:** Ruler has unlimited power and uses it arbitrarily.

- **Monarchy:** A king or queen rules and holds complete control over the subjects. Ruler sometimes claims birth and divine rights. This does not refer to a constitutional monarchy.

- **Dictatorship:** The ruler holds absolute power to make laws and command the army.

Ruled by a Few

In this system, a group of influential people controls the government. Traditionally, they appoint one of their own to function as the supreme leader of the government. Some examples of this government are:

- **Theocracy:** Ruled by a group of religious leaders, such as the Taliban in Afghanistan.

- **Aristocracy:** A group of nobles controls the economy and the government.

- **Oligarchy:** A small group of powerful and wealthy people rule the nation with the support of the military.

- **Military:** A committee of military officers or a *junta* rules.

Rule by Many

In this government, the citizens technically are the government because they make the decisions for the community being governed (e.g., cultural group, town, state, or nation). This is called a democracy. In its purest form, each person participates in voting on each decision made for the community. In practice, the citizens elect members to represent them and elected officials become the government. This is called a representative democracy. Today, most democracies are also a constitutional democracy, meaning that they are regulated by a constitution. Examples of representative governments include constitutional democracy and parliamentarian (or constitutional) monarchy.

The historical origins of democratic governance can be found in Ancient Greece where the cultures participated in pure and representational democracy and developed a court system with a jury. More information about Ancient Greece and the roots of democracy can be found online at *http://www.history.com/topics/ancient-history/ancient-greece-democracy.*

Some examples of this government are:

- **Democracy:** The citizens of the nation directly or through elected members make important decisions and become part of the government.

- **Republic:** A representative democracy is led by someone who is not a monarch, such as a president. Example: the United States of America.

- **Constitutional Democracy:** It is a democratic government regulated by a constitution. This form of government can be led by either a president or prime minister and is also referred to as a "constitutional republic."

- **Parliamentarian Monarchy:** The monarch shares the power with the parliament. Often, the powers of the monarch are ceremonial in nature, as they are in Great Britain. This government is also referred to as a "constitutional monarchy."

Government Power Structure

The structure of the governmental power can be designed so that either almost all of the decision-making capabilities are held within the centralized government (unitary government) or the power is shared between the central and local governing bodies (federal government).

- **Federal Republic:** A constitutional government in which the powers of the central government are restricted to create semi-autonomous bodies (states or provinces) with certain degrees of self-governing powers, as in the United States.

The American Government

The U.S. governmental system has been identified as a federal republic, constitutional republic, and constitutional democracy. These terms describe types of representational governments. The terms "constitutional republic" and "constitutional democracy" can be used interchangeably. The former term provides more information by identifying the leader as someone other than a monarch through the word "republic." The term "constitutional" implies that it is governed by a constitution that delineates the power of the government and its people. It is a federal republic because the U.S. government is a representative democracy that shares between a central, or national, government and smaller units of power, such as that of the states. The U.S. is a representative democracy because the citizens elect senators and representatives to Congress.

In the U.S. the national government makes decisions for the benefit of the country as a whole (e.g., laws, coin money, regulate trade and commerce, protection of rights, foreign affairs, declaration of war, banking regulations, education, taxation, postal services, etc.). The state government makes decisions pertaining to the people and businesses within its borders. These include elections, business regulations, education, taxation, transportation and communication, and so on. The national, or federal, government's powers are delineated in the U.S. Constitution. All powers not mentioned belong to the states. Local governments provide direct governance of the people in an immediate area. Many duties mirror the state (taxation, communication & transportation, business regulation, etc.) on a smaller scale. State legislatures determine local governments' power. The official White House website *http://www.whitehouse.gov/our-government/executive-branch* provides more details about the federal government. Government responsibilities and programs are largely funded by taxes. All Americans contribute a portion of their paycheck to the federal income tax. Each state decides whether to allow state and local taxes. Texas has no state and local taxes. Governments can also issue bonds, which are a mechanism to allow the government to borrow money from its citizens or from other countries. According to the U.S. Department of the Treasury, the U.S. outstanding debt was $18,087,425,445,178.53 as of Jan. 22, 2015, as stated on the website *http://www.treasurydirect.gov*.

The Constitution is the supreme law of the nation. It contains a description of the government and the rights and responsibilities of its citizens. The document can be amended with the approval of two-thirds of the House and the Senate and the ratification of individual state legislatures. Amendments to the U.S. Constitution have made it more democratic than the original document.

Effective leadership in a constitutional republic is critical for the success of the country. The leader must collaborate with opposing parties to make the best possible decisions for the nation. The following links list U.S. presidents and Texas governors and describes their term in office *http://www.whitehouse.gov/about/presidents* and *https://www.tsl.texas.gov/ref/abouttx/governors.html*. To develop a better understanding of effective leadership, teachers can ask students to compare and contrast leaders, the decisions they made, and the long-term impact of those decisions.

Executive Branch

The executive branch of the U.S. government is composed of a president and a vice president elected every four years by electoral votes. The president is the commander-in-chief of the armed forces. He or she appoints cabinet members, nominates judges to the federal court system, grants pardons, recommends legislation, and has the power to veto legislation.

Judicial Branch

The judicial branch is composed of a federal court system that includes the Supreme Court and a system of lower courts—district courts, appeals courts, bankruptcy courts, and special federal courts. Federal judges are nominated by the president of the United States and confirmed by the Senate. All federal judges are appointed for life. The Supreme Court is composed of nine judges, and their ruling is considered final. Some of the major responsibilities of this body are to interpret the Constitution, resolve conflicts among states, and interpret laws and treaties.

Legislative Branch

The legislative branch is composed of Congress, which is divided in two parts—the Senate and the House of Representatives. The Senate comprises two senators from each state, while the composition of the House is based on the population of each state. Congress makes the laws of the nation, collects taxes, coins money and regulates its value, controls appropriations, and regulates the jurisdictions of federal courts. Congress can also declare war, impeach public officials, and override presidential vetos.

System of Checks and Balances

The U.S. Constitution provides for a system of checks and balances among the three branches of the government. In this system, individual branches check the others to be sure that no one assumes full control of the central government. The legislative branch can check the executive branch by passing laws over presidential veto by a two-thirds majority in both houses. This branch exerts control over the judicial branch by refusing to confirm the president's judges. The executive can check the legislative branch by the use of the veto and the judicial branch by appointing federal judges. The judicial branch can check the other two branches through the process of judicial review, which can declare legislation unconstitutional or illegal. For example, on June 26, 2015, the U.S. Supreme Court ruled that states cannot ban same-sex marriage. With this ruling the U.S. became the 21st country to legalize gay marriage.

Judicial Review Process—*Marbury v. Madison*

A dispute that occurred as the Thomas Jefferson administration came into power fundamentally altered the system of checks and balances of the American government. In this case, the judicial branch confirmed its power to review and assess the constitutionality of the legislation passed by Congress and signed by the president. This process is now called the *judicial review*.

Bill of Rights

After the U.S. Constitution was enacted in 1783, the founders believed that additional measures were necessary to preserve basic human rights. The first 10 amendments to the U.S. Constitution came to be called the Bill of Rights. A summary of the first 10 amendments follows:

First Amendment—separation of church and state; freedom of religion, speech and press; and the right to peaceful assembly

Second Amendment—rights to keep and bear arms

Third Amendment—made it illegal to force people to offer quarters to soldiers in time of peace

Fourth Amendment—rights to privacy and unreasonable searches or seizures

Fifth Amendment—rights of due process, protection against self-incrimination, and protection from being indicted for the same crime twice (double jeopardy)

Sixth Amendment—rights to speedy public trial by an impartial jury and to counsel for one's defense

Seventh Amendment—right to sue people

Eighth Amendment—protection against cruel and unusual punishment

Ninth Amendment—enumeration of specific rights in the Constitution cannot be taken as a way to deny other rights retained by the people

Tenth Amendment—rights not delegated to the federal government by the Constitution are reserved to the states or to the people

Additional Key Amendments to the U.S. Constitution

13th Amendment—Slavery abolished

14th Amendment—Citizenship and Rights—Citizenship to African-Americans including former slaves; Reaffirmed privileges and rights for all citizens

15th Amendment—Race No Bar to Vote—Right to vote for African-American males

16th Amendment—Ratified in 1913, it gives the federal government power to levy taxes

19th Amendment—Women's Suffrage

25th Amendment—Presidential Disability and Succession

26th Amendment—Voting Age Set to 18 Years

For a detailed analysis of the U.S. Constitution and the 27 amendments see the U.S. Constitution online at *http://www.usconstitution.net/const.html*.

Power Sharing Between State and Federal Governments

One of the most significant principles of the U.S Constitution is the concept of power shared between the federal and state governments. Some of the powers reserved to the federal and state governments follow.

Powers Reserved for the Federal Government

- Regulate interstate and foreign commerce
- Print money and regulate its value
- Establish the laws for regulation of immigration and naturalization
- Regulate admission of new states

- Declare war and ratify peace treaties

- Establish a system of weights and measures

- Raise and maintain armed forces

- Conduct relations with foreign nations

Powers Reserved for State Governments

- Conduct and monitor local, state, and federal elections

- Provide for local government

- Ratify proposed amendments to the Constitution

- Regulate intrastate commerce

- Provide education for its citizens

- Establish direct taxes like sales and state taxes

- Regulate and maintain police power over public health and safety

- Maintain control of state borders

In addition to the powers reserved to the states, the 10th Amendment of the U.S. Constitution provides additional powers to the state. In this amendment, the powers not specifically delegated to the federal government are reserved for the states.

Local and State Governments

Most states follow the type of government established in the U.S. Constitution. State governments have three branches—executive, legislative, and judicial. The main difference is that the executive branch is led by a governor and the judicial branch is composed of a state court system subordinate to the federal court system. The city government is typically headed by a mayor or city manager with the support of a city council.

Citizenship

The development of civic ideas and practices is a lifelong process that begins in school by observing national holidays, learning about the contribution of historical figures, and pledging allegiance to the American and Texas flags each day. Students should develop foundational knowledge about what each pledge means as well as the history of their development and why the pledges are important to American citizens. In this way, saying the pledge will be meaningful rather than rote memorization and recitation of words that students do not understand. In first grade, encouraging good citizenship continues with the introduction of the American anthem and the mottoes of Texas and the United States. Civic education and the principles of democracy are infused through active participation in community activities. To promote civic responsibility, students can get involved in discussions about issues that affect the community. Teachers should guide students to suggest possible solutions to community problems and then to listen and analyze contribution from other students. Through this exchange, students are guided to practice principles of democracy and to value individual contributions to solve community problems.

Additionally, students should define what is a "good citizen" and to connect their definition with historical and contemporary examples from the community, state, and nation. Americans value such things as recognizing social responsibilities, helping each other, making sure everyone has food, shelter, and clothing, caring for the elderly, keeping the land clean, using things wisely, caring for others, being patriotic, respecting our men and women in uniform (e.g., military, police, firefighters), respecting our state and country flags and what they symbolize, and so on. Teachers can invite speakers from such organizations as food pantries, the Red Cross, Boys Scouts, Girl Scouts, and Meals on Wheels to show examples of good citizenship. Interdisciplinary service learning can be developed to help students explore this topic in-depth. Students can investigate ways that good citizens keep the land clean via recycling as well as with larger projects. For example, Chad Pregracke was concerned about the trash in the Mississippi River as a teenager. Realizing no one else was going to clean up the river, he began to fill his little boat with trash and haul it away. He developed an organization that now has over 70,000 volunteers who work to clean the rivers (see *http://livinglandsandwaters.org/* for more information). Inspiring stories help students realize they can be good citizens as well. Clara Harlowe Barton was a teacher who risked her life to help soldiers during the Civil War. She later founded the American Red Cross. Teachers should help students recognize the values that made these people good citizens and show students how they can also be good citizens (For more information go to *http://www.redcross.org/about-us/history/clara-barton*).

In grades K–6 students should learn the meaning and importance of national holidays. Holidays with historic significance include Memorial Day, Labor Day, Columbus Day, Independence Day, Veterans Day, and Martin Luther King Jr. Day. Memorial Day honors members of the military who died in war. Labor Day recognizes the importance of workers and labor unions. Columbus Day commemorates the arrival of Christopher Columbus to the Americas. Independence Day commemorates the adoption of the Declaration of Independence. Martin Luther King Jr. Day honors the leader of the civil rights movement. Veterans Day celebrates those who have served in the country's armed forces.

Children as early as prekindergarten can be guided to develop civic responsibility. Teachers can promote this responsibility by involving students in situations in which they practice civic responsibility. For example, teachers can make children aware of how producing trash can affect the environment. Students can be guided to examine the amount of trash they produce daily and explore ways to reduce it. Promoting a sense of responsibility to the common good constitutes the main principle in developing responsible citizenship.

American Symbols

American Patriotic Symbols

In grades EC-6, children learn what Americans value as a nation and expect from the citizenry. Patriotic symbols are visible signs of national pride. The U.S. National Flag, the Pledge of Allegiance, the Statue of Liberty, the Liberty Bell, and the White House are important examples of patriotic symbols.

- The United States of America National Flag has 50 stars representing the 50 states of the Union. The color red represents hardiness and valor, the white symbolizes purity and innocence, and the blue symbolizes vigilance, perseverance, and justice. The Congress approved a new flag with 13 red and white alternating horizontal stripes and 13 stars representing the original colonies in 1777. A star was added to the flag each time a state entered the union. The Congress set the number of stripes at thirteen in 1818 and approved to continue to add a star for each new state.

- The Pledge of Allegiance is a declaration of patriotism. It was first published in 1892 in *The Youth's Companion* and is believed to have been written by the magazine's editor, Francis Bellamy. The original purpose was that the pledge was to be used by schoolchildren in activities to celebrate the 400th anniversary of the discovery of America. The pledge was widely used in morning school routines for many years and received official recognition by Congress in 1942. The phrase "under God" was added in 1954, and a law indicating the proper behavior to adopt when reciting the pledge, which includes standing straight, removing hats or any other headgear, and placing the right hand over the heart.

- The "Star-Spangled Banner" is the national anthem of the United States. It was originally a poem written by Francis Scott Key during the Battle of Baltimore in the War of 1812 against the British. In 1931, it was made the official national anthem of the United States.

- The Statue of Liberty was a gift of friendship from the people of France to the people of the United States commemorating the United States' 100th anniversary. It is a universal symbol of freedom, democracy, and international friendship.

- The Liberty Bell is a symbol of freedom and liberty. The Pennsylvania Assembly ordered the Liberty Bell to commemorate the 50th anniversary of Pennsylvania's original constitution, William Penn's Charter of Privileges. It is traditionally believed that it was rung to summon the people of Philadelphia to hear the Declaration of Independence. It became an icon when the abolitionists adopted it as a symbol of freedom. The abolitionists changed its name from The State House Bell to the Liberty Bell.

- The White House was originally planned by President George Washington in 1791 and was completed in 1800 when its first resident, President John Adams, moved in with his wife, Abigail. It was originally called the President's House. President Theodore Roosevelt christened it with the name The White House in 1901, and for over 200 years it has been the home of the U.S. presidents and their families. It is recognized as a symbol of the U.S. presidency throughout the world.

- The Great Seal of the United States consists of a bald eagle holding an olive branch and a bundle of arrows. The olive branch represents peace and the arrows represent military strength. The eagle holds a scroll in its beak with the nation's motto: "*E Pluribus Unum*" which means "Out of many, one."

For additional information about symbols of the United States, go to *www.statesymbolsusa.org*.

Texan Symbols

Texas Patriotic Symbols

Patriotic symbols are also signs of state pride. The Texas Flag, the Texas Pledge of Allegiance, bluebonnets, longhorns, oil rigs, and the state capitol are important symbols of Texas state pride. Such places such as King's Ranch, the Alamo, cattle trails, the Capitol, Gruene Hall, and the San Jacinto battlegrounds are examples of landmarks that are meaningful symbols. For additional information about symbols of Texas, go to *http://www.statesymbolsusa.org/Texas/state_symbols.html*. For additional information about national monuments and landmarks in Texas, go to *http://texastimetravel.com/node/28774*.

References

Acosta, T. P. (2009). Raza Unida Party. *The Handbook of Texas Online. Texas State Historical* Retrieved from *Association.* Retrieved from *http://www.tshaonline.org/handbook/online/articles/RR/war1.html*.

Arends, R. (1998). *Learning to Teach*. (4th ed.) Boston: McGraw-Hill.

Barker, E. C. & J. W. Pohl. (2009). Texas Revolution. *The Handbook of Texas Online. Texas State Historical Association. http://www.tshaonline.org/handbook/online/articles/TT/qdt1.html*.

BIDC—Business and Industry Data Center. 2006. Overview of the Texas Economy. *Office of the Governor, Economic Development and Tourism*. Retrieved from *http://governor.state.tx.us/ecodev/business_research/texas_economy*

CIA World Fact Book. Central Asia: Russia. Retrieved from *https://www.cia.gov/library/publications/the-world-factbook/geos/rs.html*.

CIA World Fact Book. Nations: Forms of Government. Retrieved from *http://www.historyguy.com/nations/government_types.html*

De Blij, Harm J. & Murphy, A. B. 1999. *Human Geography: Culture, Society, and Space*. (7th Ed.) Wiley: New York.

Echevarria, J., M. Vogt, and D. Short. 2000. *Making content comprehensible for English language learners*: *The SIOP model* (4th ed.). Needham Heights, MA: Allyn and Bacon.

Fry, P. L. "Origin of Name." *The Handbook of Texas Online. Texas State Historical Association.* Retrieved from *http://www.tshaonline.org/handbook/online/articles/TT/pft4.html.*

Ganeri, A., H. M. Martell, and B. Williams. 1999. *The World History Encyclopedia.* Bath, UK: Parragon.

Kagan, S. 1985. *Cooperative learning resources for teachers.* Riverside, CA: Spencer Kagan.

Kerr, A. 2006. Temperance and prohibition. History Department, Ohio State University. Retrieved from *http://prohibition.osu.edu*

Lyman, F. T. (1981). The responsive classroom discussion: The inclusion of all students. In *Mainstreaming Digest,* ed. A. S. Anderson, 109–113. College Park: University of Maryland Press.

Marzano, R., and D. Pickering. (2005). *Building academic vocabulary*: *Teacher's manual.* Alexandria, VA: ASCD.

Mayell, H. (2004). Three high-altitude peoples, three adaptations to thin air. *National Geographic.* Retrieved from *http://news.nationalgeographic.com/news/2004/02/0224_040225_evolution.html*

Mendoza, V. (2001). Video review of *Chicano! History of the Mexican American Civil Rights Movement. The Journal for MultiMedia History,* Volume 3. Retrieved from *www.albany.edu/jmmh/vol3/chicano/chicano.html*

National Council for the Teaching of Social Studies (NCTSS) (2006). Expectations of Excellence: Curriculum Standards for Social Studies—Executive Summary. Retrieved from *www. social-studies.org/standards/execsummary*

Parker, W. C. (2001). *Social Studies in Elementary Education.* 11th ed. Columbus, OH: Merrill Prentice-Hall.

Potts, J. (1994). *Adventure Tales of America.* Dallas, TX: Signal Media.

Rosado, L., and D. Salazar. 2002–2003. La Conexión: The English/Spanish connection. *National Forum of Applied Educational Research Journal* 15(4): 51–66.

Rosado, L., Hellawell, M. & Zamora, B. E. (6/16/2011). An Analysis of the Education Systems in Mexico and the United States from Pre-Kinder to 12 Grade. Educational Resources Information Center (ERIC #ED520900). Available: *http://www.eric.ed.gov/PDFS/ED520900.pdf*

Rosales Castañeda, O. (2006). *The Chicano Movement in Washington State* Retrieved from http://depts.washington.edu/civilr/mecha_intro.htm

Rowe, M. B. 1986. *Wait Times: Slowing Down May Be a Way of Speeding Up. Journal of Teacher Education,* 37, 43–50.

Schifini, A. (1985). *Sheltered English: Content area instruction for limited English proficiency students*. Los Angeles County Office of Education.

Schifini, A., H. García, Short, D. J. García, E. E., Villamil Tinajero, J., Hamayan, E. & Kratky, L. (2004). *Avenues: Success in language, literacy and content*. Carmel, CA: Hampton-Brown.

Seattle Civil Rights and Labor History Project. (2006). Retrieved from *http://depts.washington.edu/civilr/Chicanomovement_part1.htm*

Sheppard, D. E. *Cabeza de Vaca in North America*. Retrieved from *http://www.flori-dahistory.com/cabeza.html*

Slavin, R. (1986). *Student Learning: An Overview and Practical Guide*. Washington, DC: Professional Library National Education Association.

Strayhorn, C. K. (2004), Fall. "The Rebound is Here." *Texas Economic Update*. Window on State Government. Retrieved from *http://www.window.state.tx.us/ecodata/teufall04/*

Subject Test IV: Science (804)

The National Science Teachers Association (NSTA) supports the idea that scientific inquiry should be a basic component of the curriculum in every grade in American schools (NSTA, 2002). A position paper of the organization published in 2002 emphasizes the importance of offering students early experience in problem solving and scientific thinking. The report suggests that children learn science best under the following conditions:

- Students are actively involved in firsthand exploration of scientific concepts.

- Instruction is related and built on the abilities and experiences of the learners.

- Instruction is organized thematically.

- Mathematics and communication skills are integrated.

The report also indicates that the curriculum should emphasize the contributions of people from a variety of cultures. Finally, the NSTA (2002) states that science education can be successful if teachers receive adequate professional development and school administrators show a genuine interest in science education.

COMPETENCY 001: LABORATORY PROCESSES, EQUIPMENT, AND SAFETY

The teacher understands how to manage learning activities, tools, materials, equipment and technologies to ensure the safety of all students.

Classroom and Laboratory Health and Safety

Teachers must create a safe environment for children involved in scientific inquiry. Here are some of the principles and practices that teachers can follow to reduce risks and protect children:

- Require students to use appropriate personal protective gear such as goggles, laboratory coats, and gloves.

- Use appropriate procedures for cleaning and disposing of materials.

- Adhere to appropriate disciplinary procedures to avoid accidents. For example, do not allow children to play with water or other lab materials.

- Substitute less hazardous equivalent materials when possible. For example, use cleaning products instead of chemicals in their pure form.

- Use polyethylene or metal containers in place of glass.

- Advise children to avoid tasting or ingesting substances or materials.

- Label containers appropriately to avoid confusion.

- Control the use of sharp objects that can puncture the skin.

- Supervise the use of living organisms and the cleaning of instruments.

- Avoid experimenting with human cells and bodily fluids.

- Share the responsibility for the safety of the students with the whole group; in a well-managed science lab, students should motivate each other to follow safety procedures.

- Make provisions for the movement and handling of equipment and materials for students with special needs.

- Prepare, review, and send home an age-appropriate safety contract requiring parent/guardian signature.

- Organize all materials to be used in class by placing them in separate bins for a member of each student group to pick up for use for the lab activity and for returning materials after the lab activity.

- Prepare and practice an emergency plan with students should an accident occur.

- Clearly label and demonstrate the use of safety equipment with students, such as the eyewash station and fire blanket.

- Document all accidents, regardless of how minor, and have another teacher sign as witness if possible.

- Clearly write and read to students the safety precautions for the laboratory before beginning the activity.

- Place posters around the room emphasizing the safety rules of the classroom and laboratory.

- Keep all chemicals and glassware in locked cabinets.

- Maintain regular inventory of all laboratory materials and chemicals.

- Store acids and other caustic chemicals in cabinets close to the floor in case they fall when retrieved for use.

- When using an open flame, such as lit candles, students must tie long hair back and tape or roll up loose sleeves to avoid contact with the fire.

The use of dangerous chemical substances in the elementary classroom is limited in scope. Many laboratory chemicals can be substituted with household products. However, care needs to be taken even when handling household chemicals. It is important to demonstrate safe laboratory procedures for the classroom because household products are still chemicals and pose some level of risk to students. Safety management of chemicals in the classroom requires teachers to have knowledge of those chemicals and their properties. For example, teachers need to be aware that a simple tool such as a mercury thermometer can break and pose a danger to children. In general, maintaining safety requires teachers to take the following steps:

- Assess the relative danger of each chemical used in the classroom.

- Label and store chemicals appropriately.

- Implement safety procedures for the use and handling of materials and equipment.

- Follow appropriate procedures for cleaning containers and disposing of chemicals.

Animal and animal specimens need to be treated with care and respect. In keeping live animals, it is imperative that the feeding and handling of the animal is clearly understood. Students must learn to handle the animals in a caring and humane manner. Animals found in nature should not be kept in the classroom as they pose a risk of disease and possibly a greater risk of attack such as biting, compared to those used to human interaction. Humane treatment is expected of all creatures, from mealworms to butterflies, and to rabbits and hamsters. A plan to care for the animals must be made in advance of school holidays and vacations. If hatching eggs in the classroom, be sure a farm agrees to take the chicks once hatched. Specimens of once living organisms also must be handled with care and respect. Do not allow students to take dissected organs or tissues out of the classroom or laboratory. Wash and disinfect hands and laboratory surfaces after handling live animals and/or specimens of once living organisms. Teaching the students responsibility in caring for living things is an excellent learning experience for them, and thus important for teachers to serve as models for expected behaviors.

Scientific Tools and Equipment for Gathering and Storing Data

Various tools or instruments are used in scientific experimentation in kindergarten through grade 6. The classroom can be equipped with measuring devices like graduated cylinders, beakers, scales, dishes, thermometers, meter sticks, and micrometers. They might also have anatomical models showing the body systems. Teachers need to learn to use these tools and equipment properly in order to help their students know how to use them and to collect accurate data in their inquiry investigations.

The TEKS requires students to gather information using specific equipment and tools. Examples of the tools required in kindergarten through grade 6 are presented in Table 6-1 (TEA 2013 mod.).

Table 6-1. Tools and Equipment Required in the TEKS

Tools and Equipment	Kinder-garten	1st	2nd	3rd	4th	5th	6th
Nonstandard measurements	✓	✓	✓				
Hand lenses	✓	✓	✓	✓	✓	✓	✓
Computers	✓	✓	✓	✓	✓	✓	✓
Balances	✓	✓	✓	✓	✓	✓	✓
Cups and bowls	✓	✓	✓	✓	✓	✓	✓
Thermometers		✓	✓	✓	✓	✓	✓
Clocks				✓	✓	✓	✓	✓
Meter sticks				✓	✓	✓	✓	✓
Microscopes				✓	✓	✓	✓
Safety goggles				✓	✓	✓	✓
Magnets				✓	✓	✓	✓
Compasses				✓	✓	✓	✓
Timing devices					✓	✓	✓
Calculators					✓	✓	✓
Sound recorders					✓	✓	✓
Hot plates						✓	✓
Burners						✓	✓
Beakers						✓	✓
Graduated cylinders						✓	✓
Flasks (Erlenmeyer and Florence)						✓	✓
Test tubes and holders						✓	✓

Proper Laboratory Procedures and Precision

Scientific experimentation cannot rely solely on our senses to record information. People need to extend what can be observed with their senses by using scientific instruments such as balances, microscopes, beakers, and graduated cylinders to make precise observations and measurements. Science requires the use of standard measuring devices to be sure that the information is clear, accurate, and able to be replicated in experimental settings. The metric system of measurement used by most scientists is the International System of Units, also known as Standard Units, or SI Units because it is used in most countries to maintain consistency in measurements. These SI units are based on the metric system, such as meters and kilometers to measure length, grams and kilograms to measure mass, and milliliters or liters to measure liquid volume and cubic centimeters to measure solid volume. The United States uses a combination of what is known as a non-standard unit system of measurement, or non-SI Units, along with the SI unit metric system. In fact, the United States is the only technologically developed country in the world that uses non-standard units for business transactions and for day-to-day activities. However, for international business, engineering, and natural sciences, all countries use a more standardized, precise system of weights and measurement, the SI unit metric system. The English or non-SI system uses units such as inches, feet and yards to measure length, ounces and pounds to measure mass, and fluid ounces, quarts and gallons to measure liquid amount or volume, with inches and meters used for solid amounts or volume. The SI units are a system of fractions and multiples of units related to each other by powers of 10, allowing conversion and comparison of measures simply by shifting a decimal point, and avoiding the lengthy arithmetical operations required by the non-SI English system. The TEKS requires the teaching of both the SI metric and the non-SI English systems; however, all scientific data are to be reported using the metric system.

COMPETENCY 002: HISTORY AND NATURE OF SCIENCE

The teacher understands the history and nature of science, the process and role of scientific inquiry and the role of inquiry in science instruction.

History and Nature of Science, Diversity, and Equity in Science

The history and nature of science provides an important framework for student learning. By learning the history of science, students will come to understand that science is changing and dynamic rather than fixed and tentative. They will understand that their own conceptions and understandings of science can change in light of new experimental observations and evidence. Therefore, it is important to use the history and nature of science as a tool to promote students' learning. For example, the students can learn about the Earth-centered model of the solar system that prevailed for hundreds of years before Copernicus, and then Galileo supported a new model, which is now the accepted view of a Sun-centered model of the solar system. With better tools developed through time and the extension of findings through observations and experiments, our scientific knowledge constantly shifts and changes.

It is important for students to understand the struggle of scientists in the past in conducting experiments and arriving at meaningful conclusions. These struggles are similar to those that students themselves may experience in arriving at sound conclusions, including errors in measurement, misunderstandings of information, and difficulties with interpretation. Furthermore, teachers must know and highlight for students contributions from both males and females as well as people of varied cultural and ethnic backgrounds who have contributed to scientific progress and discovery throughout history. Teaching the history of science will help students better understand how we use what has been learned to build new conclusions and make new discoveries today, and help them realize that they are the scientists of the present and future.

Important history of science topics for teachers to understand and to incorporate into their teaching are shown in Table 6.2.

Table 6-2. History of Important Science Concepts to Use in Classroom Teaching

Concept	Description	Who	Timeframe	Resource
Cell theory	All living things are made up of cells and all cells have arisen from other existing cells.	Robert Hooke Henri Dutrochet	1635–1703 1776–1847	*http://www.biologyreference.com/Gr-Hi/History-of-Biology-Cell-Theory-and-Cell-Structure.html*
Plate Tectonics	Continents on Earth today were long ago formed together in a single landmass.	Alfred Wegener	1880–1930	*http://www.scec.org/education/k12/learn/plate2.htm*
Laws of Motion	1. An object at rest will remain at rest unless acted on by an unbalanced force. An object in motion continues in motion with the same speed and in the same direction unless acted upon by an unbalanced force. This is known as the law of inertia. 2. Acceleration is produced when a force acts on a mass. The greater the mass, the greater the amount of force needed (to accelerate the object). 3. For every action there is an equal and opposite reaction.	Sir Isaac Newton	1643–1727	*http://teachertech.rice.edu/Participants/louviere/Newton/index.html*

(continued)

Concept	Description	Who	Timeframe	Resource
Universal Gravity	Every object in the universe attracts every other object with a force directed along the line of centers for the two objects that is proportional to the product of their masses and inversely proportional to the square of the separation between the two objects.	Sir Isaac Newton	1643–1727	*http://csep10.phys. utk.edu/astr161/ lect/history/ newtongrav.html*
Technology	The invention and development of systematic techniques and/or tools for making and doing things.	Various Scientists and Inventors	2.5 Million Years Ago to the Present	*http://www. historyworld. net/wrldhis/ PlainTextHistories. asp?historyid=ab11*

Planning and Implementing Scientific Inquiry

Scientific inquiry is promoted through students engaging in hands-on activities and experimentation. From their experiences conducting scientific experiments, students acquire information firsthand and develop problem-solving skills. Children in grades EC-6 are inquisitive and want to understand the environment around them. Teachers can use this interest to provide students with opportunities to use electronic and printed sources to find answers to their questions and to expand their knowledge about the topic. It is important for children to develop inquiry skills. This can only be accomplished by allowing them to experience science for themselves in hands-on investigations. By doing so, children develop important science inquiry and thinking skills (Table 6-3).

Table 6-3. Science Thinking Skills (FOSS, 2000)

- **Observing:** Using the senses to obtain information from the environment
- **Communicating:** Talking, drawing, electronic information sharing (e.g., email, texts, blogs) and acting
- **Comparing:** Pairing, judging similarities and differences, and seeking one-to-one correspondence
- **Organizing:** Grouping, seriating, and sequencing
- **Relating:** Determining cause-and-effect, connecting concepts, and grouping information
- **Inferring:** Using super-ordinate/subordinate classification, using data to make assumptions, employing if/then reasoning, and developing scientific laws
- **Applying:** Using knowledge to develop strategic plans, invent new concepts and processes

The model of inquiry that best supports science learning is a model known as the **learning cycle**, consisting of three phases: **exploration**, **concept invention**, and **application** (Lawson, Abraham, & Renner, 1989; Marek & Cavallo, 1997). Over time the learning cycle was extended with the addition of two new phases becoming what is known as the 5-E model (Bybee, 1989). What follows is some history on the development of inquiry-based teaching via the learning cycle and 5-E model.

The original three-phase learning cycle model developed by Robert Karplus in the early 1960s was based upon the following theoretical foundation:

1. Science must be taught in a way that is *consistent with the nature of science*. Science is discovery and investigation, and that means science must be taught as an active process—as something we *do*. The children need to have the opportunity to experience the true nature of science by doing science exploration for themselves through direct experiences and hands-on investigations.

2. Science teaching must be focused on promoting the main purpose of education, namely, to promote the development in our students the *ability to think*—to be critical and independent thinkers. Science must be taught in a way that promotes the students use of independent, critical, and higher-level thinking abilities (e.g., logic). Promoting this purpose of education is best accomplished by *not* giving or telling students the "answers" or information (e.g., as in giving a lecture). Instead students should be afforded hands-on, direct experiences in which they use logic and reasoning to find "answers" or explanations for themselves; further discussion and teacher guidance can follow the students' direct experiences.

3. Science must be taught in a way that *matches how students learn,* which has been described as the **mental functioning** model by Piaget (1964). How individuals learn is through mentally experiencing the following three-phase mental process: 1) **Assimilation (with disequilibrium)** 2) **Accommodation** 3) **Organization**. According to the model, in learning, individuals first *assimilate* or "take in" information with our senses from our environment and from what we are experiencing in our environment. During assimilation, we may have a sense of "disequilibrium," which is confusion or "cognitive conflict," as we try to make sense of our experiences. When in disequilibrium, we need to go back and *assimilate* more information—make more observations and gather more data. When we have assimilated enough information and made sense of the information we have gathered, our minds experience *accommodation*. That is the "aha!" moment, the point when we ultimately feel "cognitive relief" — we figured it out, or what we have observed/experienced now makes sense! Third, our minds take that newly accommodated information and we *organize* it into our mental structures. That is, we connect the new idea or what we have just figured out/made sense of to what we already know, what we experience in everyday life, and/or to new and related concepts.

The three phases of learning described by Piaget, assimilation-accommodation-organization, match the original learning cycle's three phases: Exploration-Concept Invention-Application. The logic in developing the learning cycle in these three phases was that, given what educators know about how children (people) learn, teachers should be teaching in a sequence or way that matches this learning pattern. To do so, teachers should first provide students with an **Exploration** phase in which students can assimilate information using their senses. The students may or may not experience disequilibrium, but, as teachers, we should guide them (not tell them!) through the sense-making process. Teachers should then carry out a discussion in the **Concept Invention** phase in which students share their observations and findings. With careful questioning, teachers guide students to review their data/observations toward helping them reach the "aha!" moment or accommodation. In this second phase, students write a summarizing *statement of the concept* and post it on the board, and/or read their concept statement aloud to others. In writing and stating the concept in this second phase students accommodate or gain understanding of the concept. In the final phase of the learning cycle, the teacher then helps students organize the new concept by providing experiences where they apply the concept in new contexts. In this phase, known as the **Application phase** students connect the concept with what they observe in everyday life, or what they already know.

Furthermore, by teaching via the learning cycle, teachers are teaching in a way that is consistent with the nature of science—as an active, hands-on process characterized by investigation and discovery—and teachers are teaching in a way that supports the purpose of education; that is, teachers are promoting children's development of higher-level thinking abilities. The learning cycle and its origins and theory base is more fully described in a book by Marek and Cavallo (1997) titled *The Learning Cycle: Elementary School Science and Beyond*.

Over time, science educators added some additional phases to the learning cycle, namely, the **Engage** phase, with the idea that teachers need to do something that will gain the students' attention before beginning the exploration phase. Engage can be a demonstration (without explanation) or simply posing a question, challenge, or problem. So the original learning cycle model's first phase, **Exploration**, became two phases, **Engage** and **Explore**. Though identical, the **Concept Invention** phase's name was changed to **Explain** and **Application** phase had the name changed to **Elaborate**, to sustain the alliteration. Assessment or the measurement of learning in the original three-phase model was to take place throughout the learning cycle. However, science educators at the time preferred to have assessment articulated as an additional phase labelled **Evaluate**, which was so named to keep the "E" pattern in each phase of the model. So the three-phase **learning cycle** model was expanded into a **5-E Model**: *Engage, Explore, Explain, Elaborate, Evaluate.*

The two models are basically the same and grew out of the same underlying philosophy and theoretical foundation. However, the three phases more closely follow the model of learning—assimilation, accommodation and organization—as first described by Piaget, whereas the 5-E incorporates two additional essentials of classroom teaching, namely gaining students focus and attention, and measuring student learning.

Most importantly, in both models, the learning cycle and 5-E, students are *not told* the science concept or information before beginning the inquiry, but must discover the concept themselves through hands-on investigation, observation, and collection of data. In using the *Engage* phase (from 5-E) the students' learning experience begins with the teacher posing one or more questions, giving an interesting demonstration, or providing a laboratory guide; but in all of these, this phase captures their curiosity and motivates them to learn. Whether or not an *Engage* phase is used, students next (or first) experience an *Exploration* phase—and it must be a student-centered hands-on activity, investigation, or experiment. In the *Exploration* phase, students make observations and gather data on a science idea or topic area. In this phase, students can determine the experimental design or it can be pre-determined by the teacher. The main aspect, however, is that students are doing the lab activity themselves, and have not been told the expected outcome beforehand. For example, students may grow plants in the light and in the dark, and make observations, draw and/or take photos, and measure the plants grown under the two differing conditions over a period of time. All other variables are controlled (soil, water, air); only the light received by the plants is different, which is the variable.

After the observations have been made and data has been gathered by students, the teacher begins the next instructional phase called *Concept Invention*, or in the 5-E model, the *Explain* phase. In this phase the students present and share data with their classmates in a teacher-guided discussion of findings. The teacher uses questions to guide students' thinking and encourages the use of logic and reasoning as they interpret their data. For example, students may post the photos or drawings of plants grown in the dark and in the light, make line graphs of plant height over time, or share qualitative information about how the plant appeared after grown under the two conditions (e.g., plants in the light were green, whereas plants in the dark were yellow and pale). At the end of this phase, the students construct an overall statement that summarizes their data and observations, which is the central science *concept*. The science vocabulary is then linked to the concept students "invented."

Next the teacher helps students through the *Application* (from the learning cycle) or *Elaborate* (from the 5-E model) in which students use the new concept they have learned as it is applied in new contexts. For example, students can create new questions to investigate or hypotheses to test, based on what they have just learned (the concept) and develop a way to answer their questions or test their hypotheses (e.g., what color of light is best for plants to grow?). They can also go to the Internet to learn more about the concept they have just invented. In this phase the teacher can engage students in additional hands-on laboratories, readings, discussions, field trips, and/or writing activities that extend and expand upon the concept. These models of inquiry science teaching and learning are endorsed by NSTA (NSTA, 1998, 2003).

The diagram in Figure 6-1 shows the inquiry-based learning cycle model as it corresponds to the 5-E model of science teaching. The template shown in Table 6-4 explains each phase of the learning cycle as it relates to the 5-E Model for structuring inquiry-based science teaching for all students.

Figure 6-1. The Learning Cycle and 5-E Model

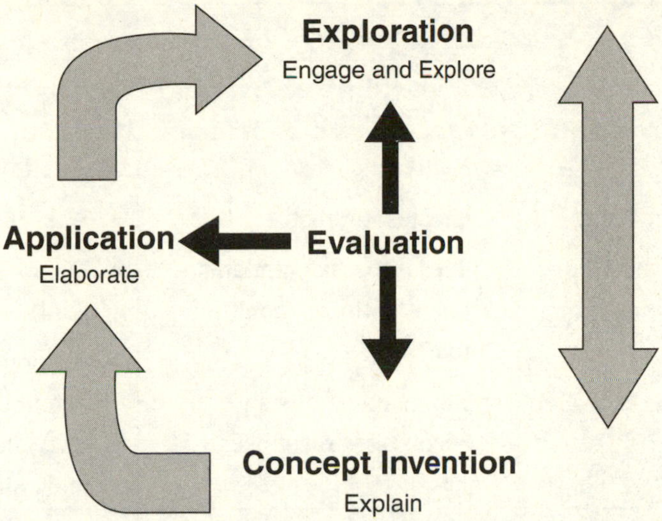

Interpreting Findings in Science Inquiry

In planning and conducting experiments, teachers should guide children to develop an appropriate procedure for testing hypotheses, including the use of instruments that can yield measurable data. Even at the early stages of scientific experimentation, the procedure must be clear and tangible enough to allow replication by other students or scientists. Help students understand the concept of controlling variables and testing only one variable at a time. Students need to learn to be precise in the collection of data and measurements. Ensure the use of the metric system in obtaining all measurement data.

The best way to promote students' critical and logical thinking abilities is to allow them to gather their own data and observations for interpretation. It also gives them experience with using appropriate tools, resources, and technology of science that will lead to accurate organization and analysis of data. The students will be able to experience and practice science skills by verifying their findings, basing findings on evidence, and analyzing sources of error. Having students collect and report their own data also brings the teacher opportunities to discuss scientific ethics with students.

In explaining data collection procedures and display of findings to English language learners, the teacher needs to demonstrate and provide a model of what the final results should look like. In using inquiry, students work in groups, which is particularly helpful for second language learners as they interpret and exchange ideas about data and scientific reasoning.

When students complete their experiments, teachers need to engage them in the process of analyzing their own, and other groups' data for similarities, differences, and variations including error. This occurs in the concept invention or "explain" phase of the learning cycle and 5-E model, and again in any application or "elaborate" activities in which data has been collected. After data

Table 6-4. The 5-E Model of Instruction

5-E Definition	Teacher Behavior	Student Behavior
Engage		
• Generate interest • Access prior knowledge • Connect to past knowledge • Set parameters of the focus • Frame the idea	• Motivates • Creates interest • Taps into what students know or think about the topic • Raises questions and encourages responses	• Attentive in listening • Asks questions • Demonstrates interest in the lesson • Responds to questions demonstrating their own entry point of understanding
Explore		
• Experience key concepts • Discover new skills • Probe, inquire, and question experiences • Examine their thinking • Establish relationships and understanding	• Acts as a facilitator • Observes and listens to students as they interact • Asks good inquiry-oriented questions • Provides time for students to think and to reflect • Encourages cooperative learning	• Conducts activities, predicts, and forms hypotheses or makes generalizations • Becomes a good listener • Shares ideas and suspends judgment • Records observations and/or generalizations • Discusses tentative alternatives
Explain		
• Connect prior knowledge and background to new discoveries • Communicate new understandings • Connect informal language to formal language	• Encourages students to explain their observations and findings in their own words • Provides definitions, new words, and explanations • Listens and builds upon discussion from students • Asks for clarification and justification • Accepts all reasonable responses	• Explains, listens, defines, and questions • Uses previous observations and findings • Provides reasonable responses to questions • Interacts in a positive, supportive manner

Extend/Elaborate		
• Apply new learning to a new or similar situation • Extend and explain concept being explored • Communicate new understanding with formal language	• Uses previously learned information as a vehicle to enhance additional learning • Encourages students to apply or extend the new concepts and skills • Encourages students to use terms and definitions previously acquired	• Applies new terms and definitions • Uses previous information to probe, ask questions, and make reasonable judgments • Provides reasonable conclusions and solutions • Records observations, explanations, and solutions
Evaluate		
• Assess understanding (Self, peer and teacher evaluation) • Demonstrate understanding of new concept by observation or open-ended response • Apply within problem situation • Show evidence of accomplishment	• Observes student behaviors as they explore and apply new concepts and skills • Assesses students' knowledge and skills • Encourages students to assess their own learning • Asks open-ended questions	• Demonstrates an understanding or knowledge of concepts and skills • Evaluates his/her own progress • Answers open-ended questions • Provides reasonable responses and explanations to events or phenomena

Based on the 5-E Instructional Model presented by Dr. Jim Barufaldi at the Eisenhower Science Collaborative Conference in Austin, Texas, July 2002.

has been collected from students' explorations, they display their data in charts and graphs, for example, and communicate their observations and, ultimately, concept statements to the class by posting them on the board and/or through an oral presentation. The data helps them develop conclusions and form new research questions or hypotheses as they evaluate their findings, setting the foundation for new explorations. Students should be able to present pertinent data by using graphic representations, and communicate their findings in written and oral forms to their peers.

In using scientific inquiry as in the learning cycle and 5-E model, scientific vocabulary is introduced *after* students have had hands-on experiences in the (engage and) exploration phase *and* have used their observations and data to construct meaning from their experiences in the *concept invention* or "explain" phase. Once students have had the hands-on direct experience with the concept, and have stated the meaning of their observations, the scientific vocabulary or terms that label the concept can be introduced by the teacher. In the application or elaborate phase, the teacher and students use the new vocabulary in extended experimentation, discussion, readings, writing, and other learning activities. Introducing terms after students have directly experienced the science inquiry and constructed meaning from their experiences by making a concept statement is especially important for second language learners in facilitating the development of understanding of science concepts. For all students, but especially for second language learners, this helps them understand concepts when terms are later *re-introduced*. By giving students the experience—something they *do*—and then allowing them to form meaning from their experience in ways that make sense to them, then when the term that labels what they learned is introduced, they are able to link it to prior knowledge and learning experiences in their minds. The terms are now able to build their background knowledge, which is critical for second language learners to understand the language of science. Making a connection between the hands-on activities and scientific vocabulary is beneficial to all students but especially to English language learners (ELLs), who can link the actions with the appropriate concept and vocabulary words without engaging in translations.

Promoting Logical Thinking and Scientific Reasoning

Interpreting results is one of the most challenging phases of scientific inquiry for children in EC-6. Students can easily discuss the observable results but might have difficulty interpreting their meaning. Teachers have to use developmentally appropriate practices to guide students to make extrapolations and infer information from the data, which involves the teachers' use of questioning.

Questioning

The use of good questions by the teacher is critical to promoting logical thinking and scientific reasoning among students. Good questioning causes students to reflect upon the logic of their data and observations with confidence and also identify possible misinformation or misunderstanding of important concepts. Through good questioning, students learn to carefully analyze their findings and prepared with experimental evidence, they can effectively use scientific argumentation and respond to questions and challenges to their findings in order to support their conclusions. In teaching science, probing questions are most effective. Probing questions are framed in a way that asks students to reveal their thinking and explain their rationale for conclusions they may draw from their experiences. Probing questions may be simple, such as "what do you think?" and "why do you think that may be true?" as examples. Overall, it is vital for teachers to use good questioning to reveal student learning and assess their progress in forming sound scientific frameworks of understanding. Questioning is clearly the hallmark of science inquiry and should be used throughout inquiry instruction. In the learning cycle/5-E model, questioning must be designed to lead students toward being able to state the concept, so it is especially critical in the concept invention or "explain" phase.

Teachers can guide students at various levels of development to observe events; and through questioning, teachers can help students develop higher-order thinking skills. For example, a teacher can lead children to make predictions while conducting experiments with objects that float or sink in water. By asking students to predict and explain why an object might sink or float, the teacher is leading students to analyze the properties of the object and the water to make an evaluative decision; that is, the children are using analysis and evaluation to complete that simple task. The following guide will help teachers best promote and elevate logical thinking abilities among students.

Taxonomy of the Cognitive Domain

Use key questioning terms aimed at the full range of the cognitive domain. (Bloom & Krathwohl, 1956; Anderson & Krathwohl, 2001).

LEVEL 1: Knowledge

Recall factual information on command.

Examples

List the five Kingdoms.

Label the parts of the cell in the diagram provided.

Write the formula for density.

LEVEL 2: Comprehension

Communicate an idea in a different form.

Examples

Explain heat transfer through conduction.

Restate what a habitat is in your own words.

Submit a definition of photosynthesis in your own words.

LEVEL 3: Application

Use what is known to find new solutions or apply in new situations.

Examples

Relate the concept of convection to lake turnover.

Utilize your understanding of burning to explain why sand works to put out a fire.

Making use of the clothes you are wearing, how can you stay afloat for several hours?

LEVEL 4: Analysis

Break things and ideas down into component parts and find their unique characteristics.

Examples

Examine blueprints of the electrical circuitry of your school building and explain how it works to bring electricity to your laboratory station.

Study the diagram of human digestion and *reason* what the organ marked #7 might be and explain its function.

Using the given laboratory materials, *deduce* the identities of the substances labeled "A," "B," and "C."

LEVEL 5: Synthesis

Use what is known to think creatively and divergently; make something new or original; pattern ideas or things in a new way.

Examples

Create a burglar alarm system for the classroom.

Build a telescope for classroom use.

Develop a plan for cleaning the pollutants in the Trinity River.

LEVEL 6: Evaluation

A. Use what is known to make judgments and ratings; accept or reject ideas; determine the worthiness of an idea or thing.

Examples

Decide whether you agree with the production of more nuclear power plants and provide justification for your decision.

Make a ruling you would give to car manufacturers on global warming and provide support for your ruling.

Rank the top five greatest discoveries in scientific history and *explain* why you have chosen those discoveries and ranked them the way you did.

B.   Avoid yes/no questions (unless part of a game) and questions with obvious answers.

Examples

Showing a picture of a cell
Not so good

Is this a cell?
Better

What is this structure and how do you know?
(Students watching a chemical reaction in which the solution turns blue)
Not so good

Did it turn blue?
Better

What happened? What did you observe? Why did this happen?

C.   Use questions beginning with the words *Why, How, What, Where,* and *When* that probe students' thinking.

Examples

How do you know? Why do you think that?

Where did you see a change?

What is your explanation for this observation? When did you notice the change occur?

What do you think?

COMPETENCY 003: IMPACT ON SCIENCE

The teacher understands how science impacts the daily lives of students and interacts with and influences personal and societal decisions.

Science in Daily Life

Students need to be aware of how science is present and plays a role in their daily lives. The functioning of their bodies, the natural environment that is around them, and their everyday use of electrical appliances, bicycles, computers, and cell phones are examples of biological and physical science in their lives. However, students tend to keep the science they learn in school separate from the science they experience in everyday life! It is important that teachers help students connect the science they are learning in school to the world around them to broaden their understandings and promote the usefulness, value, and applicability of science. In the learning cycle and 5-E models, the best time to help students make these connections is in the application/elaboration phase. After students have experienced a hands-on lab activity and constructed an understanding of the concept, the teacher should help them relate that new concept to their everyday lives and see how the concept works in differing contexts. Connecting newly-learned concepts to the students' life experiences makes the learning more meaningful for students and helps them retain understanding of the concept for later use. Relating science to what students already know and experience in life helps bridge the disconnections between "school science" and science they observe and experience in everyday life.

Science has brought society many advantages that have served to increase the health and longevity of humans, and to improve the quality of life for all. However, there may be consequences, often unforeseen, to scientific discovery and invention that impacts society and the natural environment, as well as the habitats and survival of the living organisms that share this planet. To better understand these issues, students need to gain scientific knowledge and evidence of what is known. Armed with appropriate background knowledge, students will be in the position to weigh the pros and cons of various scientific discoveries and debate issues that prevail in our global community. Students should be apprised of issues such as global warming, for example, but before taking a position on the topic, they must be prepared with accurate scientific information on the topic. When students are given opportunities to use scientific concepts as support for sound logic and reasoning to debate or evaluate a scientific issue, they are operating at a high cognitive level important to their intellectual development. Equally important is student awareness of the ethical, personal, societal, and economic implications of science, from both positive and negative perspectives. Students need to realize the trade-offs often present in scientific discovery and experimentation—for example, laboratory testing on animals. Many new and important discoveries have improved the quality of life at the cost of animals' lives. In order to best understand the complexity of how science interfaces with personal and societal issues, students need to be engaged in electronic and library research on impactful science topics and in discussion with peers and experts in the science fields. Topics such as cloning, global warming, alternative and fossil fuels, and acid rain are just a few additional topics tied to ethical, personal, societal, and economic concerns. It is important that students fully understand the scientific knowledge that underlies all such complex issues, and can formulate decisions based on the related knowledge.

Energy as a source of fuel and electricity is a major issue threatening the economic, environmental, and personal status of living in the U.S. and global society. It is important to be able to identify and know about fossil fuels, their origin, how they are obtained, and how they are used for energy consumption. These fossil fuels include coal, oil, and natural gas. These fossil fuels are nonrenewable and will one day be expended. Therefore, science must continue to develop and improve upon alternative sources of energy such as wind, hydroelectric, solar, and geothermal. Teachers must be able to identify and understand these other sources of energy and be able to guide students toward understanding how these alternative, renewable energy sources are used and how they impact our society's energy needs.

A significant impact of science on daily life relates to student fitness and health.

Childhood obesity is a serious problem in the U.S., and teachers can play an important role in educating children on the negative health issues associated with poor nutrition and a lack of exercise. Students need to learn about factors that impact physical and psychological health and about how to make good choices on such factors, including nutrition, hygiene, physical exercise, smoking, drugs, and alcohol. Understanding human biology, therefore, is important for students to realize how obesity and other factors such as substance use/abuse affect their physical and mental health. The topics of heart disease, diabetes, and cancer should be included in the curriculum as ways to help students understand the detrimental effects of unhealthy life choices.

COMPETENCY 004: CONCEPTS AND PROCESSES

The teacher knows and understands the unifying concepts and processes that are common to all sciences.

Explanatory Framework across Science Disciplines

Science is a way of knowing, a process—it is a systematic way of looking at the world and how it works. This competency focuses on how science uses a regular, consistent method of collecting and reporting data about scientific phenomena. Science is a way of organizing observations and then seeking patterns and regularity in order to make sense of the world. In science we organize evidence, create models, and explain observations in a logical form. We make predictions and hypotheses and test our predictions and hypotheses through controlled experimentation, meaning all variables of the experiment remain constant except for the variable being tested. We repeat experiments multiple times and seek constancy in our laboratory findings and in real life experiences in both form and/or function. Repeating experiments many times increases reliability of the findings. Reliability is established when the same or closely similar findings occur each time the experiment is repeated. Consistent findings from repeated experiments provide strong support for conclusions made. These patterns and consistencies in our observations and data are important for constructing evidence-based explanations and making new predictions.

Science embraces a broad spectrum of subject matter, such as life science, physical science, and earth science, all of which is interrelated. For example, in studying the ecosystem, teachers must understand the biological aspects (e.g., the living organism) and how they interact, as in predator–prey relationships and symbiotic relationships (e.g., parasitism, commensalism), as well as the chemical aspects of the ecosystem (e.g., nitrogen cycle), the geologic or earth science aspects (e.g., the landscape, the water, and the climate) and the physics aspects (e.g., energy transfer, motion). Ecosystems, for example, regardless of location on earth, share unifying components and characteristics, and teachers must understand this unity. In life science, there is unity of what makes organisms "living"—they all must carry on life functions and are composed of one or more cells. These are the criteria that unify life forms and classify something like a virus, for example, as non-living (it does not carry on the life functions and is not composed of cells).

All scientific observations can be described by their characteristics or "properties." These properties organize the observations according to commonalities, or classification. Observed properties and patterns are centered on space, time, energy, and matter.

Scientific Models

Models are representations of the natural world and universe in order to help better understand how something appears, its form and/or its function. For example, we may make models of the solar system, cells, or an atom to help us better explain its form and function and interactivity with other structures. Such models can be helpful to us in understanding the actual concept the model represents, and scientists often make models for this purpose. However, it is important to understand that, although it represents the actual science phenomena or concept and provides explanatory power, it is not the same as the actual science concept and is limited. Models in science may be physical, as in a physical model of a cell; conceptual, as in a concept map or an analogy; and/or mathematical as in a formula showing relationships, such as $d = m/v$ (formula for density).

COMPETENCY 005: STUDENTS AS LEARNERS AND SCIENCE INSTRUCTION

The teacher has theoretical and practical knowledge about teaching science and about how students learn science.

Developmentally Appropriate Practices

Exposing children to scientific inquiry can begin as early as age three or four. However, teachers must be aware of the stages of cognitive, social, and emotional development of children to appropriately introduce children to science concepts. For example, observing and experimenting with water and colors can easily be done by three- or four-year-olds, but using microscopes to observe and analyze animal or vegetable cells might be more appropriate for children in third and fourth grades. Students in EC-6 need direct experiences in order to understand concepts. According to Piaget (1964), children are transitioning through stages of development that require direct involvement to make sense of their experience. The model of teaching described earlier, the learning cycle and 5-E model, are based upon promoting the intellectual development of children. Thus, these models of teaching were designed to be consistent with the nature of science—and importantly, to match how children naturally learn (Marek and Cavallo, 1997; Renner and Marek, 1990). It is important that teachers understand the theory and research that underlie such models, as well as know how to use these models in teaching.

Misconceptions or alternative conceptions are a pervasive problem in science teaching and learning. Children tend to view the world from their own perspectives and draw conclusions based on their limited experiences. Once misconceptions are established in learners' minds, they are difficult to change. Therefore, teaching needs to allow children the opportunity for direct experience and collecting evidence. Teaching science also must begin with the teacher understanding what the students already know, and incorporate the students' every day experiences. Learning this information from students will guide instructional planning, toward designing culturally relevant, meaningful learning experiences for the students. The learning cycle has been established as a teaching model that allows teachers to learn the students' prior knowledge, promotes conceptual change, helps students resolve misconceptions, and leads to more scientifically accurate and meaningful understandings (Sandoval, 1995).

Teachers need to begin lessons with direct, concrete activities giving students experience with objects. After conceptual understandings are established in learners, then teachers can move them from the concrete to more abstract reasoning. For example, in learning the concept of density, it is important that students have objects to touch, feel, weigh (take the mass of) and measure first, as in the exploration phase of the learning cycle. From direct experience with the objects, students should construct the concept that "a certain amount of matter (mass) is packed into a given amount of space (volume)." The term that labels this concept is "density." As application, teachers help students develop their abstract-thinking abilities by having them solve problems using the formula for density, $d=m/v$. Teachers need to select instruction appropriately such that concrete experiences are used first, leading the students to later use abstract reasoning. Teachers need to select learning experiences that will promote the students scientific knowledge, skills, and use of inquiry. Further, the students are able to use the prior knowledge they have formed about density to learn more extended, related concepts such as buoyancy. This example demonstrates the instructional knowledge and skills teachers need to have to prepare the best possible science learning experiences for students. The learning cycle or 5-E model are consistent with the goals of this competency.

Science for all has long been the theme of science education's guiding documents such as Project 2061, a long-term initiative of the American Association for the Advancement of Science created in 1989, and the National Science Education Standards, published by the National Research Council in 1996. *Science for all* means that teachers need to help their students abandon stereotypes they may hold of science and scientists. For example, that science is a male-dominated profession. Teachers should help students to more appropriately view science as a field for males and females and for all cultures and ethnicities. To accomplish this goal, teachers need to be aware of their own potential, often not intentional, bias toward science and scientists that may be exclusionary. For example, teachers need to be aware of utilizing both, or alternating between "he" and "she" in examples. If discussing astronauts and doctors, for example, teachers (owing to misleading stereotypes) tend to inadvertently refer to them as "he," whereas nurses and teachers are often only referred to as "she." Teachers need to be aware of any possible gender-biased habits and regularly change the gender they may attribute to stereotypically male or female careers to the opposite gender. Likewise in using names in teaching examples given to students or in word problems. Teachers need to use names common in a variety of cultures to broaden the perception of who may be a scientist.

Teachers should design instruction to allow students of different cultures, genders, and ethnicities to work together in mixed collaborative groups. Doing so allows students to share experiences that will help broaden their understanding of differing perspectives. Vocabulary in science is particularly difficult and new to students, and should only be introduced after students have had direct laboratory experiences with particular concepts that they can later label with science terminology. This process is beneficial to English language learners because it allows them to have a physical experience of the concept before learning its scientific label. Posters of scientists displayed in the room should represent male and female scientists of diverse ethnicities and cultures while also showing the many distinct fields of science, such as environmental science, veterinary medicine, geology, engineering, and architecture, as well as the more traditionally represented physics and chemistry. Likewise, discussions of science and scientific discovery should include contributions from a diverse range of scientists. Using these measures will broaden the students' views of "who can be a scientist," with the goal that they see *themselves* as scientists. In laboratory activities it is important that all group members have the opportunity to handle the materials and perform the experiment, and that the same students are not relegated to note-taking. Varying laboratory responsibilities can be accomplished by assigning group members roles to perform when they are conducting a laboratory activity. Such roles may include materials collector, record keeper, reporter, and lab facilitator. Be sure to rotate these roles from one laboratory activity to the next to ensure all students have an opportunity to work in the various roles.

COMPETENCY 006: SCIENCE ASSESSMENT

The teacher knows the varied and appropriate assessments and assessment practices for monitoring science learning in laboratory, field and classroom settings.

Measuring Student Learning

Teaching cannot occur without student *learning*, and in order to determine that learning is occurring, student progress needs to be assessed on a regular basis. Assessment of learning should occur on some scale, large or small, every class day, and as students move through the learning of concepts, as in the learning cycle and 5-E models. Measuring learning as it is occurring is "authentic assessment" and allows teachers to adjust the instruction according to student learning and potential difficulties in learning. Alternative assessment methods, in addition to the more traditional testing formats (e.g., multiple-choice) should be used to obtain a full picture of what students know and do not know or can and cannot do. Alternative assessments include techniques such as verbal reports, laboratory practical exams, story writing, developing advertisements or brochures, constructing a concept map, writing essays, creating drawings or models, and developing a play or skit. In each assessment, the concepts to be learned are represented in alternative ways—yet clearly communicate what students have learned and understand.

It is essential that teachers monitor and assess students' understanding of concepts and skills on a regular, consistent basis and use this information to adjust instruction. The results of frequent informal and formal/traditional and alternative assessments should be used as a tool for planning subsequent instruction. Teachers must communicate progress to students so they can learn to self-monitor their own learning and understand what is needed to achieve learning goals.

Assessing the Science Curriculum

As part of the accountability system, Texas has a comprehensive assessment system to measure the state uniform curriculum—the Texas Essential Knowledge and Skills (TEKS). In this system, students take the State of Texas Assessments of Academic Readiness (STAAR) test in grades 3 through 12. However, the science component of TEKS is assessed only in grades 5, 8, and 10. The fifth-grade science test is available in Spanish; thus, Spanish-speaking ELLs can take the test in Spanish. In addition to the required science STAAR examinations, students are assessed through teacher- and district-developed tests in kindergarten through grade 12.

COMPETENCY 007: FORCES AND MOTION

The teacher understands forces and motion and their relationships.

The key universal forces included in this section are gravity, electricity, and magnetism.

Magnetism and Gravity

Magnetism is the force of attraction or repulsion between objects that results from the positive and negative ionic charges of the objects. Usually, the objects are metals, such as iron, nickel, and cobalt. Magnets have two poles that have opposing charges or forces: north (+) and south (−). When the north pole of a magnet is placed close to the north pole of a second magnet, repulsion occurs. When poles of different kinds (north and south) are placed in close proximity, they attract one another. The strength of the forces depends on the size and the proximity of the magnets. The charged area around a magnet is called a magnetic field. The Earth is like a large magnet, with opposing forces—the North Pole and South Pole, and the magnetic field of attraction of Earth. We know that magnetic field as gravity. Without gravity, all objects on Earth, including the atmosphere, would not be held onto its surface. Planets and other celestial objects that are more massive than Earth, such as Jupiter, have stronger gravitational forces, and those that are less massive and/or dense, such as our Moon, have weaker gravitational forces.

Force and Motion

Force is defined as the action of moving an object by pulling or pushing it. Force can cause an object to move at a constant speed or to accelerate. When force is applied over a distance, work is done. **Work** is the product of the force acting in the direction of movement and causing displacement. **Energy** is defined as the ability to do work; when a tow truck uses force to pull a car and move it to a different location, energy is used and work is accomplished. Newton's laws of motion are important to understand in mastering this competency. Newton's first law is that an object at rest will remain at rest unless acted upon by an (unbalanced) force, and an object in motion will continue to stay in motion with the same speed and in the same direction unless acted upon by an (unbalanced) outside force. This first law is also called *inertia*. Newton's second law is that acceleration is produced when a force acts on mass and the greater the mass of the object being accelerated, the greater the amount of force needed to accelerate that object. Newton's third law of motion is that for every action there is an equal and opposite reaction (see *http://teachertech.rice. edu/Participants/louviere/Newton/*).

Force and motion, as well as changes in motion, may be measured through hands-on activities in which variables such as time, speed, distance, and direction can be recorded and graphed, and teachers need to know how to do so. For example, teachers can have students experience and record what happens when an object with higher mass (such as a large marble or ball bearing), collides with an object with less mass (e.g., a small marble or ball bearing). Teachers should also know what happens when the rate of speed is high when the objects collide compared to when the rate of speed is low. The game of pool or billiards is a good example. When forces are unbalanced, it may cause the object to change its motion or position.

Relationships between Force and Motion: Machines, Space, and Geologic Processes

A machine is something that makes work easier. Machines can be as simple as a wedge or a screw or as sophisticated as a computer or gas engine. A **simple machine** has few or no moving parts and can change the size and direction of a force. A screw, hammer, wedge, and incline plane are examples of simple machines. Simple machines are part of our daily activities. For example, children playing on a seesaw are using a simple machine called a **lever**. Thus, teachers and their students should know the practical use of these simple machines in everyday life. A **complex machine** is two or more simple machines working together to facilitate work. Some of the complex machines used in daily activities are a wheelbarrow, a can opener, and a bicycle.

Force and motion is what keeps the Sun, Earth, Moon, and planets in their orbits and explains the structure and changes of the universe. On Earth, force and motion are found in all geologic processes, explaining phenomena such as tides and tsunamis.

COMPETENCY 008: PHYSICAL AND CHEMICAL PROPERTIES

The teacher understands the physical and chemical properties of and changes in matter.

Matter

Matter is anything that takes up space and has mass. The **mass** of a body is the amount of matter in an object or thing; **volume** describes the amount of space that matter takes up. Mass is also the property of a body that causes it to have weight. **Weight** is the amount of gravitational force exerted over an object. It is important not to confuse mass and weight. What students are measuring on their balances in the laboratory is an object's *mass*. Weight changes as an object goes from one level of gravitational force to another, for example, from Earth to the Moon, because the amount of "pull" on that object is different; but the mass of the object—how much matter or material is in the object—does not change unless we do something to actually take away or add matter to that object.

There are 118 basic kinds of matter, called **elements**, which are organized into the **periodic table**. An element is composed of sub-microscopic components called **atoms**. An element is made up of one kind of atom as listed on the periodic table. For example, Fe is the element iron, and if you had an item composed of iron, it would be composed of only iron (Fe) atoms. Atoms are made up of particles called **electrons**, **neutrons**, and **protons**. The mass of the atom is located mostly in the nucleus, which is made up of protons and neutrons. The electron contains little mass and follows an orbit around the nucleus. **Molecules** are two or more atoms bonded together in a chemical bond. The atoms of a molecule can be more than one of the same *kind* of atom, as in the naturally occurring oxygen molecule, O_2, or a molecule can be two or more different atoms as in carbon dioxide, CO_2, ammonia, NH_3, and glucose, $C_6H_{12}O_6$. **Compounds** are when you have two or more *different* kinds of atoms in the molecule and you have a given amount of that substance. In other words, compounds consist of matter composed of atoms that are chemically combined with one another in molecules in definite weight proportions. An example of a compound is water; water is oxygen and hydrogen combined in the ratio of two hydrogen molecules to one molecule of oxygen H_2O. So, you can also call it *one* H_2O a molecule.

Properties of Matter

Matter has physical, thermal, electrical, and chemical properties. These properties are dependent upon the molecular composition of the matter.

Physical Properties

The physical properties of matter are the way matter looks and feels. It includes qualities like color, density, hardness, and conductivity. **Color** represents how matter is reflected or perceived by the human eye. **Density** is the mass that is contained in a unit of volume of a given substance; it is a measure of how much *matter* is packed into a certain *amount of space*, or mass divided by volume (D=M/V). **Hardness** represents the resistance to penetration offered by a given substance. **Conductivity** is the ability of substances to transmit thermal or electric current.

Thermal Properties

Matter is sensitive to temperature changes. Heat and cold produce changes in the physical properties of matter; however, the chemical properties remain unchanged. For example, when water is exposed to cold temperature (release of heat), it changes from liquid to solid; and when water is exposed to heat, it changes from solid to liquid. With continued heat, the water changes from liquid to gas (water vapor). Water vapor can be cooled again and turned back into liquid. However, through all these states, water retains its chemical properties—two molecules of hydrogen and one molecule of oxygen or H_2O.

Electrical Properties

Matter can be classified as a conductor or nonconductor of electricity. Conductive matter allows the transfer of electric current or heat from one point to another. Metals are usually good conductors, while wood and rocks are examples of nonconductive matter.

Chemical Properties

The chemical properties of one type of matter (element) can react with the chemical properties of other types of matter. In general, elements from the same groups will not react with each other, while elements from different groups may. The more separated the groups, the more likely they will cause a chemical reaction when brought together. A type of matter can be chemically altered to become a different type of matter; for example, a metal trash will rust if left out in the rain.

States of Matter

Matter can exist in four distinct states: solid, liquid, gas, and plasma. Most people are familiar with the basic states of matter, but they might not be familiar with the fourth one, plasma. Plasmas are formed at extremely high temperatures when electrons are stripped from neutral atoms (University of California, 2006). Stars are predominantly composed of plasmas. Solids have mass, occupy a define amount of space or *volume* or have a definite shape, and are more dense than liquids. Liquids have mass, occupy a definite volume, do not have a definite shape, but instead take the shape of their container. Gases have mass, do not have a definite volume, have no definite shape but take the shape of their container, and are the least dense of the three states of matter. Plasma has no definite shape or volume, and is a substance that cannot be classified as a solid, liquid, or gas. When substances change from one state of matter to another, such as ice melting, it is a physical change, and not a chemical change.

Mixtures and Solutions

Mixtures are combinations of two or more substances, where each substance is distinct from the other; that is, made up of two or more types of molecules and not chemically combined. The two substances in the mixture may or may not be evenly distributed, so there are no definite amounts or weight proportions. Mixtures may be *heterogeneous*, which means an uneven distribution of the substances in the mixture throughout. A mixture may be *homogeneous,* which means the components are evenly distributed throughout. Examples of mixtures include milk, which is a heterogeneous mixture of water and butterfat particles. The components of a mixture can be separated physically. For example, milk producers and manufacturers remove the butterfat from whole milk to make skim milk.

Solutions are *mixtures* that are *homogeneous*, which means that the components are distributed evenly and there is an even concentration throughout. The solute is the substance in the smaller amount that dissolves and that you add into the substance that is in the larger amount—the solvent. Water is a common solvent. Solids, liquids, and gases can be solutes. Examples of solutions are seawater and ammonia. Seawater is made up of water and salt, and ammonia is made up of ammonia gas and water. In these examples, the salt and the ammonia (NH_3) are the solutes; water is the solvent.

Physical and Chemical Changes in Matter

A **physical change** is a change in a substance that does not change what that substance is made of. Examples of physical changes are melting ice (boiling water), tearing paper, chopping wood, writing with chalk and mixing sugar and water together. In the mixing of sugar with water, or salt with water, even though the sugar or salt may not be visible to the naked eye in the water, it is still there and still has the same composition—that is, the molecules that make up the sugar or salt and water are still the same as when you mixed them. You can evaporate the water and you will recover your sugar or salt crystals.

A **chemical change** is when the substances that were combined are no longer the same molecules—they have changed to new substances. For example, burning wood, mixing baking soda and vinegar, or a rusting nail, which is when the iron of the nail (Fe) combines with oxygen (in the presence of water) to form a new substance—that is, a new molecule is formed, iron oxide Fe_2O_3.

Physical changes can be reversed, whereas chemical changes generally cannot be reversed. Evidence of a chemical change includes that the combination of the substances gives off a gas (bubbles are observed), it changes color (change of color alone does not always indicate a chemical change, but may signify a chemical change if the other evidences are also present), gives off heat and becomes warmer, or absorbs heat and becomes colder (temperature change), and forms a precipitate (a solid substance). When heat is given off in a chemical change, it is an **exothermic** reaction; and when heat is absorbed in a chemical change (the combination becomes colder), it is an **endothermic** reaction. Everyday examples of exothermic reactions are firewood burning or the use of a hand warmer that many mountain climbers and snow skiers use, and examples of endothermic reactions are a cold pack used in sports injuries or the combination of baking soda and vinegar (try it with a thermometer in the vinegar during the reaction and see!).

Chemical Reactions in Everyday Life

Chemical reactions occur in everyday life and are an essential part of our physical and biological world. The burning of gasoline in automobiles is a chemical change—and burning of any kind for that matter. Burning is the combination of oxygen from the atmosphere with substances containing the carbon atom. The proper temperature has to be reached in order to begin this exothermic reaction, but once started, the chemical reaction can continue until the oxygen is used up or is prevented from entering into the reaction. When oxygen comes in contact with carbon substances at the right temperature or "activation energy" to produce a reaction, the chemical reaction we see is burning, and the reaction itself gives off heat (exothermic). So since gasoline is a fossil fuel (a once living organism), it contains carbon. When we provide the energy it needs to begin the reaction (activation energy), as long as oxygen is present, the carbon substance will burn. Burning is a chemical reaction because the carbon and oxygen combine to form new substances such as carbon monoxide (CO) and carbon dioxide (CO_2). The same reaction occurs in burning wood, candles, and even in cell respiration—the oxygen we breathe and carry through our bloodstream is combined in our cells with carbon-containing glucose molecules in a type of "controlled" burning. Our bodies give off heat from this reaction, which is why we are able to maintain a fairly high temperature of about 98.6 degrees Fahrenheit. Other examples of chemical reactions in everyday life include chemical batteries, the digestion of food, and cooking/baking. Moreover, the process of photosynthesis, where plants use sunlight to convert carbon dioxide gas and water into food for the plant known as glucose (a simple sugar), is also an important chemical reaction responsible for providing food for and sustaining all life on Earth.

COMPETENCY 009: ENERGY AND INTERACTIONS

The teacher understands energy and interactions between matter and energy.

Principles of Energy

Energy is available in many forms, including heat, light, solar radiation, chemical, electrical, magnetic, sound, and mechanical energy. It exists in three states: potential, kinetic, and activation energies. An object possessing energy because of its ability to move has **kinetic energy**. The energy that an object has as the result of its position or condition is called **potential energy**. The energy necessary to transfer or convert potential energy into kinetic energy is called **activation energy**. All three states of energy can be transformed from one to the other. A vehicle parked in a garage has potential energy. When the driver starts the engine using the chemical energy stored in the battery and the fuel, potential energy becomes activation energy. Once the vehicle is moving, the energy changes to kinetic energy. An object with high potential energy will produce high kinetic energy once it is transformed and releases this potential energy (as kinetic energy). For example, a small fire cracker has lower potential or stored energy compared to professional fireworks. This is evidenced by the amount of kinetic or released energy when it is fired off. A bicycle with its rider has more potential energy at the top of an incline than it does on a flat surface. When potential energy of the bicycle on the incline is transformed to kinetic (riding down the hill) it will have more energy released compared to the bicycle on the flat surface.

Heat and Temperature

Heat is a form of energy. Temperature is the measure of heat. The most common device used to measure temperature is the thermometer. Thermometers use heat-sensitive substances—mercury and alcohol—that expand when heated.

Heat and Light

The most common form of energy comes from the Sun. Solar energy provides heat and light for animals and plants. Through **photosynthesis**, plants capture radiant energy from the Sun and transform it into **chemical energy** in the form of glucose. This chemical energy is stored in the leaves, stems, and fruits of plants. Humans and animals consume the plants or fruits and get the energy they need for survival. This energy source is transformed again to create kinetic energy and body heat. **Kinetic energy** is used for movement and to do work, while **heat** is a required element for all warm-blooded animals, like humans. Cold-blooded animals also require heat, but rather than making it themselves through the transformation of plant sugar, they use solar energy to heat their body. Energy transformation constitutes the foundation and the driving force of an ecosystem. In addition to heat and solar radiation, energy is available in the forms of electricity and magnetism.

Heat Transfer

The transfer of heat is accomplished in three ways: conduction, radiation, and convection. **Conduction** is the process of transferring heat or electricity through a substance. Conduction occurs when heat makes the molecules move quickly; the heat is transferred from one molecule to the next and so on through the substance. Conduction occurs in solid materials, such as a metal spoon. It occurs when two objects of differing temperatures are placed in contact with each other and heat flows from the hotter object to the cooler object. A common example is leaving a spoon in a cup of hot tea. The spoon is cool, but the part in the hot tea is warmed. Eventually, the part of the spoon not itself in the hot tea will also become warm (the handle). The transfer of heat through the spoon is conduction. As another example, in the cooling system of a car, heat from the engine is transferred to the liquid coolant. When the coolant passes through the radiator, the heat transfers from the coolant to the radiator, and eventually, out of the car. This heat transfer system preserves the engine and allows it to continue working.

Radiation describes the energy that travels at high speed in empty space (that is, where there are no atoms or molecules) in the form of light or through the decay of radioactive elements. Radiation is part of our modern life. It exists in simple states as the energy emitted by microwaves, cellular phones, and sunshine or as potentially dangerous energy as X-ray machines and nuclear weapons. The radiation used in medicine, nuclear power, and nuclear weapons has enough energy to cause permanent damage and death.

Convection describes the flow of heat through the movement of liquid or gaseous matter from a hot region to a cool region. In its most basic form, the concept of convection is that warm air rises and cold air sinks, and warm liquid rises and cold liquid sinks. The colder air or liquid contracts and so is denser, thus it sinks; the warmer air spreads out or expands and so is less dense and rises. Thus, convection occurs when the heating of a substance changes the density of the substance. A good example is the heating of air over land near coastal areas coupled with the influx of cooler sea breezes offshore. The heated air inland expands and thus decreases in density, causing the cooler, more dense air to rush in to achieve equilibrium. The cold air moves underneath the warm air, causing the warm air that was over the land to rise, where it cools and sinks again. Typically the air was also holding moisture, and so a storm may occur as a result. A more common example of convection is the process of heating water on a stove. In this case, heat is transferred from the stove element to the bottom of the pot to the water. Heat is transferred from the hot water at the bottom to the cooler water at the top by convection. At the same time, the cooler, denser water at the top sinks to the bottom, where it is subsequently heated. This circulation creates the movement typical of boiling water. Convection currents created by the combining or colliding of cold and warm air masses is one factor responsible for storms and circular rotation of the air in tornados and hurricanes. Ocean currents are also caused by the collision of cold water and warm water masses in the oceans (Cavallo, 2001). See also: *http://www.physicstutorials.org/home/heat-temperature-and-thermal-expansion/heat-transfer-via-conduction-convection-and-radiation*.

Electricity and Magnetism

When you arrange an energy source, such as a battery, a wire, and a light bulb (or motor, or bell, or any electrical device) such that all *metal* parts are touching (metal is a good conductor of energy) in a *circle*—the bulb will light (the motor will run, the bell will ring, and so on). Arranging the items in this circle creates an "*electric circuit.*" The energy from the battery or other energy source is able to "flow" or be transferred through the metal wires and parts of the circuit. A **closed circuit** is when all metal parts are touching and the electrical charge is able to continue to be transferred through the circuit. A light switch or other "on button" closes the circuit and allows the electricity to flow. An **open circuit** is when there is a break someplace in the flow of electricity through the circuit. A switch or "off button" opens the circuit and stops the electricity flow. When you ring a door bell, you are closing the circuit or allowing all metal parts to touch and send electricity through it to make the bell ring; when you let go of the doorbell button, the circuit is open, and so the flow of electricity stops and so does the bell's ringing.

Lightning is a form of *static* electricity which means it is not "flowing" or being transferred in the way it is through a metal wire, but is caused by friction, much the same as walking across a carpet in socks and getting a shock when a metal doorknob is touched. In both kinds of electricity, the electrons in the atoms of the substance, which are negatively charged, are pulled away from their atom's nucleus, giving the object, or cloud, a negative charge. The negative charge is quickly attracted to a positive charge—in the case of lightning, that positive charge could be something (or someone!) on the ground. The positive charge quickly jumps toward the negative charge and the negative charge quickly jumps toward the positive charge, and a flash of lighting is seen and clap of thunder is heard; or in the case of the doorknob, a spark and a snap sound. Electric circuits are just a way to channel the electricity and the opposing charges through a conductor such as metal wires to allow us to use the energy to do work and to transform the energy into different forms such as sound (a radio), light (light bulbs), mechanical (machinery), and/or heat energy.

There is a difference between magnetic fields and electric fields. A field occurs around an object known as a magnet, which attracts and repels other magnetic objects. The strength of a magnet and its magnetic field is due to the material it is made of. In a magnet, as we mentioned, the particles (atoms, molecules) are lined up in the same direction (imagine a marching band), which creates the north and south "poles" of the magnet. Gravity is different in that its strength depends on the mass of the object (Earth, the Moon); however, the particles are still lined up in the same direction at any given time in history such to create a gravitational field with its north and south poles. The magnetic field on Earth is due to its iron core. The gravitational field surrounding Earth protects it from radiation that may bombard our planet from space, such as solar winds.

The current that moves through a wire in an electric circuit also acts like a magnet. It creates a negative and positive side to objects within the field, as in an **electromagnet.** A classroom electromagnet is created by attaching the ends of a wire to the positive and negative ends of a battery, and winding the wire on an iron nail. The nail will become an electromagnetic and be attracted to metal objects (e.g., paper clips). The more coils around the nail, the stronger the electromagnet. For more information see: *http://www.physics4kids.com/files/elec_magneticfield.html.*

Light Energy

Light energy, and all energy for that matter, travels in waves and in a straight-line path. The electromagnetic spectrum shows the different wavelengths and frequencies of energy, including the small portion that is visible light. The electromagnetic spectrum includes, for example, microwaves, X-rays, radio waves, infrared radiation, visible light waves, and ultraviolet radiation, all of which have different wavelengths and frequencies that distinguish one type of wave from another (See: *http://imagine.gsfc.nasa.gov/docs/science/know_l1/emspectrum.html* and *http://missionscience.nasa.gov/ems/01_intro.html*).

Visible light is the wavelength of light we can see, which our eyes see as white light. However, this white light is composed of a host of other wavelengths of light that our eyes cannot always distinguish, which we know as the visible light spectrum, or a rainbow. The colors of white light include red, orange, yellow, green, blue, indigo, and violet (although some sources now eliminate indigo as separate from violet), or ROYGBIV. When light, again, traveling in a straight line, hits an object or substance and is *bent*, it is called **refraction**. The bending of light waves may result in the colors of light in the spectrum becoming visible, as when we see a rainbow in the sky (the water molecules in the air bend the light) or when light travels through cut glass such as with a prism. **Reflection** is when light waves bounce back, as when looking in a mirror. The principles of reflection and refraction are used in periscopes and telescopes in order to be able to see objects we may otherwise not be able to see. They are often popular in magic shows when objects are said to "disappear." In actuality, the light of the object has been refracted or reflected to a place away from our eyes so that we can no longer see it.

Refraction is also used to our advantage through concave and convex lenses. Concave or convex lenses work such that when light passes through, the lenses change the focal point. The eye contains a lens, but when light passing through the eye cannot properly focus on the "screen" known as the retina, the object being viewed may be blurred. Concave or convex lenses are used in eyeglasses to adjust and correct the focal point. These lenses are also used in cameras, microscopes, and telescopes. A spoon is an example of both a concave and a convex lens—if you look into the concave side, you will see yourself upside down. If you look into the convex side of the spoon, you will see yourself right side up. This is due to refraction (and reflection of light). For more on this topic, see *http://www.myschoolhouse.com/courses/O/1/36.asp*.

Sound Energy

Sound also travels in waves. Sounds are caused by vibrations, such as a guitar string (or a rubber band), or banging on a drum or cymbal. Sound has a certain wavelength, frequency, pitch, and amplitude (loudness). Sound waves must travel through a medium, which may be solid, liquid, or gas. Sound travels best through solids because there are more molecules (particles) to vibrate, and least well through gases.

The types of sound waves are longitudinal and transverse. **Longitudinal waves** move parallel to the direction the wave moves, and **transverse waves** move perpendicular to the direction of the wave. For more information and animations on sound waves, see *http://www.acs.psu.edu/drussell/demos/waves/wavemotion.html*.

COMPETENCY 010: ENERGY TRANSFORMATIONS AND CONSERVATION

The teacher understands energy transformations and the conservation of matter and energy.

Electricity

Electricity is the flow of electrons or electric power or charge. The basic unit of charge is based on the positive charge of the proton and the negative charge of the electron. Energy occurs naturally in the atmosphere through light. However, it is not feasible to capture that type of energy. The electricity that we use comes from secondary sources because it is produced from the conversion of primary (natural) sources of energy like fossil fuels that are **nonrenewable** (natural gas, coal, and oil) and nuclear, and **renewable** resources such as wind and solar energy. All sources of energy are used to produce a common result—to turn a turbine that generates electricity (see: *http://www. energyquest.ca.gov/story/chapter06.html*). Electricity that is generated can then be sent through wires for human use, and can be transformed into other forms of energy, including sound, light, heat, and force.

Conservation of Energy

The main principle of energy conservation states that energy can change form but cannot totally disappear. For example, the stored energy in a battery can be used to turn on a flashlight. In this case, chemical energy stored in the battery (potential energy) is transformed into light energy being emitted from the bulb (kinetic energy). Another example of energy conservation is placing merchandise on shelves. Energy was used to do the work (placing merchandise on a shelf) and it was stored as potential energy. Potential energy in turn can be converted to kinetic energy when the merchandise is pushed back to the floor. In this case, work was recovered completely, but often the recovered energy is less than the energy used to do the work. This loss of energy can be caused by friction or any kind of resistance encountered in the process of doing the work. For example, as a vehicle's tires roll across the pavement, doing the work of moving forward, they encounter friction. This friction causes heat energy to be released, as well as kinetic energy.

In essence, energy cannot be created or destroyed, only changed in form. Likewise, matter cannot be created or destroyed, only changed in form. Thus, energy from the Sun is changed, for example, to chemical energy when plants use the energy to make glucose in photosynthesis. The energy from the Sun is stored in the chemical bonds of the glucose molecule and will be released for use by the organism—the plant itself, or any organism that eats the plant and its glucose—when the molecule's chemical bonds are "broken" by oxygen in cell respiration and/or stored in another chemical form known as ATP. Likewise, electrical energy comes from burning, or breaking the bond of carbon-based molecules as in fossil fuels. This electricity generated is then transformed to another form by first capturing and sending that electrical energy through metal wires originating at the power-generating plant, and sending it in a complete, closed circuit to homes, businesses, and industries. There the electrical energy may be transformed to sound, heat, light, and/or mechanical energy. In all cases, the energy is not lost, it is changed in form.

It is important to conserve matter and energy generated from fossil fuels as these are non-renewable sources and will one day be expended. It is also important to continue exploring alternative, renewable forms of energy and electricity generation to meet our society's energy demands and maintain our Earth's clean air and water supplies.

Key Principles of the Physical Science Competencies

- To help students develop higher-order thinking skills, teachers need to guide students to analyze research data and make extrapolations or inferences based on data analysis.

- Matter is anything that has mass and takes up space.

- Mass is the amount of matter something contains.

- Volume refers to the amount of space taken up by an object.

- The states of matter are solid, gas, liquid, and plasma.

- There are 118 basic kinds of matter called elements.

- Elements are made up of atoms. An atom is the smallest part of matter.

- A compound is a kind of matter made up of two or more elements. A chemical formula describes the kinds of elements present in a compound. The chemical formula of water is H_2O because it has two molecules of hydrogen and one molecule of oxygen.

- Physical properties of matter are the characteristics that can be seen or measured without changing the material.

- Chemical properties of matter are the characteristics that can only be seen when the material changes and new materials are formed; for example, wood burns and turns into ashes. A chemical property of wood is its ability to burn.

- Water boils at 212 degrees Fahrenheit or 100 degrees Celsius, and it freezes at 32 degrees Fahrenheit or 0 degrees Celsius.

- Weight is the amount of gravitational force exerted over an object.

- When measuring dry chemicals on a balance scale, teachers should follow these steps: (1) Place and weigh a watch glass or dish, (2) place the dry chemical inside the watch glass or dish, and (3) subtract the weight of the glass or dish from the total to obtain the real weight of the chemical.

- Energy and matter may be changed from one form to another but are not lost.

- Heat is transferred by conduction, convection, and radiation.

- Electric circuits may be open or closed.

- Potential energy is stored energy; kinetic energy is energy in motion or actively being used. Activation energy is the energy it takes to change potential energy into kinetic energy.

- Light travels in waves and in a straight line; light may be refracted or bent and/or reflected.

- Sound is caused by vibrations.

COMPETENCY 011: STRUCTURE AND FUNCTIONS OF LIVING THINGS

The teacher understands the structure and function of living things.

Structure and Function

All living things carry on life functions such as respiration, nutrition, response, circulation, growth, excretion, regulation, and reproduction, all of which characterize them as *living* as opposed to nonliving. In addition, all living things are composed of the basic unit of life known as *cells*. Organisms, as well as individual cells of an organism and single-celled organisms, carry on these life functions using specialized structures. For example, earthworms carry on respiration through their moist skin; plants excrete gases from tiny pores on the underside of leaves called stomata; a single-celled amoeba ingests food by use of a "false foot" or pseudopodia; and insects respond to chemical attractants, called pheromones, of the opposite-sex insect for mating.

Animal and Plant Cells

Animal and plant cells are similar in appearance. Animal cells contain mitochondria, small round or rod-shaped bodies found in the cytoplasm of most cells. The main function of mitochondria is to produce the enzymes for the metabolic conversion of food to energy. This process consumes oxygen and is termed **aerobic respiration**.

Plants cells contain mitochondria, which allows them to carry on respiration where they use oxygen (O_2) to burn glucose ($C_6H_{12}O_6$), and excrete carbon dioxide (CO_2) and water (H_2O) just like animals. However, plants also have specialized organelles called chloroplasts used for capturing sunlight and use this energy, along with CO_2 taken into leaves from the atmosphere and H_2O taken up from the roots, to make glucose ($C_6H_{12}O_6$), a simple sugar (food), and excrete O_2. (The $C_6H_{12}O_6$ is then burned by O_2 in respiration as already described.) Chloroplasts contain chlorophyll in the food-making process, called **photosynthesis**. Photosynthesis is the process by which chlorophyll-containing organisms convert light energy into chemical energy.

Cell System

The cell is the basic unit of living organisms and the simplest living unit of life. Living organisms are composed of cells that have the following common characteristics:

- Have a membrane that regulates the flow of nutrients and water that enter and exit the cell

- Contain the genetic material (DNA) that allows for reproduction

- Require a supply of energy

- Contain basic chemicals to make metabolic decisions for survival

- Reproduce and are the result of reproduction

Eukaryotic and Prokaryotic Cells

There are two kinds of cells—prokaryotic and eukaryotic. **Prokaryotic cells** are the simplest and most primitive type of cells. They do not contain the structures typical of eukaryotic cells. Prokaryotic cells lack a nucleus and instead have one strand of deoxyribonucleic acid (DNA). Some prokaryotic cells have external whip-like flagella for locomotion or a hair-like system for adhesion. Prokaryotic cells come in three shapes: cocci (round), bacilli (rods), and spirilla or spirochetes (helical cells). Bacteria (also called Monera) are prokaryotic cells. For more information and animated illustrations of prokaryotic cells see *www.cellsalive.com/cells/bactcell.htm*.

Eukaryotic cells evolved from prokaryotic cells and in the process became structurally and biochemically more complex. The key distinction between the two cell types is that only eukaryotic cells contain many structures, or organelles, separated from other cytoplasm components by a membrane. The organelles within eukaryotic cells are the nucleus, mitochondria, chloroplasts, and Golgi apparatus. The nucleus contains the deoxyribonucleic acid (DNA) information. The mitochondria have their own membrane and contain some DNA information and proteins. They generate the energy for the cell. The chloroplast is a component that exists in plants only, allowing them to trap sunlight as energy for the process of photosynthesis. The Golgi apparatus secretes substances needed for the cell's survival. For information and animations on eukaryotic cells, see *www.cellsalive.com/cells/3dcell.htm*.

Classifications of Living Things

Living things are divided into five groups, or **kingdoms**: Monera (bacteria), Protista (protozoans), Fungi, Plantae (plants), and Animalia (animals).

Monera consists of unicellular organisms. It is the only group of living organisms made up of prokaryotic cells—the cells with a primitive organization system. Some examples of this organism are bacteria, blue-green algae, and spirochetes.

Protista contains a type of eukaryotic cell with a more complex organization system. This kingdom includes diverse, mostly unicellular organisms that live in aquatic habitats, in both freshwater and saltwater. They are not animals or plants but unique organisms. Some examples of Protista are protozoans and algae of various types. The Amoeba, Paramecium, and Euglena are in the Protista Kingdom.

Fungi are multicellular organisms with a sophisticated organization system—that is, containing eukaryotic cells. Fungi exist in a variety of forms and shapes. Because they do not have chlorophyll, they cannot produce food through photosynthesis. Fungi obtain energy, carbon, and water from digesting dead materials. Some examples of these types of organisms are mushrooms, mold, mildews, and yeast.

Plants are multicellular organisms with a sophisticated organization system. In addition to more familiar plants, moss and ferns also fall under this category. Plant cells have chloroplasts, a component that allows them to trap sunlight as energy for the process of photosynthesis. In photosynthesis, plants use carbon dioxide from the atmospheric environment and as the by-product of this process, supply the oxygen needed for the survival of animals.

Animals are also multicellular with multiple forms and shapes, and with specialized senses and organs. The Animalia kingdom is composed of organisms such as sponges, worms, insects, fish, amphibians, reptiles, birds, and mammals. Animals are the most sophisticated type of living organisms and represent the highest levels of evolution. Animals live in all kinds of habitats, and they are as simple as flies or as sophisticated as humans.

For additional information about living things, go to the website of the Behavioral Sciences Department of Palomar College, San Marcos, California, at *http://anthro.palomar.edu/animal*.

There are relationships between the characteristics, structures, and functions of organisms and corresponding taxonomic classifications. **Homologous** structures refer to different living organisms with structural or anatomical features that look or function in a similar way. The explanation is because the organisms were inherited from a common ancestor. **Non-homologous** structures between two organisms are similar in structure and function, but arose independently and not from a common ancestor. **Parallelism** is when there are similar structures between two organisms in different species that arose after diverging from a common ancestor. The common ancestor did not have the structure, but had the beginning features of that structure. **Convergence** is when similar structures developed after diverging from a common ancestor, but the common ancestor did not have the trait or the beginnings of the trait. **Analogous** structures have the same structure or function but arose from different ancestors, for example the wings of a bird and butterfly. For more detailed information see: *http://www.majordifferences.com*.

Life Cycles

Life traditionally begins with a seed or a fertilized egg, which goes through metamorphosis until the organism is fully formed. The development and growth of organisms can take days, months, or years, but eventually they all go through similar stages: creation, short cycle, reproducing once and then dying. Others, like vertebrates, spend more time in the reproductive stage.

Different living organisms may go through either **complete** or **incomplete** metamorphosis in the transformation to adult. Complete metamorphosis has four different life stages: egg, larva, pupa, and adult. Butterflies and darkling beetles go through complete metamorphosis. Incomplete metamorphosis has three different life stages: egg, nymph, and adult. A nymph is a smaller version of the adult but does not have wings. Grasshoppers go through incomplete metamorphosis.

Some examples of living organisms and the changes that they go through are presented in Table 6-5.

Table 6-5. Life Cycles of Common Organisms

Organism	Stage 1	Stage 2	Stage 3	Stage 4	Stage 5
Darkling Beetle	Egg (fertilized by male sperm)	Larva—called "mealworm" though not a true worm	Pupa—mealworm curls up into a pupated or sleeplike state	Darkling Beetle	Reproduction—organisms lay eggs Death of the adult
Butterfly	Egg (fertilized by male sperm)	Larva—called caterpillar	Pupa—caterpillar forms a cocoon or chrysalis	Butterfly	Reproduction—organisms lay eggs Death of the adult
Frog	Egg (fertilized by male sperm)	Embryo	Tadpole	Frog	Reproduction—organism lays eggs Death of the adult
Human	Egg (fertilized by male sperm)	Embryo/Fetus	Child through adolescent	Human adult	Reproduction—organisms have live birth of offspring Death of the adult
Tree	Seed with embryo or "baby plant" inside (egg or ovule inside of flower, ovary fertilized by male sperm, nuclei inside of pollen grains)	Sprout	Growing plant	Mature tree	Reproduction—Tree produces flowers with new seeds that are dispersed Death of the adult

Some of the most spectacular metamorphoses, which is described as changes in the organism from one stage of life to another, are experienced by insects, amphibians, and humans. Insects such as the Darkling Beetle and the butterfly go through drastic changes in a period of weeks. Frogs go through similar transmutations that allow them to move from an aquatic environment to land. Humans, on the other hand, begin life as microscopic beings and after nine months develop into a six- to nine-pound physically functional individual. The TEKS emphasize that during the elementary school grades, students should be exposed to the concept of life cycles for plants and animals, including humans.

Life Cycle of Plants

The life cycle of plants generally begins with seeds. Mature plants produce the seeds, which are transported through various means: wind, water, hitchhiking on animals, or ingested as food and released as droppings or waste. For the seeds to germinate, they need air, the right amount of heat or proper temperature specific for that seed, and water. They do not need light to *germinate* or initially sprout, but do need light to grow since they need to carry on photosynthesis for their source of food, and to mature into an adult plant that can reproduce new seeds. Growing plants also need the right kind of soil, sufficient water, and heat/light from the Sun. As part of the growth process, plants develop a root system for support and to extract the water and minerals they need from the soil. It is important to understand that fertilizers are *not* food for the plant—they only provide vitamins and minerals for the plant to help it remain healthy. The only food the plant has is what it makes for itself through photosynthesis.

Through the process of **photosynthesis**, a plant containing chlorophyll captures energy from the Sun and converts it into chemical energy. Part of the chemical energy is used for the plant's own survival, and the rest is stored in the stem and leaves. As part of the growth process, some plants produce flowers, which are pollinated by insects or through the wind. That is, the pollen, which contains sperm nuclei, is transferred from the male part of the flower, the stamen, to the female part of the flower, the pistil. Once pollination occurs, the sperm leaves the pollen and travels to the ovules or eggs inside the ovary of the pistil and fertilizes the ovules. The fertilized ovules become the seeds. The ovary swells to become the fruit, and the flower itself dies because it has now served its purpose. The fruits contain, carry, and protect the seeds until they are dispersed to a place where they can sprout, and the cycle of the plant continues.

For information on how this process can be presented to children in the elementary school grades search: "The Life Cycle of Plants" ("Science Lesson for 2nd Graders") at *www.youtube. com*. For additional information about photosynthesis, visit the following site: "Exploring Photo-synthesis," at *www.botany.uwc.ac.za* and *http://biology.clc.uc.edu* (see General Biology 104). An inquiry-based curriculum on the life cycle of plants can also be found in the NSTA publication, "Science and Children" by Cavallo (2005) titled *Cycling Through Plants*.

Life Cycle of Animals

Many animals come from eggs. For some animals, the egg grows inside the female animal and is fertilized by the male. For others such as most fish species, the eggs are fertilized by the male after they have been expelled from the female's body. When fertilized internally, the fertilized egg may be laid externally from the female as in many insects, reptiles, and birds, or it may remain in the body of the female until birth. The egg has an outer lining to protect the animal growing inside. Bird eggs have hard shells, while the eggs of reptiles, like the turtle, have hard but flexible coverings. With the appropriate care and heat, an egg will hatch. After hatching, in some species, the parents protect and feed the newborn until it can survive on its own; in other species, the eggs are left on their own to survive. On reaching adulthood, females begin laying eggs, and the cycle of life continues. Mammals are also conceived through egg fertilization, but the resulting embryo is kept inside the mother until it is mature enough for life outside the womb.

Needs of Living Organisms

Living organisms like plants and animals need to have ideal conditions for their survival. They need nutrients, the appropriate temperature, and a balanced ecosystem to survive and reproduce. A healthy ecosystem must contain an appropriate system for energy exchange or a food chain. The right combination of herbivorous and carnivorous animals is necessary for a healthy ecosystem. The food chain generally begins with the primary source of energy, the Sun. The Sun provides the energy for plants; plants in turn are consumed by animals; and animals are consumed by other animals. These animals die and serve as food sources for fungi and plants. When this balance is disrupted either by the removal of organisms or the introduction of nonnative species, the ecosystem is affected, forcing animals and plants to adapt or else die. Thus, the common basic needs of all living organisms for survival are *air, water, food,* and *shelter.*

Body Structure and Function

Cells are the basic unit of all living organisms. Within cells are specialized organelles that carry on all of the life functions at a microscopic/chemical level. For example, the mitochondria carry on cell respiration, and ribosomes assemble proteins for use both inside the cell and out. Teachers should know the parts of the cell, called organelles, and their functions, particularly, the nucleus, mitochondria, chloroplasts (plants only), ribosomes, Golgi, endoplasmic reticulum, vacuoles, and cell membranes. An explanation of organelles may be found at *www.cellsalive.com/ cells/3dcell.htm.*

Moving outward from the *cell,* it is important to know that cells communicate with one another on a chemical level and work together to perform specific functions. The shape of these groups of cells and activity levels differ according to their particular function in the body; for example, muscle cells are long and narrow so they may better respond to stimuli and contract. Groups of cells with similar functions are called *tissues.* Tissues are organized together to perform a specific life function. A complex system of tissues working together to carry on one of the body's life functions is an *organ.* A group of different organs working together to support and help carry out a life function and keep the organism alive is called an *organ system.* Examples of systems include the digestive system, the respiratory system, the immune system, the muscular system, the skeletal system, the nervous system, and the circulatory system. Organ systems are organized into an *organism.* The order of organization is as follows:

Cells → Tissues → Organs → Systems → Organ Systems → Organism

For more information on the structure and function of organisms, see *http://www.neok12.com/ Cell-Structures.htm.*

Systems of the Human Body

Musculoskeletal System

The human skeleton consists of more than 200 bones held together by connective tissues called ligaments. Movements are effected by contractions of the **skeletal muscles**, and skeletal muscles are arranged in pairs, such as the biceps and triceps of the upper arm. When one of the pair contracts, it causes a certain movement of the bones; in the meantime the opposing muscle relaxes. When the opposing pair of muscle contracts, a different movement of the bones occurs, and the original muscle of the pair relaxes. For example, when the biceps (the muscle on top of the upper arm) contracts, the arm bends upwards; when the opposing muscle of the pair, the triceps, contract, the arm extends. Skeletal muscles are attached to bones with specialized connective tissue called tendons.

The specialized connective tissue that attaches bones to other bones is called ligaments. The soft spongy tissue on the ends of bones is called **cartilage**. Muscular contractions are controlled by the nervous system.

In addition to skeletal muscle, the body also has muscles that are not part of the musculoskeletal system, thus not attached to bones. One such muscle type is called **smooth muscle**. Smooth muscle forms the inner linings of our digestive system and is controlled involuntarily by our autonomic (automatic) nervous system. A third type of muscle is **cardiac muscle**, which is the muscle of the heart, and is also controlled by our autonomic nervous system.

Nervous System

The nervous system has two main divisions: the somatic and automatic. The somatic allows the voluntary control of skeletal muscles, and the automatic, or involuntary, controls cardiac and glandular functions. **Voluntary movement** is caused by nerve impulses sent from the brain through the spinal cord to nerves to connecting skeletal muscles. **Involuntary movement** occurs in direct response to outside stimulus. Involuntary responses are called reflexes. For example, when an object presents danger to the eye, the body responds automatically by blinking or retracting away from the object.

Circulatory System

The circulatory system follows a cyclical process in which the heart pumps blood through the right chambers of the heart and through the lungs, where it acquires oxygen. From there it is pumped back into the left chambers of the heart, where it is pumped into the main artery (aorta), which then sends the oxygenated blood to the rest of the body using a system of veins and capillaries. Through the capillaries, the blood distributes the oxygen and nutrients to tissues, absorbing from them carbon dioxide, a metabolic waste product. Finally, the blood completes the circuit by passing through small veins, which join to form increasingly larger vessels. Eventually, the blood reaches the largest veins, which return it to the right side of the heart to complete and restart the process.

Immune System

The main function of the body's immune system is to defend itself against foreign proteins and infectious organisms. The system recognizes organisms that are not normally in the body and develops the antibodies needed to control and destroy the invaders. When the body is attacked by infectious organisms, it develops what we know as a fever. Fever is the body's way of fighting invading molecules. The raised temperature of a fever will kill some bacteria. The major components of the immune system are the thymus, lymph system, bone marrow, white blood cells, antibodies, and hormones.

Respiratory System

Respiration is carried out by the expansion and contraction of the lungs. In the lungs, oxygen enters tiny capillaries, where it combines with **hemoglobin** in the red blood cells and is carried to the tissues through the circulatory system. At the same time, carbon dioxide passes through capillaries into the air contained within the lungs.

Animals inhale oxygen from the environment and exhale carbon dioxide. Carbon dioxide is used by plants in the process of photosynthesis, which produces the oxygen that animals use again for survival.

Digestive and Excretory Systems

The energy required for sustenance of the human body is supplied through the chemical energy stored in food. To obtain the energy from food, it has to be fragmented and digested. Digestion begins at the moment that food is placed in the mouth and makes contact with saliva. Fragmented and partially digested food passes down the esophagus to the stomach, where the process is continued by the gastric and intestinal juices. Thereafter, the mixture of food and secretions makes its way down the small intestine, where the nutrients are extracted and absorbed into the bloodstream. The unused portion of the food goes to the large intestine and eventually is excreted from the body through defecation. For a detailed analysis of each component of the body system go to the Human Anatomy Online website at *www.innerbody.com/htm/body.html*.

Reproductive System

Students in the upper elementary grades (5 and 6) should know some basic biological facts about human reproduction. They should know that the body matures and develops in order for child-bearing to occur. The menstrual cycle should be understood by students, including what occurs in ovulation to prepare the egg cell, namely, the process of meiosis. In males, the process of meiosis occurs to produce the sperm cell. Students should know that these specialized cells, called gametes (egg and sperm), unite to form a fertilized egg, which grows and develops in distinct stages to produce new offspring.

COMPETENCY 012: REPRODUCTION AND THE MECHANISMS OF HEREDITY

The teacher understands reproduction and the mechanisms of heredity.

Reproduction

An organism may consist of only one cell, or it may comprise many billions of cells of various dimensions. For example, cells are complete organisms, such as the unicellular bacteria; others, such as muscle cells, are parts of multicellular organisms. All cells have an internal substance called cytoplasm—a clear gelatinous fluid—enclosed within a membrane. Each cell contains the genetic material containing the information for the formation of organisms. Cells are composed primarily of water and the elements oxygen, hydrogen, carbon, and nitrogen.

Growth in most organisms is caused by nuclear cell division (**mitosis.**) In mitosis the chromosomes (containing DNA which is the genetic material of the cell or blueprint) first replicate—in humans the 46 chromosomes in the cell double. The cell then divides through a series of steps resulting in 2 new cells that each has the original 46 chromosomes, or the exact copy of the original. Through mitosis, new cells are made. Mitosis occurs in growth as well as the formation of scars, new bone cells, muscle cells, blood cells—in fact, any cell in the body throughout life.

However, in single-celled organisms, mitosis is the cell's form of reproduction—making exact copies of the DNA in each of the two "daughter" cells, and is often called binary fission. This type of reproduction is also called **asexual reproduction** because only one organism (the single cell) is involved and there is no exchange of genetic material or DNA. Thus, the two offspring cells, or daughter cells, are identical to the original or parent cell.

In humans and many other organisms, particularly mammals, another form of cell division occurs only in the reproductive organs (in most called the female ovaries and male testicles) where the DNA is replicated/copied; however, the cell divides *twice* in a process called **meiosis**. Meiosis is how sperm and egg cells are formed through a series of steps. The original cell in the female ovary or male testicle first duplicates (replicates) its 46 chromosomes (containing the genetic blueprint material, DNA) and then divides *twice,* the result is four cells with half the number of chromosomes, or 23 chromosomes each. In forming the egg cell, only one is a viable egg that can be fertilized and the remaining three are polar bodies that eventually dissolve. In the male, all four sperm cells that were formed by meiosis of the original cell are viable and capable of fertilizing the egg. The process is similar in other organisms; however, the number of chromosomes may be different, depending on the particular species—a similar process even occurs in plants, where the flower is the reproductive organ—the ovules are the egg cells, and the pollen contains the sperm.

This form of reproduction is known as **sexual reproduction**, because it requires the combination of DNA between two organisms of the same species (male, female). The fertilization of the egg by sperm cells occurs through copulation in vertebrates, and for fish and some amphibians it occurs through cross-fertilization. Cross-fertilization occurs outside the body; the female lays the eggs (ovum), and the males spray them with sperm to fertilize them.

Plant Reproduction

The reproduction of plants can also be divided into asexual and sexual mechanisms. Asexual reproduction of plants takes place by cutting portions of the plant and replanting them. Sexual reproduction involves seeds produced by female and male plants, which are then cross-pollinated with help from insects or other animals. As mentioned, the flower is the reproductive organ of the plant. The flower consists of several parts that are the male and female reproductive organs. Some flowers may have only the male part, and likewise, some flowers contain only the female part of the same species of plant/tree. So there actually can be a "male" tree and a "female" tree, for example. In the flower, the male reproductive organ is the stamen, which is divided into filament and anther. The filament simply holds up the anther, and the anther contains the pollen and in the pollen are the sperm nuclei. Flowers may also contain the female reproductive organ, or pistil, which consists of the ovary, style, and stigma. The ovary contains the egg cells, which in the flower are called ovules. The style is the tube above the ovary, and the stigma is the top of the style which has a sticky substance. The pollen needs to either be manually placed on the stigma, or blown there by the wind, or what usually happens, it needs to stick to the body of a bee or butterfly (who are actually in search of sugary nectar in the flower and not the pollen). When the pollen sticks to the body of the insect, it may then be transferred from the anther (male part) to the stigma (female part). In essence, the sperm nuclei then travel down the style until it reaches the ovules, where fertilization occurs. The fertilized egg then becomes the seed. The ovary of the flower may swell and become the fruit (as in a peach or apple). This process helps protect the seeds and also helps with seed dispersal (animals eat the fruit, the seed has a seed coat that protects it and is indigestible, the animals excretes the seed, unharmed, in its fecal matter). Seed germination—where the seed sprouts into a plant—requires the appropriate quantity of air, water, and heat.

Hereditary Material

Deoxyribonucleic acid or *DNA* is the hereditary material of living organisms. DNA has as its smallest complete component what is called a nucleotide. A single nucleotide consists of the sugar deoxyribose, a phosphate molecule, and a nitrogen base molecule. There are four nitrogen bases that are paired in the double-helix structure of DNA. These nitrogen bases are adenine, thymine, guanine, and cytosine. In DNA, adenine always pairs with a nucleotide having thymine as its nitrogen base (A-T); and guanine always pairs with a nucleotide having cytosine as its nitrogen base (G-C), and vice versa (T-A; C-G).

In bacteria, also called monera or prokaryotic cells, DNA is in a single strand. In more complex organisms including protista, fungi, animals and plants, which are all composed of eukaryotic cells, the DNA is arranged in **chromosomes**, and these chromosomes are located in the nucleus (though there is new evidence of DNA in other cell organelles, particularly the mitochondria). The number of chromosomes in the cells of organisms varies from one species to another—but it is the same for all members of that species. Along the strands of DNA that exist inside of chromosomes, there are certain locations that direct specific functions of cells, including hereditary traits, called **genes**. Certain genes give the cell directions, in the developing embryo, for example, for the expression of traits such as eye color, hair color, and leg shape and size. In already developed organisms, such as the human adult, other genes (sections of DNA) direct the production of substances and control specific activities and functions. The production of insulin in pancreatic cells, for example, is controlled by certain genes in the chromosomes in the cells of the organ known as the pancreas. In inheritance and cell functions, traits can be controlled or determined by more than one gene, located on the same, or even on different chromosomes. Likewise, there may be several traits influenced by one single gene.

As discussed earlier, the fertilized egg that eventually grows into the organism that then goes through its respective life cycle to adult contains half the number of chromosomes from the female egg (mother) and half the number of chromosomes from the male sperm (father). In the human, there are 23 chromosomes in the egg and 23 in the sperm, so the fertilized egg and, therefore, the offspring (baby) has 46 chromosomes—which is the normal number for all cells in all organisms of the human species. The 23 chromosomes of the egg have an exact pair or match in the sperm. That matching chromosome contains genes with DNA that direct the same traits. So along the length of chromosome number 20, for example, in the egg cell, you will find it controls the same traits that are along the length of chromosome number 20 in the male sperm. However, the 23 chromosomes in the egg contain the specific qualities or characteristics of the mother; whereas, the 23 chromosomes in the sperm contain the specific qualities or characteristics of the father. Though more than one chromosome controls eye color—we will use one chromosome as an example. In one of the egg cell's chromosomes, there is a gene that controls eye color, and in the egg this eye color could be "blue." In the corresponding chromosome in the same location in the sperm cell, there will also be a gene for eye color, but the characteristic of that eye color may instead be "brown." So traits are located on the same number chromosome whether that chromosome originated from the egg or the sperm; however, the quality or characteristic may differ (that is, the pigment color that section of DNA or gene directs the cell to make). The gene for eye color and other traits that are the paired chromosomes in the same location are called **alleles**. When the egg is fertilized, the directions coded in the DNA alleles are set. In many alleles, one of the traits directed by the gene on one chromosome is **dominant**, and the other is **recessive**. The dominant trait is the one that typically "shows" or is *expressed* in the offspring. In the case of eye color, brown is usually dominant over blue eye color, so if one of the alleles is for "blue" eyes and the other allele from the other parent is for "brown" eyes, the offspring will show the dominant trait and have brown eyes. Again, it must be cautioned that many genes may direct eye color especially in an organism as complex as humans, but it is simply used as an example here. In addition, it is important to note that **environmental factors** play an important role in the expression (showing up) of traits in the offspring as they grow and develop. Sometimes environmental stressors, for example, can cause a genetic change in an organism that otherwise may not have been expressed, such as certain food allergies or intolerances.

For more genetics information and activities go to the U.S. National Library of Medicine website at *http://geneed.nlm.nih.gov.*

COMPETENCY 013: ADAPTATIONS AND EVOLUTION

The teacher understands adaptations of organisms and theory of evolution.

Adaptations

Genetics plays an important role in the ability of organisms to be able to survive and thrive in their environment and, ultimately, produce new offspring where they can pass on similar genetic material, like that which allowed *them* to survive and thrive, and maybe survive and thrive even better. Some inherited traits, called **adaptations**, allow the organisms to best survive in their environment and others do not, and may even lead to their demise (and those prevent the prospect of future offspring). Adaptations do not suddenly arise or develop in the lifetime of organisms. They occur gradually in the species over time. For example, if a certain deer-like animal thousands of years ago was particularly fast—that is, it was born with stronger muscle tissue than most, and a better bone and muscle physical structure—perhaps it was better able to run away from predators and survive. Therefore, this deer-like animal was able to survive long enough for it to have offspring with similar genetic material. At the same time, those deer-like animals that were not born with the same muscular and structural soundness as this one were killed as prey before they could reproduce. The animal that was best adapted to its environment (needing to run from predators) was the first deer-like animal. In time, those animals that are best suited in this, as well as in other ways, are the organisms that survive, as do their offspring. Those not well adapted perish. It is also the case that the organism that survives will breed with another that also has better adapted characteristics, and was also able to survive in the natural environment. A change or **mutation** in the genetic material, that is, the genes that direct the development of a trait, may give rise to a new characteristic that either is or is not better suited for the environment. In the case that it is better suited, the organism will survive and produce offspring with this same mutation. Over the years, mutations that are better suited to the environment may make the organism appear quite different than it did hundreds, thousands, and millions of years earlier. If the environment itself changes, however, organisms that were able to survive under the previous conditions (climate, water supply, vegetation, landscape) may be unable to survive in the new environmental conditions. Thus, a catastrophic event, such as perhaps a large asteroid striking the Earth, could change the environmental conditions and leading either to the extinction of organisms, or the survival of organisms that would not have survived under the conditions before the strike. Likewise, selective breeding, which is human selection of which organisms breed with another, and thus, control of the genetic material that is passed onto offspring, also effects the change over time of organisms. The combination of genetics, adaptations, changes over time, mutations, selective breeding, and environmental conditions/changes contribute to the concept known as evolution. For more detailed information on evolution see: *http://evolution.berkeley.edu/evolibrary/article/evo_01*.

COMPETENCY 014: ORGANISMS AND THE ENVIRONMENT

The teacher understands the relationships between organisms and the environment.

Ecology

Ecology studies the relationship of organisms with their physical environment. The physical environment includes light, heat, solar radiation, moisture, wind, oxygen, carbon dioxide, nutrients, water, and the atmosphere. The biological environment describes living and nonliving organisms in the ecosystem. There are three main components of an ecosystem:

- **Producers** are green plants that produce oxygen and store chemical energy for consumers.

- **Consumers** are animals, both herbivores and carnivores. The herbivores take the chemical energy from plants, and carnivores take the energy from other animals or directly from plants.

- **Decomposers**, like fungi and bacteria, are in charge of cleaning up the environment by decomposing and freeing dead matter for recycling back into the ecosystem.

Maintaining a Healthy Balance

A successful ecosystem requires a healthy balance among producers, consumers, and decomposers. This balance relies on natural ways to control populations of living organisms and is maintained mostly through competition and predation.

Competition

When a shared resource is scarce, organisms must compete to survive. The competition, which occurs between animals as well as between plants, ensures the survival of the fittest and the preservation of the system.

Predation

Predation is the consumption of one living organism, plant or animal, by another. It is a direct way to control population and promote natural selection by eliminating weak organisms from the population. As a consequence of predation, predators and prey evolve to survive. If an organism cannot evolve to meet challenges from the environment, it perishes.

Adaptation for Survival

Changes in the environment create a situation where only those organisms with structures and functions suited to that particular environment survive and produce offspring with those same structures and functions, and those that do not have features that enable them to survive will perish before they are able to reproduce. If the environment changes, whether gradually or suddenly (e.g., a volcanic eruption that darkens the sky for a long period of time), then it may be the case that species that once could survive in the former environment can no longer survive in the current environmental conditions. Thus organisms with different structures and features are present in today's environment where they would not have survived in an earlier environment, and vice versa. For example, over thousands of years, the anteater species and its offspring were able to survive better if they had a long snout to be able to reach for ants, and frogs with a long, sticky tongue to catch flies were better able to survive and produce offspring with the same characteristics. Adaptation for animals, plants, and even humans is a matter of life and death.

Changes in the food chain of animals is another occurrence that may lead to a change in behaviors and adapt to new conditions. For example, because their habitats are destroyed when land is developed by humans, raccoons and opossums have learned to coexist with humans and to get new sources of food. Bears have managed to successfully adapt to colder climates by hibernating during the winter and living on the fat they accumulate during the rest of the year. Other animals, like the chameleon or the fox, have developed camouflage to hide from predators. Humans are not exempt from the need to adapt to new situations. For example, humans have had to adapt and use tools to produce, preserve, and trade the food supplies they needed to sustain them. All these examples represent ways in which organisms adapt to deal with challenges in their ecosystem.

One adaptation of living organisms is the ability to live together forming different kinds of relationships to one another. Living and interacting in a long-term way that in some way impacts the survival and/or well-being of one or more organism in the relationships is called **symbiosis**. There are different kinds of symbiotic relationships between organisms. When both species benefit from the relationship, the interaction is called **mutualism**. An example of mutualism is the presence of a certain kind of protozoan that lives in the guts of termites – the termites benefit by having assistance in digesting wood, and the protozoans have a living environment and food source. **Parasitism** is a symbiotic when one organism benefits but the other organism is harmed. Examples are bacteria or other organisms that cause illness or even eventual death in a living organism, such as staphylococcus bacteria invading the bloodstream or tapeworms in the intestines of animals or humans. **Commensalism** is a third type of symbiosis in which one organism species benefits and the other is neither harmed nor benefitted, basically unaffected. An example is the barnacles that attach to sea organisms, such as turtles. The barnacles have a place to anchor, yet the turtle is essentially unharmed by their presence. For more information see: *http://study.com/academy/lesson/symbiotic-relationships-mutualism-commensalism-amensalism.html.*

Key Principles of the Life Science Competencies

- When working with animals, teachers are ethically responsible for their well-being. Teachers need to provide an adequate environment for the survival and development of animals under their care.

- By observing the development of frogs and butterflies, students directly acquire information on the life cycles. Students can also observe how organisms adapt to their environment.

- Fungi obtain energy, carbon, and water from dead material. Fungi do not have chlorophyll, so they cannot produce food through photosynthesis.

- Chromosomes contain the genetic code, or DNA.

- Mitosis describes the process of a cell splitting to create two identical cells.

- Meiosis is the process of cells dividing to produce the egg and sperm cells, each with half the number of chromosomes as the parent cell so they are ready to restore the normal number of the species upon fertilization.

- Photosynthesis is the process of capturing, storing, and converting solar energy. It is also the source of oxygen in the atmosphere.

- Insects have three main parts: head, thorax, and abdomen.

- Humans have several body systems, including the musculoskeletal, nervous, circulatory, immune, respiratory, and digestive/excretory systems.

- Adaptations are features or characteristics of an organism that best help it survive in its environment.

- Organisms in the environment depend upon one another for survival and are inextricably linked in the ecosystem.

COMPETENCY 015: STRUCTURE AND FUNCTION OF EARTH SYSTEMS

The teacher understands the structure and function of Earth systems.

Structure and Composition of the Earth (Geology)

Landform Characteristics

The formation of deserts, mountains, rivers, oceans, and other landforms can be described in terms of geological processes. Mountains are formed by colliding plates. For example, the Appalachian Mountains in the United States were formed 250 million years ago when the tectonic plate carrying the continent of Africa collided with the plate carrying the North American continent

(Badder et al., 2000). Rivers and natural lakes form at low elevations where rainfall collects and eventually runs down to the sea. The sediment gathered by the rivers in turn accumulates at river mouths to create deltas. These are both constructive and destructive processes that form the Earth. Constructive processes include those that build mountains, such as the gradual (over millions of years) collision and crushing together of the Earth's tectonic plates. Destructive processes include weathering and erosion — the wearing down of mountains and rock by forces such as water, wind, and ice. For more information on these processes, go to *www.edu.pe.ca/southernkings/processes.htm*.

Layers of the Earth

The average circumference of the Earth at the equator is 25,902 miles, and its radius is about 3,959 miles. The Earth is divided into three main parts:

- The **crust** is the outer portion of the Earth where we live. The thickness of the crust varies from about 3 miles to 40 miles, depending on the location. It contains various types of soil, metals, and rocks. The crust is broken down into several floating tectonic plates. Movements of these plates cause earthquakes and changes in landforms.

- The **mantle** is the thickest layer of the Earth located right below the crust. It is composed mostly of rocks and metals. The heat in the mantle is so intense that rocks and metals melt, creating magma and the resulting lava that reaches the surface.

- The **core** is the inner part of the Earth. It is composed of a solid **inner core** and an **outer core** that is mostly liquid. The inner core is made of solid iron and nickel. Despite temperatures in the inner core that resemble the heat on the surface of the Sun, this portion of the Earth remains solid because of the intense pressure there.

For more information about the layers of the Earth, go to the following website: *www.scec.org/education*.

Continental Drift

In 1912, the German scientist Alfred Wegener proposed that all the continents were previously one large continent but then broke apart and drifted through the ocean floor to their present locations. Wegener's theory of continental drift is the basis of today's concept of plate tectonics.

Tectonic Plates

According to the theory of plate tectonics, the surface of the Earth is fragmented into large plates. These plates are in continuous motion, floating on the liquid mantle and always changing in size and position. The edges of these plates, where they move against each other, are sites of intense geologic activity, which results in earthquakes, volcanoes, and the creation of mountains. The generator for the movement of the continents and the Earth's plates is the mid-Atlantic ridge— a huge volcanic mountain range on the floor of the Atlantic Ocean that is continuously erupting and pushing the plates apart in opposite directions from each other. The plates that cover the surface of the Earth are constantly colliding because of the ocean floor spreading initiated at the mid-Atlantic ridge. The boundaries of the plates may be **convergent** or **divergent**. Convergent plates are coming together, whereas divergent plates are moving apart. When one convergent plate moves underneath another plate, it is called subduction or a **subduction zone**. A subduction zone creates a deep trench, such as that the oceanic trench located of the western coast of South America. When one convergent plate cannot move beneath another, the plates still collide, but in this case uplift occurs, which forms mountain ranges. This type of convergent zone is a **collisional boundary** and can be found, for example in Nepal where the Himalayan Mountains are the result of two plates converging/colliding. The mid-Atlantic ridge, where ocean floor spreading is occurring, is a divergent zone. For more information go to *http://science.nationalgeographic.com/science*.

Forces That Change the Surface of the Earth

Three main forces and processes change the surface of the Earth: weathering, geological movements, and the creation of glaciers.

Weathering

Weathering is the process of breaking down rock, soils, and minerals through natural, chemical, and biological processes. Two of the most common examples of physical weathering are exfoliation and freeze thaw.

- **Exfoliation** occurs in places like the desert when the soil is exposed first to high temperatures, which causes the soil to expand, and then to cold temperatures, which makes the soil contract. The stress of these changes causes the outer layers of rock to peel off.

- **Freeze-thaw** breaks down rock when water gets into rock joints or cracks and then freezes and expands, breaking the rock. A similar process occurs when water containing salt crystals gets into the rock. Once the water evaporates, the crystals expand and break the rock. This process is called salt-crystal growth.

Weathering can be caused by chemical reactions. Two of the most common examples of chemical weathering are acid formation and hydration. Acid is formed under various conditions. For example, sulfur and rain are combined to create acid rain, which can weather and change the chemical composition of rock. Hydration occurs when the minerals in rock absorb water and expand sometimes changing the chemical composition of the rock. For example, through the process of hydration, a mineral like anhydrite can be changed into a different mineral, namely gypsum.

Erosion

After weathering, a second process called erosion can take place. **Erosion** is the movement of sediment from one location to the other through the use of water, wind, ice, or gravity. The Grand Canyon was created by the processes of weathering and erosion. The water movement (erosion) is responsible for the canyon being so deep, and the weathering process is responsible for its width (Badder et al., 2000).

Earthquakes and Geologic Faults

The movement of the Earth's plates has forced rock layers to fold, creating mountains, hills, and valleys. This movement causes **faults** in the Earth's crust, breaking rocks and reshaping the environment. When forces within the Earth cause rocks to break and move around geologic faults, earthquakes occur. A fault is a deep crack that marks the boundary between two plates. The San Andreas Fault in central California is a well-known origin of earthquakes in the area. The epicenter of an earthquake is the point on the surface where the quake is the strongest. The **Richter scale** is used to measure the amount of energy released by the earthquake. The severity of an earthquake runs from 0 to 9 on the Richter scale. Small tremors occur constantly, but every few months, a major earthquake occurs somewhere in the world. Scientists are researching ways to predict earthquakes, but their predictions are not always accurate.

Volcanoes

Volcanoes are formed by the constant motion of tectonic plates. This movement creates pressure that forces magma from the mantel to escape to the surface, creating an explosion of lava, fire, and ash. The pressure of the magma and gases creates a monticule, or a small cone, that eventually grows to form a mountain-like volcano. Volcanic activity can create earthquakes, and the fiery lava can cause destruction.

Gravity

Gravity is the force of attraction that exists between objects. Gravity keeps the Earth in its orbit by establishing a balance between the attraction of the Sun and the speed at which the Earth travels around it. However, gravity is also responsible for many of the Earth's forces that change the land. For example, when ice melts on the tops of mountains, it is because of gravity that the water will form streams and rivers that flow down the mountain, eventually making its way to the lowest point. Some of the main functions of gravity are listed here:

- Keeping the Earth's atmosphere, oceans, and inhabitants from drifting into space

- Pulling the rain to the rivers and eventually to the sea

- Guiding the development and growth of plants

- Affecting the way that our bones and muscles function

For information about the Earth and space, go to the official website of the National Aeronautics and Space Administration (NASA) at *www.nasa.gov*. This site includes special sections for children, students from kindergarten through grade 12, and teachers.

Surface Water and Groundwater

Surface water is the water in streams, lakes and rivers, and all water that is on the surface of the land. Groundwater is water that seeps beneath the surface of the land and forms an underground "river" of water. The groundwater seeps into the soil until it reaches an impermeable layer of rock. The water stays on top of this layer and is a source of drinking water. This water may be tapped into via aquifers and wells. For more information, see: *http://water.usgs.gov/ogw/gwsw.html*

The Earth's Atmosphere

The Earth is surrounded by a large mass of gas called the atmosphere. Roughly 348 miles thick, this gas mass supports life on the Earth and separates it from space. Among the many functions of the atmosphere are these:

- Absorbing energy from the Sun to sustain life

- Recycling water and other chemicals needed for life

- Maintaining the climate, working with electric and magnetic forces

- Serving as a vacuum that protects life

The atmosphere is composed of 79 percent nitrogen, 20 percent oxygen, and 1 percent other gases. These other gases include argon, and also water, greenhouse gases like ozone, and carbon dioxide. The Earth's atmosphere has five layers. The layer closest to the Earth is called the troposphere, and the weather we experience occurs in this layer. For more information on the atmosphere, go to *http://csep10.phys.utk.edu/astr161/lect/earth/atmosphere.html*.

Natural and Human Influences on Earth Systems

It is important to understand that many natural processes on Earth can change its systems. For example, earthquakes and volcanoes can be destructive and change the structure and composition of the landscape. Tsunamis, an enormous wall of water that crashes into shorelines caused by earthquakes under bodies of water such as oceans, can create a dramatic change in that shoreline. However, human influences may also change Earth systems. The destruction of the rainforests, called deforestation can change the structure and composition of the land, and on a larger scale, affect the balance of atmospheric gases including carbon dioxide and oxygen levels. Carbon dioxide emissions from factories, automobiles, and airplanes, as examples, may play a role in changing the atmospheric composition as well. Carbon dioxide, called a "greenhouse gas" tends to trap heat energy and result in an overall warming of the atmosphere, which has an impact on climate and plant growth that in turn affects all living organisms on Earth. There are many natural and human influences that contribute to the increase of greenhouse gases in the atmosphere producing what is known as "global warming." Other greenhouse gases include methane (CH_4) and ozone, which is the molecule O_3, which are components of smog when at the surface of the Earth.

It is important to distinguish global warming and the ozone that is in smog from the destruction of the ozone layer (hole in the ozone layer) which is a different phenomenon. Ozone forms a layer at the top of the atmosphere that blocks harmful ultraviolet rays from the Sun from reaching the Earth's surface ("good ozone"). The "hole" in the ozone layer means there is a destruction of this ozone layer, and now harmful ultraviolet radiation is reaching Earth's surface where this hole is present. Chlorofluorocarbons, which are found in aerosols, contribute to the destruction of the ozone layer. For more information on greenhouse gases and ozone, go to *http://hvo.wr.usgs.gov*.

COMPETENCY 016: CYCLES IN EARTH SYSTEMS

The teacher understands cycles in Earth systems.

Rock Types

The hard, solid part of the Earth's surface is called rock. Rocks are made of one or more minerals. Rocks like granite, marble, and limestone are extensively used in the construction industry. They can be used in floors, buildings, dams, highways, or the making of cement. Rocks are classified by the way they are formed. Here are descriptions of the three types of rock:

- **Igneous** rocks are crystalline solids that form directly from the cooling of magma or lava. The composition of the magma determines the composition of the rock. **Granite** is one of the most common types of igneous rocks and is created from magma (inside the Earth). Once magma reaches the Earth's surface, it is called lava. The cooling lava forms different rocks depending on composition and the rate of cooling. A rock that has cooled quickly, for example, may have a glassy look, and is called **obsidian**. *https://msnucleus.org/membership/ html/k-6/pt/volcanoes/3/ptv3_3a.html*.

- **Sedimentary** rocks are called secondary rocks because they are often the result of the accumulation of small pieces broken off from preexisting rocks and then pressed into a new form. Sedimentary rock is usually formed when sediments in water settle to the floor of that body of water, and are pressed as more layers on top, compacting the sediments into different rock types according to the level of compaction and pressure applied (e.g., sandstone, shale, slate). See: *http://www.sciencekids.co.nz/sciencefacts/earth/sedimentaryrocks.html*.

- **Metamorphic** rocks are also secondary rocks formed from igneous, sedimentary, or other types of metamorphic rock. When hot magma or lava comes in contact with rocks or when buried rocks are exposed to pressure and high temperatures, the result is metamorphic rocks. For example, exposing limestone to high temperatures creates marble. The most common metamorphic rocks are slate, gneiss, and marble. For more information on rocks and the rock cycle (next section), go to *http://www.learner.org/interactives/rockcycle/types.html*.

There are three types of sedimentary rocks (also see: *http://geology.com/rocks/sedimentary-rocks.shtml:*

- **Clastic** sedimentary rocks are made when pieces of rock, mineral, and organic material fuse together. These are classified as conglomerates, sandstone, and shale.

- **Chemical** sedimentary rocks are formed when water rich in minerals evaporates, leaving the minerals behind. Some common examples are gypsum, rock salt, and some limestone.

- **Organic** sedimentary rocks are made from the remains of plants and animals. For example, coal is formed when dead plants are squeezed together. Another example is a form of limestone rock composed of the remains of organisms that lived in the ocean.

Rock Cycle

The formation of rock follows a cyclical process. For instance, rocks can be formed when magma or lava cools down, creating igneous rocks. Igneous rocks exposed to weathering can break into sediment, which can be compacted and cemented to form sedimentary rocks. Sedimentary rocks are exposed to heat and pressure to create metamorphic rocks. Finally, metamorphic rocks can melt and become magma and lava again (Badder et al. 2000). An animation of the rock cycle and forces causing the changes in rock can be found at *www.cotf.edu/ete/modules/msesc/earthsysflr/ rock.html.*

Minerals

Minerals are the most common form of solid material found in the Earth's crust. Even soil contains bits of minerals that have broken away from rock. To be considered a mineral, a substance must be found in nature and must never have been a part of any living organism. Minerals can be as soft as talc or as hard as emeralds and diamonds. Dug from the Earth, minerals are used to make various products:

- **Jewelry**—Gemstones such as amethysts, opals, diamonds, emeralds, topazes, and garnets are examples of minerals commonly used to create jewelry. Gold and silver are another type of mineral that can be used to create jewelry.

- **Construction**—Gypsum boards (drywall) are made of a mineral of the same name—gypsum. The windows in homes are made from another mineral, quartz.

- **Personal Use**—Talc is the softest mineral and it is commonly applied to the body in powder form.

Water Cycle

The hydrologic cycle describes a series of movements of water above, on, and below the surface of the Earth. This cycle consists of four distinct stages: storage, evaporation, precipitation, and runoff. It is the means by which the Sun's energy is used to transport water from the rivers and oceans to land masses, and through the atmosphere. The heat of the Sun evaporates the water and takes it to the atmosphere from which, through condensation, it falls as precipitation. As precipitation falls, water is filtrated back to underground water deposits called aquifers, or it runs off into storage in lakes, ponds, and oceans.

Tides

The word *tides* is used to describe the alternating rise and fall in sea level with respect to the land, produced by the gravitational attraction of the Moon and the Sun. Additional factors such as the configuration of the coastline, depth of the water, the topography of the ocean floor, and other hydrographic and meteorological influences may play an important role in altering the range, interval, and times of the arrival of the tides.

Nutrient Cycling

Nutrient cycling is among the most critical processes in an ecosystem. Nutrient cycling includes carbon and nitrogen cycles.

The **carbon cycle** is the capture of carbon from carbon dioxide in the atmosphere by plants to make glucose. When this glucose is used as food for the plant or other organisms, it is digested, then by respiration, broken apart again into carbon dioxide and returned to the atmosphere. The process continues in a life-sustaining process. More information on the carbon cycle can be found at *www.ucar.edu/learn*.

For the **nitrogen cycle** it is important to recognize that most of the air we breathe is nitrogen, but it is not useful to us in that form, so it is exhaled. Lightning causes nitrogen in the air to combine with oxygen. Certain bacteria that live on the roots of certain plants, called nitrogen-fixing bacteria, are able to take nitrogen in this combined form with oxygen and make it available for use by plants. The plants can incorporate the nitrogen into their plant structure, and when eaten by animals and other organisms, this nitrogen becomes available for use. The nitrogen returns to the soil when the plant or other living organism dies and decays, releasing nitrogen gas back into the atmosphere. Nitrogen is important to all living things because it is a major component of DNA, RNA, and amino acids, which are the building blocks of proteins. A good animation of the nitrogen cycle can be found at *www.classzone.com*.

COMPETENCY 017: ENERGY IN WEATHER AND CLIMATE

The teacher understands the role of energy in weather and climate.

Weather

The elements of weather include interactions between wind, water (precipitation), wind speed and direction, air pressure, humidity, and temperature. Wind is caused by air masses that have different amounts of heat (temperatures), where there may be a warm air mass that is moving toward a cold air mass. Air pressure is related to both the amount of water in the air mass and its temperature (heat content), in that warm air has higher pressure than cold air—warm, high pressure air masses move toward cold, low pressure air masses. One simple rule is that energy always moves from *warmer to colder*. So, if you open a window on a hot summer day when your air conditioning is on, the cold does *not go out*—the warm air comes in. The same is true on a larger scale with warm and cold air masses.

Humidity is a measure of the percentage of water that is in the air. Dew point is the temperature at which the air needs to be for the water to condense out of the air in liquid form as precipitation; or it may be observed as "dew." In other words, air has a certain amount of water vapor (water in the gas state) in it (the percent is measured as humidity). That water vapor will turn to liquid water as temperatures drop overnight, in which we observe dew, or when a cold front moves in that lowers the temperature, which can result in a rain or snow storm. For resources and information on weather, go to the National Weather Service education website at *www.nws.noaa.gov*.

Wind is measured by an instrument called an **anemometer**. Air pressure is measured by a **barometer**; **rain gauges** and other instruments measure precipitation. Temperature is measured by a **thermometer**. Relative humidity is measured by a **psychrometer**. For more information on these instruments, see *http://www.weatherwizkids.com/weather-instruments.htm*.

Climate

Weather is the conditions of the atmosphere at a given, relatively short period of time. Climate, however, is the weather conditions in an area on a continuous, seasonal basis. The climate is more complex and can be measured by the average variety of weather conditions, such as temperature and precipitation, that occur seasonally in that geographic region of the world over a long period of time. More information, including the contrast between weather and climate, can be found at *www. nasa.gov/mission_pages/noaa-n/climate/climate_weather.html*.

Predicting Weather

Weather can be predicted by tracking weather patterns using maps and charts. These maps have special symbols that indicate, for example, warm and cold air masses, air pressure, and relative humidity in a region. By knowing how air behaves, such as cold air goes down and warm air rises, warmer air always moves toward colder air, and high pressure always moves outward toward lower pressure, we can track the weather and make predictions. Clouds are also an indication of the type of weather occurring in an area. For a summary of predicting cloud types see: *http://scied. ucar.edu/webweather/clouds/cloud-types*. For information on predicting weather with associated cloud types, see *http://sectionhiker.com/predicting-the-weather-using-clouds/*. Interpreting weather maps is an important skill for weather prediction. Symbols that can be found on a weather map include those indicating cold fronts, warm fronts, occluded fronts, isotherm lines, high and low pressure, and wind speed and direction. It is important to know these symbols and their meanings in predicting weather. The symbols and their meanings can be found at *http://www.wikihow.com/ Read-a-Weather-Map* and *http://www.weatherwizkids.com/weather-forecasting.htm*.

The Earth's Surface and Position as a Factor in Weather and Climate

The Earth's surface is primarily water, and bodies of water affect the weather and climate of an area. Water has a high specific heat, which means that it takes longer to take in heat and longer to release the heat it has absorbed than any other material on Earth. Therefore, coastal areas tend to be warmer than areas inland or away from water, because the water moderates the temperature, even if the locations are at the same latitude. In the U.S., for example, areas in the middle of the country will have greater extreme differences in the cold temperatures in the winter and warm temperatures in the summer compared to a location at the same latitude near the ocean.

Large lakes, such as the Great Lakes also create a situation called "lake effect" in the winter—the air over the lake is relatively warm, and so can carry water vapor (evaporation). As soon as that air carrying water moves over land, however, it rapidly cools and releases its water (precipitation) in the form of snow over the land. Mountains and other landforms also have an effect on the weather. When air holding water hits a mountain side, it is forced upward which makes the air cool and therefore rain (or snow) on that side of the mountain. This is typically the western side of the mountain in the U.S. as in the mountain ranges of the Rocky Mountains. Once the precipitation is gone from that air mass and the air mass crosses the mountain to the other side, it drops back down and warms, but now it is dry air and so may result in an arid region or desert. The Gobi Desert, in Asia, is a result of this phenomenon.

On a much larger scale, the tilt of the Earth itself—as a planet—is responsible for weather and climate. The Earth is on a 23° tilt on its axis in space. This tilt means the Earth's North Pole is pointed *away* from the Sun when it is in one location in its orbit (path around the Sun), and *toward* the Sun when it is in the opposite orbital location. This tilt of the Earth results in the seasons, with extreme changes being in locations closer to the North and South poles. See more information on this topic at *www.windows.ucar.edu*.

COMPETENCY 018: SOLAR SYSTEM AND THE UNIVERSE

The teacher understands the characteristics of the solar system and the universe.

Properties and Characteristics of Objects in the Sky

Galaxies

Galaxies are large collections of stars, hydrogen, dust particles, and other gases. The universe is made of countless galaxies. The solar system that includes Earth is part of a galaxy called the Milky Way.

Stars

Stars like the Sun are composed of large masses of hydrogen pulled together by gravity. The hydrogen, with strong gravitational pressure, creates fusion inside the star, turning the hydrogen into helium. The liberation of energy created by this process causes solar radiation, which makes the Sun glow with visible light, as well as forms of radiation not visible to the human eye.

The Earth-Sun-Moon System

Movements of Planet Earth

Earth performs two kinds of movement: rotation and revolution. **Rotation** describes the spinning of Earth on its axis. Earth takes approximately 24 hours to make a complete (360°) rotation, which creates day and night. The length of daylight hours varies from 9 to 15 hours, depending on the Earth's location in its Revolution around the Sun. Thus the Earth spins on its axis or rotates, which causes day and night, and revolves in an orbit around the Sun, which causes seasons with differing hours of day and night. In the winter, and particularly at the winter solstice (around December 21) the ratio is close to 9 hours of daylight and 15 hours of darkness (night). In summer, at the Summer Solstice (around June 21) the ratio is reversed, with 15 hours of day light and 9 hours of night. In the fall and spring seasons, the day light and nighttime hours are closer to equal at 12 daylight hours, and 12 nighttime or darkness hours. The fall or "autumnal" equinox is near September 22, and the spring or "vernal" equinox is typically near March 21. For more information, visit the National Weather Service at *http://www.weather.gov/cle/Seasons*.

While Earth is rotating on its axis, it is also following an orbit around the Sun. This movement is called **revolution**. It takes a year, or 365¼ days, for Earth to complete one revolution. The tilt of Earth as it moves around the Sun and its curvature create **climate zones** and seasons. The zones immediately north and south of the equator are called the tropics— Cancer (north) and Capricorn (south). The Arctic Circle (North Pole) and Antarctic Circle (South Pole) are the area surrounding Earth's axis points. Latitude lines are imaginary horizontal lines around the Earth, and longitude lines are likewise vertical lines around the Earth from the North to the South Poles. These lines form a grid that helps us locate an object (lake, mountain, city) by its position on Earth as determined by its specific latitude and longitude.

Phases of the Moon

During each lunar orbit around Earth (about 28 days), the Moon appears to go through several stages based on the portion of the Moon visible from Earth. The Moon does not have its own source of light but reflects the light from the Sun. The shape of the Moon varies from a full moon, when Earth is between the Sun and the Moon, to a new moon, when the Moon is located between the Sun and Earth. A description of the major stages of the Moon follows:

- **New Moon**—The Moon is not visible to Earth because the side of the Moon facing Earth is not being lit by the Sun.

- **Crescent Moon**—At this stage between the half moon and the new moon, the shape of the Moon is often compared to a banana.

- **Half Moon, or First Quarter**—During this stage, half of the Moon is visible.

- **Gibbous Moon**—In this stage, about three quarters of the Moon is visible.

- **Full Moon**—The whole Moon is visible from Earth.

- The term **blue moon** describes the appearance of two full moons in a single calendar month. Because this phenomenon happens relatively seldom, the expression "once in a blue moon" represents an infrequent event.

Components of Our Solar System

Solar System

The Sun is the center of our solar system, which is composed of nine planets, many satellites that orbit the planets, and a large number of smaller bodies like comets and asteroids. Short definitions of these terms follow:

- Planets are large bodies orbiting the Sun.

- Dwarf planets are small bodies orbiting the Sun. For further explanation of the distinction between planets and dwarf planets, see *www.windows.ucar.edu*.

- Satellites are moons orbiting the planets. Earth has one moon whereas other planets may have no moons (Mercury, Venus) or many moons (Jupiter, Saturn).

- Asteroids are small dense objects or rocks orbiting our star, the Sun. The Asteroid Belt of our own solar system is located between Mars and Jupiter. Some theorize that the asteroids could be the remains of an exploded planet.

- Meteoroids are fragments of rock in space, most originating from the debris left behind by comets that burn up/vaporize upon entering Earth's atmosphere due to friction from the air molecules.

- Comets are small icy objects traveling through space in an elongated, elliptical orbit around the Sun.

Planets

The objects in our solar system revolve around our star, which we call the Sun. The **inner** solar system contains the planets Mercury, Venus, Earth, and Mars, in this order. The **outer** solar system comprises the planets Jupiter, Saturn, Uranus, and Neptune, and a number of dwarf planets, including Pluto, Ceres, Eris and others, with likely more yet to be found (see Table 6-6). More information about our solar system can be found at *http://starchild.gsfc.nasa.gov*.

Table 6-6. Planets and Dwarf Planets of our Solar System

Inner Planets	Mercury, Venus, Earth, Mars
Outer Planets	Jupiter, Saturn, Uranus, Neptune
Dwarf Planets	Pluto, Ceres, Eris, Haumea, Makemake

Key Principles of the Earth Science Competencies

- Our solar system is part of the Milky Way, one of many galaxies in the universe.

- Minerals and rocks are commonly used in our daily life.

- The movement of tectonic plates creates intense geologic activity that results in earthquakes and volcanic activity.

- The Earth's atmosphere protects and preserves life.

- The water cycles are the movement and distribution of water within the Earth's atmosphere.

- The tilt of the Earth causes the seasons, and not the distance it is in its orbit away from the Sun.

- Human activities as well as natural processes impact the landscape and processes on Earth.

- Weather is the interaction of many factors, including air temperature, air pressure, and humidity. Weather is the conditions in the atmosphere at a given location and time.

- The solar system consists of the Sun, inner planets, outer planets, dwarf planets, satellites, asteroids, comets and meteoroids.

References

American Association for the Advancement of Science (1989). *Science for all Americans: A Project 2061 report on literacy goals in science, mathematics, and technology.* Washington, DC.

Anderson, L.W., Krathwohl, D.R., & et al. (Eds.) (2001). *A Taxonomy for Learning, Teaching, and Assessing: A Revision of Bloom's Taxonomy of Educational Objectives.* Boston, MA: Allyn & Bacon (Pearson Education Group)

Badder, W., Peck, D., Bethel, L. J., Sumner, C., Fu, V. & Valentino, C. (2000). *Discovery works.* (Texas ed.). Boston: Houghton Mifflin.

Bloom, B.S. & Krathwohl, D.R. (1956). *Taxonomy of Educational Objectives: The Classification of Educational Goals, by a committee of college and university examiners. Handbook I: Cognitive Domain.* New York: Longmans, Green

Bybee, R., Buchwald, C.E., Crissman, S., Heil, D., Kuerbis, P., Matsumoto, C. & McInerney, J.D., (1989). *Science and technology education for elementary years: Frameworks for curriculum and instruction.* Washington, DC: The National Center for Improving Science Education.

Cavallo, A.M.L. (2001). Convection connections: Integrated learning cycle investigations that explore convection—the science behind wind and waves. *Science and Children, 38,* 20–25.

Cavallo, A.M.L. (2005). Cycling through plants. *Science and Children, 4,* 22–27.

Full Option Science System (FOSS). (2000). Lawrence Hall of Science, University of California, Berkeley, CA.

Lawson, A.E., Abraham, M.R., & Renner, J.W. (1989). *A theory of instruction: Using the learning cycle to teach science concepts and thinking skills.* NARST Monograph No. 1.

Marek, E.A., & Cavallo, A.M.L. (1997). *The learning cycle: Elementary school science and beyond* (Rev. ed.). Portsmouth, NH: Heinemann.

National Research Council (1996). *National Science Education Standards.* Washington, DC: National Academy Press.

National Science Teachers Association. (2003). *Standards for science teacher preparation: Skills of teaching* (Revised Version). Washington, DC: National Science Teachers Association.

National Science Teachers Association (NSTA). (2002). Elementary school science. Position paper. Retrieved, from*http://www.nsta.org/about/positions/elementary.aspx.*

National Science Teachers Association (1998). *Standards for Science Teacher Preparation: Skills of Teaching.* Washington, DC: National Science Teachers Association.

Piaget, J. (1964). Cognitive development in children: Piaget, development and learning.

Journal of Research in Science Teaching, 2, 176–80.

Renner, J.W., & Marek, E.A. (1990). An educational theory base for science teaching.

Journal of Research in Science Teaching. 27(3): 241–46.

Sandoval, J. S. (1995). Teaching in subject matter areas: Science. *Annual Review of Psychology,* 46, 355–74.

TEA (2013 mod.) *Texas Essential Knowledge and Skills by Chapter*, online: *http://www.tea.state.tx.us/index2.aspx?id=6148.*

University of California, Lawrence Livermore National Laboratory (2006). Plasma: The fourth state of matter. Retrieved from *http://FusEdWeb.llnl.gov/CPEP/.*

Subject Test V: Fine Arts, Health and Physical Education (805)

COMPETENCY 001: VISUAL ARTS

The teacher understands concepts, processes, and skills involved in the creation, appreciation, and evaluation of art and uses this knowledge to plan and implement effective and engaging visual arts instruction.

Fine Arts or Visual Arts?

Fine arts is an umbrella term used to describe artworks that appeal to people's aesthetic perceptions. The fine arts include music, theater, sculpture, painting, printmaking, and other traditional forms of art. However, the fine arts exclude applied arts or craftwork like basket weaving, ceramics, and textiles. To include more forms of artistic expression, the term **visual arts** was coined. Visual arts refers to such artistic expressions as sculpture, painting, and printmaking, but it also includes less familiar art forms. These include textiles, basket weaving, ceramics, metalworking, and jewelry-making as well as more recent art forms, such as photography and filmmaking.

Visual arts is a more inclusive term that better describes arts produced and appreciated in modern society.

Children's Artistic Development

Children's earliest experiences with visual arts are more scientific than artistic. A child making marks by moving a crayon or marker across a surface is concentrating on the sensory experience more than on self-expression or symbolism. The child is most interested in the texture of the surface, the colors that appear, and the shapes that emerge. By age three or four, however, the child may notice a similarity between an actual object and a mark that he or she has made. At this point, the child artist realizes that the colors and shapes can symbolize people, objects, and events in real life (Shirrmacher and Fox, 2009).

Drawing is one of the most basic forms of communication used across cultures. Children from diverse cultural backgrounds use a similar style and content in their attempts to express ideas graphically. Around age five, children move into drawing symbols to represent people and objects. A house, for example, may be consistently represented as a square with a triangle on top, regardless of the appearance of the house in reality. The use of symbolized drawings continues through the early elementary years, when children typically become enamored with repeating a particular theme in their drawings. A scene with a house, a tree, and hills in the background, or one with a spaceship, a planet surrounded by rings and a quarter moon may be repeated often and with little variation as the child artist works toward his or her ideas of perfection. As children move into the middle and later elementary years, they strive increasingly to achieve photographic realism in their art. They may experience frustration at this point, and this frustration may convince some children that they do not have artistic abilities. They then might become reluctant to participate in art activities.

Goals in Art Education

The goals of art education include developing children's aesthetic perception and providing experiences with many art forms. Art education also aims to facilitate children's reflections on and discussions of how they observe and respond to art. Education in the arts also provides opportunities for children to develop and extend their own artistic abilities, and it exposes children to characteristics and objects of art. Art education empowers children to analyze diverse forms of the visual arts by using informed judgment. Because of these important benefits and life skills, art education is a vital component of the Texas Essential Knowledge and Skills for grades K–12.

Texas Essential Knowledge and Skills

The state curriculum for fine arts and visual arts is organized around four main strands—**perception, creative expression, historical/cultural heritage,** and **critical evaluation**. A summary of the key elements required for children in grades K–6 is presented in Table 7-1 (TEA, 2013 mod.). Traditionally, an art teacher collaborates with EC-6 teachers to deliver these curriculum components. EC-6 teachers should understand the visual art curriculum components and know how to integrate them throughout their grade-level curriculum.

Table 7-1. Visual Arts Strands for K–6 in Texas

Grade	Perceptions	Creative Expressions	Historical/Cultural	Critical Evaluation
Kinder-garten	Identify colors, textures, and forms in the environment.	Create artwork using colors, forms, and line.	Share ideas about personal artworks and show respect for different opinions.	Express ideas about personal artworks, and the artworks of peers or professional artists.
1	Identify such art elements as color, texture, form, and line with emphasis on nature and human-made environments.	Invent images that combine color, form, and line and organize forms to create designs.	Show a basic understanding of art history. Select artwork that shows families and groups.	Make informed judgments about their own creations and the work of peers.
2	Continue using color, texture, form, line, space as well as such art principles as emphasis, patterns, and rhythm to create artworks.	Produce drawings, paintings, prints, constructions, and modeled forms using different art materials.	Develop respect for the artistic traditions and contributions of diverse groups.	Define reasons for preferences in artworks.
3	Continue emphasizing such art principles as emphasis, patterns, rhythm, balance, proportion, and unity in artworks.	Express ideas through original artworks using different media. Develop compositions using design skills; and produce drawings, print constructions, and ceramics.	Compare artworks from different cultures and link them to different occupations.	Apply simple criteria to identify main ideas in original artworks.
4	Communicate ideas about self, family, school, and community using sensory knowledge and experiences.	Invent ways to produce artworks and to explore photographic imagery using different media and materials.	Compare artworks from different groups; identify the role of art in American society.	Interpret ideas and moods in original artwork.
5	Identify in artworks basic arts elements like color, texture, form, line, space, and value.	Express ideas through original artworks, using different media with appropriate skill.	Show an understanding of art history and culture as records of human achievement.	Make informed judgments about their own creations and the artworks of others.
6	Use art vocabulary to describe the interdependence of the art elements, value and principles such as emphasis, pattern, rhythm, balance, proportion, and unity.	Express ideas through original artworks, using different media with appropriate skill.	Show an understanding of art history and culture as records of human achievement.	Make informed judgments about their own creations and the artworks of others.

Art Techniques and Materials

Painting and drawing are familiar activities to most elementary teachers, but other techniques and materials in the visual arts curriculum may be foreign to them. Some less familiar activities are:

1. **Printmaking:** This artistic process makes a print in which color (paint or ink) is applied to an object, and the object is then pressed onto a surface. When the object is lifted, a print remains on the surface.

2. **Ceramics:** The use of clay to create ceramics is one of the oldest art forms. Ceramics requires the use of a special oven to treat fresh clay with heat until it hardens. Traditionally, a special paint is used to create the desired color as well as the shine that typifies ceramics.

3. **Textiles:** The textile arts use plant, animal, or synthetic fibers to make practical or decorative objects, including stitchery, weaving, dyeing, printing, lace making, knitting, crocheting, and embroidery.

4. **Basket weaving:** This ancient art uses unspun fibers (pine straw, animal hair, hide, grasses, thread, or wood) to create baskets or other forms for artistic or practical purposes.

5. **Metalworking:** Traditional metalworking is the artistic process that shapes metals to produce individual pieces, assemblies, or structures, including jewelry.

6. **Photography and filmmaking:** This relatively recent art creates still or moving pictures by recording images on a sensitive medium, such as photographic film or an electronic sensor.

7. **Sculpture:** A sculpture is a three-dimensional artwork made by shaping or combining such hard material as marble, rock, glass, wood, or metal. Some sculptures are created directly by carving a solid material; others are assembled, built together and fired, welded, molded, or cast.

8. **Computer-generated art:** This relatively new form of art is created through the manipulation of pixels, either through drawing and painting software or through electronic images stored in the computer. The computer screen serves as the canvas, and colored light is the medium.

The Art Classroom

Whether art activities happen in an art room or the regular class, the room should allow for individual seating as well as small-group and large-group arrangements. In addition to space for learning centers, the teacher should have space to lecture and display students' work. The room also needs areas for drawing, painting, and printmaking as well as for creating computer graphics. The room also should have space for modeling and for assembling crafts. The room should have natural and artificial light, and materials should be stored in cabinets, with teachers controlling access. Safety guidelines are critical, and following them should be mandatory. Easy maintenance is a must, so sinks and surfaces must be durable and have cleanable finishes.

Visual Arts Activities for K–6

Throughout the elementary grades, students engage in such art activities as drawing, painting, designing, constructing, crafts, sculpting, weaving, and finger-painting. In grades 3 and 4, students continue developing the skills from K through 2 and work with such new techniques as printmaking, sponge painting, graphics, film animation, and environmental design. In grades 5 and 6, students should show technical skills and be able to make art based on personal experiences and direct observation.

The elementary curriculum encourages the integration of visual arts in the regular classroom with special activities in the art room. Appropriate art activities should focus first on self-expression. Because the fine motor and perceptual skills of children are still developing, their creative work may have little resemblance to reality. That's not the aim of artistic activities with children. The important goal is to encourage children to experiment, explore, and express their own ideas through their own artistic efforts. A list of strategies to engage students in art follows.

Activities to Engage Student in the Arts

1. **The Colors of the Rainbow.** Guide students to observe a rainbow and identify the colors it shows.

   • After they identify the colors of the rainbow—red, orange, yellow, green, blue, indigo, and violet—use the same activity to introduce the concept of primary and secondary colors.

2. **Experimenting with Colors.** Guide children to experiment mixing colors to discover the three secondary colors. Students can be guided later to combine colors to create tertiary colors. Use this table to guide their experimentation.

Primary Color 1	Primary Color 2	What color will result?	Actual results
Yellow	Blue		Green
Yellow	Red		Orange
Blue	Red		Purple

3. **Printmaking.** Ask children to bring artifacts that can be used in printmaking. Some common examples are leaves, pieces of fruits or vegetables, butterflies or pieces of fabrics. Establish a connection between printmaking and the concept of fossils.

4. **Art Critics.** Present paintings from different artists, and guide students to examine them based on the elements of art (line, space, value, color and texture). Guide more advanced students to analyze the artworks based on the principles of art (emphasis, balance, rhythm, contrast, movement and harmony).

5. **The Arts in Occupations.** Provide a list of occupations and guide students to determine how these occupations use the visual arts. Some of the occupations with clear connection with visual arts are: architects, plastic surgeons, engineers, advertisements, fashion designers, and photographers.

6. **Colors in Advertising and Branding.** Guide students to study the color wheel and determine how advertisers and designers use complementary colors in advertising, website development, and car designs as well as in decorating offices and buildings.

Materials for the elementary art program include scissors, wet and dry brushes, fabrics, wrapping papers, film, computers, clay, glue, construction paper, crayons, beads, and multiple household items. Safety is a primary concern, and toxic substances or potentially dangerous tools should not be allowed in the classroom. Rotating familiar materials for use in classroom art projects should help encourage artistic engagement.

Assessment in the visual arts is based on the child's attitudes and dispositions toward engaging in activities to produce and appreciate art:

- Does the child engage in art-production activities willingly and enthusiastically?
- Is the child willing to try new materials and techniques?
- Does the child express original ideas in his or her artwork?
- Does the child thoughtfully consider the art products of others and discuss the elements and principles of the exhibited art?

The EC-6 teacher and the arts specialist should consider these questions carefully during the assessment. By relating art production in the elementary curriculum to art products created by artists from other historical eras and cultures, children are introduced to art appreciation and the elements and principles of art. An analysis of the elements and principles of art follows.

Elements and Principles of Art

Art communicates and expresses ideas, emotions, and experiences. To communicate their own ideas and to understand the ideas of other artists, children must know the elements of art. Young artists use the elements and principles of art to create paintings, drawings, and designs.

Elements of Art

The elements of art are the individual components that combine to create artwork line, shape, space, value, color, and texture (National Gallery of Art, n.d.). Most works of art have at least some aspect of each. A description of the elements follows.

1. **Line** refers to marks from a pen or brush used to highlight a specific part of a painting or structure. More subtle lines can be used to accomplish the opposite effect.

2. **Shape** represents a self-contained, defined area of a two- or three-dimensional area creating a form. The two basic types of shapes are geometric and organic. *Geometric shapes* refer to squares, triangles, circles, and rectangles. *Organic shapes* describe more natural shapes like leaves, animals, and clouds.

3. **Space** describes the emptiness around or within objects. Space can be used to create perspective, to create objects or people in different planes, and to create a sense of depth. Positive space is the main area or object of focus in an artwork. Smaller objects in a painting seem farther away, while larger objects appear to be closer.

4. **Value** refers to the darkness or lightness of an artwork. Values are commonly used to create the two-dimensional quality of artwork. Values also indicate the source of light in a work and provide a three-dimensional view of figures by suggesting shadows. Values can also represent the tone of the artist and the artwork. Darker values show sadness, mystery, or formality, while lighter values usually indicate contentment and relaxation.

5. **Color** represents reflected light and the way it bounces off objects. The three primary colors are red, yellow, and blue. They cannot be created through combinations of other colors. The secondary colors are created through the combination of primary colors. The three secondary colors are green, orange, and violet. There is an unlimited number of tertiary colors. The tertiary colors fall between the primary and secondary colors. The compound colors contain a mixture of the three primary colors. There also warm colors (such as yellow, orange, and red) and cool colors (such as blue, green, and purple). There are also complementary colors. These colors go well in combination. For example, complementary colors are used to develop websites and to create PowerPoint presentations. Figure 5.1 shows the complementary colors (Ryan, 2002–2009). Artists use all these color combinations to create the environment of a painting.

6. **Texture** describes the surface quality of a figure or shape. A shape can appear to be rough, smooth, soft, hard, or glossy. Texture can be physical (felt with the hand—for example, a buildup of paint) or visual (giving the illusion of texture—for example, the paint gives the impression of texture, but the surface remains smooth and flat).

Figure 7-1. Complementary Colors

Color Wheel

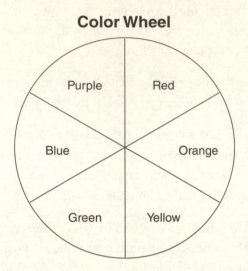

The complementary colors are those in the opposite side of each other. For example, purple is a complementary color of yellow.

Principles of Art

The principles of art describe the guidelines that artists follow to create art and to deliver their message. Artists use the elements of art to communicate the principles in their creations. The principles of art include emphasis, balance, rhythm, contrast, movement, and harmony (National Gallery of Art, n.d.). A description of these principles follows.

1. **Emphasis** is the technique of making one part of a work stand apart from the rest. It guides viewers to pay attention to specific details or components of the artwork. The lines and texture often lead viewers to the target feature. Lines in paintings and sculpture can point or lead to where to focus the attention. By making texture different from the rest of the work in one area, the artist can also make the target area stand out.

2. **Balance** refers to the positioning of objects in such a way that none of them overpower other components of the artwork. Size, space, color, shape, and lighting can be used to create balance. For example, a large shape close to the center can be balanced by a smaller shape close to the edge. A composition with a large light-toned shape can be balanced with a small dark-toned shape. The two main kinds of balance are symmetrical and asymmetrical. Symmetrical balance occurs when the two halves of a figure coincide to create a mirror image. The line of symmetry is the line that divides the figure in two. The easiest way to identify symmetrical figures is to fold the figure in half. If these two halves are identical, we can say that the figure is symmetrical. Asymmetrical balance occurs when two sides of an artwork are different. For example, the artwork of the American flag—horizontal lines of different sizes and a smaller rectangle in the upper left corner with stars—makes it asymmetrical.

3. **Rhythm** describes the patterns used in the artwork. For example, placing a repetition of objects evenly spaced presents a regular type of rhythm. Elements increasing or decreasing in size in an artwork present a progressive rhythm.

4. **Contrast** creates interest through the combination of elements. Contrast can break the monotony or repetitious pattern in a work of art. Rembrandt's paintings are known for using value (lightness and darkness) to create contrast. He also used lighter values to highlight portions of the paintings.

5. **Movement** refers to how artists produce the illusion of motion. In painting, artists use line to simulate the movement of wind or water. This technique leads viewers to perceive the effects of motion and action through the artwork.

6. **Harmony** represents a sense of completeness in the artwork. It shows the unity of the artwork. For example, texture and color can be combined to provide a sense of balance and harmony.

While the elements and principles of art provide the foundations of artwork in all media and styles, they also apply to other disciplines and contemporary occupations. **Line**, **shape**, **space**, and **balance** have parallel meanings in the mathematics, while **texture** and **color** are also basic in scientific observation. Similarly, **rhythm** and **harmony** describe synonymous concepts in both art and music. Such mathematical concepts as symmetry, angle, distance, and convergence appear in artwork and must be understood by artists. Similarly, artists explore science concepts related to light, water, and temperature in their work. Engagement in art also requires artists, whether adults or children, to problem-solve and think. Artists must consider how to communicate emotions and ideas in their work, how to convey change and movement, and how to use symbolism. Artists of all ages must also learn to evaluate their own creative work and that of others.

For an analysis of strategies and lesson plans to teach the elements and principles of art, see the website of the National Gallery of Art at *http://www.nga.gov/content/ngaweb/education/teachers.html*.

Application of Art Principles in Other Fields

The skills and dispositions required of artists apply to multiple fields and occupations. For example, architects and interior designers draw upon the elements and principles as well as other technical skills of art to create aesthetically pleasing designs for buildings, landscaping, and interior spaces. Commercial artists apply their abilities to advertising as well as to the animation of comics or cartoons and the illustrating of print media. Teachers should show students how the visual arts are present throughout daily life and guide them to identify and enjoy these artworks wherever they appear.

Identifying Characteristics of Style in Works of Art

A **style** is an artist's manner of expression. When a group of artists during a specific period, which can last a few months, years, or decades, have a common style, it is called an **art movement**.

These movements are found predominantly in Western cultures and occur in both visual art and architecture.

There are eight main historical periods, each with artistic styles and art movements within each. Although some periods have only one or two unique art styles, the 20th century has produced 36 unique styles. Descriptions of some of the widely known styles throughout history follow (Witcombe, 1995).

The **Prehistoric** period is characterized by paintings that represent the daily activities of a group of people. The best-known representation of this type of art is the Caves of Altamira in modern Spain. The Paleolithic peoples of Europe produced small, stylized stone carvings of women as symbols of fertility. These small statues have been found most often in modern France, Italy, and Austria.

The **Ancient** period produced a large number of masterpieces from such varied civilizations as the Sumerians, Babylonians, Assyrians, Egyptians, Greeks, and Romans. These civilizations carved even the hardest rocks, such as granite and basalt, into battle narratives and historical records. As they did with their architectural monuments the pyramids, the Egyptians made their statues colossal to exalt the power of their society's leaders and gods. Ancient Greek art has its roots in the Minoan civilization on the island of Crete, which flourished about 2500 to 1400 BCE. The palace at Knossos held characteristic wall paintings revealing a civilization interested in games and leisure as well as the beauty of the sea.

Mainland Greeks of the **Classical** period, which occurred about 1,000 years after the ancient period, were fascinated by physical beauty. The Greeks fashioned their Olympian gods in the human image, with a universal ideal of perfection and guided by a master plan, recreating them in idealized and gracefully proportioned sculptures, architecture, and paintings. The populace in the **Hellenistic** period (330–31 BCE) was fascinated by physical beauty and appreciated these objects of art for their beauty alone. Roman culture excelled in engineering and building, skills intended to organize a vast empire and provide an aesthetic environment for private and public use. The Romans built temples, roads, bathing complexes, civic buildings, palaces, and aqueducts. One of their greatest artistic and engineering accomplishments was the Pantheon, the massive-domed temple of all the gods. The Pantheon is one of the best preserved of all buildings from the classical period.

The **Medieval** period (500–1400 CE) also produced numerous artistic masterpieces. The Romanesque style of art and architecture was preeminent about 800 to 1200 CE. By then, many local styles, including the decorative arts of the Byzantine Empire and the German and Celtic tribes, were contributing to European culture. Common features of Romanesque churches include round arches, vaulted ceilings, and heavy walls that are ornately decorated, primarily with symbolic figures of Christianity. Gothic architecture flourished during this period with the creation of magnificent ribbed vaulting and pointed roofs. The cathedrals in this style represent some of the purest expressions of an age. They combine a continued search for improvements in engineering and structure al with stylistic features that convey a relentless verticality, a reach toward heaven, and the unbridled adoration of God. Soaring and roomy, the construction of the Gothic cathedrals employed such elements as flying buttresses (structure to reinforce a wall) and pointed arches and vaults. They also included a number of sculptures and stained-glass windows that for the worshippers were visual encyclopedias of Christian teachings and stories

Renaissance (14th to 16th century) artists developed new forms and revived classical styles and values, with realism and the belief in the importance of the human experience on Earth. Great sculptors approached true human characterization and realism as they revived elements of Greek architecture. Like the painters of the period, Renaissance architects took a scientific, ordered approach and emphasized perspective and the calculated composition of figures in space. Art became more emotional and dramatic. Because of this, the use of color and movement increased, and the compositions were more vigorous. The references to classical iconography and the pleasures of an idyllic golden age also increased. Typifying this emotional, dramatic art are Michelangelo's magnificent Sistine Chapel frescoes and his powerful sculptures of David and Moses; Leonardo da Vinci's *Mona Lisa*; Raphael's *School of Athens* fresco; and the increasingly dramatic and colorful works of the Venetian and northern Italian masters Titian, Correggio, Giorgione, and Bellini.

Baroque style emerged in the 17th century in Europe. This style used exaggerated motion and elaborate artwork. The movement produced drama, tension, exuberance, and grandeur in sculpture, painting, literature, and music.

Rococo art characterizes the art of the early 18th century. Artists of the Rococo era turned the agitated drama of the baroque style into light, pastel-toned, swirling compositions that seem placed in an idyllic land of a golden age.

Nineteenth-century art was characterized by three elements—romanticism, realism, and impressionism. In the first half of the nineteenth century, landscape painting in England reached a zenith with the works of John Constable and Joseph Mallord William Turner. Turner's awe-inspiring landscapes form a bridge between the spirit of romanticism and the expressionistic brushwork and realism of the Barbizon School in France, whose chief painters were Charles-Francois Daubigny and Jean-Baptiste-Camille Corot. Beginning with Barbizon, the French painters of the 19th century concentrated increasingly on the journalistic depiction of everyday life and the natural environment in a free, painterly (gesture and brushwork) style.

Realism rejected traditional means of composing a picture, academic methods of figure modeling and color relations, and accurate and exact rendering of people and objects. Realism instead emphasized quickly observed and sketched moments from life, the relation of shapes and forms and colors, the effects of light, and the act of painting itself. The realist pioneers were Gustave Courbet (*The Stone Breakers, A Burial at Ormans*), Jean-François Millet (*The Sower, The Angelus*), and Honoré Daumier (*The Third-Class Carriage*).

Impressionism began with Edouard Manet in France in the 1860s. French artists continually blurred the boundaries of realism and abstraction. They used light and color to capture the impression of images as opposed to the "real image." The landscapes and everyday-life paintings of impressionist artists like Claude Monet, Camille Pissarro, Pierre-Auguste Renoir, Alfred Sisley, and Edgar Degas gave way to the more experimental arrangements of form and color of the great postimpressionists: Paul Gauguin, Vincent van Gogh, Georges Seurat, and Henri de Toulouse-Lautrec. Auguste Rodin produced powerful sculptures with the freedom of impressionist style.

Twentieth-century art provided new avenues for artistic expressions:

Surrealism is one of the new trends in painting that emerged in the 20th century. Inspired by the psychoanalytic writings of Sigmund Freud and Carl Jung, artists made the subconscious and the metaphysical important in their work. The influence of psychology is especially evident in the work of the surrealist Salvador Dali. Dali created surrealistic paintings as revealed in dreams, free of such conscious controls as reason and conventions.

Cubism and the abstract paintings of Pablo Picasso also emerged during the 20th century. This art represents the most direct call for the reduction and fragmentation of realistic depiction. Artists challenged common realistic conventions to create new representations of reality or imagination. Cubism is the most important and influential movement of European paintings and sculptures in the early 20th century.

Muralists and social realists between World War I and World War II created art that was physically interesting and with subjects accessible to the average person. John French Sloan, George Bellows, Edward Hopper, Thomas Hart Benton, Grant Wood, and John Steuart Curry were among those who celebrated the American scene in paintings, frequently in murals for public buildings and through widely available fine prints. The great Mexican muralists, who usually concentrated on political themes, include Diego Rivera, José Clemente Orozco, and David Siqueiros. They brought their work to the public in both Mexico and the United States.

Photorealism also emerged as a new art form in which paintings resemble lifelike photos. They are often portraits, *still lifes* (paintings of inanimate subjects), and landscapes.

Graffiti is a new and controversial art form that emerged in inner cities in America. Part of the controversy with this art is how the expression is conducted. Traditionally, through the use of spray-painting and brushes, the artists create the work on the surface of private and public buildings and often without the approval of the owners. For some, graffiti is a nuisance or worse. For others, it represents a liberating response to authority as well as the pressure of modern life.

Art in Other Cultures

The progression of art in **China** is divided into periods according to the ruling dynasty and the development of technology. The earliest Chinese art products were made from pottery, jade, and, eventually, bronze. Porcelain art forms were introduced in early imperial China and were so refined that in English the word *china* came to mean high-quality porcelain. Buddhism arrived in China in the first century BCE and strongly influenced artists throughout the country. Calligraphy and painting were popular art forms, with artists working primarily on silk until paper was invented. Although classical sculpture was the dominant art form of the Tang dynasty, landscape painting, almost impressionistic in its portrayal of distance, dominated the Song dynasty. Color painting and printing were emphasized during the Ming dynasty and reached their peaks during the Qing dynasty when painters known as **Individualists** began to use free brushwork to express their ideas more openly. Beginning in the 19th century, Chinese artists were increasingly influenced by Western ideas and techniques. In the early 20th century, **social realism** was the dominant theme of Chinese artists. During the Cultural Revolution of the mid-20th century, art schools were closed, and exhibitions were prohibited. Following the Cultural Revolution, however, art exchanges were established with other countries, and artists experimented with themes and methods. Wang Yani, a child prodigy whose work since 1975 has exemplified *xieyi hua,* a freehand style, has received much attention (Cultural China, n.d.).

Traditional **African** art was intended to please the viewer and uphold moral values. Because traditional African art was based in religious and ethical meanings, the human figure was the primary subject. African art was most often created and exhibited or used in ritual contexts that dealt with important moral and spiritual concerns (Ray, 1997).

Native American art encompasses a mix of media and techniques that include pottery, wood-carving, weaving, stitchery, painting, beadwork, and jewelry-making. Art forms and symbols vary across Native American tribes. Tribal artisans relied on available natural resources to determine the media in which they worked, and their art often beautified common items and created objects of spiritual significance.

Integration of the Arts in the Content Areas

The arts can be easily integrated with other academic content areas. In reading, children can draw to present the main idea of a story. When they learn to write, they then can add words to their drawings. Art appreciation activities also provide an appropriate context for children to notice and discuss details in a painting. Through observation and description, children practice new vocabulary and use descriptive language. Scientific principles like light, color, and texture can be easily introduced through artwork. Likewise, art concepts of space, proportion, and balance can be introduced through mathematics. A history lesson can be enriched with a discussion of the key art movements and artists in each historical period. For example, the Goya's paintings can enhance a discussion of the Napoleonic Era in Spain. Artworks in all media can provide meaningful visual contexts to frame discussions of culture and history.

Evaluating Works of Art

To judge the quality of a work of visual art, students should be given basic criteria for evaluation. The main principle of the criteria can be derived through questions similar to the ones presented below:

- What is the artist's purpose?

- Does the work achieve that purpose?

- Has the artist spoken with a unique voice, regardless of style, or could this artwork just as easily be the work of someone else?

- Is the style appropriate to the expressed purpose of the work?

- Is the work memorable and distinctive?

- Was the work created to meet social or cultural needs?

- Has the artist used the elements and principles of art effectively?

After answering such questions, a student might determine the specific timeframe of the painting and the style in which it was painted. When addressing these questions, students should show they can describe a work of art using such technical terms as line, color, value, shape, balance, texture, repetition, rhythm, and shape. They should also be able to describe some of the major periods in the history of the visual arts. Guiding students to describe the artistic works associated with major artistic periods can provide students with an overview of human accomplishments and artistic productivity. This knowledge should help guide students to examine and enjoy the value and contribution of the arts to life in the United States and the world.

COMPETENCY 002: MUSIC

The teacher understands the concepts, processes and skills involved in the creation, appreciation and evaluation of music and uses that knowledge to plan and implement effective and engaging music instruction.

The goal of music education is to develop independent musicians through the use of conceptual teaching of musical skills. It is expected that music teachers be literate in music in much the way English teachers are literate in language. Teachers of music should be able to teach children how to sing in tune, keep a steady beat, listen to different styles of music appropriately, and perform music expressively. Teachers should also learn and use music terminology and the elements of music. Additionally, they should learn the appropriate methodology to integrate music in the content areas, and apply knowledge for evaluating and critiquing musical performances

Elements of Music

Essential to the understanding of music are the key elements upon which all music is based—rhythm, melody, harmony, form, and expression. **Rhythm** is the varied lengths of sounds and silences in relation to the underlying beat. Usually children (K–3) confuse beat and rhythm and try to make them the same thing. Beat is the pulse that is felt in the music and rhythm is typically called the melodic rhythm or word rhythm found in the song. Audiate[1] the song "Happy Birthday"; the beat is the underlying pulse and the melodic rhythm is the words to the song. Now audiate "The Star-

---

[1] Audiation is the cognitive process of hearing music inside one's head.

Spangled Banner"; the beat may or may not be faster or slower (the speed of the underlying pulse of music is called **tempo**, see Table 7-2). The beginning of "The Star-Spangled Banner" has the same melodic rhythm as the beginning of "Happy Birthday." "Happy Birthday" begins with "Happy birthday to you" and has the same melodic rhythm as "Oh say can you see." After this beginning, the two songs do not have the same melodic rhythm. Melodic rhythm is identified using musical notation (the writing of music), which includes various types of notes and rests (see Figure 7-2).

Table 7-2. Tempo Markings

Tempo Marking	Speed
Grave	Extremely Slow
Largo	Very Slow
Adagio	Slow—leisure pace
Andante	Walking pace
Moderato	Moderate
Allegretto	Moderately quick
Allegro	Fast
Vivace	Lively
Presto	Quick

Figure 7-2. Musical Notes and Rests

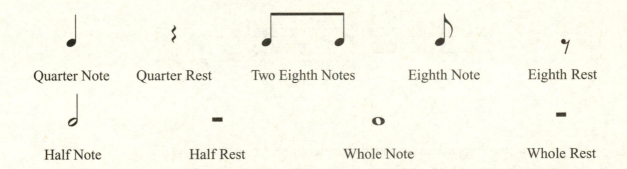

Quarter Note   Quarter Rest   Two Eighth Notes   Eighth Note   Eighth Rest

Half Note   Half Rest   Whole Note   Whole Rest

Meter refers to how musicians group the steady beats. When the beat is grouped in 2s, it is in duple meter, which can be felt as marching or walking. When the beat is grouped in 3s, it is in triple meter, which can be felt as swaying to the music or a waltz.

Melody is the succession of sounds (or pitches) and silences that may move upward, downward, or stay the same. The "tune" or the singable part of the song is the melody. A **musical staff** (see Figure 7-3), consisting of five parallel lines and four spaces, is needed to read a musical tune. The **pitches** are represented by symbols called **notes** placed on the staff. There are seven letters found in the musical alphabet (A, B, C, D, E, F, and G). The **clef signs** at the beginning of the song determine the pitch level, either higher or lower. Typically, the **treble clef** is the singing range of women and the right hand on the piano; and the **bass clef** is the singing range of men and the left hand on the piano (see Figure 7-4). A grand staff combines both treble and bass clefs and can be seen in piano music and some hymns written for singers.

Figure 7-3. Musical Staff

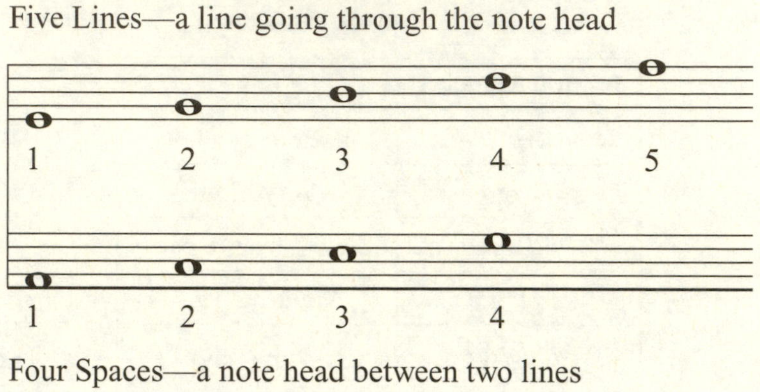

Five Lines—a line going through the note head

Four Spaces—a note head between two lines

Figure 7-4. Musical Staff or Grand Staff with Clefs and Notes

Treble Clef

Bass Clef

Most music teachers use mnemonics when teaching the names of the lines and spaces in both clefs. The way to remember the names of the lines in the treble clef is the mnemonic "**E**very **G**ood **B**oy **D**oes **F**ine." The spaces of the treble clef spell **FACE**. The mnemonic for the lines in the bass clef is "**G**ood **B**oys **D**o **F**ine **A**lways" and the spaces are "**A**ll **C**ows **E**at **G**rass."

Interval is the distance between two pitches. For example, "Twinkle, Twinkle Little Star" has an interval of a 5th between the first and second *Twinkle*. That means that the first pitch (C) and the second pitch (G) are five steps apart. All intervals are identified by a number (e.g., 3rd) except for unison and octave. Unison is two sounds of an identical pitch and an octave is the distance between one pitch and the next pitch with the same name eight steps apart. When someone is singing or playing in tune (with correct pitch accuracy), they have good intonation; however, intonation can refer to one being flat (below the pitch) or sharp (higher than the pitch).

Harmony is usually the accompaniment or supportive sounds to a melody. These accompaniments are typically played by a pitched instrument, such as a piano, guitar, or autoharp. You can teach harmony to children at a young age by singing the melody and playing the simple accompaniment on the ukulele. Harmony can also be taught by having students sing in at least two parts. For example, ostinato, which is a pattern that repeats itself, is a great way to teach harmony to first- and second-grade students. You can sing the melody and have the students sing the ostinato (see Figure 7-5) or vice versa. Another way to produce harmony is through the use of singing rounds, such as *Row, Row, Row Your Boat*. A round is where everyone sings the melody and subsequent voices enter at specific intervals after the leader. Partner songs are another example of harmony where two different songs can be sung at the same time.

Figure 7-5. Melody with Ostinato

Let Us Chase the Squirrel

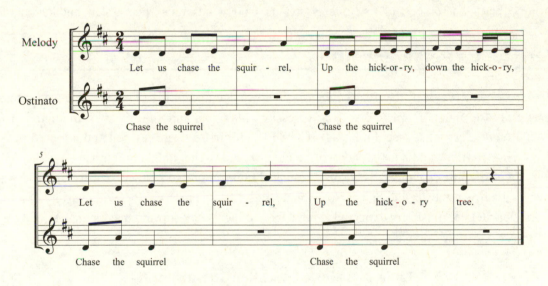

Form is the structure or design of the music. A phrase, which is a musical line that contains groups of pitches, is similar to a sentence in language. Several musical phrases make up a song just like several sentences make up a paragraph. These phrases can define a song. Musical forms are analogous to mathematical patterns. Common forms in elementary music are binary (AB), ternary (ABA), theme and variation (A A1 A2 A3 A4 etc.), and rondo (ABACA). The different musical sections determine the form. For example, if there is a song that has a verse/refrain(chorus)/verse structure, it is labeled as ABA form. If the song has one section that keeps repeating the melody, then it is called rondo form where the A section (or melody) keeps returning. These forms are easy to identify through listening to orchestral literature.

Expression consists of dynamics and timbre. **Dynamics** is a term used by musicians to represent the louds and softs in music. Typically younger children (K–2) confuse dynamics with pitch level or melodic direction. The word "up" in music is usually associated with pitch level (the music moves up or goes higher) whereas, in the home, if children are asked to turn up the music or television, the word "up" is associated with a dynamic level (louder). Dynamics are expressed using the Italian language (see Table 7-3).

Table 7-3. Dynamics

Italian Term	Dynamic Level
Piano	Soft
Mezzo piano	Medium soft
Mezzo forte	Medium loud
Forte	Loud

Timbre is defined as tone color in music. This tone color refers to the quality of sound that distinguishes one voice or instrument from another. Kindergarten children distinguish between the four human voices—speaking, whispering, calling, and singing; whereas, older students are identifying the timbre of classroom instruments (woods, metals, and skins); singing voices (soprano, alto, tenor, baritone, bass); and orchestral instruments (strings, woodwinds, brass, percussion, and keyboard).

Curriculum Requirements

Texas has developed the Texas Essential Knowledge and Skills (TEKS) for music into four basic strands—music literacy, creative expression, historical and cultural relevance, and critical evaluation and response (see Table 7-4). The TEKS for music were revised and adopted in 2013. The TEKS are designed so students will be able to read, write, and create music; perform music from diverse cultures expressively; make musical connections to history, culture and the world; listen critically to music; and be able to evaluate, describe and respond to a wide variety of musical styles. Teachers of music are expected to have their students develop and master each strand within the prescribed state curricula.

Table 7-4. Music Education Strands for K–5
TEA (2013, mod.)

Grade Level	Music Literacy	Creative Expression	Historical/ Cultural Relevance	Critical Evaluation and Response
K	Identify the difference between the voices, timbre of voices, and instruments. Identify same/different in beat/rhythm, higher/lower, louder/softer, faster/slower, and simple patterns in musical performances. Identify beat, rhythm, and simple two-tone or three-tone melodies using iconic representation.	Sing or play classroom instruments independently or in groups from diverse cultures and styles. Move alone or with others to a varied repertoire of music using gross and fine locomotor and non-locomotor movement. Perform simple part work, including beat versus rhythm, and louder/softer and faster/slower.	Sing songs and play musical games, including rhymes, folk music, and seasons music. Identify simple interdisciplinary concepts related to music.	Identify and demonstrate audience behavior during live or recorded performances. Identify steady beat in music performances, and compare same/different in beat/rhythm, higher/lower, louder/softer, faster/slower, and simple patterns in musical performances.

(continued)

Grade Level	Music Literacy	Creative Expression	Historical/ Cultural Relevance	Critical Evaluation and Response
1	Identify the singing voices of adults and children. Identify visually and aurally the instrument families. Use basic music terminology in describing changes in tempo, including Allegro/ Largo, and dynamics, including forte/piano. Identify and label representation and contrast in simple songs, such as AB, AABA, or ABAC patterns.	Sing tunefully or play classroom instruments, including rhythmic and melodic patterns from diverse cultures and styles, independently or in groups. Move alone or with others to a varied repertoire of music using gross and fine locomotor and non-locomotor movement. Perform simple part work, including beat versus rhythm, rhythmic ostinato, and vocal exploration. Perform music using tempo, including Allegro/Largo, and dynamics, including forte/piano.	Create short, rhythmic patterns using known rhythms, and melodic patterns using known pitches. Explore new musical ideas using singing voice and classroom instruments. Sing songs and play musical games, including rhymes, patriotic events, folk music, and seasonal music. Identify steady beat in short musical excerpts from various periods or times in history and diverse cultures. Identify simple interdisciplinary concepts relating to music.	Identify and demonstrate appropriate audience behavior during live or recorded performances. Recognize rhythmic and melodic elements in simple aural examples using terminology, and distinguish same/different between beat/rhythm, higher/lower, louder/softer, faster/slower, and simple patterns in musical performances. Respond verbally or through movement to short musical examples.
2	Identify choral voices, including unison versus ensemble, and instruments visually and aurally. Use music terminology to explain musical examples of tempo, including Presto, Moderato, and Andante, and dynamics, including fortissimo and pianissimo. Identify and label simple small forms such as AABA and ABAC. Read, write, and reproduce rhythmic patterns using standard notation in 2/4 meter, including half note/half rest; pentatonic melodic patterns using standard staff notation; and basic music terminology, including Allegro/Largo and forte/piano.	Sing tunefully or play classroom instruments, including rhythmic and melodic patterns from diverse cultures and styles, independently or in groups. Move alone or with others to a varied repertoire of music using gross and fine locomotor and non-locomotor movement. Perform simple part work, including rhythmic ostinato, and vocal exploration such as singing, speaking, and chanting. Perform music using tempo, including Presto, Moderato, and Andante, and dynamics including fortissimo and pianissimo. Create rhythmic phrases using rhythm, and melodic phrases using pitches. Explore new musical ideas in phrases using singing voice and classroom instruments.	Sing songs and play musical games, including patriotic, folk, and seasonal music. Examine short musical excerpts from various periods or times in history and diverse and local cultures. Identify simple interdisciplinary concepts relating to music.	Begin to practice appropriate audience behavior during live or recorded performances. Recognize known rhythmic and melodic elements in simple aural examples using terminology. Distinguish between rhythms, higher/lower pitches, louder/softer dynamics, faster/slower tempos, and simple patterns in musical performance, and respond verbally or through movement to short musical examples.

(continued)

Grade Level	Music Literacy	Creative Expression	Historical/ Cultural Relevance	Critical Evaluation and Response
3	Categorize and explain a variety of musical sounds, including voices, wood-wind, brass, string, percussion, and instruments from various cultures. Use music symbols and terminology referring to rhythm, melody, timbre, form, tempo, and dynamics. Identify and label small and large musical forms such as ABAC, AB, and ABA. Read and write and reproduce rhythmic patterns using standard musical notation and pentatonic melodic patterns using standard staff notation.	Sing or play classroom instruments, with accurate intonation and rhythm, a varied repertoire of music such as American folk songs and folk songs representative of local cultures independently or in groups. Move alone or with others a varied repertoire of music using gross motor, fine motor, locomotor, and non-locomotor skills and integrated movement such as hands and feet moving together. Perform simple part work, including rhythmic and melodic ostinato, and interpret through performance music symbols and terms referring to tempo and dynamics. Create rhythmic phrases, melodic phrases, and simple accompaniment through improvisation and composition.	Perform a varied repertoire of songs, movement, and musical games representative of American and local cultures. Identify music from diverse genres, styles, periods, and cultures. Identify the relationships between music and interdisciplinary concepts.	Exhibit audience etiquette during live and recorded performances. Recognize rhythmic and melodic elements in aural examples using appropriate vocabulary. Identify specific musical events in aural examples, such as changes in timbre, form, tempo, or dynamics using appropriate vocabulary. Respond verbally and through movement to short musical examples. Describe a variety of compositions and formal or informal musical performances using specific music vocabulary.
4	Categorize and explain a variety of musical sounds including voices, woodwind, brass, string, percussion, keyboard, electronic instruments, and instruments of various cultures. Use music symbols and terminology referring to rhythm, melody, timbre, form, tempo, dynamics, and articulation to explain musical sounds. Identify and label small and large musical forms such as ABAC, AB, ABA, and rondo. Read, write, and reproduce rhythmic patterns using standard notation in 2/4, 4/4, and 3/4 meters; and extend pentatonic melodic patterns using standard staff notation. Identify music symbols and terms referring to tempo, dynamics, and articulation.	Sing and play classroom instruments, with accurate intonation and rhythm, a varied repertoire of music, such as American and Texan folk songs and folk songs representative of local cultures, independently or in groups. Move alone and with others to a varied repertoire of music using gross motor, fine motor, locomotor, and non-locomotor skills and integrated movement such as hands and feet moving together. Perform various folk dances and play parties. Perform simple part work, including rhythmic and melodic ostinato, derived from repertoire. Interpret through performance music symbols and terms referring to tempo, dynamics, and articulation. Create rhythm phrases, melodic phrases, and simple accompaniments through improvisation or composition.	Perform a varied repertoire of songs, movement, and musical games representative of diverse cultures such as historical folk songs of Texas and Hispanic and American Indian cultures in Texas, including "Texas, Our Texas." Identify and describe music from diverse genres, styles, periods, and cultures; and examine the relationships between music and interdisciplinary concepts.	Exhibit audience etiquette during live and recorded performances. Recognize rhythmic and melodic elements in aural examples using appropriate vocabulary. Describe specific musical events in aural examples, such as changes in timbre, form, tempo, dynamics, or articulation using appropriate vocabulary. Respond verbally and through movement to short musical examples. Describe a variety of compositions and formal or informal musical performances using specific music vocabulary. Justify personal preferences for specific music works and styles using music vocabulary.

Grade Level	Music Literacy	Creative Expression	Historical/ Cultural Relevance	Critical Evaluation and Response
5	Distinguish among a variety of musical timbres, including voices, woodwind, brass, string, percussion, keyboard, electronic instruments, and instruments of various cultures. Use music symbols and terminology, referring to rhythm, melody, timbre, form, tempo, articulation, and meter to explain musical sounds presented aurally. Identify and label small and large musical forms such as ABAC, AB, ABA, rondo, and theme and variations. Read, write, and reproduce rhythmic patterns using standard notation in 2/4, 3/4, or 4/4 meters; and extend pentatonic and diatonic melodic patterns using standard staff notation. Identify and interpret music symbols and terms referring to tempo, dynamics, articulation, and meter.	Sing and play classroom instruments, with accurate intonation and rhythm, a varied repertoire of music such as American folk songs, patriotic music, and folk songs representative of local and world cultures independently or in groups. Move alone and with others a varied repertoire of music using gross motor, fine motor, locomotor, and non-locomotor skills and integrated movement such as hands and feet moving together. Perform various folk dances and play parties. Perform simple two-part music, including rhythmic and melodic ostinato, rounds, partner songs, and counter melodies. Interpret through performance music symbols and terms referring to tempo, dynamics, articulation, and meter. Create rhythm phrases, melodic phrases, and simple accompaniments through improvisation or composition.	Perform a varied repertoire of songs, movement, and musical games representative of diverse cultures such as historical folk songs of Texas and America and European and African cultures in America. Perform music representative of Texas and America, including "The Star Spangled Banner." Identify and describe music from diverse genres, styles, periods, and cultures. Examine relationships between music and interdisciplinary concepts.	Exhibit audience etiquette during live and recorded performances. Identify rhythmic and melodic elements in aural examples using appropriate vocabulary. Describe specific musical events such as changes in timbre, form, tempo, dynamics, or articulation in aural examples using appropriate vocabulary. Respond verbally and through movement to short musical examples. Evaluate a variety of compositions and form or informal musical performances using specific criteria. Justify personal preferences for specific music works and styles using music vocabulary.

Music in the Classroom

Elementary music teachers in Texas typically use two approaches to teach students music: The Kodály Method and Orff Schulwerk.

The Kodály Method

The Kodály Method developed out of Zoltán Kodály's principles and step-by-step process for Hungarian teachers. This teaching technique is rooted in Hungarian culture, but can be adapted to other cultures and is used by some Texas music teachers. The main goals of the Kodály Method are to instill the love of music into all children; to have children achieve music literacy; start music education in early childhood; teach music sequentially; use quality folk songs; and cultivate the singing voice. The 3 P's (preparation, presentation, and practice) are vital to the teaching process in Kodály. These 3 P's are similar to the whole-part-whole approach where the teacher prepares a concept, teaches the concept, and then, through repetition and review, masters that concept. The tools used in Kodály are solfege (*do, re, mi, fa, sol, la, ti, do*), hand signs (to present a visualization in space of the high-low relationships of the pitches being sung), and rhythm syllables (quarter note = ta, eighth notes = ti, etc.). Other tools include musical flash cards, stick notation (the music notation without the note head) and musical ladders that show the melodic direction of the music.

One primary goal of Kodály is to teach music literacy, and singing is the vehicle to achieve this goal. In this method, students start with simple *sol mi* songs and then expand their musical vocabulary to include all pitches in the pentatonic scale (*do re mi sol la*). Singing is the major mode of communication and is as important to the current Kodály teacher as it was to Zoltán Kodály himself. Kodály believed that music was "meant to develop one's entire being personality, intellect, and emotions" (Organization of American Kodály Educators, 2015) and used folk songs as his basis of teaching music.

Orff Schulwerk

Orff Schulwerk[2] is a "learning by doing" approach to teaching music. It is based on what is most natural to children: singing, moving, chanting, creating, improvising, and playing instruments. In an Orff classroom, every child participates and experiences all aspects of music in a noncompetitive atmosphere. Orff Schulwerk begins with speech because Carl Orff, the creator of Orff Schulwerk, believed that speech is tied to rhythm and rhythm is the strongest musical element. These speech rhythms are transferred to the body in the form of body percussion (snap, clap, patchen[3], and stamping). Special Orff instruments are used to accompany the songs or rhymes. These instruments (unpitched and barred) allow students to be creative, which leads to improvisation and later composition.

Unpitched rhythm instruments or classroom percussion (e.g., wood block, triangle, claves, drums, finger cymbals, etc.) and melodic instruments or barred instruments (xylophones, metallophones, and glockenspiels) make up the Orff ensemble. Usually the unpitched instruments play rhythmic figures and add a nice contrast to the Orff ensemble.

The barred (or melody) instruments are unique to Orff Schulwerk and can be found in classrooms all over the world. "The xylophone and metallophone are similar to traditional xylophones and vibes, but are small and have removable bars" (Lange, p. 9, 2005). The easy removal of bars enables children to set up the instruments into a pentatonic scale (see Figure 7-6). Notice that the F's and B's (half steps) are removed from the instrument. Because the pentatonic scale removes the half steps from the instrument, it allows students to have greater success during the instrumental experience because they can play anything on the instruments as a group and there is no disso-

---

[2] Schulwerk means "schoolwork" in German.
[3] Patchen means "patting legs" in German.

nance. The pentatonic scale also allows the students to play simple melodies with greater success because with bars missing, they can visually see the melody. "There are three sizes of xylophones and metallophones: bass, alto, and soprano. The bars on the xylophone are made of wood; the bars on the metallophone are made of metal and have a ringing timbre that is important in the ensemble because of the contrast in sound with xylophones" (Lange, p. 9, 2005). The glockenspiels are smaller (alto and soprano only) and have removable metal bars, similar to the xylophone and metallophone.

Figure 7-6. Pentatonic Scale on Barred Instruments

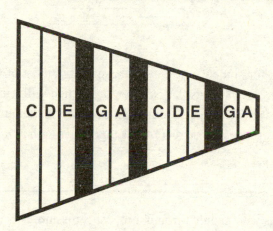

These Orff instruments are what is typically found and played in elementary music classes. They can be used to play simple songs and can accompany singing and other rhythmic and melodic instruments. Traditional band and orchestral instruments are not taught by the classroom music teacher. Usually study of these instruments begins in middle school or junior high with a specialized band or orchestra teacher. The sounds of the band and orchestral instruments are taught to the students during listening lessons by the elementary music teacher. Learning the names and aural identification of these instruments may aid in the selection of playing one of these instruments later in their musical career.

Singing

For young children to learn to sing well, they must sing songs that will not strain the undeveloped vocal chords by singing too high or too low. Typically the classroom teacher sings too low for children and as a result, children strain their voices or do not sing along with the teacher. The best singing range for students in K–2 is from D–A (see Figure 7-7). Students in grades 3–6 can sing a little higher, usually from D–D (see Figure 7-8). Children, in K–6, have a breathy tone quality and should not be asked to sing louder or project their voice. If a louder sound is necessary, add more children. If an adult asks children to sing louder, children will typically yell instead of sing and therefore damage their voice.

Figure 7-7. Singing Range of Students in K–2

Figure 7-8. Singing Range of Students in 3–6

When selecting music for students in K–6, make sure that most of the pitches fall within the desired range listed above. Avoid songs that are too low, which will cause strain and harm to the voice. There are several music collections from around the world that are appropriate for children. When choosing this music, try to choose recordings that are as authentic to the culture as possible.

Repertoire

Historically, folk songs were taught through oral transmission. Nowadays, folk songs are typically learned through written music, except in the elementary music classroom. In this environment, folk songs are taught to students by rote by echo-singing each phrase until the songs are learned. There are different types of folk songs, such as work songs, cowboy songs, and sailor songs. There are also folk songs from different cultures, such as *Sakura* from Japan and *De Colores* from Mexico. Some of the most popular American folk songs are seasonal and patriotic songs.

Singing patriotic songs is an important component in the Texas music curriculum. There are national patriotic songs, such as "The Star-Spangled Banner," "America the Beautiful," and "God Bless America." Explaining the historical significance behind each song is one of the TEKS for music. For example, the text to "The Star-Spangled Banner" was written during the War of 1812 by Francis Scott Key. He was detained on a British ship, in the harbor, while the British bombed Fort McHenry in Baltimore, Maryland. Key wrote the poem on an envelope early the next morning when he saw the American flag still flying over the fort (Star-Spangled Banner n.d.). The poem was later set to a tune written by John Stafford Smith and approved by Congress as the National Anthem on March 3, 1931.

Music has the power to heal wounds, and patriotic songs, because of their unifying nationalistic motifs, typically help in national healing. Since September 11, 2001, the singing of "God Bless America," which can be heard regularly at Major League Baseball games, has played an important part in American culture. For younger students (K–2), "America (My Country 'Tis of Thee)" is an appropriate patriotic song that allows for discussion of American history. Another patriotic song appropriate for middle- to upper-elementary students (grades 3–6) to teach history and culture is

"America the Beautiful." The text of this song was written by an American educator, Katharine Lee Bates, and describes the landscape of the country.

Texas has an amazing history that can be taught in music class through song. For example, "The Old Chisholm Trail" is a traditional folk song that teaches students about the Chisholm Trail that Texas ranchers used to drive cattle to Kansas. Also, students need to know "Texas, Our Texas," which was adopted in 1929 by the Texas Legislature as the Texas state song. It was modified once in 1959 when Alaska became a state and therefore the wording in the song needed to be changed from "largest" state to "boldest" state in the third line of the song (Texas State Libraries and Archives, 2015). Other Texas songs that should be taught in elementary school are: "Deep in the Heart of Texas," "The Yellow Rose of Texas," "San Antonio Rose" and several others that discuss the history and culture of Texas.

Music from diverse cultures is not only one of the TEKS for music, but is popular in Texas schools. For example, Tejano and Mariachi are prevalent in several districts throughout the state. Tejano music dates back to 1690 when Spain settled the area that is now known as Texas. The music developed over the centuries with new settlers from different parts of the world, thus combining several ethnic backgrounds—Mexican, Cuban, German, and Czech. The featured instrument is the accordion and the Tejano orchestra has been influenced by Mexican, Cuban, German, and Czech brass bands. In addition to the instrumentation, the roots of Tejano include various dance styles, which adds to its diversity and cultural heritage (The Roots of Tejano and Conjunto Music, 2015).

Mariachi is a traditional form of Mexican folk music that has become popular in Texas schools. The instrumentation consists of violins, trumpets, a Spanish guitar, and a guitarrón (a large deep-bodied six-stringed acoustic bass from Mexico). Typically several of the band members will sing along while playing an instrument. Usually the group all dress in the same attire with silver studded charro outfits with wide brimmed hats. The size of the group varies from three to fifteen.

Listening/Concert Etiquette

Teaching elementary-aged students how to listen to music and what to listen for in music is important for musical understanding. If students are not taught what to listen for in a piece of music, they will typically begin talking and the music therefore becomes background noise. Preparation of a listening lesson should consist of historical background of the music (e.g. time period and composer biography) followed by information of the music itself (e.g. main theme, instrumentation, musical form, dynamics, etc.). This preparation prior to listening to music, recorded music or a live performance, allows for the students to be actively engaged while listening and should ensure greater concert etiquette. Students in grades K-6 are expected to demonstrate appropriate concert etiquette. Whispering, talking, and turning around in a seat are unacceptable in most classical concert settings. The National Association for Music Education has developed "The Ten Rules for Students" (National Association of Music Educators, 2015). These rules are reproducible for distribution so inappropriate behavior at concerts does not occur. Other inappropriate behaviors, in addition to the three listed above, are dangling jewelry, watch alarms, cell phones ringing, and chewing gum loudly (National Association of Music Educators, 2015). Teaching students the expectations at a concert will benefit everyone involved—performers and audience members alike.

Evaluation

Evaluation is subjective and evaluating musical performances is no different. The way to add objectivity to evaluating music is to use **performance evaluations** (rubrics). A well-written rubric gives students positive feedback to improve their performance, and allows the teacher to measure many students performing at the same time. Rubrics identify critical components to be assessed, and communicate acceptable levels of student performance or expected behavior. Any rubric should be simple enough to allow the students opportunities for self-assessment.

The RubiStar provides opportunities for teachers to create their own rubric. This interactive site lets you choose from a list of music assessment components. Included are rubrics for judging classical concert etiquette, a general rubric for elementary standards and benchmarks, and a rubric for judging instrumental musical performance and music composition. Teachers select the area to be measured and the system provides a description of the levels of performances or the expected behavior. The system also allows the option to customize the rubric. See an example of a customized version to assess classical concert etiquette for elementary education students (see Table 7-5).

Table 7-5. Sample Rubric for Elementary Education Students

CATEGORY	4	3	2	1
Entering the Hall or Auditorium	Stands quietly outside the door, then follows usher quietly to assigned seat.	Talks in a soft voice outside the door, and then follows the usher quietly to assigned seat.	Talks in a soft voice while waiting and while being seated.	Talks in a loud voice while waiting or being seated.
Showing Appreciation	Claps at an appropriate volume at the end of all musical selections. Has pleasant expression and looks toward the performers while clapping.	Claps at an appropriate volume at the end of all musical selections. Does not look at performers when clapping.	Does not clap for all selections or claps at the wrong time.	Claps too loudly, drawing audience attention, or whistles and screams while clapping.

(continued)

CATEGORY	4	3	2	1
Attention	Listens politely to the music. Has an interested expression almost all the time.	Listens politely to the music. Looks interested some of the time. Does not distract others when not listening.	Does not appear to be listening or interested, but keeps quiet and does not distract others.	Distracts others by talking, moving, rattling things, playing with toys, etc. during the actual performance.
Stays seated	Student keeps all body parts within own seating area during entire performance, politely sharing armrest with at least one neighbor.	Student keeps all body parts within own seating area during most of the performance, politely sharing armrest with at least one neighbor. Movements do not distract or irritate others.	Student leans toward another student to talk quietly, but stays in seat and keeps hands and feet to himself/herself.	Student gets out of seat or lets arms, hands, legs stray into the space of another.

Integration

Music can easily be integrated into other subject areas. For example, music can easily be integrated into English Language Arts and Reading through the use of singing books. There are several songbooks, such as *Down by the Bay*, *Señor Don Gato*, and *The Star Spangled Banner* for various grade levels. Music also reinforces poetry when students respond to rhythm, rhyme, and repetition of simple songs and chants. Since music uses text, teachers can teach alliteration, onomatopoeia, and rhyme scheme. When integrating music and math, students use rhythm and meter to count and skip numbers when moving, playing, or singing music. Music also integrates history and culture, as explained earlier in this chapter. Music can be used to teach almost any concept and can be a useful vehicle to help students respond and retain important facts.

COMPETENCY 003: HEALTH

The teacher uses knowledge of the concepts and purposes of health education to plan and implement effective and engaging health instruction.

Enhancing Wellness

The leading causes of illness, disease, and death are not infectious by nature, but rather lifestyle related. Some common diseases such as heart disease, obesity, and cancer are influenced by people's chosen behaviors. The key to achieving good health is taking responsibility for daily actions and creating a proactive lifestyle. Many benefits result from a consistent program of diet and exercise. Improvements in cardiac output, maximum oxygen intake, and mood stabilization, as well as enhancing the blood's ability to carry oxygen, are just a few of them. Health education also includes the awareness and avoidance of risks present in everyday life. Some of the risks include smoking, using drugs, and having unprotected sex. Education is the key to minimizing such risks.

Body Systems

The body has a system of interrelated subsystems working together to keep it functioning properly. Cells are the building blocks of the body, and tissues are groups of similar cells working together to perform a specific job. An organ consists of many kinds of tissues working together for a larger purpose, and a group of organs working together is called an organ system. Several organ systems work in the human body.

Circulatory System. The heart pumps blood in the circulatory system. The blood passes through the right chambers of the heart and through the lungs, where it acquires oxygen. It then passes back into the left chambers of the heart where it is pumped into the aorta, which branches into increasingly smaller arteries, veins, and capillaries throughout the body. Beyond that, blood passes through tiny, thin-walled structures called capillaries. In the capillaries, the blood gives up oxygen and nutrients to tissues and absorbs metabolic waste products containing carbon dioxide. Finally, blood completes the circuit by passing through small veins, joining to form increasingly larger vessels until it reaches the largest veins, which return it back to the right side of the heart.

Respiratory System. Respiration results from the expansion and contraction of the lungs for gas exchange in the body. In the lungs, oxygen enters tiny capillaries, where it combines with hemoglobin in the red blood cells and is carried to the body's tissues. At the same time, carbon dioxide passes through capillaries into the air contained within the lungs. Inhaling draws air that is higher in oxygen and lower in carbon dioxide into the lungs. Exhaling forces the air that is high in carbon dioxide and low in oxygen from the lungs.

Digestive System. Food provides the energy required for sustenance of the body. After the fragmenting of food by chewing and mixing with saliva, digestion begins. Chewed food passes down the esophagus into the stomach, where gastric and intestinal juices continue the digestion process. Thereafter, the mixture of food and secretions makes its way down the alimentary canal using peristalsis (the rhythmic contraction of the smooth muscle of the gastrointestinal tract). The smallest units of food are ultimately absorbed into the bloodstream and transported throughout the body for use.

Immune System. The body defends itself against foreign proteins and infectious microorganisms by means of a complex immune system. The immune system is composed of a dual system that depends on recognizing a portion of the surface pattern of the invader and the generation of lymphocytes and antibody molecules to destroy invading molecules.

Skeletal System. The human skeletal system consists of more than 200 bones held together by connective tissues called ligaments. The bones are attached to the skeletal muscles, and contractions of these skeletal muscles affect movements.

Nervous System. The nervous system controls muscular contractions. The nervous system has two divisions: the somatic, which allows voluntary control over skeletal muscle; and the autonomic (or involuntary), which controls cardiac and glandular functions. Nerve impulses carried by cranial or spinal cord nerves that connect the brain to skeletal muscles cause voluntary movement. Involuntary, or reflex, movement occurs in direct response to outside stimulus. Nerve terminals called receptors constantly send impulses to the central nervous system. Each type of receptor directs nerve impulses to specialized areas of the brain for processing.

Diet and Exercise

Statistics show that Americans get more obese every year (Centers for Disease Control and Prevention, 2014). Although countless books and magazine articles are available on weight control, students often get reliable information about diet and exercise only in the classroom. People who are overweight on average do not live as long as those who maintain optimal weight. Being overweight has been isolated as a major risk factor in certain types of cancer, in heart and kidney disease, and in gall bladder problems. Chronic diseases such as diabetes and high blood pressure are also aggravated by, or caused by, being overweight. Maintaining a good weight and body-fat ratio can definitely affect people's quality of life.

Conversely, being underweight also presents health risks. Society often places too much emphasis on losing weight and being thin. Women are especially prone to measuring their self-worth by the bathroom scale. Young girls are particularly susceptible to these messages, and eating disorders can result (National Institute of Mental Health, 2014). Ideal weight and a good body fat ratio should be the goals when trying to lose weight. A correlation also exists between body fat and high cholesterol. Diet and exercise are the keys to maintaining a good body fat ratio. Exercise helps keep the ratio low, improves healthy cholesterol levels, and prevents heart disease.

Metabolism is a set of chemical processes that occur in the body to keep it functioning and growing as well as responding to the environment and maintaining life balance. The Basal Metabolic Rate (BMR) is the pace at which the body burns the vast majority of calories efficiently at rest. Adjustments in the BMR are slow, occur over time, and are dependent upon the demands put upon the body physically (i.e., exercise) as well as on the consumption of calories. If calorie intake is too restricted, the body goes into starvation mode and operates by burning fewer calories to conserve energy. Just a 250-calorie drop a day combined with a 250-calorie burn will result in a loss of one pound a week. Crash diets, which bring about rapid weight loss, are unhealthy and ineffective. Slower weight loss lasts longer. Aerobic exercise is a major component of successful weight loss. Exercise speeds metabolism and causes the body to burn calories efficiently. The timing of exercise may also enhance the benefits. Exercise before meals speeds metabolism and helps suppress appetite. Education should help people realize that maintaining a healthy weight is crucial to a healthy and higher quality life.

Combined with exercise, a healthy diet is vital to good health, learning, academic achievement, and longevity. The elements of good nutrition, the role of vitamins, elimination of risk factors, and strategies to control weight are all part of a healthy lifestyle. In June 2011, the USDA changed its symbol for healthy eating from a Food Pyramid to a Healthy Plate. Instead of having Americans consider their daily intake, the USDA is encouraging consumers to think about building a healthy diet one plate at a time. The colorful, four-part plate is divided into four sections (Figure 7-9). Fruit and vegetables take half of the plate while one quarter each is reserved for protein and grains. A side container represents dairy.

Figure 7-9. Choose My Plate

Source: U.S. Department of Agriculture, *MyPlate*, *www.teamnutrition.usda.gov/myplate.htm.*

Recommendations include:

1. One-half of the plate should be whole grains (e.g., bread, cereal, rice, and pasta) and proteins, which should vary between animal proteins and legumes.

2. Vegetables and fruit should comprise the other half.

3. Milk products should be low-fat (1%) or fat-free.

4. Compare sodium contents in soups and frozen foods and choose lower sodium products.

5. Drink water instead of sugary drinks.

Nutrients are divided into two main groups: macro-nutrients (carbohydrates, proteins, and fats) and micro-nutrients (vitamins and minerals). Most foods contain a combination of the two groups. Complex carbohydrates (e.g., vegetables, fruits, whole grain breads, and cereals) are the preferred energy source and should comprise up to one-half of the diet. These foods provide fiber, which helps digestion, reduces constipation, and reduces the risk of colon cancer. Proteins (e.g., milk, eggs, meat, fish, and beans) are one of the most essential nutrients because the body uses them to build and repair itself in more ways than any other food. Fats (e.g., olive and canola oils) are important to the body for regulating blood pressure, forming cell structures, transporting vitamins, and triggering immune system responses. Vitamins are essential because they perform highly specific metabolic processes in the cells and aid with many other functions, such as the growth and maintenance of the body. Minerals (e.g., calcium, iron, potassium, and zinc) help build strong bones and teeth, aid in muscle function, and help the nervous system transmit messages. Keeping a consistent balance of nutrients combined with hydration will keep systems functioning properly and thus minimize overall health risk. Much nutrition information is available to teachers at the Dietary Guidelines for Americans, published by the U.S. Department of Health and Human Services (2015).

Stress Management

Stress is the product of change, either negative or positive. Multiple components and situations can cause stress. Some of these are:

- Environmental factors such as noise, air pollution, and crowding

- Physiological factors such as sickness and physical injuries

- Psychological factors such as self-deprecating thoughts and negative self-image

Besides the normal stressors that everyone experiences, some students may live in dysfunctional families. Some also may be dealing with substance abuse and addictions, and some may be experiencing sexual abuse.

People have many sources of stress, and students and teachers should learn acceptable ways to cope with stress. The first step is to recognize the role that stress plays in daily life. A teacher might lead a class through a brainstorming activity to help the students become aware of the sources of stress that affects them. Next, the teacher could identify positive ways of coping with stress, including positive self-talk, physical exercise, proper nutrition, adequate sleep, outdoor play activities, time-management techniques, good study habits, and relaxation exercises.

Students facing stress often experience a range of emotions. They may be sad, frustrated, or afraid. Effective teachers realize that students' emotions play a significant role in students' classroom performance and achievement. Thus, they should seek to create a classroom environment supportive of students' emotional needs. They should have appropriate empathy and compassion for the emotional conflicts facing students. Teachers also should have a realistic awareness that students need to attain crucial academic and social skills that will help them control their environment as they become increasingly independent individuals and, eventually, productive citizens.

The state curriculum for health (Texas Essential Knowledge and Skills) has incorporated objectives and standards to prepare school-age children to face the multiple physical, environmental, and emotional challenges that children face in the United States. Health education teachers and teachers in general are required to teach these health objectives in formal health classes through the integration of health components in the general curricula. All Texas teachers should know the state health curriculum. An analysis of the health curriculum mandates in Texas follows.

Curriculum Requirements for Health

The Texas Essential Knowledge and Skills (TEKS) prescribed state curriculum for health education teachers (Texas Education Agency, n.d.). In conjunction with the national initiative, the TEKS curriculum provides strategies for teaching developmentally appropriate content in health education to children in grades K-12. Some key components of the TEKS require children to develop an understanding of their body as well as of proper nutrition practices and safety procedures. It also requires that children be able to use reliable information to make personal health decisions. Topics introduced in grades K–6 include:

1. Making healthy food choices.

2. Strategies to avoid health and safety risks.

3. Strategies for protection against sexual predators.

4. How media influence health decisions.

5. Assertive behaviors and strategies to deal with risky situations.

6. Gang-prevention programs.

7. Drug- and alcohol-prevention programs.

8. Knowledge of the human body.

9. Safety procedures in school and the community.

Some key skills and activities required in the state K–6 curriculum are listed as follows.

Kindergarten

Children in kindergarten should be able to:

1. Identify types of foods that help the body grow.

2. Identify the purpose of such protective equipment as a seat belt and a bicycle helmet.

3. Identify how to get help from a parent and/or trusted adult when made to feel uncomfortable or unsafe by another person/adult.

4. Demonstrate procedures for responding to emergencies, including dialing 911.

5. Demonstrate how to seek the help of parents/guardians and other trusted adults in making decisions and solving problems.

First Grade

Children in first grade should be able to:

1. Name safe play environments.

2. Describe the harmful effects of alcohol, tobacco, and other drugs as well as explain how to avoid them.

3. Identify and practice safety rules during play.

4. Identify common illnesses and diseases as well as their symptoms.

5. Name members of his/her family who help him/her to promote and practice healthy habits.

Second Grade

Children in second grade should be able to:

1. Describe and demonstrate such personal health habits as brushing and flossing teeth and exercising.

2. Identify the major organs of the body and describe their primary functions.

3. Apply practices to control spread of germs, including hand washing and skin care.

4. Demonstrate refusal skills.

5. Identify media that provide health information.

Third Grade

Children in third grade should be able to:

1. Describe ways to improve personal fitness.

2. Identify types of nutrients.

3. Explain the body's defense systems and how they fight disease.

4. Relate how protecting the environment promotes individual and community health.

5. Describe how the media can influence healthy behaviors.

Fourth Grade

Children in fourth grade should be able to:

1. Identify information on menus and food labels.

2. Explain how to develop a home-safety and emergency response plan such as fire safety.

3. Explain how sleep affects academic performance.

4. Identify the importance of taking responsibility for developing and maintaining a personal health plan for such subjects as fitness, nutrition, stress management, and personal safety.

5. Identify ways to avoid drugs and list alternatives for the use of drugs and other substances.

Fifth Grade

Children in fifth grade should be able to:

1. Apply information from the food guide plate to make healthy food choices.

2. Calculate the relationship between caloric intake and energy expenditure.

3. Explain strategies for avoiding violence, gangs, weapons, and drugs.

4. Explain the impact of neglect and abuse.

5. Assess the role of assertiveness, refusal skills, and peer pressure on decision-making and problem-solving.

Sixth Grade

Children in sixth grade should be able to:

1. Analyze healthy and unhealthy dietary practices.

2. Explain the consequences of sexual activity and the benefits of abstinence.

3. Seek the input of parents and other trusted adults in problem-solving and goal-setting.

4. Make such healthy choices as leaving a smoke-filled room or selecting healthy snacks from vending machines.

5. Describe chemical dependency and addiction to tobacco, alcohol, and other drugs and substances. (Texas Education Agency, n.d.)

Human Growth and Development

A teacher does not have to be an expert in anatomy and physiology to see the physical changes that accompany students' growth and maturity. The preschool child has trouble grasping pencils and crayons to facilitate handwriting. However, even most two-year-olds can grasp crayons well enough to make marks on papers and thus enjoy the creative excitement of art. Physiological changes play a significant role in children's development as they increase their control of bodily movements and refine their motor skills. Their ability to engage in simple to complex classroom and playground activities increases as they develop. Teachers must adjust and adapt classroom and playground activities to be developmentally appropriate for students' skill levels.

Girls typically reach maturational milestones before boys. Physical changes may embarrass girls and boys when they draw unwelcome attention. These changes usually create discomfort as adolescents find their body to be quite different, sometimes seemingly overnight. Teachers should make children aware that these changes are part of their natural development.

To build social and emotional health, teachers should understand principles of human development as well as its multiple dimensions (e.g., physical, mental, emotional, and social). Teachers also must appreciate a dynamic and interactive view of human development. This approach to understanding human development recognizes that people do not develop in a vacuum. They instead develop in an environment that, friendly or unfriendly, supportive or non-supportive, evokes and provokes reactions from individuals. Human development also is not a one-way street with the environment doing all the driving. People also act to shape and form their environment.

People constantly interact with their environments. Teachers must know and be sensitive to the personal characteristics of students (internal factors) and the characteristics of the environment. Beyond the characteristics humans share as they grow and mature, internal factors also include students' personalities as well as their self-concept and self-esteem, their self-discipline and self-control, their ability to cope with stress, and their outlook on life (attitude).

Empowerment has many components, including self-concept. A good definition of self-concept is what we believe to be true about ourselves, not what we think about others and not what they think about us. Self-efficacy is related to self-concept and refers to the confidence a person has in his/her ability to cope with challenges. Self-efficacy is the sense of control over life or over the responses to life. Ideas about self-efficacy get established by age four. Because of this early establishment of either a sense of control or a sense of having no control, classroom teachers may find that even primary grade students believe they lack control over their lives and that it makes no difference what they do or how they act. Therefore, teachers must help students gain coping skills and develop a sense of self-efficacy.

Substance Use and Abuse

Drug and alcohol problems can affect anyone, regardless of age, sex, race, marital status, place of residence, income level, or lifestyle. However, certain risk factors are identifiable for substance abuse and have individual, familial, social, and cultural characteristics.

The personal characteristics linked to substance abuse include aggressiveness, emotional problems and low self-esteem as well as the inability to cope with stress. Feelings of failure and a fragile ego can also contribute to substance abuse. Physical disabilities, physical or mental health problems, and learning disabilities can add to a student's vulnerability to substance abuse. Students at risk for academic problems are also susceptible to substance-abuse problems.

Several family characteristics are associated with substance abuse. First, the alcohol or other drug dependency of a parent or both parents may be most important. This characteristic might relate to another significant factor: parental abuse and neglect of children. Antisocial and/or mentally ill parents also put children at risk for drug and/or alcohol abuse. Family unemployment or underemployment is another characteristic. Parents with little education or who are socially isolated are also risk factors. Single parents without family or other support, as well as family instability, and a high level of marital and family conflict or violence are other risk factors. Parental absence—because of separation, divorce, or death—can also increase children's vulnerability to substance abuse. Finally, other considerations include a lack of family rituals as well as inadequate parenting, little child-to-parent interaction, and frequent family moves. These factors describe children without affiliation or a sense of identity with their families or the community. Any of these family factors could lead to a substance abuse.

Living in an economically depressed area with high unemployment, inadequate housing, a high crime rate, and a prevalence of illegal drug use are social characteristics that can put someone at risk for substance abuse. Cultural risk factors include racial discrimination, differing generational levels of assimilation, low levels of education, and low achievement expectations from society. All the recognized risk factors are indicators of potential substance abuse. They do not necessarily predict a proclivity to drug or alcohol abuse. Some children who are exposed to very adverse conditions grow up to be healthy, productive, and well-functioning adults. Yet, knowing the risk factors, teachers are better able to identify children vulnerable to substance abuse and develop prevention-education strategies. If teachers recognize the risk factors in some of their students, teachers can take action designed to increase the chances that the child will resist the lures of illegal and dangerous alcohol and drug abuse.

It can be hard to tell whether someone is using illegal drugs or alcohol. People (including young people) who abuse drugs or alcohol go to great lengths to keep their behavior a secret. They deny and/or try to hide the problem. However, certain warning signs indicate that someone is using drugs or drinking too much alcohol: (1) Lying to teachers and family members, (2) Avoiding people who are longtime friends or associates, (3) Having slurred speech, (4) Complaining of headaches, nausea, or dizziness, (5) Having difficulty staying awake in class, and (6) Bloodshot, glazed over, and/or squinting eyes. These signs alone will not confirm a substance abuse problem, but in combination and when displayed consistently over time, they are strong indicators. Teachers should record their observations and keep written reports of behavioral changes they witness. Moreover, they should report their suspicions to the appropriate school authorities.

Violence and Abuse

Child abuse is a common problem in the United States. According to the American Academy of Pediatrics, more than 2.5 million cases of child abuse and neglect are reported annually (Shelov & Remer, 2009). Half the cases involve neglect, and the other half involves physical and sexual abuse.

Abused children typically show signs of overstimulation—being "wired," unruly, and/or belligerent. By contrast, the behaviors of neglected children point to understimulation—all they want is to be left alone and typically they are unsociable, sedate, and/or withdrawn. The child learns this behavior at home during periods of neglect. The neglect may change the child's behaviors from almost flat (registering no emotion) to anger. Although poor attention, tears, violence, and apathetic behavior may indicate either abuse or neglect, neglected children usually have feelings of hopelessness and cannot adequately control their thoughts and emotions. Students either become obsessed with the neglect or refuse to acknowledge that the neglect is really happening.

Despite the media attention given to child abuse and neglect, many teachers still believe that it cannot happen to one of their students. They may think, "This is a nice neighborhood," or "Most of these students have both a mother and a father living at home." But teachers should instead keep in mind that it can happen to their students.

One of the most obvious visible signs of child abuse is red swelling or bruising caused by being hit. The appearance of marks on a child may prove child abuse, and the teacher must report the evidence immediately. Visible signs are also one way teachers can separate real abuse cases from unfounded ones. While marks from the hand, fist, or belt are usually recognizable, other marks in geometric shapes (i.e., eating utensils, paddles, coat hangers, or extension cords) can signify child abuse as well.

Besides showing the physical marks, victims of child abuse and neglect can also exhibit nontraditional behaviors. The most common documented characteristics include: (1) frequent illness; (2) hyperactivity disorders; (3) depression; (4) bowel or bladder control problems; (5) impulsivity, aggressiveness, or defiance; and (6) academic difficulties. Neglect is more common than abuse but gets less attention because it fails to show easily observable manifestations.

Teachers hope they will never have to manage a disclosure of any kind of maltreatment of a child, but such revelations are the responsibility of these trusted adults and student advocates. When a child discloses abuse, teachers should respond calmly and thank/support the child for bringing this matter to their attention. Teachers should not question the child about the details but should gather the information and follow-up with administrators, counselors, and/or nurses. The best course of action is to make an immediate referral or report of these suspicions.

Teachers in Texas are required by law to report any suspicion of child abuse or neglect to the Department of Human Services. Thus, they must be vigilant for possible symptoms or indications of child abuse. Failure to file a report of suspicion of child abuse or neglect has consequences and can result in legal action against the teacher. After reporting the abuse, the teacher should realize that the child may feel that his or her teacher has exposed the child's private life. While accepting the child's feeling of betrayal, the teacher should explain that the report was necessary and assure the child of protection against reprisals for telling about the abuse. Sometimes the child benefits from just knowing that others care about his or her well-being.

Safety and Accident Prevention

Peer counseling, peer mediation, and peer leadership programs have shown little effectiveness in reducing violence, encouraging safety in schools, and preventing accidents. Restricting promotion to succeeding grades for violent students has shown negative effects on achievement and attendance as well as behavior toward school. Research shows that the most successful programs are multifaceted and linked to a variety of services. Characteristics of such programs include: (1) early start and long-term commitment; (2) strong collaborative leadership that enforces explicit disciplinary policies; (3) ongoing staff development; (4) parental involvement and parental education (e.g., home visits); and (5) role-modeling activities designed to be culturally relevant.

School Violence

Violence is prevalent in most American schools. Some elements that contribute to school violence are: (1) overcrowding, (2) poor design and use of school space, (3) lack of disciplinary procedures, (4) student alienation, (5) multicultural insensitivity, (6) rejection of at-risk students by teachers and peers, and (7) anger or resentment at school routines.

Factors contributing to school safety include (1) a positive school climate and atmosphere, (2) clear and high performance expectations for all students, (3) practices and values that promote inclusion, (4) bonding of the students to the school, (5) high levels of student participation and parental involvement in school activities, and (6) opportunities to acquire academic skills and develop socially.

Teachers must be alert to the signs of potentially violent behavior, while acknowledging that signs can be misinterpreted and misunderstood. Warning signs should be used to get help for children, not to exclude, punish, or isolate them. Some of the imminent warning signs of school violence are: (1) serious physical violence with peers or family members; (2) serious destruction of property; (3) rage for seemingly minor reasons; (4) detailed threats of lethal violence; (5) possession and/or use of firearms and weapons; and (6) self-injurious behaviors or threats of suicide. Teachers should recognize these signs of violence and notify the appropriate authorities. Violence prevention strategies range from adding social skills training to the curriculum to installing metal detectors at the entrances to buildings. Schools should teach all students procedures in conflict resolution and anger management and should explain the school's rules, expectations, and disciplinary policies.

Mental and Emotional Health

Mental and emotional disorders present emotional and physical signs. Depression can manifest itself in an overall lack of interest in activities as well as constant crying or talk of suicide. Anxiety or obsessive thoughts also indicate a possible mental or emotional disorder. Physical signs include a disruption in eating or sleeping patterns as well as headaches, nausea and stomach pain, or diarrhea. The teacher should consider these signs as a cause for serious concerns and treatment.

Psychotic disorders, such as schizophrenia, are serious emotional disorders. These disorders are rare in young children and difficult to diagnose, although one of the warning signs for psychotic disorders is that the student experiences a complete break from the reality of his or her surroundings. Schizophrenics may have difficulty expressing themselves, resulting in unusual speech patterns or even muteness. Schizophrenics are more likely to be boys than girls and may also exhibit facial expressions that are either absent of emotion or overly active.

Infantile Autism

Infantile autism is another serious emotional disorder that appears in early childhood. Characteristics include withdrawn behavior and delayed or absent language and communication skills. Symptoms of autism can appear in children between four and eighteen months of age. Autistic children will usually distance themselves from others and may be unable to experience empathy. In addition, they often cannot distinguish or appreciate humor. Autistic children may have a preoccupation with particular objects or may perform particular activities repeatedly. While autistic children can range in intelligence, some children may have particular skills in focused areas, such as music or math. Diagnosis might inaccurately determine mental retardation, hearing/auditory impairment, or brain damage. Treatment for autistic children may involve therapy, drugs, or residential living. However, only five percent of autistic children become socially well-adjusted adults. Many of these high-functioning autistics are placed in the regular classroom, some with personal aides to facilitate their success.

Eating Disorders

Eating disorders are a real, treatable medical illness in which certain maladaptive patterns of eating take on a life of their own (National Institute of Mental Health, 2014). The main types of eating disorders are anorexia nervosa (lack of desire or interest in food, which results in starvation of the body) and bulimia nervosa (episodes of secretive excessive eating followed by inappropriate methods of weight control such as self-induced vomiting). A third problem that exhibits a total lack of control for eating is compulsive overeating or binge-eating disorder. Many professionals have suggested this condition as a formal disorder although it has not yet been approved as a formal psychiatric diagnosis. Eating disorders frequently develop during adolescence or early adulthood, but some reports indicate their onset can occur during childhood or later in adulthood. Treatments for eating disorders are complex and most often require professional help (e.g., psychotherapy, support groups, and/or hospitalization).

Healthy Interpersonal Relationships

The social domain of health is manifested in our ability to practice good social skills and maintain comfortable relationships with others. Socially, healthy people communicate respect for others, show tolerance and patience, and accept differences without compromising relationships. Successful teachers listen and recognize the needs of others. Ultimately, effective educators recognize ways they enrich and are enriched by their relationships and use these skills to role-model appropriate behaviors.

To become effective communicators, students need learning opportunities to practice interpersonal skills in situations they are likely to encounter (e.g., communicating empathy, resisting peer-pressure, managing conflicts, and asking for help). By practicing such methods, students establish a natural link to express their healthy intentions when the correct situation/environment arises. Educators should look for such ways to practice assertive communication as stating a position, offering a reason that makes sense or is healthy, and acknowledging others' feelings.

Health Care Information

The *Surgeon General's Report* on Health Promotion and Disease Prevention was first released in 1979 creating a public health revolution that emphasized disease prevention and taking personal responsibility for one's health. In 1990, the United States Department of Health and Human Services published *Promoting Health/Preventing Disease: Objectives for the Nation*, which outlined specific objectives for meeting those goals identified in the earlier *Surgeon General's Report*.

These objectives led to the development of *Healthy People 2000*, a document that aimed to reduce preventable death and disability and enhance the quality of life for American society. Today, *Healthy People 2020 (n.d.)* is setting the disease-prevention agenda for the United States, using science, technology, and education. Administrators, teachers, and health professionals must become familiar with the policy of the federal government and incorporate its principles in schools.

Health Care Professionals

School health services typically include policies and programs that assess and protect the health of students. Specifically, the school nurse leads this collaborative effort to direct patient care, screen and diagnose symptoms, promote health counseling services, participate in health promotion and disease prevention, and maintain relationships with allied health professionals and community health service providers. School administrators have the legal responsibility for the safety of all students and for the supervision of the health services program offered in school. Regrettably, many school districts have assigned these tasks to untrained teachers and/or staff, which leads to dangerous practices for the students, teachers, and school district.

Like other states, Texas has a legislative mandate requiring all children to be immunized against certain communicable diseases (e.g., polio, diphtheria, measles, mumps, rubella, chicken pox, and hepatitis) before enrolling in public school. All policies governing communicable diseases should be available to teachers and school employees to promote collaboration and risk reduction. Teachers should always be proactive in obtaining information when a child who suffers from a communicable disease can safely return to school. Besides any formal instruction in health, other teachers should integrate the content areas (e.g., social studies, science, art, and music) to health-related issues. Examples of topics that can be integrated easily into other content areas are:

1. the effects of pollution on health and occupational-related disease (e.g., "black lung" disease)

2. the health care options available to people in different parts of the world and in different economic circumstances

3. differentiation between communicable and non-communicable diseases

4. the importance of washing hands frequently

Older children should be able to explain the transmission and prevention of communicable diseases, and all children should learn which diseases cannot be transmitted through casual contact.

Students as young as kindergartners and first graders can learn how to recognize advertisements that might lead them to make unhealthy choices (e.g., for candy or sugar-laden cereal). By third or fourth grade, children should be able to show they can make health-related decisions regarding advertisements in media. Teachers can encourage students to: (1) avoid alcohol, tobacco, stimulants, and narcotics; (2) get plenty of sleep and exercise; (3) eat a well-balanced diet; (4) receive the proper immunizations; and (5) avoid sharing toothbrushes, combs, hats, beverages, and food with others.

External Influences

The school is a community agency that cannot function properly in isolation. The range of problems associated with students, results from not only school but also parents/family, neighborhoods, and the larger community (e.g., consumerism, media, and environment). Those who advocate for students must realize that the complexity of health and social problems require all community stakeholders to take responsibility and work with the schools to improve the health of students. An important step to confront these challenges is the need for local districts to establish a school health advisory council that includes members from all segments of the community (e.g., school personnel, medical professionals, nonprofit organizations, and the business sector). Such committees work to increase visibility of initiatives, increase the quantity and quality of health-promotion efforts, and reduce duplication of services.

First Aid

First aid is the immediate, temporary care of an injured or ill person. Occasionally, during physical education classes or during school hours, injuries and illnesses occur. Therefore, knowledge of first aid is important for physical education teachers and other instructors. However, a teacher should not attempt first aid if the procedures are unclear. A course in first aid is important for the classroom teacher, and they are readily available from the local American Red Cross.

The following are some common injuries and a brief description of their emergency treatments:

1. **Bone Fracture:** A fracture is a break in a bone. Fractures can be simple, multiple (many breaks in the bone), or compound (a break in the bone and the skin).

   Treatment: Immobilize, use ice to control swelling, and seek medical aid. In the case of a compound fracture, it is important to stop the bleeding.

2. **Traumatic Shock:** Traumatic shock is the severe compression of circulation caused by injury or illness. Symptoms include cool sweaty skin and a rapid weak pulse.

   Treatment: Minimize heat loss and elevate the legs without disturbing the rest of the body. Seek medical help.

3. **Sprain Injury:** A sprain is an injury to a joint caused by the joint being moved too far or away from its range of motion. Both ligaments and tendons can be injured in a sprain. Ligaments join bone to bone, and tendons join muscle to bone.

   Treatment: Guide the victim to rest, apply ice to the injury, and compression. The use of the acronym RICE—Rest, Ice, Compression, and Elevation—provides an easy way to remember the appropriate treatment for sprains.

4. **Strain Muscle:** A strain is a muscle injury caused by overuse.

   Treatment: Use ice to lessen the swelling and rest. Applying some heat after icing can be beneficial although opinion on the value of heat varies.

5. **Dislocation of a Joint:** In this injury, the bone becomes out of place at the joint. As a result, ligaments can be severely stretched and/or torn.

   Treatment: Immobilize and seek medical help. Some people advocate "popping" the dislocation back into place, but this can be risky for both the injured person and for the person giving the first aid (liability). Therefore, let the medical professionals put the joint back in place.

6. **Heat Exhaustion:** The symptoms of heat exhaustion include cold and sweaty skin, nausea, dizziness, and paleness. Heat exhaustion is not as severe as heat stroke.

   Treatment: Increase water intake, replace salt, and get out of the heat.

7. **Heat Stroke:** The symptoms of heat stroke include high fever, dry skin, and possible unconsciousness.

   Treatment: Try to cool off the body gradually, get into the shade, and seek medical attention immediately.

8. **Heart Attack:** The symptoms of heart attack include shortness of breath, pain in the left arm, pain in the chest, nausea, and sweating.

   Treatment: Elevate the head and chest, give cardiopulmonary resuscitation if indicated, and seek medical assistance. If the heart stops, apply resuscitation techniques. Resuscitation is a first-aid technique that provides artificial circulation and respiration. Remember the ABCs: A is for "airway," B is for "breathing," and C is for "circulation." Check the airway to make sure it is open and check breathing and circulation.

9. **Seizures:** The cause of seizures is often epilepsy.

   Treatment: Clear the area around the victim to avoid injury during the seizure. Do not place anything in the victim's mouth. Seek medical help after the seizure, if necessary.

COMPETENCY 004: PHYSICAL EDUCATION

The teacher uses knowledge of the concepts, principles, skills, and practices of physical education to plan and implement effective and engaging physical education instruction.

Principles of Physical Education and Physical Activity

The Society of Health and Physical Educators (SHAPE) has defined what a student should know and be able to do as a result of a quality physical education program. A quality physical education program provides learning opportunities, appropriate instruction, meaningful and challenging content, as well as regular student and program assessment. SHAPE recommends that schools provide 150 minutes of instructional physical education for elementary school children, and 225 minutes for middle and high school student per week (Society of Health and Physical Educators, 2015).

With this definition in mind, SHAPE has developed the National Standards for Physical Education:

Standard 1: The physically literate individual demonstrates competency in a variety of motor skills and movement patterns.

Standard 2: The physically literate individual applies knowledge of concepts, principles, strategies, and tactics related to movement and performance.

Standard 3: The physically literate individual demonstrates the knowledge and skills to achieve and maintain a health-enhancing level of physical activity and fitness.

Standard 4: The physically literate individual exhibits responsible personal and social behavior that respects self and others.

Standard 5: The physically literate individual recognizes the value of physical activity for health, enjoyment, challenge, self-expression, and/or social interaction.

To help students achieve these standards, physical education teachers must understand the human body and how physical activity can affect it. Knowledge of anatomy and physiology can guide teachers in the selection and implementation of games and physical activities appropriate for development. Anatomy describes the structure, position, and size of body parts and organs. Because our bones adapt to fill a specific need, exercise benefits the skeletal system. Bones that anchor strong muscles thicken to withstand the stress put on them. Weight-bearing bones can develop heavy mineral deposits while supporting the body. Because joints help provide flexibility and ease of movement, it is important to know how each joint moves. Types of joints are ball and socket (e.g., shoulder and hip), hinge (e.g., elbow and knee), pivot (e.g., head of the spine), gliding (e.g., carpal [wrist] and tarsal [ankle] bones), angular (e.g., wrist and ankle joints), partially movable (e.g., vertebrae), and immovable (e.g., bones of the adult cranium).

Muscles are the active movers in the body. To teach physical education activity, the functions and physiology of the muscles must be understood. Because muscles move by shortening or contracting, proper form should be taught so that the student gets the most out of an activity. Knowing the location of each muscle is important to help in teaching proper form while participating in physical education activities. Understanding the concept of antagonistic muscles, with the related information concerning flexors and extensors, is also vital to the physical educator. Imagine trying to teach the proper form of throwing a ball if the instructor does not understand the mechanics. Knowledge of anatomy and physiology is also necessary to teach proper techniques for calisthenics as well as all physical activities. Without applying this knowledge, exercise can harm the body.

Exploration of movement through fun activities constitutes the main focus of physical education in the early grades. However, the curriculum also can provide more organized activities like yoga or low impact aerobic exercise. Aerobic exercise involves muscle contractions and body movement. Because aerobic exercise requires large amounts of oxygen, it will condition the cardiovascular system when done regularly. Some aerobic exercises are suited to developing aerobic training benefits, with a minimum of skill and time. Good aerobic activities include walking, running, swimming, and bicycling. These activities develop fitness and can be done alone with a minimum of equipment. True aerobic conditioning means an activity must require the body to use a lot of oxygen. It also must be continuous and rhythmic, exercise major muscle groups and burn fat as an energy source. Finally, it must last for at least 20 minutes in a person's target heart rate range. Children can participate in low-impact aerobics training, but parents and teachers must monitor their performance. Children will probably try to keep up with adults, and they may not have the strength, flexibility, and/or skill to keep pace. This could lead to undue fatigue, needless muscle soreness, and/or injury.

Benefits of an Active Lifestyle

The axiom "use it or lose it" holds for the human body. Our bodies thrive on physical activity, which is any bodily movement produced by skeletal muscles and resulting in energy expenditure. Fitness enables a person to meet the physical demands of work and leisure comfortably. A physically fit person can enjoy a better quality of life and minimize the development of life-threatening diseases. Unfortunately, Americans tend to be inactive.

Lack of activity can cause many problems, including weak muscles, poor circulation, shortness of breath, obesity, coronary artery disease, hypertension, type II diabetes, osteoporosis, and certain types of cancer. Overall, mortality rates from all causes are lower in physically active people than in sedentary people. Physical activity also can help people manage mild-to-moderate depression, control anxiety, and prevent weakening of the skeletal system. By increasing physical activity, a person may improve heart function and circulation, respiratory function, and overall strength and endurance. These benefits lead to improved vigor and vitality. Exercise also lowers the risk of heart disease by strengthening the heart muscle, lowering pulse and blood pressure, and lowering the concentration of fat in both the body and the blood. It can also improve appearance, increase range of motion, and lessen the risk of back problems associated with weak muscles, weak bones, and osteoporosis. Every person should engage in regular physical activity and reduce sedentary activities to promote health, psychological well-being, and a healthy body weight. Children should engage in at least 60 minutes of physical activity every day.

Proper hydration is also important during physical activity. To help prevent dehydration during prolonged physical activity or when it is hot, people should consume water before, during, and after the activity.

Evaluating and Monitoring Fitness Levels

Two chief reasons for teaching physical education are to instill a willingness to exercise and to encourage students to make good decisions about their health. The evaluation of student performance and progress thus is an essential responsibility of the physical education teacher. In 2007, the Texas Legislature passed a law that requires all students in grades 3–12 to be measured annually on the Fitnessgram. The Fitnessgram is not a test of athletic ability but is rather a health-related fitness assessment that uses criterion-referenced standards to measure physical health (i.e., muscular fitness, aerobic fitness, and flexibility). With regular physical activity, all students should achieve a score on the Fitnessgram that will place them within or above the Healthy Fitness Zone on all test items. The idea is that all students should learn to assess their own level of fitness, interpret assessment results, plan personal programs, and motivate themselves to remain active throughout their lives.

The assessment plan for an elementary physical education program determines the degree to which students reach the identified goals. These critical objectives or "performance indicators" ensure that the teacher focuses activities on skill development and improved performance during movement games and activities. To obtain good body management skills is to acquire, expand, and integrate elements of motor control. This is done through movement experiences based on a creative and exploratory approach. Children not only manage their body with an ease of movement but also realize that good posture and body mechanics are important to their movement process and patterns. A child with good motor control is a child who is confident and graceful. This is important not only for playing games and sports but also for safety. Children without these skills are more prone to accidents and injury. The physical educator should identify and halt incorrect movement patterns, demonstrate proper forms of movement, and help learners to perform the desired movement pattern.

Development of Motor Skills

Physical changes play a significant role in children's development as they gain control of their body's movements and functions. As they develop physically, children refine their motor skills, enabling them to engage in increasingly complex movement lessons and/or activities. To identify patterns of physical development, teachers must first assess the level at which students can control specific movement patterns and then create activities that are developmentally appropriate for their students' physical abilities.

Children between three and four years have mastered standing and walking. At this stage, children are developing gross motor skills, including the ability to hop on one foot and balance, climb stairs without support, kick a ball, throw overhand, catch a ball that has bounced, move forward and backward, and ride a tricycle. Children between three and four are also developing fine motor skills, such as using scissors, drawing single shapes, and copying shapes like capital letters. By age four or five, when most children enter school, they are developing the gross motor ability to do somersaults, use a swing, climb, and skip. These skills require many movement patterns with increasing coordination. Children at this age can dress themselves using zippers and buttons, and they can possibly tie their shoes. They can also eat independently using utensils. Children at this age are increasingly capable of copying shapes, including letters and numbers. They can cut and paste and draw a person with a head, body, arms, and legs. These fine motor skills develop quickly in children at this age. By age six, children can bounce a ball, skate, ride a bike, skip with both feet, and dress themselves independently. As the student develops yearly, the physical skills (both fine and gross motor) become increasingly complex and involve more muscles and coordination. By age nine, children can complete a model kit, learn to sew, and cook simple recipes. By age ten, children can catch a fly ball and participate in all elements of a softball game.

Recognizing the TEKS milestones that most children will achieve by a certain age will help teachers make decisions about academic lessons and tasks. Teachers also may identify children who are not reaching their developmental milestones with the rest of the class. The physical ability of students to engage in simple to complex activities in school gradually increases as they develop.

Physical Educators must adjust and adapt classroom and playground activities to be developmentally appropriate for the specific skill levels of students.

During play, a child engages in meaningful movement patterns that use large muscle groups. Movement education helps a child to develop competency in those general movement patterns. Movement education has been defined as learning to move and moving to learn. Movement competency requires the student to manage his or her body through space, time, and direction with the ability to accomplish basic and specialized physical tasks and traverse obstacles. Basic movement skills are necessary for a child's daily living, whereas specialized skills are required to perform sports and other complex activities with clear techniques. Basic skills must be mastered before the child can develop specialized ones.

Perceptual motor competency is another consideration in teaching body management. Perceptual motor concepts relevant to physical education include those that give attention to balance, coordination, lateral movement, directional movement, awareness of space, and knowledge of one's body. Basic skills can be divided into three categories, locomotor, non-locomotor, and manipulative skills. A more complex movement pattern might include skills from each category. **Locomotor skills** describe the movement children must master to travel or move within a given space. These include walking, running, leaping, jumping, hopping, galloping, sliding, and skipping. **Non-locomotor skills** are used to control the body in relation to gravity. These are typically done while in a stationary position (i.e., kneeling or standing). Some of these activities include pushing, pulling, bending, stretching, twisting, turning, swinging, shaking, bouncing, rising, and falling. **Manipulative skills** are used when a child handles, moves, or plays with an object. Most manipulative skills involve using the hands and feet, but other parts of the body may be used as well. Hand-eye and foot-eye coordination are improved when manipulating objects. Throwing, batting, kicking, and catching are important skills to be developed using balls and beanbags. Starting a child at a less challenging level and progressing to a more difficult activity is an effective method for teaching manipulative activities. Most activities begin with individual practice and evolve into partner activities. When teaching throwing and catching, for example, the teacher should emphasize skill performance, principles of opposition, weight transfer, eye focus, and follow through. Some attention should be given to targets when throwing because students need to be able to catch and throw to different areas and levels. For detailed information on physical education activities for K–6 children, visit the PE Central website at *www.pecentral.org*.

Promoting Physical Fitness

Children in early childhood are not concerned with physical fitness. They are interested in having fun. Based on this premise, a physical education program for this age group should reflect this interest. The child who participates in fun physical activities will get the same benefits as children in a highly structured physical fitness program. It is thus important for K–6 physical educators to understand that programming activities that focus on the students' enjoyment of moving their bodies is much more important than grooming them for success at an event or sport.

Movement education enables children to choose the activity and the method they wish to use. Teachers can structure learning situations so that the child can be challenged to develop his or her own means of movement. The child becomes the center of learning and is encouraged to be creative in carrying out the movement. In this method of teaching, the child is encouraged to progress according to his or her abilities. The teacher is not the center of learning but offers suggestions and stimulates the learning environment through guided discovery. Student-centered learning works well when there is a disparity of motor abilities. If the teacher sets standards too high, the less talented students may become discouraged and lose motivation. Conversely, if the teacher sets standards too low, the more talented students will become bored and also lose interest. Providing options for learners is the best way to facilitate movement games and activities. Learners can identify which option or challenges are most appropriate and perform up to their developmental level with little help and/or cues from the teacher. Movement education tries to develop children's awareness not only of what they are doing but how they are doing it. Each child is encouraged to succeed in his or her own way according to his or her own capacity. If children succeed at developing basic skills in elementary school, they will have a much better chance at acquiring the specialized skills required for sports, events, and specific activities later in secondary school.

To teach a basic or specialized movement to a variety of learners, the instructor must present and use explanation, demonstration, and drill. Students can do demonstrations if the teacher monitors the demonstration and gives cues for proper form. Drills are excellent to teach specific skills but can become tedious unless they are done creatively. Using simulated games to practice skills can also work to maintain interest during a practice. Teachers should use observation and feedback when teaching a skill or activity. Positive feedback is more conducive to skill acquisition than negative feedback. The "old school" intimidation tactics of physical education coaches will not work for children at this age. Appropriate feedback means correcting with suggestions to improve. A student who continually misses the ball or kicks the ball out of play during kickball is aware that something is not right. The teacher should indicate what the problem is and show the student how to succeed when kicking the ball (and, of course, practice, practice, practice . . . time on task).

Many physical education professionals advocate the Teaching Games for Understanding model as a sound philosophy for teaching movement games. It is a socio-constructivist teaching and learning approach to physical education that emphasizes the learners' engagement in the construction of knowledge, skills, and experience. This student-centered model builds upon critical thinking, problem-solving, observation, and debriefing the experience for specific learning outcomes (i.e., teamwork, sportsmanship, and skill performance). Strategies of this model can be used across the physical education curriculum and include adventure education, cooperative learning, fitness education, tactical games, and sports education.

Curriculum Requirements for Physical Education

The TEKS comprises all the curriculum components in physical education. Physical education teachers are expected to use the prescribed state curriculum (Texas Education Agency, n.d.). In conjunction with the national initiative, TEKS requires children to show knowledge and skills for movement that provide the foundation for enjoyment, continued social development through physical activity, and access to a physically active lifestyle. All children are expected to develop muscular strength and endurance of the arms, shoulders, abdomen, back, and legs. They are also expected to become aware of how the muscles, bones, heart, and lungs work in physical activity. The activities and skills for children in K–6 are designed to keep children active, to develop the fitness necessary for appropriate physical development, and to maintain a healthy body and mind. Some of the key skills and activities required in the state K–6 curriculum are listed below (Texas Education Agency, n.d.).

Kindergarten

Children in kindergarten should be able to:

1. Play with other children within boundaries during games and activities.

2. Develop muscular strength and endurance of the arms, shoulders, abdomen, back, and legs in such activities as hanging, hopping, and jumping.

3. Demonstrate such relationships as under, over, behind, next to, through right, left, up, down, forward, backward, and in front of.

4. Roll sideways (right or left) without hesitating.

5. Toss a ball and catch it before it bounces twice.

First Grade

Children in first grade should be able to:

1. Show proper foot patterns in hopping, jumping, skipping, leaping, galloping, and sliding.

2. Demonstrate the ability to work with a partner in such activities as leading and following.

3. Clap in time to a simple rhythmic beat; create and imitate movement in response to selected rhythms; jump a long rope; and demonstrate on cue key elements in overhand throw, underhand throw, and catch.

4. Describe how muscles and bones work together to produce movement.

5. Demonstrate control in balancing and traveling activities.

Second Grade

Children in second grade should be able to:

1. Demonstrate skills of chasing, fleeing, and dodging to avoid or catch others.

2. Show mature forms of walking, hopping, and skipping.

3. Display good sportsmanship and treat others with respect during game play.

4. Demonstrate simple stunts that exhibit personal agility, such as jumping with one- and two-foot takeoffs and landing with good control.

5. Demonstrate on cue key elements of hand dribble, foot dribble, kick and strike, such as striking a balloon or ball with a hand.

Third Grade

Children should be able to:

1. Show mature forms in jogging, running, and leaping.

2. Demonstrate control and appropriate form, such as curled position and protection of neck in rolling activities.

3. Transfer their bodies on and off equipment with good body control with such items as boxes, benches, stacked mats, horizontal bar, and balance beam.

4. Clap echoes in one measure rhythmical patterns.

5. Demonstrate key elements in such manipulative skills as underhand throw, overhand throw, catch and kick.

Fourth Grade

Children in fourth grade should be able to:

1. Change speed during straight, curved, and zigzag pathways.

2. Catch a football pass on the run.

3. Jump and land for height and distance absorbing force such as bending knees and swinging arms.

4. Perform basic folk dance steps such as schottische (German folk dance), and step-together-step.

5. Demonstrate key elements in such manipulative skills as volleying, hand dribble, foot dribble, and punt, also, striking with a body part, racquet, or bat.

Fifth Grade

Children in fifth grade should be able to:

1. Show smooth combinations of such fundamental locomotor skills as running and dodging and hop–step–jump.

2. Demonstrate the ability to contrast a partner's movement.

3. Identify common phases such as preparation, movement, follow through, or recovery in such movement skills as a tennis serve, handstand, and free throw.

4. Self-monitor the heart rate during exercise.

5. Identify potentially dangerous exercises and their adverse effects on the body.

Sixth Grade

Children in sixth grade should be able to:

1. Use relationships, levels, speed, direction, and pathways in such complex group and individual physical activities as crouching low for volleyball digs, stretching high during lay-ups, positioning for a soccer pass, or passing ahead of a receiver.

2. Move in time to such complex rhythmical patterns as ¾ time or ⅝ time.

3. Hand and foot dribble while preventing an opponent from stealing the ball.

4. Practice in ways appropriate for such learning skills as whole/part/whole; shorter practice distributed over time is better than one long session; or practicing is best in game-like conditions.

5. Select and use proper attire that promotes participation and prevents injury.

Managing Instruction

Managing a large class of children in a loud gymnasium or outdoor learning environment is no easy task. Therefore, a major goal of the physical education teacher is to have all students listen to directions before activity. The instructions should be short, to the point, and as clear as possible. A teacher who talks longer than 20 seconds during any single instructional period will soon find the class losing interest. This leads to an environment difficult to manage. Teachers thus should alternate short instructional episodes including one or two points of focus with longer periods of activity. Minimizing instructional content will reduce student frustration and difficult situations. Most students and teachers enjoy an organized and efficient learning environment that devotes maximum class time to physical activity and learning skills.

Especially early on, the instructor must regularly enforce management behavior routines. Otherwise, the environment will be chaotic and difficult to manage. Effective physical educators identify a consistent keyword to use with learners to start a new activity (i.e., "Begin" or "Ready Go"). This implies encouraging youngsters to listen to the entire set of instructions before preparing for the next exercise. Since the keyword is not given until all directions have been issued, students cannot begin until they hear the keyword. Similarly, a consistent signal should be established for stopping an activity (i.e., "Freeze" or "Clap once . . . Clap twice . . . Clap three times . . ."). The signal must be practiced daily so that the signal becomes second nature to the learners. Using an audio signal (i.e., whistle blast) with a visual signal (i.e., raising the hand overhead) may also be effective, since some youngsters may not hear the audio signal if they are engrossed in loud activity. A loud audio signal may be used to stop a class, but a voice command should always be used to start the class. If children do not respond to these signals, the procedure must be practiced. If a teacher settles for less than full attention, students will fulfill expectations of being chaotic and unmanageable.

Physical education teachers should also know how to divide students into teachable groups quickly. Simple games can accomplish this, such as "Back to Back" or "Foot to Foot," in which individuals get back to back (or foot to foot, etc.) with a partner as fast as possible. Students without a partner are instructed to go to the center of the teaching area (marked by a cone or spot) to find someone else without a partner. If students are staying near a friend, teachers can tell the class to move throughout space using a locomotor skill and then find a different partner each time the body part is called. If arranging students in groups larger than two people, Whistle Mixers work well. When the whistle is blown a certain number of times, students form groups corresponding to the number of whistle blows and sit to signify that they have the correct number of people in their group.

Physical education teachers need to use a consistent approach for dealing with undesirable behavior, and "Time-Out" is generally used. The time out approach moves youngsters out of the class setting and places them into a designated area when they misbehave. Placement in the time-out area does not imply that the student is a "bad person." It just means he or she has forgotten to follow the rules. When placing students in time-out, teachers should communicate to children that they are loved, but their misbehavior is unacceptable. Hence, they are in time-out.

To minimize undesirable behavior, teachers should develop a set of expectations and rules for the class. The expectations should be no more than five items, posted in the teaching area for easy reference. The rules should be discussed regularly so that children understand the expected behaviors and consequences. A set of consequences might be as follows: First misbehavior—the student is warned quietly to avoid embarrassment. Students sometimes are unaware they are bothering others, and a gentle reminder is all that is needed to refocus the behavior. Second misbehavior—the student is told to go to a designated time-out spot. The student must stay there until ready to reenter the activity and show the desired behavior. The student might to go to the area for a short period and return almost immediately to the activity. The assumption is that the student has agreed to stop misbehaving. Third misbehavior—the student goes to time-out for a longer period or the remainder of the period. Besides negative consequences, teachers also should identify positive consequences. The reward system is used to acknowledge students who follow the rules and comply with instructions and to motivate others to exhibit appropriate behavior.

Adaptive Physical Education

The Americans with Disabilities Act (n.d.) requires the placement of students in the least restrictive environment. For most "handicapped children," the least restrictive environment is the regular classroom, which includes participation in physical education activities. The challenge in teaching physical education to handicapped children is tailoring activities to fit each child. For example, blind or partially sighted students can participate in dance and some gymnastic and tumbling activities. These students can also participate in other activities with modifications. A beeper ball together with verbal cues can be used for T-ball or even for softball. If a beeper is unavailable, the teacher can put the student in position and assist in aiming and cueing when to hit the ball. Students using assistive devices like walkers or crutches can be allowed to hit the ball from a seated position and use the crutch to bat. If the child is unable to run, allow a substitute runner. Many games and activities can be modified for the handicapped child. Sometimes all it takes is a little ingenuity to change activities so handicapped students can enjoy participating.

COMPETENCY 005: THEATRE

The teacher understands the concepts, processes and skills involved in the creation, appreciation and evaluation of theatre, and uses that knowledge to plan and implement effective and engaging theatre instruction.

Introduction

The term **theatre** describes a dramatic theatrical live performance in front of an audience. The origin of this kind of performance has been highly debated; however, wall paintings, hieroglyphics, and artifacts suggest that the creation of theatre was heavily influenced by religious ceremonies and public celebrations as well as by the art of storytelling (Robinson, n.d.). The available evidence suggests that theatre/drama originated in Ancient Greece (and indeed the word *theatre* is rooted in the Greek *theaomai*, "to see") around the 6th century BCE, as part of the celebration of Dionysus, the god of fertility and wine (Gascoigne, n.d.). Thespis, a Dionysus priest, allegedly introduce the first form of theatre in Greece. In this initial play, Thespis engaged in a dialogue with the chorus. With this performance, he became the first actor in these types of theatrical performances.

Most plays of the time were performed by a single actor and staged in improvised outdoor scenarios with little or no technical support. For many years, theater was a one-actor show. Later, additional actors were added to the performance.

From its humble beginnings, theatre is now a well-established industry with multiple actors and large crews. Modern performances require large financial investments, with multimillion-dollar revenues. In the United States alone, several venues offer multiple performances year-round. Most major U.S. cities and universities have some form of theatre activity. The most successful locations for theatre in the United States are New York and Las Vegas.

When students are introduced to theatre and its inherent creative and critical aspects, a gateway to a new world of perception and experience opens to them. These perceptual experiences include the physical, emotional, intellectual, aesthetic, social, moral, and spiritual aspects of what it is to be human.

When they act in plays, students shift their perceptions from self to others through voice and physical action as well as through interaction with other performers. Perceptions of reality expand as youngsters interpret the characters in the play.

Genres of Theatre

Traditionally, theatre productions were classified in two main areas—comedy and tragedy. The symbol of theatre, the laughing and weeping masks, represents this historical association. The literature also talks about *drama* as a theatre classification. In its narrow sense, drama refers to a play that deals with a serious topic but cannot be classified as tragedy or comedy. However, modern theatre has developed beyond these classifications. An analysis of some of the key categories of drama follows:

- **Tragedy** is one of the original forms of theatre, developed in Ancient Greece around the 6th century BCE. A tragedy is a dramatic composition of serious and often somber themes. It generally portrays the life and misfortunes of the main characters, leading to their downfall and destruction. Two of the best-known tragedies are: *Oedipus the King* by Sophocles, and *Hamlet* by Shakespeare. In each case, the play has a tragic ending. In *Oedipus the King* the protagonist—Oedipus—killed his father, married his mother, and finally blinds himself as punishment. In *Hamlet*, the protagonist deals with disloyalty, murder and finally, he is killed.

- **Comedy** is another form of theatre developed in Ancient Greece. This type of play uses humor to represent simple topics of daily life. It always ends happily. One of the first comedies produced in Greece is *Wasps* by the Greek playwright Aristophanes, considered to be the father of comedy. This play satirizes an Athenian government official and his demagogic practices.

- **Melodrama** represents the struggle between good and evil. It uses such theatrical elements as music, dialogue, pantomime, and acting to lead to a moral conclusion. One of the first melodramas was *Pygmalion* from the French philosopher Jean-Jacques Rousseau. In this story, a sculptor falls in love with one of his sculptures, and Venus, the goddess of love, feeling his pain, brings the sculpture to life. Modern melodramas adapted or created for television are characterized by extravagant theatricality and oversimplifies and often one-dimensional characterization. Both Spanish and U.S. soap operas fall within this tradition.

- **Satire** uses irony and exaggeration to ridicule such targets as unquestionably held beliefs, extreme religious positions, and human vices to teach a moral. A modern example of a satirical play is *The American Dream* by the playwright Edward Albee, who uses the play to critique the American family.

- **Farce** is a comedy in which the plot is developed around a situation instead of the characters. In lay terms, it has been called situational comedy, or sitcom and has been among the most durable and popular forms of teleplay. Popular television sitcoms that have also earned critical acclaim have included *I Love Lucy, All in the Family, M*A*S*H,* and, more recently, *Seinfeld* and *Frasier*.

Elements and Conventions of Theatre/Drama

To appreciate theatre, teachers should understand the components of a play as well as the elements and conventions of drama and theatre. The playwright, with the support of the stage manager and the actors, uses all the elements of theatre to create a play. Besides the elements of theatre, the playwright uses the conventions of theatre to communicate with the audience. An analysis of these components follows.

Basic Elements of Theatre

Theatre has four main elements: script/scenario, the process, the product, and the audience (Adair-Lynch, n.d.).

1. **Script/scenario** is the foundation of a theatrical performance. The playwright writes the script and conceptualizes the scenario for it. The script and details about the scenario are used to produce the actual performance.

2. In the **process,** the director becomes the artistic visionary who brings to life the ideas of the playwright. The *director,* in consultation with such specialists as the casting director, movement coach, custom designer, vocal coach, and choreographer, designs the structure and the process to lead the play to completion.

3. The **product** is the result of all the efforts and the collaboration of the production crew (producer, director, production manager, stage manager, designers, sound engineers, stage crew, the actors, etc.). It includes every aspect of the performance, including casting, sound and light effects, and the creation of the scenario for the play.

4. The **audience** is the most important component of the theatrical experience. They decide the fate of the play. To engage the audience, modern productions often allow opportunities for actors to interact directly with the audience. Involving the audience in the actual play provides a different experience for both the actors and the audience. This strategy has been used extensively in such modern theatrical presentations as the *teatro campesino*, a theatrical production developed by artistic director Luis Valdez. This type of theatre for the masses emerged as a cultural tool of Cesar Chavez's United Farmworkers strikes of the 1960s (El teatro campesino, n.d.). Eventually, it became a national form of theatre and a tool for the development of Mexican-Americans' consciousness of their social, political, and economic position in society (Library USB, n.d.).

Elements of Drama

The elements of drama or a play are the stagecraft, plot, conflict, mood, music, and theme as well as characters and the form of communication.

- **Stagecraft/Spectacle**

  The stagecraft, or spectacle, describes the creation and preparation needed to stage a play. It includes the special effects, lighting, set, and props as well as the make up, hairstyle, and costumes for the performers.

  The stage manager, together with the costume and scenic designers, creates the stagecraft for the performance.

- **Plot**

  The plot is the storyline. Traditionally, the play has an introduction that sets up a complication that comprises the main action and entwines the characters. The rising action leads to a climax, and the falling action then leads to a resolution.

- **Conflict**

  A struggle between opposing forces. The struggle may be internal (within a character) or external (between characters or between a character and an idea or entity).

- **Mood**

  The feeling or atmosphere of both the physical space and the dramatic action stemming from the characters' performance as well as special effects.

- **Music**

  The music encompasses not only the musical composition for the play but also the rhythm of the dialogues and speeches. It can also include sound effects and the actors' voices as well as songs and instruments.

- **Theme**

  The theme is the central idea of the play. The theme should be thoroughly and consistently integrated into the plot and the dialogue.

- **Characters**

  The characters are the central figures of a play. Through them, the playwright introduces the plot, the theme, and the mood of the play.

- **Communication/Language**

  Communication encompasses all the information presented verbally and nonverbally to stage the play. It includes the design of the stagecraft, the interaction among the characters, and the interaction of the characters with the audience. For oral communication, the playwright can use dialogues, monologues, and soliloquy—in which a character talks alone to convey thoughts to the audience—to communicate the information and create the dramatic mood of the play.

Conventions of Theatre

The conventions of theatre refer to the rules established by the playwright, the director, and the actors to replicate reality and communicate with the audience. Some of these conventions are:

1. Use of a narrator or a chorus to provide information about the scene

2. Using the stage curtain to signal the end of scene, to make changes to the stage, or to allow actors to change costumes

3. Use of realistic or expressionistic costumes

4. Use of strategies for sequencing time—change of lights, change of scenery, change of characters, or the use of make up

5. Use of flash backs and flash forwards to clarify and present information

6. Use of music and songs to set up scenes and provide information to the audience

7. Use of pantomime and exaggerated movement to provide details of a scene

8. Control of the tempo (speed) of the scenes

9. Use of split scenes/conversations—two separate scenes presented concurrently

10. Use of light or sounds to replicate the time of day

11. Use of costumes, sounds, or artifacts to represent a symbol (Example: The use of howling to create a sense of mystery.)

How to Teach Element and Conventions of Theatre

Dramatic play is a natural process that children use to cope with problems and to help them understand the world. It represents one of the earliest manifestations of symbolic thought, which is one of the foundations for the development of language and creative thinking. Dramatic play helps children make sense of the world and practice the language skills needed for further development.

One of the key components of the Texas K-6 state curriculum (TEKS) is to begin developing *self-awareness*, especially in early childhood. Dramatic play gives children opportunities to develop self-awareness in the controlled and protected classroom environment. Through these activities, children also develop problem-solving and socialization skills and improve their understanding of human behavior and conflicts. Dramatic play also lets children practice expressive movement, voice, and characterization. To accomplish these goals, teachers provide opportunities for children to initiate dramatic play in a non-restrictive environment. For students in early childhood, these activities should be spontaneous, as opposed to having the students memorize a script or mimic a structured behavior. Dramatic play offers an effective way to teach these components.

What are the key features of dramatic play?

The Center for Best Practices in Early Childhood (September 2002) identified the following key features of dramatic play:

1. It is a form of pretending that includes role-playing, the use of puppetry, and fantasy play.

2. It can be part of solitary play, which gives children the option of using toys or artifacts to play on their own.

3. It can also become social play, including interaction with the teacher and other students.

4. It can include reading stories to children or showing video presentations to them. In these cases, children can interpret and recreate the story.

5. It can also include props and costumes to provide a framework for the activity, or it can be spontaneous improvisation and child-generated.

Moreover, dramatic play lets children create their own voices to represent different characters of a story. For example, in the Norwegian fairy tale *The Troll and the Three Billy Goat Gruff,* children can practice their theatrical voices by imitating a timorous voice to represent the fear of the first two goats and a more assertive voice for the third goat. They can also recreate a strong and menacing voice to represent the troll. In the same story, children can practice *expressive movement* by walking nervously over the bridge and *characterization* by using facial expressions to show the fear of the first two goats and the challenging behavior of the third goat. Moreover, they can practice *sound effects* with music and the sound of the goat walking over the bridge. All these components of theatre can be practiced in the relaxed and controlled environment of the elementary school classroom.

Older students can be exposed to theatre in a more in-depth fashion through mature and structured play. They can be exposed to play that requires holding auditions, memorizing a script, organizing a crew, setting up the stage, and presenting the play to an audience. Some of the key steps in presenting a theatrical production are:

- **Running a production.** Teachers coordinate scheduling and organize resources. It helps to list the resources available to the production. The teacher may need to check with school administrators and other teachers about the budget and equipment as well as the availability of school facilities. The teacher can then set priorities about the choice of play, auditions, rehearsals, and performance.

- **Selecting a play.** The play should be age-appropriate for the students and approved by school administrators. The stage also should have the necessary technical capabilities for the production.

- **Holding auditions.** Teachers should encourage students to try out for the roles in the play. Teachers often will steer leading roles to older students capable of performing the parts, but this is optional. Students not selected for the play can be encouraged to become part of the production, such as working on the stage crew. The key goal is to involve all students who want to participate.

- **Organizing a stage crew.** The production will require crew members capable of handling sound, lighting, props, costumes, and other technical details. Students who act in one production may take stage crew positions in another.

- **Rehearsing.** The teacher should oversee all the details of preparing the production, from holding rehearsals with the actors to arranging for the stage crew to practice their duties. The teacher must also monitor the students who are acquiring props, building sets, and creating costumes. For a musical play, the teacher should also insist that the musicians join several rehearsals.

Brief History of Theatre

As long as humans have been capable of communication, they have probably employed some form of drama and performance. Cave paintings supply evidence for the early use of costumes and masks to bolster mimetic performances. As either magic or prayer, these performances hoped to encourage nature's productivity. A historical analysis of theatre follows (Adapted from Life 123, n.d.; Educational Portal, n.d.).

Ancient History

Greek plays began around 700 BCE with seasonal ritualistic performances celebrating their multiple deities (Robinson, n.d.). During the festivities different groups competed against each other to win the challenge. Later, Thespis, known as the founder of classical **tragedy,** brought these early performances to the level of drama. He is credited with inventing a new breed of performer, the actor, who would engage the audience by impersonating one or more characters between the dances of a chorus. From the connection of the founder of classical tragedy, the word *thespian* was coined to refer to actors in theatre.

Some of the greatest accomplishments in theatre during this period were (Educational Portal, n.d.):

1. The production of plays by Aeschylus (*Agamemnon*), Sophocles (*Antigone* and *Oedipus the King*), and Euripides (*Medea*).

2. The introduction of dance as part of plays. Euripides is considered the first choreographer in the history of theatre.

3. During the Hellenistic (350-250 BCE) period, *comedy* replaced *tragedy* as the preferred form of theatre. The themes for drama move from politics and philosophy to portrayals of the follies and daily life of people.

Middle Ages

With the fall of the Roman Empire in 476 CE, popular theatre practically disappeared from public view. A new form of play emerged in its place: the **morality** play. Morality and religious plays became the main representation of drama during the dark ages. Medieval theatre in Europe began as a springtime religious observance. This communal and public event drew large audiences to celebrate the teachings of the Old and New Testaments of the Bible. Religious theatre was restricted by such elements as the liturgy, church calendar, and ecclesiastical dress. **Morality** plays were also performed then, and they show the conscience of the Middle Ages. After approximately 200 years, drama moved out of the church to the streets and theatre halls. Historians document that women never performed in medieval plays for two reasons. First, male-dominated, rigidly hierarchical groups like clergy, craftsmen, and merchants predominated. Second, it was believed that boys with trained voices could produce more volume than women.

Contributions of Chinese Theatre

One of the first theatrical performances in China was recorded during the Shang Dynasty (618-907 CE) (Miettinen, n.d.). These original plays used dance, masked performers, and music to develop the plot. They also used puppetry in street performances. The developments of stringed and shadow puppetry are two of the greatest contributions of China to European and world theatre. Early evidence of this type of art goes back to the Han Dynasty (206 BCE to 220 CE).

Renaissance

The European Renaissance began in Italy, where theatre experienced key changes in production and content. The use of music, songs, acrobatics and dance were incorporated as part of theatrical productions. One of the greatest contributions of Italy was the development of commedia dell'arte or Italian comedy around the mid-1500s. This was a popular form of entertainment akin to street theatre, designed to appeal to a mass audience. The home page of the Commedia dell'arte describes it as a colorful theatrical production that uses masks with exaggerated features. It also uses acrobatics to entertain the audience and support the comic plot (n.d.) This type of comedy is one of the greatest contributions of Italian playwrights to theatre.

In France similar changes were taking place. Molière was the chief French playwright among those who changed the world of comedy and drama. Costumes, hairstyles, and makeup on the French stage mirrored popular fashions on the streets and among the nobility. The comedy of Molière stands as one of the most remarkable contributions of France to world theatre. In Spain, dramatists Lope de Vega, Pedro Calderón de la Barca, and Miguel Cervantes helped create the Golden Age of Spanish literature. However, by 1700 Spain's world influence was declining, and its influence on European theatre declined as well.

England joined the movement during Queen Elizabeth I's reign, a period known as the *Elizabethan Era* (1558-1603). In England, theatre was used for the first time as a commercial enterprise.

The stage became lavish with detailed scenery and colorful costumes. The two basic types of costumes were contemporary and symbolic. Symbolic costumes were worn to distinguish the important characters from the ordinary people. This period produced world-renowned playwrights such as Christopher Marlowe and Ben Johnson as well as William Shakespeare, the author who best represents the era. Shakespeare created enduring characters and addressed timeless questions that resonate today. Through his plays, Shakespeare also provided an interesting historical overview of the monarchy because his plays often represented real historical characters and periods.

Romanticism

The Romantic period began in Germany around 1800 CE. During this period, the plot of the drama focused on a hero fighting for justice and against the forces of evil. Melodramas became the preferred form of this artistic movement. Special effects were used to provide the emotion that typifies this form of drama. During this period, women also began acting in plays. Some of the best known plays of the time are:

1. The German Wolfgang von Goethe's tragic play *Faust*, and

2. The French playwright Alexander Dumas' script for the novels *The Three Musketeers* and *The Count of Monte Cristo*.

Modern Era

Political and economic forces of the early 19th and early 20th centuries changed the view of theatre. Theatre became a source of communication with the masses and often a source of political voices. This period also saw the development of technological innovations to facilitate and improve theatre. Some of these were: revolving stage or elevator stage to change scenes, electric lights, and voice amplification technology to communicate with spectators.

The modern era also brought the use of radio, movies, and television. As new technologies took hold, the interests of the audience shifted to the new media. During the first part of the 20th century, radio theatre became the most popular form of theatre in the United States and in the world. Through radio, producers recreated the theatrical experience for larger audiences. Radio delivered live performances with actors, music, and special effects. Radio required listeners to use their imagination to "see" the story unfold before a national audience. Popular stories in drama, mystery, and comedy motivated families to regularly congregate around the radio.

Later, television sought to recreate the theatrical experience through different types of drama, comedy, and mystery shows. The television and movie industries now represent some of the most successful enterprises in the world. People around the world can choose from hundreds of specialized channels presenting their version of theatre. Due in part to the plethora of entertainment options available electronically and the cost for attending theatre performances, today theatrical performances are largely an entertainment for the upper classes.

Despite these changes, the theatre industry has prevailed and continues expanding. Musical dramas have become popular and, in fact, one of the key exponents of modern theatre. Musical productions have become very elaborate, with large casts and extensive ensembles, and the use of sophisticated choreography. In the United States, one of the most memorable musicals of the mid-20th century was Leonard Bernstein's *West Side Story.* In the latter part of the 20th century, musical productions became even more elaborate, with productions like *Cats* and *The Lion King,* which became huge box office successes on Broadway.

Realism in Theatre

As a result of the Realism Movement of the 20th century, drama instruction moved from the exaggerated acting style of the past to a more realistic and natural performance. Improved acoustics in modern theatres and the use of voice amplification technology made this transition possible. In this movement, the characters are real, and the costumes are authentic. The stage in this type of theatre is simple. with three physical walls and a fourth imaginary wall facing the audience (Cash, 2014). The dialogues use everyday speech, including the use of the vernacular to provide a natural view and to identify with the audience. Modern drama is still strong in the United States and the world. However, the high price of admission associated with the costs of production has helped make theatre less accessible to a mass audience.

Modern Acting Theory

Russia's Konstantin Stanislavsky (1863–1938) is a major force in the development of modern acting theories. He developed a technique that became standard for acting classes. He maintained that actors should bring to the play their personal emotions and experiences to prepare for the role. If the character requires a show of anger, for example, the actors should search deep in their subconscious to find when they experienced the emotion. They then should use that experience and the emotion it creates to add realism and credibility to their character. Stanislavsky's theories of acting today provide the main way to teach acting in the United States and perhaps the world.

Texas Essential Knowledge and Skills (TEKS) for Theatre

Theatre, or drama, falls under the umbrella of the fine arts curriculum of the Texas Essential Knowledge and Skills (TEKS). The TEKS for theatre are organized around four main strands—perception, creative expression/performance, historical and cultural heritage, and critical evaluation (TEA, 2013 mod.). These strands constitute the core components of the EC-6 state curriculum.

The key components of the EC-6 curriculum can be summarized as follows (TEA, 2013, mod.):

(1) Through perceptual studies, students increase their understanding of self and others and develop clear ideas about the world. Through theatrical experiences, students com-

municate in a dramatic form, make artistic choices, solve problems, build positive self-concepts, and relate interpersonally.

(2) Students increase their understanding of heritage and traditions through historical and cultural studies in theatre. The study of theatre can promote thinking and further discriminating judgment, developing students who are appreciative and evaluative consumers of live theatre, film, television, and other technologies.

The goal of theatre arts in the elementary grades is to guide learners to use their imagination, improvise dramatization, and use short stories or historical events to foster original thoughts and creativity (Center for Educator Development in Fine Arts, 2013). These key components of the TEKS are introduced in kindergarten and continue to increase in complexity from the early grades to sixth grade and beyond. The expectations are that by the sixth grade, students develop a strong foundation in the elements and conventions of theatre and can analyze and evaluate theatrical performance.

Traditionally, a fine arts teacher in collaboration with EC-6 teachers delivers these curricular components. However, EC-6 teachers often lack the preparation to deliver and integrate quality theatre instruction in school.

Table 7-6 shows an example of how these strands can be integrated in the kindergarten curriculum to promote original thought among students (Adapted from Center for Educator Development in Fine Arts, 2013).

Table 7-6. Theatre Arts Kindergarten Strand Content

Theatre Arts Strands	Content/skills	Activities
Perception	listening and observation skills	• Guide children to arrange illustrations from a story in the correct sequence. • Allow students to use movement to imitate objects and actions from their environment. • Ask children to imitate such sounds as wolves howling, dogs barking, birds singing, or, say, a dripping faucet or the sound of the wind.
Creative Expression/ Performance	Add sounds and movement to a story	• Children stage a simple play after reading the story of the Three Little Pigs. They imitate the walk of the characters and the sounds they make. • They can also practice facial expressions to express surprise, fear, and other emotions.

(continued)

Theatre Arts Strands	Content/skills	Activities
Historical/ Cultural Heritage	Recreating tales from other cultures to better understand people's point of view.	• After listening to the story: The Legend of the Blue-bonnet (Tomie DePaola)—students recreate the story to explore the concept of sacrifice. • After reading about the Columbus voyage and contacts with the natives of America, students can stage a play to represent this initial contact.
Response/ Evaluation	Analyzing and evaluating a performance	• Students view a live or video presentation of a play. While watching the presentation, they model the appropriate behavior of an audience.

For further details on the Theatre TEKS, go to *http://ritter.tea.state.tx.us/rules/tac/chapter117*.

Integration of Theatre in the Content Areas

Theatre can be easily integrated with multiple content areas. Integration of content with the arts has been linked to increased student achievement (De Moss & Morris, 2002). In social studies, teachers can guide students to improvise conversations between and among historical characters. For example, students might improvise conversations among the defenders of the Alamo and leaders of the Mexican Army. In science class, teachers can guide students to represent the life and accomplishments of key scientists. Teachers can also use actors to represent and perform how these scientists use the scientific process.

In language arts, one of the most widely used activities to integrate theatre education is **Readers' Theatre**. In this activity, a story is modified so that characters read portions of the text. Students rehearse their reading part and then create a theatre format to present the reading. Although Readers' Theatre does not require setting up a stage, students can still practice stagecraft, develop costumes, and set up lights and the stage to improve the quality of the performance. On stage, students can also use drawings to represent the background of the story. Children enjoy this approach, and it improves reading. This activity can be especially appropriate for English language learners (ELLs) at different stages of development because the script can be changed to address individual differences. Teachers can modify the script to include non-English speakers through the use of onomatopoeia—sounds of a rooster, a cat, an explosion—that require minimum linguistic development. Table 7-7 presents examples of additional activities to integrate theatre with the content areas.

Table 7-7. Integration of Theatre Arts and the Content Areas

Social Studies	• Guide students to improvise conversations among historical characters. • Develop mock elections in class and guide students to represent political figures. • Guide students to analyze ways in which social and cultural values are expressed throughout history (MLDE, 2006). • Identify the types of jobs available in theatre—actors, producers, stage crew . . .
Arts and Music Education	• Guide students to develop a stage for a performance, using drawing and artifacts. • Select the music for a performance.
Science	• Role-play the life of important scientists and their contribution to society. • Link the scientific principles and manipulation of light, sound, and space in theatrical productions (MLDE, 2006).
Mathematics	• Apply mathematical concepts in the set design and stage directions in theatrical enactment (MLDE, 2006).
Language Arts	• Interpret literary texts. • Identify characters and use of terms like protagonist, villain, etc. • Identify the elements of theatre.

For more information about Readers' Theatre and free scripts, visit Aaron Shepard's Readers' Theatre website at *www.aaronshep.com/rt/RTE.html*.

Benefits of Theatre

Good dramatic experience develops reading in all curriculum areas. Reading with expression and with performance gestures, stage presence and concentration can carry over for the rest of a student's life. The arts involve the use of multiple skills and abilities and can lead students to explore issues in an integrated fashion in authentic situations (Champions of change, n.d.). Moreover, learning expands when students can represent concepts from the content areas through the arts (Seidel, n.d.).

The American Alliance for Theatre and Education (AATE) provides an overview of research on the benefits of participation in theatre arts programs (n.d.). Among the most relevant findings are:

1. Drama promotes student engagement in school and improves reading comprehension.

2. Participation in drama has also been linked to improved attendance.

3. Participation in drama also improves social interaction and communication skills. This interaction improves self-esteem among participants in drama programs.

Drama also can give students opportunities to take risks with language, to connect with their emotions, and to enhance their cognitive abilities. Drama also provides students with opportunities for social interaction, and lets them practice academic content in non-threatening situations. The commitment required from participation in drama and the skills practiced by the participants supports the linguistic and academic performance of all students. It especially can support the performance of diverse student populations.

Visual Arts References

American Orff Schulwerk Association (AOSA). Retrieved from *http://www.aosa.org/index.html* (accessed July 6, 2009).

Cultural China (n.d.) The main artistic features in the development of Chinese paintings, from *http://arts.cultural-china.com/en/23Arts9838.html*.

National Gallery of Art (n.d.). Washington, D.C. Retrieved from http://www.nga.gov

Organization of American Kodály Educators (OAKE). Retrieved from *https://www.oake.org/default.aspx*.

Public Domain Information Project. Retrieved from *http://www.pdinfo.com/index.php*.

Ray, B. C. 1997. *African art: Aesthetics and meaning.* Retrieved from http://static.lib.virginia.edu/artsandmedia/artmuseum/africanart/

Ryan, V. (2002 – 2009). Primary, secondary and complementary colours. Retrieved from *http://www.technologystudent.com/designpro/pricol1.htm*.

Shirrmacher, R., and Fox, J. E. (2009). *Art and creative development for young children.* 6th ed. Upper Saddle River, NJ: Cengage Learning.

TEA (2013 mod.) Texas Essential Knowledge and Skills by Chapter. Retrieved from *http://ritter.tea.state.tx.us/rules/tac/chapter117/index.html*.

Witcombe, C. L. (1995). Art history resources. Retrieved from *http://arthistoryresources.net/ARTHLinks.html*.

Music References

Lange, D.M. (2005). *Together in harmony: Combining Orff Schulwerk and music learning theory.* Chicago: GIA Publications.

Mariachi. (n.d.) Retrieved from *http://www.mariachi.org/history.html*.

National Association of Music Educators. (n.d.). Retrieved from *http://musiced.nafme.org/resources/concert-etiquette-home/*.

Organization of American Kodály Educators (n.d.) Retrieved from *http://www.oake.org/about-us/who-was-kodaly/*.

The Roots of Tejano and Conjunto Music. (n.d.). Retrieved from *http://www.lib.utexas.edu/benson/border/arhoolie2/raices.html*.

RubiStar: Create rubrics for your project-based learning activities (n.d.). Retrieved from *http://rubistar.4teachers.org/index.php?screen=ShowRubric&rubric_id=1837253&*.

Star-Spangled Banner. (n.d.). Retrieved from http://amhistory.si.edu/starspangledbanner/

Texas State Libraries and Archives. (n.d.). Retrieved from *https://www.tsl.texas.gov/ref/abouttx/statesong.html*.

Health and Physical Education References

Americans with Disabilities Act. *Search ADA (n.d.)*. US Department of Justice, Retrieved from *http://www.usdoj.gov/crt/ada/adahom1.htm*.

Centers for Disease Control and Prevention (2014). *Overweight and Obesity.* Retrieved from *http://www.cdc.gov/obesity/data/index.html*.

Fitnessgram (n.d.). *Activity and fitness assessment.* The Cooper Institute, Retrieved from *http://www.fitnessgram.net/*.

Healthy People 2020 (n.d.). *Search Healthy People.gov Homepage.* Office of Disease Prevention and Health Promotion. Retrieved from http://*www.healthypeople.gov/*.

National Institute of Mental Health (2014). *Eating Disorders.* US Department of Health and Human Service. Retrieved from *http://www.nimh.nih.gov/health/topics/eating-disorders/index.shtml*.

PE Central. *The Premier Website for Health and Physical Education* (n.d.). Retrieved from *http://www.pecentral.org/*.

Shelov, S., & Remer. T. (2009). *Caring for baby and young child: Birth to age 5.* American Academy of Pediatrics. New York City, Bantam Books.

Society of Health and Physical Educators (2015) *National Standards.* SHAPE America. Retrieved from *http://www.shapeamerica.org/standards/*.

Texas Education Agency (n.d.). *Texas Essential Knowledge and Skills.* Retrieved from *http://tea.texas.gov/index2.aspx?id=6148/*.

U.S. Department of Agriculture (n.d.). *Search ChooseMyPlate.gov.* USDA Center for Nutrition Policy & Promotion. Retrieved from *http://www.choosemyplate.gov/about.html.*

U.S. Department of Health and Human Services (2015). *Dietary Guidelines.* Office of Disease Prevention and Health Promotion. Retrieved from *www.health.gov/DietaryGuidelines/.*

Theatre References

AATE (n.d.). The effects of theatre education. Retrieved from *http://www.aate.com/?page=effects.*

Adair-Lynch, T. (n.d.). Elements of theatre and drama. Retrieved from *http://homepage.smc.edu/adair-lynch_terrin/ta%205/elements.htm.*

Cash, J. (2014). Realism and naturalism theatre conventions. The Drama Teacher. Retrieved from *http://www.thedramateacher.com/realism-and-naturalism-theatre-conventions/.*

Center for Best Practices in Early Childhood (2002). Dramatic play in early childhood. Retrieved from *http://dramaticplay.wordpress.com/.*

Center for Educator Development in Fine Arts (CEDFA)(2013). Theatre curriculum framework. Retrieved from *http://www.cedfa.org/wp-content/uploads/theatreframework.pdf.*

Champions of change (n.d.). The impact of the arts on learning (Edward B. Fiske, ed.). Retrieved from *http://artsedge.kennedy-center.org/champions/pdfs/champsreport.pdf.*

DeMoss, K. & Morris, T. (2002). How arts integration supports student learning: Students shed light on the connections. Chicago, IL: Chicago Arts Partnerships in Education (CAPE).

Educational Portal (n.d.) *History of Drama: Dramatic Movements and Time Periods.* Retrieved from *http://education-portal.com/academy/lesson/history-of-drama-dramatic-movements-and-time-periods.html.*

El Teatro Campesino (n.d.) Retrieved from *http://www.elteatrocampesino.com/About/missionhistory.html.*

Home page of *commedia dell'arte* (n.d.) A brief history of *commedia dell'arte.* Retrieved from *http://shane-arts.com/commedia-history.htm.*

Library USB. El teatro campesino. Online: *http://www.library.ucsb.edu/special-collections/cema/etc.*

Life 123 (n.d.). A brief history of drama. Retrieved from *http://www.life123.com/parenting/education/drama/history-of-drama.shtml.*

Miettinen, J. O. (n.d.). Early history of Chinese theatre (n.d.). Retrieved from *http://www.xip.fi/atd/china/the-early-history-of-chinese-theatre.html.*

MLDE (2006). Benefits of integrating fine arts across the curriculum. Maryland Department of Education. Retrieved from *http://www.mfaa.msde.state.md.us/source/MDFAintegrating_3d.asp.*

Robinson, S. R. (n.d.) Theatre and Drama in Ancient Greece. CWU Department of Theatre Arts. Retrieved from *http://www.cwu.edu/~robinsos/ppages/resources/Theatre_History/Theahis_2. html.*

Seidel, S. (n.d.). Stand and unfold yourself: A monogram on the Shakespeare & Company— Harvard Program Zero. Retrieved from *http://artsedge.kennedy-center.org/champions/pdfs/ Shakespe.pdf.*

TEA (2013 mod.) *Texas Essential Knowledge and Skills by Chapter, Retrieved from http://www. tea.state.tx.us/index2.aspx?id=6148.*

TExES Core Subjects EC–6 Practice Test Battery

TExES Core Subjects EC–6 Practice Test:
English Language Arts and Reading & the Science of Teaching Reading

ELA and Reading Practice Test Answer Sheet

1. (A) (B) (C) (D)   26. (A) (B) (C) (D)   51. (A) (B) (C) (D)
2. (A) (B) (C) (D)   27. (A) (B) (C) (D)   52. (A) (B) (C) (D)
3. (A) (B) (C) (D)   28. (A) (B) (C) (D)   53. (A) (B) (C) (D)
4. (A) (B) (C) (D)   29. (A) (B) (C) (D)   54. (A) (B) (C) (D)
5. (A) (B) (C) (D)   30. (A) (B) (C) (D)   55. (A) (B) (C) (D)
6. (A) (B) (C) (D)   31. (A) (B) (C) (D)   56. (A) (B) (C) (D)
7. (A) (B) (C) (D)   32. (A) (B) (C) (D)   57. (A) (B) (C) (D)
8. (A) (B) (C) (D)   33. (A) (B) (C) (D)   58. (A) (B) (C) (D)
9. (A) (B) (C) (D)   34. (A) (B) (C) (D)   59. (A) (B) (C) (D)
10. (A) (B) (C) (D)   35. (A) (B) (C) (D)   60. (A) (B) (C) (D)
11. (A) (B) (C) (D)   36. (A) (B) (C) (D)   61. (A) (B) (C) (D)
12. (A) (B) (C) (D)   37. (A) (B) (C) (D)   62. (A) (B) (C) (D)
13. (A) (B) (C) (D)   38. (A) (B) (C) (D)   63. (A) (B) (C) (D)
14. (A) (B) (C) (D)   39. (A) (B) (C) (D)   64. (A) (B) (C) (D)
15. (A) (B) (C) (D)   40. (A) (B) (C) (D)   65. (A) (B) (C) (D)
16. (A) (B) (C) (D)   41. (A) (B) (C) (D)   66. (A) (B) (C) (D)
17. (A) (B) (C) (D)   42. (A) (B) (C) (D)   67. (A) (B) (C) (D)
18. (A) (B) (C) (D)   43. (A) (B) (C) (D)   68. (A) (B) (C) (D)
19. (A) (B) (C) (D)   44. (A) (B) (C) (D)   69. (A) (B) (C) (D)
20. (A) (B) (C) (D)   45. (A) (B) (C) (D)   70. (A) (B) (C) (D)
21. (A) (B) (C) (D)   46. (A) (B) (C) (D)   71. (A) (B) (C) (D)
22. (A) (B) (C) (D)   47. (A) (B) (C) (D)   72. (A) (B) (C) (D)
23. (A) (B) (C) (D)   48. (A) (B) (C) (D)   73. (A) (B) (C) (D)
24. (A) (B) (C) (D)   49. (A) (B) (C) (D)   74. (A) (B) (C) (D)
25. (A) (B) (C) (D)   50. (A) (B) (C) (D)   75. (A) (B) (C) (D)

Practice Test: ELA and Reading & the Science of Teaching Reading

TIME: 1 hour and 45 minutes
75 questions

> **Directions:** Read each item and select the correct response or responses. Most items on this test require you to provide the one best answer. However, some questions require you to select all the options that apply.

1. During the pre-reading stage of the shared book experience, teachers can increase interest in the story by

   A. encouraging students to make predictions based on the title and the pictures.

   B. encouraging students to draw a picture representing the main idea of the story.

   C. encouraging students to draw pictures representing the characters of the story.

   D. introducing students to the author's biography and other books written by the author.

2. Luke's mother has commented that her two-year-old is constructing sentences with only two or three words at a time. For instance, she says that Luke responds by saying, "no more play" and "mommy milk more." She suggests that he has heard his brothers use phrases like these. Luke uses these two phrases frequently. Based on the information above, in which stage of language acquisition is Luke at this point?

   A. Babbling stage

   B. Holophrastic stage

   C. Two word stage

   D. Telegraphic stage

3. Identify the main benefit of using a thesaurus.

   A. It helps in the recognition of words in print.

   B. It can expand the vocabulary repertoire of the child.

   C. It can identify the appropriate definition of words.

   D. It can identify various definitions of words.

4. Mr. Michel provides guiding questions to guide Tamara's writing. A couple of the questions are "What evidence do you need to prove your thesis to skeptics?" and "What would you say to convince them?" Based on this information, what type of writing is Tamara developing?

   A. Narrative writing

   B. Expository writing

   C. Descriptive writing

   D. Persuasive writing

5. Identify the factor that most likely can affect the development of early literacy among preschool children.

   A. Parents read frequently to their children and have books available at home.

   B. Parents teach children to use the dictionary and guide them to select the best definition based on the context of the words.

   C. Parents have available reference materials and electronic translation programs to promote early bilingualism among children.

   D. Parents take their children to the library and bookstores to obtain books.

6. Identify the most appropriate strategy to meet the needs of children at the emergent stage of writing development.

   A. Identify errors in the writing sample and guide children to self-correct.

   B. Provide a prompt and guide children to write a composition based on it.

   C. Provide a shared writing or language experience in which the teacher writes what the child says.

   D. Allow the child to read for at least 30 minutes every day.

7. Which of the following summaries best describes aspects of the writing process of competent writers?

   A. Completing an initial draft and proofreading for errors in spelling, punctuation, and usage.

   B. Completing an initial draft, revising for the accuracy of the content, and publishing.

   C. Brainstorming for ideas, completing an initial draft, revising content, proofreading for errors in spelling, punctuation, and usage, and writing a final draft.

   D. Writing an initial draft, sharing it with peers, reviewing it for errors, and publishing.

8. Mrs. London frequently leads students in choral reading to promote reading fluency. What is the main purpose of the activity?

   A. To emphasize listening and speaking skills

   B. To teach the intonation pattern of the language

   C. To integrate music through choral singing

   D. To make the class more enjoyable

9. Mr. Chapman is a third-grade teacher at a school that is implementing a balanced reading program. Which of the following TWO sets of learning experiences will he include to provide the major components of a balanced literacy program?

   A. Having students read fiction and nonfiction

   B. Reading aloud, shared reading, guided reading, and independent reading

   C. Shared writing and independent writing

   D. Having students complete worksheets to check comprehension of stories students read

10. Dan is an eight-year-old whose oral communication has significantly improved over the past two months. He is beginning to use relative pronoun clauses when speaking and more sophisticated constructions. However, his teacher has discovered that he still struggles when using subordinate clauses. Based on this current limitation, Dan might have problems with the following type of sentence:

   A. I like the cars, but I dislike motorcycles.

   B. He wants to sleep until late in the morning.

   C. If you want me to go, I will need to start getting ready now.

   D. My mom and my dad are real Texans.

11. Marcus can separate a word into syllables by tapping as he says the word. However, he has problems telling what the word is when the teacher says "th-at" or "b-ed." Based on this description, Marcus needs additional support with what type of phonological skill?

    A. Blending onset and rime

    B. Rhyme recognition

    C. Phoneme segmentation

    D. Syllable deletion

12. Connectors are used in writing to create cohesive and coherent compositions. Connections like "on the contrary," "conversely," and "on the other hand" are commonly used in compositions addressing

    A. opinion.

    B. sequencing.

    C. contrast.

    D. results.

13. English writing samples from Spanish-dominant ELLs may contain which key feature?

    A. The stories are simple in content and written in a linear fashion.

    B. The stories might have complex sentence patterns and sophisticated words from Spanish.

    C. The stories might be perceived as disjointed and lacking a logical sequence.

    D. The stories might switch from Spanish to English within the same sentence.

14. Mr. Martínez is going to be introducing the Dolch words to his first-grade students. Before showing the list of words to his students, Mr. Martínez explains that these words are the most frequently used words in English. Which of the following words should not be included in the list that Mr. Martínez is going to show to his students?

    A. a

    B. had

    C. but

    D. awesome

15. Identify the statement that *best* describes the advantages of using the language experience approach to teach reading to language-minority students.

    A. When students' language is the basis of what they read, students are more apt to be able to say the words and learn words as they read what they dictated.

    B. It uses the vocabulary and the experience common to both language-minority and mainstream students.

    C. It minimizes the possibility of errors due to idiomatic expressions from both L1 and L2.

    D. It facilitates reading by ensuring a positive match between L1 and L2.

16. Identify the strategies that lead the child from the stage of *learning to read* to the stage of *reading to learn*.

    A. Expose children to different kinds of stories.

    B. Introduce children to different kinds of texts, and teach how to scan to locate and retrieve information.

    C. Allow students to read without interruptions for at least 20 minutes a day.

    D. Introduce the concepts of connotation and denotation in words and phrases.

17. Mrs. Thompson has directed her students to create a PowerPoint presentation on the history of visual media. Before working on such a presentation, students need to pick a topic to create their presentation. Which of the following would be the most appropriate topic for such a presentation?

    A. The evolution of billboards on the highway

    B. Using Twitter in school

    C. The internet is a superhighway

    D. You email me, I email you

18. In the context of a comprehensive or balanced literacy program, which of the following are the THREE main benefits of the shared reading experience?

   A. Children can gain in sight vocabulary as the teacher points to words and the students read with the teacher.

   B. Children will be better able to complete worksheets about the story when they read with the teacher.

   C. Emergent readers can gain in concepts of print.

   D. As children read with the teacher, they receive scaffolding, experience success, and are able to see that they can become stronger as readers.

19. Effective writing requires students to tailor compositions to their audience or to the purpose of an occasion. To accomplish this, the writing portion of the Texas basic skills exam uses

   A. multiple-choice questions.

   B. specific instructions to guide children in the writing sample.

   C. writing prompts.

   D. a series of questions to guide the development of the writing sample.

20. Daniele is a third grader having problems identifying prefixes and suffixes in the words she reads and writes. When asked to identify the free morpheme of the word *predetermined*, she identified the segment *mine* as the answer. Based on the scenario, what might be the rationale for her answer?

   A. She is confused with suffixes and prefixes.

   B. She did not understand that the segment *mine* is not a free morpheme in that context.

   C. She does not understand the concept of free morpheme.

   D. She did not understand that free morphemes constitute the main component of the word.

21. Identify the number of syllables and the number of phonemes present in the word *thought*.

   A. Two syllables and three phonemes

   B. One syllable and three phonemes

   C. Three syllables and six phonemes

   D. Two syllables and three phonemes

22. Knowledge of the two words used to create compound words can help students in the interpretation of the compound word. However, there are examples of compound words in which the meaning of the two components does not contribute to, and often interferes with, the interpretation of the new word. Identify the set of compound words that fall into this category.

   A. Doghouse, autograph, and boathouse

   B. Greenhouse, White House, and mouthwash

   C. Butterfly, nightmare, and brainstorm

   D. Horseshoe, birdhouse, and underground

23. Identify the number of phonemes in the word *through*.

   A. Seven

   B. Two

   C. Four

   D. Three

24. In addition to the intelligibility of the communication, what should teachers take into account when assessing the speaking ability of native English speakers?

   A. The role of language interference in the oral production of the child.

   B. The impact of socio-economic status and the influence of the students' first language.

   C. The impact of regional and social dialectical variations.

   D. The value of speech therapy in the development of native pronunciation.

25. The development of academic vocabulary is best introduced in contextualized situations, and it should be presented

   A.   in isolation.

   B.   in context.

   C.   explicitly.

   D.   in school.

26. Students eventually have to be familiar with the types of media used in school. These types of media available in school can be organized into the following three major categories:

   A.   Print, social, and electronic

   B.   Visual, electronic, and social

   C.   Electronic, social and print

   D.   Print, electronic, and visual

27. If a child is reading an average of 90 to 94 percent of the words correctly, he or she is reading at the

   A.   independent level.

   B.   frustration level.

   C.   comprehension level.

   D.   instructional level.

28. Identify the instructional activity for viewing and representing for first-grade students that also involves higher-order thinking.

   A.   Sketching an image of what a character might be thinking or feeling during a story

   B.   Developing a PowerPoint presentation with embedded clip art

   C.   Creating a video response to a story

   D.   Designing a newsletter related to a social studies unit

29. Identify the statement that *best* describes sight words.

   A.   Sight words are prevalent in environmental print.

   B.   Sight words can occur frequently in print.

   C.   Children decode sight words using semantic and structural clues.

   D.   Children have difficulty spelling sight words.

30. Ali is a sixth grade advanced English learner experiencing problems with some English sounds. These problems often make his pronunciation incomprehensible to native speakers. Ali tells the teacher that he can conceptualize the standard pronunciation in his mind, but when it comes out, it comes out wrong. What strategy can the teacher use to address this pronunciation problem?

   A.   Ask the student to spend more time in the language laboratory, listening to authentic discourse.

   B.   Guide the child to read a list describing all the pronunciation problems typical of English learners.

   C.   Isolate key pronunciation problems, identify the sounds involved, and describe how the sounds are produced.

   D.   Describe the articulators involved in the production of each English phoneme.

31. Chang, a Mandarin speaker in second grade, has difficulty understanding how phonemes are put together to create words in English. He struggles when the teacher asks him to sound individual phonemes, and to identify syllables in words. What might be a rationale for this kind of problem?

   A.   English is a syllabic language, while Mandarin is a pictorial language.

   B.   English is a very difficult language for Chinese speakers.

   C.   The native language of the student does not use English phonemes.

   D.   Phonemic and phonological awareness is not an important feature of the native language of the child.

32. During a literature-circle discussion, a group of fourth graders produces a response journal with ideas about the short story they have read to share with their peers. In small groups, the students share their ideas about the text in an open-ended discussion. The purpose of having students bring the written response journal to the group is to develop their ability to do which of the following?

    A. Express their thoughts in an imaginative way with others.

    B. Plan and organize their thinking in writing before sharing their thoughts with the group.

    C. Use grammar, spelling, and punctuation in conventional ways.

    D. Share ideas, especially for the less talkative students.

33. Identify the most appropriate strategy to promote oral language development among kindergarten children.

    A. Use dramatic play, songs, and rhymes.

    B. Introduce activities where students listen for comprehension.

    C. Lead students to memorize and to recite poems.

    D. Help students in the preparation of formal presentations using technology.

34. Identify the strategy that teachers can use to foster development in phonological awareness.

    A. Repeated reading

    B. Oral retelling

    C. Tongue twisters

    D. Think-pair-share

35. Mara is a fifth grade ELL without prior schooling in L1. She is having problems connecting the letters of words with the sound they represent. She can recognize the name and logos of stores and a few sight words, but she cannot decode written communication as such. Based on this information, Mara is having problems with which of the following?

    A. Morphemic analysis

    B. Letter-sound correspondence

    C. Morpheme-allomorphs correspondence

    D. Sound system in L2

36. When teaching the grapheme-phoneme correspondence of the English alphabet, teachers must:

    A. Make the activity interesting to all students.

    B. Monitor the children so they do not pronounce the letters with a foreign accent.

    C. Create an atmosphere of cooperation among students from diverse ethnic and linguistic backgrounds.

    D. Control the inconsistency of the grapheme-phoneme correspondence of English by presenting consistent sounds first.

37. Identify the set of words that does not adhere to typically used phonic generalizations.

    A. Green, meat, feet

    B. Said, come, break

    C. Hope, road, blow

    D. Car, stir, blow

38. Identify one common strategy used to guide students to retrieve prior knowledge and to link it with new knowledge.

    A. KWL charts—Know, wants to know, and has learned

    B. Semantic mapping and dictionaries

    C. Brainstorming discussions about future topics

    D. Lecturing about the topic for the day

39. Jeannie reads and understands words in books written for students well above her chronological age. However, she does not write on grade level and does not use words she can read. What statement can explain this discrepancy?

    A. She has problems communicating with other students.

    B. Her productive vocabulary is lagging behind her receptive vocabulary.

    C. She does not have a chance to practice book words in her daily speech.

    D. Her listening vocabulary is smaller than her speaking vocabulary.

40. One of the advantages of Tier 3 vocabulary words is their historical connection with the Greek and the Latin languages. A large number of these words have affixes that have meaning on their own, and can guide students in the words' decoding and comprehension. Which of the following words best represents this example?

    A. Smiles

    B. Reviewed

    C. Phonology

    D. Cooking

41. During writing workshop instruction, fourth-grade students have been writing personal narratives. Now the teacher wants to introduce students to the process used to write research reports. What initial instruction does the teacher need to provide to make the transition to learning a new form of writing?

    A. The teacher needs to remind students to use the Internet responsibly.

    B. The teacher needs to make sure English learners have another assignment because it might be too difficult for them.

    C. The teacher needs to make sure the students can spell words they might use in the report.

    D. The teacher needs to provide instruction and examples of the format and content required in a research report.

42. Mr. Travolta uses DRTA (Directed-Reading-Thinking-Activity) regularly during his guided reading groups. The main purpose of this instructional activity is to

    A. make predictions about a text, and confirm or correct predictions as one reads.

    B. interpret the text according one's own background knowledge.

    C. pose questions to students related to the themes of the text.

    D. develop oral language abilities.

43. In a writing workshop lesson, Mrs. Romero writes the phrase, "My dog, Marly," and then she adds lines extending from the phrase as she talks briefly about the following: finding him at the shelter, favorite treats, bath time, play time. Why would Mrs. Romero primarily use this approach?

    A. Mrs. Romero wants the students to know about her dog.

    B. Mrs. Romero is modeling using phonics by talking as she says words.

    C. Mrs. Romero is categorizing information about a topic.

    D. Mrs. Romero is showing students how to proofread work.

44. A teacher is listening to one student read aloud while other students are reading silently during the guided reading group instruction. The student hesitates in reading the last word of this sentence: I will eat something. The teacher covers the word, *thing,* and asks the student to read the first part of the word, *some,* and then the second part, *thing.* What is the teacher primarily teaching the child?

    A. The teacher is showing the student how to use word parts/structural analysis/morphemic analysis to identify an unknown word.

    B. The teacher is showing how to use syntax to identify an unknown word.

    C. The teacher is showing the child how to use semantics to identify an unknown word.

    D. The teacher is helping the student apply phonics generalizations.

45. A teacher is taking a running record. An English learner has made a miscue or word substitution as indicated below. What can the teacher learn from analyzing the student's miscue?

    Student: The children pulled the wagon across the street.

    Text: The children pulled the wagon along the street.

    A. The student does not understand what a wagon is, so the teacher needs to address that.

    B. The student is using knowledge of English syntax, but the teacher needs to help the student learn to read and distinguish the differences of *along* and *across*.

    C. The student is not paying attention to the initial position of letters in words.

    D. The student's miscue does not interfere with meaning, so the teacher does not need to address this.

46. Mr. Rosales is working with a group of students having reading comprehension problems. He notices that students often start reading a text but lose their concentration and abandon the task. They frequently fail to understand the main idea and details of the story. Which of the following is the most effective strategy to support students with this type of reading behavior?

    A. Rereading

    B. Evaluating

    C. Judging

    D. Inferring

47. Mrs. Henao is working with a group of third-grade students who are below grade level in reading. She wants to assess their progress every six weeks to get a comprehensive measure of both their decoding and comprehension skills. Which of the following assessment tools would be most appropriate to assess their reading skills in these domains?

    A. An informal reading inventory

    B. A timed one-minute oral reading test

    C. A running record

    D. A phonics screening tool

48. Mr. Maduro developed a social studies test for third grade English learners. The test had illustrations to improve students' comprehension. For beginner ESL children, he read the questions to be sure that language did not interfere in the process. These testing modifications are an example of

    A. formative evaluation.

    B. effective test-taking skills.

    C. content validity.

    D. accommodations.

49. Identify the statement that best describes the connection between reading and writing.

    A. The development of reading and writing is sequential.

    B. The development of reading and writing skills are interrelated and developed concurrently.

    C. The development of reading and writing is controlled by the structure of the language.

    D. The development of reading and writing is controlled by the age of exposure to the language and the type of strategies used to teach them.

50. Mrs. Davis shared a quality wordless picture book that conveys an Aesop fable. Which statement provides an accurate description of this teaching practice?

    A. All students can gain from having the opportunity to understand and interpret a story through looking at high-quality illustrations.

    B. The teacher should not let advanced students read that book because it is too easy.

    C. Less advanced students need to learn words, not read a wordless text.

    D. Students do not need to know about an Aesop fable, and should be reading textbooks.

51. In her science class, Ms. Navas teaches her fifth graders Greek and Latin affixes as an advanced organizer for daily lessons. Today she is working on inventions and their contribution to society. Based on that, she introduces and defines the following affixes and stems: *micro*, *tele*, *scope*, *phone*, and *graph*. Then, she guides students to create words with the affixes. What is the main purpose of this activity?

    A. To use phonemic awareness as a foundation for learning

    B. To use the structural clues to recognize words

    C. To use semantic clues to improve decoding skills

    D. To use phonics to decode words

52. Running records, teacher observations, and speaking checklists are examples of what type of assessment?

    A. Teacher-developed assessment instruments

    B. Informal literacy assessment

    C. Formal literacy assessment

    D. Objective literacy instruments

53. Ms. Jefferson has guided first-grade students to read polysyllabic words until they can read them fluently. Later, students are asked to separate the words into syllables, and finally she guides students to identify the main stress in each word. What skill is Ms. Jefferson emphasizing?

    A. Alphabetic awareness

    B. Reading fluency

    C. Phonological awareness

    D. Syllabication

54. Newly fluent readers can read with relative fluency and comprehension. Which cueing system is NOT one they would use to obtain meaning from print?

    A. Semantic cueing systems

    B. Structural cueing systems

    C. Visual cueing systems

    D. Kinesthetic cueing systems

55. Introducing the multiple versions of stories like *Cinderella* can help students understand how a theme can be developed from different points of view. Moreover, this kind of literature can help students in the development of

    A. critical reading.

    B. literal recall.

    C. repairing understanding.

    D. retelling checklist.

56. Mr. Jennings presented his sixth grade students with the documentary *An Inconvenient Truth*, which features former U.S. Vice President Al Gore. After the movie, students gathered in groups and conducted an Internet search to read critiques of the film and to learn more about the topic of climate change. Later, students were asked to use the information gathered to determine if global climate change is scientific fact or fallacy. Which of the following is the main purpose of this kind of activity?

    A. To guide students to interpret data based on a variety of sources

    B. To guide students to use the Internet to support their education

    C. To guide students to understand the positions of the two leading American political parties regarding climate change

    D. To guide students to understand that this type of film is an example of valueless propaganda

57. Kindergarten students can identify the main idea of a story by

    A. drawing a picture representing the story.

    B. writing a short paragraph summarizing the story.

    C. verbalizing the main points of the story and writing a chronology of events in the story.

    D. developing a detailed analysis of the story line.

58. In upper elementary grades, reading becomes more challenging and meaningful for students because at this stage,

    A. interest in reading fades as students find other activities they prefer.

    B. students are still developing skills in fluency and decoding.

    C. children use reading to obtain information to be successful in the content areas.

    D. students have a harder time self-selecting books to read on their own.

59. Informal reading inventories are used to

    A. measure reading proficiency.

    B. read short stories and poems.

    C. motivate children to enjoy reading.

    D. create an inventory of new words learned daily.

60. Identify the rationale for the popularity of onset and rimes to teach spelling skills in English.

    A. It is used to take advantage of common spelling patterns in English.

    B. It is used to teach words as sight words.

    C. It is the best approach to teach words with multiple syllables.

    D. It is the best approach to teach the spelling pattern for prefixes and suffixes.

61. Speakers of Romance languages have advantages when decoding and understanding English words derived from which of the following languages?

    A. Greek

    B. German

    C. English

    D. Latin

62. In addition to grouping vocabulary words based on their levels of sophistication (Tier 1–4), others have organized vocabulary based on

    A. the nomenclature of the content areas.

    B. speech acts and semantic clusters.

    C. sight words and decodable words.

    D. word origin.

63. Kindergarten students who are not reading yet can use media to represent ideas about a story read to them. Identify the example that best represents this example of media:

    A. A photograph of the teacher reading the story

    B. A picture representing a favorite part of the story

    C. A short video describing events of a story

    D. A cartoon presenting a critique of the story

64. During his guided reading lesson, Mr. Diaz is pointing out to his first graders the question mark at the end of a sentence as he prepares the students to read the story. How could this teaching foster fluency?

    A. Fluency involves rate of reading.

    B. Fluency involves accuracy.

    C. Fluency involves intonation.

    D. Fluency involves phonemic analysis.

65. Convergent research on linear versus curvilinear rhetorical patterns shows that Spanish-speaking English language learners and young children in general have a tendency to follow a curvilinear approach in writing. What strategies can teachers use to support these students?

   A. Teach pronunciation and application of grammar structures.

   B. Guide children to develop an outline for the story and provide them with guiding questions to keep them focused on the topic and the audience.

   C. Provide a speaking checklist to help students stick to the topic.

   D. Provide examples of stories written in a linear fashion and ask students to modify them by adding their own information.

66. Print media is one of the oldest and more consistent forms of media. Identify the key element that makes this type of media unique.

   A. It is more formal and interesting than visual media.

   B. It is static and permanent.

   C. It is visually pleasing and easy to produce.

   D. It is one of the oldest and more interesting than visual media.

67. Ken Goodman used the term *miscues* in reading to describe the type of

   A. variation that occurs when children attempt to put words into writing.

   B. variation that occurs when children try to decode and guess the meaning of printed words.

   C. errors that occur when children try to communicate orally in their native language.

   D. discrepancy that occurs between the schemata of the child and the one intended by the author.

68. Miscue analysis was developed by Kenneth Goodman to assess

   A. the performance of children in silent sustained reading.

   B. the performance of children in their development of writing.

   C. the performance of children in their ability to speak.

   D. the performance of children in oral reading.

69. Identify the statement that best represents the rationale for the implementation of initial reading instruction in the student's native language.

   A. Reading skills are transferable from L1 to L2.

   B. Reading skills are identical in L1 and L2.

   C. Reading skills are confusing for English language learners (ELLs).

   D. Reading skills affect the cognitive process in bilingual students.

70. Mr. Cheng uses monosyllabic words to present the concept of onset and rimes. Identify the pair of words that best represents this concept.

   A. want-ed—walk-ed

   B. very—berry

   C. think-ing—eat-ing

   D. s-ank—b-ank

71. Identify the set of words representing the concept of antonyms.

   A. small—smaller

   B. small—large

   C. bear—bear

   D. small—little

72. Mrs. Romero models a mini-lesson on how to add information to a rough draft. The teacher projects an example of her own writing, and proceeds to read it aloud. Mrs. Romero tells the students about a sentence she needs to add to write more clearly. She then shows the students how that can be done by writing the sentence at the bottom, and using an arrow to show where the sentence should go. What might be the advantage of presenting this kind of lesson?

   A. The students are learning about conventions of writing.

   B. The teacher is showing students that writing rough drafts can entail making revisions to write more clearly, and how to make revisions.

   C. The teacher is demonstrating topic selection.

   D. The teacher is helping students expand their vocabulary.

73. Which of the following is not a characteristic of emergent writers?

   A. Dictating an idea or a complete story

   B. Using initial sounds

   C. Using pictures and scribbles

   D. Using conventional spelling

74. Mrs. Jones has three fourth graders who are at the early stages of their reading development. She wants to help her students move from the emergent stage of reading to understanding some basic sight words and the conventions of print. She uses a technique called "shared writing," in which students dictate their thoughts orally and she writes them down. This is followed by the group of students doing a repeated reading aloud of the shared text. Which of the following is the *primary* purpose of this activity with these students?

   A. Demonstrating the conventions of writing such as punctuation, spelling, and grammar rules

   B. Engaging students with a high-interest activity that will motivate them to want to write more

   C. Developing the students' ability to engage in listening, speaking, reading, and writing to further their reading development

   D. Fostering a sight-word vocabulary that will help the students improve their spelling in future writing

75. Ms. Gandhi guided her first graders to read a passage multiple times until they read the passages effectively. What skill is the teacher promoting?

   A. Phonemic awareness

   B. Reading fluency

   C. Phonological awareness

   D. Syllabication

ELA and Reading Practice Test Answer Key

1.	A.	26.	D.	51.	B.
2.	D.	27.	D.	52.	B.
3.	B.	28.	A.	53.	C.
4.	D.	29.	B.	54.	D.
5.	A.	30.	C.	55.	A.
6.	C.	31.	D.	56.	A.
7.	C.	32.	B.	57.	A.
8.	B.	33.	A.	58.	C.
9.	B. and C.	34.	C.	59.	A.
10.	C.	35.	B.	60.	A.
11.	A.	36.	D.	61.	D.
12.	C.	37.	B.	62.	B.
13.	C.	38.	A.	63.	B.
14.	D.	39.	B.	64.	C.
15.	A.	40.	C.	65.	B.
16.	B.	41.	D.	66.	B.
17.	A.	42.	A.	67.	B.
18.	A., C., and D.	43.	C.	68.	D.
19.	C.	44.	A.	69.	A.
20.	B.	45.	B.	70.	D.
21.	B.	46.	A.	71.	B.
22.	C.	47.	A.	72.	B.
23.	D.	48.	D.	73.	D.
24.	C.	49.	B.	74.	C.
25.	C.	50.	A.	75.	B.

ELA and Reading Practice Test
Detailed Answers

1. A.

The correct answer is (A). By guiding children to notice the title, major headings, and pictorial clues, they can make predictions about the story. Approaching the story content in this way can increase a child's interest in reading because they want to corroborate their predictions with the actual content of what they read. Options (B), (C), and (D) are incorrect because they describe activities typical of the post-reading stage, not the pre-reading stage. **(801-007 Reading Comprehension and Applications)**

2. D.

The correct answer is (D). As seen in the scenario, Luke is clearly in the telegraphic stage. He is using chunks of words and phrases he has heard others use and is including them in his linguistic repertoire. Based on this explanation, options (A), (B), and (C) are incorrect. **(801-002 Phonological and Phonemic Awareness)**

3. B.

The correct answer is (B). A thesaurus presents synonyms and can help students in using a variety of words, thus enhancing students' receptive and productive vocabulary. Thesauri are not designed to help students recognize words in print (A). In addition, it would be tedious to find a word by trying to look up its synonyms. Options (C) and (D) describe the function of dictionaries, not thesauri. **(801–008 Vocabulary Development)**

4. D.

The correct answer is (D). In trying to convince the reader of something, posing a question relating to reasons why the argument might be convincing will help the writer to see the reader's point of view. In narrative writing (A), expository writing (B), and descriptive writing (C), the need to convince may be present; however, it is more essential in the very nature of persuasive writing. **(801-011 Written Communication)**

5. A.

The correct answer is (A). Reading to children and having books available for them provide children with reading readiness skills and can promote interest in reading. Option (B) is incorrect because the use of dictionary skills is not developmentally appropriate for preschool children. Option (C) is incorrect because the children might not be ready for electronic translation programs, and translation is not the best strategy for promoting literacy development. Option (D) is incorrect because getting books for children without additional support will not develop early literacy among children. **(801-004 Literacy Development)**

6. C.

The correct answer is (C). The most appropriate strategy to use at the emergent stage of writing is to provide a shared writing or language experience in which the child dictates and the teacher writes what the child says. When the teacher writes down the dictated story, the child can see the connection of oral and written work. Options (A) and (B) are incorrect because the children at the emergent stage don't have sufficient command of written language to correct their own writing or write a composition based on prompts. Option (D) is incorrect because reading for 30 minutes a day without any kind of explicit or implicit writing support might not be effective for children at the emerging stage for writing. **(801-010 Writing Conventions)**

7. C.

The correct answer is (C). Brainstorming for ideas, completing an initial draft, revising content, proofreading for mechanical errors (in spelling, punctuation, and usage), and writing a final draft—these are all aspects of what a competent writer does to produce a piece of writing. Options (A), (B), and (D) are incorrect because they do not contain all the facets necessary to carry out and complete the writing process. **(801-011 Written Communication)**

8. B.

The correct answer is (B). Mastering correct word identification and the intonation patterns of the language and practicing choral reading can lead to reading fluency. Reading fluently in turn can improve reading comprehension because students do not have to struggle decoding words. Students also pay attention to meaning as they read with appropriate intonation, letting all students participate. Emphasizing listening and speaking skills (A) is not the primary purpose of this activity. There is no connection between choral reading and choral singing (C). Making the class more enjoyable (D) is important, but is not the main intent of the activity. **(801-006 Reading Fluency)**

9. B. and C.

Options (B) and (C) are correct. A balanced reading program is one in which the teacher provides reading to students (reading aloud), reading with the students (shared reading and guided reading), and reading by the students (independent reading). The teacher also provides writing with students (shared writing) and writing by students in the nature of independent writing or a writing workshop.

Students do need to read both fiction and nonfiction, but that relates to providing an array of types of reading materials toward establishing a literate environment, and these could be a part of shared reading, guided reading, and independent reading (A). However, having students complete worksheets is not considered to be a cornerstone of such a program, but teachers would have

discussions about stories students read (D). **(801-004 Literacy Development)**

10. C.

The correct answer is (C). A subordinate clause is a dependent clause that needs the information of a second clause to present the entire message. In option (C), the phrase "If you want me to go" does not convey a complete message; it needs the second part of the sentence ("I will need to start getting ready to go now") to make sense. Option (A) represents an example of coordinate clauses—two clauses joined by a coordinated conjunction. Options (B) and (D) contain main, or independent, clauses, which can stand alone as sentences. That is, they contain a subject and a verb, and express a complete thought. **(801-002 Phonological and Phonemic Awareness)**

11. A.

The correct answer is (A). The child is having problems with blending an onset (such as *b* in bed) and a rime (such as *ed* in bed), which is part of phonological skill development. Option (B) is incorrect because the scenario described does entail the child providing or identifying a rhyming word. Option (C) is incorrect because the task described requires blending, not segmenting. Option (D) is incorrect because the task does not require the child to say a word again and delete one of the syllables. **(801-002 Phonological and Phonemic Awareness)**

12. C.

The correct answer is (C). The connectors are guided to compare and contrast ideas and to identify the preference of the author. Options (A), (B), and (D) are incorrect because the connectors presented do not call for opinions, sequencing, or results. **(801-010 Writing Conventions)**

13. C.

The correct answer is (C). The English writing samples of ELLs from a Spanish background often follow a curvilinear progression and might include multiple stories embedded within the narrative. This deviation from the linear progression expected in English writing creates the impression that the story is disjointed and lacks coherence. Based on the previous explanation, option (A) is incorrect—children might not produce compositions following a linear progression. The compositions of children might contain complex sentences and an occasional use of Anglicized words or even Spanish words, but these features do not represent the main characteristics of English compositions of Latino children. Based on this explanation, choices (B) and (D) are incorrect. **(801-011 Written Communication)**

14. D.

The correct answer is (D). The introduction of sight words can expedite students' decoding skills and it can also help develop fluency among early readers. From the options presented, the only word that is not in Dolch's list is (D) *awesome*. **(801-005 Word Analysis and Identification Skills)**

15. A.

The correct answer is (A). Through the language experience approach (LEA), a student dictates and the teacher writes what the student said. Because the written text is what the student said, the student is familiar with the words and can more easily read with the teacher and then independently. Option (B) is incorrect because the student may or may not use words common to mainstream students. Option (C) is incorrect because students will use their own vocabulary in the story. Option (D) is incorrect because the main purpose of LEA is not to contrast L1 and L2. **(801-004 Literacy Development)**

16. B

The correct answer is (B). The main purpose of *reading to learn* is to obtain content information efficiently and effectively. One way to accomplish this task is to make students aware of the format used in the content areas and to guide them to retrieve the information by reading for the main idea or scanning for informa-

tion. Option (A) is incorrect because it addresses reading stories, which, while important in literacy development, fails to embrace students' need to acquaint themselves with informational texts of content areas and to learn how to read to gain content effectively. Option (C) is incorrect because it does not address the issue of helping students learn how to read and retain information through strategies, such as note-taking. Option (D) is incorrect because it addresses only the issue of vocabulary development—connotation and denotation. **(801-009 Reading, Inquiry and Research)**

17. A.

The correct answer is (A). The most appropriate topic would be for students to research the evolution of billboards on the highway. Options (B), (C), and (D) are incorrect because they represent examples of electronic media, not visual media. **(801-012 Viewing and Representing)**

18. A., C., and D.

Options (A), (C), and (D) are correct. Option (B) is incorrect because asking students to complete comprehension questions on a worksheet is not an objective of shared reading. Students are more apt to comprehend a story if they can read the words accurately, but discussing the story is a more authentic way to foster comprehension and build upon the interactivity of shared reading. **(801-004 Literacy Development)**

19. C.

The correct answer is (C). A state writing exam provides a prompt to guide children to produce the writing sample. In responding to the prompt, students have to address the audience, purpose, and occasion implied in it. Option (A) is incorrect because the multiple-choice portion of a test does not require the student to actually write or compose. Option (B) is incorrect because this type of test item assesses proofreading skills, not the ability to compose or establish content. Option (D) is incorrect because the instructions do not contain specific questions to guide the writing. **(801-011 Written Communication)**

20. B.

The correct answer is (B). The word *mine* is a free morpheme when used in isolation; however, it is not a free morpheme in the word *predetermined* (B). There is no evidence to suggest that the student is having problems with suffixes or prefixes (A). Since she recognized that the segment *mine* can be classified as a free morpheme in certain conditions, there is no evidence to suggest that she does not understand the concept of free morphemes (C and D). **(801-001 Oral Language)**

21. B.

The correct answer is (B). The word *thought* is a long word, even though it is monosyllabic. It has three phonemes. The word contains two consonant digraphs, *th* and *ght*, and a vowel digraph, *ou*, representing one sound each for a total of three sounds. Options (A), (C), and (D) are incorrect based on the previous explanation. **(801-001 Oral Language)**

22. C.

The correct answer is (C). The words *butterfly*, *nightmare*, and *brainstorm* may confuse students because they do not provide a reliable point of view to comprehend their meaning. Options (A), (B), and (D) are incorrect because they contain information to help children in the comprehension process. Words such as *doghouse*, *underground*, and *mouthwash* provide clear indications of the intended meaning. **(801-005 Word Analysis and Identification Skills)**

23. D.

The correct answer is (D). The word contains seven graphemes (letters), but only three phonemes (sounds). Based on this explanation, the rest of the options are eliminated. **(801–006 Reading Fluency)**

24. C.

The correct answer is (C). Teachers often fail to take into account the role of dialectical variations in the speech of children, when assessing their speaking ability. For example, the speech of West Texas speakers might appear nasalized and slow for speakers from, say, New York City or Boston. However, this type of variation should not be used against the child when assessing language development. Options (A) and (B) are both incorrect because both make reference to second language learners, and the question is dealing with native English speakers. Option (D) is irrelevant because teachers assess the pronunciation of all children, without taking into account whether they have had speech therapy. **(801-001 Oral Language)**

25. C.

The correct answer is (C). Because of its complexity, academic vocabulary should be presented through direct instruction (explicitly) and in contextualized situations, so students develop a better understanding of the word and the concept(s) it represents. Presenting language in isolation (A) has not been successful. This activity is often boring and lacking the rigor necessary for the children to internalize the meaning of the words. **(801-008 Vocabulary Development)**

26. D.

The correct answer is (D). Media can be organized into three large categories: print, electronic, and visual. The remaining three options refer to social media as a separate classification; however, social media fall under the broader category of electronic media. **(801-012 Viewing and Representing)**

27. D.

The correct answer is (D). When a child can read 90% to 94% of the words in a text, he or she is reading at the instructional level. If the child can read 95% to 100% of the words, then the child is reading at the independent level (A). If the child is reading less than 90% of the words correctly, he or she is at the frustration level (B). The term *comprehension level* (C) is not a technical descriptor used to describe the concept of word recognition. **(801-013 Assessment of Developing Literacy)**

28. A.

The correct answer is (A). Sketching a character is developmentally appropriate for students in first grade for viewing and representing and involves creating a visual depiction of a character that can then be discussed. Options (B), (C), and (D) are more appropriate activities for students in grades 3–6. **(801-011 Written Communication)**

29. B.

The correct answer is (B). Sight words occur frequently in writing, and often the best way to teach them is by instant recognition. Option (A) is not correct because environmental print does not necessarily contain sight words. Street signs and store names can have long and very unique names that cannot be taught as sight words. Option (C) is incorrect because sight words are taught to be recognized instantly. Students may analyze their structural or semantic representation when encountering an unknown sight word, but high-frequency words need to be taught so students can read a text fluently. Option (D) is incorrect because some sight words are short and easy to spell. Because they occur so frequently in reading, spelling is facilitated. **(801-005 Word Analysis and Identification Skills)**

30. C.

The correct answer is option (C) because the student is having problems with specific sounds; teachers can isolate those sounds and introduce the place and manner of articulation used to produce them. This strategy works better with mature students (such as 6th graders). For younger learners, the best strategy is to model the pronunciation. Guiding students to spend time in the language laboratory (A) is a generic strategy that does not address the immediate problem of the child. Developing a list of all problems typical of ELLs (B) is not necessary, since the child is having problems with specific sounds only. Describing the articulators involved in each English sound (D) might be too cumbersome for the child. **(801-001 Oral Language)**

31. D.

The correct answer is option (D) because English is an alphabetic language that uses phonemic and phonological awareness to introduce reading. In phonemic awareness, the letters (graphemes) are used to connect to the individual sounds (phonemes) of the language. Option (A) is a false statement: English is an alphabetic language, not syllabic. Additionally, Mandarin is a logographic language that uses some pictographs and ideographs in its writing system. Syllabication is part of the process of phonological awareness, which constitutes a key process to introduce reading. English or any other new language is difficult for anyone new to the language (B). Option (C) is a true and obvious statement: Mandarin does not use English phonemes, but it does not qualify as the best answer. **(801-001 Oral Language)**

32. B.

The correct answer is (B). The primary purpose of having a response notebook is to organize thinking about the key ideas and themes relating to the book. Organizing written notes also connects to students' ability to share these ideas orally. Option (A) is incorrect because expression, while important, is not the primary purpose of the writing component and its connection with sharing ideas orally in the literature circles. Option (C) is incorrect because grammar development and a focus on mechanics and conventions are not the primary objectives of a literature response activity. What is key is the ability to express ideas. Option (D) is incorrect because writing and planning don't necessarily assist shy students in their ability to express themselves. **(801-001 Oral Language)**

33. A.

The correct answer is (A). The use of games and fun activities is ideal to engage and promote oral language development among young learners. Introducing listening activities (B) can also be used, but students at this age respond better to dramatic play and fun activities. Memorizing (C) and preparing formal presentations

(D) might not be appropriate for students at this early stage of development. **(801-001 Oral Language)**

34. C.

The correct answer is (C). Phonological awareness involves listening and the ability to hear and make distinctions in oral language. It includes the ability to hear distinct sounds, use alliteration and recognize rhyming words. Tongue twisters foster development in phonological awareness because they involve the use of rhyming words, along with the ability to hear and use words that begin with the same initial sound (alliteration). Repeated reading (A) primarily develops fluency, whereas oral retelling (B) and think-pair-share (D) help students develop comprehension skills. **(801-002 Phonological and Phonemic Awareness)**

35. B.

The correct answer is (B). The student is having problems connecting the letters or letter strings with the appropriate sound. This is a typical problem for students who have not mastered the alphabetic principle in English. Options (A) and (C) are incorrect because the scenario does not highlight problems in identifying morphemes (basic units of meaning) or with an alternate pronunciation of morphemes (allomorphs). These problems crop up when the past-tense morpheme has alternate pronunciations, such as in the words *wanted*—/əd/, *walked*—/t/, and *reviewed*—/d/. Having problems with the sound system (D) is too broad and does not address the real issue in the scenario. **(801-003 Alphabetic Principle)**

36. D.

The correct answer is (D). The grapheme-phoneme correspondence in English is not consistent. English uses 26 letters to represent 44 sounds. Consonants are more consistent than vowel sounds. For that reason, we introduce consonants before vowels or consonant digraphs. Making instruction interesting (A) to students or promoting cooperation (C) among students are not the primary reasons for teaching the grapheme-phoneme correspondence of English. Teaching pronunciation (B) is not the key purpose of teaching the grapheme-phoneme connection. The real purpose is to guide students to see the connection between the two components. **(801-003 Alphabetic Principle)**

37. B.

The correct answer is (B). The words *said*, *come*, and *break* represent irregular spellings because they do not adhere to phonics generalizations. Two vowels are together in *said* and *break*, but the two vowels together do not make the long vowel sound as they do generally or in the patterns of words, such as in *wait* and *meat*. The pattern of vowel-consonant-silent *e* signals the long vowel sound, such as in *home*, so *come* is irregular. The two vowels together do make the long vowel sound as they do generally for the words of option (A). The two vowels together do make the long vowel sound as they do generally for words of option (C) because in *blow*, the *w* is a vowel and *ow* represents the long *o* sound in many words, such as in *snow* and *know*. The words in the set in option (D) also are regular in presenting *r*-controlled vowels, another phonics generalization. **(801-005 Word Analysis and Identification Skills)**

38. A.

The correct answer is (A). KWL charts have been used effectively to link prior knowledge with new knowledge. Semantic mapping and dictionaries (B) are not the best options to link current knowledge with new knowledge. Brainstorming about the topic of the day can help, but is less effective when linked to future topics. Lecturing about the topic should be part of the lesson, not part of the initial activity to discover how much students know about the topic. **(801-007 Reading Comprehension and Applications)**

39. B.

The correct answer is (B). The receptive vocabulary describes those words that people understand but rarely use in conversation (productive vocabulary). Having a larger receptive than productive vocabulary is a common characteristic even among native English speakers. The information does not indicate that the student is having communication problems with other students (A). Option (C) focuses on speaking, not writing. The scenario does not provide information about the student's speaking vocabulary. Option (D) focuses on oral language, not written language. Typically, listening vocabulary development comes before speaking, but the scenario focuses on reading and writing. **(801-008 Vocabulary Development)**

40. C.

The correct answer is (C). The Greek word *phonology* is composed of two graphemes—*phone* (sound) and *logy* (study of a subject). The rest of the options represent words that contain inflectional morphemes only (*ed, s, ing...*). **(801-008 Vocabulary Development)**

41. D.

The correct answer is (D). The teacher will need to provide demonstrations and guided practice of each aspect of writing a report, such as how to select a topic, locate information, take notes without copying, organize information, and write drafts. If the teacher simply tells students what to do, the students will not have a clear understanding of how to engage in the various aspects of writing a report, so reminding is not sufficient (A). English learners need to engage in academic writing, and they can participate if the teacher provides ample scaffolding through mini-lessons, and lets students work together in productive ways (B). Students can check for accurate spelling through publishing conferences when students write their final draft of the report, so teaching words initially is not the best way to use instructional time (C). **(801-009 Reading, Inquiry and Research)**

42. A.

The correct answer is option (A) because the purpose of the DRTA is to guide students to become active readers. Making predictions about a story guides them to read to confirm or reject predictions. Interpreting the text (B) is part of the outcome of the DRTA, but the main benefit of the strategy guides the learner to read with a purpose. The student must read first to understand the text and perhaps ask questions about the themes (C) represented. Developing oral language (D) could take place as students discuss what they read, but it does not constitute the main idea of the activity. **(801-009 Reading, Inquiry and Research)**

43. C.

The correct answer is (C). The teacher is categorizing information about a topic, using webbing. Through a web, she is breaking down a topic by categories, modelling the selection and identification of components of a writing. Mrs. Romero may want to share her experiences, and this shows students how she draws upon her life in writing (A), but using a web is primarily being done to show how to help students organize their writing, and not use phonics (B) nor proofread (D). **(801-012 Viewing and Representing)**

44. A.

The correct answer is (A). The teacher is showing the student how to use word parts/structural analysis/morphemic analysis to identify an unknown word, because the teacher is showing the student how to examine the two words of a compound word. Option (B) be ruled out because syntax relates to the way words can be put together in English, and the teacher's prompt did not focus upon syntax. Option (C) is also out because semantics relates to meaning, and the teacher's prompt did not focus upon meaning or what would make sense. Finally, option (D) is incorrect because the teacher's prompt did not focus upon letters and their sounds. **(801-013 Assessment of Developing Literacy)**

45. B.

The correct answer is (B). The student is using knowledge of English syntax because what the student said can be said in English. However, the teacher needs to help the student learn to read and distinguish the differences between *along* and *across* because the student did not recognize the word *along*. Option (A) is incorrect because the student's miscue does not indicate that the student does not know what a wagon is. A wagon can be pulled across a street, so the student's miscue is logical. Option (C) can also be ruled out because the student's response shows that he/she is paying attention to the initial position of the letter *a* in *along* and *across*. Finally, option (D) is incorrect because the miscue does change the description of what took place in the story. Also, the student needs to know how to read the word *along*, so the teacher should not ignore the miscue even though what the child said could be said in English. **(801-013 Assessment of Developing Literacy)**

46. A.

The correct answer is (A). Rereading is a common and widely used comprehension strategy with students that lose concentration when reading unfamiliar text. Expanding on pre-reading activities and guiding them to reread the story can improve comprehension and their confidence to deal with the text. Through repeated exposure to the text, students can repair comprehension and develop a better understanding of the story. Options (B), (C), and (D) all focus on higher-order thinking skills that first assume the reader has a good literal understanding of the text. Rereading is more effective in terms of repairing or fixing comprehension at a more basic level. **(801-013 Assessment of Developing Literacy)**

47. A.

The correct answer is (A). A variety of measurement tools are used to assess reading growth and progress in decoding and comprehension. The correct choice is an informal reading inventory because it specifically measures accuracy in decoding and comprehension of text at both the literal and inferential levels. A timed test (B) is used to measure the fluency rate (accuracy and rate) of decoding but doesn't specifically measure comprehension. A running record (C) is used more for beginning readers and usually measures just the decoding aspect of reading, although it can also give insight

into the comprehension of content. Similarly, a phonics screening tool (D) might help the teacher to assess the decoding aspect, but would not let the teacher know how well the student is developing comprehension skills. **(801-013 Assessment of Developing Literacy)**

48. D.

The correct answer is (D). When testing for content, teachers need to be sure that language does not interfere in assessing the content objectives. To minimize the effect of language in comprehension, teachers provide linguistic accommodation. Technically, teacher-made examinations are generally part of formative evaluation; however, the scenario provides information to go beyond this simple concept. The teacher is not providing specific test-taking skills (B). He is not addressing the content validity of the test (C) either. Content validity is a term to suggest that the test questions assess the content covered in class. **(801-013 Assessment of Developing Literacy)**

49. B.

The correct answer is (B). There is a close connection between decoding (reading) and encoding (writing). Skills from reading can transfer to writing and vice versa. Contrary to popular belief, the skills of reading and writing are developed concurrently, as opposed to sequentially (A). The structure of English (C) does not regulate the development of reading and writing. Instead it reinforces concepts in both skills. Age of exposure (D) to the language does not play a vital role in establishing the connection between reading and writing. **(801-011 Written Communication)**

50. A.

The correct answer is (A). Visual literacy is important to develop, and an Aesop fable represents a type of literature students should know, contrary to option (D), so this is a valuable learning opportunity. Students do need to make gains in reading words, (B) and (C), but students also need to learn how to interpret illustrations. **(801-012 Viewing and Representing)**

51. B.

The correct answer is (B). The teacher is using the meaning of morphemes as a foundation for improving word identification and vocabulary development in the content areas. She is taking advantage of the multiple morphemes common between the Greek and Latin languages, and English. The use of phonemic awareness (A), semantic clues (C), and phonics (D) is minimal in this type of analysis and most likely unnecessary for the fifth graders. **(801-005 Word Analysis and Identification Skills)**

52. B.

The correct answer is (B). All three instruments, running records, teacher observations, and the checklist, are examples of informal assessment. Option (A) is incorrect because at least one of the instruments, running records, is not a teacher-developed instrument. Option (C) is incorrect based on the information previously stated. Option (D) is incorrect because all three instruments require some level of subjectivity. **(801-013 Assessment of Developing Literacy)**

53. C.

The correct answer is (C). Syllabication and word stress are part of the concept called phonological awareness. Option (A) is incorrect because the activity goes beyond establishing the connection between letters and sounds typical of the alphabetic principle. Option (B) is incorrect because the development of fluency goes beyond the analysis of individual words. The development of phonological awareness is a prerequisite for the development of fluency. Option (D) is incorrect because the concept of syllabication is only one of two elements presented in the scenario—syllabication and word stress. **(801-003 Alphabetic Principle)**

54. D.

The correct answer is (D). Semantic, structural, and visual cueing systems are all used by newly fluent readers to aid in their comprehension of texts. Punctua-tion does need to be observed by readers and clarifies what is presented in a text, but when identifying words, readers rely upon the visual cues based upon the look of the letters or the word, structure cues based upon whether a word would sound correct according to language structure or syntax, and meaning cues based upon what would make sense. **(801-004 Literacy Development)**

55. A.

The correct answer is (A). Comparing and contrasting variations of a fairy tale, such as *Cinderella*, can foster higher-order thinking skills and critical reading. Students will have to analyze the new story to determine how it related to the traditional version, and how the theme is treated. Options (B), (C), and (D) are not focusing specifically on such higher-level reading as it relates to comparing and contrasting across multiple texts. **(801-007 Reading Comprehension and Applications)**

56. A.

The answer is (A). Students are viewing and studying a variety of sources to compare different points of view to arrive at conclusions. The use of the Internet (B) to support education is just one component of the purpose of the lesson. Studying the position of the two leading political parties (C) and how propaganda works (D) are also by-products of the project, but they do not constitute the main purpose of the lesson. **(801-012 Viewing and Representing)**

57. A.

The correct answer is (A). Since students cannot write in conventional ways in kindergarten, drawing becomes an alternate means to express their understanding of the story. Options (B) and (C) are incorrect because children at this level of literacy development cannot write well. Option (D) is also incorrect because children in kindergarten might not have the cognitive maturity to develop a detailed analysis of the story line. They are generally able to present the gist of the story and identify meaningful events. **(801-010 Writing Conventions)**

58. C.

The correct answer is (C). One of the key challenges children in upper elementary experience when moving from the stage of *learning to read* to *reading to learn* is the need to read to obtain information from academic writings. There is no evidence to suggest that interest in reading fades out in upper elementary (A). Students might be developing skills in fluency and decoding (B) but the main challenge now is to understand text format to obtain content information. Problems selecting books (D) should not be an important aspect when the real task is to obtain information to be successful in the content areas. **(801-007 Reading Comprehension and Applications)**

59. A.

The correct answer is (A). Informal reading inventories are designed to identify reading proficiency levels in children. Teachers or reading specialists administer this instrument. Based on this explanation, options (B), (C), and (D) are ruled out. **(801-013 Assessment of Developing Literacy)**

60. A.

The correct answer is (A). English has a large number of words with specific spelling patterns. These patterns are labeled rimes. If children are able to recognize onsets and rimes when listening, they should be able to recognize and spell words. Contrary to sight words, in onset and rimes the onset is changed to create new words. In sight words (B), specific units are introduced for instant recognition—and no changes or recombinations are done to generate new words. Onset and rimes are traditionally used with monosyllabic words to introduce word patterns to children, not polysyllabic words (C). Prefixes and suffixes (D) are not traditionally taught as onset and rimes. Since they can have meaning on their own, they are taught individually and as part of words. **(801-005 Word Analysis and Identification Skills)**

61. D.

The correct answer is (D). Romance languages evolved from Latin, which can make it easier to recognize words with this origin. Romance languages have multiple cognates (similar words) among these languages. Modern Greek is the only world language that evolved from ancient Greek (A). German (B) and English (C) are both Germanic languages. **(801-008 Vocabulary Development)**

62. B.

The correct answer is (B). Some researchers such as Margarita Calderón organized the lexicon based on speech acts or language functions, while others such as Robert Marzano organized them based on semantic clusters or topics. Organizing the nomenclature or terminology (A) of the content areas only has not become a practical way to introduce vocabulary due to the complexity and number of words that such organization encompasses, but students do need to gain in academic vocabulary. There is the Dolch list of sight words (C), but these are used only to emphasize initial reading instruction—Tier 1 only. Dictionaries of word origins (D) are available; however, these are not commonly used to introduce vocabulary. Instead, they are used to expand on the knowledge of terms and to prepare students for spelling bees. **(801-008 Vocabulary Development)**

63. B.

The correct answer is (B). Young children can use a drawing to represent a favorite part of stories read to them. A picture (A) or a video (C) of the teacher reading the story will not provide evidence that the child understood the story. Creating a cartoon (D) to critique a story is well beyond the cognitive capabilities of kindergarten students at this level of development. **(801-012 Viewing and Representing)**

64. C.

The correct answer is (C). Mr. Diaz is pointing out that a sentence ends in a question mark, which signals to the reader that the sentence should be read differently than a statement, with the appropriate change in intonation. If the child is aware that the statement is actually a question, sh/e can provide the appropriate intonation pattern, which can improve fluency. Fluency involves rate, accuracy, and prosody (intonation, stress and pauses), but rate and accuracy, in options (A) and (B), are not emphasized in the lesson. Phonemic analysis (D) relates to hearing and manipulating the sounds of words, not reading fluently. **(801-006 Reading Fluency)**

65. B.

The correct answer is (B). During the prewriting stage, students should be guided to develop an outline that reflects the order of the ideas in the composition. They also can benefit from guiding questions to keep them focused on the topic and the intended audience. Choice (A) is incorrect because learning about grammar structures and pronunciation will not necessarily affect the organization and coherence of the composition. Choice (C) is incorrect because it addresses speaking ability as opposed to the writing process. Choice (D) is a strong distractor but not the best answer. Modeling effective writing is always a good strategy, but using only examples might not provide the necessary guidance to make permanent changes in the students' writing style. (B) is a better choice because it provides a strategy that, once learned, can be used in multiple future situations. **(801-011 Written Communication)**

66. B.

The correct answer is (B). Print is permanent. Once something is printed, it cannot be changed unless and until the publisher produces a second printing. Print media can be formal or informal, and it can also be interesting or dull (A). It can also be visually pleasing ro displeasing, and easy or difficult to produce (C). Option (D) is out because it was already stated in the scenario. **(801-012 Viewing and Representing)**

67. B.

The correct answer is (B). Miscue analysis describes the variation that students produce in their attempts to read or decode words. Goodman suggested that only those miscues affecting meaning should be taken into account. Option (A) is incorrect because miscues is a term to describe reading not necessarily writing attempts. Option (C) is incorrect because Goodman does not identify miscues as errors, plus the concept does not apply to attempts to communicate orally, such as conversation. Option (D) is incorrect because there is no connection between miscues and the schema theory. **(801-004 Literacy Development)**

68. D.

The correct answer is (D). Miscue analysis was designed to assess how well children read aloud. Choice (A) is incorrect because during silent reading miscues cannot be identified. Option (B) is incorrect because miscue analysis was designed to understand the reading process, not the development of writing. Option (C) is incorrect because miscue analysis was not designed to assess the oral performance of children speaking but of reading aloud. **(801-006 Reading Fluency)**

69. A.

The correct answer is (A). Research on second language acquisition suggests that a strong literacy development in L1 can facilitate the acquisition of similar levels of proficiency in L2. Some language-specific variables together with literacy and metacognitive strategies can also transfer from L1 to L2. Reading skills are not identical in L1 and L2; option (B) does not explain the rationale for implementing instruction in L1. Option (C) is probably an accurate statement: reading can be confusing for ELLs, but this statement does not address the question. Option (D) represents an opinion that fails to provide the rationale for the implementation of initial reading instruction in L1. **(801-007 Reading Comprehension and Applications)**

70. D.

The correct answer is (D). Onsets represent the first phoneme of a syllable or a monosyllabic word like the words presented in choice (D). Rimes follow the onset and are linked to the concept of word families. The rime *ank* can be used to create multiple words, such as *blank*, *tank*, *rank*, and *flank*. Choices (A) and (C) are generally used to represent verb tenses and cannot be considered the typical rime or word family. Choice (B) is incorrect because the two words do not represent onset and rimes. Instead, the example of *very* and *berry* represents a minimal pair—two words that differ in only one phoneme. **(801-003 Alphabetic Principle)**

71. B.

The correct answer is (B). Antonyms are words that indicate "opposites." The only pair that does so is (B), small—large. The set of words in (A), *small* and the comparative, *smaller*, represent two different words. The words in (C), *bear—bear*, represent an example of homonyms — words with the same pronunciation and spelling, but with different meanings. (D) represents an example of synonyms, words with equivalent meaning. **(801-002 Phonological and Phonemic Awareness)**

72. B.

The correct answer is (B). Students are learning that rough-draft writing can provide writers the opportunity to revise content, and by modeling for the students, the students will better understand how they can apply a revision technique of using arrows. The students learn about spelling, punctuation, and usage primarily in publishing conferences for writing the final draft (A). Helping students select a topic to write about in developing a rough draft (C), and helping students learn about word choice (D) can be effective mini-lessons, but that is not the focus of this mini-lesson. **(801-011 Written Communication)**

73. D.

The correct answer is (D). Students who are becoming literate are not yet writing conventionally. However, options (A), (B), and (C) all represent features and characteristics of emergent writers. As young writers grasp the concept of the alphabetic principle and are able to better map speech onto print in conventional ways, their spelling will more closely approximate conventional spelling. **(801-010 Writing Conventions)**

74. C.

The correct answer is (C). Shared writing is also known as the language-experience approach. Its main purpose is to integrate reading, writing, listening, and speaking in a holistic way to allow students to make connections between speech and print. By engaging in this activity, students can learn about both the reading and writing processes in an authentic and holistic way. Options (A), (B), and (D) are incorrect because they focus on more narrow and specific aspects of the activity's purpose. The broader, primary reason to do shared writing is option (C). **(801-002 Phonological and Phonemic Awareness)**

75. B.

The correct answer is (B). Guiding students to read passages repeatedly while providing guidance can lead to reading fluency. Students who are reading to improve reading fluency most likely have already mastered phonemic awareness (A), phonological awareness (C), and syllabication (D). All three of these components are prerequisites to mastering reading fluency. **(801-006 Reading Fluency)**

TExES Core Subjects EC–6 Practice Test: Mathematics

Mathematics Practice Test Answer Sheet

1. Ⓐ Ⓑ Ⓒ Ⓓ
2. Ⓐ Ⓑ Ⓒ Ⓓ
3. Ⓐ Ⓑ Ⓒ Ⓓ
4. Ⓐ Ⓑ Ⓒ Ⓓ
5. Ⓐ Ⓑ Ⓒ Ⓓ
6. Ⓐ Ⓑ Ⓒ Ⓓ
7. Ⓐ Ⓑ Ⓒ Ⓓ
8. Ⓐ Ⓑ Ⓒ Ⓓ
9. Ⓐ Ⓑ Ⓒ Ⓓ
10. Ⓐ Ⓑ Ⓒ Ⓓ
11. Ⓐ Ⓑ Ⓒ Ⓓ
12. Ⓐ Ⓑ Ⓒ Ⓓ
13. Ⓐ Ⓑ Ⓒ Ⓓ
14. Ⓐ Ⓑ Ⓒ Ⓓ
15. Ⓐ Ⓑ Ⓒ Ⓓ
16. Ⓐ Ⓑ Ⓒ Ⓓ

17. Ⓐ Ⓑ Ⓒ Ⓓ
18. Ⓐ Ⓑ Ⓒ Ⓓ
19. Ⓐ Ⓑ Ⓒ Ⓓ
20. Ⓐ Ⓑ Ⓒ Ⓓ Ⓔ
21. Ⓐ Ⓑ Ⓒ Ⓓ
22. Ⓐ Ⓑ Ⓒ Ⓓ
23. Ⓐ Ⓑ Ⓒ Ⓓ
24. Ⓐ Ⓑ Ⓒ Ⓓ
25. Ⓐ Ⓑ Ⓒ Ⓓ
26. Ⓐ Ⓑ Ⓒ Ⓓ
27. Ⓐ Ⓑ Ⓒ Ⓓ
28. Ⓐ Ⓑ Ⓒ Ⓓ
29. Ⓐ Ⓑ Ⓒ Ⓓ
30. Ⓐ Ⓑ Ⓒ Ⓓ
31. Ⓐ Ⓑ Ⓒ Ⓓ
32. Ⓐ Ⓑ Ⓒ Ⓓ

33. Ⓐ Ⓑ Ⓒ Ⓓ
34. Ⓐ Ⓑ Ⓒ Ⓓ
35. Ⓐ Ⓑ Ⓒ Ⓓ
36. Ⓐ Ⓑ Ⓒ Ⓓ
37. Ⓐ Ⓑ Ⓒ Ⓓ
38. Ⓐ Ⓑ Ⓒ Ⓓ
39. Ⓐ Ⓑ Ⓒ Ⓓ
40. Ⓐ Ⓑ Ⓒ Ⓓ
41. Ⓐ Ⓑ Ⓒ Ⓓ
42. Ⓐ Ⓑ Ⓒ Ⓓ
43. Ⓐ Ⓑ Ⓒ Ⓓ
44. Ⓐ Ⓑ Ⓒ Ⓓ
45. Ⓐ Ⓑ Ⓒ Ⓓ
46. Ⓐ Ⓑ Ⓒ Ⓓ
47. Ⓐ Ⓑ Ⓒ Ⓓ

Practice Test: Mathematics

TIME: 60 minutes
47 questions

> **Directions:** Read each item and select the correct response or responses. Most items on this test require you to provide the one best answer. However, some questions require you to select all the options that apply.

1. The concept of the zero evolved in India but was also developed, disconnectedly, by the

   A. Babylonians.

   B. Mayans.

   C. Arabs.

   D. Romans.

2. While students in a sixth-grade class work in small groups on an ungraded discovery activity involving linear functions, the teacher circulates through the class asking individual students questions such as, "Why did you choose to assign the height variable to the vertical axis?" and "What happens to the graph if you use different-sized cups for the experiment?"

   Based on the scenario, which of the following is a primary purpose of these questions?

   A. To provide a formal assessment that can be used to encourage students to work harder.

   B. To gauge student progress in developing conceptual understanding in a way that will not penalize the student.

   C. To show the students that the teacher cares about the work they are doing.

   D. To provide an informal summative assessment that can be used to determine each student's grade for the assignment.

3. Carlos wants to bring cookies for each student in his entire elementary school. He knows there are 800 students in the school. His teacher asks him to make sure he buys enough bags to carry all of the cookies, assuming each bag can hold 38 cookies. Carlos goes to the store and buys 20 bags, then brings the cookies to school the next day. He finds out that he doesn't have enough cookies for all the students at the school. Which of the following is Carlos most likely to have done to obtain the incorrect number of bags?

   A. Rounded 38 to 40

   B. Neglected to count 2 classrooms of students

   C. Baked at 375 degrees for too long

   D. Used plastic bags

   > Word problem: Tripti has 10 apples and 20 oranges. Tripti's mother doubles the total number of apples and oranges she has. Meanwhile, Gahn's mother gives Gahn twice as many apples and twice as many oranges as Tripti started with.

4. A teacher creates the word problem shown above for a math lesson. Based on the word problem, the lesson will most likely cover which of the following mathematical properties?

   A. Associative property

   B. Distributive property

   C. Commutative property

   D. Dissociative property

5. Simplify: $6 \cdot 2 + 3 \div 3$.

   A. 18

   B. 5

   C. 10

   D. 13

6. Which of the following is an expression that represents the following statement: three times one-half of a number less eighty percent?

   A. $3 \times \dfrac{4}{2} - 0.8$

   B. $3 \times \dfrac{x}{2} - \dfrac{8}{100}$

   C. $3 \times \dfrac{x}{2} - 0.8$

   D. $3 \times \dfrac{x}{2} - 80$

7. Divide 6.2 by 0.05.

   A. 124

   B. 1.24

   C. 12.4

   D. 0.124

8. Multiply $\dfrac{3}{4}$ by $\dfrac{2}{3}$. Show your answer in simplified form.

   A. $\dfrac{5}{7}$

   B. $\dfrac{5}{12}$

   C. $\dfrac{1}{2}$

   D. $\dfrac{6}{12}$

9. What is the mode of the following data set? 4, 12, 3, 15, 8, 3, 9, 9, 8, 10, 12, 14, 3, 2.

   A. 3

   B. 9

   C. 8

   D. 14

10. A card is drawn from a standard deck of cards, what is the probability that the card is a queen or a black four?

    A. $\dfrac{6}{52}$

    B. $\dfrac{8}{25}$

    C. $\dfrac{25}{52}$

    D. $\dfrac{12}{52}$

11. A pair of 6-sided dice is rolled. What is the probability the sum of the dice is less than 13?

    A. $\dfrac{1}{12}$

    B. $\dfrac{35}{36}$

    C. 1

    D. $\dfrac{1}{18}$

12. What is the formula for the relationship between the number of faces, vertices, and edges of a cube?

    A. $F + E = V + 2$

    B. $E + V = F + 2$

    C. $F + V = E - 2$

    D. $F + V = E + 2$

13. What is another way to write $4 \times 4 \times 4$?

    A. 4^3

    B. 3^4

    C. 4×3

    D. 12

14. An isosceles triangle is a polygon with two equal sides. What else does this imply?

    A. It is equilateral.

    B. Its angles sum to greater than 180°.

    C. It is also scalene.

    D. It has two equal angles.

15. Two fair two-sided coins are tossed at the same time. What is the probability that only one head is obtained in each of the tosses?

    A. 0.25

    B. 0.75

    C. 0.5

    D. 0.1

16. The main advantage of using hands-on activities in mathematics is to

    A. enhance students' ability to think abstractly.

    B. make the lesson more enjoyable.

    C. lead the students to active learning and guide them to construct their own knowledge.

    D. promote equity, equality, and freedom for the diverse ethnic groups in the nation.

Use the figure below to answer the question that follows.

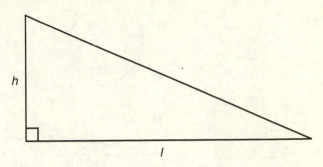

17. Which formula can be used to find the area of the triangle?

    A. $A = \dfrac{(l \times h)}{2}$

    B. $A = \dfrac{(l + h)}{2}$

    C. $A = 2(l + h)$

    D. $A = 2(l \times h)$

18. If a can weighs 14 oz., how many cans would you need to have a ton? (Round your answer to the nearest ones place and pick the best answer.)

    A. 2285

    B. 2286

    C. 2287

    D. 2300

19. How many faces does a cube have?

    A. 7

    B. 6

    C. 5

    D. 4

Use the figures below to answer the question that follows.

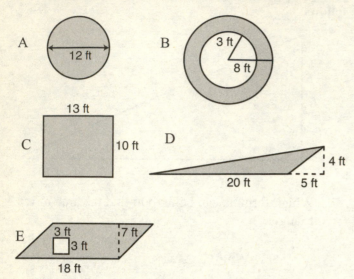

20. In each of the figures shown above, made up of circles, rectangles, triangles, and parallelograms, the shaded area represents a region in which flowers will be planted costing $2.50 per square foot. Which of them costs under $300 to plant the flowers?

Select *all* that apply.

A. Figure A

B. Figure B

C. Figure C

D. Figure D

E. Figure E

21. Students in Ms. Lopez's class are solving this problem by the discovery method:

A sheet of paper 16 by 30 inches has squares of side x cut out from the corners as shown in the diagram below. The paper is folded on the dotted line to create a rectangular solid. The volume of the solid is $V = x(30 - 2x)(16 - 2x)$.

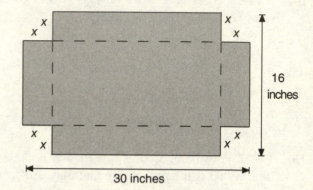

Which of the following activities is most effective in helping students understand how length, width, and height contribute to the volume of a rectangular solid?

A. Have students cut out squares of various sizes and determine the area of the resulting piece of paper.

B. Have students cut out squares of various sizes, bend up the sides, and determine the volume of the resulting shape.

C. Have students plug in various values of x into the given formula.

D. Have students watch a YouTube video of the problem.

22. For what value of x is the expression $\dfrac{5}{x}$ undefined?

A. 9

B. 1,000,000,000.1123

C. 0

D. 1E − 14

23. Which of the following sets of numbers is not an integer followed by its square?

   A. −8, 64

   B. 8, 64

   C. 6, 32

   D. −9, 81

24. Which of the following statements best represents the value of manipulatives as part of an instructional strategy?

   A. Manipulatives are more appropriate for students at the preoperational stage of cognitive development.

   B. The use of manipulatives should be restricted to children in kindergarten to fourth grade.

   C. The use of manipulatives is more appropriate for teaching computation skills and geometry.

   D. Manipulatives can be used to teach mathematics in grades Pre-K to high school.

25. Which of these numbers or number representations are irrational numbers? Select *all* that apply.

   A. π

   B. $\sqrt{2}$

   C. $e \approx 2.71828182845...$

   D. $\dfrac{5}{8}$

26. What measurement principle do children in Pre-K through kindergarten sometimes have difficulty with?

   A. Conversation

   B. Conservation

   C. Condensation

   D. Conversion

27. Which of the following would be the best set of units to use when measuring a football field?

   A. Centimeters

   B. Inches

   C. Meters

   D. Miles

28. Which of the following were the first mathematicians to impact the development of modern-day mathematics?

   A. Greeks and the Aztecs

   B. Egyptians and Babylonians

   C. Hindus and Aztecs

   D. Arabs and the Mayans

29. Perform the indicated operation: $(-36) - 11$.

   A. 47

   B. 25

   C. −47

   D. −25

30. In the problem, $5 + 6 \times \dfrac{3}{2}$, what is the first operation which should be performed according to the order of operations?

   A. Exponent

   B. Multiply

   C. Subtract

   D. Add

31. A local Brownie troop uses the model $y = 2x - 25$ to calculate the money earned in a bake sale, where x is the number of cookies sold. If the troop sold 75 cookies, how much money did the troop earn?

   A. $75

   B. $150

   C. $175

   D. $125

32. Which of the following is not a critical step to take when solving a problem?

    A. Understand the problem.

    B. Choose a strategy and/or making a plan.

    C. Make a diagram of the problem situation.

    D. Think critically about the solution.

33. Mr. Anderson tells his class that in a two-week period (including weekends and holidays), Max spends $71.47 on lunch. Two students in Mr. Anderson's class, Dave and John, are asked to state the approximate average value Max spends on lunch over this time. Dave says Max spent $4.50 on average per day. John says Max spent $5 on average. What concept needs to be addressed further in Mr. Anderson's class?

    A. Multiplication

    B. Integration

    C. Differentiation

    D. Rounding

34. In Ms. Leal's class, there are 18 blondes, 17 brunettes, and 5 redheads. Rodrigo is asked to determine the probability of Ms. Leal randomly selecting a redhead from her class to answer a question. His answer is 8. Which of the following best describes how Rodrigo went wrong in finding the solution?

    A. He divided 40 by 5.

    B. He divided 5 by 40.

    C. He added 7 and 1.

    D. He subtracted 1 from 9.

35. Two paper bags are each filled with four blue marbles and four red marbles. What is the probability of selecting a blue marble from the first bag and a blue marble from the second bag?

    A. $\dfrac{1}{4}$

    B. $\dfrac{2}{16}$

    C. $\dfrac{1}{2}$

    D. $\dfrac{4}{8}$

36. An example of a prime number is

    A. 9

    B. 682

    C. 49

    D. 67

37. Which of the following numbers cannot be used to express probability?

    A. −0.004

    B. 0.2

    C. 0

    D. 0.99

38. Solve the following problem. Express the answer as a mixed number. $1.6 - \dfrac{3}{8} =$

    A. $\dfrac{49}{40}$

    B. 1.225

    C. 1.23

    D. $1\dfrac{9}{40}$

39. There are 16 more apples than oranges in a basket of 62 apples and oranges. How many oranges are in the basket?

    A. 23

    B. 39

    C. 32

    D. 30

40. Valerie has a bathtub that she needs to fill with water. To fill the tub, she first needs to fill a bucket with water and then dump this into the bathtub. If the bucket is a cylinder with a radius of 6 in. and a height of 12 in., how many buckets will it take to fill the 5 ft. × 3 ft. × 3 ft. tub?

    A. 50 buckets

    B. 48 buckets

    C. 57 buckets

    D. 62 buckets

41. Dan and Stacy live on a farm where they are no longer allowed to let their cattle roam free. They need to add a fence around their land, which has a rectangular shape like the figure below. How many feet of fence do they need to buy in order to fence in all of their land?

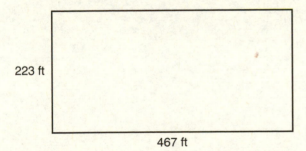

223 ft

467 ft

    A. 103,341 ft.

    B. 104,141 ft.

    C. 1,380 ft.

    D. 690 ft.

42. Simplify to a single term in scientific notation: $(2 \cdot 10)^3 \cdot (6 \cdot 10^4)$.

    A. $0.12 \cdot 10^7$

    B. $12 \cdot 10^7$

    C. $4^8 \cdot 10^8$

    D. $4.8 \cdot 10^8$

Use the figure below to answer the question that follows.

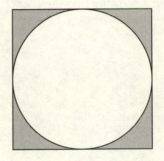

43. Given that the radius of the circle shown is 6 units and that the circle is inscribed in the square, which of the following is the approximate area of the shaded region?

    A. 106 square units

    B. 31 square units

    C. 77 square units

    D. 125 square units

44. Identify the next logical pattern of shapes that comes in ths sequence:
    ○○♦○○♦ ♦○○♦♦♦○○ …

    A. ○♦♦○

    B. ○♦○♦

    C. ♦♦○○

    D. ♦♦♦♦

45. Which of the following is equivalent to $17(64 + 8^2) - 4^3$?

    A. $64(17 + 82) - 46$

    B. 64×34

    C. 64×33

    D. $17(128) - 12$

46. Jamie rolls a pair of 6-sided dice hoping to get an odd number. What is the probability that the sum of the dice will show an odd number?

    A. 0.625

    B. 0.75

    C. 0.25

    D. 0.5

47. How many lines of symmetry does the following figure have?

    A. 1

    B. 2

    C. 3

    D. 0

Mathematics Practice Test Answer Key

1. B	17. A	33. D
2. B	18. B	34. A
3. A	19. B	35. A
4. B	20. A, D, E	36. D
5. D	21. B	37. A
6. C	22. C	38. D
7. A	23. C	39. A
8. C	24. D	40. C
9. A	25. A, B, C	41. C
10. A	26. B	42. D
11. C	27. C	43. B
12. D	28. B	44. D
13. A	29. C	45. C
14. D	30. B	46. D
15. C	31. D	47. D
16. C	32. C	

Mathematics Practice Test
Detailed Answers

1.   B.

The correct answer is (B). The Mayans developed the concept of the zero around 700 CE. However, there is no evidence to suggest that its discovery has any connection with the development of the same concept in India. Choice (A) is incorrect because there is no evidence to suggest that the Babylonians developed the concept of the zero as part of their numeric system based on 60. Choice (C) is incorrect because most historians agree that the Arabs used information from the Hindus to develop our modern numeric system, which includes the zero. Choice (D) is incorrect because there is no evidence to suggest that the Romans developed the concept of the zero as part of their numeric system. **(802-003 Patterns and Algebra)**

2.   B.

The correct answer is (B). Because no grades are being assigned, the students will not be penalized if they cannot answer the question. The questions themselves are focused on key concepts in linear functions such as the meaning of the y-intercept (question No. 1) and the linear function as a model of the physical world (question No. 2). Choice (A) can be ruled out because the fact that the teacher is asking the questions in a conversational tone without mention of grades being assigned makes this an informal assessment. Choice (D) can be ruled out because the teacher is assessing the students as they work on the content. This means the teacher is using a formative, not summative, assessment. Though choice (C) may initially seem appealing, it is not correct because a teacher who maintains a neutral relationship with his or her students can still perform these tasks effectively; thus, the notion of caring in itself is not integral to this test item. **(802-001 Mathematics Instruction)**

3.   A.

The correct response is (A). It is most likely that Carlos rounded 38 to 40 in order to make his division process easier. This would then explain how he came to purchase 20 bags because 800 students divided by 40 yields 20. **(802-006 Mathematical Processes)**

4.   B.

The correct response is (B). The distributive property best describes the statement. Tripti initially had $(10 + 20)$ apples and oranges and then the amount is doubled: $2 \times (10 + 20)$. Gahn was given twice as many apples and oranges from the beginning: $(2 \times 10 + 2 \times 20)$. Choice (A) is a play on the associative property and therefore is incorrect. Answers (C) and (D) do not apply. Therefore, the best answer is choice (B). **(802-006 Mathematical Processes)**

5.   D.

The correct answer is (D). The order of operations must be obeyed here. Remembering the saying "Please Excuse My Dear Aunt Sally (PEMDAS)" allows us to remember the order in which mathematical operations must be carried out: Parentheses Exponent Multiply Divide Add Subtract. Following this, multiply 6 by 2 to obtain 12. Then, divide 3 by 3 obtaining 1. Finally, add the two results together to obtain $12 + 1 = 13$. **(802-001 Mathematics Instruction)**

6.   C.

The correct answer is (C). The statement "three times one-half of a number less eighty percent" implies that we do not know the actual number. Therefore, it must be represented by a variable. This fact eliminates choice (A). Knowing that 80% is equivalent to $\frac{80}{100}$ or

0.8 eliminates choices (B) and (D). Therefore, the only choice that is left happens to be choice (C). **(802-006 Mathematical Processes)**

7.   A.

The correct answer is (A). The traditional whole number division algorithm (method) is helpful when dividing decimals longhand. The work can be set up like this:

$$0.05\overline{)6.2}$$

Dividing (while temporarily ignoring the zeros and decimal points) gives

$$
\begin{array}{r}
124 \\
0.05\overline{)6.2} \\
\underline{5} \\
1\,2 \\
\underline{1\,0} \\
20 \\
\underline{20} \\
0
\end{array}
$$

Next, you count the number of digits to the right of the decimal point in the divisor (two). Two, then, is the number of places that you shift the "inside" decimal point to the right, and then "up" into the answer:

$$0.05\overline{)6.2} \longrightarrow 0.05\overline{)6.2}$$

Because the answer is a whole number, the decimal point does not have to be shown. **(802-002 Number Concepts and Operations)**

8.   C.

The correct answer is (C). The useful, traditional approach to multiplying simple fractions (those between 0 and 1) is to first multiply the numerators together and then to multiply the denominators together to find the product. In this case, $\frac{3}{4} \times \frac{2}{3} = \frac{6}{12}$. That fraction is then shown in simplest form, $\frac{1}{2}$. Based on the explanation, choices A, B, and D are incorrect. **(802-002 Number Concepts and Operations)**

9.   A.

Choice (A) is the correct answer. The mode is the number that occurs most often. From looking at the data we see that the number 3 occurs 3 times, the most of all the numbers. **(802-005 Probability and Statistics)**

10.   A.

The correct answer is (A): $\frac{6}{52}$. In a standard deck of cards there are 52 total cards. Of the 52 cards, there are four suits and 13 cards per suit. Therefore, there are four queens in the deck. Additionally, of the four suits, two are black and two are red. So, there are two black fours giving a grand total of six cards of 52 that meet the criteria. **(802-005 Probability and Statistics)**

11.   C.

The correct answer is (C): $\frac{36}{36} = 1$. On a single die there are six numbers, 1–6. On a pair of dice, the values of the sums range from 2–12. All values are clearly less than 12. Therefore, all rolls will be less than 13. Additionally, with a pair of dice, there are 36 possible outcomes (6 each) and, therefore, the answer is (C). **(802-005 Probability and Statistics)**

12.   D.

The correct answer is (D): $F + V = E + 2$. Recall that the Face (F) of a cube is a plain region of a geometric body, the Edge (E) is a line segment where two faces of a three-dimensional figure meet, and a Vertex (V) is the union of two segments or the point of intersection of two sides of a polygon. Knowing this we can see that for a cube there are 6 faces, 8 vertices, and 12 edges. Substituting these numbers into the appropriate spot in each formula allows us to determine option (D) as the only correct answer. **(802-004 Geometry and Measurement)**

13.   A.

Recalling that exponential notation is used when numbers are multiplied by themselves numerous times, try to simplify the expression. Option (B) is not correct because this implies 3 is multiplied by itself 4 times. Options (C) and (D) are the same answer in different representations, but both are incorrect. Since 4 is multiplied by itself 3 times in this problem, we know the answer should be option (A). **(802-002 Number Concepts and Operations)**

14. D.

In any triangle, the sum of the angles must equal 180°. If a triangle has two equal sides, the third side cannot be unique and must be a set length. The lines associated with the equal sides will intersect the third side at the same angle. Therefore, the only answer that can be determined to be true from the information is option (D). **(802-004 Geometry and Measurement)**

15. C.

Since tossing two separate coins does not affect the outcome of the other coin, we know that the probability of getting heads on either coin is $\frac{1}{2}$. The probability of the outcome is thus $\frac{2}{4}$ or 0.5. Alternatively, the possibilities are HH, HT, TH, and TT. Since there are 4 possibilities and 2 of them have only one H, the probability is $\frac{2}{4} = \frac{1}{2} = 0.5$. **(802-005 Probability and Statistics)**

16. C.

The correct answer is (C). Hands-on activities can make the curriculum more relevant and guide children to construct their own knowledge. Hands-on activities can probably lead children to think abstractly (A), but the activity is not designed exclusively to accomplish this goal. Hands-on activities can make the class more interesting and enjoyable (B), but they are not the reasons for the activities. (D) is incorrect because there is no evidence to suggest that hands-on activities can promote equity, equality, or freedom among students. **(802-001 Mathematics Instruction)**

17. A.

The area of any rectangle is equal to the measure of its length times the measure of its width (or to say it differently, the measure of its base times the measure of its height). A right triangle can be seen as half of a rectangle (sliced diagonally). Choice (A) represents, in effect, a rectangle's area cut in half (i.e., divided by 2). Based on this explanation, choices (B), (C), and (D) are incorrect. **(802-004 Geometry and Measurement)**

18. B.

The correct answer is (B), 2286. An easy way to solve this problem is to use basic algebra. Knowing that there are 16 oz. in a pound and that there are 2,000 lbs. in a ton helps ease the difficulty of the problem. We want to find out the number of cans x it will take to obtain a ton. Therefore, we have $\frac{14}{16}x = 2000$. If both sides of the equation are multiplied by 16 and then we divide both sides by 14, we will obtain the approximate number of cans it will take to obtain one ton. $x = \frac{16 \times 2000}{14} = \frac{32000}{14} \approx 2285.7$. We see that many of the answers are close to this value. When we round this number, we will obtain 2,286. **(802-003 Patterns and Algebra)**

19. B.

The correct answer is (B): 6. Remembering that a face is a plane region of a geometric body, one can determine that since there are six sides to a cube, there are also six faces. **(802-004 Geometry and Measurement)**

20. A., D., E.

The correct answers are (A), (D), and (E). This problem tests the area of regular polygons.

A. Area = $\pi(6^2) = 36\pi$. Cost = $36\pi(2.5) = 90\pi$ dollars = \$282.74, which is less than \$300

B. Area = $\pi(64) - \pi(9) = 55\pi$. Cost = $55\pi (2.5) = 137.5\pi$ dollars = \$431.97, which is not less than \$300

C. Area = 13(10) = 130. Cost = 130(2.5) = \$325, which is not less than \$300

D. Area = $\frac{1}{2}(20)(4) = 40$. Cost = $40(2.5) = \$100$, which is less than $300

E. Area = $18(7) - 9 = 117$. Cost = $117(2.5) = \$292.50$, which is less than $300

(802-004 Geometry and Measurement)

21. B.

The correct answer is option (B) because having students cut out the squares gets them to see that the larger the square, the smaller the length and width. Being able to have a physical model of these solids allows students to see readily which ones are obviously larger in volume than others. Option (A) is incorrect as cutting squares out and examining the area tells students nothing about the volume. Option (C) is incorrect because although plugging different values of x will give different volumes of V, students do not see how the size of x affects the length and the width. Option (D) is incorrect because unless this video shows someone performing option (B), it cannot be as effective a learning tool. **(802-001 Mathematics Instruction)**

22. C.

Until more advanced mathematics are incurred, the standard definition of division states that an expression is undefined if it contains division by 0. Option (D) is a number very close to zero. Although option (D) will make the expression a huge number, it is still not undefined. Therefore, the response that best corresponds to the question is choice (C). **(802-003 Patterns and Algebra)**

23. C.

An integer number is a whole number that is either positive or negative. Remembering that a negative times a negative gives a positive means that any of the answers could be possible and we cannot rule any out by process of elimination. Knowing that 8 times 8 gives 64 and –8 times –8 gives 64 means both choices (A) and (B) are true. Similarly, –9 times–9 results in 81 (D), meaning 81 is true. However, 6 times 6 gives 36, not 32. This means

that choice (C) is not a true statement and is the solution to the problem. **(802-003 Patterns and Algebra)**

24. D.

The correct answer is (D). Manipulatives can be used to simplify the teaching of mathematics in all grade levels—Pre-K to high school. Choices (A) and (B) are incorrect because the use of manipulatives does not have to be restricted to early childhood (pre-kindergarten through fourth grade). Choice (C) is incorrect because manipulatives can be used to teach concepts including computation skills and geometry but its use is not limited to these two components. **(802-001 Mathematics Instruction)**

25. A., B., and C.

The correct answers are (A), (B), and (C). An irrational number is a number that cannot be expressed as a fraction. π is one of the most well-known irrational numbers. Additionally, the square root of 2 and Euler's number (e) are well-known numbers that are irrational (at no known point does a pattern appear in the decimals of these numbers). Choice (D) is not correct because any number that can be written as a fraction is a rational number. **(802-006 Mathematical Processes)**

26. B.

Children that are four and five years old may not understand that changes in the appearance do not necessarily change the characteristics of an object. For example, if an apple is cut in half the children may not understand that there are two pieces of one apple. Instead, many students may say that there are now two apples. The difficulty these students face is with the concept of conservation (B). **(802-001 Mathematics Instruction)**

27. C.

While all of these units will accurately express the length of the football field, centimeters and inches would not be a convenient scale to use, as the resolution of the measurement would be too great resulting in an extremely large number (or a long time to measure). Miles are another inconvenient method to measure a football field, as a mile is much larger than a single football field. **(802-002 Number Concepts and Operations)**

28. B.

While other groups made significant contributions to mathematics, choice (B), the Egyptians and Babylonians (third millennium BCE) were the first groups to make an impact on the development of modern-day mathematics. **(802-006 Mathematical Processes)**

29. C.

When subtraction involves any negative numbers, a good rule to use is, "Don't subtract the second number. Instead, add its opposite." Using that rule, the original expression, (–36) – 11, becomes (–36) + –11. To be "in debt" by 36, then to be further "in debt" by 11, puts one "in debt" by 47, shown as –47. **(802-002 Number Concepts and Operations)**

30. B.

Using the acronym PEMDAS as a mnemonic device to remember the order of operations, it allows us to see that the first operation required in the problems is multiplication. That is, the acronym calls for the following order: parenthesis, exponents, multiplication, division, addition, and subtraction. However, since the problem does not contain parenthesis or exponents, the first operation required in the problem is multiplication. **(802-006 Mathematical Processes)**

31. D.

(D) is the correct answer. The Brownie troop sold $125 worth of cookies. The amount of money, y, is found by substituting the number of cookies sold, 75, for x in the given equation: $y = 2x - 25 = 2(75) - 25 = 150 - 25 = 125$. **(802-006 Mathematical Processes)**

32. C.

In order to solve a problem we must understand the problem, choose a strategy and/or make a plan, carry out the plan, and think about whether the answer makes sense in the context of the problem. The only response option that is not a critical component of the process is to make a diagram of the problem situation (C). This is because not all problems lend themselves to diagrams. **(802-006 Mathematical Processes)**

33. D.

The correct answer is (D), rounding. Choices (B) and (C) are related to calculus, and are not involved in the problem. Multiplication (A) is not needed as the problem asks to find the average value spent on lunch, which implies division. Based on the outcomes of Dave's and John's answers, both being relatively close to each other and less than the true average, it appears that rounding should be addressed further. **(802-006 Mathematical Processes)**

34. A.

The correct answer is (A). Choices (C) and (D), while matching Rodrigo's answer, would seemingly come from nowhere which is highly unlikely. Choice (B) would produce a number less than 1, the correct answer for the problem asked of Rodrigo, and therefore would not match Rodrigo's answer. It is most likely that Rodrigo divided 40, the number of students in the class, by 5, the number of redheads, to obtain his answer of 8. **(802-005 Probability and Statistics)**

35. A.

There are equal numbers of blue and red marbles in each bag. For a single bag on a single draw, the probability of pulling a red or a blue marble is equal to $\frac{4}{8}$, or $\frac{1}{2}$. Selecting a marble from one bag does not affect the probability of selecting a specific marble from the other bag, therefore these events are said to be independent. When dealing with the probability of independent events, one may multiply the probabilities together to obtain the overall probability. In this case, we know the probability of selecting a blue marble is $\frac{1}{2}$ for the first bag and it is also $\frac{1}{2}$ for the second bag. Therefore, the overall probability of the independent events is $\frac{1}{4}$. **(802-005 Probability and Statistics)**

36. D.

A prime number is a number whose only factors are one and itself. Even numbers greater than 2 can always be factored by 2, eliminating (B). (A) can be factored as 3 times 3 and (C) can be factored as 7 times 7. Therefore, (D) must be the right answer as it only has factors of 1 and 67. **(802-002 Number Concepts and Operations)**

37. A.

A probability can be expressed as a number from 0 to 1, or with percentage or decimal numbers. A percent is a representation of a decimal number relative to 100. Therefore, the only number shown which does not fit is the negative number. **(802-005 Probability and Statistics)**

38. D.

This problem can be solved by converting the decimal to a fraction, or the fraction to a decimal and then subtracting. If the decimal is converted to a fraction, 1.6 becomes $1.6 - \frac{3}{8}$ becomes $\frac{16}{10} - \frac{3}{8}$. In order to subtract, we should now get a common denominator. The lowest common denominator between 8 and 10 is 40. Therefore, the answer becomes $\frac{64}{40} - \frac{15}{40} = \frac{49}{40}$. Since the problem asks for a mixed number, the answer is $1\frac{9}{40}$. **(802-002 Number Concepts and Operations)**

39. A.

This problem is easily solved by using some basic algebraic reasoning. Since we are interested in deter-

mining the number of oranges that are in the basket, we will set this as a variable called r. The number of apples, a, and the number of oranges, r, sum to a total of 62. We also know that there are 16 more apples than oranges ($a = r + 16$). This gives $r + (r + 16) = 2r + 16 = 62$. Solving for r yields 23 oranges in the basket. **(802-003 Patterns and Algebra)**

40. C.

This problem requires critical thinking and some basic knowledge of math. Solving for the volume of the bathtub, one obtains 45 ft³ and the volume of the bucket is $\pi \cdot 0.5^2 \times 1 \approx 0.7854$ ft². To find how many buckets of water it will take to fill the tub, we must divide 45 by 0.7854. This gives approximately 57 buckets (C). **(802-003 Patterns and Algebra)**

41. C.

This problem deals with finding the perimeter of the rectangle. Since the two short legs of fence have the same length and the two long legs have the same length, we know $P = 2l + 2w$. This gives us a value of $2 \cdot 223 + 2 \cdot 467 = 1380$ ft. So you should have chosen option (C). **(802-004 Geometry and Measurement)**

42. D.

First simplify the expression $(2 \cdot 10)^3 \cdot (6 \cdot 10^4)$; rewrite as $(2^3 \cdot 10^3) \cdot (6 \cdot 10^4) = 8 \cdot 10^3 \cdot 6 \cdot 10^4$. Rearrange the terms so they appear as $(8 \cdot 6) \cdot (10^3 \cdot 10^4)$ to assist in multiplying the "like" numbers. The first group results in 48. To calculate $(10^3 \cdot 10^4)$ we use a specific rule for exponents. To multiply quantities with the same base (in this case 10), add the exponents: $10^3 \cdot 10^4 = 10^{(3+4)} = 10^7$, which produces a value of $48 \cdot 10^7$. To place this into scientific notation, the first number's absolute value should be between 0 and 1. For the leading number, move the decimal point one place to the left and add 1 to the exponent of the 10. Our final answer would then be $4.8 \cdot 10^8$. **(802-002 Number Concepts and Operations)**

43. B.

First, it is helpful to view the shaded area as the area of the square minus the area of the circle. With that in mind, you simply need to find the area of each simple figure, and then subtract one from the other. You know that the radius of the circle is 6 units in length. That tells you that the diameter of the circle is 12 units. Because the circle is inscribed in the square (meaning that the circle fits inside of the square touching in as many places as possible), you see that the sides of the square are each 12 units in length. Knowing that, you compute that the area of the square is 144 square units (12×12). Using the formula for finding the area of a circle (πr^2), and using 3.14 for π, you get approximately 113 square units. ($3.14 \times 6 \times 6$). Then, you subtract 113 (the area of the circle) from 144 (the area of the square) for the answer of 31. Based on the explanation given, choices (A), (C), and (D) are incorrect. **(802-004 Geometry and Measurement)**

44. D.

In the presented pattern we see two circles followed by one diamond. Then, there are two circles followed by two diamonds. Next, we see two circles, three diamonds, and then two circles again. We take note that every time circles appear they only appear in pairs. Therefore, we know the next set should not be a circle right away. If we look at the diamonds, we see that at first we had one diamond, then two, and finally three. They are increasing by 1 each time they appear. Therefore, we should expect to see four diamonds. **(802-003 Patterns and Algebra)**

45. C.

In this problem it is necessary to perform the order of operations as well as look at equivalent representa-tions of numbers. Since there are no exponents in any of the solutions, it may be beneficial to carry this out within the problem before proceeding further. Doing so results in $17(64 + 64) - 64$. This may also be written as $17 \times 64 \times 2 - 64$. Since 64 appears in the first multiplica-tion sequence as well as being a subtrahend, it may be factored to produce $64(17 \times 2 - 1) = 64(34 - 1) = 64 \times 33$. Thus, you should have selected option (C). **(802-002 Number Concepts and Operations)**

46. D.

Knowing that with a pair of dice there are 36 pos-sible outcomes allows us to view all of the possible out-comes. Of the possible outcomes, half are odd and half are even as shown by the following table:

Sum	1	2	3	4	5	6
1	2	3	4	5	6	
2	3	4	5	6	7	8
3	4	5	6	7	8	9
4	5	6	7	8	9	10
5	6	7	8	9	10	11
6	7	8	9	10	11	12

(802-005 Probability and Statistics)

47. D.

(D) is the correct answer. The shape in question does not have any lines of symmetry since any lines cre-ated would not produce mirror images. **(802-004 Geom-etry and Measurement)**

TExES Core Subjects EC–6
Practice Test:
Social Studies

Social Studies Practice Test Answer Sheet

30/41

✓ 1. (A) (B) (C) (D)

✓ 2. (A) (B) (C) (D)

✓ 3. (A) (B) (C) (D)

C ✗ 4. (A) (B) (C) (D)

✓ 5. (A) (B) (C) (D)

✓ 6. (A) (B) (C) (D)

A ✗ 7. (A) (B) (C) (D)

8. (A) (B) (C) (D)

9. (A) (B) (C) (D)

B ✗ 10. (A) (B) (C) (D)

✓ 11. (A) (B) (C) (D)

✓ 12. (A) (B) (C) (D)

✓ 13. (A) (B) (C) (D)

✓ 14. (A) (B) (C) (D)

✓ 15. (A) (B) (C) (D)

D ✗ 16. (A) (B) (C) (D)

D ✗ 17. (A) (B) (C) (D)

✓ 18. (A) (B) (C) (D)

✓ 19. (A) (B) (C) (D)

C 20. (A) (B) (C) (D)

✓ 21. (A) (B) (C) (D)

C 22. (A) (B) (C) (D)

✓ 23. (A) (B) (C) (D)

✓ 24. (A) (B) (C) (D)

D 25. (A) (B) (C) (D)

✓ 26. (A) (B) (C) (D)

✓ 27. (A) (B) (C) (D)

✓ 28. (A) (B) (C) (D)

C ✗ 29. (A) (B) (C) (D)

✓ 30. (A) (B) (C) (D)

A,C,E ✗ 31. (A) (B) (C) (D) (E)

32. (A) (B) (C) (D)

✓ 33. (A) (B) (C) (D)

✓ 34. (A) (B) (C) (D)

✓ 35. (A) (B) (C) (D)

✓ 36. (A) (B) (C) (D)

✓ 37. (A) (B) (C) (D)

C ✗ 38. (A) (B) (C) (D)

✓ 39. (A) (B) (C) (D)

✓ 40. (A) (B) (C) (D)

✓ 41. (A) (B) (C) (D)

Practice Test: Social Studies

TIME: 35 minutes
41 questions

> **Directions:** Read each item and select the correct response or responses. Most items on this test require you to provide the one best answer. However, some questions require you to select all the options that apply.

1. Which of the following best describes how elementary teachers should prepare students for their roles as citizens of the United States?

    A. They lay the foundation of American core values, citizenship, democracy, and patriotism.

    B. They have students in upper elementary grades prepare reports on the values and beliefs of America's forefathers.

    C. They ask students in lower elementary grades to role-play key historical figures in school plays and other events.

    D. They provide basic information when they can, so students can fit social studies content into their daily schedules.

2. Which of the following best describes the women's suffrage movement in Texas?

    A. Women activists in Texas became involved when the suffrage movement was popular in the United States.

    B. Many women in Texas embraced change and sought an equal status in all parts of society.

    C. Texas women believed that the suffrage movement was a natural extension of the work they did at home.

    D. The suffrage movement was a long fight, lasting nearly 60 years, to convince the male-dominated political establishment and other women of the merit of enfranchising women.

3. The Virginia House of Burgesses was established in Jamestown to

    A. function as the official body of the U.S. government.

    B. regulate trading among colonies.

    C. function as a form of representative government.

    D. regulate the establishment of religions.

4. Identify the order of the products that have supported the Texas economy through its history.

    A. Petroleum, cotton, oranges, and cattle

    B. Cattle, corn, petroleum, and education

    C. Cotton, cattle, petroleum, and computers and electronics

    D. Cattle, petroleum, beef, venison, and poultry

5. The Imperial Forces of Japan attacked Pearl Harbor on Sunday, December 7, 1941. Once the attack began, the officer in charge called President Roosevelt and notified him of the attack. During the communication, the president was able to hear the noise of the bombs exploding and the struggle of the battle. Recently, a reporter from the *Dallas Morning News* was researching the details of the attack and found a transcription of the official diary of Emperor Hirohito, in which he indicated the following: "The Imperial forces of Japan destroyed the American fleet in Hawaii Monday, December 8, 1941." If the attack occurred on December 7, why did the official document from the Japanese government indicate that the attack happened on December 8? Select the statement that best explains this discrepancy.

A. The Americans knew that the attack was going to happen and assumed that it had happened the day before.

B. The U.S. government had spies in Japan who knew when the attack was going to take place.

C. There is a one-day difference between the two regions.

D. Emperor Hirohito learned about the attack the day after, and he assumed that it happened on the same day he was apprised of it.

6. The U.S. Constitution was designed so that no single branch of the government—executive, judicial, or legislative—could exert full control over the other two. This unique feature of the Constitution is known as

A. judicial review.

B. the pocket veto.

C. checks and balances.

D. habeas corpus.

Advanced organizers and graphic representations are commonly used in social studies. What is the advantage of using these strategies to teach content?

A. They make content accessible to all children.

B. They make learning more interesting.

C. They can be used to teach other content areas.

D. They can be used to teach higher-order thinking skills.

8. The Mayflower Compact was one of the earliest agreements to

A. establish a political body and to give that political body the power to act for the good of the colony.

B. establish rules for farming and trading.

C. establish a plan to implement plantation systems.

D. establish a policy for settlement.

9. What is the function of the lines of latitude and longitude on a map?

A. They form a grid system that emphasizes a cylindrical projection.

B. Together, they provide the coordinates for the absolute location of a place.

C. They form a grid system that measures distance in meters.

D. Together, they are used to explain the relative location of a place.

10. A globe is a scale model of the Earth shaped like a sphere. A globe shows sizes and shapes more accurately than

A. a compass rose.

B. a Mercator projection map.

C. a map scale.

D. a thematic map.

11. The Sumerians, Akkadians, Babylonians, and As-syrians were some of the civilizations that flour-ished in Mesopotamia—the land between the rivers. What rivers are being alluded to in this statement?

    A. Nile and Amazon

    B. Tigris and Euphrates

    C. Nile and Indus

    D. Volga and Danube

12. A compass rose is a design printed on a chart to

    A. show the orientation of a map of Earth.

    B. show the distance between two places in the world.

    C. represent features such as elevations and divisions.

    D. show the distance between two corresponding points.

13. The tallest mountains in the world are part of the

    A. Andes Range.

    B. Himalayas Range.

    C. Karakoram Range.

    D. Kunlun Range.

14. The Battle of Gettysburg was the most disastrous episode of which of the following?

    A. American Civil War

    B. American Revolution

    C. Second World War

    D. Texas Revolution

15. The economic theory that states that prices vary based on the balance between the availability of a product or service at a certain price and the desire of potential purchasers to pay that price is known as

    A. free enterprise.

    B. the law of supply and demand.

    C. the interplay of inflation and deflation.

    D. economic interdependence.

16. What is the main purpose of the Federal Reserve System?

    A. To promote fiscal stability and provide stimulus money to balance the economy

    B. To promote economic growth

    C. To create inflation and deflation

    D. To keep the banking industry strong enough to ensure a supply of currency

17. The Texas state curriculum officially introduces children to U.S. history in

    A. second grade.

    B. third grade.

    C. fourth grade.

    D. fifth grade.

18. There are two categories of maps: reference maps and thematic maps. An atlas is an example of

    A. a reference map.

    B. a thematic map.

    C. a physical map.

    D. a population map.

19. The New England colonies consisted of

    A. Virginia, North Carolina, South Carolina, and Georgia.

    B. Massachusetts, Connecticut, Rhode Island, and New Hampshire.

    C. New York, New Jersey, Delaware, Maryland, and Pennsylvania.

    D. North Carolina, Rhode Island, Delaware, and Maryland.

20. To apply the concept of time zones, students need to have a clear understanding of

    A. the international date line.

    B. the Earth's yearly revolution.

    C. the concept of the meridians of longitude.

    D. the concept of the parallels of latitude.

Use the photograph below to answer the question that follows.

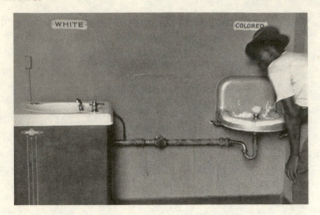

21. Which of the following court cases saw the U.S. Supreme Court rule that the conditions of segregation illustrated in the photograph above violated the Fourteenth Amendment?

   A. *Plessy v. Ferguson*

   C. *Brown v. Board of Education of Topeka*

   B. *Marbury v. Madison*

   D. *Dred Scott v. Sandford*

22. The earliest European colonization efforts in North America began with the founding of which of the following?

   A. Virginia and Massachusetts

   B. Texas and New Mexico

   C. Saint Augustine and Roanoke

   D. New York and New Jersey

Use the information below to answer the question that follows.

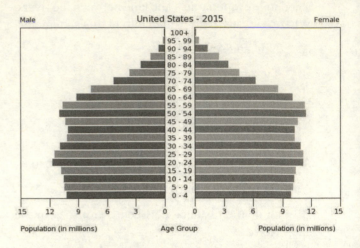

Source: United States Census Bureau

23. A population pyramid as seen above is a complex example of what type of chart, diagram, or graph listed below?

   A. Bar graph

   B. Pie graph

   C. Pedigree chart

   D. Dot plot

24. The first 10 amendments to the U.S. Constitution are known as the

   A. doctrine of the separation of church and state.

   B. Bill of Rights.

   C. Right to Privacy.

   D. Right to Due Process.

25. Students are expected to have received how many years of daily social studies instruction before entering middle school (grades 7–8)?

   A. As much as possible

   B. Two years

   C. Four years

   D. Seven years

26. Why are Indian tribes from the Central and Great Plains of Texas better known than their counterparts from the Coastal Plains?

    A. They had a more advanced civilization.

    B. They were sedentary and built better ceremonial sites and permanent structures.

    C. They domesticated the horse, which made them better hunters and warriors.

    D. They had an abundance of food sources and were stronger.

27. The United States has 50 states and at least four territories. Based on these figures, what is the maximum number of senators who can serve in the U.S. Senate?

    A. 50

    B. 100

    C. 54

    D. 435

Revere, Paul, engraver. "The BLOODY MASSACRE perpetrated in King Street BOSTON on March 5th 1770 by a party of the 29th REGT." 1770. Courtesy of Prints and Photographs Division, Library of Congress.

28. The Paul Revere engraving of the Boston Massacre (1770), pictured above, is taught at what grade level?

    A. 6th grade

    B. 5th grade

    C. 4th grade

    D. 3rd grade

29. Cinco de Mayo is a holiday commemorating the victory of the Mexican army over the French forces of Napoleon III on May 5, 1862. This event is important to Mexican Americans because

    A. the Mexicans defeated a ragtag army.

    B. it led to Mexican Independence Day.

    C. the general who led the Mexican forces was born in present-day Texas.

    D. President Benito Juarez joined forces with the United States to defeat France.

30. The Fifteenth Amendment to the U.S. Constitution was ratified in 1870 to grant

    A. black women and men the right to vote.

    B. citizenship for blacks.

    C. freedom of slaves.

    D. black men the right to vote.

31. Determining globes for a first grade classroom should be based on which of the following characteristics? Select *all* that apply.

    A. Three or fewer colors to represent land.

    B. At least seven colors to represent land.

    C. Two or fewer colors to represent water.

    D. Three or more colors to represent water.

    E. A 12-inch globe.

32. Probably as a response to the war in Iraq and Afghanistan, the Organization of Petroleum Exporting Countries (OPEC) cut the production of oil. As a result of this action, the cost of gasoline increased to almost $3.00 per gallon in 2005. What is the economic principle or statement that best represents this scenario?

    A. During war, the prices of fossil fuels increase.

    B. The American economy is dependent on foreign oil.

    C. The law of supply and demand determines the prices of goods and services.

    D. OPEC was boycotting the United States.

33. Identify the statement that best describes the country of Iraq.

A. It is a linguistically and ethnically homogeneous Muslim nation.

B. It is a Muslim nation with multiple ethnic groups within its borders.

C. It is located in Southeast Asia.

D. It is a province of Pakistan.

Use the information below to answer the question that follows.

**Texas GDP Ranking among Nations
Gross Domestic Product, 2014
(in billions of U.S. dollars)**

Rank	Nation	Billion $
1	United States*	$17,418
2	China	$10,380
3	Japan	$4,616
4	Germany	$3,859
5	United Kingdom	$2,945
6	France	$2,846
7	Brazil	$2,353
8	Italy	$2,147
9	India	$2,049
10	Russia	$1,871
11	Canada	$1,788
12	**TEXAS****	**$1,648**
13	Australia	$1,444
14	Korea	$1,416
15	Spain	$1,406
16	Mexico	$1,282
17	Indonesia	$888
18	The Netherlands	$866
19	Turkey	$806
20	Saudi Arabia	$752

*Includes Texas
**If Texas were a nation

Sources: International Monetary Fund and the U.S. Bureau of Economic Analysis. Based on data provided by the Texas Comptroller of Public Accounts staff. Published June 2015.

34. Based on the table above, if Texas were an independent nation, its annual economic output would be which of the following? Select *all* that apply.

A. Ahead of Canada by approximately US$140 billion

B. More than double the GDP of Saudi Arabia

C. More than half the GDP of the United Kingdom

D. One notch above Australia

35. The Spaniards Francisco Pizarro and Hernán Cortés conquered, respectively, which of the following two civilizations?

A. Mayan and Aztec

B. Inca and Aztec

C. Toltec and Olmec

D. Taino and Quechua

36. Identify the statement that best describes the relationship between the eight social studies strands and the TEKS in the implementation of the Texas curriculum.

A. There is no connection between the TEKS and the social studies strands.

B. The social studies strands have been used as a foundation for the development of the state curriculum.

C. The strands apply to programs at the university level and the TEKS applies to K–12 curricula.

D. The strands apply to programs at the high school level, while the TEKS applies to all grade levels.

37. Why might children in prekindergarten and kindergarten have problems understanding how the Earth is represented in globes and flat representations?

   A. They might not be developmentally ready to understand symbolic representations.

   B. They might pay more attention to the colors and features of globes and maps than the concepts being taught.

   C. They might not be interested in maps and globes.

   D. They might have problems recognizing the Earth's features presented on a 12-inch globe representation.

38. Which of the following has a government that is an example of a theocracy?

   A. Jordan

   B. China

   C. Iran

   D. India

39. A census of the population of the United States is conducted every 10 years. Based on census results, which of the following can be affected by population changes?

   A. U.S. House of Representatives

   B. U.S. Senate

   C. Justices of the Supreme Court

   D. The Executive Branch

40. In Texas, the course that focuses on human or cultural geography is introduced in which of the following grades?

   A. third

   B. fourth

   C. fifth

   D. sixth

41. The English colonies were established in three regions: the New England Colonies, the Middle Colonies, and the Southern Colonies. The economy of the Southern Colonies was based on

   A. farming, shipping, fishing, and trading.

   B. farming and very small industries such as fishing, lumber, and crafts.

   C. trading.

   D. crops of tobacco, rice, indigo, and cotton.

Social Studies Practice Test Answer Key

1. A	15. B	29. C
2. D	16. D	30. D
3. C	17. D	31. A, C, and E
4. C	18. A	32. C
5. C	19. B	33. B
6. C	20. C	34. B, C, and D
7. A	21. C	35. B
8. A	22. C	36. B
9. B	23. A	37. A
10. B	24. B	38. C
11. B	25. D	39. A
12. A	26. C	40. D
13. B	27. B	41. D
14. A	28. B	

Social Studies Practice Test Detailed Answers

1. **A.**

The correct answer is (A). All elementary teachers play an important role in students' civic education. They introduce and instill the core values and ideals of what it means to be an American. Additionally, they provide foundational understanding of concepts upon which subsequent grade levels build. Social studies education also teaches students to consider events and situations from different points of view and to connect information learned in other disciplines, such as science or English language arts. Option (B) may occur; however, writing such reports is not central to preparing students for their role as citizens. Option (C) is correct in that students in lower elementary do learn about key historical figures. Some teachers may ask them to role-play. However, the answer does not specifically describe the elementary teacher's responsibility to prepare students for their role as citizens of the United States. Option (D) is incorrect. It is expected in the state of Texas that students will receive daily instruction in social studies. **(803-001 Social Science Instruction)**

2. **D.**

The correct answer is (D). After being left out of the 15th Amendment (right to vote), women across the United States, and in Texas and other states, began to fight for equal rights. Option (A) is incorrect because women in Texas were involved in the suffrage movement from the mid-1800s to the early 1900s. As it turns out, many women had to be persuaded that equal rights would not detract from their role and responsibility as wife and mother (C). The suffrage movement was a long struggle in Texas that required the dedication of great numbers of women and men to see it through to fruition. In 1919, Texas became the ninth state in the Union to ratify the Nineteenth Amendment, which guaranteed all American women the right to vote. **(803-002 History)**

3. **C.**

The correct answer is (C). Established in 1619, the Virginia House of Burgesses was the first democratically elected legislative body in the British American colonies. Option (A) is incorrect because the U.S. government did not exist during this time (1619). Option (B) is incorrect because England regulated trading with the colonies. Option (D) is incorrect because there was no official entity in the colony to regulate the establishment of religions. **(803-005 Government and Citizenship)**

4. **C.**

The correct answer is (C). Cotton and eventually cattle were the main products produced in Texas during the nineteenth and early twentieth centuries. Later, with the discovery of petroleum in the twentieth century, it became one of the most important exports for Texas. In the latter part of the twentieth century, computers and electronics replaced oil as the main products of the state. Based on this explanation, options (A), (B), and (D) are eliminated. **(803-004 Economics)**

5. **C.**

The correct answer is (C). There is a difference of one day from Honolulu to Tokyo. Honolulu is located east of the International Date Line (IDL), while Japan is west of the line. That is, if we travel from Honolulu toward the west on December 7, crossing the IDL to get to Tokyo, we would get there on December 8. The attack was recorded on December 7, 1941, in Honolulu, but the equivalent date for Japan was December 8, 1941. Options (A), (B), and (D) are incorrect because they do not explain the real reason for the date confusion. Additionally, the scenario does not provide information to support the position that Emperor Hirohito was confused about the dates. **(803-003 Geography and Culture)**

6. C.

The correct answer is (C). The U.S. Constitution set up a system so that each branch of the government has the power to control or regulate the power of the other two. Option (A) is incorrect because judicial review addresses only the power of the judicial branch. Judicial review is the power to review legislation enacted by Congress and signed by the president. If the legislation is unconstitutional, it can be invalidated. Option (B) is incorrect because it addresses the power of the president to veto or refuse to sign legislation approved by Congress. Option (D) is incorrect because habeas corpus is one of the civil rights that guarantees people the right to a quick trial by jury. **(803-005 Government and Citizenship)**

7. A.

The correct answer is (A). Information in social studies can be presented in graphic form through the use of graphs and charts. This makes the content accessible to all children, including ELLs. Options (B), (C), and (D) describe possible ways to use advanced organizers and graphic representations, but individually these options do not fully explain their value. **(803-001 Social Science Instruction)**

8. A.

The correct answer is (A). The Mayflower Compact was drawn up and signed by the Pilgrims aboard the *Mayflower*. They pledged to consult one another to make decisions and to act by the will of the majority. It is one of the earliest agreements to establish a political body and to give that political body the power to act for the good of the colony. Options (B), (C), and (D) are incorrect because these were aspects of colonial life but not the purpose of the Mayflower Compact. **(803-005 Government and Citizenship)**

9. B.

The correct answer is (B). The coordinates provide the precise, or absolute, location of any place, thing, or person on Earth. The coordinates provided from the latitude/longitude grid system support all map projections, not just cylindrical projections (A). The lines of latitude and longitude support all units of measure for distance, not only meters (C). The combination of latitude and longitude provide the exact or absolute location of something on Earth. Relative location is the description of the general location of a place in relation to another geographic point. **(803-003 Geography and Culture)**

10. B.

The correct answer is (B). A globe is a scale model of the Earth shaped like a sphere. Because a globe is the same shape as the Earth, it shows sizes and shapes more accurately than a Mercator projection map (a flat representation of the Earth). Option (A) is incorrect because a compass rose is a design used to show the relative position of the cardinal points (north, south, west, and east) and not a representation of the Earth. Option (C) is incorrect because a map scale is used to show the distance between two places in the world. Option (D) is incorrect because thematic maps are not used to show the size and shape of the Earth. **(803-003 Geography and Culture)**

11. B.

The correct answer is (B). The convergence of the Tigris and the Euphrates created a fertile region where some of the greatest civilizations of the world emerged. This part of the world has been called the Fertile Crescent, and it is part of the area called the Cradle of Civilization. Option (A) is incorrect because the Nile gave birth to the Egyptian civilization, and the Amazon River is located in South America, far away from Mesopotamia. Option (C) is incorrect because the Indus River is located in modern-day India. Option (D) is incorrect because the Volga and Danube rivers are located in Europe. **(803-002 History)**

12. A.

The correct answer is (A). A compass rose is a design printed on a chart or map for reference. It shows the orientation of a map on Earth and shows the four cardinal directions (north, south, east, and west). A compass rose may also show in-between directions such as northeast or northwest. Option (B) is incorrect because a map scale shows the distance between two places in the world. Option (C) is incorrect because features such as elevations and divisions are represented by different colors. Option (D) is incorrect because the ratio of the distance between two points on the Earth and the distance between the two corresponding points on the map is represented by a scale and not by a compass rose. **(803-003 Geography and Culture)**

13. B.

The correct answer is (B). With the exception of peak K2, the top 10 mountain peaks are all part of the Himalayas Range. Choice (A) is incorrect, because, despite the fact that the Andes Range contains several high mountains, none of them ranks within the top 50 in the world. Choice (C) is incorrect because only three of the top 20 mountains in the world are part of the Karakoram Range. Choice (D) is incorrect because only one mountain from the Kunlun Range ranks within the first 25. **(803-003 Geography and Culture)**

14. A.

The correct answer is (A). The Union and the Confederate armies fought from July 1 through July 3, 1863, southwest of Harrisburg, Pennsylvania, in the Battle of Gettysburg. More than 50,000 soldiers were casualties— killed, wounded, captured or missing in what the Gettysburg Foundation terms "the largest battle ever fought in North America." In November 1863, President Lincoln dedicated the National Cemetery at the site of the battle by delivering his Gettysburg Address. In 1895 the battlefield became a national military park. **(803-002 History)**

15. B.

The correct answer is (B). The economic theory that states that prices vary based on a balance between the availability of a product or service at a certain price and the desire of potential purchasers to pay that price is

known as the law of supply and demand. Free enterprise (A) is a generic term to describe capitalism and entrepreneurship. Inflation and deflation (C) are, respectively, the prevailing rate at which prices for goods and services are rising or declining. Economic interdependence (D) characterizes the relationship between people, regions, nations or other entities that has each dependent on the other. **(803-004 Economics)**

16. D.

The correct answer is (D). The main purpose of the Federal Reserve System is to keep the banking industry strong enough to ensure a supply of currency. When the banking industry is strong and there is an adequate supply of currency, fiscal stability and economic growth are more likely to occur. However, the direct role of the Fed is not to provide stimulus money to balance the economy (A), promote economic growth (B), or create inflation and deflation (C) in the country. Policies adopted by the Fed can lead to a healthy economy—or a weak economy resulting in inflation or deflation. **(803-004 Economics)**

17. D.

The correct answer is (D). The TEKS introduces the history of the United States in fifth grade. Option (A) is incorrect because in second grade the social studies curriculum covers local communities. Option (B) is incorrect because in third grade the curriculum centers on how individuals change their communities and the world. Option (C) is incorrect because in fourth grade students are familiarized with the history of Texas. **(803-001 Social Science Instruction)**

18. A.

The correct answer is (A). Reference maps show the locations of places, and boundaries of countries, states, counties, and towns. Atlases or road maps are examples of reference maps. Option (B) is incorrect because thematic maps show a particular topic such as population density, distribution of world religions, or physical, social, economic, political, agricultural, or economic features. Option (C) is incorrect because a physical map is a thematic map that shows the topography of the land including land features and elevations. Option (D) is incorrect because population maps are thematic maps that are used to show where people live in a particular region. **(803-003 Geography and Culture)**

19. B.

The correct answer is (B). The New England Colonies consisted of Massachusetts, Connecticut, Rhode Island, and New Hampshire. Option (A) is incorrect because Virginia, North Carolina, South Carolina, and Georgia formed the Southern Colonies. Option (C) is incorrect because New York, New Jersey, Delaware, Maryland, and Pennsylvania formed the Middle Colonies. Option (D) is incorrect because this answer represents a combination of some of the Southern Colonies and some of the Middle Colonies. **(803-002 History)**

20. C.

The correct answer is (C). The Earth is divided into 24 zones based on the meridians of longitude, which are determined using the rotation of the Earth and its exposure to sunlight. This rotation creates day and night, and consequently the concept of time. Option (A) is incorrect because the international date line is only one of 24 meridians of the Earth. Option (B) is incorrect because the term *revolution* describes the movement of the Earth around the Sun, which affects the seasons but not necessarily the time zones. Option (D) is incorrect because the parallels of latitude do not affect the time zones. **(803-003 Geography and Culture)**

21. C.

The correct answer is (C). The conditions represented in the photograph, which shows separate drinking fountains for whites and for African Americans, were ruled unconstitutional by the U.S. Supreme Court in *Brown v. Board of Education of Topeka* in May 1954. The case struck down *Plessy v. Ferguson* (A), the 1896 case in which the High Court had established the "sepa-

rate but equal" doctrine for determining the constitutionality of racial segregation laws. The High Court's ruling in *Marbury v. Madison* (B) in 1803 established the doctrine of judicial review, but did not touch on issues of racial segregation. In contrast, race was central to the thesis put forth in the Supreme Court's *Dred Scott* decision (D) in 1857: that African Americans, regardless of whether they had been slaves or been granted their freedom, were not protected by the U.S. Constitution and could never become U.S. citizens. **(803-002 History)**

22. C.

The correct answer is (C). The Spaniards established Saint Augustine, the first permanent European colony in North America, in 1565 near what is today Jacksonville, Florida. Subsequent to this, the English made an attempt to establish a colony off the coast of North Carolina—Roanoke. Choice (A) is incorrect because Virginia, Massachusetts, and all the other American colonies were established in the seventeenth century. Choice (B) is incorrect because New Mexico was established a few years later, in 1598, to become the first European colony west of the Mississippi. The first mission in Texas was established more than one hundred years later, in 1682. Choice (D) is incorrect because the Dutch did not begin bringing families to the area of New York and New Jersey until 1624. **(803-002 History)**

23. A.

Option (A) is correct. A population pyramid uses a series of bar graphs to represent the population of males and females at different ages. A population pyramid is a critical resource in social studies education. Elementary teachers should use them often to help students stay in practice with reading and interpreting the data on these graphs as they apply to different cultures and/or time periods in history. Option (B) refers to a circle divided into parts to represent data. Option (C) is a diagram that looks like a flow chart and is used to show lineage, or a family tree. Option (D) is a type of graph that is often seen in mathematics. It is like a bar graph except that it uses a dot to identify data. For example, if the bar graph extends a bar, or thick line, to the number 9, the dot plot uses a dot at the number 9 to represent the same information. Elementary teachers should use this commonality to help students transfer skills for reading and analyzing data in multiple forms. **(803-001 Social Science Instruction)**

24. B.

The correct answer is (B). Civil rights are the legal and political rights of the people who live in a particular country. In the United States, the Constitution and the Bill of Rights guarantee civil rights to American citizens and residents. The first 10 amendments to the U.S. Constitution are known as the Bill of Rights. Choices (A), (C), and (D) are incorrect because these name certain rights included in the Bill of Rights, but fail to address the question. **(803-005 Government and Citizenship)**

25. D.

The correct answer is (D). In Texas, teachers are required to teach social studies in every grade level. Therefore, by grade 7 students are expected to have seven years of social studies (kindergarten through 6th grade). Because the answer hinges on the amount of instruction to be received by middle school, response options (A), (B), and (C) can be ruled out. **(803-001 Social Science Instruction)**

26. C.

The correct answer is (C). The Apache and the Comanche domesticated the horse and became skillful hunters and warriors. These skills allowed them to fight the whites for many years for control of the Central and Great Plains of Texas. Choice (A) is incorrect because the tribes from the plains were nomads and did not develop an advanced civilization. Choice (B) is incorrect because both the Comanche and the Apache were nomads and did not leave permanent constructions. Choice (D) is incorrect because the tribes from the area had to hunt for survival and they had to move continuously to find adequate food supplies. **(803-002 History)**

27. B.

The correct answer is (B). The U.S. Constitution provides for two senators to represent each of the 50 states, for a total of 100. Territories are not represented in the U.S. Senate. Choice (D) is incorrect because it represents the current number of members of the U.S. House of Representatives. **(803-005 Government and Citizenship)**

28. B.

Option (B) is the correct answer. Students are taught U.S. History in grade 5. The Boston Massacre was an important part of the Revolutionary War. Option (A) refers to World Cultures. Option (C) refers to Texas History. Option (D) refers to the social studies topic, "How Individuals Change their Communities and their World." **(803-001 Social Science Instruction)**

29. C.

The correct answer is (C). General Ignacio de Zaragoza was one of the leaders of the Mexican Army. He was born south of the city of Goliad, when this region was part of Mexico. Because the region is now part of Texas, Mexican Americans celebrate the accomplishment of this "Mexican American" hero. In the Battle of Puebla, the Mexican forces faced anything but a ragtag army (A); Napoleon III's French troops represented one of the world's best fighting forces, so the victory took on symbolic significance. Cinco de Mayo has nothing to do with Mexican Independence Day (B), which was established in 1810, a full half-century before the Battle of Puebla. Option (D) is incorrect because the United States did not participate in this war. The U.S. was fighting its own war—the American Civil War (1860-1865). **(803-002 History)**

30. D.

The correct answer is (D). The Fifteenth Amendment granted black males the right to vote. Option (A) is incorrect because the voting right was given to black males only, not women. Option (B) is incorrect because the Fourteenth Amendment granted citizenship to former slaves. Option (C) is incorrect because the Thirteenth Amendment granted freedom to slaves. **(803-005 Government and Citizenship)**

31. A., C., and E.

Options (A), (C), and (E) are correct because lower elementary grades (PreK–3) should use a smaller, simpler globe than upper elementary grades (4–6). Options (B) and (D) are characteristics of a globe for older elementary students. **(803-001 Social Science Instruction)**

32. C.

The correct answer is (C). Reducing the production of oil while keeping the same demand for the product creates an imbalance between supply and demand. This imbalance results in a price increase. Options (A) and (B), while potentially and flatly true, respectively, do not articulate an economic principle, as the question requires. Option (D) presents an opinion that fails to address the true question. **(803-004 Economics)**

33. B.

The correct answer is (B). Iraq is a Muslim nation with multiple ethnic groups within its borders. The largest groups are the Arabs, consisting of Shiite and Sunni Muslims. The Kurds are the largest minority group. (A) is incorrect. The multiple groups living in Iraq speak Arabic, Kurdish, Turkish, Assyrian, and other languages. (C) is incorrect because Iraq is located in the Middle Eastern part of Asia. (D) is incorrect because Pakistan is a Muslim country from the region, but there is no political association between the two nations. **(803-003 Geography and Culture)**

34. B., C., and D.

Options (B), (C), and (D) are correct. Option (B) is correct because Texas's US$1.65 trillion GDP in 2014 was more than double Saudi Arabia's US$752 billion. Option (C) is correct because the United Kingdom chalked up approximately US$2.95 trillion in GDP in

2014, half of which would be US$1.48 trillion. Option (D) is correct because Texas ranks 12th while Australia ranks 13th, according to the table. Option (A) is incorrect because the statement is actually the inverse of the reality: the figures show Canada in 11th place in terms of GDP, a notch above Texas. **(803-003 Economics)**

35. B

The correct answer is (B). Francisco Pizarro conquered the Incas of Peru, and Hernán Cortés conquered the Aztecs of Mexico. Choice (A) is incorrect because the Maya had virtually disappeared before the arrival of the Spaniards in America. Choice (C) is incorrect because these Mesoamerican groups, the Toltec and Olmec, disappeared before the Spanish colonization. Choice (D) is incorrect because the Tainos were from the Caribbean, an area that was under Spanish control before the intervention of Cortes and Pizarro. Additionally, the word *Quechua* refers to the language spoken by the Incas and other groups in the Andes Mountains. **(803-002 History)**

36. B.

The correct answer is (B). The social studies strands are systematically integrated throughout the social studies state curriculum in grades K-12. Option (A) is incorrect based on the previous explanation. Options (C) and (D) are incorrect because the social studies strands are used in public education as well as in higher education. **(803-001 Social Science Instruction)**

37. A.

The correct answer is (A). Maps use symbolic representation, and children at that age (PreK and kindergarten) rely mostly on concrete experiences for learning. The abstraction typical of maps' legends and other symbolic representations might not be developmentally appropriate for this age group. Choice (B) is a plausible statement but not the best answer. Children initially will be inclined to use the globe as toys and pay attention to colors, but eventually they will understand its function through classroom instruction. Choice (C) is incorrect because it presents an opinion not supported in the scenario. Choice (D) is probably a true statement: Children will have problems conceptualizing how the Earth can be represented in a small 12-inch globe, but this choice is not the best answer because it addresses only one component of the question—globe representation. **(803-001 Social Science Instruction)**

38. C.

The correct answer is (C). Iran is a theocratic Islamic republic ruled by a supreme religious leader, a president, and a parliament. Jordan (A) is a constitutional monarchy. China (B) is ruled by a strictly hierarchical, highly centralized government led by the Chinese Communist Party. India (D) is a constitutional democracy led by a president, a prime minister, and a parliament. **(803-005 Government and Citizenship)**

39. A.

The correct answer is (A). The number of members of the House of Representative is adjusted to reflect a proportion of the total U.S. population; thus, every time there is a census, the number can change. Choices (B), (C), and (D) are incorrect because population changes do not affect the composition of the Senate, the Supreme Court, or the Executive Branch. **(803-005 Government and Citizenship)**

40. D.

The correct answer is (D). The course designed to introduce students to cultural or human geography is introduced in sixth grade. Unfortunately, some teachers teach this from a world history perspective, not from a geographic perspective. A geographic perspective includes history as well as other information such as culture, geopolitics, demographic, and human-environment interaction. Geographic concepts and skills are taught at each grade level. However, the World Cultures course is designed to teach basic understanding of cultural geography in preparation for World Geography at the high school level. **(803-001 Social Science Instruction)**

41. D.

The correct answer is (D). The economy of the Southern Colonies was based on the crops of tobacco, rice, indigo, and cotton. Plantations produced agricultural crops in large scale and exploited workers as well as the environment. Choice (A) is incorrect because it was the economy of the Middle Colonies that was based on farming, shipping, fishing, and trading. Choice (B) is incorrect because it was the economy of the New England colonies that was based on farming and very small industries such as fishing, lumber, and crafts. Choice (C) is incorrect because trading was a part of the Middle Colonies economy. **(803-004 Economics)**

TExES Core Subjects EC–6 Practice Test: Science

Science Practice Test Answer Sheet

1. (A) (B) (C) (D)   19. (A) (B) (C) (D)   37. (A) (B) (C) (D)

2. (A) (B) (C) (D)   20. (A) (B) (C) (D)   38. (A) (B) (C) (D)

3. (A) (B) (C) (D)   21. (A) (B) (C) (D)   39. (A) (B) (C) (D)

4. (A) (B) (C) (D)   22. (A) (B) (C) (D)   40. (A) (B) (C) (D)

5. (A) (B) (C) (D)   23. (A) (B) (C) (D)   41. (A) (B) (C) (D)

6. (A) (B) (C) (D)   24. (A) (B) (C) (D)   42. (A) (B) (C) (D)

7. (A) (B) (C) (D)   25. (A) (B) (C) (D)   43. (A) (B) (C) (D)

8. (A) (B) (C) (D)   26. (A) (B) (C) (D)   44. (A) (B) (C) (D)

9. (A) (B) (C) (D)   27. (A) (B) (C) (D)   45. (A) (B) (C) (D)

10. (A) (B) (C) (D)   28. (A) (B) (C) (D)   46. (A) (B) (C) (D)

11. (A) (B) (C) (D)   29. (A) (B) (C) (D)   47. (A) (B) (C) (D)

12. (A) (B) (C) (D)   30. (A) (B) (C) (D)   48. (A) (B) (C) (D)

13. (A) (B) (C) (D)   31. (A) (B) (C) (D)   49. (A) (B) (C) (D)

14. (A) (B) (C) (D)   32. (A) (B) (C) (D)   50. (A) (B) (C) (D)

15. (A) (B) (C) (D)   33. (A) (B) (C) (D)   51. (A) (B) (C) (D)

16. (A) (B) (C) (D)   34. (A) (B) (C) (D)   52. (A) (B) (C) (D)

17. (A) (B) (C) (D)   35. (A) (B) (C) (D)

18. (A) (B) (C) (D)   36. (A) (B) (C) (D)

Practice Test: Science

TIME: 40 minutes
       52 questions

Directions: Read each item and select the correct response or responses. Most items on this test require you to provide the one best answer. However, some questions require you to select all the options that apply.

---

1. Which of the following instruments should be used to most accurately measure a liquid in milliliters in a laboratory investigation?

   A. Flask

   B. Beaker

   C. Graduated cylinder

   D. Test tube

2. Which of the following scientists first proposed the theory of plate tectonics, which maintains that the Earth's continents were formed long ago as part of a single landmass?

   A. Robert Hooke

   B. Sir Isaac Newton

   C. Charles Darwin

   D. Alfred Wegener

3. Which of the following is a non-renewable source of energy?

   A. Wind

   B. Solar

   C. Natural gas

   D. Hydroelectric

4. In which of the following ways does deforestation (cutting down) of the rainforests in South America impact residents of the United States?

   A. Deforestation does not impact the U.S. population.

   B. Deforestation results in a decrease in the amount of carbon dioxide in the atmosphere, which decreases the threat of global warming.

   C. Deforestation results in contaminated food crops that may be consumed by U.S. residents.

   D. Deforestation results in an increase in the amount of carbon dioxide in the atmosphere, which contributes to the threat of global warming. *we need trees to take CO_2 out of the air*

5. Which of the following gases comprises the majority of the air in Earth's atmosphere?

   A. Oxygen

   B. Carbon Dioxide

   C. Nitrogen

   D. Water vapor

6. Which of the following is the most effective, concrete way to teach elementary students the concept of diffusion for the first time?

  A. Present a lecture giving the definition of diffusion for students to write in their notebooks.

  B. Make a drawing of diffusion on the board showing how diffusion happens while at the same time providing the definition.

  C. Give students a clear, plastic cup of water and ask them to place one drop of food coloring in the water without stirring and observe; then follow up with discussion on their observations.

  D. Assign students a textbook reading on diffusion, with review questions to complete when finished reading.

7. Mr. Garcia spends three weeks teaching students about ecosystems. At the end of the unit, he gives students a 45-minute unit exam consisting of a variety of question formats, such as short-answer, multiple-choice, and essay. After grading the exam, he is surprised and disappointed that his students did not perform well on the exam, with most students failing. What is the most important thing Mr. Garcia should have done to prevent this disaster?

  A. He should have used different assessments throughout the unit instead of waiting until the end to measure his students' learning.

  B. He should have spent another week lecturing students on ecosystems.

  C. He should have made his assessment all multiple-choice items.

  D. He should have made the test longer than 45 minutes by adding more test items.

8. What is the usefulness of informing students of their results on a test or project?

  A. It creates a competitive environment in your classroom for students when they take tests or work on projects.

  B. It provides both the student and teacher with information on the extent to which the students have learned the material.

  C. It creates anxiety among students that negatively impacts future performance on tests and projects.

  D. It allows administrators to report scores to the state education agency.

9. The students in Ms. Johnson's class are rolling a toy convertible car down a slanted ramp with a brick at the end of it. They place a small stuffed animal in the convertible, unrestrained, and then let the car roll down the ramp. The car hits the brick and stops. What happens to the stuffed animal as soon as the car hits and is stopped by the brick? Why?

  A. The stuffed animal stays in the car because an object at rest stays at rest unless acted upon by a force.

  B. The stuffed animal flies out of the car backwards because for every action there is an equal and opposite reaction.

  C. The stuffed animal flies out of the car forward because an object in motion will continue to stay in motion unless acted upon by a force.

  D. None of the above is correct.

10. A rocket burns fuel in bursts out of a nozzle, allowing it to maneuver and turn in the vacuum of space. Which of Newton's Laws of Motion explains how this maneuvering is able to occur?

  A. An object in motion stays in motion unless an outside force acts on it.

  B. For every action there is an equal and opposite reaction.

  C. Fast-moving air has low pressure.

  D. An object at rest stays at rest unless an outside force acts on it.

11. What does using two pulleys in a single system (movable pulley) to lift an object do to the force required compared to lifting the object without the movable pulley?

Select from the following.

A. The use of the movable pulley reduces the amount of force required by one-half.

B. The use of the movable pulley increases the amount of force required by one-half.

C. The use of the movable pulley changes the amount of force required to 5 Newtons.

D. The use of the movable pulley changes the amount of force required.

12. Which of the following is a chemical change in matter?

A. Ice melting

B. Paper tearing

C. Paper burning

D. Crushing chalk

13. The chemical formula for water is H_2O, making water which of the following?

A. Element

B. Compound

C. Atom

D. Ion

14. When does cellular respiration occur in plants?

A. Cellular respiration does not occur in plants, only photosynthesis.

B. Cellular respiration occurs only at night, because photosynthesis occurs during the day.

C. Cellular respiration occurs only during the day, because photosynthesis occurs at night.

D. Cellular respiration occurs all day and night, the same as in animals.

15. What is the proper sequence of energy transformations that occurs in ringing a doorbell?

A. Mechanical, electrical, sound

B. Electrical, mechanical, sound

C. Sound, electrical, mechanical

D. Electrical, sound, mechanical

16. In Ms. Sullivan's class, the students measured the starting temperature of two thermometers. They used one thermometer to measure the temperature at the surface of a pond. The second was attached onto a sinker on an eight-meter rope and was dropped to near the bottom of the pond. They repeated the experiment several times, recording their findings. The students' results revealed that the temperature at the surface was on average four degrees higher than the temperature near the bottom of the pond. Which of the following forms of energy transfer best explains their findings?

A. Conduction heat → solid

B. Radiation heat → space

C. Convection heat → liquid + gas

D. Evaporation

17. Jorge and Rita were working on a laboratory activity where they connected one end of an electric wire to the positive node of a new 6-volt battery, then wound the wire around an iron nail with 20 twists, then attached the other end of the wire to the negative node of the battery. The students then plunged the point of the nail into a pile of small paper clips and made observations. They repeated this experiment three more times. The two students then changed the number of times the wire was wound around the nail to 10 twists, and plunged the point of the nail in the paper clips again. The students made observations and again repeated this experiment three more times. What did the students observe happen in the first trial with 20 twists of the wire around the nail compared to the second trial with 10 twists of the wire around the nail, and why?

A. The first trial with 20 twists attracted and "picked up" fewer paper clips than the second trial with 10 twists because the electric field was weaker with 20 twists compared to 10 twists of the wire.

B. The first trial with 20 twists attracted and "picked up" more paper clips than the second trial with 10 twists because the electric field was stronger with 20 twists compared to 10 twists of the wire.

C. The first trial with 20 twists attracted and "picked up" and equal number of paper clips as the second trial with 10 twists because the electric field was equally strong with 20 twists and 10 twists of the wire.

D. Neither trial produced an electric field and could not attract and "pick up" the paper clips.

18. What do green plant leaves do with green wavelengths of visible light in the electromagnetic spectrum, and what is the evidence?

A. Green plants absorb green wavelengths, and the evidence is that the leaves are green in color.

B. Green plants refract green wavelengths, and the evidence is that the leaves may be green or yellow in color.

C. Green plants absorb green wavelengths, and the evidence is that the leaves turn red and yellow in the fall.

D. Green plants reflect green wavelengths, and the evidence is that the leaves are green in color.

19. What causes sound waves?

A. Vibration of air molecules

B. Vibration of objects such as strings on a piano

C. Light waves colliding with sound waves

D. Force equaling mass times acceleration

20. What is the energy source for each of the following nonrenewable and renewable energy types used to generate electricity for human use, listed in the same order as the energy type?

Nonrenewable and Renewable Energy Types:

Hydroelectric – Nuclear – Fossil Fuel – Geothermal – Solar

A. Heat from beneath Earth's surface – Coal – Moving Water – Soil – Sun

B. Soil – Uranium – Wind – Volcanoes – Heat from beneath Earth's surface

C. Moving Water – Uranium – Coal – Heat from beneath Earth's surface – Sun

D. Moving Water – Sun – Heat from beneath Earth's surface – Sun – Uranium

21. Mr. Littlejohn hands his students a seed, and then hands them a log from a tree. He discusses with students that somehow this tiny seed becomes a great tree, part of which the students are holding in their hands as a log. He asks the students, "Where does all the mass come from that allowed this tiny seed to grow into a tree?" What is the correct response to this question?

A. The mass that made the tree came from nutrients in the soil.

B. The mass that made the tree came from the soil itself.

C. The mass that made the tree came from nitrogen in the soil.

(D.) The mass that made the tree came from carbon dioxide in the air.

22. The students in Mrs. Leone's class are studying mealworms. They fill the bottom of a petri dish with oatmeal for food and tiny slices of apple for moisture, and then place three mealworms in the dish and replace the cover (which allows air in). The students observe the mealworms over several days, drawing their observations. After several days the students notice their mealworms are shorter, curled up, and no longer moving. The students are concerned but continue to draw and write observations of their three mealworms. After several more days, the students observe that there are three black beetles in their petri dishes and no curled up mealworms. What is the best explanation for what happened?

Select from the following:

A. The mealworms became ill and the beetles got inside the petri dishes and ate them.

(B.) The mealworms underwent metamorphosis, changing from larva to pupa to adult.

C. The mealworms underwent metamorphosis, changing from egg to pupa to larva.

D. The mealworms underwent metamorphosis, changing from adult to larva to pupa.

23. The forest and pond area inhabited by wildlife including raccoons was demolished to build a large restaurant. It so happens the restaurant disposes of uneaten meals in an open dumpster in the far end of the parking lot behind the building. Which of the following basic needs specifically among the raccoons likely changed the *least* due to the construction of this building?

A. Shelter

B. Water

C. Food

(D.) Air

24. The arm of a human and the front legs of a cat have the same structure, and function in a similar way. They were inherited from the same ancestor. Which of the following describes these structures?

(A.) Homologous

B. Non-homologous

C. Analogous

D. Heterozygous

 dif would be

25. In sexual reproduction, what is the process that occurs in specialized cells to produce the gametes before fertilization, and the process that then occurs in the fertilized egg or zygote to begin development of the embryo?

A. Mitosis occurs to produce the gametes, and then meiosis occurs in the zygote.

B. Binary fission occurs to produce the gametes, and then meiosis occurs in the zygote.

C. Asexual reproduction occurs to produce the gametes, and then sexual reproduction occurs in the zygote.

(D.) Meiosis occurs to produce the gametes, and then mitosis occurs in the zygote.

26. Black fur (B) in guinea pigs is dominant over white fur (b). If a homozygous black-furred female guinea pig mates with a heterozygous black-furred male guinea pig, what percentage of their offspring will have white fur?

A. 25% white

B. 50% white

C. 75% white

(D.) 0% white

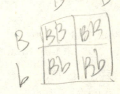

27. Which of the following options explains why some species of animals may be unable to adapt and no longer survive in its environment? Select *all* that apply.

   A. The environment changed from forest to industrialized city.

   B. The amount of water in lakes and marshlands in the environment significantly decreased.

   C. The predator population in the environment significantly increased in number.

   D. The population moved to urban areas and became dependent on humans.

28. Giraffes with long necks have survived over time because they can reach treetop leaves, which they eat for nourishment. What is one reason giraffes developed long necks over time?

   A. Giraffes in the past constantly stretched their necks to reach leaves on tall trees and thus developed long, strong muscles in their necks.

   B. Trees grew taller over time, so giraffes grew longer necks to accommodate this tree growth and reach their food.

   C. Genetic mutations occurred over time, resulting in some giraffes developing longer necks than others; these giraffes were more likely to survive than those with shorter necks.

   D. The types of leaves giraffes fed on consisted of rich sources of calcium that strengthened and lengthened their vertebrae over time.

29. Which of the following is a learned characteristic rather than an inherited trait in humans?

   A. Having brown eye color like one or both parents

   B. Having interest in being a runner like one or both parents

   C. Having attached ear lobes like one or both parents

   D. Having high cholesterol like one or both parents

30. Working in groups, the students in Ms. Rosa's class plant three seeds in a pot of soil, then water them, and place the pot in a tall, narrow cardboard box with a half-dollar-sized circular hole cut out on one side near the top of the box where light can enter. The students only briefly open the box each day to measure their plant's growth and add water, then close it again. They keep their boxes on the window sill with the hole-side facing the outside light. After several weeks, what will students most likely observe happening to the plant, and why?

   A. Students will observe the plant stem bending toward the hole in the side of the box due to the stimulus produced by light, called phototropism.

   B. Students will observe the plant stem bending away from the hole in the side of the box due to the stimulus produced by the dark, called anti-phototropism.

   C. Students will observe the plant stem bending toward the bottom of the box due to the stimulus produced by the water, called hydrotropism.

   D. Students will observe the plant stem bending toward the bottom of the box due to the stimulus caused by gravity, called geotropism or gravitropism.

31. Which of the following organisms in a food chain or food web absorbs and holds the most energy?

   A. Producers

   B. Secondary consumers or carnivores (2nd level)

   C. Primary consumers or herbivores (1st level)

   D. Decomposers

32. Which of the following represents the order of the layers of the Earth if one were to travel from the surface to its center?

   A. Crust, outer core, mantle, inner core

   B. Mantle, crust, inner core, outer core

   C. Outer core, inner core, crust, mantle

   D. Crust, mantle, outer core, inner core

33. Which of the following is a rocky planet?

    A. Jupiter

    B. Neptune

    C. Mars

    D. Uranus

34. Which of the following *best* describes the transpiration in the water cycle?

    A. The evaporation of water from the surface of lakes

    B. The condensation of water on the leaves of green plants

    C. The evaporation of water from the leaves of green plants

    D. The precipitation of water on the leaves of green plants

35. Which of the following is a property of water?

    A. When water freezes to ice it expands

    B. When water freezes to ice it contracts

    C. Water is a nonpolar molecule

    D. Most water on Earth is freshwater

36. What is relative humidity and what instrument is used to measure it?

    A. Relative humidity is a measure of the wind speed in a specific region and time, and is measured by an anemometer

    B. Relative humidity is a measure of the amount of moisture in the air in a specific region and time, and is measured by an anemometer

    C. Relative humidity is a measure of the moisture in the air in a specific region and time, and is measured by a psychrometer

    D. Relative humidity is a measure of the air pressure in a specific region and time, and is measured by a barometer

37. Which of the following is the symbol for a stationary front on a weather map?

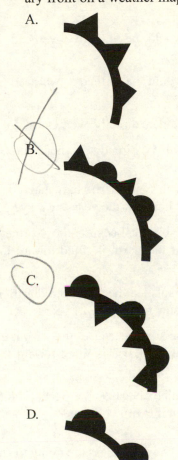

    A.

    B.

    C.

    D.

38. Which of the following regions of the U.S. will experience lake effect snow in the winter?

    A. The Northeast states next to the Atlantic Coast

    B. The Northeast states just east of the Great Lakes

    C. The Midwestern states located in the Great Plains

    D. The Western states just east of the Rocky Mountains

459

39. What time of day or night would the New Moon phase be as close to directly overhead as possible for your location?

   A. The Moon would be directly overhead at midnight

   B. The Moon would be directly overhead at dawn

   C. The Moon would be directly overhead at noon

   D. The Moon would be directly overhead at dusk

40. What day in the Earth's Northern Hemisphere has the longest daylight hours of the year and why?

   A. The summer solstice because the Northern Hemisphere of the Earth is tilted toward the sun

   B. The summer solstice because the Earth is closest to the sun at this time of year

   C. The winter solstice because the Northern Hemisphere of the Earth is tilted toward the sun

   D. The vernal equinox because the Earth is closest to the sun at this time of year

41. The students in Mr. Lawson's class are going to engage in an inquiry-based laboratory investigation in which they will be placing a glass thermometer in a beaker of ice and heating it on a hot plate so they can graph the heating curve of water. What is the first and most important thing Mr. Lawson should do before students begin this investigation?

   A. Provide students with the materials needed to conduct the investigation and let them begin

   B. Give students a review sheet that explains and shows a completed graph of the heating curve of water before they begin the investigation

   C. Read aloud and discuss all safety precautions of the investigation, including wearing safety goggles and the use of glassware and heating surfaces

   D. Instruct students on the clean-up procedures to follow after the investigation, including where to store the glassware

42. Which of the following indicates the type of questioning used to gain the most participation from students?

   A. Calling the name of the student to respond first, then asking the question

   B. Asking students to raise their hands

   C. Asking the question first, then calling on students at random to respond

   D. Asking students to "call out" the response

43. Which of the following types of rock is formed from other types of rock listed below after it has been subjected to extreme pressure and temperature over time?

   A. Igneous Rock

   B. Metamorphic Rock

   C. Sedimentary Rock

   D. Conglomerate Rock

44. The students in Mr. Gonzales's class are reading about a research scientist who believes she has found the cure for lung cancer tumors with a new medication that needs to undergo further research. Her research involves 200 lung cancer patients. Half are given the new medication and half are given a "placebo" pill, which is simply a sugar pill. None of the patients know whether they are receiving the actual medication or the placebo. After three months of recording data measuring the size of cancer tumors in the lungs of all patients, the scientist finds that the size of the cancer tumor has not grown in about 3% of the patients receiving the new medication. However, all patients receiving the new medication are exhibiting severe and unusual mental side-effect reactions, including fits of rage and physical violence toward others and themselves. Which of the following is the ethical course of action for this scientist to take in testing this cancer medication?

   A. Stop the experiments immediately and return to the laboratory for more testing, without using humans, on the mental side effects it has caused.

B. Continue the experiments with humans because it is helping some of the cancer patients, and wait to see if the mental issues resolve themselves.

C. Provide the placebo group with the new medication because it is helping a few of the patients in the group who are receiving the medication.

D. Recruit another sample of 200 patients and repeat the same experiment with new groups receiving either the medication or the placebo.

45. In using the 5E (learning cycle) inquiry model in teaching, which of the following is the best way to introduce new science-concept vocabulary to students and English language learners in particular?

A. List, define, and review the science vocabulary words and definitions before students begin the exploration.

B. Have students read the textbook definitions of new science vocabulary the day before class and quiz them before beginning the exploration.

C. Introduce science vocabulary that labels the science concept after students have conducted an exploration, but before the students state the concept.

D. Introduce science vocabulary that labels the science concept after students have conducted an exploration and have stated the concept.

46. Which is longer, three yards or 25 decimeters?

A. 3 yards

B. 25 decimeters

C. Both distances are the same

D. The answer cannot be determined

47. In an inquiry lesson, the teacher noticed Keysha as she was conducting an experiment in which she obtained two thermometers and recorded the starting temperatures of each. Keysha then placed one thermometer near the ceiling and the second near the floor. After 15 minutes, she observed the thermometers and again recorded the temperature. In comparing the temperature change on the thermometers in the two locations, Keysha observed that air near the ceiling was 2 degrees warmer than the air near the floor. She concluded that warmer air rises and stays near the ceiling, while cooler air sinks and stays near the floor. Although her conclusion is scientifically accurate, what was the major flaw the teacher should have noticed with Keysha's experimental procedures?

A. She cannot use two different thermometers in the experiment.

B. She did not repeat her measurement multiple times before drawing a conclusion.

C. She should not have recorded the starting temperatures before the experiment.

D. She needed to graph her results before drawing a conclusion.

48. What is true about using models in teaching to represent the natural world in science?

A. Models are exact in their representation of the actual phenomena.

B. Models only work as a representation of actual phenomena if computer generated.

C. Models will always differ from the actual phenomena they represent.

D. Models of natural phenomena will always lead students to form misconceptions.

49. In an exploration activity, the students measure 50 ml of water and pour it into one cup, and 50 ml of isopropyl alcohol and pour it into a second cup. They then drop one ice cube in the cup of water and one ice cube in the alcohol. The students observe that the ice cube floats in the water but sinks in the isopropyl alcohol. Why?

Select from the following.

A. The ice cube is less dense than the water and denser than the alcohol.

B. The ice cube is denser than the water and less dense than the alcohol.

C. The ice cube has a density equal to that of the water and is denser than the alcohol.

D. The ice cube has a density equal to that of both the water and the alcohol.

50. What is the proper instrument to use in measuring the mass of an object?

A. Meter Stick

B. Graduated cylinder

C. Triple beam balance

D. Sling psychrometer

51. Which of the following is the best way to evaluate whether students are able to determine the density of an irregular object?

A. Give them a multiple-choice test item to demonstrate their knowledge.

B. Provide them with a true-false test to demonstrate their knowledge.

C. Give them a fill-in-the-blank test to demonstrate their knowledge.

D. Have students conduct a hands-on lab practical test to demonstrate their knowledge.

52. Which of the following is a physical change?

A. Mixing an acid and base to form a salt and water

B. Pouring salt (NaCl) in a glass of water to form a mixture

C. Cars forming rust from salt and ice on roads in winter

D. Burning sugar in a crucible in the laboratory

Science Practice Test Answer Key

1. C	19. A	37. C
2. D	20. C	38. B
3. C	21. D	39. C
4. D	22. B	40. A
5. C	23. D	41. C
6. C	24. A	42. C
7. A	25. D	43. B
8. B	26. D	44. A
9. C	27. A, B, C, and D	45. D
10. B	28. C	46. A
11. A	29. B	47. B
12. C	30. A	48. C
13. B	31. A	49. A
14. D	32. D	50. C
15. A	33. C	51. D
16. C	34. C	52. B
17. B	35. A	
18. D	36. C	

Science Practice Test
Detailed Answers

1. C.

Option (C) is correct because a graduated cylinder precisely measures liquid amounts in milliliters. Options (A), (B), and (D) are not used to measure precise amounts of liquid, but actually are vessels mainly used to carry out various experiments, such as mixing liquids to produce a chemical reaction. Flasks and beakers can measure liquids in larger units of volume, whereas graduated cylinders are used to measure liquids in smaller standard units with greater precision. **(804-001 Lab Processes, Equipment and Safety)**

2. D.

Option (D) is correct. Alfred Wegener first described the theory of plate tectonics in the early 1900s. Options (A), (B), and (C) are incorrect. Robert Hooke (A) first described cell theory: that all living things are composed of cells. Sir Isaac Newton (B) is known for discovering the Laws of Motion and Gravity. Charles Darwin (C) described natural selection, which led to the theory of evolution. **(804-002 History and Nature of Science)**

3. C.

Option (C) is correct. Natural gas is a non-renewable source of energy because it is a fossil fuel. Natural gas, which is a gas mixture of methane and other hydrocarbon compounds, comes from deep in the Earth, as does oil and coal. Natural gas is formed when ancient buried plants and the gases they produce are exposed to intense heat and pressure over many thousands of years. Once the natural gas is used to produce energy (e.g., electricity), it cannot be replaced. Options (A), (B), and (D) are all renewable sources of energy. These sources are not depleted upon use. The wind produces energy (generates electricity) whenever it blows, solar power results from the capture of energy from the sun, and hydroelectric energy uses the forces of moving water—as in a waterfall—to produce electricity. **(804-003 Impact on Science)**

4. D.

Option (D) is correct because the high quantity of trees and massive foliage in South America carry on photosynthesis, which utilizes carbon dioxide gas to produce glucose, thus decreasing the amount of carbon dioxide in the atmosphere. Carbon dioxide gas in excess has been shown to absorb heat and increase warming of the atmosphere. If the foliage is removed, there will be fewer plants to take carbon dioxide out of the atmosphere, and it will accumulate in ever-increasing amounts. Global warming impacts the growth of food plants elsewhere across the globe, including the U.S., and these food plants have optimal growth within particular temperature and climatic ranges, which could be detrimental to their growth if conditions change. Option (A) is incorrect because there are interactions and interrelationships between what happens in one part of the globe and another. Option (B) is incorrect because the carbon dioxide in the atmosphere will increase rather than decrease. Option (C) is incorrect in that deforestation is not related to crop contamination. **(804-003 Impact on Science)**

5. C.

Option (C) is the correct response. Nitrogen comprises most of the Earth's atmosphere. The percentages are: Nitrogen at 78 percent, Oxygen at 21 percent, Argon at 0.93 percent, and Carbon dioxide at 0.038 percent. Even smaller percentages of water vapor and other gases are also in the atmosphere. Therefore, options (A), (B), and (D) are incorrect. **(804-015 Structure and Function of Earth Systems)**

6.   C.

Option (C) is correct because elementary school children are in the concrete stage of intellectual development, meaning they need hands-on, direct experiences with objects and phenomena. Options (A) and (D) will be mundane, negatively affect student motivation, cause confusion, and likely lead to significant misconceptions of the concept. This is because lecturing and reading are abstract, which is beyond what these students are ready for the first time they are learning a new concept. Drawing by the teacher (B) should be done after the students experience and observe a form of diffusion as described in option (C). An even better teaching strategy is for students to draw and develop a definition themselves. **(804-005 Students as Learners and Science Instruction)**

7.   A.

Option (A) is correct because it is important to monitor and measure student learning throughout the unit using various assessment techniques. In doing so, the teacher can adjust teaching to match what students are and are not learning during the unit. Assessments throughout the unit reveal difficulties and misconceptions students may be forming. Such knowledge of student learning throughout the unit will allow the teacher to better help all students achieve success. Option (B), teaching the unit for a longer period of time, would not help the students because even more time would have passed in the unit without monitoring student learning. Option (C) is incorrect because using only one testing format does not fully reveal what students have learned. Many students have difficulty, and even anxiety, with multiple-choice questions but do well with short answer and essay. Using only short-answer and essay formats may cause such stresses for other students. Therefore, using a variety of testing formats gives all students an opportunity to express their knowledge. Option (D) is incorrect because more test items would have produced the same result. **(804-006 Science Assessment)**

8.   B.

Option (B) is correct because it allows the teacher to adjust instruction according to the needs of the students, and for the students to gauge their levels of learning of the concepts. Options (A) and (C) indicate that not informing the students may lead to a negative learning environment in the classroom. Reporting scores (D) is typically done within school districts on standardized tests *after* learning has taken place; the scores achieved do not provide information on students' understandings and potential difficulties as learning progresses throughout the school year. **(804-006 Science Assessment)**

9.   C.

Option (C) is correct because the stuffed animal and car become one object. The stuffed animal is in motion with the car as it rolls down the ramp. The stuffed animal is unrestrained, however, so when the car stops, the stuffed animal remains in motion, flying forward out of the car until gravity acts upon it and it lands on the floor. Option (A) is incorrect because the object is or was in motion and so the stuffed animal will not remain in the car when it hits the brick unless it is attached to the car (as with seatbelts in actual cars). Option (B) is incorrect because the stuffed animal will continue its forward motion when it suddenly stops by hitting the brick and cannot reverse its motion and fly backwards. Option (D) is incorrect because there is indeed a correct answer in option (C). **(804-007 Forces and Motion)**

10.   B.

Option (B) is the correct answer because burning the fuel causes the gases released to be expelled at a very high speed out of a nozzle, which is computer controlled in the desired direction to push the rocket in the opposite direction. This is Newton's third law—that for every action there is an equal and opposite reaction. Options (A) and (D) are incorrect because the force is not from outside of the rocket in this case. Option (C) is incorrect as it is a simplified version of Bernoulli's principle of lift. **(804-007 Forces and Motion)**

11. A.

Option (A) is correct. A single pulley and movable pulleys are classified as simple machines. The amount of force required to lift an object with two pulleys in a single system reduces the force required to lift the object by one-half. Option (B) is incorrect because the movable pulley will not increase but rather decrease the amount of force required. Option (C) is incorrect because the force will not be changed to a definite value of force; the reduction of force to be applied depends on the weight of the object to be lifted and the number of pulleys in the system. Option (D) is incorrect because the use of a movable pulley does reduce the amount of force required to lift the object. **(804-007 Forces and Motion)**

12. C.

Option (C) is correct because burning is when oxygen in the air chemically combines with the hydrocarbon molecules in the paper, which are long connected chains of glucose ($C_6H_{12}O_6$) molecules. Burning the hydrocarbons results in new substances, including carbon dioxide (CO_2), carbon monoxide (CO), and water (H_2O). The new substances are no longer hydrocarbon molecules, but new products; thus the reaction is not reversible. The reaction also showed classic signs of chemical reactions, including a change in color, heat produced, and gas released. The changes listed in Options (A), (B), and (D) indicate physical changes because the substances do not change their chemical compositions; the liquid water is still H_2O after it melts; the paper is still made up of the hydrocarbons and possible other molecules in the torn pieces; and the chalk is still made up of the same molecules of chalk (typically calcium carbonate, $CaCO_3$) only now it is in tiny pieces. **(804-008 Physical and Chemical Properties)**

13. B.

Option (B) is correct because water is made up of two or more different kinds of atoms: hydrogen (H) and oxygen (O), which is a compound. Option (A) is incorrect because elements are made up of only one kind of atom. Option (C) is incorrect because water is made up of more than a single atom. Option (D) is incorrect because ions are positively or negatively charged atoms or molecules and water is a stable molecule. **(804-008 Physical and Chemical Properties)**

14. D.

Option (D) is correct because cellular respiration is a life function that uses oxygen to burn glucose to produce energy as an end product. Just as in animals, cellular respiration must occur during the day and night, for the entire 24-hour cycle. If cellular respiration were to stop, the plant would die. Option (A) is incorrect because respiration does occur in plants, very much the same as in animals. Options (B) and (C) are incorrect because cellular respiration occurs all day and night. **(804-008 Physical and Chemical Properties)**

15. A.

Option (A) is correct because mechanical energy pushed the doorbell and closed the circuit. The closed circuit allowed for the transfer of energy from mechanical to electrical energy. The electrical energy was transferred into sound energy. Options (B), (C), and (D) indicate an incorrect sequence in the transformation of energy. **(804-009 Energy and Interactions)**

16. C.

Option (C) is the correct answer because convection is the transfer of heat energy through liquids and gases. In convection, warmer air or liquid expands and rises, and cooler air or liquid contracts and sinks. Convection explains why the water at the surface was slightly warmer than the water near the bottom of the pond. Convection also explains why a home's attic is warmer and its basement is cooler than the rest of the house; it also explains ocean currents and lake turnover in the spring in cold climates. Option (A) is incorrect because conduction is the transfer of heat energy through solids, such as through a metal spoon placed in a hot liquid—the heat from the liquid travels through the spoon to the handle, and the handle soon becomes hot. Option (B) is incorrect because radiation is the transfer of heat energy through space, as with the sun's radiation. Option (D) is incorrect because evaporation is the phase change in which a liquid changes to a gaseous state of matter. **(804-009 Energy and Interactions)**

17. B.

Option (B) is correct because the laboratory activity described is transforming the nail into a temporary magnet or electromagnet. The more twists of the wire around the nail, the greater the electric field produced, and the stronger the electromagnet. Thus, the trials with 20 twists of the wire around the nail would pick up more paper clips than the trials with 10 twists of the wire around the nail. Option (A) is incorrect because the trials with 20 twists of wire around the nail would have a stronger rather than weaker electric field and would thus pick up more paper clips compared to the trials with 10 twists. Option (C) is incorrect because the different number of twists produces stronger and weaker electric fields and the strengths of these fields would not be equal. Option (D) is incorrect because a 6-volt battery or any battery would create an electric field and therefore attract some number of paper clips in the example given. **(804-009 Energy and Interactions)**

18. D.

Option (D) is correct because the colors we see around us are the wavelengths of light reflected by that object or substance. Green plants, therefore, do not absorb green light waves, but this color of visible light of the electromagnetic spectrum reflects off the plant's surface and our eyes see the color green. Option (A) is incorrect because if the plant absorbed green wavelengths, the color green would not be seen by our eyes because it would be absorbed into the substance of the leaves. Option (B) is incorrect because refraction is the bending of light rather than reflection, so the color would be bent rather than reflected to our eyes. Option (C) is incorrect because green plants in the growing season reflect and do not absorb green wavelengths of light, so the color we see is green. However, in the fall, deciduous trees, which are plants in which the leaves change color and fall off in the winter, stop producing chlorophyll (the green pigment in plants), and instead produce other pigments, including red and yellow, as they become dormant. The red and yellow colors taken on by these leaves indicate a shift in the wavelengths of light reflected. If our eyes see the color red, then the leaves are reflecting light in the red wavelength region of the electromagnetic spectrum. **(804-009 Energy and Interactions)**

19. A.

Option (A) is correct because although sound is initiated with the vibration of an object, the sound waves are caused by the vibration of the air around the object, not the object itself. The vibrating air reaches the human eardrum, causing it to vibrate, which is sensed by the auditory nerve and carried to the brain for interpretation as sound. Option (B) is incorrect, as previously explained, in that it is not the object itself vibrating that causes sound, it is the movement or vibration of the air molecules in the vicinity of the object. Option (C) is incorrect because light colliding with sound waves is not the cause of sound, and, in fact, light waves travel much faster than sound waves. Option (D) is incorrect because this is the formula for Newton's Second Law of Motion. **(804-009 Energy and Interactions)**

20. C.

Option (C) is correct in that hydroelectric energy produces electricity through fast-moving water as in Niagara Falls. Nuclear energy utilizes the radioactivity of uranium. Fossil fuel energy produces electricity through the burning of coal, oil, and/or natural gas. Geothermal energy produces electricity by harnessing the energy beneath the Earth's surface to produce electricity. Solar energy captures the energy of the sun to produce electricity. Options (A), (B), and (D) are listed in the incorrect order and/or are incorrect sources of energy. **(804-010 Energy Transformations and Conservation)**

21. D.

The correct answer is (D). Photosynthesis is the process by which plants take carbon dioxide (CO_2) from the air and combine it with water (H_2O) to make glucose with the formula $C_6H_{12}O_6$. Glucose is a simple sugar that joins together with other glucose molecules to form starch or carbohydrates—long chains of sugar molecules. These carbohydrates become the substance of plants—the roots, stems, leaves, and in angiosperms (flowering plants), also the flowers and fruits. Carbohydrates, for example, form the cellulose in the stems of plants. Plants, therefore, are basically made from "air"—namely, the carbon dioxide gas in the air. Option (A) is incorrect. The nutrients in the soil or fertilizers we apply only provide vitamins for the plants; they do not form the structure or substance of the plant. Option (B) is incorrect as plants do not absorb the soil itself. This can be demonstrated by measuring the mass of the soil in a pot before planting seeds in that soil, and again after the seeds grow into plants (ensuring approximately equal moisture is in the soil at both measurement times). The measures will reveal that the soil has the same mass before and after plant growth. Option (C) is incorrect because although nitrogen is an element plants do utilize, it accounts for only a small percentage of the mass of a plant. **(804-010 Energy Transformations and Conservation)**

22. B.

The correct answer is (B). The mealworm is not actually a worm, but instead the larva stage in the life cycle of a darkling beetle. The larva feeds on the oatmeal, uses the moisture from the apple, and grows. After gaining the necessary nutrition, the mealworm will undergo metamorphosis and change into a pupa. In this stage the mealworm shortens, curls up, and does not move, yet many changes are taking place. The pupa undergoes metamorphosis and changes into the adult, which is the darkling beetle. The only stage not observed in this life cycle is the egg stage; however, if the adults are left to remain together long enough in the petri dish, there likely will be eggs, and the four-stage life cycle will begin again with new offspring (egg, larva, pupa, adult). Option (A) is incorrect, and though students may believe this to be what happened, the beetles did not come into the petri dish from outside, but were the mealworms after undergoing complete metamorphosis into the adult stage. Options (C) and (D) are incorrect because the correct sequence in the life cycle of a mealworm that undergoes complete metamorphosis is egg to larva (mealworm) to pupa to adult, then back to new eggs as the offspring. **(804-011 Structure and Function of Living Things)**

23. D.

The correct answer is option (D). The air likely changed the least as the concentration of oxygen in the atmosphere remains relatively constant and will be sufficient for the survival of the raccoons. All three remaining options would have been likely to undergo a greater change. In the case of option (A), the shelter likely changed because the raccoons, a nocturnal animal, no longer have the trees and shrubs to inhabit. In the case of option (B), the water likely changed because the pond was taken out or filled in to construct the restaurant. In the case of option (C), the food likely changed because the raccoons now had the uneaten food to forage upon rather than seeking insects, frogs, and other food typical of its diet in a forest environment. **(804-011 Structure and Function of Living Things)**

24. A.

Option (A) is correct because homologous structures are those of different living organisms that share a common structure and function and were inherited from the same ancestry. Option (B) is incorrect because non-homologous structures are similar in structure and function but were inherited independently and not from common ancestors. Option (C) is incorrect because analogous structures have the structure or function but arose from different ancestors. Option (D) is incorrect because heterozygous refers to chromosomes and gene expression and not taxonomic classifications of organisms. **(804-011 Structure and Function of Living Things)**

25. D.

The correct answer is (D). Meiosis forms the gametes or the egg and sperm cells. In this process the beginning primary sex cells, called oocytes in the female and spermatocytes in males, undergo various stages of division in which chromosomes are replicated followed by two cell divisions. The result of meiosis is half the number of chromosomes (haploid) in each of the four resulting sperm and egg cells, although only one of the four cells in females is the true egg capable of being fertilized. Fertilization is the union of the single viable egg cell produced in meiosis and a single sperm cell. Fertilization of the haploid egg and sperm cells restores the chromosome number (genetic material) to the proper number for that organism, which is double (diploid), and where each chromosome has a pair from the opposite cell that codes for the same types of traits. After fertilization of the egg cell has occurred, the resulting zygote now divides by mitosis to make exact copies of the chromosomes it contains and maintain the full diploid number of chromosomes necessary for the organism's growth, development, and by and large, its survival. Mitosis also goes through a series of distinct stages where the first step is the duplication of chromosomes, followed by one cell division that produces two new cells from the original cell—each an exact copy. Option (A) reverses the process that occurs to produce the gametes and to form the embryo after fertilization. Options (B) and (C) are incorrect to explain the process that occurs to produce the gametes and the embryo after fertilization. **(804-012 Reproduction and the Mechanisms of Heredity)**

26. D.

Option (D) is correct: None of the offspring will have white fur. If the female is homozygous black, then her gene combination is BB, and if the male is hetero-zygous black, he has a gene combination of Bb. That is, for the female, both chromosomes that code for fur color code for the dominant trait, black fur (BB). For the male, only one of the chromosomes out of the pair codes for black fur, and the second inherited chromosome codes for white fur color (Bb). In using a Punnett square diagram to determine the offspring, the result will show 100% of the offspring have black fur, and 0% have white fur. However 50% of the offspring carry the hidden trait for white fur color, so white color is still carried on in future generations. The Punnett square for this genetic cross is shown below. Options (A), (B), and (C) are incorrect because none of the offspring will have white fur. **(804-012 Reproduction and the Mechanisms of Heredity)**

	Father (sperm cell) B	Father (sperm cell) b
Mother (egg cell) B	BB	Bb
Mother (egg cell) B	BB	Bb

27. A., B., C., and D.

The correct answer requires that you select all four options because options (A), (B), (C), and (D) are all experienced by animals as stresses that may displace them, cause a significant decline in population, or lead to extinction. Adaption requires time and generations of chance genetic mutations in animals, with some of those mutations proving beneficial to the animal and the offspring in the new environment. Those animals with the mutation would survive and produce more offspring, whereas those animals without the mutation would perish. Moving to urban areas sometimes results in the decline or even extermination of animal populations. **(804-013 Adaptations and Evolution)**

28. C.

Option (C) is correct because genetic mutations randomly occur over time. If the genetic mutation happens to be beneficial to the organism in the environment, such as a giraffe having a longer neck than others within the species, then the organism with that mutation is more likely to survive, thrive, and produce offspring with the inherited mutation compared to those organisms without the mutation. Over time, the offspring that have the mutation and generations that follow are likely to continue to prosper and reproduce in this environment; and those organisms without the mutation are more likely to die off. Options (A) and (D) are both incorrect because stretching the neck in the past or eating calcium would not produce the result described, nor would offspring inherit this same trait as their parents. Option (B) is incorrect because organisms cannot choose to change in ways to match the environment. **(804-013 Adaptations and Evolution)**

29. B.

Option (B) is correct because interest in running was learned by the offspring watching and likely participating in running with his or her parents from a young age. Perhaps the size and potential strength of the leg and heart muscles, for example, was inherited, but the interest was learned. Many individuals who inherited similar genetic characteristics are not runners. Option (A) is incorrect because eye color of the offspring is inherited from the parents. Eye color is determined by the DNA codes at specific gene locations on one or several pairs of chromosomes that were inherited in fertilization from the original egg and sperm cells of the parents. These particular egg and sperm cells, with their genetic codes on each matching chromosome, joined in fertilization and produced that offspring. The particular eye color was immedi-

ately determined in the fertilized egg, and the color expressed by the genes for eye color in the offspring depends on the laws of dominance. Option (C) is also incorrect as this trait is inherited in the same way as described for eye color. Option (D) is incorrect as high cholesterol has been found to be inherited. The genetic mutation in the chromosomes in this disorder for high cholesterol is a dominant trait. **(804-012 Reproduction and the Mechanisms of Heredity)**

30. A.

The correct answer is (A). The plant stem and leaves will grow toward the light. The plant responds to the stimulus of light as its means for initiating photosynthesis, which produces the plant's food or glucose. Hormones within the plant called Auxins respond to stimuli and produce this result. Option (B) is incorrect because plants will grow toward light rather than away from light. Options (C) and (D) are incorrect because the plant would not respond in these ways to water or gravity. **(804-014 Organisms and the Environment)**

31. A.

Option (A) is correct because producers are plants that receive the energy directly from the sun to produce food in the form of glucose. Option (C) is incorrect because primary consumers obtain their food from producers; however, some of the energy it receives has already been lost because it was used by the plant to maintain its own life functions. Option (B) is incorrect because secondary consumers are carnivores that obtain food from primary consumers; however, even more of the energy has been lost due to it being utilized to maintain life functions of the producers and the primary consumers. Decomposers are the final stage; however, much of the energy has already been lost through the various consumers in the food chain or web, so decomposers receive the least amount of energy. **(804-014 Organisms and the Environment)**

32. D.

Option (D) shows the correct order of the layers of the Earth from surface to center: crust, mantle, outer core, inner core. Options (A), (B), and (C) show an incorrect sequence of the layers of the Earth. **(804-015 Structure and Function of Earth Systems)**

33. C.

Option (C) is correct. Mars, Earth, Venus, and Mercury are rocky planets, whereas Jupiter, Saturn, Uranus and Neptune are gaseous planets. Therefore, options (A), (B), and (D) are incorrect. **(804-018 Solar System and the Universe)**

34. C.

Answer (C) is correct. Transpiration is the evaporation of water from the stomata located on the underside of leaves on plants. Liquid water is absorbed through the roots, is carried through the plant in small vessels called the xylem, and water that is not needed or excreted evaporates, meaning it changes from liquid to gas (water vapor) as it leaves the stomata. This moisture in the air from transpiration contributes to humidity and to cloud formation along with water evaporated from lakes, rivers, and oceans, which is eventually precipitated to Earth again in the water cycle. Option (A) is incorrect because evaporation from lakes and other bodies of water is simply evaporation—molecules of liquid water on the surface leave the surface in the form of water vapor. Option (B) is incorrect because condensation is water changing from water vapor (gas) to liquid water. Option (D) is incorrect because precipitation is water falling to Earth from clouds in the form of rain, snow, sleet, or hail. **(804-016 Cycles in Earth Systems)**

35. A.

The correct answer is (A). When water freezes, its molecules arrange in crystalline form because it is a polar molecule (has a positive and negative end). The arrangement of molecules in ice takes up more space than it does in liquid form. This property explains why potholes in roads are caused by freezing and thawing (melting) of water in the cracks of roads in winter, and why the ice cubes in an ice cube tray in a freezer are larger than the liquid water that was originally poured into the tray. Option (B) is incorrect because water expands when it freezes. Option (C) is incorrect because water is a polar molecule. Option (D) is incorrect because most water on Earth is saltwater, with only 2.5 percent freshwater. **(804-016 Cycles in Earth Systems)**

36. C.

Option (C) is correct because relative humidity is the percentage of water in the air and is measured by a psychrometer. Options (A) and (B) are incorrect because an anemometer measures wind speed. Option (D) is incorrect because humidity is not a measure of air pressure. **(804-017 Energy in Weather and Climate)**

37. C.

Option (C) is the correct symbol for a stationary front. Stationary fronts occur when a cold front or warm front stops moving. Stationary fronts result from warm and cold air masses that are in the same region pushing against each other, but they are of equal power. Option (A) is incorrect because it is the symbol for a cold air front. The spikes are facing the direction the cold air mass is moving. Option (B) is incorrect because it is the symbol for an occluded front. An occluded front is when a cold air mass is trailing right behind a warm air mass, and there is already a cold air mass ahead of the warm front that the warm front is pushing into. The cold front that is following the warm air mass overtakes the warm front and connects with the cold front that is ahead of the warm front. The warm air mass rises and there is usually precipitation when this happens. Option (D) is the symbol for a warm front. As with the cold front, the warm air mass is behind the curved line and the half-circles represent the leading edge of the front. **(804-017 Energy in Weather and Climate)**

38. B.

Option (B) is correct because those states just east of the Great Lakes, such as New York and Pennsylvania, experience the most lake-effect snows. The air contains water evaporated over the Great Lakes, such as Lake Erie and Lake Ontario. As the air mass moves east it cools, which causes precipitation in the form of snow if the air is below the freezing temperature of water. Option (A) is incorrect because large bodies of water tend to keep the areas near the coast warmer than land. This is because water has high specific heat, meaning it cools off and warms up more slowly than any other substance on Earth. This is why coastal areas have comparatively warmer winters and cooler summers compared to inland regions at the same latitude. In addition, storms in the U.S. tend to travel from west to east. Options (C) and (D) are incorrect because these regions are not located near significant bodies of water. **(804-017 Energy in Weather and Climate)**

39. C.

The correct answer is (C). The New Moon phase is when the Moon is not visible because it will be daytime, likely near or at 12 noon. The spatial position of the New Moon phase is between the Sun and Earth, so it will not be visible because the light from the Sun conceals it from view. Options (A), (B), and (D) are incorrect because the New Moon is only out and "visible" (although not typically seen with the naked eye) during the daytime. **(804-018 Solar System and the Universe)**

40. A.

The question addresses the beginning teacher's knowledge of "how to guide students in making systematic observations and measurements and posing questions tto guide investigations. Option (A) is correct because at the location in the Earth's orbit that is the summer solstice, the tilt of the Earth in the Northern Hemisphere is facing toward the Sun, making the daylight hours longer than at other times of the year. On the date of the summer solstice, typically June 20 or 21, or the first day of summer, the Northern Hemisphere has approximately 15 hours of sunlight and 9 hours of darkness. Option (B) is incorrect because first, the Earth's distance does not impact daylight hours, and second, the Earth is actually farther away from the Sun at the summer solstice than it is at the winter solstice (on or around December 21). Option (C) is incorrect because the Northern Hemisphere is tilted away from the Sun at the winter solstice, with 9 hours of daylight, and 15 hours of darkness. So the winter solstice has the shortest number of daylight hours of any day of the year. The Vernal Equinox occurs in the spring in the Northern Hemisphere, typically around March 20 or the first day of spring, and has an equal number of daylight hours and darkness hours (12 hours each). **(804-018 Solar System and the Universe)**

41. C.

Option (C) is correct because presenting the safety precautions is the first step in any laboratory investigation. The safety procedures should be in printed form on the students' laboratory sheets, posted on the walls of the classroom, and read aloud to students before beginning any investigation. Option (A) is incorrect because giving students the materials should not be done prior to a thorough explanation and discussion of both the safety precautions and the laboratory procedures. Failure to do so before allowing students to begin could have disastrous results and cause harm to students. Option (B) is incorrect because providing the "answers" and giving away the concepts to students should not be done before an inquiry investigation—students are to discover the concepts based on their own experiences and data. Option (D) is incorrect because although clean-up instructions are important, these instructions should not precede a discussion on safety. Safety precautions must be implemented throughout the investigation, including during clean-up activities. **(804-002 History and Nature of Science)**

42. C.

This question addresses the beginning teacher's knowledge of "how to guide students in making systematic observations and measurements and posing questions to guide investigations," as stated under TExES Core Subjects Science Competency 002. Option (C) is correct because by asking the question first and then randomly calling the name of a student to respond, the students do not know who will be called on to respond. Therefore, more of the students will be attentive and prepared to respond compared to other styles of questioning. Option (A), in which the name of student is called before the question, may promote a situation where other students do not feel they need to listen to the question or answer; only the student called upon needs to respond. Options (B) and (D) are incorrect because students who do not want to participate can simply choose to not raise their hand or refrain from calling out a response. **(804-002 History and Nature of Science)**

43. B.

Option (B), metamorphic rock, is correct because this type of rock is formed from igneous or sedimentary rock that is deep in the Earth and has been subjected to extreme pressure and temperature. Metamorphic rock may also exhibit signs of the Earth's folding due to plates colliding, which may also bend and twist the rock. Igneous rock (A) is the rock produced from hot lava or magma prior to exposure to pressure and/or folding. Sedimentary rock (C) is rock formed from eroded rock carried in bodies of water as sediments such as clays and sand. The sediments settle out of the water and form rock such as sandstone and shale. Conglomerate rock (D) is coarse grained sedimentary rock. In conglomerates, rocks of different shapes and sizes are cemented together. **(804-016 Cycles in Earth Systems)**

44. A.

Option (A) is the correct response because the new medication is causing harm to the patients receiving it and to others. Options (B), (C), and (D) are incorrect because it is unethical to continue and/or expand upon experiments with patients knowing it is also causing them harm. The benefits of the new medication are not significant enough to place all patients in danger. **(804-003 Impact on Science)**

45. D.

Option (D) is correct because all students, including ELLs, will best understand new terminology/vocabulary after they have experienced the concept in a concrete, hands-on manner. The new terms that label the new concept they have defined through their explorations will have meaning to them because they experienced it. Options (A), (B), and (C) are incorrect because they force students to learn new vocabulary words and definitions before they have experienced their meanings through their own explorations. The students will tend to simply memorize the terms, which will have little to no meaning to them, and will likely form misconceptions about those terms, or they will not retain their meanings. **(804-005 Students as Learners and Science Instruction)**

46. A.

The correct answer is (A). First, calculate how many meters are in a yard. To do this, you have to know the following: 1 yard = 0.9144 meters and 0.9144 meters = 9.144 decimeters. The measurement known as the yard is an imperial, U.S. length unit. It equals 3 feet, or 36 inches. The meter is a length unit of the metric system with a base-10 structure. The measurement of 0.9144 meters = 9.144 decimeters. First convert decimeters to meters. In this problem, 25 decimeters = 2.5 meters. Since 1 yard = .9144 meters, then 3 yards is calculated as .9144 x 3 = 2.7 meters. So 3 yards is a slightly longer distance. Option (B) is incorrect because it is a shorter distance than 3 yards as previously shown. Option (C) is incorrect because the lengths are not equal. Option (D) is incorrect because the answer can be found by knowing the conversion of non-standard units to standard units. **(804-001 Lab Processes, Equipment and Safety)**

47. B.

The correct answer is (B). Experiments must be repeated many times in order to increase reliability and obtain more accurate results. If only one trial was conducted, it is not known if results would hold up after repeated trials, or if the data would change. The thermometer could have been faulty, or there could be other explanations for the results. Repeating experiments many times and finding the same results is necessary to produce reliable, supportable results. Option (A) is incorrect because as long as the starting temperature was recorded on each thermometer, then only the change in temperature after placement is relevant to the findings. Option (C) is incorrect because it is necessary to record the starting temperatures in order to observe the change at the two locations. Option (D) is incorrect because, although graphing is valuable and helps students observe the data in a more visual way, it is not a *necessary* step in the experiment. **(804-002 History and Nature of Science)**

48. C.

Option (C) is correct because it is not possible to create a model that is exactly the same as the actual scientific phenomena or object being represented. For example, a ball-and-stick model of molecules is only a representation of an atom; the ionic or covalent bonding is due to the charges in the atoms, particularly electrons, which cannot be adequately represented by a stick. Option (A) is incorrect because no model is exact in its representation; it is impossible to represent every detail of a phenomenon with a model—it would simply have to end up being the real phenomenon instead. For example, you can make a marsh ecosystem in the classroom in an aquarium to represent an actual marsh, but it could not possibly have all of the elements of the actual marsh ecosystem in nature. Option (B) is incorrect because although computer-generated models are often useful, many physical models are equally or more useful than computer-generated ones. Making and flying an actual paper airplane to represent real airplane flight gives learners a different experience than making virtual paper airplanes on the computer. Option (D) is incorrect because, although sometimes students may develop misconceptions through the use of models, if models are implemented correctly, they will actually help students build more sound understandings of natural phenomena. In using models, teachers should ask the students to point out differences between the actual phenomena and the model. Students should understand that the model is simply a tool to help us visualize the natural phenomena, and that models have inherent limitations in their applicability. **(804-004 Concepts and Processes)**

49. A.

Option (A) is correct because for something to float, it must be less dense than the liquid it is in, and for an object to sink it must be denser than the liquid it is in. Density is a measure of how tightly packed the matter is (mass) within a given amount of space (volume), or $D = M/V$. Water is unique with respect to its density because it is the only substance on Earth that is less dense in solid form (ice) than in liquid form (water); therefore, the solid form floats in its own liquid. Alcohol is less dense (molecules are less tightly packed) than water, so the ice cube sinks. Option (B) is incorrect because if the ice cube was denser than liquid water it would sink in the water, and if less dense than the alcohol it would float in this liquid. Option (C) is incorrect because if a substance has equal density as the liquid it is in, it would be suspended in the middle of the liquid. This statement is incorrect even though the second part of it—which states that the ice is denser than the alcohol—is correct. Option (D) is incorrect because again, equal density means the ice cube would be suspended (i.e., neither sink nor float) in both the water and in the alcohol. **(804-008 Physical and Chemical Properties)**

50. C.

Option (C) is correct because in science the triple beam balance is the instrument or piece of equipment used to measure mass. Option (A), the meter stick, measures length. Option (B), the graduated cylinder, measures liquid amount or volume. Option (D), the sling psychrometer, measures relative humidity. **(804-001 Lab Processes, Equipment and Safety)**

51. D.

Option (D) is correct because the best way to evaluate a laboratory skill such as determining density is to ask students to perform the skill. This evaluation measures learning and skill as authentic, alternative assessment—in this case, the laboratory practical. Demonstrating skill is superior to any other method of evaluation in this particular example because the teacher can observe students performing the technique and students can earn a grade for successful performance. Choices (A), (B), and (C) are not the best evaluation methods because although students may be able to learn the correct answers on how to measure density, knowing the correct answers does not mean the students know how to perform the laboratory technique. **(804-006 Science Assessment)**

52. B.

Option (B) is correct because mixing salt (NaCl) in water does not change the substance in any way and it is reversible. The substance in the water is still salt, and if the water is evaporated, salt crystals will again be restored. Option (A) is incorrect because mixing an acid and base is a neutralization reaction—a chemical reaction that forms new substances, namely a salt and water. For example, mixing hydrochloric acid (HCl) with the base sodium hydroxide (NaOH) produces NaCl and H_2O. Option (C) is incorrect because rust is the chemical reaction between oxygen in the atmosphere and iron (FeO). The salt and ice spread on roads in the winter are electrolytes that wear away the protective finish on automobiles, exposing the metal to oxygen so rust can form (FeO). Option (D) is incorrect because burning is a chemical reaction in which oxygen combines with the substance to form a new substance. Burning sugar, a hydrocarbon-based substance, will form carbon dioxide and water. **(804-008 Physical and Chemical Properties)**

TExES Core Subjects EC–6 Practice Test: Fine Arts, Health, and Physical Education

Fine Arts, Health, and Physical Education
Practice Test Answer Sheet

1. Ⓐ Ⓑ Ⓒ Ⓓ
2. Ⓐ Ⓑ Ⓒ Ⓓ
3. Ⓐ Ⓑ Ⓒ Ⓓ
4. Ⓐ Ⓑ Ⓒ Ⓓ
5. Ⓐ Ⓑ Ⓒ Ⓓ
6. Ⓐ Ⓑ Ⓒ Ⓓ
7. Ⓐ Ⓑ Ⓒ Ⓓ
8. Ⓐ Ⓑ Ⓒ Ⓓ
9. Ⓐ Ⓑ Ⓒ Ⓓ
10. Ⓐ Ⓑ Ⓒ Ⓓ
11. Ⓐ Ⓑ Ⓒ Ⓓ
12. Ⓐ Ⓑ Ⓒ Ⓓ
13. Ⓐ Ⓑ Ⓒ Ⓓ
14. Ⓐ Ⓑ Ⓒ Ⓓ
15. Ⓐ Ⓑ Ⓒ Ⓓ
16. Ⓐ Ⓑ Ⓒ Ⓓ
17. Ⓐ Ⓑ Ⓒ Ⓓ
18. Ⓐ Ⓑ Ⓒ Ⓓ

19. Ⓐ Ⓑ Ⓒ Ⓓ
20. Ⓐ Ⓑ Ⓒ Ⓓ
21. Ⓐ Ⓑ Ⓒ Ⓓ
22. Ⓐ Ⓑ Ⓒ Ⓓ
23. Ⓐ Ⓑ Ⓒ Ⓓ
24. Ⓐ Ⓑ Ⓒ Ⓓ
25. Ⓐ Ⓑ Ⓒ Ⓓ
26. Ⓐ Ⓑ Ⓒ Ⓓ
27. Ⓐ Ⓑ Ⓒ Ⓓ
28. Ⓐ Ⓑ Ⓒ Ⓓ
29. Ⓐ Ⓑ Ⓒ Ⓓ
30. Ⓐ Ⓑ Ⓒ Ⓓ
31. Ⓐ Ⓑ Ⓒ Ⓓ
32. Ⓐ Ⓑ Ⓒ Ⓓ
33. Ⓐ Ⓑ Ⓒ Ⓓ
34. Ⓐ Ⓑ Ⓒ Ⓓ
35. Ⓐ Ⓑ Ⓒ Ⓓ
36. Ⓐ Ⓑ Ⓒ Ⓓ

37. Ⓐ Ⓑ Ⓒ Ⓓ
38. Ⓐ Ⓑ Ⓒ Ⓓ
39. Ⓐ Ⓑ Ⓒ Ⓓ
40. Ⓐ Ⓑ Ⓒ Ⓓ
41. Ⓐ Ⓑ Ⓒ Ⓓ
42. Ⓐ Ⓑ Ⓒ Ⓓ
43. Ⓐ Ⓑ Ⓒ Ⓓ
44. Ⓐ Ⓑ Ⓒ Ⓓ
45. Ⓐ Ⓑ Ⓒ Ⓓ
46. Ⓐ Ⓑ Ⓒ Ⓓ
47. Ⓐ Ⓑ Ⓒ Ⓓ
48. Ⓐ Ⓑ Ⓒ Ⓓ
49. Ⓐ Ⓑ Ⓒ Ⓓ
50. Ⓐ Ⓑ Ⓒ Ⓓ
51. Ⓐ Ⓑ Ⓒ Ⓓ
52. Ⓐ Ⓑ Ⓒ Ⓓ

Practice Test:
Fine Arts, Health, and Physical Education

TIME: 40 minutes
52 questions

> **Directions:** Read each item and select the correct response or responses. Most items on this test require you to provide the one best answer. However, some questions require you to select all the options that apply.

1. Identify an activity that can guide children to see the tangible value of the visual arts in our lives.

    A. Present a picture and guide children to notice the concept of perspective.

    B. Present examples of sculpture and guide children to determine the materials used to create it.

    C. Prepare a list of occupations and guide students to link them with skills taught in visual arts.

    D. Post students' drawings in the school hallways, so people can appreciate their accomplishments.

2. What is the glycemic index?

    A. A list of foods that illustrate carbohydrate impact on blood sugar

    B. The usable energy part of the Krebs Cycle

    C. The amount of sugar grams on a food label

    D. The rate at which a person's metabolism burns glycogen

3. Which of the following developed a teaching method that emphasizes rote learning?

    A. Gordon

    B. Orff

    C. Suzuki

    D. Jaques-Dalcroze

4. Ceramics is an art form that is accessible to elementary-level students. However, it is also a form that is highly specialized because it requires

    A. an understanding of the concepts of perspective and color.

    B. the use of an oven and a specialized type of paint.

    C. an awareness of tridimensional figures and details of human form.

    D. the application of highly flammable paint to create a shiny look.

5. Fifth grade students are singing a song accompanied by the piano. The piano is playing which part?

   A. Rhythm

   B. Melody

   C. Form

   D. Harmony

6. A high male voice is classified as which of the following?

   A. Soprano

   B. Tenor

   C. Bass

   D. Baritone

7. Count Basie, a jazz pianist and band leader, employed which style of playing in his accompaniment?

   A. Comping

   B. Scat singing

   C. Riffs

   D. Figured bass

8. Horseshoe making and jewelry making are examples of which of the following?

   A. Art forms developed in the United States

   B. Metalworking

   C. Functional art

   D. Forms developed in China

9. What is Basal Metabolic Rate (BMR)?

   A. How efficient the body is at burning calories at rest

   B. How the body regulates hormone production

   C. The level at which metabolism burns calories best

   D. How diet impacts metabolic functions

10. After the game has started, which of the following would be the least advisable method for modifying a physical activity or game?

    A. Switching out equipment to increase/decrease the difficulty level

    B. Changing the rules to accommodate large groups

    C. Altering the size of the playing environment

    D. Applying rules of elimination from game play

11. Flashbacks and flash-forwards are used to do which of the following?

    A. Clarify and present important information

    B. Establish differences among the characters

    C. Lead the audience to the climax of the play

    D. Add realism to the drama

12. Dramatic play includes a variety of activities, but it rejects

    A. interaction with the teacher and students.

    B. the option of having children-initiated activities.

    C. the use of solitary play.

    D. memorization of lengthy dialogues.

13. Dramatic play is commonly used to introduce students to theatre arts. This strategy is most appropriate for which of the following?

    A. Children in upper elementary grades

    B. Children with prior experience in theatre

    C. Children in early childhood education

    D. Children learning English as a second language

14. Inactivity can increase the risk factor of contracting which of the following diseases or conditions?

    A. Heart disease

    B. Anemia

    C. Sleep apnea

    D. Psoriasis

15. Which of the following characteristics of a quality physical education (PE) program would the Society of Health and Physical Education (SHAPE) advocate most to policy makers regarding elementary PE?

A. Curriculum stressing lessons that keep students happy and busy

B. Student involvement in moderate-to-vigorous physical activity for at least 90% of class time

C. The number of students in physical education class should be the same as the number of students in a regular classroom

D. Students participating in physical education and physical activity every school day

16. Which of the following identify key arts movements of the 19th century?

A. Romanticism and Impressionism

B. Impressionism and Idealism

C. Cubism, Realism, and Surrealism

D. Rococo and Baroque

17. Which of the following statements describes the key characteristic of a farce in theatre? *situational comedy*

A. It is shorter than a traditional drama.

B. The plot is developed around a situation.

C. The plot is developed around the main characters.

D. The characters sing their lines instead of saying them.

18. Which of the following sets of symptoms best describes heat stroke?

A. Cool, moist, pale skin

B. Red, hot, dry skin, unconsciousness

C. Nausea and dizziness

D. Headache and excessive sweating

19. Fourth grade students are singing a song where they all sing the melody and come in at specific intervals after group No. 1. What type of song are they singing?

A. Round

B. Partner Song

C. Call and Response

D. The speed of the underlying pulse in music

20. A physical education teacher is planning a skipping and galloping lesson based on the TEKS requirements. These requirements suggest this type of lesson is most appropriate for which of the following age groups?

A. Children 5–6 years of age

B. Children 8–9 years of age

C. Children 11–12 years of age

D. Children 14–15 years of age

21. During Ancient History and again during the Renaissance, artists sought to perfect representation of the human body. To accomplish this goal in sculpture, artists studied

A. pictures or drawings representing the human body.

B. the skin texture of models.

C. the human anatomy.

D. the type of bones and composition of human tissue.

22. In music, the words "up" and "down" are usually associated with which of the following?

A. Fast and slow

B. Loud and soft

C. High and low

D. Strong and gentle

23. Which of the following statements about human metabolism is inaccurate?

   A. More total calories are expended during rest (Basal Metabolic Rate) than exercise

   B. "Fasting" (not eating for long periods of time) speeds up metabolism

   C. Exercise stimulates metabolism

   D. Adjustments in metabolism are slow and take place over long periods of time

24. Based on the Individuals with Disabilities Education Act (IDEA), children with crutches or any other types of assistive devices should

   A. not be allowed to participate in physical education activities.

   B. be allowed to participate like any other student.

   C. be provided with appropriate modification for participation in physical education activities.

   D. be provided with a special physical education class designed for them.

25. When teaching students the structure of music, to which of the following could a musical phrase be likened in terms of the structure of language?

   A. A letter

   B. A word

   C. A sentence

   D. A paragraph

26. Gothic architecture, which spawned magnificent churches with pointing arches and towers reaching to the sky, flourished in Europe during which of the following?

   A. The Roman Empire

   B. The Greek Empire

   C. The Middle Ages

   D. Ancient Civilization

27. Which of the following enable the playwright, the director, and the actors to establish the guidelines and limitations to deliver a realistic and convincing play?

   A. Elements of theatre

   B. Stagecraft and the plot

   C. Conventions of theatre

   D. Theme and communication

28. In the pre-kindergarten and kindergarten reading classroom, children use drawings to

   A. represent the main idea of a story.

   B. communicate their emotions.

   C. practice muscular coordination.

   D. practice with primary and secondary colors.

29. Nine-year-old Jesse is having difficulty hitting a ball with a bat. Which of the following activities is likely to be most effective for helping him learn how to hit a ball successfully?

   A. Working cooperatively with another learner who has similar difficulties hitting the ball

   B. Striking whiffle balls on the ground with a short-handed hockey stick

   C. Participating in games that require fast reflexes and advanced eye–hand coordination skills

   D. Hitting a larger ball placed on a batting tee

30. Select the letter that contains the correct sequence of Kodály rhythm syllables for this song line, "Twinkle, Twinkle Little Star."

   A. Ta Ta Ta Ta Ti ti Ta

   B. Ta ti Ti ti Ta Ta Ti

   C. Ti ti Ti ti Ti ti Ta

   D. FACE

31. Which of the following systems is most affected by aerobic activity?

    A. Muscular system

    B. Digestive system

    C. Cardiovascular system

    D. Skeletal system

32. One of the most famous scenes in Hamlet is when the main character speaks to himself and shares with the audience his internal thoughts and indecisions: "To be or not to be, that is the question." What element of drama was William Shakespeare using in this performance?

    A. A farce

    B. A satire

    C. A dialogue

    D. A soliloquy

33. In traditional theatre, actors use which of the following to communicate directly with the audience?

    A. Artifacts and non-verbal communication

    B. A monologue

    C. Questions and answers before the play

    D. A soliloquy

34. From a learner's perspective, what sequence (from start to finish) best represents the progression for learning a motor skill?

    A. Student Demonstration > Transfer of Knowledge & Information > Assessing that Knowledge & Information > Summary

    B. Stating Objectives > Providing Examples > Teaching Rules of the Game > Playing the Game > Closure & Summary

    C. Clear Idea of the Task > Motivational Disposition to the Skill > Practice > Feedback > More Practice > Skill Utilization

    D. Introduction Using Visual Aids > Demonstration of All Related Modifications > Assessment & Evaluation of Skill

35. Which of the following instruments is not a member of the brass family. Select *all* that apply.

    A. Piccolo

    B. Trumpet

    C. Tuba

    D. Alto saxophone

36. A build-up of paint on canvass can be used to create a sense of which of the following?

    A. Energy

    B. Texture

    C. Intensity

    D. Empty space

37. What are the letter names of the spaces on the musical staff?

    A. FACE

    B. ABCD

    C. ACEG

    D. FGAB

38. The state song of Texas is

    A. "Home on the Range."

    B. "Deep in the Heart of Texas."

    C. "The Yellow Rose of Texas."

    D. "Texas, Our Texas."

39. A web developer is trying to select the appropriate colors for his client's new website. He knows this type of work requires the use of complementary colors; however, his client specifically requested that he use blue. What color best complements blue?

    A. Orange

    B. Green

    C. Red

    D. Yellow

40. A teacher asked a health class to complete a written homework assignment involving an analysis of the physiological effects of participating regularly in physical activity as well as the risk factors associated with inactivity. For which of the following is physical inactivity a risk factor?

    A. Heart disease

    B. Anemia

    C. Sleep apnea

    D. Psoriasis

41. A teacher notices multiple bruising marks on a child. The teacher should then do which of the following?

    A. Ask the child about their home life for more information

    B. Do nothing, it is not a teacher's responsibility

    C. Talk with the parents about child abuse

    D. Report the evidence immediately

42. By ages four and five, children are generally able to stack cups in a pyramid, dribble a small ball, and tap their foot to a rhythm. They also begin dressing themselves using buttons and zippers. These kinds of activities represent an example of which of the following?

    A. Gross motor skills

    B. Required curriculum components of school

    C. Fine motor skills

    D. A transition point from early childhood to adulthood

43. Flying buttresses, pointed arches, and stained glass windows are characteristic of which historic style of architecture?

    A. Romanesque

    B. Renaissance

    C. Byzantine

    D. Gothic

44. Aristophanes is to comedy as _____ is to tragedy.

    A. Aristotle

    B. Sophocles

    C. Socrates

    D. Oedipus

45. Most televised situation comedies are a form of which of the following?

    A. Farce

    B. Drama

    C. Soap opera

    D. Satire

46. Which of the following is least likely to lead to illness and disease?

    A. Stress

    B. Hydration

    C. Dietary sugar

    D. Isolation

47. Roughly what percentage of a daily diet should be composed of carbohydrates?

    A. 5-10%

    B. 15-25%

    C. 35-50%

    D. 70-90%

48. Activities that develop gross motor–visual skills almost always involve the use of a

    A. ball.

    B. balance beam.

    C. trampoline.

    D. exercise mat.

49. The "E" in the acronym RICE, a treatment process for sprains, represents which of the following?

   A. Exercise

   B. Elevation

   C. Evaluation

   D. Exposure

50. European artists of the _____ attempted to recreate the themes and the prolific development of art of the Ancient period.

   A. Middle Ages

   B. Modern Era

   C. Renaissance

   D. Prehistoric era

51. Which of the following is a poem set to music?

   A. A madrigal

   B. An art song

   C. An opera

   D. An aria

52. Artists Edouard Manet, Camille Pissarro, Auguste Renoir, and Edgar Degas were the leading painters of which of the following movements?

   A. Impressionism

   B. Romanticism

   C. Realism

   D. Surrealism

Fine Arts, Health, and Physical Education Practice Test Answer Key

1. C	19. A	37. A
2. A	20. A	38. D
3. C	21. C	39. A
4. B	22. C	40. A
5. D	23. B	41. D
6. B	24. C	42. C
7. A	25. C	43. D
8. B	26. C	44. B
9. A	27. C	45. A
10. D	28. A	46. B
11. A	29. D	47. C
12. D	30. C	48. A
13. C	31. C	49. B
14. A	32. D	50. C
15. D	33. B	51. B
16. A	34. C	52. A
17. B	35. A and D	
18. B	36. B	

Fine Arts, Health, and Physical Education Practice Test
Detailed Answers

1. C.

    The correct answer is (C). Linking visual arts with actual occupations (e.g., architecture or advertising) can guide students to appreciate its practical value. It can also spark interest in the arts. Bringing notice to the concept of perspective (A) and posting students' art on the wall (D) will not significantly establish a connection between the arts and its impact in our lives. Knowing about the materials (B) used in different types of sculpture may be interesting to children, but it falls short in tangibly connecting the visual arts with our daily lives. **(805-001 Visual Arts)**

2. A.

    The glycemic index is a system that ranks a variety of foods on a scale from 1 to 100 based on their effect on blood sugar levels. Thus, option (A) is the correct answer. The glycemic index has nothing to do with the Krebs Cycle (B) or glycogen utilization in the body (D). Although the amount of sugar intake can directly affect blood sugar levels (C), the glycemic index has nothing to do with the amount of sugar, only the body's response to a particular food with sugar in it. **(805-003 Health)**

3. C.

    The correct answer is (C). Dr. Shinichi Suzuki developed a teaching philosophy called "Talent Education," which used the so-called mother-tongue method. This means that music is taught in a similar fashion to the way children learn their native language: by rote. The use of imitation, repetition, and observation are stressed. Edwin Gordon emphasized audiation, the use of inner hearing, making option (A) incorrect. Carl Orff's approach employed the use of rhythm, ruling out choice (B). Émile Jaques-Dalcroze is primarily recog-

    nized for his use of eurythmics and improvisation. **(805-002 Music)**

4. B.

    The correct answer is (B). Ceramics requires the use of an oven and specialized paints to create the final glossy shine of the work. Traditionally, the pieces are bought raw and students are guided to paint them. The firing of the pieces is generally done in a specialized shop. Understanding colors (A) is not required to begin creating ceramic work. The paint used in ceramics changes drastically once the piece is fired in the kiln. Because ceramics is traditionally part of the elementary school art program, knowledge of tridimensional figures and human forms is not required to create this type of art (C). The materials and the paint used in ceramics are generally not flammable (D). Glaze is typically used to create the shiny appearance. **(805-001 Visual Arts)**

5. D.

    The correct answer is (D). Harmony is the accompaniment or supportive sounds to a melody. Choice (A) is incorrect because rhythm is varied lengths of sounds and silences. Choice (B) is incorrect because melody is the singable part of a song. Choice (C) is incorrect because form is the structure of the music analogous to mathematical patterns. **(805-002 Music)**

6. B.

    A tenor (B) is a high male voice. The range of voices is classified from high to low; that is, soprano, alto, tenor, baritone, bass. A soprano (A) is a high female voice. A bass (C) is the lowest male voice. A baritone (D) has a range between the tenor and the bass. **(805-002 Music)**

7. A.

The correct answer is (A). Comping, short for accompaniment, is the style of playing that Count Basie mastered. Often used in jazz, comping has a bounce, syncopation, and flexibility that allows soloists the freedom to improvise. Scat singing (B) is also used in jazz; it is a vocal technique, popularized by Louis Armstrong, that does not use words. Riffs are short phrases often used as accompaniment. Figured bass is a notation below the bass line that tells the performer which chords to follow. **(805-002 Music)**

8. B.

The correct answer is (B). Both horseshoe making and jewelry making are forms of metalworking. The first is an instrumental and highly functional form of art, while the second is focused on the creation of adornments (C). There is no conclusive historical evidence to identify a country where horseshoe making was developed (A) and (D). Though horseshoe making was used extensively in the United States during the 18th and 19th centuries, both it and jewelry making long predated the founding of the U.S. **(805-001 Visual Arts)**

9. A.

The correct answer is (A). BMR is the basic rate at which the body burns calories at rest (A). It may have peripheral effects on certain kinds of hormone function (B), but is not defined by this. Diet may also affect the BMR slightly (D), but is not defined by this either. Option (C) is a distractor answer: It sounds good, but there is no "best" way for the body to burn calories; there is just the rate at which it does so. **(805-003 Health)**

10. D.

The correct answer is (D). You never want to design, modify and/or play games in which students are eliminated from participation during a lesson, game or physical activity (e.g., dodgeball). Inevitably the highest-skilled kids will receive all the activity/opportunity provided and the lowest-skilled kids will become spectators. Options (A), (B), and (C) are all appropriate modifications a teacher could use to bring out the best in students, activity levels, and game play. **(805-004 Physical Education)**

11. A.

The correct answer is (A). The use of flashbacks and flash-forwards is a strategy to present information and clarification of the plot. Whereas this two-pronged strategy can theoretically be used to establish distinctions among the characters (B), to lead the audience to a climax (C), or to add realism (D) to the drama, it was not designed for that purpose. **(805-005 Theatre)**

12. D.

The correct answer is (D). Dramatic play can include interactions with teachers and students (A), or it can be a form of solitary play (C), or it can be teacher- or student-initiated (B). However, since this activity is designed mostly for younger children, the use of memorization of dialogues is not recommended. **(805-005 Theatre)**

13. C.

The correct answer is (C). Dramatic play is a spontaneous activity in which students are allowed to recreate scenes based on their interpretation of the world. It is not scripted, and it does not require memorization because the target group is students in early childhood. Dramatic play can be used for upper elementary (A) and for English language learners (D), but it was not expressly designed for these groups. Option (B) should be cast aside because no prior experience in theatre is required to participate in dramatic play. **(805-005 Theatre)**

14. A.

Sedentary lifestyle behavior is a primary risk factor for heart disease as well as other preventable diseases. (B), (C), and (D) are not directly caused by inactivity. **(805-003 Health)**

15. D.

Option (D) is the best answer for physical education in EC-6 settings. The No. 1 issue physical education professionals face (and advocate for) at the elementary school level is that students receive structured physical activity and exercise every school day. This is how lifestyle patterns are shaped and formed; thus, the goal of PE is to create lifelong movers. Currently, the vast majority of elementary children receive physical education only once or twice per week. Option (A) is vague and does not ensure any kind of structured physical activity that is beneficial to the student for health purposes. Option (B) is unrealistic, even the best physical education classes struggle to keep students motivated to exercise at a moderate-to-vigorous level for more than half of the class time. Option (C) applies more to PE at the secondary level, where multiple regular-sized classes are combined into one large class, making it more difficult for a teacher to manage and teach. **(805-004 Physical Education)**

16. A.

The correct answer is (A). Romanticism and Impressionism were key art movements of the 19th century. Cubism and Surrealism (C) were two movements of the 20th century. Baroque and Rococo (D) were two European movements of the 17th and 18th centuries. Baroque paintings and sculptures were characterized as extravagant, beautiful, and complex. This movement is best represented in the sculptures of Bernini, and the paintings of Caravaggio, Rubens, and van Dyck. In painting, the Rococo (later Baroque) portraits representing pastoral life—relaxing, playful scenes. One of the best representations of the Rococo paintings is *The Swing* by French painter Jean-Honoré Fragonard. **(805-001 Visual Arts)**

17. B.

The correct answer is (B). A farce can be identified as "situational comedy," where the plot develops around a situation, not necessarily around the characters (C). There are not strict guidelines to determine the length of a farce versus other forms of theatre (A). Option (D) describes opera instead of farce. **(805-005 Theatre)**

18. B.

The correct answer is (B). Heat stroke is best recognized and described by red, hot, dry skin due to lack of hydration, leaving the body unable to cool itself efficiently. Unconsciousness is another sign of heat stroke in extreme situations. Option (A) does not include the typical signs of heat stroke rather heat exhaustion which is not as severe. Options (C) and (D) may accompany heat stroke but are not by themselves primary indicators of the problem. **(805-003 Health)**

19. A.

The correct answer is (A). A round is a musical form that creates harmony, which consists of simultaneous combination of tones. Typically when thinking of harmony, one thinks of melody and accompaniment. However, when singing a round, everyone sings the melody and then the students break into groups and enter at different intervals creating musical harmony. A famous round is "Row, Row, Row your Boat." Option (B) is incorrect because a Partner Song consists of two songs that have the same harmonies that can be sung together. Option (C) is incorrect because a Call & Response is having one leader sing in solo and the rest of the class sings a response. Option (D) is incorrect because a Play Party Song is a song that is sung at social events and contains movements, similar to folk dancing. **(805-002 Music)**

20. A.

Skipping and galloping are basic locomotor skills that can first be introduced at the kindergarten level and then practiced throughout the elementary grade levels and beyond. Most children are ready to learn skipping and galloping skills at age 5, which makes option (A) the correct answer. **(805-004 Physical Education)**

21. C.

The correct answer is (C). During the Renaissance, painters and sculptors studied the human body, even using cadavers to see muscle formation. While it's true that some studied the drawings of others (A), and the texture of the skin (B), and the structure of bones (D) to do their work, the study of cadavers was instrumental in developing the drawings and information to recreate human-like paintings and sculptures. **(805-001 Visual Arts)**

22. C.

The correct answer is (C). Pitch describes how high and low sounds, or up and down, are produced. Option (A) is incorrect because it describes characteristics of rhythm. Option (B) is incorrect because it describes characteristics of dynamics. Option (D) is incorrect because it describes characteristics of weight. **(805-002 Music)**

23. B.

The only inaccurate answer about metabolism is choice (B). Fasting does not speed up metabolism but rather shuts metabolism down in order to conserve energy due to little or no calories fueling the body. Choice (A) is true because your basal metabolism (basal metabolic rate) is constantly burning calories and converting energy. Choice (C) is correct because physical activity always stimulates metabolic function. Choice (D) is correct in that metabolism slowly adjusts to the demands placed on the body over long periods of time. **(805-003 Health)**

24. C.

The correct answer is (C). The ADA required school districts to place special education children in the least restrictive educational environment; thus, an orthopedic-handicapped student would be placed in mainstream classrooms. Students are required to receive physical education using appropriate accommodations to allow their successful participation. Choice (A) is incorrect because only in extreme cases are special education children excluded from participating in the school curriculum. Choice (B) is only partially correct, as it fails to mention the need to make accommodations for successful participation in physical education activities. Choice (D) is incorrect because it adopts an extreme position not applicable to limited mobility. **(805-004 Physical Education)**

25. C.

The correct answer is (C). The form or structure of music is analogous to the structure or design in language. A letter in language is equivalent to a pitch in music. A word in language is equivalent to a musical pattern. A phrase is a group of musical patterns, which is similar to a sentence in language. Several musical phrases are similar to a paragraph in language. **(805-002 Music)**

26. C.

The correct answer is (C). Gothic architecture spanned a period from the mid-12th century to the 16th century. The Middle Ages gave birth to an architectural style with religious themes brought to life with the help of the rib vault, flying buttress, and pointed, or Gothic, arch – all of which made it possible to create vast expanses while allowing for natural light. The church spires symbolically reached for God. The Greek (B) and Roman (A) empires as well as the Ancient Period (D) all preceded the Middle Ages. **(805-001 Visual Arts)**

27. C.

The correct answer is (C). The conventions of theatre describe all the details needed to deliver a realistic performance. Some of the conventions of theatre are: the use of a narrator, costumes, sequencing time, lights and makeup, and flashbacks. The stage and the plot (B) and theme and communication (D) are four of the six elements of theatre (A). **(805-005 Theatre)**

28. A.

The correct answer is (A). Since children in kindergarten and below may have problems answering comprehension questions in written form, the teacher guides them to draw to represent their understanding of a story. It is difficult to determine if in the reading class, students will use drawing just to represent their emotions (B) or to practice muscular coordination (C). Practicing with primary and secondary colors (D), might be more appropriate in art class rather than in reading class. **(805-001 Visual Arts)**

29. D.

In order to create opportunities for success with a physical task, educators need to find creative ways of making the task easier for student of varying skill levels. By placing a larger ball on a fixed tee, the task becomes much easier and doable for a less skilled student like Jesse. Therefore, option (D) is the best answer. Option (A) is incorrect because two low-skilled students are not going to be able to help each other progress with the skill. Options (B) and (C) may be indirectly helpful in the process but will not directly train the muscles needed to accomplish the task at hand. **(805-004 Physical Education)**

30. C.

The correct answer is (C). The question addresses the basic understanding of the Kodály rhythm syllables. The two syllables included in this example are ta, which would be notated as a quarter note on the staff; and ti, which would be notated as an eighth note on the staff. If a person were to keep the beat and sing the song "Twinkle, Twinkle Little Star," it should be apparent that the answer is C. Options (A) and (B) begin with the wrong note (ta), and option (D) ends with the wrong note (ti). **(805-002 Music)**

31. C.

The correct answer is (C). Although options (A) and (D) are largely necessary for participating in aerobic kinds of activity, it is the cardiovascular system that works the hardest to support and sustain the energy and oxygen utilization necessary for continuous activity (via blood circulation). Option (B) is not directly relevant to aerobic activity. **(805-003 Health)**

32. D.

The correct answer is (D). A soliloquy is a form of a monologue in which the character engages in introspection, expressing intimate thoughts and emotions. The term *soliloquy* comes from the Latin—*solus* (alone) and *loqui* (to speak). Soliloquy is similar to a monologue, but in a monologue the actor presents a speech directly to the audience. This indirect communication with the audience provides information about his/her state of mind and indecisions. A farce (A) is comedy, and a satire (B) has features of comedy. In a dialogue (C) two characters share information through a conversation. **(805-005 Theatre)**

33. B.

The correct answer is (B). In a monologue, a single actor presents a speech directly to the audience. Artifacts and non-verbal communication (A) are used to present information in an indirect fashion to the public. Traditionally, actors do not engage the audience prior to the play (C). In a soliloquy (D), the actor engages in a conversation with himself/herself in which the actor provides insights into emotions the character is experiencing internally. **(805-005 Theatre)**

34. C.

The correct answer is (C). In order to learn a motor skill, learners need to have a clear idea of what the task is before they can begin to practice and improve that task or activity. In order to account for diverse learning styles, good teaching includes visual, auditory, and kinesthetic exemplars to the task at hand. In addition, a focus on practice with feedback is fundamental to mastering a motor skill. Thus, option (C) is the progression that clearly makes the most sense for learning psychomotor skills. **(805-004 Physical Education)**

35. A. and D.

The clarinet (A) and alto saxophone (D) are in the woodwind family, and thus are not members of the brass family. Woodwind instruments once were all made of wood, but today are made of wood, metal, plastic, or some combination thereof. The trumpet (B) and tuba (C) are members of the brass family, as they are made of brass. The clarinet and alto saxophone use a thin reed that vibrates when you blow through the mouthpiece. In contrast, brass instruments produce sound by the vibration of the airstream as you blow through the mouthpiece. **(805-002 Music)**

36. B.

The correct answer is (B). Building up paint with thick brushes is generally used to create texture, even if the surface appears flat. A build-up of paint generally is not used exclusively to create a sense of energy (A) or intensity (C). An empty space (D) is generally not created through a build-up of paint, either. **(805-001 Visual Arts)**

37. A.

The correct answer is (A). The spaces in the treble clef spell FACE. It is easy to remember because space and face rhyme. **(805-002 Music)**

38. D.

The correct answer is (D). In 1929, the Texas State Legislature adopted "Texas, Our Texas" as the state song. Choice (A) is incorrect because the song "Home on the Range" is the state song of Kansas. Choice (B) is incorrect because the song "Deep in the Heart of Texas"

is a well-known song elaborating on the qualities of the state. Choice (C) is incorrect because the song "The Yellow Rose of Texas" is a well-known song in the state. It is a patriotic song popularized by Texan soldiers during the American Civil War. **(805-002 Music)**

39. A.

The correct answer is (A). Blue and orange are complementary colors. Other complementary pairings are green (B) and red (C), and yellow and violet (D). **(805-001 Visual Arts)**

40. A.

The correct answer is (A). Sedentary lifestyle behavior is a primary risk factor for heart disease as well as other preventable diseases. Options (B), (C), and (D) are not directly caused by inactivity. **(805-003 Health)**

41. D.

The correct answer is (D). If a teacher notices abuse or neglect with a child, he or she should calmly and immediately report it to the proper authorities at the school (i.e., principal or assistant principal). Although options (A) and (C) may appear to be natural choices for humanistic educators, it is not a good course of action for a variety of reasons. First, the teacher is not trained in the field(s) of counseling or psychology. Second, the teacher will not be as familiar or knowledgeable with the leadership policies and procedures regarding abuse as an administrator should be. Third, the teacher no longer remains anonymous and/or protected by the school district in case of legal issues that may result. Option (B) is not an option as the teacher has a responsibility to advocate for (act on behalf) of the child. **(805-003 Health)**

42. C.

Option (C) is the correct answer. Stacking cups, dribbling a small ball, and tapping their foot to the rhythm, as well as dressing themselves are all activities that require children to master fine motor skills. Based on this explanation, option (A) is incorrect because gross motor skills include the use of large muscle groups in the body to perform big movements like running and jumping. Choice (B), while broadly plausible, is too generic and does not directly address the question. Choice (D) also is incorrect because all of the skills outlined in the question should be achievable long before any transition into adulthood. **(805-004 Physical Education)**

43. D.

The correct answer is (D). The flying buttress was a device invented specifically to support the high vaults of Gothic churches. Flying buttresses, pointed arches, and stained glass windows appear together only on Gothic style buildings, most of which were built between 1150 and 1500. Choice (A) is incorrect because buildings of the Romanesque period (c. 1050–1150) usually employ wall buttresses and rounded arches, with only a few having pointed arches. Choices (B) and (C) are also incorrect because Byzantine and Renaissance buildings are often characterized by domes and rounded arches. **(805-001 Visual Arts)**

44. B.

The correct answer is (B). Aristophanes is the father of comedy and Sophocles is one of the most prolific tragic playwrights. Aristotle was a Greek philosopher (A) who provided the guidelines for the development of theatre in Ancient Greece. He believed that Sophocles' Oedipus the King was a perfect example of a tragedy, and wrote six principles of drama based on this play. These principles still inform modern theatrical performances. Socrates (C) was a Greek philosopher who often found himself the object of parody in the plays of comic dramatists of his day (e.g., Aristophanes' *Clouds*) and Oedipus (D) was a character in Sophocles' tragedy Oedipus the King. **(805-005 Theatre)**

45. A.

The correct answer is (A). A farce is a comedy that revolves around a situation or a plot rather than around a specific character. Drama (B) is a generic term that describes a play that presents a serious topic, but which cannot be classified as a tragedy. The term *soap opera* (C) describes a form of melodrama commonly shown on television in which emotions are overdrawn. Satire (D) uses irony and exaggeration to criticize and devalue a position, situation, or people. Satirical cartoons are commonly used in newspapers and magazines to achieve the same purpose. **(805-005 Theatre)**

46. B.

The only answer that is not risky behavior for causing illness and disease is option (B), keeping the body hydrated by drinking sufficient quantities of water. All the remaining options put the body at risk for illness and/or disease. **(805-003 Health)**

47. C.

The correct answer is (C). Complex carbohydrates should comprise at least half of the calories consumed for the healthy diet of an active person (a little less for an inactive person). Carbohydrates are the primary and most efficient source of energy for the body. Based on this, options (A), (B), and (D) are incorrect. **(805-003 Health)**

48. A.

The correct answer is (A). Gross motor-visual skills involve movement of the body's large muscles as visual information is processed. A ball is always used to perfect these skills. In some cases a bat or racquet will also aid in developing these skills. Choices (B), (C), and (D) are incorrect because they address motor skills, but fail to include a visual component in the activity. **(805-004 Physical Education)**

49. B.

The correct answer is (B). Elevation is a key component to the RICE treatment process for sprains. The other components are Rest, Ice, and Compression. Elevating the sprained limb allows for better circulation of blood to the affected area which leads to less swelling and faster recovery. Option (A) is incorrect because one should not return to exercise until significant healing has been achieved; although bearing a tolerable amount of weight on the sprain periodically has been shown to help quicken the healing process slightly. Option (C) is incorrect because evaluation is not a technical term used in the treatment of sprains. Option (D) is incorrect because the sprain should be bandaged properly to achieve compression of the surrounding area and support the injured joint. **(805-003 Health)**

50. C.

The correct answer is (C). The term *renaissance* means revival: Artists from this period attempted to re-create the themes and the artistic accomplishments of the Greek and Roman civilizations. The Middle Ages (A) began with the fall the Roman Empire in 476 CE. In this historical period, artistic productivity was limited, and the themes were mostly religious in orientation. In the Modern Era (B), artists developed multiple movements, but there was no marked interest in recreating the past. Since the Prehistoric Era preceded the Ancient period, option (D) is incorrect. **(805-001 Visual Arts)**

51. B.

An art song (B), or lieder, is a poem set to music, for solo voice and piano. A madrigal (A) is verse set to music for two or more voices which often follows a prescribed form. An opera (C) is a theatrical drama that is sung, often with instrumental accompaniment. An aria (D) is a solo for voice with accompaniment, and takes place during a longer form such as an opera. **(805-002 Music)**

52. A.

The correct answer is (A). Impressionism was a movement of the 19th century which shifted away from the realistic and detailed paintings of the Realism movement (A) of the late 1800s to a new way to represent an impression of reality. Impressionism used bright and vibrant colors to capture the impression of the images. Surrealism (C) is a movement of the 20th century. Romanticism (B) was a movement of the 18th century that tried to depict an escape from the pressures of the industrial period and the scientific rationalization of life. Its adherents communicated strong emotions and liberalism in their paintings. **(805-001 Visual Arts)**

Index

English Language Arts and Reading Practice Test

Practice-test questions are sorted here by competency. To get an idea of your level of mastery, check the box under the question numbers that you answered correctly.

801-001 Oral Language

20	21	24	30	31	32	33

801-002 Phonological and Phonemic Awareness

2	10	11	34	71	74

801-003 Alphabetic Principle

35	36	53	70

801-004 Literacy Development

5	9	15	18	54	67

801-005 Word Analysis and Identification Skills

14	22	29	37	51	60

801-006 Reading Fluency

8	23	64	68	75

801-007 Reading Comprehension and Applications

1	38	55	58	69

801-008 Vocabulary Development

3	25	39	40	61	62

801-009 Reading, Inquiry and Research

16	41	42

801-010 Writing Conventions

6	12	57	73

801-011 Written Communication

4	7	13	19	28	49	65	72

801-012 Viewing and Representing

17	26	43	50	56	63	66

801-013 Assessment of Developing Literacy

27	44	45	46	47	48	52	59

Total: _____/75

Mathematics Practice Test

Practice-test questions are sorted here by competency. To get an idea of your level of mastery, check the box under the question numbers that you answered correctly.

802-001 Mathematics Instruction

2	5	16	21	24	26

802-002 Number Concepts and Operations

7	8	13	27	29	36	38	42	45

802-003 Patterns and Algebra

1	18	22	23	39	40	44

802-004 Geometry and Measurement

12	14	17	19	20	41	43	47

802-005 Probability and Statistics

9	10	11	15	34	35	37	46

802-006 Mathematical Processes

3	4	6	25	28	30	31	32	33

Total: _____/47

Social Studies Practice Test

Practice-test questions are sorted here by competency. To get an idea of your level of mastery, check the box under the question numbers that you answered correctly.

803-001 Social Science Instruction

1	7	17	23	25	28	31	36	37

40

803-002 History

2	11	14	19	21	22	26	29	35

803-003 Geography and Culture

5	9	10	12	13	18	20	33

803-004 Economics

4	15	16	32	34	41

803-005 Government and Citizenship

3	6	8	24	27	30	38	39

Total: _____/41

Science Practice Test

Practice-test questions are sorted here by competency. To get an idea of your level of mastery, check the box under the question numbers that you answered correctly.

804-001 Lab Processes, Equipment and Safety

1	46	50

804-002 History and Nature of Science

2	41	42	47

804-003 Impact on Science

3	4	44

804-004 Concepts and Processes

48

804-005 Students as Learners and Science Instruction

6	45

804-006 Science Assessment

7	8	51

804-007 Forces and Motion

9	10	11

804-008 Physical and Chemical Properties

12	13	14	49	52

804-009 Energy and Interactions

15	16	17	18	19

804-010 Energy Transformations and Conservation

20	21

804-011 Structure and Function of Living Things

22	23	24

804-012 Reproduction and the Mechanisms of Heredity

25	26	29

804-013 Adaptations and Evolution

27	28

804-014 Organisms and the Environment

30	31

804-015 Structure and Function of Earth Systems

5	32

804-016 Cycles in Earth Systems

34	35	43

804-017 Energy in Weather and Climate

36	37	38

804-018 Solar System and the Universe

33	39	40

Total: _____/52

Fine Arts, Health, and Physical Education Practice Test

Practice-test questions are sorted here by competency. To get an idea of your level of mastery, check the box under the question numbers that you answered correctly.

805-001 Visual Arts

1	4	8	16	21	26	28	36	39

43	50	52

805-002 Music

3	5	6	7	19	22	25	30	35

37	38	51

805-003 Health

2	9	14	18	23	31	40	41	46

47	49

805-004 Physical Education

10	15	20	24	29	34	42	48

805-005 Theatre

11	12	13	17	27	32	33	44	45

Total: _____/52